Beyond the Dream Syndicate

Beyond the Dream Syndicate: Tony Conrad and the Arts after Cage

(A "MINOR" HISTORY)

Branden W. Joseph

ZONE BOOKS · NEW YORK

2011

Lyrics to "Why Don't You Smile Now" (John W. Cale, Terry Philips, Lou A. Reed, Jerry Vance), "The Ostrich" (Terry Philips, Lou A. Reed, Jimmie Sims, Jerry Vance), "Johnny Won't Surf No More" (Terry Philips, Lou A. Reed, Jimmie Sims, Jerry Vance), and "Sad Lonely Orphan Boy" (Terry Philips, Jerry Vance), quoted by permission of The Music Goes Round, BV, administered by Third Tier Music, LLC.

ZONE BOOKS
1226 Prospect Avenue
Brooklyn, NY 11218

First Paperback Edition

Printed in the United States of America.

Distributed by The MIT Press,
Cambridge, Massachusetts, and London, England

Library of Congress Cataloging-in-Publication Data

Joseph, Branden Wayne
Beyond the Dream Syndicate: Tony Conrad and the arts after Cage / by Branden W. Joseph.
p. cm.
Includes bibliographical references (p.) and index.
ISBN 978-1-890951-87-0
1. Conrad, Tony — Criticism and interpretation. 2. Avant-garde (Music) — United States — 20th century — History and criticism. 3. Avant-garde (Music) — United States — History — 20th century. 4. Postmodernism — United States — History — 20th century. I. Title.
ML410.C7515J87 2008
780.92—dc22 2007061965

Contents

For, of course, Tony

Preface

I first met Tony Conrad in the mid-1990s, in the context of his *Early Minimalism* project and its astute and trenchant critique of the concepts of authorship and the composer. This book derives and takes its inspiration from that moment in Conrad's thinking and career. Hence my attempt in the pages that follow to, in essence, turn the monograph inside out. As the project grew from the small study into its final form (and particularly as Chapter 3 separated from Chapter 2), I several times considered jettisoning the monographic focus entirely to write a broader history of a particular moment in New York's artistic underground. Yet, as not only the connections made (from La Monte Young to Mike Kelley), but also my own critical perspectives on them had been opened by following Conrad's particular artistic trajectory, I decided to retain the book's original focus, however expanded. The result, which I have termed a "minor history" for reasons explained in Chapter 1, is nonetheless offered in a spirit of speculation, meant to distance, trouble, and hopefully open up new avenues of study without replacing or shutting down the many other productive investigations of the period and its protagonists.

My thanks, first of all, to Tony Conrad, who entrusted me to tell a version of his story when he could, without a doubt, very well tell it himself. Thanks also to: Alex Alberro; Tim Barnes and Quakebasket; Barry Bergdoll; Bud Bynack, Meighan Gale, and

Gus Kiley at Zone Books; John Cale; James Conlon, Cassy Juhl, and Caleb Smith at the Columbia University Visual Media Center; Jonathan Crary; Arnold Dreyblatt; the Getty Research Institute, Research Library and Special Collections; Joe Gibbons; Jon Hendricks; Hannah Higgins; Mike Kelley; Alison Knowles; Kevin Kushel; Bliss Cua Lim; Reinhold Martin; Jonas Mekas, Robert Haller, and Anthology Film Archives; Anthony McCall; Duncan McCorquodale; Mondo Kim's, New York; Billy Name; Anna Neimark; Other Music, New York; Tony Oursler; Jon Pestoni; Dawson Prather and Locust Music; Jay Reeg; Julia Robinson; Paige Rozanski; Jay Sanders; M. M. Serra and the New York Filmmakers' Co-op; P. Adams Sitney; William S. Strong; Lynne Tillman; and Michael at Subterranean Records, New York. Special thanks are due to Callie Angell, Karen Beckman, David E. James, David Grubbs, Ben Piekut, and Felicity D. Scott, all of whom read the manuscript for this book in whole or in part. Additional, very special thanks are due, as always, to Felicity Scott.

Work on this book was supported, in part, by a residency at the American Academy in Berlin. Reproductions were supported, in part, by a research grant from the University of California, Irvine and research funds from Columbia University.

Portions of Chapters 2, 3, and 4 have appeared in abbreviated and altered forms as "The Tower and the Line," *Grey Room* 27 (Spring 2007); and "Concept Art and Instrumental Reason," *Texte zur Kunst* 15, no. 60 (Winter 2005).

Chapter One

What Is a Minor History?

> There is nothing that is major or revolutionary except the minor.
> —Deleuze and Guattari

In the summer of 1997, Tony Conrad made an appearance, *in imago*, at the multinational art fair Documenta, then in its tenth iteration, in Kassel, Germany, as part of Mike Kelley and Tony Oursler's multimedia installation *The Poetics Project, 1977–1997*. It was not the first time Conrad had been included in Documenta as part of another's work. Twenty-five years earlier, he had been present, in person, as part of La Monte Young and Marian Zazeela's Dream House, a room in which a single complex chord filled a space tinted by Zazeela's specially designed lighting, an environment that would now be understood as a species of "sound art."

In 1972, Conrad had signed on to oversee the Dream House's electronics, making sure the installation's sine-wave generators were functioning and in tune for the duration of the exhibition. Conrad also played violin in the concerts presented in the Dream House by Young's reincarnation of the Theatre of Eternal Music, a group that, in its original form, Conrad had helped found and in which he had integrally participated throughout the 1960s. By the 1970s, Conrad was more widely known as a filmmaker, his reputation having been made by *The Flicker* (1965–66), an infamous "structural film" consisting of alternating black and white frames that formed stroboscopic patterns upon projection. After Documenta, he and his wife and collaborator, Beverly Grant, spent several weeks accompanying *The Flicker* to screenings across Europe, along with the equally abstract films *Straight and Narrow* (1970), *Four Square* (1971), and the fantastic transvestite narrative *Coming Attractions* (1970). One particularly noteworthy visit was to filmmakers Birgit and Wilhelm Hein's avant-garde/porno theater, X-Screen, in Cologne, where Conrad heard stories about Viennese Aktionist Otto Muehl (who would later visit him in the United States), encountered Austrian filmmaker, Kurt Kren, and eventually, via Wilhelm's brother Karlheinz and his wife Renate in Munich, encountered the films of Muehl, Otmar Bauer, and others in their circle (an experience Conrad recounted at length in the article "The Eye and the Asshole").[1]

Another significant travel that fall took Conrad to the farmhouse commune in Wümme where producer Uwe Nettlebeck had set up the pioneering Krautrock band, Faust. The recordings made on that occasion would be released the following year as the now famous, but at the time almost entirely overlooked album *Outside the Dream Syndicate* (Figure 1.1). As has been recounted by David Fricke, Conrad had by then come to feel that the reformed Theatre of Eternal Music was no longer performing the same music that he, Young, Zazeela, and John Cale had created in New York during the period that Conrad termed the "Dream Syndicate."[2] The title Conrad chose for the Faust recording clearly referred to that period and more specifically his article "Inside the Dream Syndicate," published in *Film Culture* half a dozen years before.[3] "Inside the Dream Syndicate" was the closest thing to a manifesto that any member of the group would produce at the time, an outline of what Conrad, at least, held to be their shared aesthetic goals. Although, according to Conrad, he approached the recording of *Outside the Dream Syndicate* without malice or contention, its release resolutely declared that era to be closed.

• • •

Five Documentas later, Conrad was once again incorporated into an art and music installation, Kelley and Oursler's *The Poetics Project*. This work was vastly different from the staid, meditative,

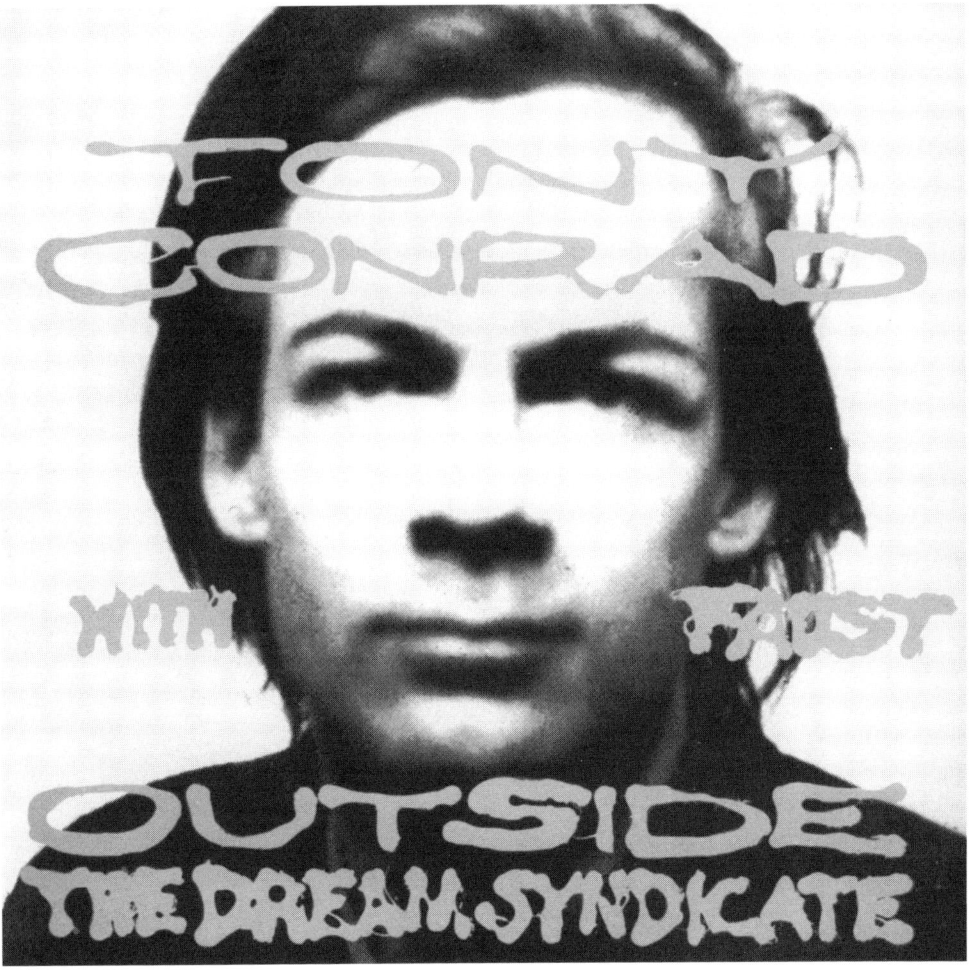

Figure 1.1. Tony Conrad with Faust, *Outside the Dream Syndicate* LP cover, Caroline Records C 1501, recorded October, 1972, released 1973. Courtesy Tony Conrad.

almost organic unification to which the Dream House aspired (Figures 1.2 and 1.3). It was instead a digressive, cacophonous, multimedia conglomeration that staunchly resisted totalization. Paintings, sculptures, free-standing architectural panels, video projections, and audio tapes competed for the visitor's attention, interrupting and overlapping one another in apparently chaotic fashion.[4] On closer inspection, almost all of the installation's components revealed themselves to be further diversified, even fractured, on the level of artistic medium. A painted canvas, for instance, turns out to be the reproduction of an old letter that recounted Kelley's impressions of a rock concert, specifically one put on by the industrial music group Throbbing Gristle, fronted by former visual artists Genesis P-Orridge and Cosi Fanni Tutti.[5] Other paintings were enlargements of notebook sketches, reproductions of book covers, or reconstructed props from early Oursler videos and performances, all of which functioned as screens for other video projections or walls for the installation's labyrinthine structure. Still other canvasses housed speakers that "battled" one another with raucous guitar and drum solos.[6] As an ensemble, *The Poetics Project* formed not only a vast collage, but an internally differentiated media *mise-en-abyme*; the closer one's inspection, the more diversified its content.

The primary subject of the work was the Poetics, an "art band" formed by Kelley and Oursler while attending CalArts (the California Institute of the Arts), which included fellow student and founding member Don Krieger and, eventually, John Miller (Figure 1.4). Before settling into the form of a band, the group experimented with prop comedy and Bauhaus or Judson Dance–like performance activities, most notably the Pole Dance, reconstructed on video with different dancers for the installation. Though "the Poetics, initially, was designed to be a dysfunctional nightclub comedy act," Kelley recalled, "the call of the band format was too strong to resist and the nightclub version of the Poetics merged with some of the ex–Polka Dot musicians to form a more Rock-song-oriented version of the band."[7] Kelley's "Polka Dot" reference was to his pre-Oursler CalArts band, Polka Dot and the Spots, inspired by the originator (and prolific recorder) of "Chicago-style" polka, Li'l Wally. Previously, Kelley had been part of an earlier (and now revived) artistic and musical collective, Destroy All Monsters, founded while he was an undergraduate at the University of Michigan, Ann Arbor.[8] Arising out of an even earlier set of guerillalike, chaotic, and confrontational performances, the group's core consisted of Kelley, Cary Loren, Niagara, and Jim Shaw (an occasional musical collaborator with Kelley and Oursler at CalArts, as well). Inspired by the aesthetic ideas of futurist simultaneity, Cagean indeterminacy, and eccentric jazz musician Sun Ra's whiplash-inducing shifts from one style to another, Destroy All Monsters produced collagelike performances that refused to cohere on either a formal or an ideological level. When Kelley asked Loren – who had studied and emulated the equally heterogeneous trash aesthetic of Jack Smith – "How do you think that all these different ideas that everyone in the band has work together?" Loren summed up their aesthetic concisely: "It doesn't work together."[9]

In the Poetics, Oursler served as front man, and their sound, at least during their "organ period," often recalls the sound tracks to his video tapes of the time.[10] In part, the group's preference for the organ (and its smaller cousin, the toy orgatron – which Oursler personified and addressed, at times, as Mr. Orgatron) resulted from the associations it had for two ex-Catholics who, as Kelley put it, "had spent a good part of our youths in mass sniffing incense and listening to death-lyrics accompanied by organ music."[11] More than Mass, however, the foregrounding of the organ by the Poetics brings to mind sound tracks for B-grade and foreign films, from those of Ennio Morricone to those of Nino Rota, as well as Korla Pandit–type kitsch, carnival rides, and soap-opera melodrama, all of it run through a sensibility attuned to early Kraftwerk. Oursler has also recalled the importance of seeing Martin Rev on organ in the legendarily confrontational New York band Suicide.[12] Certain of the Poetics "concerts" could be similarly, though perhaps inadvertently, confrontational.[13] Despite such a legacy, the fact that you could make punk rock out of essentially

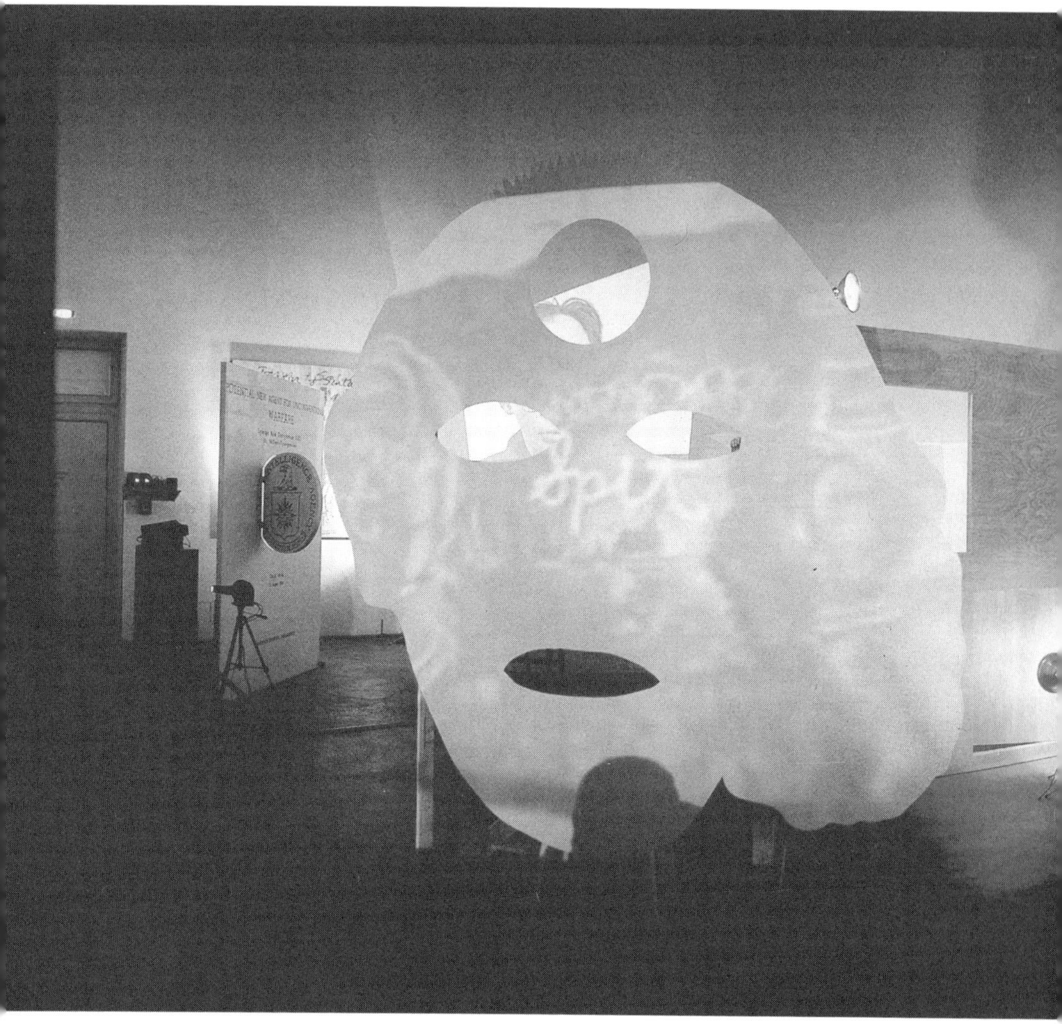

Figure 1.2. Mike Kelley and Tony Oursler, *The Poetics Project: 1977–1997* (Documenta version), as installed at Documenta X, Kassel, Germany, 1997. Courtesy Tony Oursler.

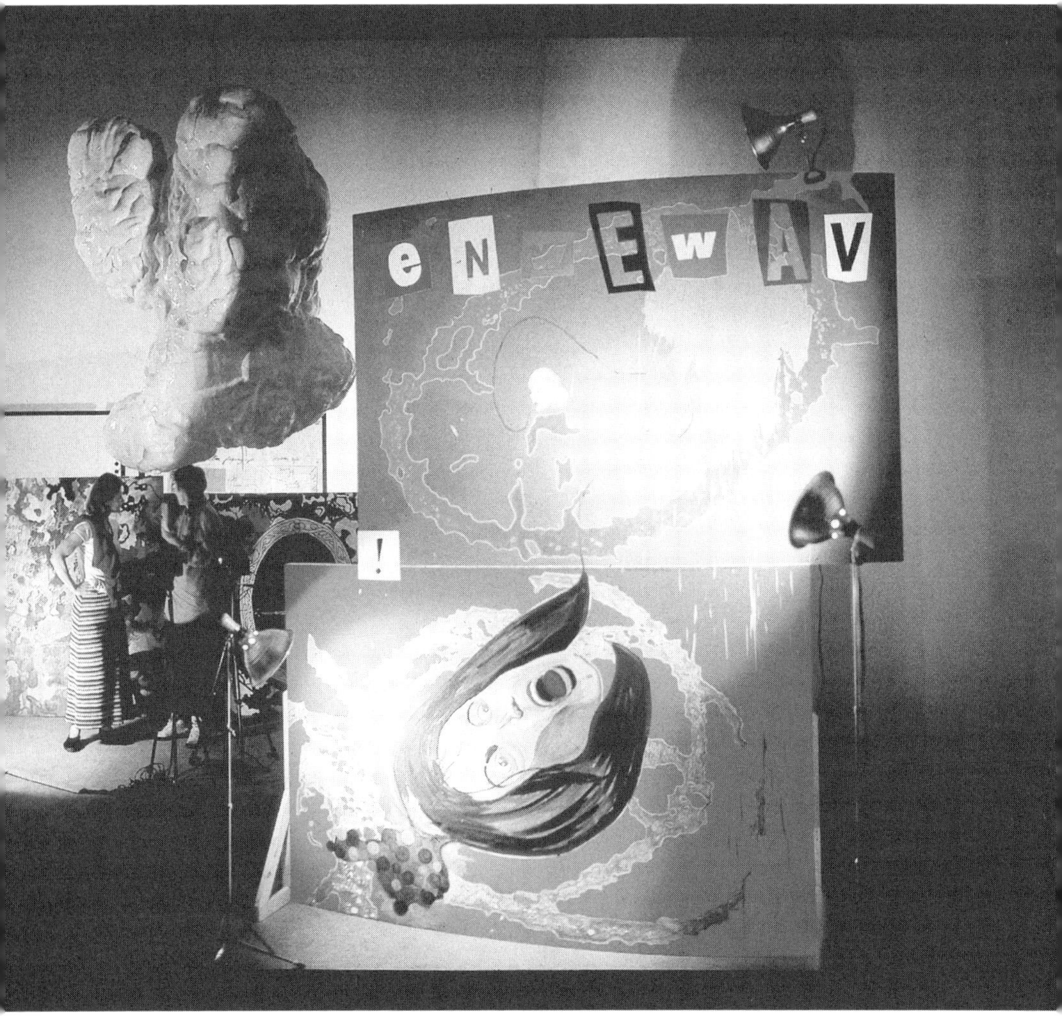
eN EwAV
!

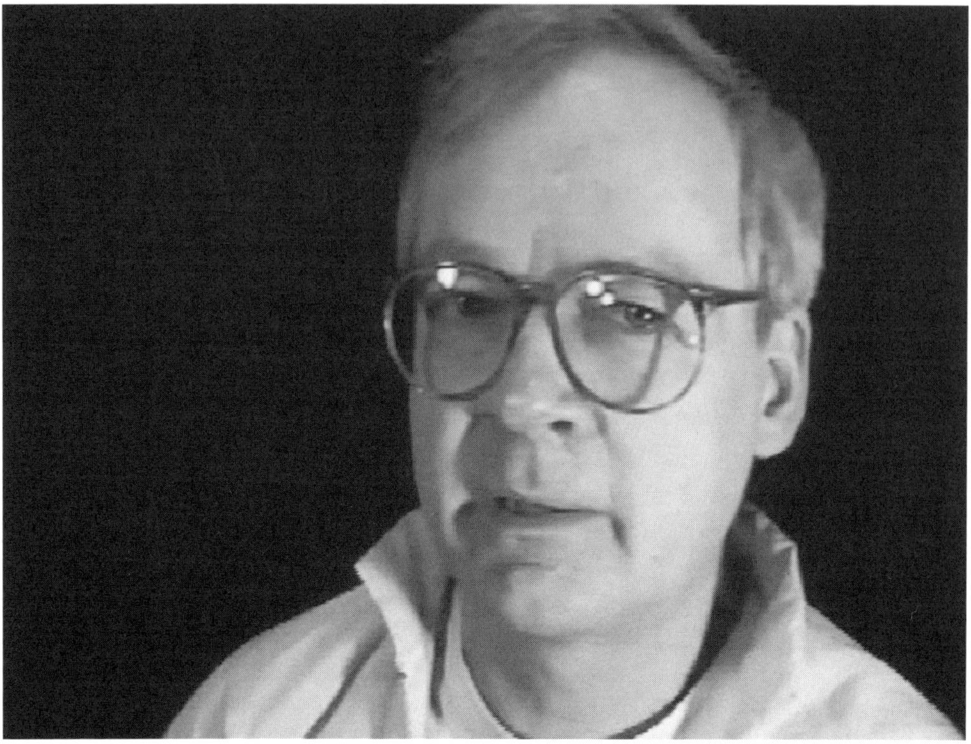

Figure 1.3. Tony Conrad in Tony Oursler, *Synesthesia: Tony Conrad*, 1997–2001, originally shown as part of Mike Kelley and Tony Oursler, *The Poetics Project: 1977–1997* (Documenta version), 1997.

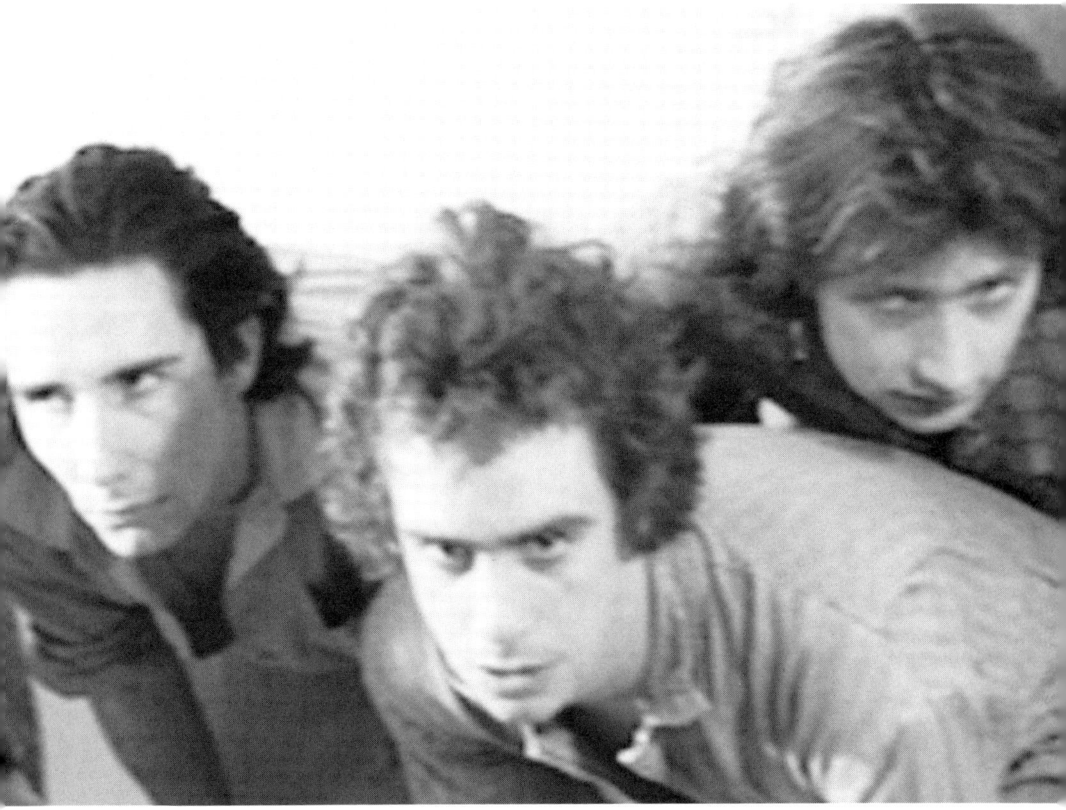

Figure 1.4. The Poetics (Mike Kelley, Tony Oursler, John Miller), ca. 1977–78. Photographer unknown. Courtesy Kelley Studio.

the same materials played by the guy in the organ store at the mall must also have appealed to Oursler and Kelley out of sheer perversity.

The Poetics developed within the context of an emergent post-pop, postconceptual, poststudio art practice in which different artistic and nonartistic formats were understood as interchangeably available for useful exploitation. "The conceptualist motto about form following content and the privileging of idea over craftsmanship changed the way we thought about what we could make," recalls Oursler. "For me, the energy of the time can be summed up in the concept of the crossover.... In the seventies, artists were escaping the studio; they were interested in making art in more popular, public forms like music, performance, film, and video."[14] Laurie Anderson taught a course on sound and performance at CalArts while Kelley and Oursler were students and at a moment when she was moving from more restrained conceptual performances to the combination of art and popular music for which she would become most known. The Poetics were founded to explore the cross-media and cross-genre borrowings examined in Anderson's class, as well as in the work of David Askevold and the school's generally conceptualist milieu. "But in retrospect," Oursler recalled, "Laurie Anderson was the only one who could make the crossover leap as a total media artist. It's strange that only one is allowed to carry on, instead of op[e]ning up a new field."[15]

Unlike Anderson, the Poetics would be all but forgotten, ignored by the histories of music and performance art alike. The group didn't "take"; it proved unassimilable to the categories existing within both the art institution and institutionalized art history. As an art band, the Poetics were a Gnostic or Manichean mixture of disciplines and genres, a strange hybrid resting comfortably within neither the realm of art nor that of music, implicitly questioning and bifurcating the cultural and intellectual assumptions about both. The best appreciation of their interests seems to have come from fellow CalArts student Bill Vex of the Suburban Lawns, who once told Oursler "that [they] were a fake rock band."[16]

In *The Poetics Project*, such unassimilability was to be understood according to the context established by dissident surrealist Georges Bataille. The amorphous fiberglass sculptures *Nondescript God* and *Spineless Sack of Flesh* – one hanging from the ceiling, the other slumping in a chair and addressing the visitor with a litany of abject apologies – were intended to invoke the idea of the *informe* as put forth by the "excremental philosopher," with whose thinking Kelley had been explicitly involved since at least as far back as the project *Plato's Cave, Rothko's Chapel, Lincoln's Profile* (1986, performed with assistance of the band Sonic Youth).[17] Specifically, Kelley and Oursler invoked Bataille's notion of "heterology" and the unequal dialectics of appropriation and excretion encompassed by it. Unlike more conventional philosophical approaches, which assimilate only those phenomena that can be rendered commensurable – via abstract conceptualization or categorization – heterology addresses what remains "completely other," constitutively unassimilable within general cognitive systems, whether they be advanced philosophical speculation or common sense. In a passage that sheds light on *The Poetics Project*'s material prolixity as well as its intellectual pretensions, Bataille noted: "The process of appropriation is thus characterized by a homogeneity (static equilibrium) of the author of the appropriation, and of objects as final result, whereas excretion presents itself as the result of a heterogeneity, and can move in the direction of an ever greater heterogeneity, liberating impulses whose ambivalence is more and more pronounced."[18] In Kelley and Oursler's view, the Poetics remained a heterological presence within contemporary art and cultural history. To take them seriously within that history, as the installation proposed, would be to question, expand, and possibly undermine the existing categories and trajectory of artistic activity, making them other than themselves.[19]

With *The Poetics Project*, Kelley and Oursler's intentions – in equal parts hubristic and humorous – went beyond reviving the reputation of the Poetics as a performance group, no matter how challenging or complex the issues involved. Their broader ambition was to intervene in the emerging histories of popular music would cause. It was a device that, as an actor, he had used to great effect in Oursler's largest video mannequin sculpture, *Keep Going* (1995), where he improvised his role as a demanding, though maddeningly inconsistent movie director (Figure 1.7). *Keep Going* was not the first time Conrad had appeared in an Oursler piece. He turned up briefly as the "sperm doctor" in Oursler's *EVOL* (1984) and had a larger role in Oursler and Joe Gibbons's collaborations *ONOUROWN* (1990) and *Toxic Detox* (1992), where he played a cut-rate videotape psychiatrist. (The parodic plots of the latter two videos hinge on the Reagan-era devastation of social services that cut costs by simply pronouncing numerous mental patients able to care for themselves. After feigning interest in Gibbons's and Oursler's characters for a couple of minutes, Conrad, as the prerecorded Dr. Conrad, spends most of the time attempting to convince them to shut off and rewind the tape for the next day's "session.")[22]

The second distinguishing feature of Conrad's interview was its content. Conrad had, in fact, been central to the development of the art-band phenomenon in several ways. He had been a member of the Primitives, the short-lived rock group with Cale, Lou Reed, and Walter De Maria that existed for a brief moment during the winter of 1964–65 and eventually morphed into the Velvet Underground (of which Conrad was not a part, but which he inadvertently named, finding Michael Leigh's soft-core paperback of that title and bringing it to the apartment he used to share with Cale).[23] He also played a role in Rhys Chatham's development into a minimalist rock composer by inviting the young musical director of the performance space The Kitchen to play "long-string drone" in his sound and video performance *Ten Years Alive on the Infinite Plain* (1972). (The next month would find Conrad, Chatham, and Charlemagne Palestine "manifesting" *The Fundamental D Flat Group* together at Antioch College.)[24] Rather than discussing such relations, however, Conrad, hardly pausing for questions, entered into a long, not entirely unrelated exposé on the history of the capitalist exploitation of the youth market through music and the wider historical relations of art, music,

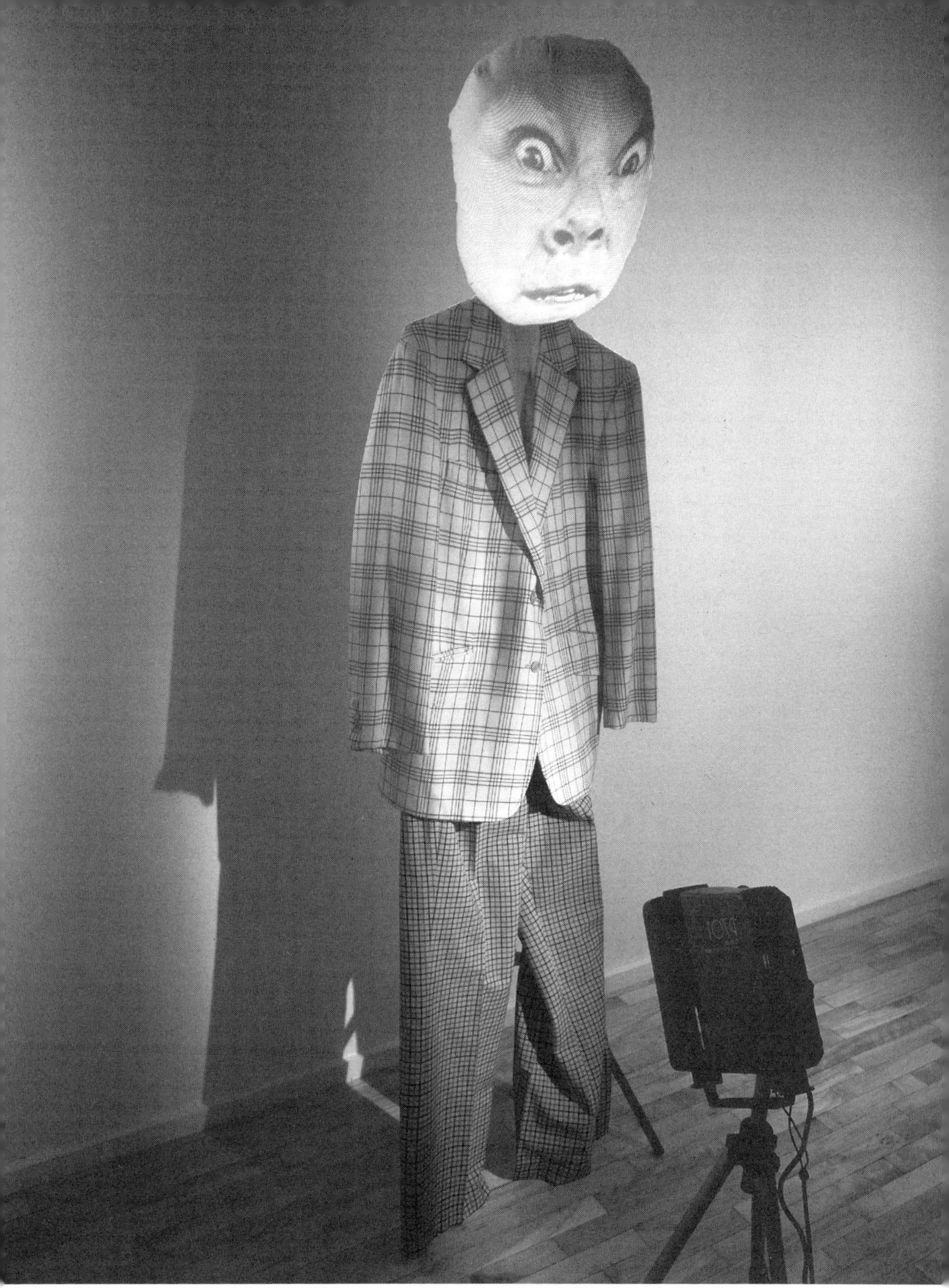

Figure 1.7. Tony Oursler, *Keep Going*, 1995. Tony Conrad plays the part of a movie director. Courtesy Tony Oursler.

technology, and culture.[25] As though to avoid a repeat of his experience at Documenta in 1972, Conrad made his participation in *The Poetics Project* into a sort of collaboration; rather than remain appropriated material, he gently, but resolutely detourned Kelley and Oursler's agenda to match his own.

That Conrad would do so is not, perhaps, surprising, given that 1997 marked a sort of culmination of his own aesthetico-historical project with the release of the four-CD boxed set *Early Minimalism, Volume One*.[26] Although the project of which it is a part is, in some sense, ongoing, the release bracketed a period begun ten years earlier with the New York premiere of the composition *Early Minimalism: December 1964*.[27] It was enabled and in some sense overdetermined by the continued differences between Conrad and Young, which over the quarter-century since Documenta V had become a much-publicized conflict over the nature and meaning of their earlier interactions — one that led most infamously to Conrad's picketing of Young's appearance in the North American New Music Festival in Buffalo in 1990 (a type of aesthetic/political action with a long history, as we will learn in Chapter 4).[28]

• • •

The first Theatre of Eternal Music in which Young and Conrad performed together was so named in February 1965 and continued until the summer of 1966 (Figure 1.8).[29] Shortly before Conrad joined him, Young, who already had an impressive jazz and avant-garde pedigree, had been improvising a sort of blues, alternately with Terry Jennings and Henry Flynt, as well as working with Zazeela, poet and drummer Angus MacLise, and Billy Linich (later to become, in the ensemble around Andy Warhol and the Velvet Underground, Billy Name). At a series of concerts at the 10-4 Gallery in July and August, 1962, Young, Zazeela, MacLise, and Linich performed an improvisatory amalgam of jazz and Indian music, producing an ecstatic din lasting for hours: Linich strumming guitar, MacLise polyrhythmically beating hand drums,

Zazeela intoning a voice drone (occasionally joined by Linich), and Young, in the middle of it all, executing lightning-fast permutations on a sopranino saxophone in a style partially inspired by the contemporary soprano sax playing of John Coltrane. It was this ensemble that elicited Conrad's desire to join the group: "The music was formless, expostulatory, meandering; vaguely modal, arrhythmic, and very unusual," Conrad recalls; "I found it exquisite."[30] Conrad began working with the group soon afterward, making his first public appearance with them at the Third Rail Gallery on June 14, 1963. His violin playing ultimately joined Zazeela in the production of an underlying drone, reinforcing that dimension of the group's sound. The wildly ecstatic, proto-psychedelic direction of the group was further disciplined that fall with the addition of John Cale on viola. In recordings from this time, Conrad, Cale, and Zazeela form a sort of iron triangle, a structured harmonic drone against which MacLise, on the one hand, and Young, on the other, perform incendiary permutations. Young's modal sopranino sax playing, which shimmers atop the continually held pitches of Conrad, Cale, and Zazeela, aspired to a similar (though apparently paradoxical) stasis: performing changes so rapidly that they would virtually meld, hanging in the air as a sort of cloud.[31]

After having played in this configuration for some time, Young began to change his style, first experimenting with more sustained notes on the saxophone, but soon joining Zazeela on voice. Abandoning the saxophone allowed the group to adopt what is known as "just intonation," a means of tuning to simple mathematical ratios without the fudging necessary in the equal-tempered Western scale, hegemonic since the time of Bach. Though Young's and Cale's musical training outweighed that of Conrad, the latter's mathematical background and interest in acoustics were crucial to the group's subsequent development of the new tuning.[32] In just intonation, each harmonic relationship can be represented by whole-number fractions. The tonic or key note within any given scale—for example, the standard middle A on a piano keyboard, which is physically tuned to a wavelength of 440

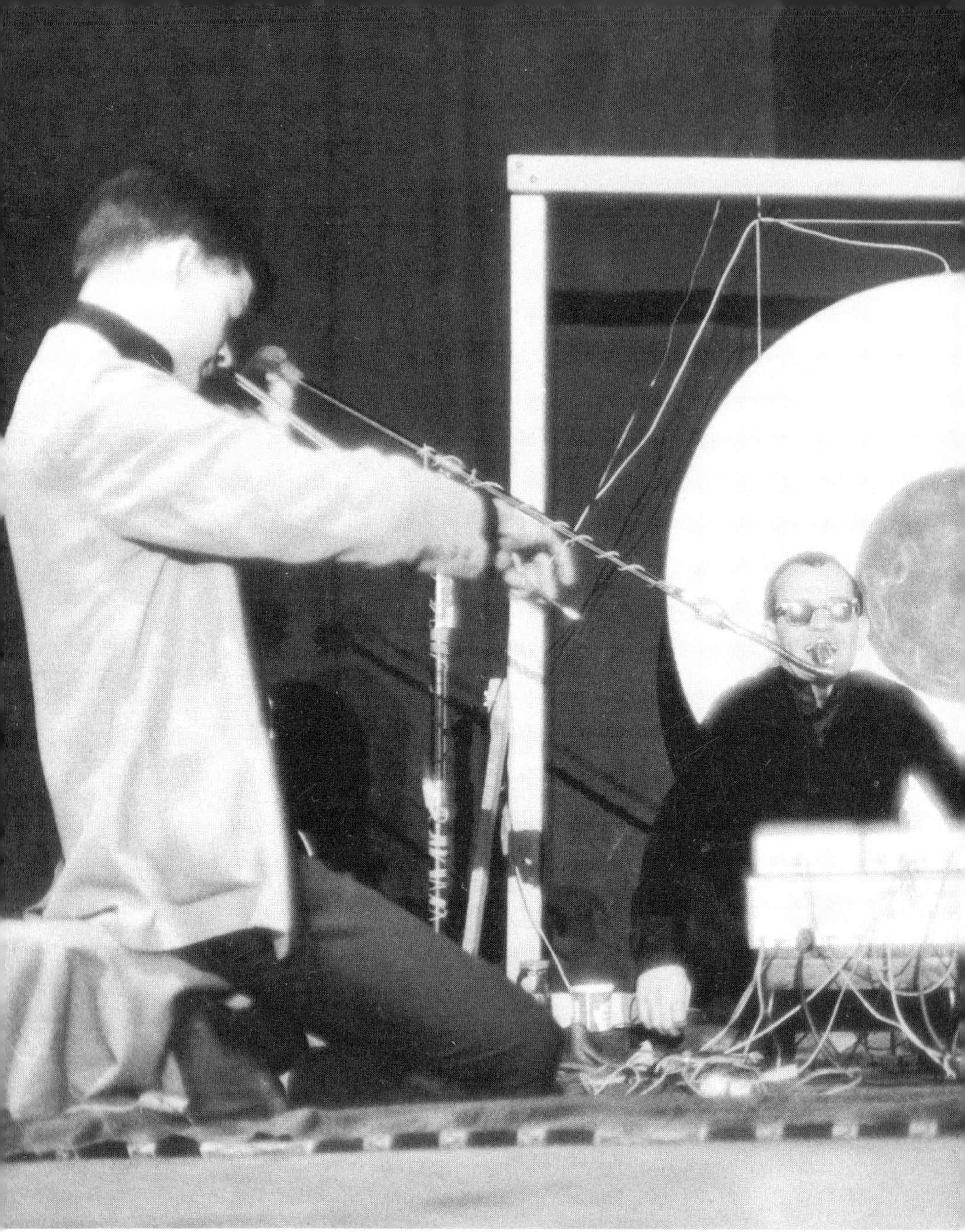

Figure 1.8. Fred W. McDarrah, *The Theatre of Eternal Music* at the New York Film-makers' Cinematheque, 1965. (Left to right: Tony Conrad, La Monte Young, Marian Zazeela, John Cale) Photo: Fred W. McDarrah. Copyright © by Fred W. McDarrah.

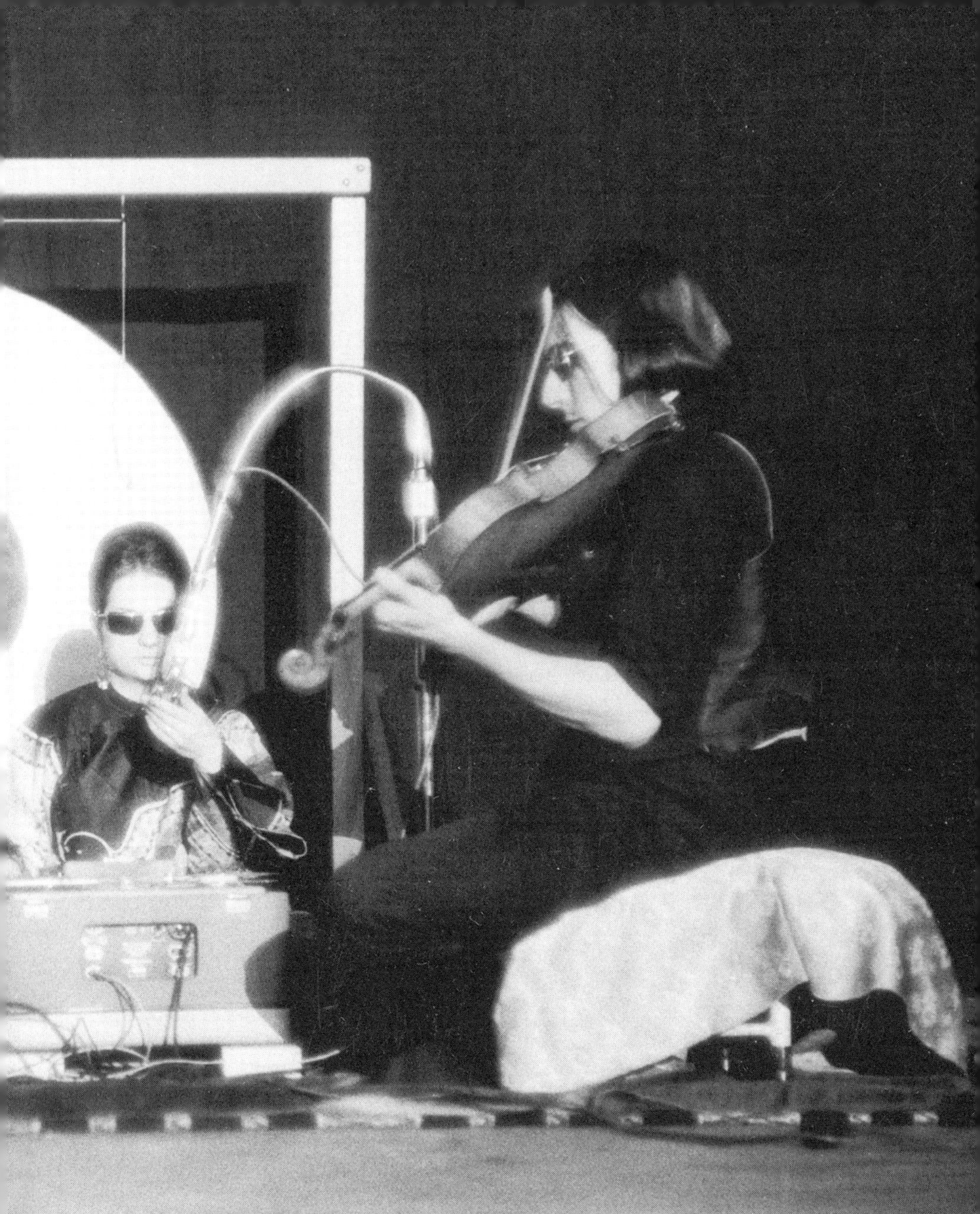

cycles per second — can be represented by the integer 1. The note exactly an octave above this note, also an A, but at a physical wavelength of 880 cycles per second, would then be represented by the integer 2, which corresponds to the ratio of 880 over 440 or 2:1. Likewise, the other major Western harmonic relationships can be represented in similar fashion: the fifth, for example, can be represented as the ratio 3:2, the fourth as 4:3 or 2^2:3, a major sixth as 5:3, and so on.[33]

Once all members of the group had begun producing sustained tones (rather than the rapid modulation of Young's blistering saxophone playing), discussions and decisions had to be made about which notes or tones to sustain. On account of his prior experience and personal taste, Young did not want to perform the major third (that is, the ratio 5:4), to which, up to that time, in fact, Conrad had been somewhat partial. When Young suggested the slightly flat "blues" seventh, Conrad assimilated it to and performed the seventh harmonic (that is, the integer 7). It is beyond the scope of the present study to investigate the intricacies of the group's harmonic practices, ones that drew from Conrad's extensive earlier investigations of harmonics and that Young, in his later work and theorizations of it, has elaborated to extraordinarily complex and precise degrees.[34] Nevertheless, it is important to note that the group's decision to exclude the major third and to embrace the seventh harmonic led in effect to the replacement of the dominant Western scale, which is based upon the integers 2-3-5 (the octave, the perfect fifth, and the major third), with an alternate harmonic system, equally mathematically rational, based upon the integers 2-3-7 (the octave, the perfect fifth, and the seventh harmonic). "So I started playing this note," Conrad recalls about his adoption of the seventh harmonic, "but this led to much discussion because, for one, La Monte wanted to know, 'What's with this note?' 'Where's this note coming from?'... But as that began to happen, it became apparent to all of us that there was a possibility here of using 7 instead of 5 as a basis of elaborating a harmonic structure" (Figure 1.9).[35]

Putting aside for the moment the contentious issue of who

was responsible for the decision that set the Theatre of Eternal Music on this path (whether Young, Conrad, both, or the group as a whole), this revelation and the initiation of the ensuing project of exploring and developing its implications would prove crucial for both Conrad and Young. For Young, it provided a basis on which to elaborate and build upon the strategy of minimal reduction and temporal expansion he had explored since *Trio for Strings* (1958). For Conrad, it promised a system of alternate tuning that was in a sense more rational and better justified than the relatively arbitrary equal-tempered scales of Edgar Varèse and Alois Hába that had previously attracted his attention.[36] For both, it represented a viable strategy for surpassing John Cage, turning away from the older composer's foundational futurist embrace of an art of noises (which, for Cage, was a means of getting around the impassible "wall" of harmony, as his one-time teacher Arnold Schoenberg had described it).[37] A swipe in Cage's direction can be discerned in Conrad's assertion in "Inside the Dream Syndicate" that "noises are not *ever* pitchless, to say the least."[38] Whereas the young Cage had criticized the prejudices of Western harmonic music in favor of his own time structures (which, unlike harmonic structures, could allow the inclusion of any sound, whether pitched or—as in noise or percussion music—pitchless), the Theatre of Eternal Music would rely on the mathematical rigor and "correctness" of just intonation to counterpose and relativize the comparatively approximate and compromised scale of Western equal temperament. In so embracing a music entirely predicated on harmony to the virtual exclusion of rhythm (with the exception of the beats and pulses produced by harmonic interactions), the Theatre of Eternal Music could situate itself as at the opposite pole from Cage within the musical avant-garde.

The result of the Theatre of Eternal Music's transformation of instrumentation and scale was a mosaiclike set of harmonic tones within which the musicians modulated to form different interlocking auditory structures. The harmonics produced were greatly augmented by electronic amplification; Conrad and Cale added contact mikes to their instruments, Cale further filing down the

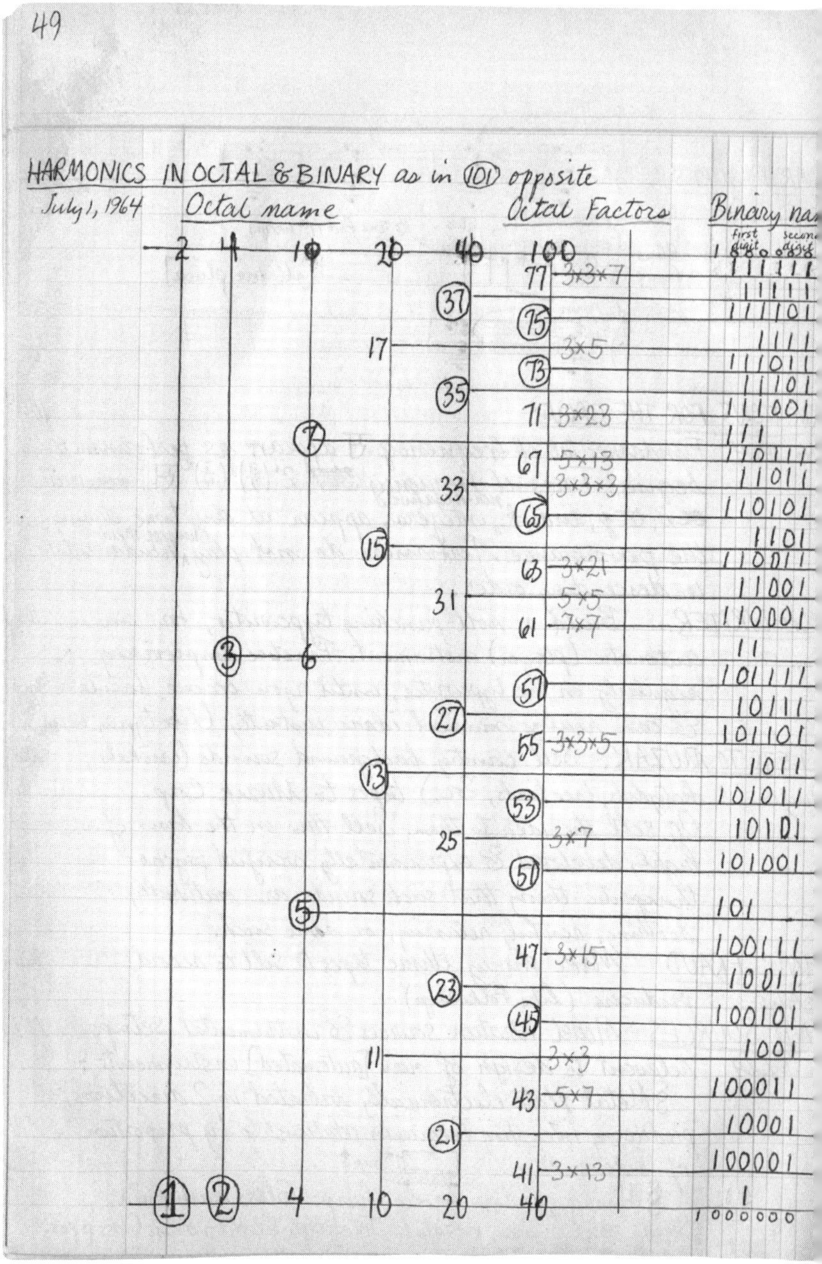

Figure 1.9. Tony Conrad, "Table of Harmonics" and "Harmonics in Octal and Binary," July 1, 1964, from Tony Conrad's unpublished notebook "Music Notes II," pages 48 and 49 (pages numbered in reverse order in original).

LE OF HARMONICS below 64, transposed to one octave: 101

Size in Cents	Harmonics	Factors	Divided by: 3	5	7
1200	4 8 16 32 ~~65~~ 64	~~5·13~~			
1173	63	3·3·7	3·7		9
1145	(31)				
1117	(61)				
1088	15	3·5	5	3	
1059	(59)				
1030	(29)				
999	57	3·19	19		
969	(7)				
938	55	5·11		11	
906	27	3·3·3	9		
874	(53)				
841	(13)				
807	51	3·17	17		
772	25	5·5		5	
738	49	7·7			7
702	(3) 6				
666	(47)				
628	(23)				
590	45	3·3·5	15	9	
551	(11)				
512	(43)				
471	21	3·7	7		3
429	(41)				
386	(5)				
342	39	3·13	13		
298	(19)				
251	(37)				
204	9	3·3	3		
155	35	5·7		7	5
105	(17)				
53	33	3·11	11		
0	(2) 4 8 16 32				

rimes are circled.

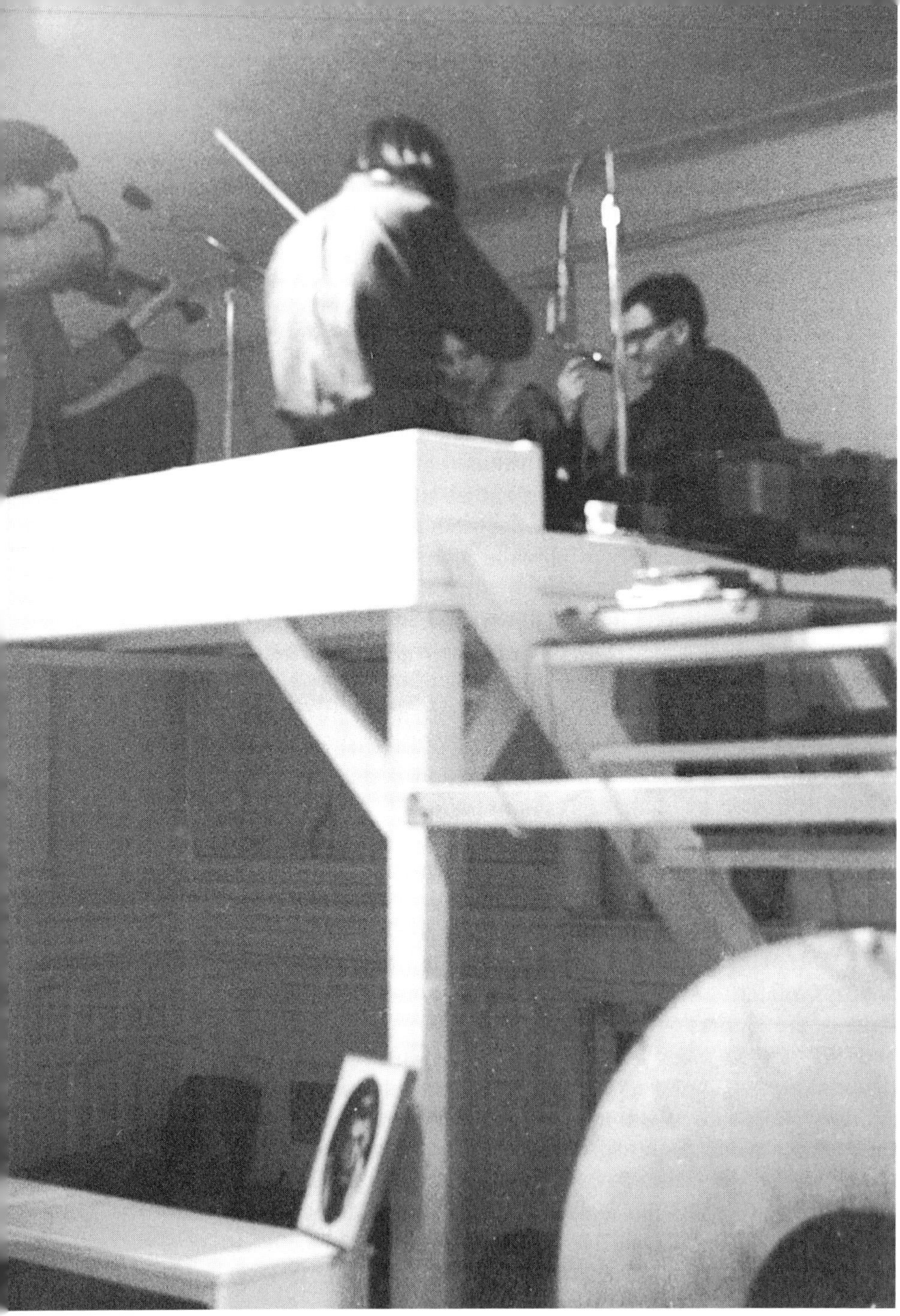

Figure 1.10. The Theatre of Eternal Music at Henry Geldzahler's loft, New York, March 7, 1965. (Left to right: Tony Conrad, John Cale, Marian Zazeela, La Monte Young) Photo: Billy Name.

marketplace and its commodities, the pressure that economic circumstances nonetheless continue to exert shifts emphasis from the commodity status of the object to the persons responsible for its making. Therefore, within this paradigm, it is the immaterial and process-based work, which is by nature refractory to the conventional categories of authorship, that requires an unambiguous author."[46] In the case of Young and Conrad, though, it would be misleading to understand or to characterize their differences in purely personal or professional terms, as a "feud" between two individuals.[47] Upon examination, it becomes clear that we are dealing in this instance not just with differences of opinion, but with opinions that are different *in kind*, situating themselves on opposite sides of a whole series of interrelated questions of authorship, history, the institution, and, ultimately, power.

Since 1983, Young's role and position within the development of musical minimalism has been the subject of several major studies, from Wim Merten's *American Minimal Music* to Keith Potter's *Four Musical Minimalists*.[48] As the subtitles of these two books indicate — both being *La Monte Young, Terry Riley, Steve Reich, Philip Glass* — the history of musical minimalism is also a canonization. Despite increasingly detailed and sophisticated archival research and musicological analyses (particularly in Potter's authoritative study), certain methodological assumptions about the writing of history remain largely unquestioned, narrating the development of musical minimalism according to the tropes of authorship, influence, expression, linear progression, and disciplinary specificity.[49] Such an approach can be characterized as what Michel Foucault (following Nietzsche) referred to as "historian's history," a form of historical analysis that actually annihilates time and the contingencies of historical circumstance in favor of atemporal understandings of individual subjects (historical actors) and eternal truths.[50]

Young's claim to authorship, both in its tenacity and in the manner in which it is expressed, is integrally, if unconsciously, aligned with such a historical perspective, one that seeks stable points of origin and unchanging verities, mediated only by the vicissitudes of biography. Most accounts of musical minimalism follow suit, locating the origin of the minimalist style or genre in Young's childhood recollection of the sound made by the wind whistling though the cracks in the walls of the Bern, Idaho, log cabin in which he was born. This primordial sound is then understood to be referred to and reiterated later by related acoustical experiences such as buzzing electrical wires, train whistles, and the humming of lathes and drills in a machine shop in which Young worked as a teenager.[51] Young's innate affection for long tones thus acts as minimalism's original "form of content," which will find its "form of expression" in various compositions, most notably Young's justly celebrated *Trio for Strings*, a serial piece remarkable for its sparse stretching of single chords for minutes at a time.[52] "The telephone poles in Bern," relates Potter, "produced a continuous chord from which, much later, [Young] recalled the four pitches he named the 'Dream Chord,' basing many of his mature works on it."[53]

It need not detract from the importance, innovation, or quality of works such as Young's *Trio* to question the manner in which such a "history" of minimalism – presented as a linear trajectory almost entirely cut off from cultural forces and enshrined in myth – subsequently projects this form of content both backward and forward: back past even Young's childhood, to the Greek mathematician and philosopher Pythagoras and the eternal harmony of the spheres;[54] forward, with equal autonomy, as a content expressed again and again in pieces from Young's *Trio* to his *Composition 1960* #7 (the famous perfect fifth to be held "for a long time") to the Theatre of Eternal Music, *The Well-Tuned Piano*, the "melodic" versions of *The Four Dreams of China*, and beyond. This "history" of minimalism is really a metaphysics and at its most extreme finds in each work's particular manifestation a recollection (and container) of an unchanging, universal essence.[55] Within the larger history of minimalism, this originary content, variously modified and inflected, continues through the canonic lineage connecting Young to Riley to Reich to Glass, a trajectory that is presented, both collectively and in each individual case, as illustrative of the increasing sophistication and establishment of minimalism, a trajectory that ends in opera and appearances at the Brooklyn Academy of Music.[56]

It is against the backdrop of such an institutionalizing history – a history of minimalism's development as a style *of* the institution – that Conrad's *Early Minimalism* developed. And it is against this historical construction, much more so than against Young as an individual, that Conrad's aesthetico-historical position attains a significance that exceeds him as an individual, as well. The stakes of this position are nonetheless articulated through the notion of authorship, the role and standing of the composer within minimalism's development. There is little doubt that something occurred in Conrad's mind (and Cale's, as well) around 1965 that was evident to him even then: In letters of that November, Conrad unequivocally terms Young "the leader of our group," yet pointedly characterizes the Theatre of Eternal Music in terms of a "collaboration."[57] It is also fairly clear that Young acknowledges having been confronted with some understanding of Conrad and Cale's position as early as 1964, a situation that led to the compromise agreement of presenting the names of each of the group's members in the hierarchical, diamond-shaped arrangement that appeared on announcements at the time: Young receiving "top billing," Conrad and Cale below and to each side of him, and Zazeela directly below.[58] Young, however, is also within his rights to maintain that he never accepted Conrad and Cale's claims as legitimate (the mere fact of there being a compromise would indicate that he never fully relinquished his position). Perhaps, as he later argued, he always considered improvisation as a form of composition, one that could be attributed to a composer by name.[59]

The particulars of this conflict, now doubtlessly compounded on both sides by years of antagonism, may never be resolved. In any event, to remain on the level of such intentions and (mis)-understandings does not get one very far. Though it may have been enabling for Conrad's own artistic project, the personal nature of the conflict between Conrad and Young confronts the historian as more of a debilitating block, albeit one perhaps too easily bypassed in the canonical and linear historical trajectory described above. Nevertheless, this "war for control of meaning" (as Kelley would call it) between Young and Conrad exemplifies a situation in which, as Foucault has argued, the origin, the historical origin, is never a point, locatable or not, never a single moment in time, but rather an interstice, a gap, a "non-place," a site of confrontation between "originating" forces, the "adversaries" within the situation, which do not occupy or operate on the same level or realm: "Consequently, no one is responsible for an emergence; no one can glory in it, since it always occurs in the interstice."[60] The differences between Young and Conrad, as we noted earlier, are differences in kind. Though Conrad has recently engaged in aspects of his own mythologization,[61] his claim, at its most productive and radical, is not that he is the author, or that he, Cale, and Young are coauthors, or even that the music in dispute is entirely authorless. His claim, rather, is that in some profound and significant manner, the musical legacy of minimalism was to put the institution of authorship into question. If on one side of this "conflict" is located the construction of the author, a composer who guards all of his or her traditional attributes, on the other is a very different instance of what Foucault has called an "author-function."

• • •

It is Foucault, in fact, to whom Conrad attributes the theoretical perspective that enabled *Early Minimalism*. Conrad had previously been interested in various aspects of Foucault's thought — in 1988, he produced a video installation, *Panopticon*, based on *Discipline and Punish* (Figure 1.11) — but *Early Minimalism* achieved a new level of sophistication and focus by connecting the issues of history to those of power.[62] The most important reference for *Early Minimalism* is no doubt to be found in the essay "What Is an Author?" in which Foucault outlines the role played by the notion of authorship in the functioning of a discourse. Specific to a discourse, as opposed to an oeuvre, is that it is *initiated* by a

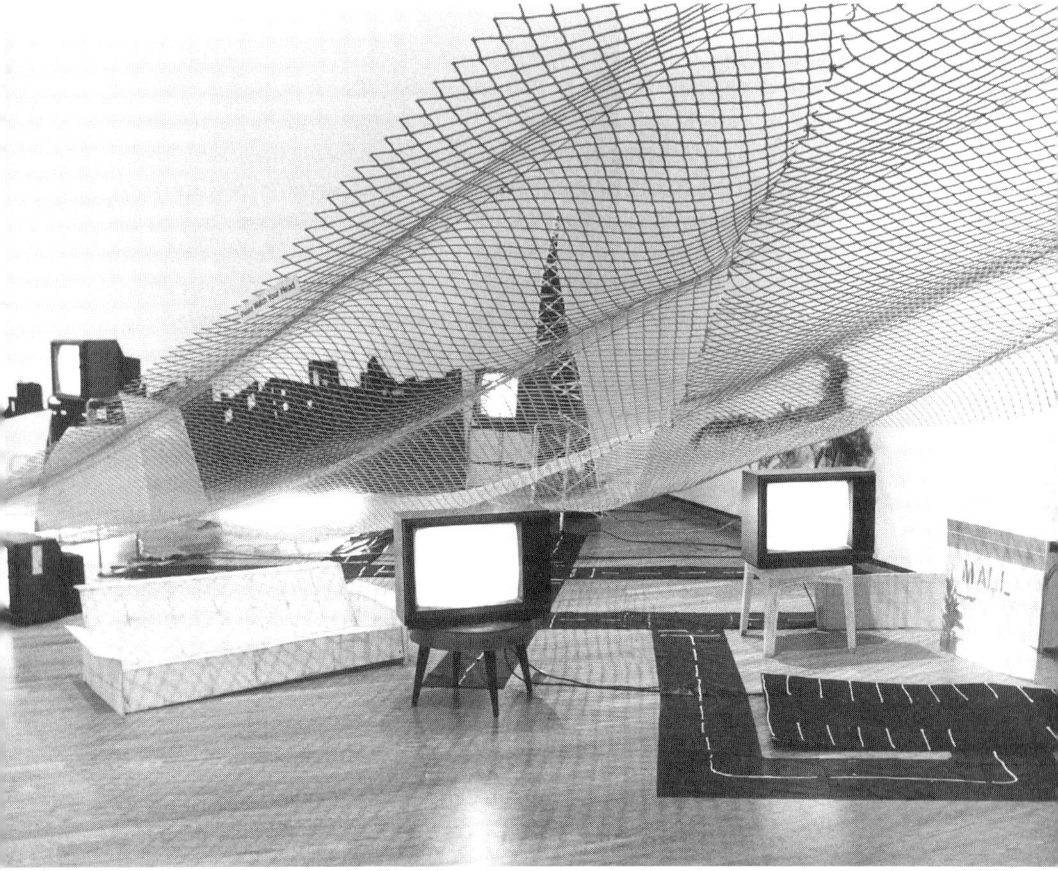

Figure 1.11. Tony Conrad, *Panopticon*, 1988. Herbert F. Johnson Museum of Art, Cornell, New York. Courtesy Tony Conrad.

enabled a certain type of historical construction, not only an attribution of authorship, intention, and expression, but a positioning of the very cultural and historical stakes of the discourse as a whole, stakes that were for Conrad, as we will see, ultimately and from the outset political in nature.[66] With *Early Minimalism*, Conrad set about a return by which to shift the discursive center of gravity from Young's *Trio for Strings* or the wind in his Bern, Idaho, log cabin to the moment of the Theatre of Eternal Music that Conrad would now term "the Big Bang of minimalism."[67]

• • •

If it was Foucault who provided the theoretical basis for Conrad's *Early Minimalism* project, it was the contemporary postmodern practices within the visual arts that indicated the means by which Conrad would carry it out. Conrad had long known artists such as Cindy Sherman and Robert Longo and saw in their work and that of others of the "Pictures" generation, such as Jack Goldstein, a type of appropriation he could develop within music.[68] In the years before embarking on *Early Minimalism*, Conrad had already begun practicing a form of musical postmodernism in his seven-year piano project, *Music and the Mind of the World* (1976–83), which resulted in some three hundred hours of recordings. Conrad included within the "finished" work aspects of practice, qualitatively "bad" technique, and the appropriation of "folk-classical-pop-'ethnic' sources."[69] For Conrad, *Music and the Mind of the World* was an attempt to claim for Western piano music not only a diversity of styles and tropes, but also facets of music's social and cultural contexts, and it might be seen as a sort of counterpoint to the increasingly mystical framework surrounding Young's *The Well-Tuned Piano*. Whereas Young, for instance, claimed that when playing the partially improvised *The Well-Tuned Piano* he opened himself up to higher powers that channeled through him, Conrad, in the *100 Songs* section of *Music and the Mind of the World* (1980), subjected his playing to a litany of withering insults recorded by himself and filmmaker Beth B—

instigating an equal, but more evident and contestatory power relation in the performance.[70]

In *Early Minimalism*, Conrad was willfully putting himself into a paradoxical position, becoming the "author" or "composer" by means of appropriating practices he claimed challenged the notion of author or composer. Somewhat like Cindy Sherman's *Untitled Film Stills*, *Early Minimalism* founded authorship on the appropriation of an authorless "source"—although in Conrad's case, a source that was more actively suppressed than the diffuse and ubiquitous cinematic tropes that Sherman distilled from the cultural imaginary.[71] Conrad's *Early Minimalism* performances would take place behind a scrim, backlit so that the musicians appear in silhouette, connoting (as in Plato's parable of the cave) the concerts' function as a "shadow," a representation of an absent event. Conrad's presentation worked to sunder the moment allegorically in a manner reminiscent of Goldstein's performances: "They appeared as if déjà vu, remote, spectral, yet just as certainly, present."[72]

On an acoustical register, Conrad's *Early Minimalism* "compositions" also acknowledged and instituted a certain temporal and historical differentiation from their "source":

> As a *present* performance, EARLY MINIMALISM stands before you on its own; but paradoxically, it somehow also trails a shadow—a question (unexpounded and therefore unanswered, but forever posed) of what "might have been." What if the Dream Music had never stopped, and instead had moved in the direction that EARLY MINIMALISM signifies? What if EARLY MINIMALISM is an overdue return on a forgotten promise? In calling upon a lost time, EARLY MINIMALISM is a sign of that time's passing, and a measure of that absence.[73]

Although recalling and largely maintaining the structure and materials of the earlier Theatre of Eternal Music, the act of recovery itself, as Conrad maintains, has the possibility of indicating or activating alternative receptions—paying attention, as it were, to "those things registered in the interstices of the [musical] text" to which Conrad had returned: "The 'accurate reconstruction' of the past does not access a real (non-recoverable) past, but it does represent this recoverability. Our image of the past *is* the 'real' past; and this past is always a 'reconstructed' one, albeit not a unique one."[74] This transformation in the understanding and reception of the original group's music was specifically vectored not only against the "unrecoverability" of the unreleased tapes in Young's archive, but also against the built-up mythos of the music's relation to the ahistorical and eternal harmony of the spheres to which their legacy had been (and continues to be) attached by Young and those historians who follow him.[75] By contrast, Conrad's perception and presentation of the music of the Theatre of Eternal Music resembles, to a certain extent, the texture of history as described by Foucault: disparate, fabricated structures beyond any finality. For Conrad, just intonation gave rise to a set of harmonic ratios that opposed the accepted conventions of Western harmony, not via a more correct, rational, or universal form of harmony, but through a "dissonant but not discordant" multiplicity, one that opposes an unquestioned hegemony to model and open up a contestatory and contradictory social space.[76] "*Heterophony* is the sound of radical democracy," Conrad exclaimed to his imaginary interlocutor, Pythagoras: "interwoven individual voices, in their full multiplicity."[77] In this way, Conrad's *Early Minimalism* project did not hide and in fact foregrounded the fact that history is a site of interpretation and contestation, a wrestling with contemporary issues and stakes.

What *Early Minimalism* thus brought forward was not merely an usurpation or alternate claim to authorship, but a reformulation of the originary moment of minimal music along the lines called for by Foucault's "What Is an Author?"—an interrogation of the acknowledged and particular construction of the connection between a named individual and his or her attributed works. In this, the contested moment within the development of the Theatre of Eternal Music—the moment from 1964 to 1966 when the attribution of authorship is in question—stands as a particular, but far from exceptional case within the more general problematic of constructing *any* oeuvre. A shift in emphasis in the particular practices and assumptions that underlie authorship further opens up questions relevant to the understanding, place, and relative valorization of those works in which authorship—as the attribution of a piece to a name—remains uncontested. What is included or excluded within the corpus of Young's or Conrad's work? What or who is included or excluded from the history of minimalism? What divides or determines the boundaries of that history as musical composition, artistic practice, or, perhaps, both? Ultimately, as much as *Early Minimalism* posits a particular place for Conrad within the historical record, it implicitly, but profoundly reformulates the place and importance of minimalism itself, not primarily by devaluing Young, but on the contrary, by opening both Young's and Conrad's work up to a broader and more significant (or at least different) set of questions and concerns.

• • •

It is in this manner and on this set of issues that Conrad's *Early Minimalism* comes into contact with the "minor history" that Kelley and Oursler put forth in *The Poetics Project*. Both younger artists were well aware of Conrad's project at the time they initiated their own, and Kelley's description of the type of historical recovery undertaken in *The Poetics Project* resonates strongly with issues broached in *Early Minimalism*. The questions of historical constructedness discussed in Kelley's *Short Guide* statement (quoted above) similarly follow a Foucauldian genealogical outlook, refusing the ascription of stable origins in favor of a field of historical contingencies, an archive always in contestation as an effect of power. As Kelley explained further, "the critical analyses which accompany [*The Poetics Project*], though reflective of period issues, [are] colored by hindsight," and it is in this sense that the history it presents was, according to Kelley, a specific type of "fiction."[78] (Conrad's and Kelley and Oursler's projects may perhaps best be understood as parts of an extended dialogue or discussion.

Before Conrad turned his attention from piano back to violin, reopening a chapter of musical history that he had all but considered closed, Kelley had asked him to take up violin to play a segment of *The Anvil Chorus* as part of his performance *The Monitor and the Merrimac* at Hallwalls in Buffalo in 1981 [while Oursler appeared on snare drum] [Figure 1.12]. The following year, a letter from Conrad recounts his enthusiastic reaction to Kelley's first one-person exhibition at Metro Pictures gallery in New York.[79])

It is not, however, merely in its insistence on its nature as a construction that *The Poetics Project* takes on the character of a "minor history" that Kelley attributes to it, but more importantly in a certain opposition to existent historical forms. "Minor histories," Kelley declared, "are ones that have yet found no need to be written. Thus they must find their way into history via forms that already exist, forms that are considered worthy of consideration. Thus minor histories are at first construed to be parasitic."[80]

Kelley's notion of minor history is provocative and can be extended via analogy with Gilles Deleuze and Félix Guattari's ideas of "minor science" and "minor literature" that, no doubt, to some extent lie behind it. According to Deleuze and Guattari, "major" and "minor" are not simply quantitatively opposed, nor are they qualitatively opposed, when quality is judged on a commensurate scale: higher or lower, better or worse, more or less significant.[81] The major is rather what can be made to serve as an idea, category, or constant against which, whether explicitly or implicitly, other phenomena are measured. As an ideal, form, or standard that arises out of concrete phenomena, the major doubles and is therefore never entirely coincident with any manifestation from which it is derived or to which it is applied.[82] Deleuze and Guattari's examples are major languages and major sciences, standardized and homogenized in the interests of regulation by a king, a state, or an institution – allied, in other words, with sovereignty, instituted in every case in the interests of erecting or maintaining a hierarchical power. This is true even if that power is an avowedly revolutionary one, as in a revolutionary party that wants to claim

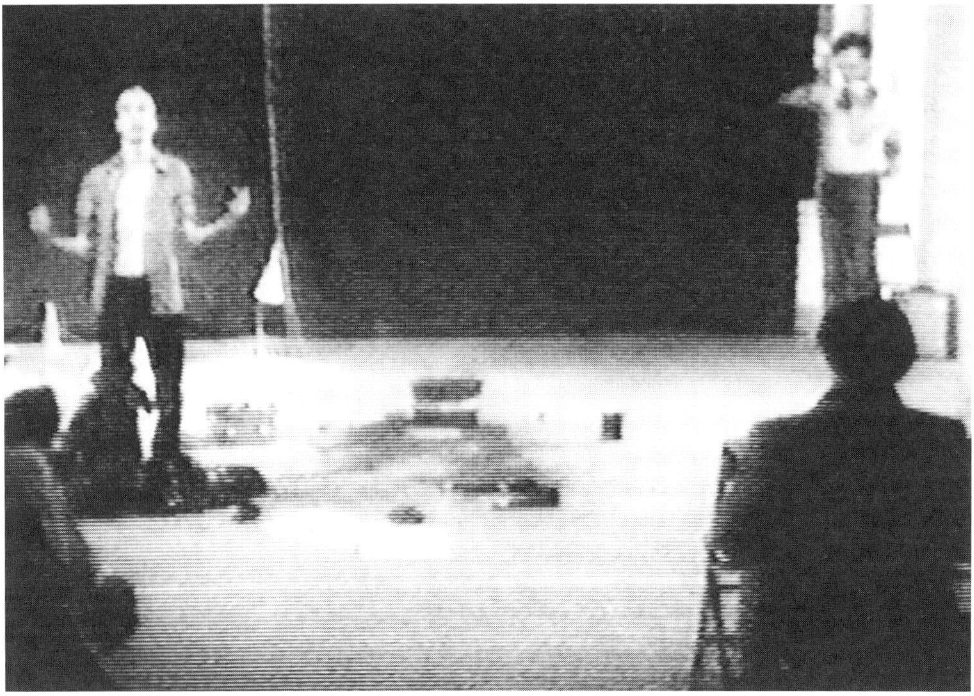

Figure 1.12. Mike Kelley, *The Monitor and the Merrimac*, 1981, performed at Hallwalls Contemporary Art Center, Buffalo, New York. Tony Conrad on violin. Video still courtesy of Kelley Studio.

power or substitute one hierarchy for another. Against this, the "minor" is not the qualitatively or quantitatively inferior, but what is marked by an irreducible or uncontainable difference. It is not a subcategory or subsystem in a conventional sense, but what Deleuze and Guattari term at one point an "outsystem" (*hors-système*).[83]

When Deleuze and Guattari put history and minority into opposition, declaring in *A Thousand Plateaus* that "there is no history but of the majority," they are discussing major history, what Foucault designated "historian's history," history, as they sometimes write it, with a capital "H." It is history allied with "macropolitics . . . in which it is a question of knowing how to win or obtain a majority."[84] Such a history is told according to the constants, even temporally changing constants, that it can extract: authorship, movement, period, style, genre, medium, discipline, and so on. It retains of variable and heterogeneous historical developments only what it can thereby appropriate into major categories and tells of minor figures and developments only in relation to such constants. All the rest it turns into a set of ancillary names and facts without impact; it renders them "context" or else simply represses or ignores them.

A minor history, on the other hand, does not rise out of its discursive context in such a manner as to pose or narrate such categorical standards. It is more immanently related to the archive, so as to be extractable only incompletely and with difficulty. In this, it relates to the gray meticulousness of Foucault's genealogy and the author-function that, "partially at the expense of themes and concepts that an author places in his work . . . could also reveal the manner in which discourse is articulated on the basis of social relationships."[85] Thus, it does not proceed from point to point in clearly articulated relations of development (from minimalism, say, to postminimalism) or of opposition (as in the dialectics of pop and minimalism or expanded cinema and structural film). Nor is it concerned primarily with adding figures to movements, making great authors out of them, or posing them as aesthetic models to be followed.

Yet although it eschews any attempt to take on a major role or function, a minor history, or a history of "minor" figures, does not lack all relation to major categories, historical transformations, movements, or individuals. On the contrary, a minor history is always in a relation to such categories. It is, however, as Kelley noted, in a "parasitic" relation to them. A minor history should not be confused with a history of isolated developments, the idiolects of a naïve artist or practitioner of a sort of *art brut*. Neither is a minor history devoted to those figures that strive for self-containment, movements unto themselves (figures in art history such as Joseph Cornell, perhaps, or Lucas Samaras, or Lee Bontecou). Even less is it an anonymous history. "Minor" figures have a tendency to remain known; they do not pass entirely out of the historical record. But their trajectory through history takes a different direction from that of "major" artists. A minor history represents a different sort of development, which impacts or passes by each categorical point, each acknowledged grouping. "The line," as Deleuze and Guattari state, "does not go from one point to another, but runs *between points* in a different direction that renders them indiscernible."[86] If "minor" artists retain a place within major history — sometimes a central place — it is on account of their relation of proximity to the movements and categories engendered by major history and because of the unceasing pressure that they exert upon them. Their persistence within the historical record, as a remainder (via preterition or slightly awkward footnotes), is a mark or acknowledgment of their effect. (This is the case, for example, with Henry Flynt's "concept art" in relation to conceptualism, as discussed in Chapter 4.) It is for this reason that "minor" figures often appear from the point of view of major history to be an unruly and indistinct mob (as Fluxus, for example, is often treated), misguided or underdeveloped practitioners, members of "transitional and limitrophe" movements, inhabitants of aesthetic "zones of indiscernibility."[87] Appearing at the fringes of major movements or styles, their relation to them is one of deterritorialization, opening these categories up to heterological connections and interactions. These fringes or margins, however, are sometimes found at the very center of major categories or movements; a "minor" figure may — perhaps fleetingly, perhaps not — become essential to the development of a major category or movement without, however, being fully contained. (Conrad's *The Flicker* holds such a place within the category of structural film, as we will see in Chapter 6.) Though minor artistic activities or practices can and do appear within movements or categories (again, a minor history is not an anonymous or isolated history), they often do so in a matter that is seemingly too prolix, too heterogeneous, too variable, too undeveloped for major histories to account for. Sometimes they exist within several (even incompatible) categories at once; sometimes they move through them too quickly; sometimes they appear within them too early or too late. In all cases, however, they take the category out of itself (if they are considered seriously), make it other than it is, transform it beyond recognition.

In so doing, a minor history opens categories to their outside, onto a field of historical contingencies and events that is never homogeneous and that is always political. A minor history, in its deterritorializing relation to major categories, does not dissolve them into a space in which all developments would be equal or equivalent: a weak version of cultural studies, material culture, or visual culture in which everything is equally as worthy of attention as everything else, in which mere generality is the manner in which relations are made. (This is a type of homogeneity that, as Deleuze and Guattari make clear, is also related to institutional forms of power.)[88] Against both extreme antinomies and homogeneous leveling, a minor history poses a field of continual differentiation: specific networks and connections. Like each minor language, each minor history delimits "a properly dialectical zone of variation."[89] Against the major history's extraction of constants and their linear or oppositional enchaining ("even if those constants are only relations between variables"), the role of a minor history is to engage in a "process of deterritorialization [that] constitutes and extends the territory itself."[90] "The figure to which we are referring," Deleuze and Guattari write of the minor, "is continuous variation, as an amplitude that continually oversteps the representative threshold of the majoritarian standard, by excess or default."[91]

• • •

It is from this perspective that I propose to turn the notion of minor history found in Kelley and Oursler's *Poetics Project* back onto an examination of Conrad's production and interactions in the 1960s and to consider him as a "minor artist": minor, not in the sense of a judgment of quality — any such misreading should quickly be dispelled by the fact that Deleuze and Guattari's primary example of a "minor" author is Franz Kafka — nor, of course, to attempt to claim him as a member of a minority, but as an indicator of a certain trajectory through and within an artistic and historical milieu. Conrad is precisely the type of figure whose work's historical reception has thus far been hindered by its appearance in seemingly incompatible contexts, its crossing of medium and disciplinary boundaries, and its developmental precocity and prolixity. Conrad broached the issue himself in 1975: "I tend to fear at times for the world's perception of my own work: though *I* find my own oeuvre impeccably consistent and directed, its diversity (I realize) obscures the plane of this consistency from any but the most careful analyst."[92]

Although integrally related to Conrad's own Foucauldian project outlined above, this book will not stage exactly the same historical return as *Early Minimalism*. *Early Minimalism* located the initiating point of a minimalist discourse in the Theatre of Eternal Music's adoption of just intonation and the elaboration of the drone-based music of its Dream Syndicate phase. Emboldened in part by Conrad's heterogeneous deployment of strategies deriving from both visual art and music, the return proposed here will aim at a slightly earlier historical moment: the period around 1959 when Young and Conrad first met in California, when Conrad made his first forays into composition, and when Young began to put the very notions of "composition" and "music" into question with his first post-Cagean scores. To see this moment as the initiation of the discourse of minimalism fundamentally transforms the nature of that discourse, the rules of formation that it implicitly and not so implicitly proposes — and it does so not least by putting into question not just the role of the author or composer, but also the distinction between the disciplines of music and the visual arts at this time. Struggling above all with the legacy of John Cage, whose impact on art and music is still little understood, minimalism in its widest ramification arose from the beginning, or so it will be my contention, as an audio-visual movement. And in the particular network of interactions and developments to be traced through and around Conrad — who will serve less as the monographic subject of this book than as the Orpheus guiding our return to minimalist prehistory and a certain facet of the New York underground (Figure 1.13) — minimalism will also be seen as an interaction of major and minor forces, deriving from and cathected onto different modes and models of power.

To designate and examine Conrad as "minor" in this way is to acknowledge the manner in which he problematizes the terms "musician," "composer," "artist," "filmmaker," and so on. Something of what is at stake has been raised by French art historian Hubert Damisch when discussing the related case of multiple-media artist Michael Snow. "Michael Snow," writes Damisch of the Canadian painter/sculptor/photographer/filmmaker/ musician,

> is no more a musician doing photography or a painter doing films than Joseph Conrad was a Pole who wrote in English.... But neither is he, to use a hallowed expression, a "multimedia" artist employing concurrently, or even simultaneously, different means of expression. Such a notion ... ignores the distinction that ought to be made between *media* understood as a means of transmitting signals bearing a written, aural or visual message and *mediums* as designating the very fabric or substance of which signals and messages are made. And finally it smacks of that literally totalitarian notion of the *Gesamtkunstwerk*, and although we know only too well to which ends the "total artwork" myth lent itself, at Nuremburg and elsewhere, a whole century will not have sufficed to take the winds out of its sails.

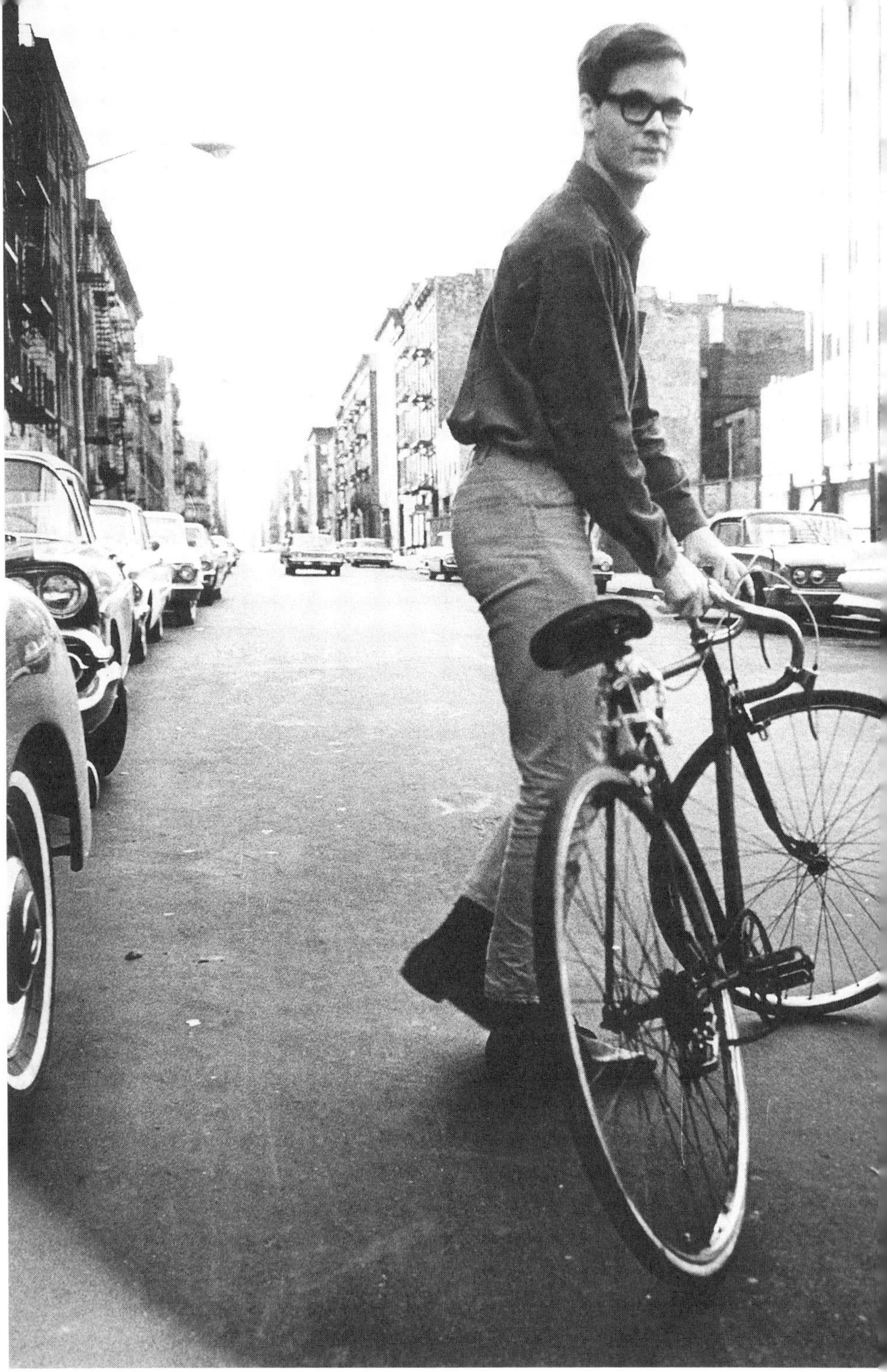

Figure 1.13. Tony Conrad, 1966. Photo: Frederick Eberstadt, used by permission.

> If an "artist" exists in the form or name of Michael Snow, it is in a strictly differential way, having found no better place to settle down and operate than in the gaps, in the distances between the different *mediums* that he puts into play, the various *media* to which he has recourse, and the practices that correspond to them. The effect (or Should I say the issue or the aim?), in terms of both "object" and "subject," has less to do with translation or transposition than with dialogue and exchange.[93]

There is much in Damisch's characterization that would be as applicable to Conrad as to Snow: the caution against totalization of either artist or body of work, for instance, as well as the related insistence on a differential or internally divided artistic subjectivity. If anything, the distinctions — both "mediumistic" and "mediamatic" — within Conrad's production are starker and more apparently irreconcilable than those Damisch describes. For it is not just the variety of mediums, media, and even disciplines that Conrad has practiced, but the broad distinctions in style and underlying structural tenets that make his output appear so diverse. Whereas there is a certain independence and consistency to Snow's production, despite its diversity (signaled, for example, in his recurring "Walking Woman" motif), particular to Conrad's career has been not only internal differentiation, but also an immersion into seemingly incompatible collaborative enterprises: playing in the minimal Theatre of Eternal Music while also doing sound production for Jack Smith's most extravagant films, for example, or producing the starkly abstract *Straight and Narrow* in the same year as the flagrantly narrative *Coming Attractions* (both with Grant).

Part of the reason that Conrad has not received wider recognition is that his production has not been containable within the various cultural movements or categories by which the period is commonly charted. Although they are alternately more central or peripheral to minimalism, Fluxus, early conceptualism, underground and structural film, paracinema or expanded cinema, artistic performance, video, and more, addressing his contributions within any one of these areas singly (to which the writing on Conrad has, to date, largely been confined) does little to provide an understanding of either his work or the historical textures from which and in which it was produced. Instead, Conrad's work has to be understood through the situations and dialogues, the networks and interconnections, of which it was a part. Any "consistency" in his oeuvre will be located in the specifics of his interlocutions.

Thus, although what follows will give some measure of Conrad's activities during the 1960s and beyond, fleshing out a startlingly diverse but underresearched figure, the challenge of addressing an artist such as Conrad is unavoidably a methodological one, a challenge not only to the role or concept of authorship, but also to the practice of writing history and particularly to the practice of writing a monograph. Those who desire no more than facts should be able to glean them easily from the chapters that follow. The text, however, will diverge for long periods from any linear narration of Conrad's development, exploring the contiguous networks and connections of the downtown New York scene, losing Conrad at times to explore others' work and ideas (most notably in Chapter 3) – sometimes to return to their importance for Conrad or Conrad's response to them, sometimes to illustrate the nearly Herculean task of dealing with the legacy of John Cage, sometimes merely to explore other avenues within the cultural network.[94] Like *The Poetics Project*, *Beyond the Dream Syndicate* aims to be a somewhat digressive account of Conrad's work, role, and importance. Though it acts, to some extent, as a bildungsroman, following Conrad from his earliest artistic endeavors to his first widely recognized autonomous production, *The Flicker*, it devotes nearly as much time and material to those in his cohort, including Young and Zazeela, Cale, Grant, Robert Morris, Cornelius Cardew, Henry Flynt, Jack Smith, and others. Its aim is to open up Conrad as an author in a manner analogous to that explored by his own *Early Minimalism* project, to chart through him a minor history of perhaps the most important decade in contemporary American culture.

But more than that, following from the perspectives opened by Foucault and Deleuze and Guattari, the aim of this book is to elucidate a transformation in the manner in which cultural practices relate to models, means, and structures of power. Conrad's trajectory, as we will see, crossed and intersected with a number of aesthetic practices by which an artistic generation that still considered itself avant-garde modeled and struggled against (whether explicitly or implicitly) formations or regimes of power that were not monolithic (despite what the practitioners themselves may have thought), but multiplicitous, heterogeneous, and mixed. Conrad's first film, *The Flicker*, with which the period covered by this book will end, will be seen to model one aspect, perhaps the most advanced, of contemporary power—"control"—but to get to it, we will necessarily have to pass through many others, charting and understanding the important residual refunctionings and imbrications of both sovereign and disciplinary power as they were modeled and engaged in related artistic practices. It is in this way that our minor history will attempt to open onto one of the major questions of our time.

Chapter Two

The Social Turn

Our history begins, not arbitrarily, but nonetheless contingently, in 1959 in Berkeley, California, where Tony Conrad and La Monte Young first met. A mathematics major at Harvard, Conrad had a job doing technical illustrations and writing that allowed him to spend the summer in California after his sophomore year.[1] Through a classmate, Conrad was introduced to Ralph Costa, a Chilean poet, who helped him find an apartment on Haste Street, just around the corner from where Young and Dennis Johnson were living on Telegraph Avenue. When Costa introduced him to Conrad, Young was a master's composition student who had already played in jazz ensembles for a number of years and who had produced several pieces in the drawn-out serial style that had become his signature: *for Brass* (1957), *for Guitar* (1958), and *Trio for Strings* (1958). Always extremely confident in his abilities, Young already held *Trio for Strings* in particularly high esteem, lauding it to Conrad the next spring as one of the best works of music ever written.[2]

Conrad had by then already come to know Henry Flynt, whom he befriended at Harvard during their freshman year, in part because they both played violin. Conrad had studied violin for a number of years before college at the Peabody Conservatory of Music in Baltimore and privately with Ronald Knudson, a future member of the Boston Symphony Orchestra whom he credits with introducing him to the acoustical principles of frequencies and harmonics. Conrad also played for a time in the Harvard student orchestra—"You know, hacked away at second violin, and never practiced, and so forth"—before becoming disillusioned with it and with his studies in general.[3] At the time they met, Flynt, Conrad avers, was a "much better, much more studied" violinist than he was. More importantly, it was Flynt, according to Conrad, who pushed him toward an appreciation of modern and contemporary music, to which he had not yet been exposed:

> He challenged my musical taste and said that if I thought Tchaikovsky was the greatest, or whatever, that actually Bartók was greatest, and asked "What's the greatest?" and all of this.... While we were freshman, he would say, like, "Look at the art structure in this, the use of themes...." All this formal machinery was brought into play in his insistence that this modern music was much better.

Conrad would recall an epiphany one day when he realized that the tune in his head, which he could not quite place, was none other than the Bartók that Flynt had insisted he procure and study.[4]

As a result of what soon became a good-naturedly competitive inquiry into the most avant-garde developments, Conrad keyed into Harvard's burgeoning new-music scene, supported partly by the Music Department, but much more so by graduate students such as David Behrman and Frederic Rzewski and the young classics professor and Cage protégé, Christian Wolff. Under the auspices of the Harvard-Radcliffe Music Club, this group offered regular concerts of new music, performing and premiering their own compositions, as well as those of Cage, Karlheinz Stockhausen, Aaron Copland, Anton Webern (an old master in this context), and more.

> I did go back and tell Henry that there were these concerts going on [and] that he should check into this stuff. And when he did, he was amused and astonished that I, who obviously had no understand-

> ing of the "superior matters" with which he was involved (laughs), had somehow found my way into a circle where he had been left in the dust with Bartók — because this was *much* more advanced than Bartók!

Among the most important events that Conrad recalls attending during his first two years was a lecture by Stockhausen titled "New Instrumental and Electronic Music" and a lecture and demonstration by Cage and David Tudor.[5]

While at Berkeley, the eighteen-year-old Conrad accompanied Young and Johnson to several of the seminars offered that summer by Rudolf Kolisch, brother-in-law of Arnold Schoenberg and founder of the famous Kolisch Quartet, who analyzed Pierre Boulez's *Structures* (1951–52) and Luigi Nono's *Varianti* (1957) in detail.[6] Conrad was also particularly keen to hear Young's and Johnson's recordings of contemporary music, still at that time a relatively rare commodity. Conrad had already begun to think of himself as a composer, or was at least making inroads in that direction, as was Flynt. Flynt, who was simultaneously developing his own version of concrete poetry, had in fact premiered an experimental composition entitled *Trio* (1959) at Harvard in his sophomore year. According to Flynt, the work, now destroyed, was "largely imitative of Cage, with an elaborate chance and chronometric structure, a pointillist sound realization, and bizarre instrumental techniques and movement of performers in the theatre space."[7] (The effect of Flynt's piece was immediate. After having witnessed it, the next musician, who was supposed to play Webern, left, rather than appear on the same bill.) Although Conrad had also been influenced by the generally Cagean atmosphere surrounding Harvard's graduate music students, his own reception of Cage at the that time was largely confined to the more general avant-garde notion of extending one's taste toward the acceptance and incorporation of nontraditional musical materials. In this, Cage's Harvard lecture served to confirm, rather than to initiate, the attitude that Conrad had already received from Flynt's challenge to understand, accept, and even like modern compositions.

From Bartók, Conrad progressively extended this attitude to the more contemporary avant-garde compositions he heard at Harvard and, eventually, to a more specifically Cage-like appreciation of the nonmusical sounds of nature and the environment.

More important than Cage for Conrad's initial forays into composition, however, seems to have been the example set by Stockhausen, whose Harvard demonstration had included several of his own compositions—perhaps *Studie I* (1953) and *Studie II* (1954) and probably, according to Conrad's recollection, *Gesang der Jünglinge* (1955–56)—as well as György Ligeti's *Artikulation* (1958). At Berkeley, Conrad was already experimenting with his own tape music, making loops from as many as several hundred bits of one-sixteenth-of-an-inch lengths of magnetic tape. One of Conrad's interests at the time and afterward was the liminal or threshold relationship between pitch and rhythm, accessible through the tape recorder's ability to alter playback speed. Conrad explored this phenomenon, in part, by manipulating recordings of metronomes, speeding their clicking, rhythmic beat until it blended into a what could be perceived as a continuous "tone." Conrad later incorporated a variation of this interest into a sextet that he wrote for three violins and three metronomes, the score for which he mailed to Young in the spring of 1960 (*Sextet for Metronomes and Violins: Variations on a Theme of K. Stockhausen*, revised as *Sextet for Violins and Metronomes* [both ca. 1959]).

Already by 1959, Conrad understood the avant-garde incorporation of nontraditional musical materials to include not only noise, percussion, magnetic tape, and electronics, but also alternate tuning systems for stringed instruments such as his violin. This idea had been motivated, in part, by his discovery in the Harvard music library of the scordatura violin works of seventeenth-century composer Heinrich Ignaz Franz von Biber. (Scordatura works employ alternate tunings for the open strings of a string instrument to achieve their effects.) "Biber astonished me; the whole idea of finding polyphonic—that is two-note—music for my instrument, where I put the violin out of tune and then it did these amazing things, and I heard resonances in the instrument...

it was very stirring for me."[8] Some time before April 1960, Conrad retuned a piano and taped a set of improvisations that he sent to Young, a potential precedent for Young's own semi-improvisational opus *The Well-Tuned Piano*, for which Young retuned a piano in just intonation in March 1964.[9]

After the summer of 1960, which Conrad spent as a computer-programming trainee at Copenhagen's Universitets Fysik-Kemiske Institut (from which he continued to correspond with Young), he decided to pursue both facets of his musical interests. Taking a leave of absence from Harvard, Conrad spent the next academic year traveling through Europe, particularly in Germany, searching out scores for both seventeenth-century polyphonic music and contemporary works and spending a month at the Darmstadt Institute studying scores and recordings of the contemporary avant-garde. Notebooks kept from this time reveal Conrad putting himself through a rigorous self-tutoring. He was particularly interested, at first, in the work of Edgar Varèse and particularly that of Alois Hába, who had developed, respectively, alternative twenty-four-note and forty-note microtonal tuning systems, though he also studied the work of George Antheil, Luigi Nono, Richard Maxfield, Bruno Madera, Bo Nilsson, Henri Pousseur, and others.

At Darmstadt, Conrad visited Hermann Heiß's electronic-music studios and eventually obtained an introduction to Stockhausen, whom he tracked down at the electronic-music studios in Cologne. Conrad stayed in Cologne for a week (April 13–20, 1961), studying and receiving copies of additional recordings, discussing work with Stockhausen, Ligeti, Herbert Eimert ("a very jovial business-man type German"), and Gottfried Michael König, and generally hanging around the studio, observing.[10] Conrad's notebooks contain observations on all aspects of Stockhausen's production, revealing a particular interest in the effect of combination tones and the relation of pitch to rhythm that he found in some of Stockhausen's plans for using interrelated loudspeakers. (Conrad's notes also include the time of day of Stockhausen's arrival and details of his habitual sartorial appearance: "green corduroy peg pants, billowy shirt," an occasional red, white, and green knit tie, and an ubiquitous leather jacket.)[11] Among the things that, according to Conrad, Stockhausen explained to him was the means by which the auditory reception of regular mechanical pulses is stereophonically related to a listener's proximity to the speakers. If, while standing at an equal distance between the right and left channels, the clicking seemed the same as the actual emission of pulses (at a frequency, for example, of forty cycles, i.e., forty pulses per second), moving toward the speaker on one side would cause the perceived "tone" of the pulses to shift, such that, when directly in front of one speaker, the "tone" would sound as though it were a full octave higher:

> If you stand over to one side and the speakers are far enough apart, [and] the sound from one speaker takes an eightieth of a second longer to get to you than the sound from the other speaker... *then* you hear the sounds from the far speaker *in between* the sounds from the near speaker, which means that the frequency you'll hear will be *eighty* pulses per second.[12]

(Actually, Stockhausen only partially demonstrated the phenomenon to Conrad, who worked out the underlying acoustical principles for himself.)[13] Unbeknownst to Conrad, such "musical" insights were directly related to the type of technology deployed in range-finding equipment for bomber pilots in the German Air Force in World War II. As Friedrich Kittler summarizes it:

> Radio beams emitted from the coast facing Britain, for example from Amsterdam and Cherbourg, formed the sides of an ethereal triangle the apex of which was located precisely above the targeted city. The right transmitter beamed a continuous series of Morse dashes into the pilot's right headphone, while the left transmitter beamed an equally continuous series of Morse dots—always exactly in between the dashes—into the left headphone. As a result, any deviation from the assigned course resulted in the most beautiful ping-pong stereophony (of the type that appeared on the first pop records but has since been discarded). And once the Heinkels [bombers] were

> exactly above London or Coventry, then and only then did the two signal streams emanating from either side of the headphone, dashes from the right and dots from the left, merge into one continuous note, which the perception apparatus could not but locate within the very center of the brain. A hypnotic command that had the pilot — or rather, the center of his brain — dispose of his payload.[14]

It was also in Cologne that Conrad first heard Stockhausen's *Kontakte* (1959–60), one of the most important results of the researches Stockhausen had discussed at Harvard, a prominent feature of which was the continuous relation of pitch and rhythm with which Conrad was already so fascinated. Not surprisingly, Conrad recalls being "particularly stunned" by the piece.[15]

The result of Conrad's year of investigations was *(Prelude and) Fugue for Strings for 18 Solo Instruments*, which he completed at the beginning of April, 1961 and dedicated to "my friend and teacher Henry Flynt" (Figures 2.1 and 2.2). The composition, written in Darmstadt, combined a series of gamelike dependencies (players perform one of a number of passages, depending on how they are cued by other players fulfilling certain preset criteria), with scordatura tunings and a passage in "the 'just' diatonic scale of C."[16] The idea of using dependency relations in *Fugue* seems partly to have been derived from Stockhausen's solo percussion piece, *Zyklus* (1959), the score for which allowed the performer to begin at any page and move successively through the spiral-bound score back to the beginning point. In any case, the impact of *Zyklus* on Conrad seems to have been immediate: His notes continue for only two pages after the analysis of *Zyklus* (and a meticulous hand copy of the score), indicating that he turned at this moment to the composition of *Fugue*.

Although Conrad's *Fugue* was never performed, after he returned for his senior year at Harvard, he would succeed in presenting his next composition, *Three Loops for Performers and Tape Recorders*, at a Harvard-Radcliffe Music Club concert, thereby joining Flynt among the ranks of the university's avant-garde. The premiere and sole performance of Conrad's *Three Loops* (featuring

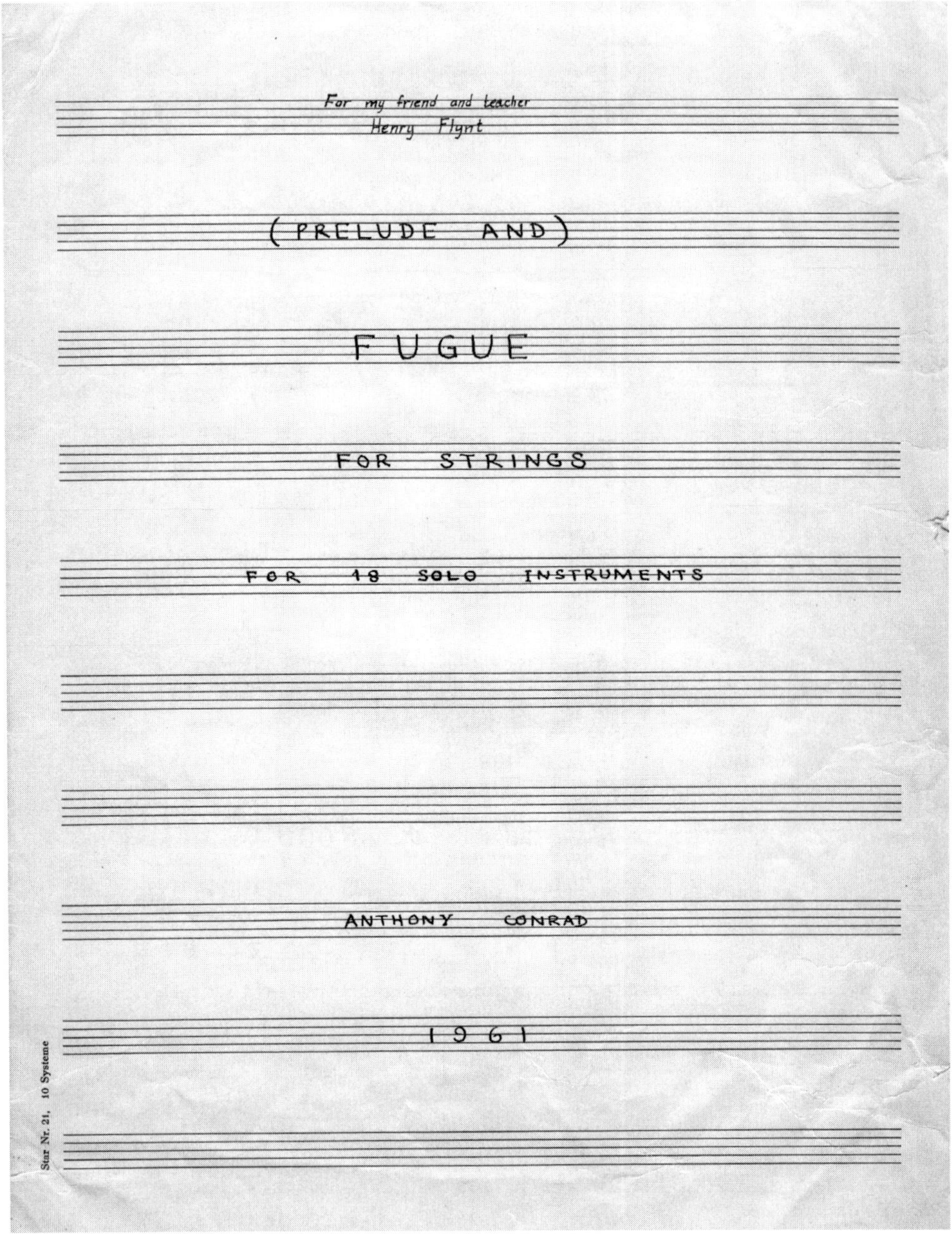

Figure 2.1. Tony Conrad, *(Prelude and) Fugue for Strings for 18 Solo Instruments,* March 24 – April 9, 1961. Cover. Courtesy Tony Conrad.

(PRELUDE AND) FUGUE FOR STRINGS ANTHONY CONRAD

For 18 Solo Instruments:
6 Violins
4 Violas
5 Cellos
3 Basses

Preliminary Note.

The *Fugue for Strings* comprises two sections. The first of these is the composition, *Fugue for Strings*, and the second is a note providing suggestions for performances. Perhaps, in view of the relatively informal style of the second section, it should at this point be made clear that, whatever (if anything) is accepted in the way of suggestion from the second section in any performance of the *Fugue for Strings*, the first section is to be approximated as closely as possible in every detail (intonation, dynamics, etc.).The suggestions of Section II may either be adopted literally, altered to suit the taste or inventiveness of the reader, taken only as stylistic suggestions, or abandoned altogether, so long as in an actual performance all the requirements of Section I are followed. If Section I is neglected or altered in any way, the performance can not be considered a faithful realization of this work.

Section I.

Each player is to be in posession of three parts: the sequence of 18 musical lines, one of the sequences of letters used in ordering the musical lines, and one of the sequences of dependencies. As well, each player is to be made familiar with the Legend and other parts of Section I that may help him comply with the instructions contained therein.

The 18 performers are assigned numbers according to the location they occupy during the performance, which should be according to the following scheme:

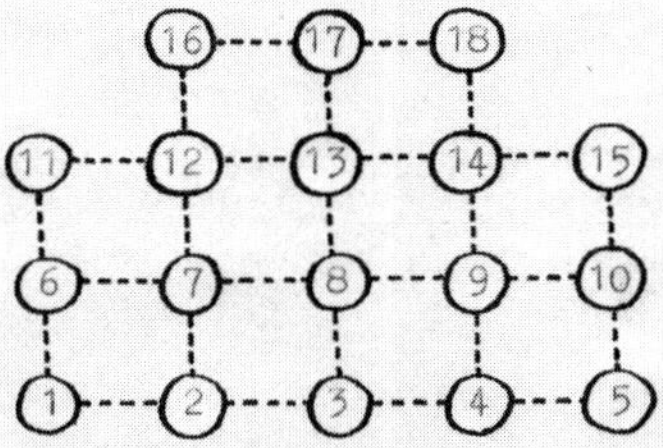

AUDIENCE (if any)

This plan should be easily descernable, with the intermediate distances great enough so that each performer will have more than sufficient space to perform, but not so great that instruments on opposite sides of the array will present strikingly different intensities or tone colors to the listener in the audience. Each performer should be thoroughly fami-

Figure 2.2. Tony Conrad, *(Prelude and) Fugue for Strings for 18 Solo Instruments*, March 24 – April 9, 1961. First page of score. Courtesy Tony Conrad.

Conrad and Christian Wolff among its eight performers) took place on December 18, 1961 (Figure 2.3). John Cage later included a fairly conventionally notated page from the "Aria" section of the work (the second of the three movements) in his edited collection of scores, *Notations*.[17] The most innovative aspect of Conrad's piece, however, was not in the notation, but in Conrad's deployment of two tape recorders that, rather than playing a prerecorded passage of electronic music, were connected as a primitive tape delay to record and play back what occurred on stage, including what had previously been recorded and played back (Figure 2.4). From a certain perspective, *Three Loops* can be seen to take the dependency relations Conrad explored in *Fugue* and mechanize them, absorbing the performance and playing it back as a feedback loop.

Conrad had sketched out the idea behind the tape delay in his notebooks earlier that fall: "*RESONANCE.* Use tape-recorder resonance (3 recorders...) during a concert to give a canonic effect. Perhaps use more than one resonance unit; n-mike systems. Vary length of tape loop, initialization of contents of tape loop, resonance settings, mike distances. Have (n?) tape recorder 'performances' (à la Cage radios)."[18]

In an appendix to the *Three Loops* score, Conrad elaborated on the final setup and effect of his recorders:

> In general, two tape recorders are used, arranged so that one plays what has been recorded some interval of time (referred to as the "tape loop length") previously by the other; the other also records all that is played by the former. Thus sound events occurring at intervals equal to the tape loop length are superposed, to within the fidelity of the recording and playback apparatus.
>
> Various kinds of distortion will more or less rapidly accumulate, depending on the level settings and fidelity of the various components. Although these effects may generally be minimized, they provide an intrinsic part of the performance, and need not be deplored.[19]

I

Chant

Two tape recorders are used (see appendix), with speaker-microphone distance and constant intensity settings so arranged that the relative intensities of the playing recorder and the performers are roughly equal for the audience (preferably at forte level) and the recording tape recorder.

Each performer selects a pitched instrument on which to play within a single pitch band 1/3 tone wide* centered on one of the following (just) intervals above a given frequency: †

Perfect unison
" octave
" fifteenth
" twenty-second
" twenty-ninth

Perfect twelfth
" nineteenth
" twenty-sixth

Major seventeenth
" twenty-fourth
" thirty-first

Minor seventeenth
" twenty-fourth
" thirty-first

Major twentieth
Minor twenty-third
Minor twenty-eighth
Perfect thirty-second

The performing order is ruled by changes (on attack times, as in bells), beginning with any order of the performers. Intensities and durations are free, but at least 1/3 change should be performed during each tape loop. The loop length should not be greater than 1/3 minute.

Performers continue as long as they wish; they may drop out individually, so long as they indicate by a prearranged silent signal that they are doing this. The piece continues until all drop out.

A conductor may be used to direct or call out the changes.

† Example:

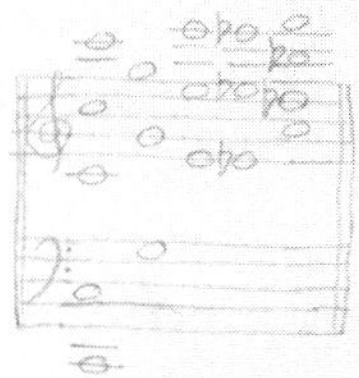

*(Roughly)
—Feb 23, '63

1

Figure 2.3. Tony Conrad, *Three Loops for Performers and Tape Recorders*, November 8–21, 1961. Page 1 ("Chant") of score. Courtesy Tony Conrad.

Appendix

In general, two tape recorders are used, arranged so that one plays what has been recorded some interval of time (referred to as the "tape loop length") previously by the other; the other also records all that is played by the former. Thus sound events occurring at intervals equal to the tape loop length are superimposed, to within the fidelity of the recording and playback apparatus.

Various kinds of distortion will more or less rapidly accumulate, depending on the level settings and fidelity of the various components. Although these effects may generally be minimized, they provide an intrinsic part of the performance, and need not be deplored.

Level settings should be high enough to give the recordings as much body as the live playing, except as otherwise indicated.

Diagram of Tape Recorder Setup

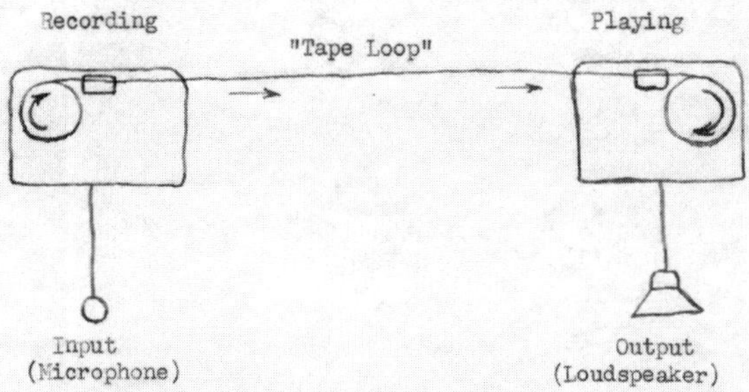

If stereophonic recording equipment is used, interesting effects may be obtained through various arrangements of the speakers and microphones; the general scheme used will still be that of the diagram above.

Moving the microphone(s) and speaker(s) during the performance, correcting the intensity settings appropriately if noticeable intensity variation is caused thereby, may be allowed (and offers, in fact, many good possibilities) so long as this does not directly introduce new sounds (as moving a microphone however usually does).

Throughout, the word "instrument" has been used very liberally to refer not only to the usual musical instruments, but to the voice and more generally to any source of (audible) sound whatever.

8

Figure 2.4. Tony Conrad, *Three Loops for Performers and Tape Recorders*, November 8–21, 1961. Page 8 ("Appendix") of score. Courtesy Tony Conrad.

While not exactly "deploring" the effect made by Conrad's tape recorders, a reviewer from the *Christian Science Monitor* described the resulting sound as "like an air-raid siren inside an oil drum, an anarchy of sound that was highly amusing."[20]

In actual fact, Conrad's performance sounded, in its most ruthlessly fed-back passages, like nothing so much as musique concrète. Particularly in the final section, "Din," in which the tape recorder's volume controls are actively manipulated according to a preset diagram, the rapid changes in amplitude and the audible recurrence of previously played snippets of instrumentation on the tape player (which ultimately overwhelms and subsumes the notes played by actual performers) resemble an edited recording more than a live performance. Although the initial section, "Chant," builds more slowly, with the performers engaged in something like a game—each one, starting in the order in which they are lined up on stage, playing spontaneous changes from a predetermined selection of intervals in just intonation, giving a silent signal to the others when they decide to drop out—it also ultimately ends in a sustained, enveloping, dronelike cacophony of feedback distortion. In the "Aria" section that Cage chose to publish, a single performer (likely, though not necessarily a pianist, according to the score) plays each of six somewhat sparse lines, repeating each one as many times as he or she pleases before moving on to the next (somewhat in the manner of a glacial solo version of Terry Riley's *In C* [1964]). Each line is timed to coincide with the length of the loop of magnetic tape, thus redoubling the performed repetitions in a human-machine duet. While this section takes the longest to build into noise, continuous high-pitched feedback is audible as background to the sounded piano notes, and it, too, ends in resonant cacophony.

Conrad's early exploration of tape delay brings to mind Riley's use of the "time-lag accumulator," another tape-delay device, initially fabricated by a sound engineer in Paris for the production of Riley's *Music for the Gift* (1963).[21] The resemblance is even clearer in another of Conrad's speculative notes, dated to the fall of 1961, which recalls more closely the improvisatory musical technique that Riley later perfected with the time-lag accumulator: "Or use recorders to play a *canon* (adding a part each time through the loop). Each time could change the character, and older lines can be allowed to die out. 'Improvise' to fit in."[22] Another interesting note from the time finds Conrad experimenting with swinging a microphone in front of speakers to produce feedback in the manner of Steve Reich's *Pendulum Music* (1968).[23] Such observations are not, of course, meant to imply that Conrad was the sole originator of either of these techniques, but rather that he understood as well as any of his generation the technical aspects and possibilities of amplification and magnetic tape on which musical minimalism is necessarily dependent.

Such artistic and technical concerns reveal the direction Conrad would likely have followed were he not dialogically engaged with Young, Flynt, and others. Indeed, notes from the time reveal Conrad's desire to engage in the kind of musical researches taking place in Cologne.[24] Nearly all of his formal concerns from this moment would subsequently become integral components of the aesthetic developed by the Theatre of Eternal Music and in other pieces that Conrad realized at the time, such as *Four Violins* and John Cale's *Dream Interpretation* (1969).[25] Once Conrad and Cale were "inside" the Dream Syndicate, alternate tunings, in particular just intonation, would play a major part, as would the threshold relationship of pitch and rhythm, how and where those two phenomena might meld or transform into one another. In the Theatre of Eternal Music, very low, even subsonic pitches and harmonic beating would be understood, at least by Conrad, as contributing an almost subliminal rhythmic element to the group's overwhelming harmonic environment. In the article "Inside the Dream Syndicate," Conrad – referring back, no doubt, to Stockhausen – described the group's exploration of "a synchronous pulse-beat that is the first coherent usage of rhythm-pitches or microtonal intervals outside of isolated electronic pieces."[26] The type of dependency relations found in *Fugue* might also be understood to recur, transposed, in the manner in which each member of the Theatre of Eternal Music could modulate to other frequencies only in relation to and by taking into account what frequencies all the others were playing (one of the aspects that Young maintains was part of the composition, but that Conrad maintains was determined by democratic deliberation). Later, Conrad's concerns with technology, with magnetic tape, and with rhythm/pitch interactions would all recur, albeit somewhat transformed, in the sound track to *The Flicker*, his first major production outside the Dream Syndicate. As he explained to George Henry Romney:

> The soundtrack consists primarily of homemade electronic music composed indissolubly of tones (pitches) bordering closely on the lower range of audibility and of very rapid rhythms, rhythms whose speed is comparable in frequency to the tones. The confusion of pitch and rhythm that occurs in this range gives unexpected birth to a sense of aural vastness and spaciousness. The pitch-rhythm ambiguity has also enabled me to treat the tones as primitive rhythms and vice versa, so that there turns out to be a correlation here with some of the work that La Monte and I (and John Cale and Marian Zazeela) have done in harmony at slightly higher frequencies. This correlation is actually after-the-fact, since the electronic music arose in an independent context [i.e., Conrad's 1959 experiments at Berkeley], but the advantage of the relationship is the suggestion of a working concept of rhythmic harmony.[27]

Without doubt, it is via or through such tropes—understood as aspects of a consistent Conrad "style"—that a continuous linear history, a major history, of Conrad's development from 1959 to 1966 would be written. Indeed, it would even be possible, were one so inclined, to locate the kernel from which all minimal music derived in, say, rhythm/pitch interaction, this being arguably a more characteristic and encompassing trait of the genre as it stretches from Young to Glass than sustained tones. Or, instead of an interstice, the summer of 1959 could be understood as a point of synthesis or conjunction between two artistic predilections that, unbeknownst to either Young or Conrad at the time, foreshadowed their later, mutual development of a musical genre.

Either approach, however, would again verge on a metaphysics, eliminating the historical contingencies by which Conrad's (and minimalism's) development actually transpired. Conrad's route from Stockhausen to *The Flicker* was not linear or direct, but defined by swerves and detours, conflicts and alliances, emulations and collaborations. If a major history would render them as *in*fluences, turning or folding them into the construction of a consistent, stable, and unified artistic subject, the role of a minor history is to turn them *out* in order that the larger network of intersecting positions can be mapped, realized, and understood. The first and perhaps most important of these intersections is to be found in Young's and Conrad's working though and development of the legacy of John Cage (Figure 2.5).

• • •

It was only a few weeks after he and Conrad met that Young headed to Darmstadt for Stockhausen's summer session, where he would encounter Cage's music and ideas in depth for the first time.[28] Whereas Conrad had already been exposed to a number of recent pieces by Cage and associates at Harvard, Young had been familiar only with Cage's *Sonatas and Interludes for Prepared Piano* (1948) and *String Quartet* (1949–50), recordings of which were owned, respectively, by Johnson and another of Young's composer friends, Terry Jennings.[29] At Darmstadt, Young had the opportunity to hear good recordings of the *Concert for Piano and Orchestra* (1958), Cage's most significant chance composition to date, as well as to study his scores and writings. Most important among the latter seem to have been Cage's "Lecture on Nothing" and "Indeterminacy" (first published as "Unbestimmtheit" in Stockhausen's journal *Die Riehe*), the randomly arranged collection of stories that exemplified more than it explained Cage's notion of all things able to come together in an interaction more complex than any predetermined order. As Cage explained in the liner notes to the *Indeterminacy* LP, "My intention in putting 90 stories together in an unplanned way is to suggest that all things, sounds,

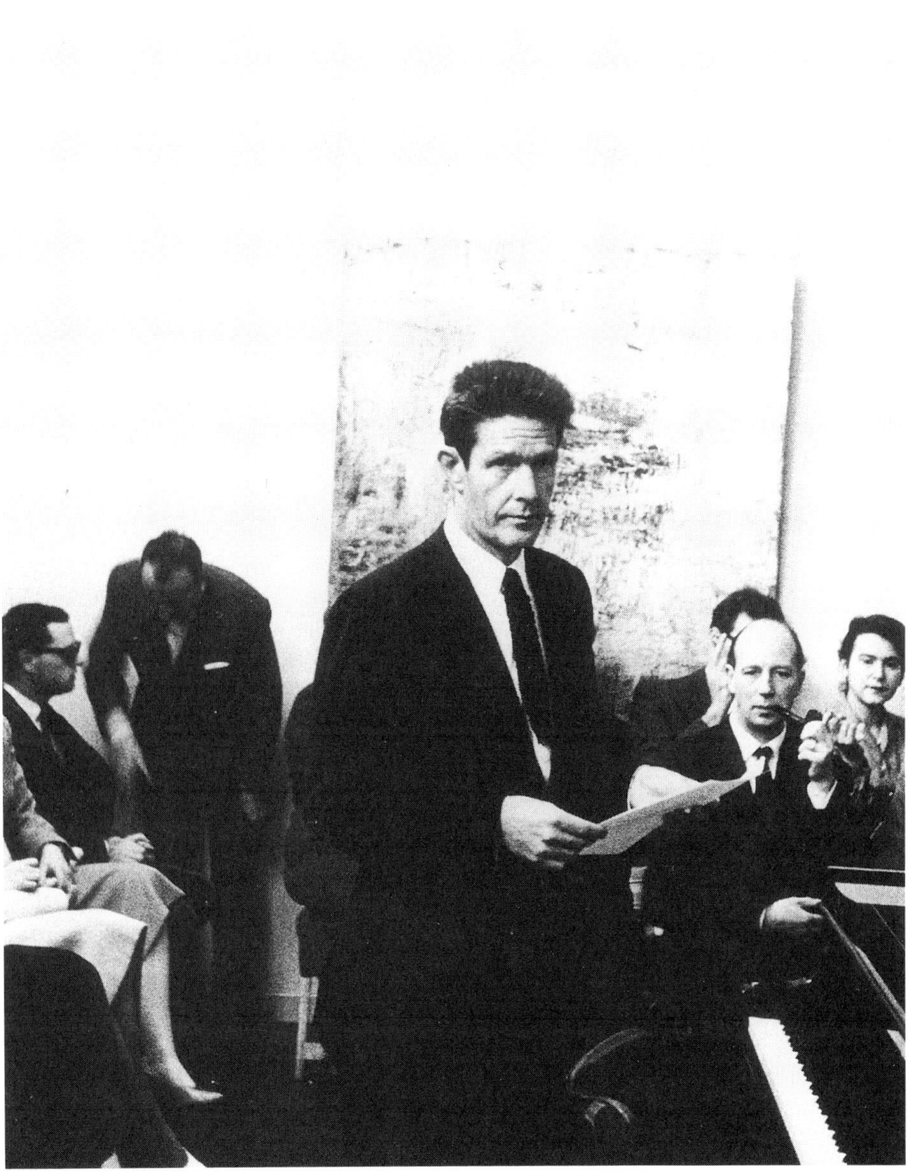

Figure 2.5. John Cage in Düsseldorf, Germany, c. 1959. Photo: Manfred Leve. Courtesy of the John Cage Trust.

stories (and, by extension, beings) *are* related, and that this complexity is more evident when it is not over-simplified by an idea of relationship in one person's mind."[30] Upon returning from Germany, Young recommended both articles to Conrad. Declaring them by far the most inspirational texts on music he had ever encountered, Young urged Conrad to read them, capitalizing the word "must" and underlining it five times.[31]

When Young arrived in Darmstadt, the best-known and most significant phase of Cage's aesthetic had already been thoroughly developed. Situated roughly between the *I-Ching*-derived chance techniques of the *Music of Changes* (1951) and the complete indeterminacy of *Variations II* (1961), this period in Cage's work has long been recognized as central, indeed, fundamental, to the breakdown of the modernist project and the advent of postmodernism.[32] Despite its multidisciplinary importance, which had profound consequences for art, music, dance, and film, Cage's impact on the period outside the discipline of music (and sometimes within) is more often minimized or dismissed than explored. Frequently, the idea of chance, aside from any specific understanding of Cage's deployment of it, is hypostatized as the sole content of his aesthetic and equated with an attitude of complete relativism. Caricaturing him as some type of holy fool, dismissing him as a mere imitator of dada, or disparaging him as a religious reactionary on account of his invocation of Zen, critics consistently overlook the logical, self-reflexive, and utterly consistent development of the first two decades of Cage's career. Individual quotes and compositions are routinely cited or analyzed out of context (a practice, to be sure, abetted by Cage's decomposition of his own writings via chance procedures and typographic experiments), while the specifics of both his scores and his performances are usually simply ignored.

Such off-hand treatment by critics and historians, however, differs markedly from the reception of Cage by the artists (in the widest sense of the term) who interacted with him on an almost daily basis in New York or at Black Mountain College, encountered his work at Darmstadt (like Young), took his composition courses at the New School for Social Research, or studied his scores in Robert Dunn's choreography workshop, out of which the Judson Dance Theater would arise. While it would be impossible to chronicle the evolution of Cage's project in detail here, it is nonetheless important to analyze certain of its most significant implications, for they formed the backdrop against which the aesthetic positions developed (variously) within the network of which Young and Conrad were a part would play themselves out.[33]

The first implication of Cage's work is the production of an aesthetic of immanence. For the better part of two decades, Cage had pursued a thoroughgoing disarticulation of any and all abstract or transcendent connections between sounds or between the individual components of a sound, such as frequency, amplitude, timbre, duration, or other morphology. In this, he opposed the direction of his European contemporaries, most notably Stockhausen and Boulez, who sought an aesthetic of integral serialism by which all aspects or parameters of a composition would be interrelated. Beginning with the investigation of chance procedures, Cage worked to detach sounds from traditional, illustrative, or other preestablished meanings, as well as to disconnect composition (the arrangement of sounds) from continuity, whether produced by melody or by rhythm, and any form of structure: harmonic, atonal, and eventually even the neutral time structures he himself had produced and lauded throughout the 1940s. "It is thus possible," Cage argued, "to make a musical composition the continuity of which is free of individual taste and memory (psychology) and also of the literature and 'traditions' of the art. The sounds enter the time-space centered within themselves, unimpeded by service to any abstraction, their 360 degrees of circumference free for an infinite play of interpenetration."[34]

Going beyond the disarticulation of a priori connections between sounds, Cage also sought to undercut the production of any determinate a posteriori interconnections between them, as well. Quickly realizing that, once fixed, a chance-derived score such as *Music of Changes* (which was indeterminate with regard to *composition*) was still as determinate upon *performance* as if it had been intentionally produced,[35] Cage sought to insert indeterminacy into the relation between composer and performer, by allowing, for example, for multiple realizations of any compositional notation, as well as into the relation between performer and listener, by means, for instance, of arranging loudspeakers and musicians around the audience so that no two listeners would hear the same "mix" of sounds – so that there was no longer any "best seat in the house" (one of the aspects of Cage's work Flynt replicated in 1959). Cage's goal, in all such endeavors, was to eliminate as much as possible from the acoustical experience the creation of any abstract form that could be received as existing on a level above, beyond, or outside the immanent realm (what Deleuze and Guattari, discussing Cage, among others, would term a "plane of immanence").[36]

Such an embrace of immanence does not, as is often charged, amount to a quietistic acceptance of "life" or "nature" (two of Cage's favorite terms) as unchanging or eternal realms, or as ones that are identical to the actually existing social structure as it unreflexively appears from what Cage called an "anthropomorphic" point of view. "Nature," for Cage, or more properly, nature's "manner of operation," was understood as an ongoing process of ateleological and nonhierarchical transformation. At his most specific, Cage described the purpose of music as "an imitation . . . of nature in her manner of operation as, in our time, her operation is revealed," further explaining that "art changes because science changes – that is, changes in science give artists different understandings of how nature works."[37] Always attentive to contemporary scientific and technological developments (the one-time futurist was famously the son of an inventor), Cage's notions of complexity and chaos ultimately, perhaps, have more resonances with cybernetics and chaos theory than with Eastern religion. For Cage, the idea of "identifying with nature" was above all a reconfiguration of the avant-garde technique of estrangement, the most important aspect of which, arguably, was the disidentification with overly reductive (but not all) ideas of causality: "The life situation from a natural, rather than anthropomorphic, view is more complex than art or putting arts together tastefully . . . the really important problems require greater earnestness."[38]

The second component of the Cagean aesthetic concerns the relation between the listener and the indeterminate musical production. Instead of confronting the composition as a totality — unified by its derivation from or representation of an abstract (nonimmanent) structure or form — listeners were to encounter sonic events as a "field" or "constellation" that not only potentially surrounded them, but that opened onto and interpenetrated with random acoustical occurrences "outside" and therefore beyond any single intentionality. (Hence Cage's quip that "a cough or a baby crying will not ruin a good piece of modern music.")[39] Like a glass house, to use one of Cage's favorite metaphors, or an auditorium with the windows left open, Cage's compositions emulated a type of acoustical "transparency" to external events that undermined their separation and autonomy. To this end, many of Cage's compositions could be performed simultaneously, allowing for a kind of superimposition or audio collage effect through which they melded into one another and further blurred their status as discrete works. With neither determinable formal nor "spatial" limitations, Cage's compositions were to be grasped not as discrete, acoustical "time-objects," but as temporally changing, yet ateleological ("purposeless") "processes."[40] The listener, then, instead of following pregiven structures or attempting to comprehend the work as a message (whether intentionally implanted or not), was to assume an attitude of attentiveness within a differentiated, but nonhierarchical field of sonic occurrences: "to approach them as objects is to utterly miss the point."[41] For Cage, this reconfiguration of the traditional subject-object/listener-work relation into an almost topographical situation of a listener within a multidimensional transformational field (i.e., a field of more than two dimensions) was an explicit challenge not only to abstraction, but to dialectics:

> Where a single operation is applied to more than one notation, for example to those of both frequency and amplitude characteristics,

> the frequency and amplitude characteristics are by that operation common to both brought into relationship. These relationships make an object; and this object, in contrast to a process which is purposeless, must be viewed dualistically. Indeterminacy when present in the making of an object, and when therefore viewed dualistically, is a sign not of identification with no matter what eventuality but simply of carelessness with regard to the outcome.[42]

According to Cage, seeing the composition as an ateleological process or focusless, but differentiated field produces an additional transformation in the listening relationship, which is the third relevant point of his aesthetic: Interpretation gives way to "experimentation." In place of the attempt to comprehend the meaning of a composition or any of the sounds in it as signs with unilaterally determinable (i.e., bi-univocal) meanings – whether pregiven or a posteriori and even if multiple or ambiguous – the listener was to experience the process as without ulterior signification, structure, or goal. Cage sometimes groped for terms to describe this relationship: "awareness," "curiosity," "use," even "an entertainment in which to celebrate unfixity."[43] Nevertheless, "experimentation," as developed within the Cagean project, was the process of interpretation, of reading and receiving signs, in the absence of pregiven signifieds.[44] Such was not conceived by Cage as an embrace of negation (no received meaning whatsoever), or of irrationality or mystical oneness (though, combined with Zen, both were almost unavoidable receptions), but at least at its most radical, as a death of the composer that was also a liberating birth of the listener. As Liz Kotz has observed, the more celebrated notion of the "death of the author" put forward by Roland Barthes in 1968 was likely a reimportation of the idea into literature and art from the context of contemporary music.[45]

In this reconfigured listening experience, neither the unavoidably *perceived* connections between sounds nor the listener's thoughts or feelings about them were denied or eliminated. "Hearing sounds which are just sounds," Cage stated, "immediately sets the theorizing mind to theorizing."[46] However, the locus of the meaning of the acoustical experience is transferred to the listener, who is thereby allowed to "become their own center," rather than submit to the will or thoughts of either composer or performer. "Of course, there are objects," Cage declared about the visual analogue of his aesthetic in Rauschenberg's Combines. "Who said there weren't? The thing is, we get the point more quickly when we realize it is we looking rather than we may not be seeing it."[47]

The dissolution or dismantling of transcendent structures was understood as a subversion of power. This was the fourth relevant point of Cage's aesthetic. For Cage, the traditional, determinate passages from composer to score, score to performer, and performer to listener were understood in terms of power relations. Thus, to disarticulate them as necessary, bi-univocal relations meant that neither performer nor audience had to be subservient to the will of another; they could instead work from their own centers, not by doing whatever they want, but nonetheless without being "pushed," as Cage put it, in any one direction.[48] As he explained about one such musical relation, "Giving up control so that sounds can be sounds (they are not men: they are sounds) means for instance: the conductor of an orchestra is no longer a policeman."[49] This (ultimately utopian) attempt to dissolve or to eradicate all forms or effects of power was essentially an anarchist position, and it would be explicitly labeled as such by Cage in 1960 in a brief statement published in *Art News*: "Emptiness of purpose does not imply contempt for society, rather assumes that each person whether he knows it or not is noble, is able to experience gifts with generosity, that society is best anarchic."[50]

The final component of the Cagean legacy to be drawn out at this point is its challenge to the disciplinary status of the separate arts. Beginning with a quest to undermine the separation between music and noise in his futurist-inspired percussion work of the 1930s and 1940s, Cage moved, at the outset of the 1950s, to undo the distinction between sound and silence. Following upon his experience in an anechoic chamber at Harvard in 1951, Cage famously redefined silence as inherently and unavoidably filled with sounds, the production of which is simply unintended.

There is thus no such thing as silence. Instead, there are only two kinds of sounds: "those intended and those others (so-called silence) not intended."[51] By 1954, Cage would go further, extending the progressive disarticulation of "abstract" categories such as sound and silence to the distinction between the auditory and the visual. The inevitable combination of these two components in any and all performed actions, which implicitly questioned the distinction between the visual arts and music, Cage described as "theater."[52] As he wrote in "45′ for a Speaker" (a lecture carefully scripted to incorporate, via chance determinations, such activities as coughing, brushing his hair, blowing his nose, and banging his fist on the table), "Music is an oversimplification of the situation we actually are in. An ear alone is not a being; music is one part of theatre. 'Focus' is what aspects one's noticing. Theatre is all the various things going on at the same time. I have noticed that music is liveliest for me when listening for instance doesn't distract me from seeing."[53]

All five aspects of Cage's aesthetic would have been available to an attentive student in 1959 and would become progressively more so up to the publication of *Silence*, the first volume of his collected writings, in 1961. And, as we will see, the group around Young and Conrad would respond in various ways to them all. For our purposes, however, it is worthwhile to pause for a moment to understand more clearly how the points sketched above, in particular, the final two, interact, and what some of the implications of that interaction might be.

Since the publication of Michael Fried's "Art and Objecthood," art historians, in particular, have largely accepted an idea of "theatricality" as the undetermined area outside the traditional arts or mediums. Outside or beyond the "modernist arts," from Fried's perspective, is a vast no-man's land, "some kind of final, implosive, hugely desirable synthesis" that has been all too easily accepted and conflated with the idea of postmodernism as a relativisitic, potentially indistinguishable heterogeneity in which, as Fried argued, standards of neither quality nor progressive status could hold.[54] Fried provided this undetermined area (where, in the words of

Clement Greenberg, which he quotes, "everything material that was not art also was") with a veritable topography, referring to the architect and sculptor Tony Smith's infamous ride on the New Jersey Turnpike.[55] Theatricality was seen as a mundane spatial and cultural expanse without discernible boundaries that continues for an "endless or indefinite *duration*."[56] Despite the fact that many of the most significant artistic movements of the latter part of the twentieth century arose precisely from within this realm, the anxiety associated with the dissolving specificity of modernist mediums has never entirely dissipated. And it is this anxiety, one might suppose, that stands in large measure behind the failure to contemplate the full importance and scope of the Cagean legacy, certainly within the visual arts and potentially within music, as well.

Fried was, of course, right to note the manner in which "theater" questions the distinction between mediums or disciplines such as art and music.[57] However, Cage's notion of theater might be seen as opening up something quite different from the naively euphoric and boundless dissolution of any and all distinctions that Fried's analysis of theatricality foresaw or implied. Rather, Cage's theater opened onto a situation in which *certainty* about the disciplinary status of the aesthetic object (even that it was necessarily "aesthetic") was effectively dissolved. This, of course, did not imply that there was, magically, no longer any such thing as a painting or a sculpture or that the different institutions of concert hall, gallery, or museum were no longer relevant or recognizable. What it implied, as Fried in fact observed and argued, was that the disciplinary and medium-based distinctions between the arts as traditionally handed down could no longer be received as akin to ontological facts or even mutually accepted conventions, but had to be reiterated in each instance.[58]

For the generation of artists in Cage's wake, however, as opposed to those championed by Fried, the issue was not one of seeking to restore the validity of medium-based or disciplinary distinctions through what Fried called "conviction." Rather, for a certain group of artists at a certain time, not only could such distinctions not be taken for granted, but the very idea of producing an "advanced" work seemed to imply precisely that the question of a work's status — the disciplinary, institutional place of the work as art or music — almost necessarily had to come into play. That is, for a certain group of artists roughly associated with minimalism (which would include Conrad, Young, Robert Morris, Walter De Maria, Simone Forti, and Yvonne Rainer, for example, but not necessarily Frank Stella, Carl Andre, Dan Flavin, or Donald Judd), the very notion of being "advanced" meant that the status of the work (which might be an object or a process or, as we will see, might be both) was not only already constitutively problematized, already *in* question, but had to take up that question and keep it in question. Not eradicating, but continually questioning the notion of medium or disciplinary specificity was, in other words, a primary condition of being "advanced" after Cage. This is different from Judd's positioning of what he termed a "specific object" in the formal space between (but no longer part of) painting and sculpture. For a more radical group of minimalists, whether coming from a lineage historically rooted in music or in visual art, a work could not be advanced, could not be "new," unless it took up the question posed by Cage's idea of "theater."

Furthermore, the question or issue of the problematization or breakdown of formal and disciplinary distinctions was — particularly after Cage's linking of his aesthetic to anarchism — an unavoidably political question. Indeed, it was a directly political question, a question of politics without mediation. According to Cage, the relations between composition, score, performance, and audition were directly political to the extent that they involve the imposition of something like semantic force. Hence the conductor, enforcing (his or her idea of) the dictates of the composer, was understood to act as a "policeman." For Cage, form and power appeared intimately connected to such a degree that form was politics; an abstract or transcendent connection or relation was, for Cage, an imposition of power.

More specifically, we could say that, by 1960, at the latest, Cage conceived form as a particular *technique* of power, a moment within a micropolitics. To disarticulate, unstitch, or undermine form, to produce an aesthetic of immanence, was therefore to dismantle that technique. Rather than obscuring or avoiding a political project (a charge, for instance, routinely advanced about Cage's relationship to dada), what Cage put on the table was precisely the connection or articulation of politics and form. For the generation coming of age with Cage in their sights, a certain relation was thereby posed between aesthetics and politics — an understanding that an aesthetic is, in some way and without mediation, equal to a politics or to a political position or model. Thus, the situation from which the arts were approachable after Cage was no longer evidently and unquestionably that of "objects" (even if musical performances) within a discipline or institution, but of specific techniques enacted within a field or realm of power effects. (Cage's decomposition of form, his production of an aesthetics of immanence, therefore also opens onto a historiographic project.)[59] To examine how this was played out in Young's work and what it means for an understanding of the artistic production of the time will be one of the primary goals of the remainder of this (and the following) chapter.

• • •

Perhaps because Young at Berkeley was relatively less familiar with Cage's work than Conrad had been at Harvard, exposure to Cage's ideas at Darmstadt had an immediate impact on his production, most notably in *Vision* (November 12, 1959) and *Poem for Chairs, Tables, Benches, etc.* (January 21, 1960). Both compositions employed chance techniques to determine the duration, arrangement, and, in *Poem*, number of sounds, as well as other aspects of instrumentation and performance. Determinations were to be made by drawing pieces of paper out of a hat (a technique Diane Wakoski, Young's partner at the time, also used to produce poems)[60] and by using a random-number table or, the poor man's equivalent, the last four or five digits in any column of the telephone directory.

In *Vision*, musicians are spread around the audience in "Cagean" fashion to produce a field, rather than an object, disarticulating the performers' actions (and the sounds produced by them) from dependence upon others' and allowing them to act, in Cage's terms, "from their own centers." Somewhat unexpectedly, given its title, *Vision* was to take place in a darkened auditorium, a feature it shared with a contemporaneous piece by Johnson entitled *Din* (ca. 1960). In later conversations, Young emphasized both how the sounds in *Vision* arose individually from unexpected places and how casting the audience in darkness served not only to put a certain focus on listening, but to separate each performer from the others, as well as from the ego-inflating experience of conventional performance.[61]

Although the duration and arrangement of sounds in *Vision* and *Poem* were chance-derived, Young rather meticulously specified their unconventional means of production. This was especially true of *Vision*, where the major portion of the fourteen-page score is devoted to describing how to make the work's eleven different sounds. The sounds include scraping a glass ashtray on the strings of a piano while intermittently sounding the key (a technique probably inspired by Tudor's performing on the insides of the piano at Darmstadt), growling or howling into wind instruments, blowing into a bassoon without a reed, producing a "herd-of-elephants sound" on twin bassoons, drawing the bow down the strings of a violin or other instrument to produce a grating white noise, and making various other instrumental glissandi. Young's interest in long durations, manifest already in *Trio for Strings*, was further evinced by the stipulation to use aerophones to sustain tones of any duration that, by chance, had been determined to exceed what a brass or woodwind player could normally achieve without drawing a breath. Extended duration was even more of an issue in *Poem*. While the overall length of *Vision* was set at thirteen minutes, the score for *Poem* explicitly allowed for performances lasting from ten seconds to ten or more days.

In contrast with Conrad's already-developed interest in just intonation and other tuning systems, Young's work of 1959–60 was primarily devoted to irregular, atonal noises. According to the score for *Vision*, the pianist should strike the key at "irregular intervals"; the growling and howling into the instruments were explicitly to be of inconstant frequencies; the elephant noise made by the bassoons was to be out of tune with regard to the standard Western scale (and not in any prescribed alternate tuning); bows were to be dragged down the strings of stringed instruments in a manner that was irregular and so as to eliminate any pitch properties normally associated with them.[62] Such concerns continued in *Poem for Chairs, Tables, Benches, etc.*, the original instrumentation of which, as indicated by the title, consisted of pushing or dragging different types of furniture across a floor. The inherent properties of the materials – wooden or metal furniture and the slight unevenness of the floor – would produce irregular noises, even if performers' actions remained constant. Young thereby achieved a type of indeterminate relation between performance and sound that was distinct in emphasis from Cage's more elaborately chance-derived decompositions and recompositions of a sound's various components. This interest continued in Young's *2 Sounds* (April 1960), in which the improvised sounds of wood and metal scraped on glass by Young and Riley were recorded and played back with great amplification on magnetic tape. (Young's friend and fellow composer Cornelius Cardew quoted one less than sympathetic listener's description of the piece: "When the first sound starts you cannot image that any more horrible sound exists in the whole world. Then the second sound comes in and you have to admit you were wrong.")[63]

Although *Vision* might be understood as resisting Cage's idea of the inevitably theatrical nature of all musical performances by turning out the lights to eliminate any visual component, Young's interests soon turned in the other direction, toward full-fledged happenings. In a letter to Conrad in the spring of 1960, Young lauded Allan Kaprow's article "One Chapter from 'The Principles of Modern Art,'" published in 1958 in the small artists' periodical *It Is*.[64] In it, Kaprow explained the various procedures used for scoring his first happening, *18 Happenings in 6 Parts*, which premiered at the Reuben Gallery in October of 1959 but had largely been worked out in Cage's composition course at the New School for Social Research before classmates George Brecht, Dick Higgins, Al Hansen, Robert Whitman, Jackson Mac Low, and others.

Kaprow's happening was both a direct descendent and a partial repudiation of Cage's idea of theater, which it extended to include touch and smell in addition to vision and hearing. To this end, as his article detailed, Kaprow not only adopted chance techniques but also variants of the Schoenbergian tone row, which made clear the genealogical derivation of the happening as a multisensory extension of "musical" composition.[65] However, like Judd's specific object, which was to exist as neither painting nor sculpture, but within a new aesthetic sphere, Kaprow's happenings were to be understood, not as midway between art and music, or as somehow both art and music, but as a new, autonomous art form: "A separate kind of art is proposed here which is not to be confused with the others, nor is it in competition with them. Neither is it a combination of already existing disciplines."[66] In this, Kaprow's position differed not only from Cage's, but also from that of his contemporaries in Fluxus, with which he is sometimes associated and that also had evolved out of the context of Cage's New School classes.

Unlike happenings, Fluxus activities maintained a less distinct or autonomous position vis-à-vis art and musical performance, being in a "minor" relation to them both.[67] This is perhaps clearest in the work and words of George Brecht, who coined the term "event" to describe the performative aspect of a "non-musical" occurrence. "Every object is an event anyway and every event has object-like quality," he explained to Michael Nyman. "So they're pretty much interchangeable."

> So you'd have the piece from 1961, *Play Incident*. It's not only an object. It looks static but when you drop the pingpong ball through one of the two holes above and it strikes the nails inside, it has a musical aspect. And it has a time aspect not only while the ball is making music within the piece, but if it falls out through one of the apertures at the side and you put it back, or you leave it where it

> is, it's already a performance. Or there's the solitaire game, or the medicine chest where the spectator is invited to change the pieces around or even exchange them with other pieces. These were both in the "Towards Events" show in 1959.[68]

For Young, by now thoroughly familiar with Cage and, before that, with Schoenberg, the significance of Kaprow's call to abandon "the limits of a single medium" was instantly understood.[69] While he specifically did not follow Kaprow's claim of a new, autonomous art, within a month he had revised and enlarged *Poem* into a fully multisensory, theatrical version. Titled *Poem, a Chamber Opera in one act* (possible variants included *Poem, an Event* or *Poem, a theater Piece*), the work was performed on May 11, 1960, as part of the Berkeley noon concert series that Young organized.[70] With Walter De Maria, then a graduate art student, billed as "artistic collaborator," the performance included female students cooking eggs and bacon and sleeping in sleeping bags, Young walking around and yelling the word "green" into a bucket, performers asking audience members if they had a "tame octopus" or informing them of (evidently nonexistent) leftover mashed potatoes, and a class full of music students reading aloud from their texts and lecture notes as they moved throughout the aisles. There was also blues singing, dragging a shoe on a string, cradling celery like a child, teeth brushing, moving a piano and threatening it and some loudspeakers with a saw (originally intended for use on some inadvertently forgotten boxes), "electronic" music (possibly another tape improvisation like *2 Sounds*), and even some Beethoven – all of it strictly timed according to the procedures dictated by the score.[71] Tape of the Berkeley concert sent by Young to Conrad is not as chaotic as one might imagine. Until the eruptions of piano playing and taped noise, the predominant acoustical impression is of the scattered, disparate voices of the students reading from the aisles, with Young's repeated call of "gree-een" providing continuity as it rings out at even intervals throughout the performance. At the end, the audience erupts in appreciative applause and laughter. Announcer Glen Glasow can be heard on the tape declaring, "I don't think I can begin to describe what happened."

That July, Young sent Tudor a list of all the actions he and De Maria had tried, as well as several others they had only considered.[72] Tudor, who had already staged a performance of the original version of *Poem* at The Living Theater in New York (April 11, 1960) and at Mary Bauermeister's atelier in Cologne (June 15, 1960), was considering using the Chamber Opera version at a festival in Venice as a double bill with Cage's *Theatre Piece* (1960), itself an "audio-visual" realization of the materials from his score for *Fontana Mix* (1958). Young had staged the theatrical version of *Poem* at least twice more, first at a student composers' forum at Brigham Young University in April and then, that May, at Stanford University, where what appears in retrospect as an all-star cast included Young, Terry Riley, Joseph Byrd, Charles MacDermed, and Bruce Conner.

Despite the obvious traces of influence, Young and his circle, eventually including Conrad, would not be content to remain in Cage's shadow for long. Although historians have focused almost exclusively on the impact on Young of having encountered Cage at Darmstadt, he had in fact already been drawn to the work of younger colleagues clearly set on besting Cage at his own game. On the first page of his letter to Conrad in September 1959, Young proclaimed that the best two composers he had encountered there were Cornelius Cardew and Sylvano Bussotti. At the time, both were producing scores as graphs or charts, almost entirely devoid of conventional musical notation. Young found Bussotti, whose *Five Piano Pieces for David Tudor* had just been published by Universal Editions, particularly interesting, and he was still praising and pursuing the young Italian's work a year later.[73] He also recommended to Conrad Cardew's *Piano Piece* (February 1959), published in the first issue of the magazine *New Departures*. Cardew, who would be similarly impressed with Young, subsequently played a major role in introducing Young's work to Great Britain (not least to his younger colleague, John Cale).

Both the influence of and struggle against Cage's legacy would become evident in Young's "Lecture 1960," parts of which were first delivered in July 1960 at Ann Halprin's summer workshop before a group that included Rainer, Morris, Riley, Forti, and others.[74] The impact of Cage can be discerned both in the lecture's form, that being a collection of stories and observations clearly patterned on "Indeterminacy," and in its content – evident, for instance, in the shared antipathy to Cage's longtime rhetorical nemesis, Beethoven: "Once I tried lots of mustard on a raw turnip," Young noted. "I liked it better than any Beethoven I had ever heard."[75] Two of the major ideas explored in Young's lecture – decoupling musical materials from composers' intentions (letting sounds "be themselves") and relinquishing the dictates of taste and quality – were staples of Cage's own writings. Declarations of Young's such as "if... we are interested in what is good, it seems to me that we will always be interested in the same things (that is, the same things that we already like)" are in large part extrapolations of Cage's thinking about expanding acceptable acoustical tastes and the definition of music. Young's conclusions, however, were sometimes decidedly un-Cagean and evinced his interest in overtaking Cage's status at the forefront of the avant-garde. "I am not interested in good," Young explained at the end of the statement above; "I am interested in new – even if this includes the possibility of its being evil."[76] Young's conundrum, how to go beyond Cage while going through him, was typical of his generation. Their situation, in the shadow of Cage and to some extent suffering the anxiety of his influence, was neatly summed up by Young's declaration: "It is often necessary that one be able to ask, 'Who is John Cage?'"[77]

• • •

Conrad, as already noted, spent the 1960–61 academic year in Europe studying Biber and Stockhausen. Although he devoted little of his time to Cage, notes indicate that he had listened to the recording of "Indeterminacy," reflecting upon it in passages written possibly around the time he visited the Staatsbibliothek in East Berlin.[78] His interest in the Cagean legacy would, however, be progressively rekindled by its continued reception in Young's work, as well as in that of his old friend and "teacher," Flynt, who was also responding to Cage as filtered through Young. Conrad had put Young and Flynt in contact after the summer of 1959, conveying their dialogue in part though his and Young's correspondence. At one point, Young attempted, apparently without success, to extract the score for a piece that Conrad described as entitled *IS* (ca. 1960) from Flynt for performance at one of the Berkeley noon concerts, chastising the reticent undergraduate for being so aloof.[79]

The most significant aspect of Young's reception and transformation of the Cagean legacy would be found in the "word pieces" he developed, beginning in May of 1960, and that he published three years later in the famous compendium *An Anthology*, which he edited and copublished with Jackson Mac Low (full title: *An Anthology of Chance Operations Concept Art Anti-Art Indeterminacy Improvisation Meaningless Work Natural Disasters Plans of Action Stories Diagrams Music Poetry Essays Dance Constructions Mathematics Compositions*).[80] Eschewing the complex, collagelike multiplicity of Cage's indeterminate scores, which were analogous to intricate, multipart puzzles for which there was no preset solution, Young's 1960 compositions (like the contemporary "event scores" of George Brecht and "instructions" of Yoko Ono) took the form of short verbal directives, as, for instance, in *Composition 1960 #13 to Richard Huelsenbeck* (November 9, 1960), which instructs the performer to prepare and perform a composition as well as he or she is able. Young has emphasized that such pieces sought to go beyond Cage's example by "delimit[ing] the work to be a single event or object" and has pointed to certain formal continuities between these works and the reductive or minimal focus on musical materials evinced in compositions such as *Trio for Strings*.[81] Almost without exception, historians have reiterated Young's perspective on these works (first voiced in 1966), tending thereby to prioritize *Composition 1960 #7* (July 1960), the sustained open fifth, and, to a lesser degree, *Composition 1960 #9* (October 1960), the horizontal line on a card that – as in Young's collaboration with Andy Warhol at the 1964 New York Film Festival at Lincoln Center — has been realized as a sustained tone.[82] By contrast, Young's twelve other published word scores have been largely marginalized, often on disciplinary grounds. Their dismissal can sometimes be quite high-handed, as when Edward Strickland writes of *Composition 1960 #15 to Richard Huelsenbeck* (December 25, 1960) — which simply indicates the existence of small "whirlpools" somewhere amid the sea, "I personally do not believe it is music any more than this sentence, although it is a more interesting sentence."[83] Even so assiduous and insightful a scholar as Keith Potter has downplayed the period in which Young worked through the Cagean legacy, including the word scores, as a "sidetrack" that temporarily led away from the main line of Young's musical development.[84]

Yet rather than a formal reaction to Cage's influence, one based on "minimal" reduction, Young's word scores might more productively be understood in terms of an almost epistemological inquiry. Taken as an ensemble, they amount to a multifaceted probing into various tenets of Cage's work, not all at once and in its entirely, but particularly, part by part. Each of Young's word scores isolates, emphasizes, questions, and usually demonstrably attempts to surpass one or another aspect of Cage's position. The emphasis on sustained tones found in *Compositions 1960 #7* and *#9* thus proves to be only one node in, or line issuing from, a more diverse, expansive, variegated, and overlapping set of responses. *Composition 1960 #15 to Richard Huelsenbeck* and the enigmatic two-line *Piano Piece for David Tudor #3* (November 14, 1960) — "most of them/ were very old grasshoppers" — might, for example, be seen as bids to outdo Cage in the realm of indeterminacy, not only by removing any explicit directive to the performer, but by confounding any implicit one, as well.[85] With its haikulike cadence and reference to the grasshopper, *Piano Piece for David Tudor #3* also foregrounds, as the composition's sole content, the connections to Oriental culture continually broached in Cage's writings.

Piano Piece for David Tudor #1 (October 1960) and *Piano Piece for Terry Riley #1* (November 8, 1960) both highlight the audio-visual aspect of Cagean theater. In *Piano Piece for David Tudor #1*, a piano is to be fed a bale of hay and provided a bucket of water, the realization of which, particularly in concerts put on by Fluxus, pushed the work into a more explicitly (and sometimes traditionally) theatrical direction than most of Cage's work. Equally theatrical was the piece dedicated to Riley, which instructs the performer to press a piano flat against a wall, pushing it as hard as possible for as long as possible (even if one managed to knock down the wall), until the point of exhaustion.[86] *Composition 1960 #2*, which instructs the performer to build a fire, the sound of which might be amplified by a microphone, emphasizes both a theatrical quality (explicitly dictating that the performer should not block the audience's view) and the use of a "musical" material that endorses and extends Cage's acceptance of the sounds of nature and, like the furniture sounds in *Poem*, is largely indeterminate.[87] Much the same combination of nature, indeterminacy, and theater is also found in *Composition 1960 #5* (June 8, 1960), in which one or a number of butterflies are released into the performance area. Here, the theatrical combination of sound and vision is complicated by the butterflies' (possible) production of sounds only on a register inaudible to human hearing, an extension of Cage's "nonanthropomorphic" stance beyond any point Cage had yet envisioned. Young's response to Wakoski's questioning of the "musical" content of *Composition 1960 #5*, as related in "Lecture 1960," emphasizes precisely this perspective: Young criticized "the usual attitude of human beings that everything in the world should exist for them," adding that "it didn't seem to me at all necessary that anyone or anything should have to hear sounds and that it is enough that they exist for themselves."[88]

In addition to interrelating the Cagean notions of nature, material, and theatricality, *Composition 1960 #5* also seems to respond to Cage's infamous notion of silence, extending it beyond sounds that are not intended to "sounds" that cannot even be heard, at least by human ears. Several other of Young's 1960 compositions seem to relate even more specifically to *4′33″* (1952), Cage's manifesto presentation of his redefined idea of silence, in which a performer sits at his or her instrument for the designated amount of time without sounding a note, thereby allowing unintentionally produced sounds to take center stage. Young's *Piano Piece for David Tudor #2* (October 1960) evidently refers to the premiere of *4′33″*—a performance in which Tudor signaled the composition's three silent "movements" by closing and opening the keyboard cover to the piano. Young's composition challenges Tudor (or any other performer) to attain an additional level of virtuosity in the avoidance of sound production by instructing him to attempt the opening and closing of the keyboard cover without making any sound audible, not only to the audience, but to the performer as well. (The piece ends once the performer has succeeded or given up trying.)[89]

When taken as a collection, rather than selected for continuity with earlier and later developments, Young's word pieces point in diverse, even opposing or contradictory directions, the silence and indeterminacy of *Composition 1960 #5*, for example, being largely at odds with the auditory control embodied in *Composition 1960 #7*. Furthermore, in that they are discursively predicated on and responding primarily to the existing aesthetic precedent set by Cage, each work is never complete in itself and does not refer back to the composer as the sole or even primary source or repository of meaning. Young's word pieces thereby question any idea of authorship as a consistent, cohesive, stylistic unity or development.[90] The same is largely true of all such word pieces or event scores as they developed into the characteristic artistic morphology of Fluxus.

Rather than expression, the content or meaning of a word piece might be seen to reside in something like the structural transformation of the discourse in which it appears. Each one can be and in some sense demands to be read as paradigmatic, at one and the same time setting forth a general proposition about composition—an implicit challenge to the definitions and/or limitations of the discipline—as well as instructing a realizable, performable act.[91] Like Young's word pieces, each Fluxus score evidently derives from a preexisting artistic and historical milieu and opens onto an intersubjective, collective reception and response. The definition of a "good" word piece, one might contend, does not reside in the successful expression of authorial intent, but in the transformations precipitated and relayed by means of the responses that the work evokes. Within the wider context of Fluxus, such responses, significantly, tended to operate in a specific and particular, rather than general manner, as was indicated by the habit of dedicating particular word scores to other artists. As Strickland has noted, "it was common practice for one . . . artist to 'answer' a composition [word score] with another composition."[92] As Dick Higgins once noted in correspondence with George Maciunas about the typical Fluxus attitude toward word scores, "In the early sixties, when the first generation of Fluxus artists were doing and giving away their experiences, it mattered little which of us had done which piece. The spirit was: you've seen it, now — very well, it's yours. Now you are free to make your own variation of it if you like, and the piece and the world will be a little richer for all that."[93]

Sometimes these responses were quite explicit. Robert Bozzi's *Choice #12* (1966), for instance, responds to Young's *Piano Piece for Terry Riley #1* by making the activity of pushing a piano into a competition ("Two teams of performers compete against each other by pushing a piano from opposite sides"), while his *Piece for Chieko Shiomi* (1966) incorporates Brecht's *Drip Music* (1959).[94] Mieko (Chieko) Shiomi's *Boundary Music* (1963) reworks the manner in which Young's *Piano Piece for David Tudor #2* repositioned the division between silence and sound: "Make the faintest possible sound to a boundary condition whether the sound is given birth to as a sound or not. At the performance, instruments, human bodies, electronic apparatus or anything else may be used."[95] Alison Knowles's *Chair Piece for George Brecht* (winter 1965) relocates the context of Brecht's *Three Chair Events* (spring 1961) from the gallery to the performative and social situation of an audience: "Locate an empty chair, before the performance, in the center of the center aisle, equipped with a reading light and a book. If nobody has taken this seat by the intermission, one of the performers should do so."[96] Such interconnections among the word pieces do not give rise to a "movement" (not even Fluxus), but set up a network of particular interactions that resist or evade totalizations into an overall "genre" with an easily generalized meaning or significance.

• • •

In addition to those already discussed, at least two other of Young's 1960 compositions can be understood as responding explicitly to *4′33″*. In *Composition 1960 #3* (May 14, 1960), the announcer declares to the audience the piece's beginning and end points (if there is a limit on duration). Instead of sitting at an instrument, however, the announcer states only that members of the audience can do whatever they like for this amount of time. *Composition 1960 #4* (June 3, 1960) is largely the same, except for the fact that the audience is both literally and figuratively kept in the dark. They are told at the beginning about the piece's duration and that the lights will be extinguished for the length the performance. Only at the end of the piece (and then only at the discretion of the announcer) is the audience to be informed that their actions were the composition's sole content.

4′33″ was Cage's clearest presentation to date of the death of the composer, transferring the locus of the meaning of the sounds, if there were any, in some sense onto the audience. Yet, in *4′33″*, the audience was not supposed to become the work's primary performers, at least not intentionally or exclusively. There was no announcement that the audience could do whatever they wanted, nor was this what Cage desired. They were not to improvise or act out, to "go crazy," as Young's audiences had done, particularly when cast into the dark.[97] For Cage, such purely improvisational activities served merely to reiterate and thereby reinforce the habitual or ideological limitations of the audience members' existing states of consciousness.

With performers, Cage provided the means, first, to take into account each individual's particular capabilities and, then, to allow (indeed, in a certain sense, to push) each individual to produce something new, an "experimental" action preconceived neither by them nor by the composer. Because the components of each performer's actions were inductively based upon their individual performative capabilities, Cage regarded this procedure as not violating the principle of allowing people to work from their own centers while also compelling the expansion of their capabilities in ways they had not foreseen. Rather than reproduction, performance was a means of discovery, of producing sounds as yet unconceived: "here the word 'experimental' is apt, providing it is understood not as descriptive of an act to be later judged in terms of success and failure, but simply as of an act the outcome of which is unknown."[98] If habit is a form of ideology, as Cage seemed to believe, a limiting factor on the transformation of consciousness, then such experimental actions, understood almost as a form of ethics, were means of experiencing freedom. It was a notion of freedom, not as a stable, static state, but as the smallest act of self-transformation, the opposite or undoing of a technique of reproductive power.

For the audience of *4′33″*, the goal was similarly to get outside themselves, to open their minds and egos to external influences that – in interacting with their current states of consciousness, not by overpowering or subjugating them – would allow or move their minds toward change, toward new individual perceptions and ideas.[99] With *4′33″*, Cage intended to turn listeners out of themselves, to allow them to hear all sounds, both audience-created and ambient or environmental, on the same level, thereby opening the self-enclosure of the listening subject onto the immanent plane that Cage identified as "nature."[100] The locus of activity was therefore transferred to the audience only insofar as the latter was an interpenetrating part of the larger "natural" environment. As Cage explained in 1956 to the music critic Paul Henry Lang:

> We live in a world where there are things as well as people. Trees, stones, water, everything is expressive. I see this situation in which I impermanently live as a complex interpenetration of centers moving out in all directions without impasse. This is in accord with contemporary

> awarenesses of the operations of nature. . . . Life goes on very well without me, and that will explain to you my silent piece, *4′33″*.[101]

Although predicated on *4′33″* to the extent that they leave sound production completely undetermined, Young's *Compositions 1960 #3* and *#4* do not position the audience as part of the larger and more expansive continuum of nature, but as a closed set or delimited group that produces all of the work's sounds. At the time, as Young explained to Richard Kostelanetz, he "was really intrigued with the audience as a social situation," and pieces such as *Composition 1960 #3* and *#4* were "specifically related" to it as such.[102] Young was cognizant of Cage's political position and even quoted Cage's *Art News* statement about anarchy on the program for a performance of sound improvisations by himself, Riley, and De Maria at the California School of Fine Arts in May, 1960.[103] Throughout that summer, if not longer, Young continued to profess his affinity with Cage's position, most notably in the one-word endorsement of "Anarchy" in "Lecture 1960."[104] As a political program, anarchy is, of course, distinct from mere individualism, implying collectivity as a vision of people living together without hierarchy, subjugation, or foregoing their individual freedoms. *Compositions 1960 #3* and *#4*, however, pointed toward a much more precise and detailed vision of the audience's awareness of themselves as an ensemble or group than *4′33″* had encouraged or allowed. In retrospect, this aspect of Young's production opened up one of the most significant lines of escape from Cage's aesthetics. Instead of identifying with nature or the outside, Young's audience was placed in a situation more conducive to a certain degree of self-reflexive consciousness of their actions as a collective. One of the implications of *Composition 1960 #3* was therefore replacing the primacy of the composer by a collective, improvisational, deskilled performance practice, an aesthetic of the audience as producer that would, in some sense, be brought to its logical conclusion in the work of Cardew and the Scratch Orchestra.

This line out of a Cagean problematic would be developed

further, or made more explicit, in Young's *Composition 1960 #6* (July 2, 1960), in which performers are to occupy the stage in a manner that effectively mimics the audience's actions and physical environment. Rows of seats, like those in the auditorium, were to be erected on stage for the performers to sit in, or, "if in a bar," the score stipulates, "the performers might have tables on stage and be drinking as is the audience." Effectively reversing roles, performers are further instructed to watch and listen to the audience. Such mirroring situates the audience and performers as equals, eliminating any distinction predicated on skill. An optional instruction allows for the selling of tickets to those in the "audience" who wish to purchase entry onto the stage, further blurring the distinction between audience and performers (and leading some, potentially, to pay a second time). In *Composition 1960 #6*, the traditional distinction between audience and performer (based on preparation or skill) is almost entirely supplanted by conventional and institutional factors: the architectural division between stage and floor, on the one hand, and the transgression of this division, on the other, the latter now made an effect of relocating the concert's customary financial threshold from the door to the foot of the stage.

The resonance and legacy of *Compositions 1960 #3, #4,* and *#6* would echo throughout the period, giving rise to variants such as Yoko Ono's *Audience Piece* (1962), in which performers stare at individual audience members until the latter avert their eyes, Robert Bozzi's *Choice #18* (1966) ("Performers use mirrors to show the audience to itself"), and Ben Vautier's numerous *Audience Pieces* (1964–65), including *Concerto for Audience by Audience* (1965): "The audience is invited to come to the stage, take instruments that are provided to them, sit on the orchestra seats and play for 3 minutes. If the audience does not respond to the invitation, instruments should be distributed to them."[105]

Young's work would not, of course, be the sole or even the clearest presentation of a collective consciousness to arise within the art world at large during the 1960s. Nevertheless, by so specifically marking a line out of Cage's aesthetic (that is, by providing one possible means by which his generation would be able to ask "Who is John Cage?"), *Compositions 1960 #3, #4*, and *#6* formed an important, if consistently underacknowledged touchstone for the transformation from a "natural" to a "social" and potentially collective point of view, a social turn that would come to characterize the general ethos of both minimalism and Fluxus, as well as the more overtly communist projects of George Maciunas, Henry Flynt, and others, eventually including Cardew.

• • •

While Conrad was not himself a member of Fluxus (though he would, as we will see, produce his own word scores), it might be surmised that these developments had an effect on his understanding of authorship. In any case, his own understanding of the Cagean legacy would develop in an ongoing dialogue with Young. Their dialogue was initiated in June of 1960, when Young mailed copies of his recently completed *Compositions 1960 #2–#5* to Conrad, who received them by forwarded mail in Denmark. In his response, Conrad, like Wakoski, expressed a certain bafflement at the butterfly piece, which Young duly noted in "Lecture 1960."[106] Conrad reacted more positively, however, to *Composition 1960 #2*, to which he devoted a paragraph describing his own affinity for sounds of the natural environment, including those made by a fire, which he had also contemplated including in one of his own compositions. As previously noted, Conrad regarded the acceptance and inclusion of such nontraditional sound sources as the primary lesson to be derived from Cage. Conrad would also have understood well the manner in which such a piece relocated indeterminacy within the material, rather than within the manner in which such materials were put together. In the fall of 1961, when Conrad's return to Cambridge pushed him toward further contemplation of Young's work, he considered other similarly nontraditional sound sources. As he dictated in a notebook entry dated November 15: "*MATTRESS.* Compressing mattress slowly with ear close to: many very good interesting sounds, some almost threshold intensity (apparently). Especially tiny pings of the compressing springs, at all pitches + very low intensity. Can all of this be picked up by a mike?"[107]

Conrad responded more critically and equivocally, however, to Young's *Compositions 1960 #3* and *#4*. He astutely noted the derivation of *Composition 1960 #4* from *Vision*: It virtually replicated a paragraph on the second page of Young's score that dictated turning off the lights (*Composition 1960 #4* is, in fact, largely *Vision* emptied of all intentional sounds). He also perceptively surmised Young's dialogue, not only with the legacy of Cage, but also with Dennis Johnson's response to it. Johnson's response arose from the context of a conversation between him, Young, and Richard Maxfield concerning the inherent limitations on Cagean indeterminacy: "We generally agreed," Young recalled, "that the composer was always left with some choices of one sort or another. At the very least, he had to decide what chances he would take or what he would leave to indeterminacy in his composition."[108] Later that fall, however, Johnson contended that he had conceived of a work that "was entirely indeterminacy and left the composer out of it." He then handed Young a piece of paper on which he had written "LISTEN."[109] Although Cage's typographic score for *4′33″*, which reads simply "I. Tacet/ II. Tacet/ III. Tacet," arguably serves as a precedent for both Young's word pieces and Brecht's event scores, I would suggest that Johnson's *LISTEN*, which succeeded in eliminating the very last traces of a specifically musical language, was a more proximate and powerful impetus toward Young's particular development of these works.[110]

The most radical component of Johnson's work, its sole "compositional" act, had been to relinquish any further compositional activity and give the composer and performer a place on the side of the audience. Writing or composing was, if not wholly eradicated, seemingly supplanted in importance by listening. If indeterminacy was relocated within the material, then even when manipulating the means of sound production, as in lighting a fire, pressing a mattress, dragging furniture across the floor, or scraping glass with wood and metal, the performer was primarily listening to the result. Conrad pressed Young on just this point, responding to Young's return of explicit directives and the designation of a time structure in *Composition 1960 #3* by calling it a "cluttered" rendition of *LISTEN*.

A little over a year later, in the fall of 1961 (well before explicit responses by Vautier or Bozzi), Conrad further considered the implications of Cage, Young, and Johnson's production, exploring for himself the means by which to question the relation between performer and audience: "Define 'audience.' Is it those who listen only or is it those who do not perform in addition? In which case is a performance by the audience (coughing, etc) part of the piece? A basic revolution here of Cage's is seen to be merely a redefinition of 'audience' to include performers."[111]

Conrad's rumination is in some sense the equal opposite of Young's *Compositions 1960 #3* and *#4*, which had redefined the audience as performers. Here, Conrad redefines performers (somewhat in the sense of *Composition 1960 #6*) as listeners, that is, as members of the audience of the work. This leads Conrad to sketch out possible pieces or scores that develop this insight further:

> §Turn some of the audience into performers: "Those in even-numbered seats are performers," or some such. Then instructions for them. Perhaps ask them to be as quiet as possible....
>
> Make directions for audiences + performers consistent (or, for a "concept artish" touch, inconsistent). Or, have each person individually an audience, with the others performing, or conversely each individual a performer with the others as audience; this gives n simultaneous performances for n persons attending. If performers or audiences are not a function of the other (multi-valued), there may be up to n! performances of this kind at once with people attending.[112]

Conrad, who was working at the time on *Three Loops*, extended the issues of blurring the distinction between the performers' and the audience's actions to the operation of his tape delay: "*AUDIENCE RES.* In (66) above [i.e. *RESONANCE*], put mike near audience: audience reaction becomes part of the performance + will recur on recording. Do only in last of canons performed, for public relations reasons."[113] At the Harvard performance of *Three Loops*, short moments of audience laughter are distinctly audible, caught on the tape recorder and rebroadcast in the first and third movements, adding to the musique concrète–like nature of the piece.

• • •

In his response to Conrad, Young acknowledged that all four of *Compositions 1960 #2–#5* did in some way imply *LISTEN*.[114] But he contested Conrad's reading, saying that he would never want to reproduce Johnson's work and that his own "involves more." What Conrad saw as "clutter," Young seems to have insisted upon as an aspect of composition. Although Young did get rid of all structure in fully indeterminate pieces such as *Piano Piece for David Tudor #3*, the retention and designation of a time structure in *Composition 1960 #3*, even if it could be an unlimited duration, clearly held on to a notion of compositional action, however minimal. Indeed, it was the exact same intervention to which Cage had reduced "composition" in the residual time structure of *4′33″* and that he would not fully relinquish until the early 1960s.

In what was at the time a good-natured disagreement – and the first time the two had discussed issues related to the legacy of Cage – can be found the kernel out of which the later dispute between Young and Conrad would grow. For Young, a certain conceptual apparatus still existed for the work of the Theatre of Eternal Music, an understanding, whether written or not, of the parameters and rules within which the group operated and that governed the choice and combination of frequencies used. For Conrad, in contrast, this was all an inductive result, one that followed from the elimination of composition as "a 'conceptual' activity" and the advent of a performance practice that "would instead be structured around pragmatic activity, around direct gratification in the realization of the moment, and around discipline."[115] (We will come to understand, in the next chapter, the importance of this final word.) "The function of [the] composer becomes one of participating at the site of the origin of the sound," Conrad explained further:

> We just started off playing, you see, and *then* we had discussions and interactions about which kind of things we might do. Somebody would want to play the gong, or bow guitar, or play another note, or try something. Then maybe it would happen and maybe it wouldn't, and there would be discussion about that. Everything would be hashed over endlessly. And so my sense of what was valuable, in that whole complex of an evolving, dynamic, active engagement with the sound, was that we were composers who positioned ourselves in the midst of the work, which after all was largely sort of, like, one note or sound....
>
> The Sound! Returning to the sound as the substance of music; returning to the sound, sitting in the midst of it, and then manipulating it or becoming engaged actively in a discursive context in relation to the music; a group in a real time situation where the function of the score is replaced by consensus and immediate intentionality that's at the level of the fingertips and millisecond hearing relationships: this, in my sense of it, was a very, very important part of what it was that we were about.... [We had a]bsolute conviction and understanding that this was *way*, way out in front of anything else that was going on and that we wanted to do this because it was very, very clearly the direction to pursue all of these different efforts.[116]

In this, Conrad's perspective, far from idiosyncratic, proves to be close to an understanding of group activity found, for example, in the contemporaneous functioning of the Judson Dance Theater—which, as Sally Banes emphasizes, operated via democratic, deliberative decision-making processes—as well as improvisational musical ensembles such as AMM, which Cardew joined in 1965.[117] For AMM and a host of other groups of the time, such as Group Ongaku (which included Fluxus artists Takehisa Kosugi and Mieko [Chieko] Shiomi), Musica Elettronica Viva (MEV), Gruppo

Di Improvvisazione Nuova Consonanza, portions of the Los Angeles Free Music Society (LAFMS), and more, the step beyond Cagean indeterminacy was to embrace pragmatic improvisational activity (despite, or rather in the face of Cage's reservations about improvisation). Indeed, Cardew would describe the activities and goals of AMM in terms that resonate very closely with Conrad's:

> Informal "sound" has a power over our emotional responses that formal "music" does not, in that it acts subliminally rather than on a cultural level. This is a possible definition of the area in which AMM is experimental. We are *searching* for sounds and for the responses that attach to them, rather than thinking them up, preparing them and producing them. The search is conducted in the medium of sound and the musician himself is at the heart of the experiment.[118]

As Young has insisted, the Theatre of Eternal Music never engaged in improvisation in the manner of free-jazz or free-noise ensembles such as AMM.[119] Nevertheless, it is interesting to note that most of the components of Conrad and Cale's understanding of the Dream Syndicate fully accord with Cardew's more overtly politicized development of the Cagean legacy in AMM and certain moments of the Scratch Orchestra: the end of the score as a source of compositional authority,[120] the rise of collective improvisation, the direct impact of music as a powerful, affective force, and the radical democracy of group-made decisions. It is thus not difficult to assume that Cale, who was in contact with Cardew throughout the 1960s, visiting him in 1966 and bringing a tape of the Theatre of Eternal Music, not only influenced Cardew's development, but also understood his work in Cardew's terms, ones that he and Conrad shared.[121]

The distinctions made by Conrad and Young are, to a certain extent, ones of emphasis, which no doubt allowed the various opinions of the group's members to coexist during the early years. It is not a question, once again, of adjudicating the correctness of one side or the other, but of understanding that, from the very beginning, both were in tension, even though they implied different directions or lines of development. For Conrad, the pragmatic situation of the performance and the material nature of the sound undermined, eroded, or, in his terms, "corrupted... in a terminal way" the function of an abstract, written score.[122] To this end, his perspective remained close to Cage's aesthetic of immanence, even while it was inflected by the "social turn" represented in Young's *Composition 1960 #3* in the manner in which Conrad understood it. Elsewhere in the interview quoted above, Conrad attributed this perspective directly to "the lesson of Cage":

> I would say that this idea about going into the sound and becoming—rather than a composer who offers the directions for what to do—a composer-performer, sitting in the environment of the ongoing sound and examining and manipulating and adjusting and devising that sound as an environment and as a condition in which the hearing and listening is taking place: this had a great deal for me to do with the way in which you would move beyond Cage's impact. Not the Cage who was the modernist who was dealing with the position of the composer and the activity of the composer, but, in this instance, the Cage who is teaching you about listening.[123]

Neither Conrad nor Cale would develop as explicitly a political aesthetic within music as Cardew, at least not until much later, when, in such pieces as *Slapping Pythagoras* (1995), Conrad sought to desublimate some of the implications of his work with the Theatre of Eternal Music along the lines of a radical democratic project.[124] It will not, however, be primarily via the notion of a radically participatory democracy that we will explore the political consequences of Young's social turn or Conrad's production in the pages that follow. Rather, it will be through the way in which the avant-garde arts of their time modeled, implicitly and explicitly, the multiple and mutually imbricated regimes of power within which and on which they operated. In order to do so, we will have to take leave of Conrad momentarily and explore aspects of the work of Young, Robert Morris, Cardew, and others that evolved during the time Conrad was still in Denmark and

Germany. In their work, we will find in play some of the same questions of transcendent form and immanent practice as found in the differences between Conrad and Young we have encountered above.

Chapter Three

The Tower and the Line

What about the *Box with the Sound of Its Own Making*? Shouldn't that also be part of the history of minimal *music*?

—Tony Conrad

Of all of La Monte Young's word scores, the most infamous and influential was *Composition 1960 #10 to Bob Morris* (October 1960).[1] Reading simply "Draw a straight line and follow it," Young's piece was responded to and modified many times. Milan Knizak's *Line* (1965) made it into a competition: "A line is drawn on the sidewalk with chalk. The longest line wins."[2] Knizak had already been trumped or countered, in a way, by George Maciunas's *Homage to La Monte Young* (January 12, 1962), which instructed the performer to "Erase, scrape or wash away as well as possible the previously drawn line or lines of La Monte Young or any other lines encountered, like street dividing lines, rulled [sic] paper or score lines, lines on sports fields, lines on gaming tables, lines drawn by children on sidewalks etc."[3] Yoko Ono included three variant *Line Pieces* from the spring of 1964 in her book *Grapefruit*, including an injunction to draw a line with yourself "until you disappear."[4] Nam June Paik didn't rewrite Young's piece, but did a performative interpretation that became known as *Zen for Head* by dipping his head (or tie) in a bowl of paint and marking a broad line down a long sheet of paper (Figure 3.1). In his notebook, Conrad would propose another performance variant: "'draw' = 'pull'; 'line' = 'string': pull a string around in a circle."[5] In a different type of response, John Cale, in his eighth *Outdoor Piece for Robin Page* (summer 1962), echoed Young's piece in syntax, rather than in form: "Follow the wind and listen to it."[6]

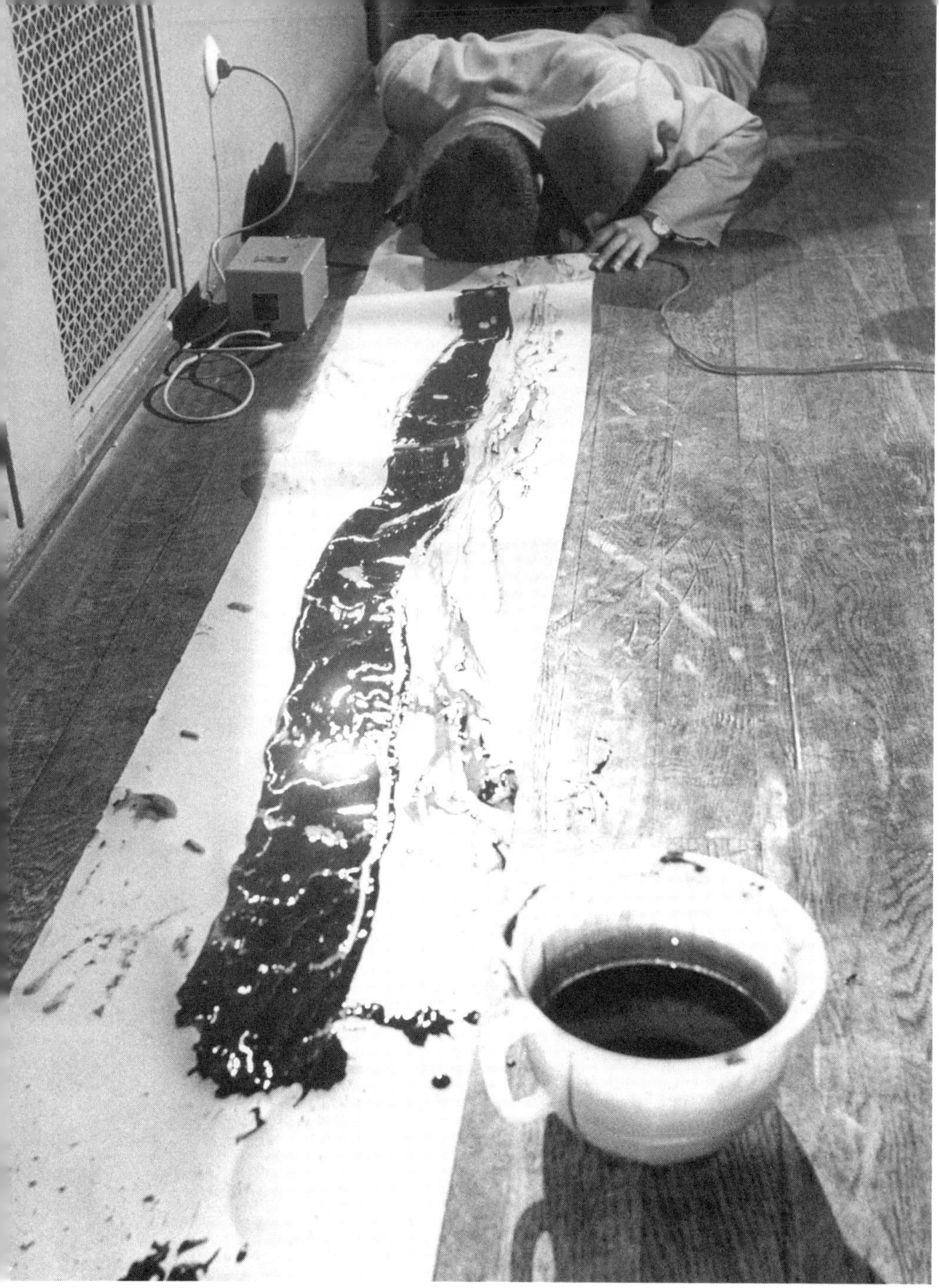

Figure 3.1. Nam June Paik performing La Monte Young's *Composition 1960 #10 to Bob Morris* as "Zen For Head," Wiesbaden, West Germany, 1962. Photo: © picture-alliance/dpa.

Young himself returned to *Composition 1960 #10* the next year in a series of works entitled *Compositions 1961*. By averaging out his previous production, Young calculated that he completed approximately twenty-nine works per year and decided to finish off a year's worth at one time in early 1961, being careful, however, to assign each composition an appropriate compositional "date," equally spaced between January 1 and December 31. Having further decided that originality need not be a criterion for a legitimately "new" work, Young simply repeated the brief instruction for *Composition 1960 #10* for each of the 1961 compositions.[7] The results were later issued by Maciunas as a small booklet in 1963.

Unlike *Composition 1960 #9*, which Young realized "musically" as a sustained tone, *Composition 1960 #10* was performed by Young in a "theatrical" manner on a bill with all twenty-nine of his *Compositions 1961*. The works were premiered on March 31, 1961, at a Harvard-Radcliffe Music Club concert organized by Henry Flynt while Conrad was still out of the country. Assisted by Robert Morris (who appropriately performed the first piece, *Composition 1960 #10*, alone), Young used plumb lines and yardsticks to draw a straight line across the length of the stage – being careful to stay behind it, thereby following it at the same time – and repeated this action once for each of the compositions, all the time trying to repeat the drawing as precisely as he could.[8] In the Harvard *Crimson*, a student reporter quoted Young as declaring that he "does not call such proceedings music, but rather 'art' in general."[9] As Flynt later commented: "*Art in general; ideas which are interesting in themselves.* Music had become an arena for a transformation which did not need to be about music."[10]

John Cage was in the audience when Young reprised the Harvard performance, this time assisted by Robert Dunn, on May 19 and 20, 1961, at the famous concert series that Young curated at Yoko Ono's loft. "We had a beautiful program by La Monte Young," Cage wrote to David Tudor: "He and Bob Dunn drew 30 straight lines using a string with a weight in the manner somewhat of surveying. By the time La Monte finished, not only had all the audience left, but Bob Dunn too had left exhausted. The next evening the project was shortened by shortening the line. Even then it took 3 hours."[11]

In his own letter to Tudor, Young emphasized the performance's intentionally workmanlike character (including matter-of-fact verbal instructions exchanged between performers), a relationship to labor later echoed in Morris's performance *Site* (1964).[12] Aside from this aspect of workmanlike diligence and the incidental creation of sounds, the primary interest in the realization of *Compositions 1961* lay in the inadvertent and thus indeterminate differences in the paths traced by the chalk lines. Although some years later (tellingly, as we will see), Young characterized the performance primarily in terms of the approach to an ideal – informing Richard Kostelanetz that there were deviations only because "the technique I was using at the time was not good enough" – nearly all of the work's appeal lies in the conflict between intention and result.[13] Being performed was a dialectic, executed in time, between the ideal of a straight line (as the shortest distance between two points) and the inevitable alterations that arise in actual, real-world production.

Composition 1960 #10 was not the first time Young had broached such a dialectical relation within his work. It had been preceded that same year by his exploration of loud sounds of sustained duration in *2 Sounds* (April 1960) and other improvised works presented in 1960 in the context of Ann Halprin's dance workshop. Long interested in noise, Cage responded to this aspect of Young's work immediately and positively, most notably by choosing *2 Sounds*, which he heard at Richard Maxfield's New York studio, as the accompaniment to Merce Cunningham's dance, *Winterbranch* (1964).[14] Instead of surrounding the audience with a multiplicity of different sounds, as in much of Cage's work or in his own *Vision*, Young so amplified a limited number of sounds that he effectively rendered them environmental, creating a sort of sonic architecture. To Cage's mind, such works opened up something like an "acoustical unconscious": "Listening to these pieces has been for me an experience that has changed my way of hearing, of hearing everything. It is like when one sees something through a microscope: afterward, one sees differently, even without a microscope. With Young's music, you can say that you hear in the interior of the sound, in the interior of the action."[15]

For Walter Benjamin, who theorized an "optical unconscious" in relation to photography and film, the camera's ability to capture spaces and events not "informed by human consciousness," particularly through its capacity for enlargement (as in a microscope) or slow motion, was a means of revealing previously unseen possibilities for comprehension, interpretation, and action:

> Photography reveals in this material [enlarged "details of structure, cellular tissue," and the like] physiognomic aspects, image worlds, which dwell in the smallest things—meaningful yet covert enough to find a hiding place in waking dreams, but which, enlarged and capable of formulation, make the difference between technology and magic visible as a thoroughly historical variable.[16]

> On the one hand, film furthers insight into the necessities governing our lives by its use of close-ups, by its accentuation of hidden details in familiar objects, and by its exploration of commonplace milieux through the ingenious guidance of the camera; on the other hand, it manages to assure us of a vast and unsuspected field of action [*Spielraum*].[17]

Cage related to this period of Young's work in much the same way as Benjamin: getting to the "interior of the action" via amplification opened up, as he explained elsewhere, "a veritable world of possibilities and events" in what formerly appeared a single, immutable sound object.[18] However, whereas Benjamin emphasized the manner in which a technological unconscious reveals the historical nature of all events, thus making possible political action and change, Cage—who tended to regard form itself as a necessity that "governs our lives"—saw opening up the sound to reveal its components to be processes free of neither contingencies nor time (another facet of the move from abstraction to immanence) as potentially liberating on its own.[19] Nevertheless, for Cage, much as for Benjamin, the importance of works such as *2 Sounds* was the manner in which they burst sound asunder:

> When I listen to La Monte Young, I conduct the experience in my way rather than in his. It's just that, in his music, you are free to discover a veritable world of possibilities and events. You can settle down within a single sound. At that moment, listening reverts to placing a particular object under a microscope so that the object becomes an entire universe, simply because it is enlarged to that extent. It ceases to be an object.[20]

As indicated by Cage's quote ("I conduct the experience in my way"), his understanding of Young's work differed from Young's own. Young's point of view was most specifically explained in the largest section of "Lecture 1960," where he described the effect of being able "to get inside of a sound":

> When the sounds are very long, as many of those we [Young and Terry Riley] made at Ann Halprin's were, it can be easier to get inside of them. Sometimes when I was making a long sound, I began to notice that I was looking at the dancers and the room from the sound instead of hearing the sound from some position in the room. I began to feel the parts and motions of the sound more, and I began to see how each sound was its own world and that this world was only similar to our world in that we experienced it through our own bodies, that is, in our own terms.[21]

In this passage, as in the section as a whole (in which Young is concerned to develop and transform Cage's idea of allowing sounds to "be themselves"),[22] Young introduces two important ideas. The first – highly important for Young's work here and with Conrad in the Theatre of Eternal Music but, in this passage, less evolved – is found in the manner in which sound is experienced through the body: that is, not apprehended discretely through the ears, but via a more evidently phenomenologically complex interaction in which the listeners not only potentially feel the movement of the air molecules on account of amplification, but also hear different parts (or partials) of the sounds, depending on their place within and movement through its acousticized space.[23] Hence Young's discussion of experiencing the sound "through our own bodies ... in our own terms."

The second and more pronounced idea in Young's passage concerns the manner in which the sound space constitutes "its own world," a separate or separable sphere. Whereas Cage, listening to Young's work in his own way, initially saw its importance as blowing up the sound, enlarging and fragmenting it so that it became perceivable as a realm of continually transforming processes, for Young, the fullness and singularity of the now nearly architectural sound returned precisely the totality and objecthood that Cage sought to dissolve into an open, multiplicitous field. Young, in other words, sought to restore the transcendence Cage sought to dismantle. Cage would come to label this aspect of Young's work "fixation" and juxtapose it to the "transparency" by which he described his own production.[24] For Cage, the goal of music is not to isolate the listener within an acoustic space (Young agreed that being "inside of sounds" was "like being alone"),[25] but to dissolve the boundaries of the ego that, to Cage's mind, already separate the individual as a self-enclosed, monadic being from the environment and from others. Such, for Cage, was the path both to enlightenment and political liberation. The "purpose of music," as he often declared, is to "sober the mind, thus making it susceptible of divine influences."[26] As he clarified in 1966, however, this had little to do with transcendence, for "we learned from Oriental thought that those divine influences are, in fact, the environment in which we are."[27]

Young, on the other hand, was expressly interested in restoring transcendence. As he continued in "Lecture 1960,"

> I could see that sounds and all other beings in the world were just as important as human beings and that if we could to some degree give ourselves up to them, the sounds and other things that is, we enjoyed the possibility of learning something new. By giving ourselves up to

> them, I mean getting inside of them to some extent so that we can experience another world. This is not so easily explained [we're back, in some sense, within Benjamin's realm of magic] but more easily experienced.[28]

As Cage pointed out to Jacqueline and Daniel Caux some time later, Young's idea of being inside a sound was, in many ways, the direct opposite of his own: "I would like that you consider, as you can consider it in Zen Buddhism, that 'I am where I must be,' but Young finds that where you must be is 'elsewhere.'..."[29] That Cage came to consider this aspect of Young's aesthetic not merely different, but (literally) regressive and potentially oppressive was implied by a story in *A Year from Monday*: "In the lobby after La Monte Young's music stopped [the reference is almost certainly to the Theatre of Eternal Music], [Henry] Geldzahler said: 'It's like being in a womb; now that I'm out, I want to get back in.' I felt differently and so did Jasper Johns: we were relieved to be released."[30]

If Cage criticized Young's "fixated" acoustical environment (as he would also the physical environments of Allan Kaprow) as a regression from the aesthetic of multiplicity, transparency, and immanence that he pursued, it was not only for its separation from the plane of immanence, but for its reintroduction of a type of power dynamic that Cage wanted to avoid.[31] Whereas Cage sought to place the listener into a nonhierarchical field with which he or she could interact as a disinterested equal, Young reinscribed a dialectical relation between subject (the listener) and object (the environmental, nearly overwhelming, sound). As Cage pointed out, once again to the Cauxs, he found Young's point of view "dualistic."[32] Furthermore, in so amplifying the sound, both literally and figuratively, Young exacerbated this interaction to such a degree as to make the inherent power relationship palpable. (In so doing, he may in fact merely have desublimated a dialectic inherent in Cage's work.)[33] Markedly different from the situation in *Composition 1960 #3*, where the audience was free to do whatever they wanted, in work from *2 Sounds* up to the Theatre of

Eternal Music, Young's listener and sound were engaged in a type of struggle, the phenomenological particularities of hearing in "one's own terms" fighting, in some sense, for autonomy against the nearly overwhelming pressure exerted by the sound.

• • •

Although not listed on the flier for the concert Flynt organized at Harvard, Robert Morris, in addition to assisting in the execution of *Compositions 1961*, figured on the evening's bill along with Richard Maxfield. Originally slated to present *Water Sculpture* – possibly an early version of *Fountain* (1963) or a relative of the unrealized *Wind Ensemble* (ca. 1959–60) – Morris ultimately debuted *Box with the Sound of Its Own Making* (1961) (Figure 3.2), Flynt having made the mistake of asking permission for the performance of *Water Sculpture*, which was denied.[34] That Morris's *Box* would appear in this context, as a sort of "musical" performance (though already redefined by Young as "art in general") was not without precedent. As Morris recalls, that had been how Cage received the work in New York at around the same time. Morris had described his piece to Cage at a concert, most likely Flynt's appearance at Ono's loft, and in a letter dated February 27, 1961, he invited the composer to come see it and other works at his apartment.[35] When Cage arrived at Morris's studio, he reacted to the *Box* as to a private concert, seating himself and listening to the entire tape. "He was the first person in New York that I asked to come see the *Box with the Sound of Its Own Making*," Morris recounted to Jack Burnham. "When he came I turned it on. I said this is something I made. I turned it on, and he wouldn't listen to me. He sat and listened for three hours. And that was really impressive to me. He just sat there."[36]

Burnham would brush off Cage's response as "sort of a perverse graciousness," and it has always seemed the idiosyncrasy of a composer avowedly interested in nonmusical sounds. Yet Cage's interest in Morris's *Box* likely also stemmed from the work's "theatricality," which it distilled into a discrete thing, one

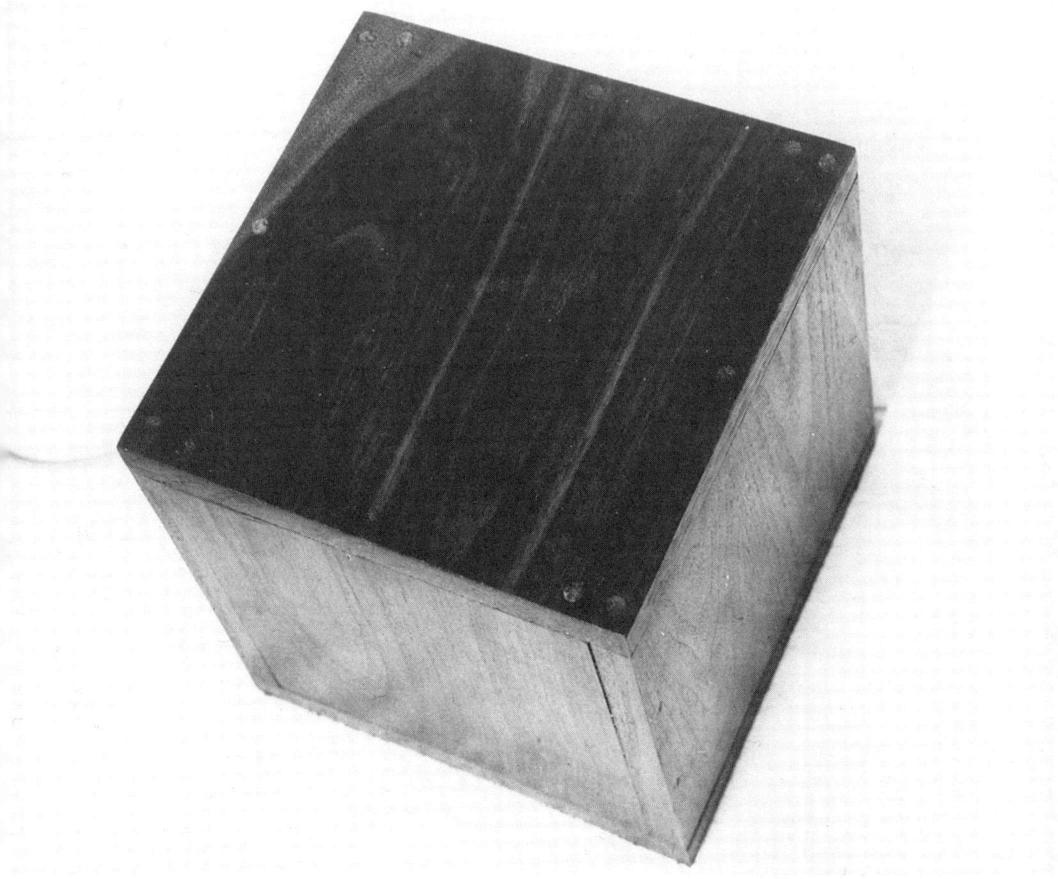

Figure 3.2. Robert Morris, *Box with the Sound of Its Own Making*, 1961. © 2000 Robert Morris / Artists Rights Society (ARS), New York.

that problematized process and object, temporality and form, art and music, and, potentially, performance and score. For although the *result* of a process, Morris's walnut box, in its simple and evident construction (note the visible wood screws), also acts as instructions on how to produce a subsequent "performance." Such a reversal, in which the score comes afterward and as a result of the performance, would be taken up by Cage himself in such works as *Variations V* (1965).[37] Thus, both in New York and at Harvard, at least for a time, Morris's *Box* existed simultaneously as sculpture and music, hybridizing and problematizing the two "major" categories in a manner that (as described in Chapter 2) served to keep them both in play – and at bay.

Something similar can be said of the *Performer Switch* and *Game Switch* that Morris constructed in the same year, which – much like Walter De Maria's *Boxes for Meaningless Work* (1960–61) – are, in essence, interactive, three-dimensional realizations of the type of word pieces that Morris submitted to and then withdrew from *An Anthology*, pieces such as *Make an object to be lost* (1961) or *Tomorrow 8 am to 12 pm* (1961).[38] Embossed on a brass plaque on the inside lid of the *Performer Switch* were the instructions: "To begin turn on – continue doing what you are doing – or don't – do something else. Later switch may be turned off – after a second, hour, day, year, posthumously."[39] In fact, nearly all the work Morris described to Cage that February was decidedly hybrid, moving the traditional genres of sculpture, painting, drawing, and writing into a determinately performative direction without, however, entirely relinquishing genre or medium interrelations for a realm in which "anything goes." Works such as *Litanies* (1961) would be described as "drawings, writings" and also "a two and one half hour graphic recitation" (Figure 3.3).[40] Morris's lesser-known *Frugal Poem* (1961; also known as *Words*) consisted of the repetition of the word "words" filling an entire page. "When read aloud," Morris explained to Cage, "one substitutes the word 'talk' for 'words.' A tape was made of the scratching of the pencil as it was written – it is intended to be several superimposed images, i.e., drawing and/or poem and/or musical score

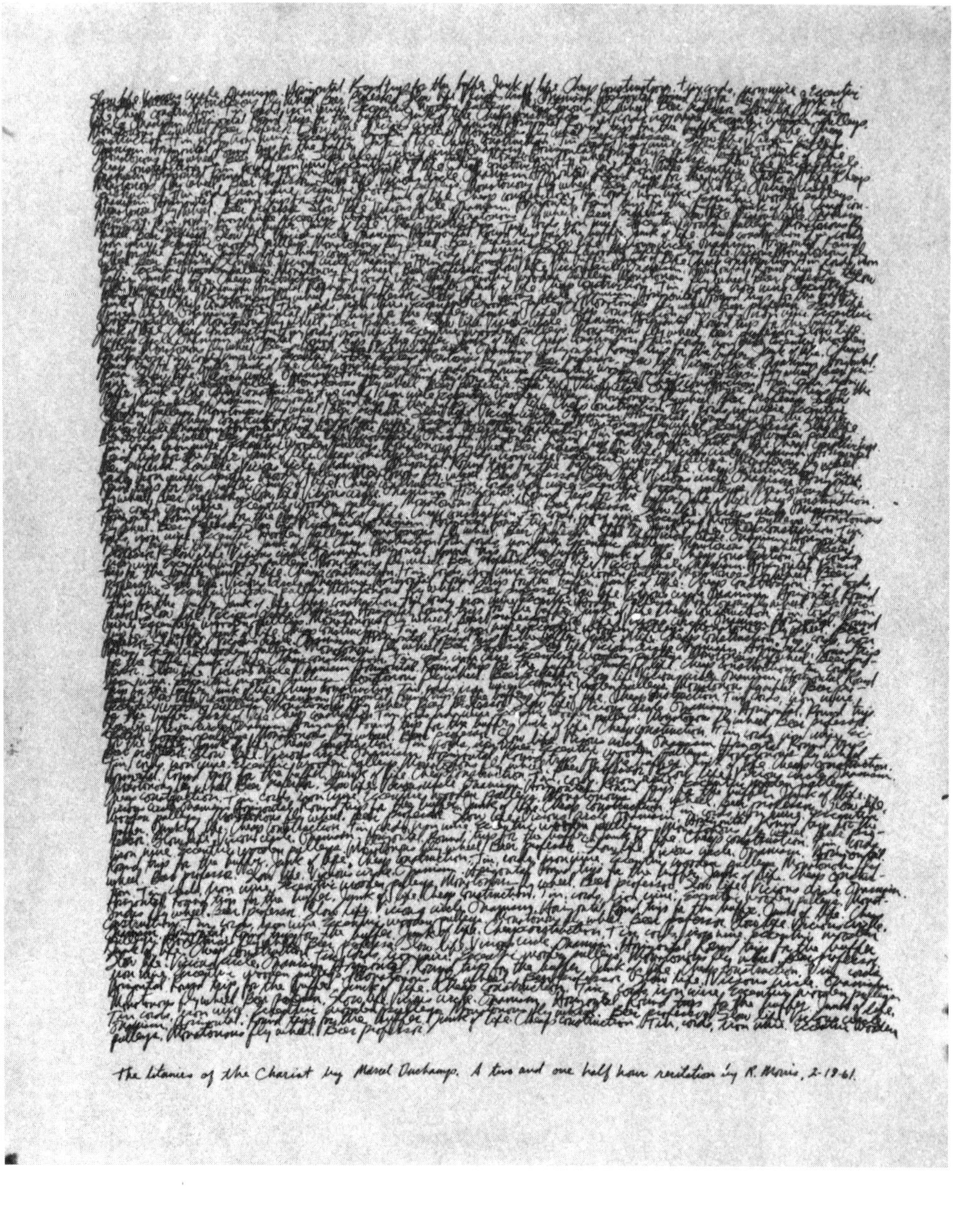

Figure 3.3. Robert Morris, *Litanies*, 1961.

and performance."[41] Young would perform *Words* in 1962 at the ONCE Festival in Ann Arbor, with compositions by himself, Maxfield, De Maria, Terry Riley, Toshi Ichiyanagi, and Christian Wolff.

Such intermedia hybridity is, of course, common to all the art forms that evolved in Cage's immediate wake and to which Morris's development is genealogically related: Fluxus performances and objects, Judson Dance, and what would come to be minimal music and sculpture.[42] And it would continue in a longer lineage of art/music hybridizations such as De Maria's *Cross* (1966), a sculpture meant to operate as an instrument (making the title a double entendre), Riley's gazebo-like glass sculptural *Time-Lag Accumulator* (ca. 1968),[43] Bruce Nauman's various violin pieces,[44] Charlemagne Palestine's performance and video works, Laurie Anderson's early conceptualism, and so on. Within the larger history of the period, both Ann Halprin's summer workshops and the Judson Dance Theater would play pivotal roles in the development of what would come to be known as the minimal aesthetic. Halprin's experiments with building up dances inductively on the basis of collective, improvisational activities, rather than formal, authored choreography; Forti's investigation (and literalization) of the conflict between abstract intentions and actual results, as in *Instructions for a Dance* (ca. 1961); Yvonne Rainer's pursuit of a choreography of the body's "*actual* time" and "*actual* weight" against the inherent illusionism of both traditional and modern dance; and more—all pursued in various important ways an engagement with the immanent realm as the site or location of anti-idealized aesthetic practice.[45] Without denying the importance of such a context, what I would like to examine in what follows is the comparatively lesser-known relationship of Morris's work to Young's, the manner in which they both instantiated, in their own way, the same dialectical relation between temporality and form, contingency and abstraction, process and object, immanence and transcendence.

• • •

Nearly a year after the Harvard "performance" of the *Box*, Morris further explored the theatrical dimension of his aesthetic in his first gray plywood *Column* (1961), which debuted at a concert organized by Young at the Living Theater on February 5, 1962 to raise money for publication of *An Anthology* (Figure 3.4). As is well known, the two-by-two-by-eight-foot *Column* stood upright for three and a half minutes before being toppled by means of an attached string tugged from offstage by Morris — who had injured himself in rehearsal when he knocked the column over by standing inside it. (An earlier version of *Column* was to "perform" in a more mechanical [and implicitly sexual] manner: "a pillar 2′ x 8′ which telescopes out two more feet. It is to be motorized and geared in such a way that it has a 48 hr. cycle — 24 up and 24 down.")[46] Rosalind Krauss has described the place of the Living Theater event in the development of Morris's aesthetic:

> Although the column was devised for an expressly theatrical setting, there is very little visual difference between it and the subsequent work that Morris showed in gallery or museum contexts as sculpture.... the large obdurate forms that Morris went on to make possessed a kind of stage presence, like the column's. His later works did not withdraw themselves into an aesthetic space, separate from that of the spectator but, instead, were clearly dependent upon a situation in which the beholder of the works was actually their audience.[47]

Maurice Berger has similarly explored the performance's paradigmatic critical importance in resituating the space of sculpture from the purely aesthetic realm to that of an interaction with an actual, real-world audience:

> In its literal fall from illusionism, its rejection of formalist sculpture's defiance of gravity, *Column* reasserted the anti-illusionism that would become central to Morris's transgressive strategy.... The notion of temporality and passage would contribute to the dissolution of formalism's romance with idealized form and time. In the end, Morris's metaphoric toppling of the pillars of late modernism announced an

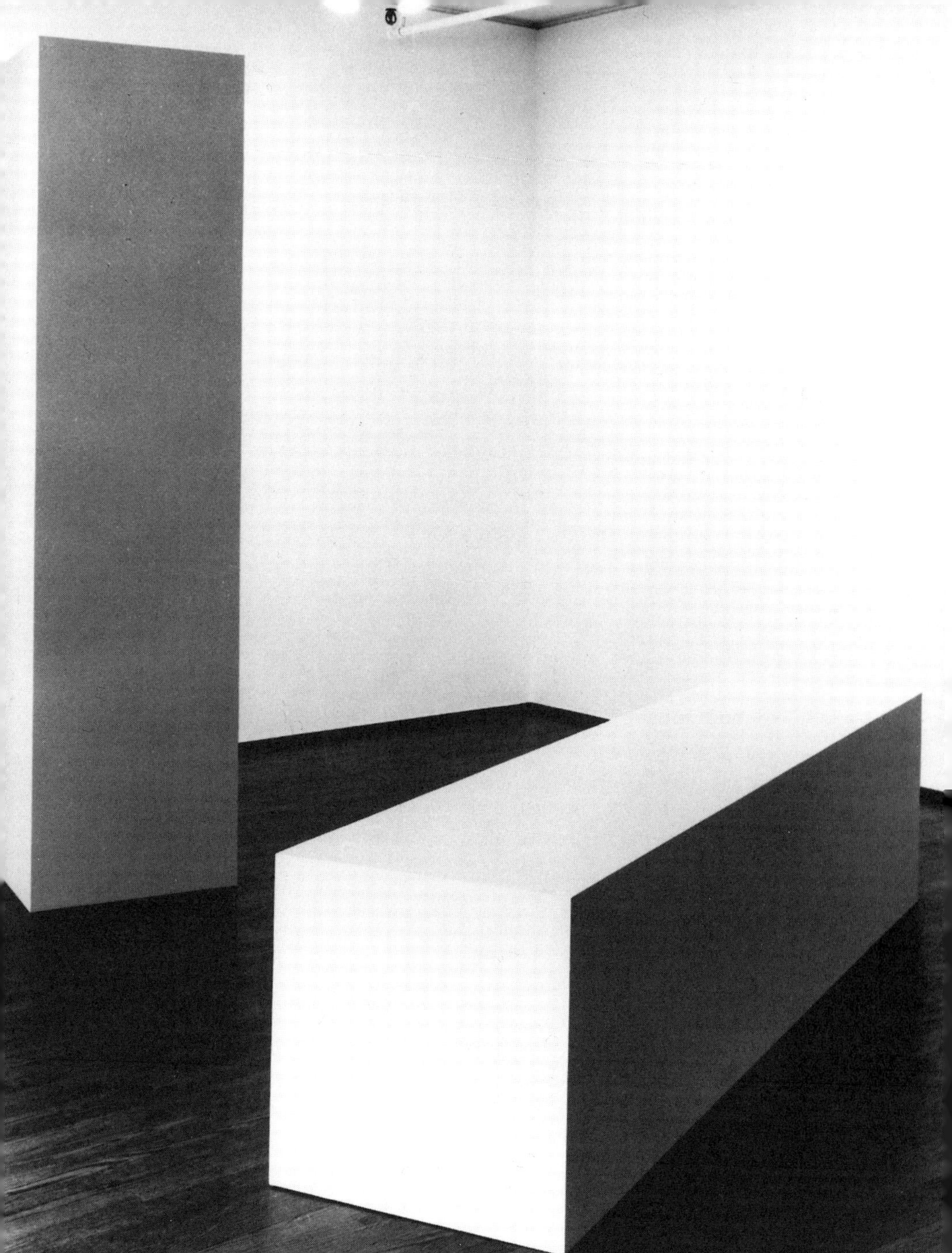

Figure 3.4. Robert Morris, *Two Columns*, 1973 refabrication of a 1961 original. © 2000 Robert Morris / Artists Rights Society (ARS), New York.

important shift within the American cultural scene as the art object appeared to be dissolving into a field of choreographic gestures.[48]

For Morris, the most important artistic precedent for the relation between contingency and ideal ("A beam on its end is not the same thing as the same beam on its side")[49] was found in the work of Marcel Duchamp, to whom Young – though he comprehended and commented on dada in general – has never revealed much interest or affinity.[50] Duchamp had most explicitly invoked the interaction between an ideal and its subversion in *Three Standard Stoppages* (1913–14), in which he dropped three threads, each one meter in length, from a height of one meter, fixing each in the configuration in which it fell in order to produce a new (non)-standard of measurement, which he made into templates and traced in paintings such as *Network of Stoppages* (1914) and *Tu m'* (1918).[51] Morris's *Three Rulers (Yardsticks)* (1963) forms an obvious homage to Duchamp. Each one numerically counts out the same thirty-six inches, while all, in actuality, measure different physical distances. (Note the title's pun relating measurement and political power. As we will see, for Morris, a ruler is a ruler is a ruler.)

By 1965, with works such as the *Untitled (Battered Cubes)* (1965) and *Untitled (Two L-Beams)* (1965) (Figure 3.5) – and the critical delineation of "minimalism" – the interaction of contingency and ideal at work in *Composition 1960 #10*, *Compositions 1961*, and *Box with the Sound of Its Own Making* would be firmly connected to the category and legacy of modernist sculpture. As Morris explained in "Notes on Sculpture, Part 2":

> Some of the best of the new work, being more open and neutral in terms of surface incident, is more sensitive to the varying contexts of space and light in which it exists. It reflects more accurately these two properties and is more noticeably changed by them. In some sense it takes these two things into itself, as its variation is a function of their variation. Even its most patently unalterable property, shape, does not remain constant. For it is the viewer who changes the shape constantly by his change in position relative to the work. Oddly, it is

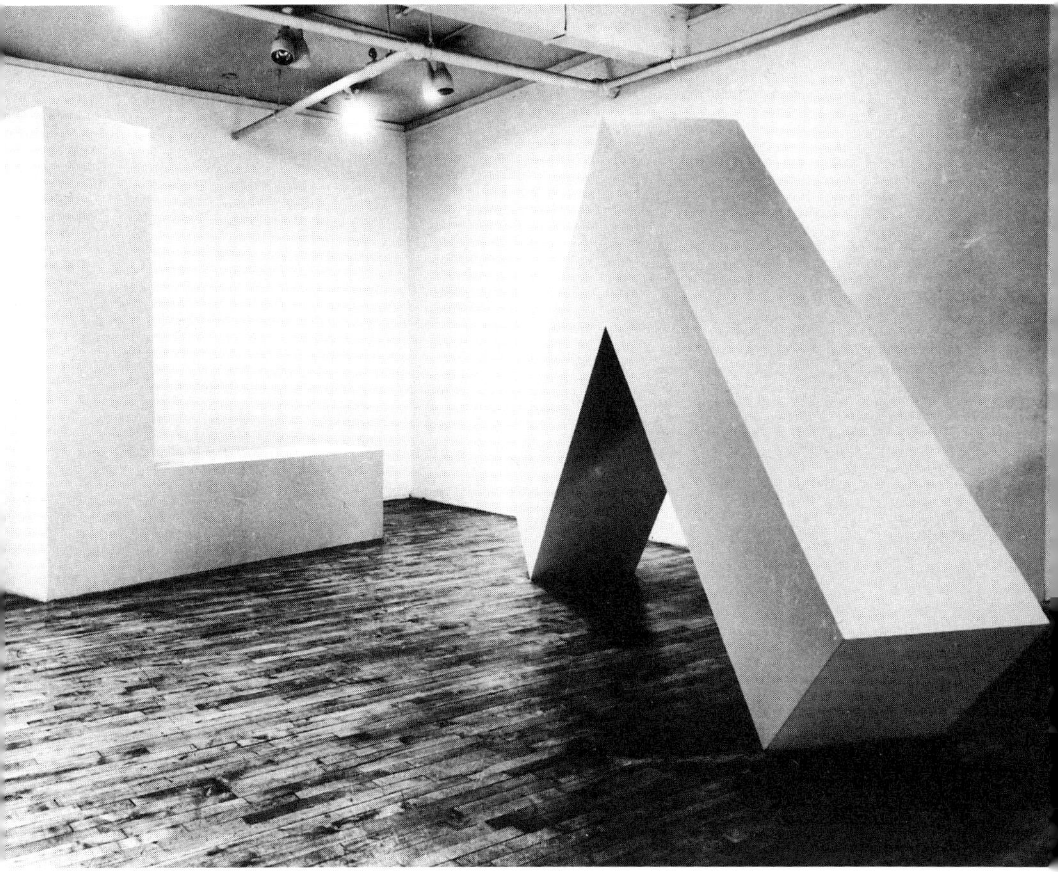

Figure 3.5. Robert Morris, *Untitled (Two L-Beams)*, 1965. © 2000 Robert Morris / Artists Rights Society (ARS), New York.

> the strength of the constant, known shape, the gestalt, that allows this awareness to become so much more emphatic in these works than in previous sculpture. A baroque figurative bronze is different from every side. So is a six-foot cube. The constant shape of the cube held in the mind, but which the viewer never literally experiences, is an actuality against which the literal changing perspective views are related. There are two distinct terms: the known constant and the experienced variable.[52]

The genealogical relation between this type of interaction and Young's nearly architectural sounds – in which the unornamented sound is transformed by taking environmental factors "into itself," as well as by the listener's movement in space – should be evident. It is as though the morphology of the two-dimensional line in *Composition 1960 #9* or *#10* (an indication, for Young, of duration) becomes in Morris's work the three-dimensionality of the cube or other regular polygon: an almost a priori degree zero of sculptural form. As Morris wrote in "Notes on Sculpture, Part 3," "The most obvious unit, if not the paradigm, of forming up to this point is the cube or rectangular block. This, together with the right-angle grid as method of distribution and placement, offers a kind of 'morpheme' and 'syntax' that are central to the cultural premise of forming."[53]

However, rather than being actively performed in time by the artist or object (as was the case with *Compositions 1961* or *Column* at the Living Theater), the performative aspects of circumnavigating Morris's minimalist polygons, approaching and apprehending them from all angles and sides in the continually changing conditions caused by such perambulation, is entirely delivered over to the receptive activities of the gallery-going "audience." In this, even more so than in *2 Sounds* (which, as a tape recording, still dictated the experience temporally), Morris's gray plywood sculptures allowed viewers to experience the work through their own bodies and in their own terms, displacing the dialectic of ideal and contingency fully into the observer as thought and experience. As Krauss has most perceptively written with regard to

Morris's *Untitled (Three L-Beams)* (1965): "No matter how clearly we might *understand* that the three Ls are identical (in structure and dimension), it is impossible to see them as the same. Therefore, Morris seems to be saying, the 'fact' of the objects' similarity belongs to a logic that exists *prior* to experience; because at the moment of experience, or *in* experience, the Ls defeat this logic and are 'different.'"[54]

Or, as Morris explained to Cage: "by reducing the stimulus to next to nothing (some of us really are trying to say nothing in an elegant manner) one turns the focus on the individual, as if to say, 'whatever you got in the past you brought along anyway, so now really work at it.'"[55] By putting the focus on the spectator, in the implicit power relation being staged between subject and object, Morris—in a way much different from Young's thinking, if not always from the actual effect of Young's work—emphasized *resistance* over identification or capitulation ("giving oneself up to the sound").

Since the publication of Annette Michelson's "Robert Morris: An Aesthetic of Transgression" in 1969, all analyses of Morris's work have stressed its subversion, the manner in which its phenomenological involvement of the viewer's body serves to challenge and undermine the purportedly atemporal "presentness" of late modern painting and sculpture.[56] And this aspect of Morris's production has been linked to the political climate of the 1960s (most notably by Berger), as well as to the revival of the revolutionary aspirations of the historical avant-garde movements of the 1910s and 1920s. For Hal Foster, the "crux" of minimalist sculpture both culminates a formal modernism and recovers the strategic, transgressive legacy of the avant-garde. "What the transgressive avant-garde sought to *transform*," he writes, is "the institutional autonomy of art": "We arrive, then, at this equation: *minimalism breaks with late modernism through a partial reprise of the historical avant-garde*."[57]

Foster's analysis is crucial, particularly regarding the influence of Duchamp as it was recovered by Morris. Yet the role of the early avant-garde as it figures within Morris's early thought and production must itself be seen as dialectical, particularly where it concerns constructivism. For what Morris emphasized in his only invocation of the historical avant-garde in "Notes on Sculpture, Part 1" (and in practically his only reference to constructivism anywhere) are the qualities of form, autonomy, and an uneasy negotiation with transcendence much more than any clear insistence upon subversion:

> Tatlin was perhaps the first to free sculpture from representation and establish it as an autonomous form, both by the kind of image, or rather non-image, he employed and by his literal use of materials. He, Rodchenko, and other Constructivists refuted Apollinaire's observation that "a structure becomes architecture, and not sculpture, when its elements no longer have their justification in nature." At least the earlier works of Tatlin and other Constructivists made references to neither the figure nor architecture. In subsequent years Gabo, and to a lesser extent Pevsner and Vantongerloo, perpetuated the Constructvist ideal of a non-imagistic sculpture that was independent of architecture.[58]

Although Morris soon enough emphasized the transgressive nature of his project ("*At thirty I had my alienation, my Skilsaw, and my plywood. I was out to rip out the metaphors, especially those that had to do with 'up,' as well as every other whiff of transcendence*")[59] the main thrust of "Notes on Sculpture, Part 1" (somewhat in contrast to its insistence that sculpture is literal, material, and concrete) was to establish as a legitimate morphology for an autonomous sculpture those nearly unitary shapes ("the simpler regular polyhedrons") that produce "strong gestalt sensations" in the viewer.[60] As noted by Foster, for Morris, the ideal form is often primary; it comes first.[61] It is perhaps enough to examine Morris's *Corner Piece* (1964), which stands clear of the wall and floor, asserting an autonomy even as it moves into the room, to realize that it is not about actual space, mass, weight, and materiality so much as it is about, as James Meyer has put it, "actual" *volume* (Figure 3.6).[62] Primary for Morris, as opposed, for example, to Carl Andre (who critiqued this

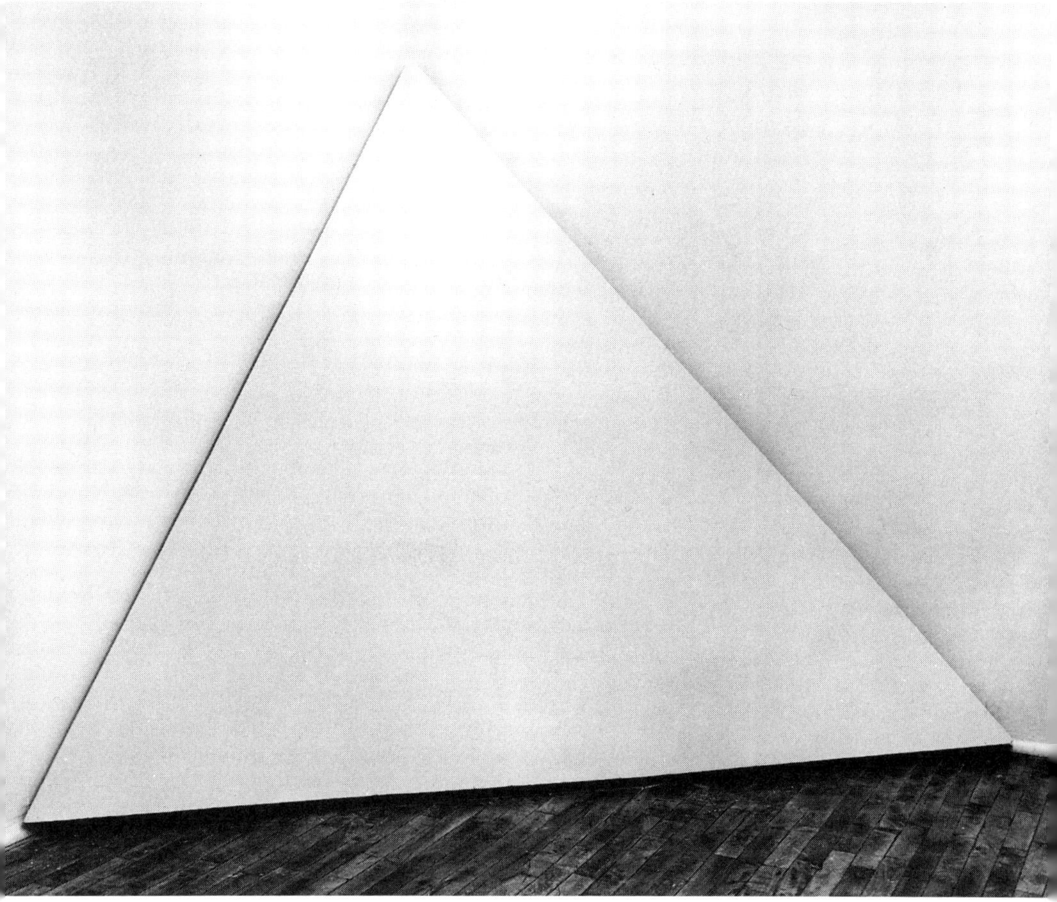

Figure 3.6. Robert Morris, *Corner Piece*, 1964. © 2000 Robert Morris / Artists Rights Society (ARS), New York.

aspect of constructivism), was shape and opticality, rather than tactility or mass, as revealed in his use of textureless fiberglass, wire mesh, and mirrors.[63] Indeed, in the above-quoted passage from "Notes on Sculpture," Morris equated Vladimir Tatlin and Aleksandr Rodchenko with Naum Gabo, Antoine Pevsner, and Georges Vantangerloo, constructivist sculptors whose work is hardly tactile, generally not in real space, and largely mathematically based. As Morris later reflected, "What was relevant to the 1960s was the necessity of reconstructing the object as art. Objects were an obvious first step away from illusionism, allusion, and metaphor. They are the clearest type of artificial independent entity, obviously removed and separate from the anthropomorphic. It is not especially surprising that art driving toward greater concreteness and away from the illusory would fasten on the essentially idealistic imagery of the geometric."[64]

This places Morris in an analogous position vis-à-vis the Cagean legacy as that characterized by Young's *Composition 1960 #10* and experiments with sustained, spatially enveloping sounds (which, as a participant in Halprin's summer workshop, Morris knew well). Against the background of a Cagean aesthetic practice, already thoroughly allied with the plane of immanence, the initial project of the minimalist generation seems to have been to reconstruct or to recover transcendent structures—or, in the case of the visual arts, to articulate a (Cagean) investigation of immanence with, or vector it against late modern abstraction.[65] When approached from an interdisciplinary, "theatrical" perspective, one leading out of Cage's aesthetic, rather than that of Clement Greenberg or Michael Fried, Morris's link to constructivism provokes an opposite, but equally true, counterpart to Foster's minimalist equation: minimalism, we can say, reconnects with transcendent form through a partial reprise of the historical avant-garde.

• • •

In the close amalgam of aesthetics and politics put forth in the Cagean program, Morris's move to restore transcendence had effects on both sides of the issue. For one reason to restore a dynamic engagement with transcendent form was, no doubt, the desire to model certain relations of power – power that, in Cage's work, was understood as potentially absent or eradicable once transcendent, hierarchical structures had been dismantled. Morris's reengagement with such structures, then, can be understood not as a regression (as even Morris, at times, seems to have judged),[66] but as a refusal of Cage's utopianism, his (to some extent typically anarchist) hope that power could simply be dissolved. That Morris's position was not merely personal is well characterized by Fredric Jameson, who has described the general political consciousness of the 1960s:

> It was as though the protracted experiences of the earlier part of the decade gradually burned into the minds of the participants [in social struggles] a specific lesson. In the United States, it was the experience of the interminable Vietnam War itself; in France, it was the astonishing and apparently invincible technocratic dynamism, and the seemingly unshakeable inertia and resistance to deStalinization of the French Communist Party; and everywhere, it was the tremendous expansion of the media apparatus and the culture of consumerism. This lesson might well be described as the discovery, within a hitherto antagonistic and "transparent" political praxis, of the opacity of the Institution itself as the radically transindividual, with its own inner dynamic and laws, which are not those of individual human action or intention, something which Sartre theorized in the *Critique* as the "practico-inert," and which will take the definitive form, in competing "structuralism," of "structure" or "synchronic system," a realm of impersonal logic in terms of which human consciousness is itself little more than an "effect of structure."[67]

Understood in accordance with Morris's combined reception of the linguistics of Charles Sanders Peirce and Ferdinand de Saussure (along with the phenomenology of Maurice Merleau-Ponty and the liberationist politics of Herbert Marcuse), the relationship between an indissoluble, repressive, transpersonal structure or form and its liberating subversion would become the overriding manner in which he approached and modeled power relations throughout the decade.

At this stage in his career, Morris understood power as a transcendental, autonomous form that operates in an exclusively "sovereign" manner: a mode of repression exerted by a hierarchical authority that, even if impersonal, acts from on high, a superior law that governs the distribution and combination of bodies and desires. Repression was, for Morris, necessarily a top-down affair, a vertical imposition, a standard, a rule, a "tower." Such a model of power as a sovereign, repressive form or structure was, in fact, much the same as what Cage himself had been confronting since his earliest work: what he described nearly thirty years earlier as "the cumbersome, top-heavy structure of musical prohibitions."[68]

Operating from the perspective of an interconnected semi-autonomy, Morris extended his position by analogy to the larger realm of New Left political struggles.[69] As such, the formal model established by his gray plywood sculptures could be extrapolated to a variety of situations: transcendent ideal and contingent perception, sexual repression and desublimation, institutional constraints and their subversion, and so on. "As calls for the 'desublimation' of Western society and the liberation of human sexuality resounded in the 1960s, Morris sought to liberate the art object from the repressive control of galleries, museums, and the media – the imprisoning iron triangle of the art world."[70] From Morris's perspective, the topography of contemporary power was one of isomorphic towers. The gallery, the museum, the bedroom, the factory, the university, the government, the media: each one is the purview of a despotic, repressive law; each one resembles the others, is homologous with the others, but is discontinuous from them – autonomous, abstract, reified structures. Berger goes so far as to characterize Morris's project as "a continual dialectic between the repressive, overpowering verticality of urban spaces and the more expansive, liberating realm of the Peruvian plain."[71]

Morris's aesthetic and political project, however, was dialectically and therefore inextricably connected to the towers that he would subvert. Circling around the gestalt or near-gestalt sculpture, the viewer is, as Morris wrote, "both free of the shape and bound to it."[72] His is a version of a "paranoiac avant-garde" – the "infinite paranoiac spiral" that Gilles Deleuze and Félix Guattari saw in the rotating chambers of Tatlin's *Monument to the Third International* (1920) and, even more, in László Moholy-Nagy's unrealized 1922 project for a tower wherein bodies would circulate endlessly on spiral ramps and athletes' paths (Figure 3.7). Morris's viewer, like Moholy-Nagy's, is always "a part of the function of the tower."[73] Indeed, Morris never sought to escape or to destroy the towers that he on all levels confronted, but rather to occupy them.[74] Whereas Cage argued for a strategy of exodus, escape, or acceding to the "outside" of hierarchical or institutional power structures ("Let them build whatever walls," he wrote; "someone will always be getting out"), Morris sought, according to Berger, "empowerment through a subversive relation to these institutional connections."[75] The difference is between a "minor" and a "major" politics, the latter operating within a restricted, Oedipal economy predicated on there being one, immutable mode of power's operation.

Morris was not wrong, of course, to oppose the repressive spires of sovereign power. The era of the late twentieth and early twenty-first century is filled with oppressive, hierarchical structures. Indeed, recent years have even seen the emergence of an overarching neosovereignty.[76] Yet power is not, nor was it in the 1960s, univocally or exclusively sovereign, but multiple – always existing within the mutual penetration of regimes: "*archaisms with a contemporary function*," on the one hand, and "*neoformations*," on the other.[77] Correspondingly, any analysis of cultural production must also proceed on a differential basis, examining its imbrication and mutual implication within multiple regimes.[78]

Seeing Morris's viewer's corporeal engagement within the act of perception as inherently "subversive" functions only to the extent that power is understood to operate exclusively in a sovereign, transcendent form. As Morris himself would later understand, however, the body is not a site of desublimated freedom

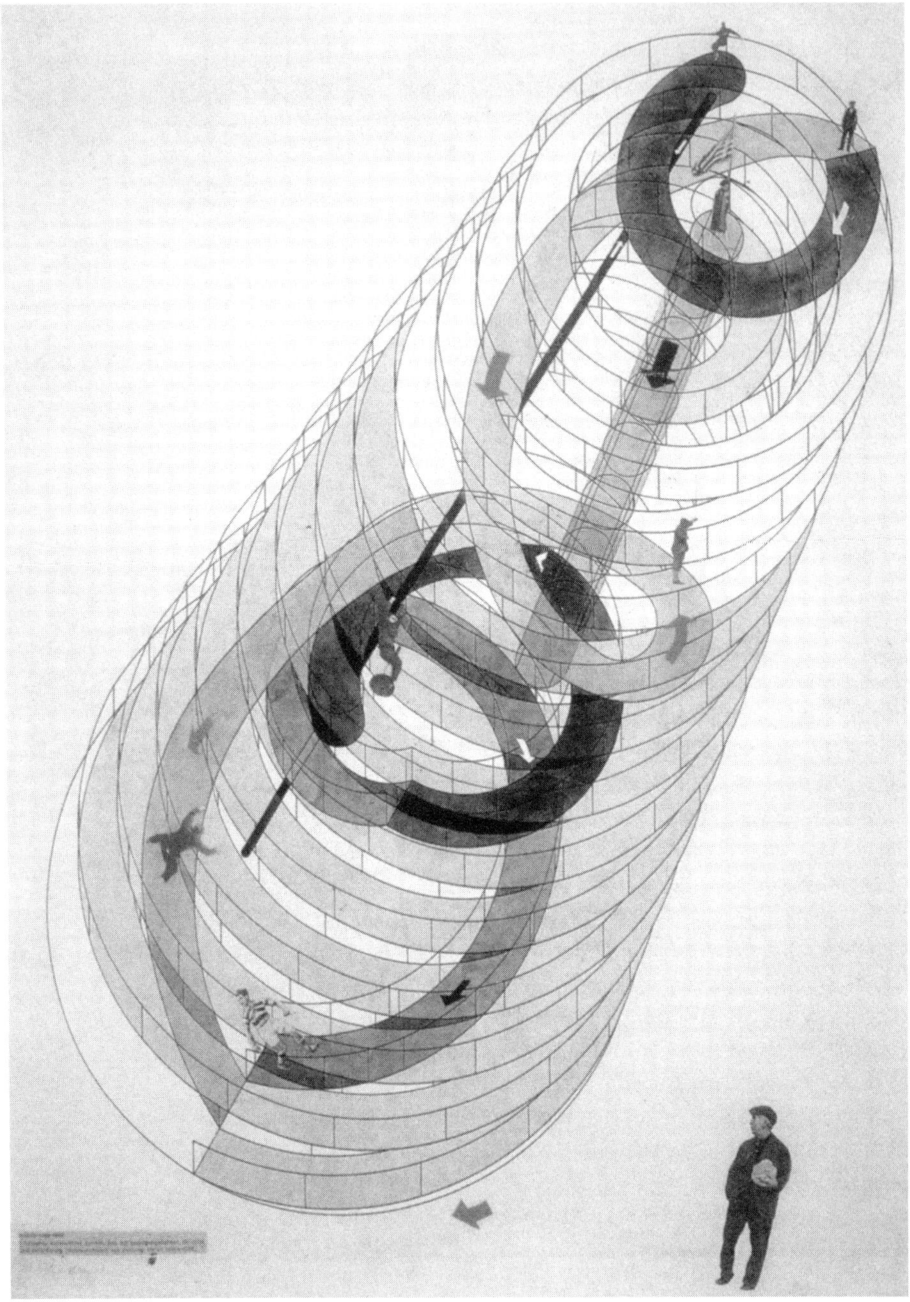

Figure 3.7. László Moholy-Nagy, *Kinetic-Constructive System*, 1922–28. © 2000 Artists Rights Society (ARS), New York / VG Bild-Kunst, Bonn.

(even, indeed especially, when dealing with sexuality), but itself a site of power effects. The physical participation and kinesthetic demands on the body that Morris understood as subversively engaging or transgressing ideal form may in fact be better understood as limitations on or inherent structurings of actions and behaviors — precisely, that is, as aspects of the disciplinary regime Morris would later explicitly invoke in the series of graphic meditations entitled *In the Realm of the Carceral* (1978) (Figure 3.8).[79] What comes into play (and into consciousness) in the kinesthetic interactions that Morris's minimal sculpture commands — the incorporation into the act of aesthetic perception of the body, its gestures, its placement, its movements, its forces, its time — is none other than the level or layer of subjectivity in which discipline infiltrates, operates, and inheres. Discipline, as Michel Foucault has explained, is precisely what accommodates itself to the exact contours of the "somatic singularity" that is the body, what makes of the body both a "subject" *and* subject to power: a "subjected body."[80] What was being modeled, then, even in Morris's earliest gray plywood sculptures, was not so much a dialectic of subversion as an oscillation between two distinct but coterminous loci of power: the despotic form and the disciplined body. Thus it is a type of mapping of the interactions between sovereignty (already in the 1960s a neosovereignty) and discipline that forms the subject of Morris's work.[81]

It is perhaps not surprising, therefore, to find it argued that the trajectory that began with *Column* culminates with *Voice* (1974): a largely objectless, chance-derived, "schizoid" acoustical field.[82] Such immersion in process and temporality was not, however, a simple return to Cage. Far from it. Once Morris had (once again) undermined the stability and self-evidence of the artwork as object, what he realized (in a way that Cage never would entirely) was that the dissolution of transcendent form did not effect or guarantee the dissolution of power, but only (and at best) the dissolution of a certain type of sovereign power. Within other regimes or modes, however, power operates on an immanent level, coursing through and even producing subjects out of

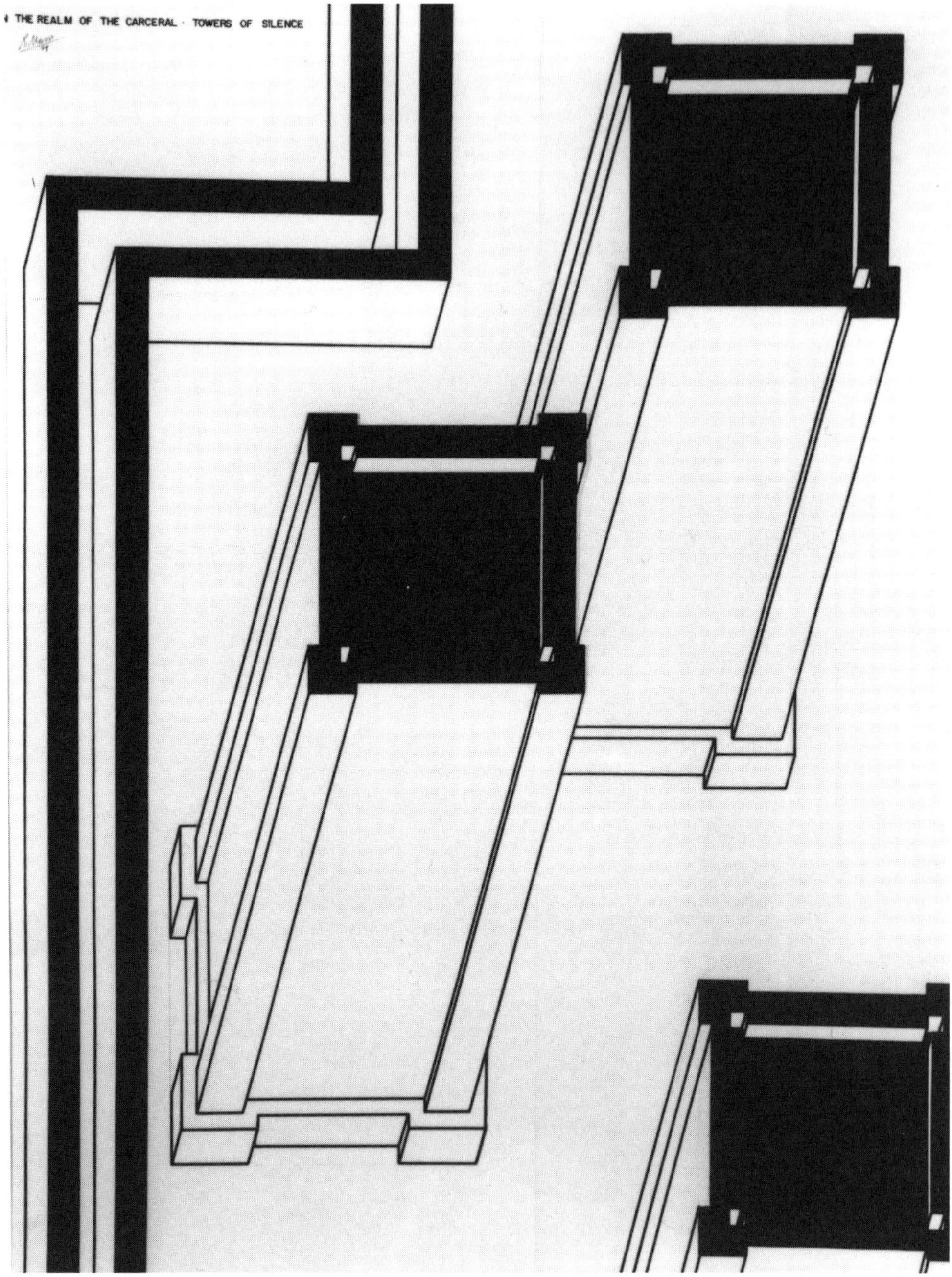

Figure 3.8. Robert Morris, *Towers of Silence*, 1978. From the series *In the Realm of the Carceral*. © 2000 Robert Morris / Artists Rights Society (ARS), New York.

bodies. (As we will see, it is on this level that Conrad's work, in the Theatre of Eternal Music and elsewhere, would develop and, most notably with *The Flicker*, push well beyond the aesthetico-political project inherited from Cage.)

• • •

This aspect of minimalism, the manner in which it evolved at the intersection of sovereign and disciplinary power, was certainly not unique to Morris's work and would likely be found to manifest itself in various guises in the work of many of his associates in art, music, and dance. In any case, it can be found to play a large part in the work and outlook of Young. This much was surmised by none other than Cage, who intuited the disciplinary aspect of Young's production by likening his approach to that within a "monastery" or "school," two of the primary sites of disciplinary formation.[83] Whereas Morris initially saw the interaction of the body and the gestalt or near-gestalt sculptural form as an analogue of resistance — a continual subversion of the ideal form that, in the end, one could never leave (an endless circulation about the tower) — Young embraced a more overtly disciplinary understanding on the interaction of body and ideal.

For Young, giving oneself up to the sound, in practice and over the long term, meant adopting and engaging in an intense, disciplinary practice (in the most literal sense of the word), by which the body is trained toward more and more precise tunings, an ever more exacting stability of tones, and so on. To his mind, the dialectic in play is one of ever greater approximation to an ideal.[84] Young's desire, the motor of his performance practice, is wholly vectored *toward* or sublimated *to* the "tower," not concerned with its subversion. (Hence his response to Kostelanetz's question about the lines in each of the 1961 compositions at Harvard being slightly different only because the technique he used at the time was "not good enough.") Young's model and analogue are those Eastern disciplines such as yoga or meditation where one seeks the identity of the body and the ideal, the achievement, through discipline, of a state of transcendence on earth.[85] This ideal, which is posited by Young in a spiritual fashion as "the good," is to be manifest for identification by the audience, as well. "My own feeling," Young explained to Kostelanetz, "has always been that if people just aren't carried away to heaven I'm failing. They should be moved to strong spiritual feeling."[86] In adopting this perspective, perhaps needless to say, Young turned away from his previous adherence to anarchism (from which perspective he had told the Harvard *Crimson* that "standards external to the artist are regimentation and therefore anathema"), explicitly distancing himself from it as he and Cage came to see themselves as opposite poles of the avant-garde.[87]

Although a need for performative rigor can be found in Young's work from as early as the *Trio for Strings* or realizations of *Composition 1960 #7* (such as the uninterrupted three-hour performance at the AG Gallery by Joe Byrd, George Maciunas, Jackson Mac Low, Toshi Ichiyanagi, Yoko Ono, and others on July 2, 1961), the disciplinary aspects of getting inside a sound were developed most extensively within the context of the Theatre of Eternal Music. Over the course of its existence, the Theatre of Eternal Music evolved an exacting, even ascetic practice regimen that took place several days a week for nearly three years. On this point, all of its members are in agreement. As Conrad has recently explained, the necessities of playing in just intonation, in which minute imprecisions in tuning can produce extremely audible results, called for that type of inhabitation of the sound described by Young (Figure 3.9):

> I found that just when I thought I was playing in tune, I would listen again, and I would hear even more miniscule inner artifacts in the tone that would be moving around. Maybe they're beats between harmonics, for example, and you know that way up the harmonic series, if you have a little inaccuracy, you're gonna be generating beat tones that are going to be quite off. So the more you get closer and closer, the more you begin to hear things lining up and then things not lining up. And a kind of hearing became necessary which I can only describe as going into the sound, going into the interstices of

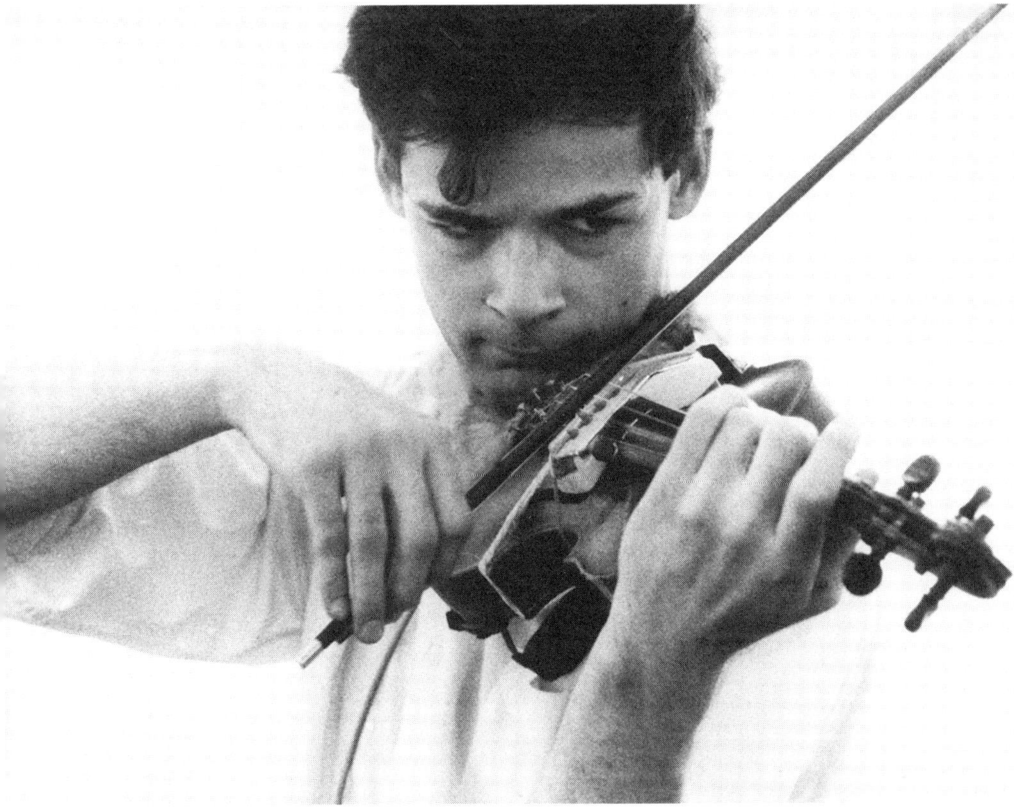

Figure 3.9. Tony Conrad, 1966. Photo: Frederick Eberstadt, used by permission.

> listening more carefully in the way that you can learn to discriminate like when you hear that there's a number of pitches in one note.... Entering into a very, very attentive relation to the sound and listening to the subtleties very carefully, in the same way as you might look at a picture and begin to see that there are inflections in the overall color, I had discovered that it was possible to align some of these inner events in such a way that you would have a lot of coincidence in the delivery of the energy.[88]

In the 1960s, it would also be Conrad who most directly and eloquently wrote about the disciplinary aspects of the Theatre of Eternal Music, most notably in a remarkable passage from the article "Inside the Dream Syndicate," which is worth quoting at length:

> The genius of conglomerate action raises the overall harmonic operative level beyond what is rationally controllable without great care in any case; machines suggest the patterns potentiated by manipulation and selection of high harmonic-content timbre complexes, but infinitesimal control has to be used to get the precisely wanted range of interrelations. Variation by extremely minute degrees, as well in fact as rates of variation, spring flagrantly into vivid distraction, creating almost the need for a new kind of instrumentalist. It seems to take a new year of listening to begin to obtain the control that comes only with the self-corrective semiautomatic control of the tiniest beat-elements of the single instrument. The string fingerer fights to find the right spot to press a motionless digit for months before noticing the demands of the right arm for microscopic fingerboard digit-rockings, compensating periodically for the tiny variations in string tension with each change of bow. More and unforseen months and years demand the developing of the keenness of static control to bring the effective minutiae to the performance surface of a group, though these efforts are constantly rewarded by slow coordinative growth that fills the communicative gap jazz calls swinging. All this sounds like the mythical rigor of Eastern mysticism, perhaps, but far from this, it is the world-wide demand made upon the exacting and significant

> musical communicant. The state of drive that has produced a 3-year drive in this direction by the four who play the dream music has come not from the sensational or ludicrous, as . . . have . . . put it to us, but from the excitement of a continuing growth, welling up constant richness and always approaching an ideal and limitless serenity which breathes on us each time we play and with each step forward. The exhaustion of changes is improbable and the exhaustion of stasis is impossible. The music has now gone on for years and opens up, with each new eye-opening of new sonar involution, into the world at large, both through us and collaborative awareness of the machines.[89]

As indicated by Conrad's rather blunt refusal of "Eastern mysticism," his view of the ends toward which the group's coordinated practice was directed differed from that conceived and expressed by Young. As Conrad explained more recently, "Our 'tradition' was centered in this constructed fiction: that the sound we made had flowed, and would flow on, forever. Young's elitist temperament was much abetted by this absolutist conceit, which for others of us was always usably picaresque precisely to the extent that it was unthinkable."[90]

It is an integral aspect of disciplinary practices that the "goal" can never, ultimately, be reached, but only be approached in an asymptotic manner. The difference between Young and Conrad on this point comes down to whether the goals are set transcendentally (by Young, as composer and further as conduit for a true, universal harmony of the spheres) or socially (by the group, as a deliberative, democratic collective whose decisions have no higher source, though they form and adhere to a system) – whether, that is, the end is eternally (and authoritatively) pregiven or an unlimited and unending set of temporary, contingent goals. This we have already encountered in the previous chapter. Important here is to note the manner in which the Theatre of Eternal Music both engaged with and effectively detourned the techniques and operations of disciplinary power. (As we will learn, however, in Chapter 6, Conrad's use of the term "control" is far from unimportant.)

It would be wrong to dismiss the practice of the Theatre of Eternal Music, as Cage seemed at least at one point to have done, as inherently or inescapably regressive. Far more so than the work of Cage or Morris (though it is also implicit in Morris's work), the Theatre of Eternal Music manifests the immanent operations of power in their productive guise. With the Theatre of Eternal Music, we enter upon a realization that appears all the more dangerous or disturbing for being true: that, as against any clear-cut separation of repression and freedom, power and desire are inextricably intertwined, not opposed, but inherently ambivalent, caught up in different assemblages and made to move toward different ends and different goals — crystallized in transcendent form or moving out ever further in different directions (which is why, among other things, it is not possible to simply oppose Young and Conrad to each other).[91] The project engaged in by the Theatre of Eternal Music must be recognized as a form of "counter-conduct" analogous to those movements of resistance that arose alongside the Christian pastoralism that, according to Foucault, was the initial incubator of disciplinary power.[92] The Theatre of Eternal Music engaged in a self-imposed form of communal self-regulation turned toward ends (whether understood from Conrad's perspective or Young's) that were almost entirely other than those of conventional Western music and harmony. It was a direction Young and Zazeela would later pursue in their infamous adherence to a twenty-seven- or thirty-three-hour day and the alteration of their domestic (and affective) environment by the constant playing of continuous tones and that Conrad developed differently in relation to the Bohemian New York underground, the politics of Henry Flynt, and the radically queer socialist heterotopia of Jack Smith.

• • •

Before we turn our attention back to Conrad's trajectory, however, we should make one more swerve to examine the distinct and in some ways divergent implications of another of Young's most notorious works from the beginning of the decade: *arabic numeral (any integer)* (April 1960) to H.F. [Henry Flynt], colloquially known as *X for Henry Flynt*. The score, as written out by Young in 1960, instructs the performer to bang out cluster chords on a piano every one to two seconds, with the forearms centered on the keyboard covering both black and white keys, an allowable alternative being to strike a gong with the drumstick from a snare drum.[93] Although potentially realizable with any integer – the choice of which becomes the work's title on that occasion, i.e. *62 (to Henry Flynt)* – in practice and by Young's preference, it was to be realized through the choice of a large integer that would take half an hour or more to perform.

The list of the work's early recitalists forms an impressive and select contingent of the musical avant-garde: Toshi Ichiyanagi premiered the piece at Carnegie Hall on May 14, 1961, choosing the integer 566. The next month, Cornelius Cardew performed it five times, in Paris and Cologne, twice choosing 1698 repetitions (exactly three times 566), and twice an incredible 6198. Young himself, in February 1962 at the ONCE Festival in Ann Arbor, clocked in at 923 repeated bangs. By the spring of 1963, Tudor, Nam June Paik, and Peter Yates had all performed the work, as well. Tudor chose to perform it using a cymbal on September 6, 1961, at the Darmstadt summer institute; Young realized the alternate version on a gong as an accompaniment to Morris and Robert Huot's jousting duet, *War*, at the Judson Church on January 30, 1963, and at some point decided the piece could also be performed with an orchestra or a group of more than forty-five instruments with identical tone colors (neither version, to my knowledge, ever having been realized).[94]

Like *2 Sounds* and *Poem for Chairs, Tables, Benches, etc.*, *arabic numeral* succeeded in capturing Cage's attention. In the same letter to Tudor in which he recounted the concert of *Compositions 1961* at Ono's loft, Cage described Ichiyanagi's performance of *X* as "a magnificent piece by La Monte: a single cluster (both arms) fortissimo, utterly regular, for nine minutes or so!"[95] By 1961, Cage had gone public with his admiration, saying that Young "is able . . . through the repetition of a single sound . . . for a period like twenty minutes, to bring it about that after, say, five minutes, I discover that what I have all along been thinking was the same thing is not the same thing after all, but full of variety."[96] Undoubtedly, Cage's understanding of *arabic numeral* (comparable to his reception of *2 Sounds*) was a key factor in his decision to stage the entirety of Erik Satie's *Vexations* (1893), the one-page score for which instructs that it be repeated 840 times.[97]

This more than eighteen-hour event, which took place between September 9 and 10, 1963, would prove to be John Cale's introduction to the leading edge of the New York avant-garde. Cale was particularly well prepared to take a place among the relay team of ten pianists, having corresponded with Cage, having long known of Young's work though his friendship with Cardew, and having just given the British premiere of *arabic numeral* at the University of London on July 6. (Cale recalls Cardew's helping him maintain a regularity of tempo as the unruly audience attempted to pull the piano away from beneath his arms.)[98] Almost immediately after the *Vexations* concert, Cale sought out Young and joined him, Conrad, MacLise, and Zazeela.

It would not, in fact, be Cage or Cale, but Cardew, in an article entitled "On the Role of the Instructions in the Interpretation of Indeterminate Music" dated February 12, 1965, who most extensively analyzed *arabic numeral*, breaking down the various layers of difference and repetition that it put into play. For our purposes, the most interesting and germane aspect of his discussion concerns the composition's implicit requirement of "uniformity and regularity":

> What is the model for this uniformity? The first sound? Or does each sound become the model for the one succeeding it? If the former, the first sound has to be fixed in the mind as a mental ideal which all the remaining sounds are to approach as closely as possible. (In practice the first sound too is an attempt to approach a mental image that exists already before the piece began.) If the latter method is chosen, constant care has to be taken to assimilate the

> various accidental variations as they occur. David Tudor has approached the piece in this way and tells how, on noticing that certain keys in the centre of the keyboard were not being depressed it became his task to make sure that these particular keys continued to be silent. This task of assimilating and maintaining accidental variations, if logically pursued, requires superhuman powers of concentration and technique. (It also presents the possibility that the piece might come to a "natural end" before the decided number of repetitions has been accomplished.) It must be remembered that although uniformity is demanded ("as far as possible"), what is *desired* is variation. It is simply this: that the variation that is desired is that which results from the human (not the superhuman) attempt at uniformity.[99]

The implications of the two possibilities Cardew outlines for performance in this passage are quite different. According to the first option, the initial sound becomes the transcendent ideal to which all subsequent sounds in the sequence will be related. Raised to "major" status, the first-sounded cluster is immediately doubled, existing once as an actual, material sound and again as an ideal form, a new category that, as Cardew makes clear, exists even before the performance begins. This first sound, then, as a mental image, assumes the place of an eminent, sovereign authority – the tower about which the performer circles throughout the remainder of the concert, weaving closer or veering further away as the factors of concentration and fatigue vary and intervene. The dynamic that results is largely identical to the one put into play between the ideal line and its subsequent realizations in the performance of *Compositions 1961*.

According to the second option, however, notably attributed to Tudor, the first sound never assumes a stable, transcendental form akin to a gestalt. Rather, the function of model devolves onto the actually immediately preceding cluster and changes – minutely, perhaps, but nonetheless continually – as "accidental variations" are assimilated. The transformation of the sounded cluster over the course of the performance, as Cardew is at pains to make clear, is not merely the result of being sloppy or inattentive (quite the opposite), but necessitates a different kind of attentiveness on the performer's part: a concentration not on a single ideal, unchanging over the course of the performance as much as possible, but on a mobile model in which a comparison is made only once between any two sounded clusters (a cluster with the one before it, and then, as temporarily remembered ideal, with the one that follows). There is no longer, in this case, a single, transcendental ideal, but a segmentary connection between contiguous points: x_1, x_2, x_3, and so on to x_{566}, x_{1698}, or whatever the case may be. The result is a repetition that—unlike that of a theme and variations (even a theme of a single sound)—allows difference to overcome the "model," each contiguous cluster tone not only approximating, but at one and the same time overturning and replacing the one before. As differences such as those noted by Tudor accumulate, are accreted one upon the other, change becomes cumulative, and the performer strays further and further from the tower or ideal, not in an infinite paranoiac spiral, then, but in an "unlimited schizoid line."[100]

The engine of these transformations is still indeterminacy: There is no teleology, no preconceived or foreseeable endpoint, no goal. "These elements occur rather *in spite of* the instructions," Cardew noted, "although naturally they are the *result* of them. What the listener can hear and appreciate are the *errors* in the interpretation. If the piece were performed by a machine this interest would disappear and with it the composition."[101] As Cardew's final sentence makes clear, he saw the conflict between transcendent ideal and contingent performance as located in the human body (as opposed to a machine) and, particularly in the case of *X*, in the factor of endurance. In Cardew's characterization, performance of the work increasingly becomes a conflict between the willing mind and the unwilling or incapable flesh, a case of bodily discipline breaking down or being destroyed by its own excess: "Truly this piece is gladiatorial; what the audience comes to witness is a rosy crucifixion."[102]

Cardew's interest in the relation between sound production

and the performer's body preceded his account of *X*. In the article "The Unity of Musical Space," published in *New Departures* in 1959 alongside *Piano Piece* (which Young recommended to Conrad), Cardew noted that in order truly to regulate the tension within a performance, "the composer would have to compose not only music but menus for a considerable period before his concert, and a tempered scale of sleeping-hours, relative to age, weight, sex, etc." It would be less difficult, he drolly suggested "to extract, before a short piece, one tooth from each in the audience who possesses any, thus ensuring at least the dominating tendency in the majority's experiential time."[103] As we have seen, a not dissimilar relation to the body (of the performer, rather than the bodies of the audience) and physical endurance would be invoked, in an equally improbable manner, in Young's *Piano Piece for Terry Riley #1* (November 8, 1960), which instructs the performer to push a piano into a wall (and beyond if the wall comes down) for as long as possible until overcome by exhaustion. Such interactions with performers' physical endurance seem quixotic, perhaps, in a conventional musical context, but not at all in the music-related performance art that followed: Fluxus performances by Paik, for example, famous for their physicality; Nauman's *Violin Tuned D.E.A.D.* (1969) – an adaptation, of sorts, of *X for Henry Flynt*, in which Nauman draws a quick, short bow stroke across the (detuned) violin strings approximately once a second over the course of an hour; or Palestine's *Body Music I* (1973), in which the voice – often understood as an ideal expression of metaphysical presence – conflicts with the contingencies of the body's movement, wavering and breaking for increasingly long breaths as rhythmic slapping gives way to an ever more rapid and exhausting circling and shaking of the arms until, finally, Palestine confronts the architectural (and implicitly institutional) boundaries of the gallery by literally running into them, and exhaustion leads him, and the voice, to collapse to the ground.

If the first option in Cardew's discussion of *X* entails a similar dialectic of body and ideal as that instituted in the performance of *Compositions 1961* and the phenomenological reception of the *L*-

Beams, the second differs, not only in practical application, but in its implicit modeling of or interaction with regimes of power. The move that it effects — from the hierarchy and eminence of the tower to the segmentalization of the line — is none other than a move from the plane of transcendence to the plane of immanence. As such, it is not unconnected to the turn from sculptural form to the viewer's body that we saw most clearly in Morris's minimalist dialectic. However, unlike the case with Morris, Cardew's performer (or Cardew's presentation of Young's performer) is no longer tied to the ideal, except through the contiguity that takes him or her ever farther away on a line of escape.[104]

Yet as in the case of Morris, it would be wholly insufficient to present or understand this "escape" as any type of pure and simple liberation. As Cardew's description alone should make clear, although the second option for performing *X* forms a line of escape from the original, transcendental ideal, it nonetheless does so as a technique, connection, line, or operation in which the body is fully implicated, both as a productive force and as a captured, engaged, or even subjugated one. Evincing itself as both escape and subjugation at one and the same time, the "performance" of the body makes evident the ambivalent, dual nature of power.

Cardew, himself, put the performer's body into play in "Paragraph 2" of *The Great Learning*, which he began composing in 1968 and recorded with the Scratch Orchestra in 1971. "Paragraph 2" was scored for a large number of voices singing against the ringing background of a number of drums all simultaneously beating out different polyphonic patterns. As with all Scratch Orchestra pieces, Cardew's composition sought to incorporate the different abilities of a number of individuals regardless of skill level:

> We wanted to break the monopoly of a highly-trained elite over the avantgarde, so we made a music in which "anyone" could participate regardless of their musical education. We wanted to abolish the useless intellectual complexity of the earlier avantgarde, and make music which was quite concretely "simple" in its assault on the

> senses. We wanted to devise a kind of music that would release the initiative of the participants.[105]

(Such a perspective, as we have seen, follows the implications of the "social turn" discernible in Young's *Composition 1960 #3*.)

What united the Scratch Orchestra beyond their diversity was not only unity of purpose (which became more explicit as they pursued more orthodox Marxist-Leninist-Maoism), but the experience of fatigue. Though Cardew does not describe it as such, the liner notes to the Deutsche Grammophon recording of "Paragraph 2" make it clear that he was enlisting the group in a collaborative form of "rosy crucifixion" not unrelated to his description of the lone performer of Young's *X*: "Occasionally a voice may seem equal to the situation, but due to the long duration they increasingly prove inadequate. Singers may justifiably feel proud of surviving to the end, but in my own experience of singing the piece I come away feeling drained and exhausted: I've given everything I've got and it has not proved adequate – I have failed."

A few sentences later, Cardew turns this perspective into a not so implicit critique of Young's development, siding with the immanence of failure over pursuit of the transcendence of the ideal: "the composer La Monte Young says that if his music does not transport you to heaven he is failing. Everyone's failing: our entire experience is this side of perfection. . . . Failure exits in relation to goals. Nature has no goals and so can't fail. Humans have goals, and so they have to fail."[106]

• • •

Seventeen years earlier, in "45′ for a Speaker," Cage had observed that "an error is simply a failure to adjust immediately from a preconception to an actuality."[107] Two years after that, in the letter to Paul Henry Lang, he specifically invoked the productive nature of "error," calling it "an excellent thing" that might bring about "an 'adventure in ideas'" or a new composition.[108] As early as 1960, Conrad had absorbed Cage's lesson, similarly embracing failure and error. In the *Sextet* that he mailed to Young, he included provisions for retaining mistakes in performance—expressly calling for "no violin performer . . . to have studied the violin for more than one year"—precisely for the reason that they accounted for the majority of interesting musical innovations.[109] According to the type of thinking we have been examining in this chapter, Conrad was already siding with immanence over transcendence, practice over the ideal.

We have already seen how certain aspects of Conrad's more overtly political aesthetic would ultimately prove close to that of Cardew. Years later, as mentioned in Chapter 1, Conrad would once again prove his affinities by understanding the type of music developed by the Theatre of Eternal Music as implicitly allied with a notion of "radical democracy" (akin to the "ultra-democracy" that Cardew perhaps too rapidly denounced when, in 1974, he renounced *The Great Learning* on orthodox Marxist grounds), a notion that appeared in the guise of "heterophony": "*Heterophony*; each person sounding their own voice; *no* blending into one; *no* overarching sound packaging; *no* universal understanding; *no* authoritative 'way to do it.'"

> Pythagoras's idealism has torpedoed our language and the structure of our thought: "philosophy"—"mathematics"—"cosmos." "Harmonia" is his term that cements each of these words into a *social vision*; a vision of a "harmonious" esoteric master-order which is set in rigid opposition to Greek democracy. . . .
>
> *Heterophony* is the sound of radical democracy. But this is more than a symbolic thing; heterophony is *doing*, where homophonic performance is *always* just *trying*. Homophonic "perfection" debases the performer—*all* performers. Not only that; what about some respect for the *listener?* Can a listener feel that they have any dignity, when the values in music are registered against "ideals?" After all, the work and the joy of listening are in the internal refraction between what *is* and what is *imagined*. And there ain't no respect in a prefigured imaginary.[110]

It would be on the level of immanence — against that of "a prefigured imaginary" — that Conrad's project would develop in the 1960s, as well. However, as we will see, it would not be within the body exactly, not entirely or as such, that Conrad would locate the operation of an immanent power (as "control," rather than as discipline). Far less categorical than Cardew in his adherence to human performers, Conrad would locate the operation of power (to crib from the track titles of *Outside the Dream Syndicate*) somewhere between "the side of man and womankind" and "the side of the machine." We are still, however, at some distance from that point.

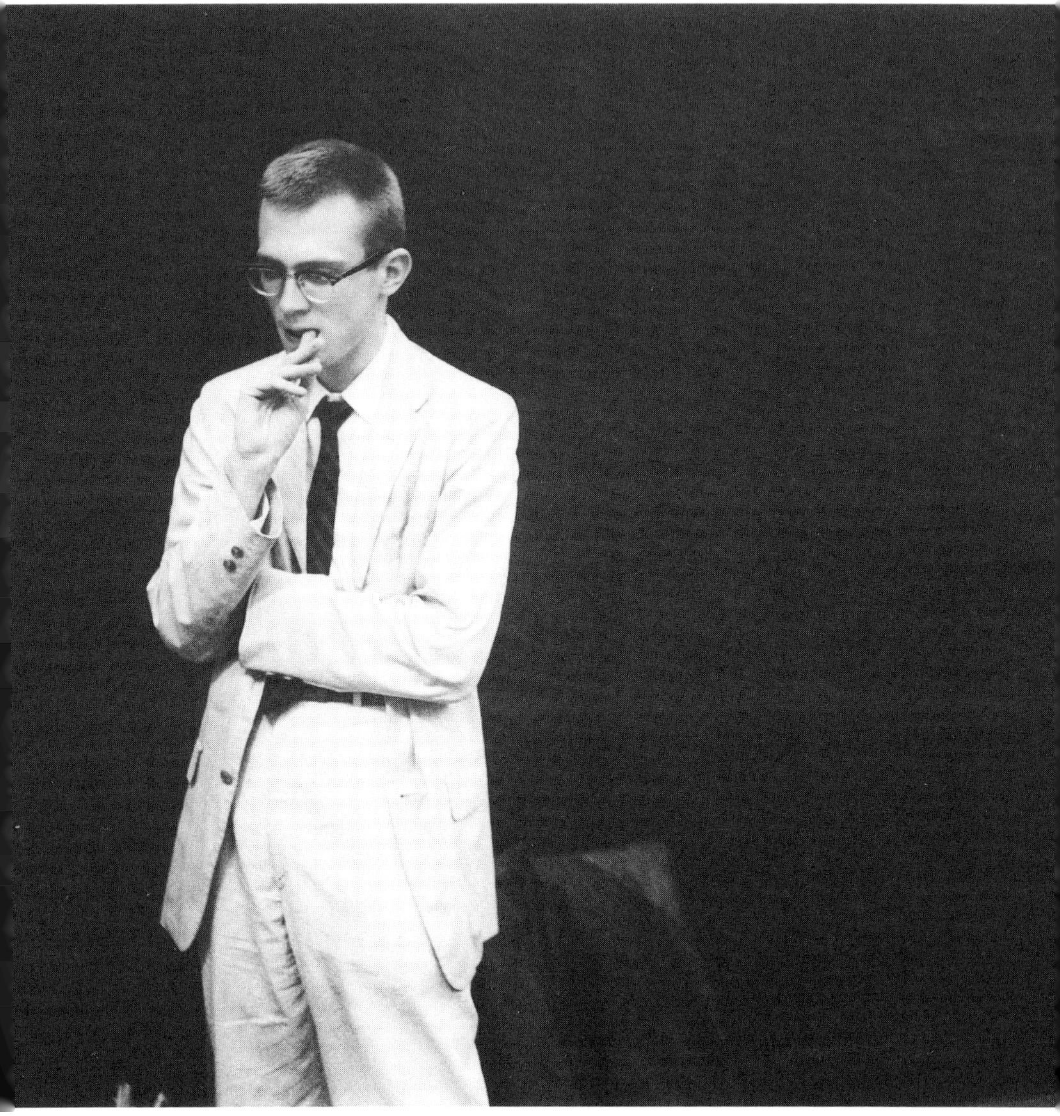

Figure 4.1. Henry Flynt, ca. 1963.
Photograph by George Maciunas.
The Gilbert and Lila Silverman Fluxus
Collection, Detroit.

Chapter Four

Concept Art

> Most of my writings are really collaborations with Tony Conrad. I often find that I do not understand my own position until I know how it appears to him.
>
> — Henry Flynt

When Conrad finally returned to Harvard in the summer of 1961 for his senior year, he found himself confronted most immediately not by Young's work, but by the transformations Henry Flynt's aesthetic had undergone while he had been away (Figure 4.1). That Flynt had given up modern composition he already knew (having communicated this in a letter to La Monte Young the previous summer, who responded with the news that Dennis Johnson had done the same), but "when I ran into Henry," Conrad recalled, "he just completely astonished me by saying that he wasn't listening to classical music anymore. He was only listening to Elvis Presley!"[1] Ultimately, Presley would be among the least of Flynt's enthusiasms, which encompassed aspects of jazz, blues, rhythm and blues, rock and roll, and an increasingly wide range of non-Western musics. Flynt had also already begun to improvise his own form of "popular" music with Young, their first session taking place in Boston a few days after Young's appearance at Harvard. After the Harvard concert, Young played his repetitive, rhythmic version of blues piano. "My musical interests had already shifted to 'jazz' (or American ethnic music, a term I sometimes prefer)," Flynt recalled, "and I was enthusiastic about supplying lines to Young's rhythm-piano composition."[2]

Conrad was certainly not averse to such enthusiasms. Before heading to Europe, he had discovered Indian music through Flynt, who obtained a copy of Ali Akbar Khan's first release on Angel records. "I went up the stairs to Henry's room," Conrad recalls,

> and as I approached the door I heard this amazing sound that I'd never heard anything like before. And it just went on and on like this. I couldn't place it. I thought I'd just never heard anything like this sound before. I couldn't knock on the door; I knew the moment I knocked on the door the sound would stop and Henry would come to the door and say, "Oh, uh, hi," you know. And so I stood outside the door and the whole piece went on and on and on – it lasted about twenty-five minutes. And then it ended, and I knocked on the door and I said "What was that?!" . . . I thought it was incredible music.[3]

Conrad's exposure to Indian music had an immediate effect, leading him to track down more examples in the collection of one of the university's professors and marking his own nineteen-tone piano improvisations so clearly that Young (who also knew the Khan disc) noted and remarked on it.[4] Interestingly, despite Flynt's own enthusiasm and absolute conviction of the importance of Khan's recording (the first-ever LP release of Indian music), it struck him somehow as not being sufficiently different: "I remember saying to Tony Conrad," he later recalled of that day, "'I wonder if that was really done in a basement in Brooklyn with, like, the kettle drum player from the New York Philharmonic and. . . .' He actually had passage work, Ali Akbar Khan. I mean sometimes it sounded like Bach to me."[5]

Ironically, given the current nature of Young and Conrad's authorship dispute, it was Conrad, in 1961, who proved most resistant to abandoning conventional composition. As he wrote to himself that October, "Now is a continuing aesthetic struggle, with Henry and the (indirect) return to Music in music. I understand him and La Monte, but what to DO? as usual. The Fugue is still good."[6] Although he persisted in completing and premiering *Three Loops for Performers and Tape Recorders*, Conrad realized that, given the developments that took place while he was gone, "it would be a cold day in hell before the pieces I'd worked on in Europe got performed."[7] Conrad soon began visiting New York, stopping on his way between Cambridge and his parents' home in Maryland, meeting with Young and encountering such denizens of the underground as Billy Linich, Robert Olivo (aka Ondine), and The Turtle (a somewhat infamous drug dealer, so-named because he never arrived on time). Before Conrad moved to New York permanently in 1962, however, it was Flynt who continued to serve as his closest and most consistent interlocutor.

Flynt had been indirectly in touch with Young through Conrad since the summer of 1959. They first met in person, however, in December 1960, when Young invited Flynt to New York for Terry Jennings's concerts at Yoko Ono's loft.[8] It was there over the next couple of days that Flynt discovered Young's word scores, a genre that immediately captured his attention. Flynt's take on such pieces was informed by his undergraduate interests in philosophy and his studies in mathematics. For him, the most remarkable aspect of Young's concert of *Compositions 1961* was not their performative dialectic of ideal and real, but the conceptual conundrum underlying their dates. As he explained:

> Young had been threatening to present the most avant-garde pieces in the world. I remember when he told me over the telephone how the works were to be listed in the program. As he dictated, he came to *Composition 1961 #8*, dated April 2, 1961! [The concert was to take place on March 31.] He was going to perform 22 compositions before they were composed. In logical terms, he was going to follow a rule which he had planned, but which did not yet exist. From the point of view of the conventionalist explanation of the existence of abstractions, Young was introducing time travel at the level of whether given abstractions existed or not.[9]

Flynt would produce a series of his own word scores that January. Some, such as the *Concerto for Kitchen Sink and Monkey Orchestra* (January 2, 1961; somewhere between a music score and a word piece proper) were intentionally written as dadaist (or proto-Fluxus) pranks.[10] Instructing the soloist to bang on a sink with an iron pipe at a steady tempo (100 times per minute) and at an amplitude that was loud and unchanging, Flynt's *Concerto* parodies Young's *arabic numeral*. As absurd as it was, the accompanying monkey orchestra – to consist of fourteen caged chimpanzees whose musical instruments were amplified and broadcast in stereo – also had a precedent as a noisier example of the type of indeterminacy Young delivered over to the animal kingdom via the butterfly in *Composition 1960 #5*. Another of Flynt's early works responded to Young's *Composition 1960 #9*, the straight line on a card. Underneath his own line, Flynt noted: "Each point on this line is a composition" (January, 1961).

Flynt's more characteristic word pieces, or at least those more consequent for Conrad, posed unperformable logical conundrums. This was the case, for example, in Flynt's two versions of *The Instructions for This Piece Are on the Other Side of This Sheet* (January, 1961), one of which had nothing but a blank page as the verso, the other a verbatim repetition of the original statement. Such concerns were ultimately developed into a word piece on a Möbius strip that read: "The instructions for this composition are on the other side of this strip" (January 1961).

Young included Flynt in both the Chambers Street concerts at Ono's loft and the subsequent series of events at George Maciunas's AG Gallery, on which Young and Jackson Mac Low advised. Flynt's performances were diverse. According to Maciunas, in addition to exhibiting the Möbius strip piece, Flynt's evenings at Ono's loft included: "ran around the room, recorded watch ticking, bad viennese violin music, banged on wood of piano."[11] During the first night's performance, Simone Forti memorably bested Flynt in one of his own quixotic logic games. "I asked the audience to propose a contest," he recalled: "If I liked the contest, then the audience would compete and whoever won would get to perform on a clamp and rubber band (which I had picked up and announced made an instrument). Simone Morris (now Simone Forti) said: 'Let the contest be who can think up a good contest the quickest.' I accepted this as a good contest. She said: 'I win.'"

Flynt's disappointment led to a sort of recovery: "Feeling that she had somehow cheated, I paced the floor trying to discern the trick. Finally I announced that her contest violated one of the principles of logic announced by Russell."[12]

Though it may seem today like little more than a dead end, at the time such gamelike exercises appear to have been treated (or at least indulged) as a legitimate line of inquiry for a group grappling with the legacies of John Cage and Young. Flynt recalls the impetus behind his pursuits as being "engrossed in the competition to be newest as Young conceived it and crusaded for it."[13] (Indeed, Flynt felt so sure that his Chambers Street concert had established him as the most avant-garde that his only contribution to Young's Harvard concert was the program listing, "possibly Henry Flynt." The idea was that Flynt, if he felt his position at the vanguard challenged by Young, Richard Maxfield, or Robert Morris, "would create a work on the spot which would top theirs.")[14] At the time, Flynt's activities were also not as far from Young's production as they may now seem. The program for the first Jennings loft concert listed the final piece as Young's *an invisible poem sent to Terry Jennings for him to perform*. The score, dated February 1960, consists of nothing more than the empty space in an envelope alongside a letter. (Jennings responded with an unannounced, invisible, and inaudible performance.)[15] Flynt's answer to this work, in a sense, was *Work Such That No One Knows What's Going On* (1961), which Young prominently included at the ONCE Festival in Ann Arbor on that same bill with *923 to Henry Flynt*, and *Words* by Morris. As listed on the program, the content of Flynt's work was that "one just has to guess whether this work exists and if it does what it is like." Flagged by four asterisks on the next line, Young provided a "realization" particularly attuned to Flynt's interest in quizzical self-referentiality: "My guess," Young's program note continued, "is that this work exists and that it is of such a nature that one just has to guess whether this work exists and if it does what it is like."[16]

Conrad, who had received Young's first word scores in Denmark, was particularly interested in Flynt's versions and immediately reacted by producing a series of closely related works (Figure 4.2). Conrad must particularly have appreciated Flynt's Möbius strip, because he was working at the time with a more complex, but not dissimilar topological structure, the Flexagon. Conrad published a mathematical paper titled "The Theory of the Flexagon" in February 1960 before leaving for Europe and coauthored another, longer work, "Flexagons," in May 1962.[17] One of Conrad's earliest word pieces would rework Flynt's Möbius strip into a circular transcription that read (in an infinite loop): "The instructions for performing this piece follow."[18]

Like Flynt, Conrad's background in mathematics predisposed him to logic games, investigations into composition as a form of self-referentiality that ends by negating and ultimately annihilating itself. Many of his word pieces, like his Ouroboros-like circle, took the form of paradoxes or tautologies that were either not realizable at all or else fully realized in their composition. "To perform this piece," one of his scores instructed, "do not perform this piece" (variants included: "To perform this piece perform this piece" and "To perform this piece do not compose this piece"). *Null Piece* (1961) declared: "This is the piece that is no piece." As Conrad later explained:

> The short pieces that I wrote for myself at the time were pieces that I jotted down because I felt that it was interesting to imagine work which hypostatized its own status as composition into a realm of logic or simple relationalism, so that it no longer had any relation to performance or any real-world anything. In other words, work that so problematizes its own status as a composition, or its own capability of performance, that it becomes simply an abstract work, in the sense that "abstract," as a category, represents a hypostatization into a metaphysical realm—a realm which, now, I recognize as having to do with a kind of religious impulse, but at that time because of my background in mathematics I identified with purity and mathematics and all of these kinds of things.... The way in which the score could become an object which lost its connectivity to performance altogether—and to all of the projects of a grounded and traditional craft

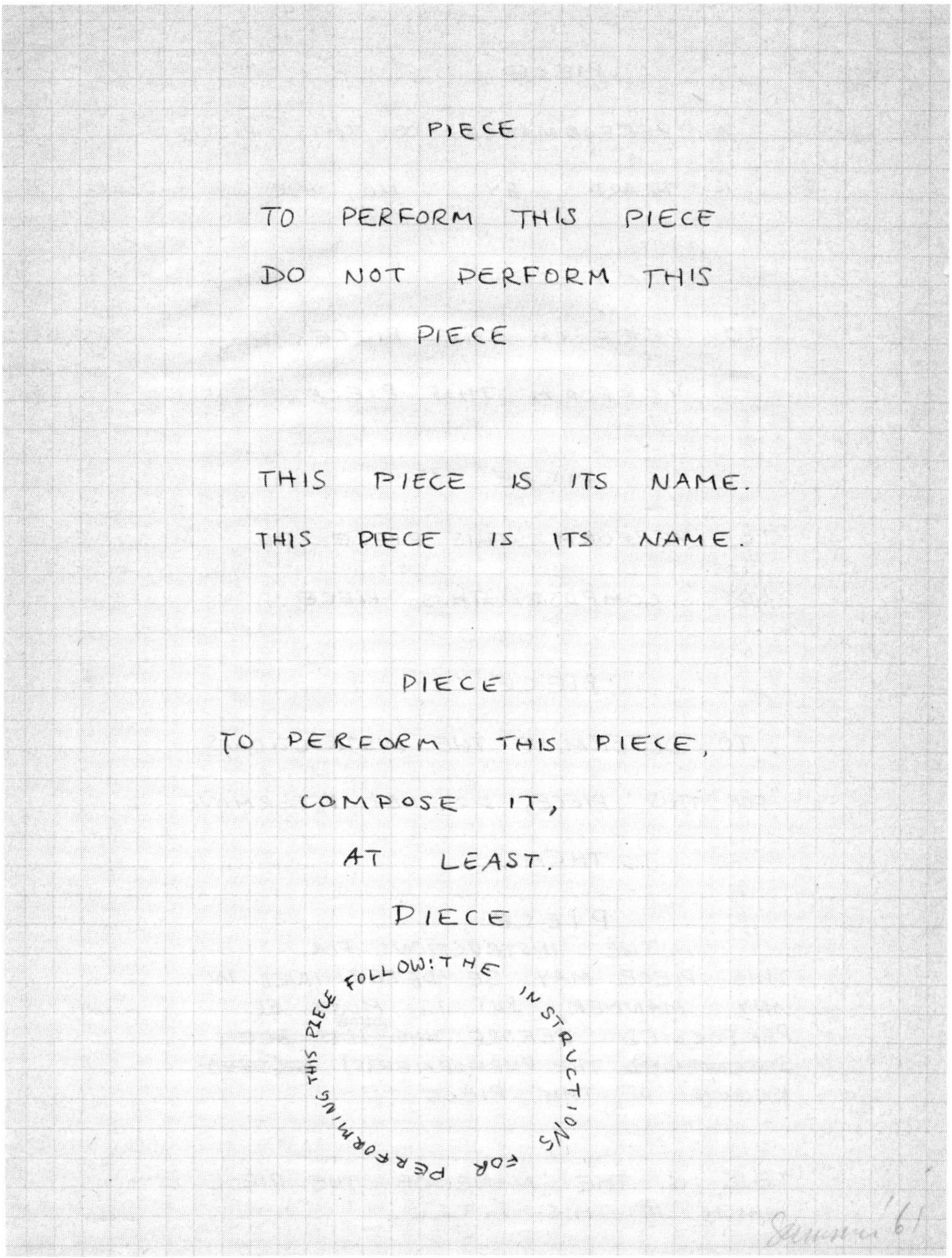

PIECE

TO PERFORM THIS PIECE
DO NOT PERFORM THIS
PIECE

THIS PIECE IS ITS NAME.
THIS PIECE IS ITS NAME.

PIECE

TO PERFORM THIS PIECE,
COMPOSE IT,
AT LEAST.

PIECE

FOLLOW: THE INSTRUCTIONS FOR PERFORMING THIS PIECE

Summer '61

Figure 4.2. Tony Conrad, page of four word scores, summer 1961. Courtesy Tony Conrad.

> of composing and music making: that seemed like a valuable sort of jump to go for. So a piece called *This Piece Is Its Name*, in which the substance of the piece is "This Piece Is Its Name," problematizes whether you have a piece.[19]

Nearly all word scores, as we have already posited, challenge traditional artistic tropes of authorship, composition, and intention. Conrad's and Flynt's, however, more specifically emulated a type of analytic demonstration derived from mathematics. As such, they proved no more expressive than a mathematical equation, which can be run through identically by anyone who accepts the axioms and moves through the logical steps.[20]

While closely related in both form and content (or what content they had) to Flynt's production, Conrad's word scores, true to the genre, also made reference to the presuppositions or instructions of other specific works. "A performance of this piece is heard by no one" evidently inscribes itself within the growing tradition of reworking Cagean silence. Another of Conrad's compositions reworked Flynt's interest in the "time travel" virtually effected by the Harvard performance of *Compositions 1961*:

> PIECE
>
> THE INSTRUCTIONS FOR THIS PIECE MAY BE DETERMINED IN ANY MANNER, BUT IT MUST BE PERFORMED BEFORE THE PERFORMER(S) KNOW(S) OF THIS PIECE.
>
> (Summer 1961)

Conrad later revisited the idea in the title-only *This Is the Piece That Is Performed Only Before It Is Written* (November 7, 1961). In perhaps the most developed of Conrad's productions in this vein, *Work Which Is Its Title* (1961, an elaboration of *This Piece Is Its Name*), Conrad reworked as a word piece the dependency relations first explored in *Fugue*. Dedicated, as *Fugue* had been, to Flynt, *Work Which Is Its Title* consists of a mazelike array of words and arrows that provide nothing more than a means of deriving alternate titles for the piece: "Concerto for Henry Flynt," "Work for Henry Flynt," "Concerto for Henry Flynt, Tie, Rat, and Orchestra," and so on (Figure 4.3).

Although neither Flynt's nor Conrad's word pieces were published in *An Anthology*, they would not be without echoes, whether directly connected or not. Conrad's *This Is the Piece That Is Any Piece That Is Performed Only When It Is Written* (November 7, 1961), for example, anticipates Cage's writing out the score for *0′00″* (1962; also known as *4′33″ No. 2*) as the sole content of the composition's initial performance.[21] And Fluxus works such as Ken Friedman's *Mandatory Happening* (1966) would evince a similar type of self-referential abstraction as that Flynt and Conrad explored:

> You will decide to read or
> not to read this instruction.
>
> Having made your decision,
> the happening is over.[22]

• • •

Flynt's and Conrad's word pieces were related to Flynt's newly defined genre, "concept art." Indeed, in his final and most extensive diagram of postwar art, George Maciunas listed Conrad as Flynt's only follower in this regard (Figure 4.4).[23] Concept art was one of five cultural categories that Flynt defined in 1961, alongside the much lesser-known "audart," short for "auditory art," which was to replace music; "linart," from "linguistic art," meant to replace poetry; "visart," the replacement for painting and sculpture; and "strange culture description," an investigation into alternate reality states inspired by science fiction. Later, Flynt would replace "art" with the suffix "-act" (short for "acognitive cultural activity") to derive the terms "concact," "audact", "linact," "visact," and "strange culture description." Conrad was impressed enough with Flynt's ambitions to collect, type, and publish examples of all these forms as Flynt's *Anthology of Non-*

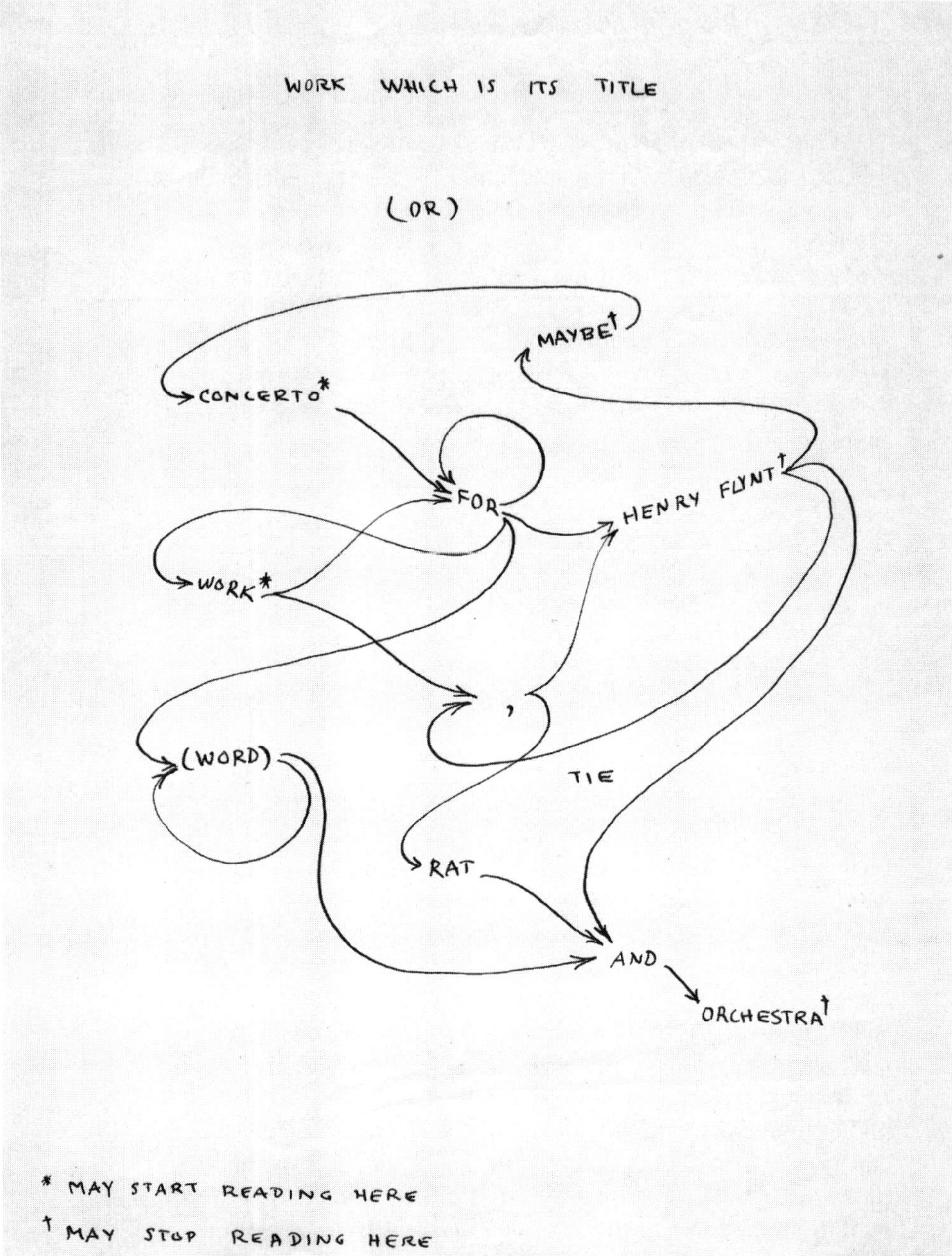

Figure 4.3. Tony Conrad, *Work Which Is Its Title*, 1961. Courtesy Tony Conrad.

Figure 4.4 (right). George Maciunas, *Diagram of Historical Development of Fluxus and Other 4 Dimentional* [sic]*, Aural, Optic, Olfactory, Epithelial and Tactile Art forms. (Incomplete)*, 1973. Detail.

monomorphic, cond

JAMES WARING

LA MONTE YOUNG

LONG TONES

for brass 27.06.1957

fugue in c min. 6.10.57

ROBERT WATTS

1ST EVENT BOX
RANDOM LIGHT WORK
AUDIENCE PARTICIPATION

1958
programmer for random light
1ST BOTANICAL PIECE

'Project in Multiple Dimensions'
statement by Watts, Brecht,
Kaprow, citing new trends.

CONCEPT ART

HENRY FLYNT

1954 first concept art:
replace words of sentence
with dictionary definition.

1958-60
structure compositions

1959-60
postage stamp dispenser
heat & light pieces
light, sound, kinetic constr.
MULTIPLE OBJECTS

GEORGE BRECHT

READY-MADES
NEO-HAIKU EVENTS
CHANCE OPERATIONS

spanish card piece,
time table music,
drip music,
comb music.

trio for strings. 5.09.58

studies for piano 18.01.59
vision 12.11.1959

NOISES
CHANCE OPERATIONS
FRICTION SOUNDS

RIS
RPHISM

DE MARIA
03.1960
work boxes,
ball on top,
l box, etc.

PHICAL ART
1960

MULTIPLE OBJECTS

ENZO MARI
milan
cubes 1959
reflex 1962
etc.

MAN RAY
blue bread 1960

1960
Motor Vehicle
Sundown (event)

READY-MADES
NEO HAIKU EVENTS
MONOTONISM:

21.01. poem for chairs, tables, benches,etc.
00.04. (any integer) for H. Flynt (repeat)
05.05. comp. no. 2 (fire)
14.05. comp. no. 3 (nothing)
03.06. comp. no. 4 (lights off)
08.06. comp. no. 5 (butterflies)
02.07. comp. no. 6 (performers watching)
00.10. comp. no. 7 (5th interval held)
00.10. piano piece for david tudor no.1 (feed)
00.10. piano piece for d.tudor no. 2 (cover)
00.10. comp. no. 10 (draw straight line)
09.11. comp. no. 13 (perform any piece)

02.05.1960
L.M.YOUNG,
TERRY RILEY,
WALTER DE MARIA:
collaboration event
univ. of cal. berkeley

CHIEKO SHIOMI

1959-61
GROUP
ONGAKU.
impo
improvisations
sound fragments
actions.

YOKO ONO

1960 PAINTINGS:
to be stepped on,
kitchen piece,
burning piece

1961 PAINTINGS:
decollage poem,
wind, see the skies,
cut piece, smoke,
shake hands,
word dispencer.

00.12.1960
CONCEPT ART defined

01.01.1961
1st mathematical concept ar

1961 CONCEPT ART:
frictionless floor,
piece by another composer,
nondenumerable infinity
optical audiorecorder, etc.

25/26.02.1961
at la monte young series:
ran around the room, recorde
watch ticking,
bad viennese violin music,
banged on wood of piano,
moebius strip (instructions
on other side)

00.04.1961
lecture on newness
(1st use of creep rules)

S at AG gallery
A. MEKAS, etc.
STLER: vaudeville
: butterflies '58
ugh music 1959
it music 1960
eripateie '61, wind, persp.
adio, water, clarinet music,
isica antiqua, for l.m.y.'61
williams, fontana mix, etc.
: journey around a zero
I: music for piano 1 to 7.
C LOW: various works.
ph.3, in memoriam,
everything its season,
of animals dying,
oncerto for politics, etc.
etry, music for voices,
, strata II.
water, breath, water.
sic for a while
bagatelles, music for tape
companied voice.
LA DAVIES, E. BROWN.
OUNG: composition no.7
OUNG: composition no.3
excercise, awareness, states
boxes, ropes,
demonstrations.
N: nothing.
O: paintings & drawings
yourself paintings)

READY-MADES
CONCEPT ART:

3 aqueous events,
tea event,
3 lamp events,
mallard milk,
incidental music,
2 exercises,
impossible effort.

LA MONTE YOUNG SERIES
at YOKO ONO studio, 18.121960–30.06.1961
18/19.12.1960 T. JENNINGS: piano pieces etc.
07/08.01.1961 T. ICHIYANAGI: strings,
music for piano 3,4,5, music for electric metronome,
kaiki for koto for j.c. mudai 1,2, ibm for m.c.
25/26.02,1961 H. FLYNT: jazz, flynt-music,
compositions, contest, improvisation, poetry, etc.
04/05.03.1961 J. BYRD: music
08/09,04 J. MAC LOW: biblical poems '55,
rush hour '55, 4 pianissimo pieces '55, dona rita '58
peaks & lamas '59, sade suit '59, sept. pack '59
verdurous sanguinaria, ode to iris, night walk,
stanzas for iris lezak '60, asymmetries, thanks,
gatha, piece for s. dienes, sermon, etc.
28/29/30.04. R. MAXFIELD: electronic music.
19/20.05. L. M. YOUNG: compositions '60
no.10 & all 1961 compositions (1 to 29)
26/27.05 SIMONE MORRIS:
3–7.06 BOB MORRIS: environment (spiral corridor)
28/30.06. D' LINDBERG: lights

03.04.1961, concert of
contemporary japanese
music and poetry:
MAYUZUMI: various pieces
ICHIYANAGI: kaiki 3,
strings 2, piano 7, aos '61
YOKO ONO: grapefruit in
the world of park: with
tudor, forti (voice), alsop,
glick, kobayashi, mayuzumi,
soyer, la monte young.

YOKO ONO, 24.11.1961
a grapefruit in the world of park,
a piece for strawberries and violin,
aos – to david tudor
at carnegie recital hall.
assisted by: maxfield, ayo, brecht,
byrd, corner, jennings, mac low
mekas, rainer, young, brown etc.

30.11.1961 ICHIYANAGI:
IBM perf. by: kosugi, tone,
shiomi, takemitsu, takahashi,
mayuzumi, tokyo.

TONY CONRAD
CONCEPT ART:

Sum. 1961
to perform this piec
do not perform it.
this piece is its nam
this is the piece tha
is any piece.
watch smoke.

09.06.1962
neo-dada in new york:
B.PATTERSON: bass & duo
G.MACIUNAS: olivetti
T.RILLEY: ear music
D.HIGGINS: constel. no.2
J.CURTIS:
gal. parnass, wuppertal

L, 14 concerts: 01–23.091962, staedtischen museum.
ne, flute, piano, quartet, comb, voice, card piece, incidental.
pping, CAGE: williams, fontana mix. CHIARI: gesti.
red piano), S. FORTI: dance structures. EVANGELISTI,
2,118, danger 2,17, 2 contributions, construct 7, requiem.
WLES: cream, proposition, KOSUGI: anima I, micro I.
crophone, piano pieces, music for sich man.
nce, biblical, piece for dienes, MERCURE: struct. met.
o, danger music for higgins, young: no.10 (with head),
astoral, night, concert. RILEY: ear piece for audience.
olo, septet, wash hands. SCHNEBEL: conductor solo.
events, WILLIAMS: counting, voice for young, litanies,
, german opera, etc. COLLECTIVE IMPROVISATION.
nds, comp. nos: 3,4,7,9,10, tudor no.2, 566 to flynt.
ik, patterson, maciunas, vostell, williams, welin. etc.

05.01.1962
G.BRECHT:
dithyramb
henry st. playhouse

12.06.1962
G.BRECHT:
nactarine
80 jefferson st.

24.03.1962
variety:
brecht, young,
r.johnson.
maidman
playhouse.

08.01.1962
AN ANTHOLOGY
BRECHT: 3 events, comb.
BREMER: 2 poems
BROWN: folio
BYRD: pattern
CAGE: 45 for a speaker
DE MARIA: objects
FLYNT: afro-amer. music
YOKO ONO: chair no.1
HIGGINS: symphony 4
ICHIYANAGI: mudai 1
JENNINGS: song
the living theatre, nyc.

05.02.1962
AN ANTHOLOGY II
johnson, ray johnson,
maclow, maxfield
r.morris, s.morris, paik,
riley, rot, waring,
williams, wolff, young.
the living theatre, nyc.

JASPER JOHNS

BALLANTINE
ALE CAN 1962

MIMMO
ROTELLA

shell oil
CAN

05.06.1962
HENRY FLYNT:
my new concept of
general acognitive
culture (lecture)
49 ave D nyc

Philosophical Cultural Works, a four-page mimeograph printed and distributed no later than September, 1961.

Although Flynt's *Anthology* contained an example of concept art (*Work Such That No One Knows What's Going On*), the genre's definition would appear only in *An Anthology* (after which Flynt's own publication was named). The opening lines of Flynt's essay "Concept Art" characterized the newly developed category:

> *Concept art* is first of all an art of which the material is *concepts*, as the material of e.g. music is sound. Since *concepts* are closely bound up with language, concept art is a kind of art of which the material is language. That is, unlike e.g. a work of music, in which the music proper (as opposed to notation, analysis, etc.) is just sound, concept art proper will involve language.[24]

Concept art evolved out of Flynt's musings on "structure art" as developed in an earlier essay, "Structure Art and Pure Mathematics."[25] "Structure art" was Flynt's term for highly elaborate, formally architected artworks, most particularly integral serialist compositions of the type analyzed and promoted in Karlheinz Stockhausen's journal *Die Riehe*, but also encompassed visual art and poetry. For Flynt, such works were on the order of metaworks, works about their own structure and analysis, which had little relation, in fact, to their material realization and as such were akin to formalist mathematics.

> The purpose through all this art is dual; structure or concept art [perhaps the first use of this term, but here as a slightly derogatory description, rather than a new category] tries to be, first, music, visual art, or whatever (which suggests that it is to be listened to, or looked at), *and*, something else entirely, to be valuable for its structure or conceptual cleverness.... In general, logic, and experience (with the results of the artists' efforts), show that the dual purpose of structure art consists of irreconcilable objectives; that one can be attained only at the other's expense. Which objective are the structure artists trying to attain? – they obviously have no idea.[26]

The impetus behind Flynt's new cultural categories was to rectify what he saw as a confused situation, his solution being simply to divide each art form in two. Thus, music would become, on the one hand, audart (or audact) when it dealt primarily or exclusively with acoustical material – Young's *2 Sounds* was an example, as was Flynt's own astounding series of "Central Park Transverse Vocals" (1963) – and, on the other hand, concept art when it relinquished composition's by now merely vestigial relation to sound and accepted its role as pure structure.[27] To Flynt's mind, both halves could now develop without compromise or dilution. This prefigured the idea of concept art: "Structure (or concept) music, for example, needs straightening out, first, by ceasing to call it 'music,' and starting to say that the sound (or activity) is used only to carry the structure or conceptual cleverness, and that the real point is the structure or conceptual cleverness – the categorization – and then it will be seen how limited, impoverished the structure of these productions trying to be music are."[28]

It was then only a short step to valorize a concept art that took up such formal activities consciously, including (and thereby, to Flynt's mind, superceding) the analytic side of nearly all cultural forms, from musical composition to traditional math (concept art's other main precedent, which, in its "pure" form, Flynt argued, was already primarily of aesthetic value). From this more encompassing point of view, many of the word scores that he, Young, Conrad, and others had been producing were rendered a less significant subgenre: "art involving play with the concepts of the art such as, in music, *the score, performer vs. listener, playing a work*," and so on, was described as "another, less important kind of art which when straightened out becomes concept art."[29]

Conrad was explicitly interested in Flynt's proposal. Notes and compositions reveal him addressing the issue of concept art specifically, most notably in his *Universal Metacomposition* (November 6, 1961):

> To compose this { piece/artwork }, form the logical union of all possible permutations of { words in your vocabulary/concepts of your acquaintance }.
>
> [N.B. – May also be appreciated as concept art.][30]

In a notebook entry a couple of weeks later, Conrad muses on a somewhat strange type of "intermedia" formed by recombining the two facets of music and concept art that Flynt had severed:

> *COMPLEX-ABSURD.* Write a piece with an infuriatingly complex long traditionally modern score, but with playing instructions completely annihilating import of the score. Conceive of art both in terms of concept art + music, or, similarly, as dada per se.
>
> *Example:* Long piano work, to be recorded on tape which is then cut to length of "performance"; tape is placed on windup spool of tape recorder + performance of the piece consists in letting the end of the tape flap when recorder is set to "play." Length of "performance" (of score) then gives type of performance. ["'performance'" here = "preparation"].[31]

Although such a piece, never realized, reconnected music's conceptual and experiential components, the result had almost nothing to do with modern composition and much more in common ("as dada per se") with activities later defined as Fluxus.

Although concept art derived from Flynt's discussion of structure art and mathematics, it was not merely or even primarily allied with the type of abstraction they represented. Or, rather, it was, but only once one had jettisoned any and all claims to equate such abstraction with rationality, truth, or any idea of objective discovery. Such pretensions on the part of aesthetic production (primarily, once again, the rhetoric surrounding integral serialism) were regarded by Flynt as little more than "a vestige of the time when e.g. music was believed to be knowledge, a science, which had important things to say in astronomy etc."[32] (Flynt's 1968 essay "Art or Brend?" opened with an even more strongly worded observation: "Perhaps the most diseased justification the artist can give of his profession is to say that it is somehow scientific." It was a critique that, in an important precedent to Conrad's opposition to Pythagorean interpretations of just intonation, Flynt at the time explicitly extended to Young.)[33]

That such pretensions to knowledge were "obsolete," disprovable, indefensible, and should be "discredited" was the main point behind "Structure Art and Pure Mathematics." And it was the confusion of epistemological claims and aesthetic experience (which Flynt described in highly traditional terms as "meaning, expression, and emotion") that Flynt also criticized in "Concept Art": "Now there are two things wrong with structure art. First, its cognitive pretensions are utterly wrong. Secondly, by trying to be music or whatever (which has nothing to do with knowledge), and knowledge represented by structure, structure art both fails, is completely boring, as music, and doesn't begin to explore the aesthetic possibilities structure can have when freed from trying to be music or whatever."[34]

In place of any such cognitive claims (which Flynt, it seems, simultaneously overestimated and one-dimensionally reduced) was to be a larger activity of formal relations derived from a type of mathematics based on "aesthetic theorems, without considering whether they are true."[35] As he explained further in "Concept Art": "The category of *mathematics*, a vestige of Platonism, is an *unnatural*, bad one. My work in mathematics leads to the new category of *concept art*, of which straightened out traditional mathematics (mathematics as discovery) is an untypical, small but intensely developed part."[36]

Hence the logical, but not rational character of Flynt and Conrad's concept art pieces, where self-canceling or self-problematizing conundrums undermined (nearly) any possibility of realization as music or any other traditional art form as well as any pretension to objective truth. (Conrad would find additional justification for this position in Duchamp's statement that "art has absolutely no existence as veracity, as truth. People always speak of it with this great religious reverence, but why should it be so revered? It's a drug, that's all.")[37]

Flynt and Conrad later collaborated in taking the deconstruction of traditional mathematics to the discipline itself. In November 1967, they launched a (failed) project to found *The Journal of Indeterminate Mathematical Investigations.*[38] Declaring "We want the most experimental papers we can get" (and, additionally, "We are not afraid of papers we can't understand"), they announced forthcoming articles such as "Cybernetics of Controlled Brain Inputs"—by Dennis Johnson, then a mathematics Ph.D. candidate at UCLA—and "Infinite-Dimensional Erections in Sexual Freak Space," by one Philip Anthony. Announcing that the first issue was scheduled to appear in 1968, the editors invited submissions on one of Flynt's favorite topics: "We would particularly like to receive an article on time travel." Conspicuously embracing "aesthetic" statements of the type that would, for example, "defin[e] 'proving a theorem' as bouncing a ball on one's head," the project was a direct descendant of concept art.

• • •

Although concept art is frequently mentioned, in passing, in discussions of the conceptual art of the late 1960s and 1970s, both practitioners and historians alike generally exclude it from the genealogy of the latter movement.[39] Nevertheless, it would seem that, no matter how idiosyncratically formulated, many aspects of conceptualism were clearly put forward by Flynt: the turn to language as a material and the subsequent "dematerialization" of the work of art; the emphasis on structure over content; the move from specific artistic mediums to the category of art in general; an appeal to certain aspects of mathematics, including irrational ones; a move from aesthetic to analytic propositions (and associated philosophical pretensions); even, as we have seen in the work of both Flynt and Conrad, an engagement with tautological structures, the significance of which for conceptual art has been analyzed by Benjamin Buchloh.[40]

To take note of such correspondences, however, is not to claim for Flynt the status of originator or precursor of conceptualism.[41] Although concept art pieces such as *Implications* and *Innperseqs* (both 1961) involved a certain relation to the visual (the first designating a series of manipulations of photographs and photographic negatives, the second a complex manner of observing light effects), they more closely related to Flynt's (expanded) mathematical project than to the conventions or institutions of visual art with which conceptual artists were primarily concerned.[42] Flynt showed no perceptible interest in issues of the context or contingent nature of the exhibition venue (as in the work of Robert Barry or Lawrence Weiner); in questioning modes of artistic display, documentation, and distribution (as with Dan Graham, Mel Bochner, Adrian Piper, or the curatorial practices of Seth Siegelaub and Lucy Lippard); in the artwork's role as a commodity (one of the primary questions raised by the legacy of Duchamp); or in other signature strategies of conceptual art.

Yet whether Flynt should or should not be taken into account in the mainstream history of conceptualism is not our concern. Ultimately, his development traces a very different trajectory. Indeed, from the beginning, as put forward in "Concept Art," Flynt questioned the validity of the category "art" — in a manner diametrically opposed, for example, to Joseph Kosuth's retrenchment of conceptualism onto art's very definition.[43] Although Flynt recognized the historical precedents in art (widely put) that led to concept art, his initial essay concluded that "perhaps it would be better to . . . recognize my activity as an independent, new activity, irrelevant to art (and knowledge)."[44] Which is exactly what Flynt would do, first by renaming concept art "concact" and then by repudiating it altogether in favor of what he termed "acognitive culture."[45] The trajectory through concept art thus led to an attempt to be rid of art entirely. But just as conceptual art, as Buchloh among others has argued, would lead to artistic practices now known as institution critique (in the work, for instance, of Morris), concept art would evolve, in a kind of historical parallel, into a different and in many ways more radical critique of both cultural institutions and institutionalized culture.

• • •

On May 15, 1962, after Flynt suspended his university enrollment to pursue philosophical projects (though still living close by in Harvard Square), Conrad organized an opportunity for him to present his most recent investigations at the university's Adams House (Figure 4.5). It was not Flynt's first stint as a lecturer. A year earlier, he had presented "The Supererogatory, Misleading Notion of 'Newness'" – in which he renounced the type of vanguardism he previously pursued – at La Monte Young's Bank Street apartment in New York (June 3, 1961), and just the previous month, he had delivered "The Cognitive (A Newly Defined Field): Its Present Situation" at Harvard for Christian Wolff (April 17, 1962).[46] Either Flynt or Conrad contacted Young about the new lectures, and he traveled to Cambridge for the event with two companions (one of them being future Warhol superstar Ondine; the three arrived late, near the beginning of the second of the evening's two presentations).

The first of Flynt's two lectures was entitled "My New Concept of General Acognitive Culture."[47] In it, Flynt developed one of the earliest manifestations of his concept of uncodified "cultural" experiences, later developed under the headings "Veramusement" and, ultimately, "Brend." Flynt's presentation was predicated on his having repudiated all forms of art, "Serious Culture," and traditional mathematics. Flynt thus presented his concept as a theory of recreation. Flynt's "old" concept of general acognitive culture seems to have been merely that: an endorsement of recreation, including, in Flynt's listing, "games, possibly athletics 'for fun,' conventional entertainment and recreation, and children's play." With his new concept, however, Flynt sought to develop something like a theory of *pure* recreation, actions not beholden to any existing social, objective, or intersubjective category. "As ('mere') recreation," such activities, Flynt explained, "are not supposed to have cognitive value (and in particular are without associated cognitive pretensions, so that they cannot be Serious Culture)."

Acognitive culture was, in some sense, concept art's opposite. Concept art had been a hypostatization of pure structure, extracted

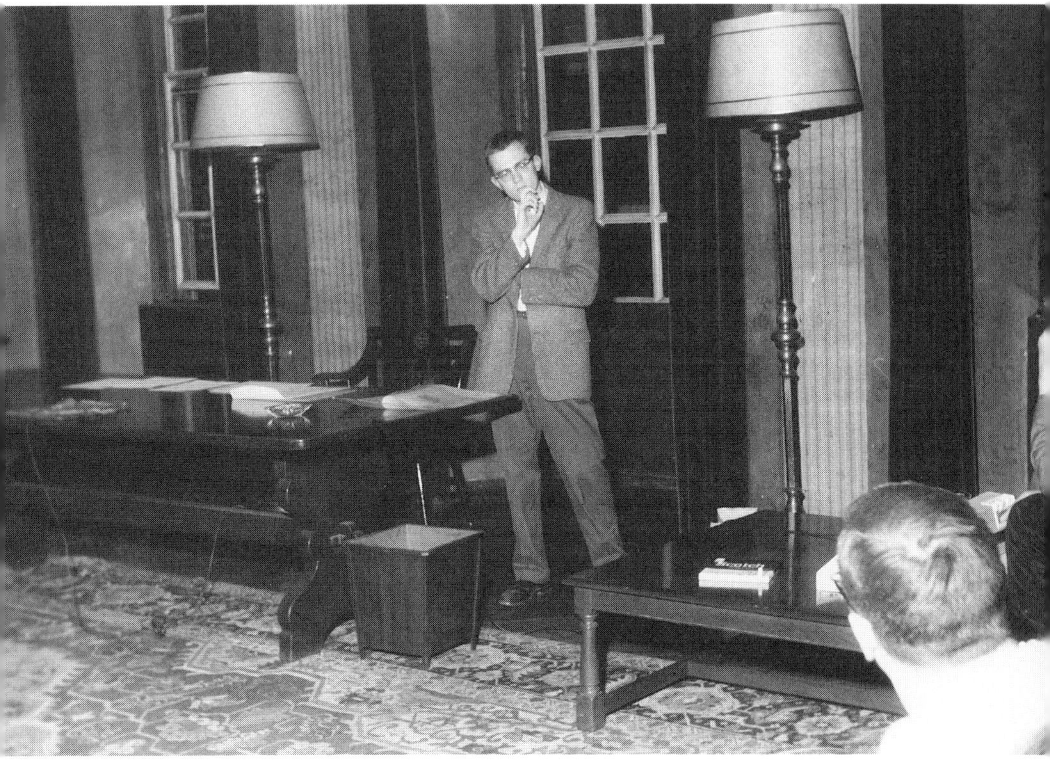

Figure 4.5. Henry Flynt, delivering the lectures "My New Concept of General Acognitive Culture" and "Creep," May 15, 1962. Adams House, upper common room, Harvard University. Photo: Tony Conrad. © Henry A. Flynt, Jr. Used by permission of Henry A. Flynt, Jr.

from recognized artistic activities (the "structure art" tendency in all mediums) and then expanded away from any pretensions to truth, objective value, or discovery. Acognitive culture developed out of the other half of Flynt's artistic redefinition, being closer for example to audart: a dwelling in the material of the sound or sound creation in which the forms or rules are so intrinsic as to be inseparable from production and experience. As Flynt later wrote of his 1963 audart pieces, "This music has a definite structure as opposed to its physical-acoustical character, but the structure is so complex and subtle that it only has an *intuitive* existence."[48] Flynt's new concept of general acognitive culture continued in this vein, specifically vectoring itself against "'objective' or 'intersubjective standards of value.'" "It is obvious, then," wrote Flynt, "that Serious Cultural institutionalized activities, doing things in Serious Cultural institutional Forms, such as the Fugue, cannot be [pure] recreation, acognitive culture. What is not obvious, a point of this analysis, is that the whole institution of society's providing Forms (for the individual to do things in) supposedly for his recreation and self-expression, such as Science Fiction and Pole-Vaulting... is absurd. The notion that the Forms are the real right ones, represent the real right thing to do, are objectively valuable, inevitably grows up around them."

Flynt's true enemy – what his lecture was, in its dry, academic way, railing against – was the notion of form as any component of an action (we are well beyond artworks in even the largest sense by now) that can be extrapolated from the material existence of the action itself. All forms, which Flynt likened to "work," even forms of thought, were understood as a type of oppression; one is, Flynt stated, "pretty much forced" to adhere to them. Flynt aimed to undermine the acceptance of this fact as common sense:

> Then there is the notion that given a Form, such as I am considering, one should do things in it whether one likes to or not, until one "understands" the Form, because one will like to then; and that the Form is objectively good if this happens. This has no place in recreation, acognitive culture. People who do things in these Forms all do

> so largely because they have acquired the notion that the Forms are the real right ones, are objectively more valuable than just anything. A proof of this is that the Forms are so extremely "objective," common, impersonal. This is why one can be unable to tell anything about the people themselves from what they do in the Forms. People have no idea of the extreme extent to which they are socialized even in what they do for recreation, self-expression. Even being a writer of any kind, a maker of objects, a creator of works, in the traditional, established, and common sense, is already extremely objective, impersonal, and indicates that one is extremely socialized.

Acognitive culture was to be the strict and tireless opposite of intersubjective or socially sanctioned forms: "an excellent determining principle is that it's pure recreation, acognitive culture, only if it's what one would have done, would do, are doing, 'anyway'; 'prior' (to being 'advanced' enough) to 'know' the real, right, objective, the impersonal things to do.... One does it 'anyway' 'first,' and 'then' it turns out to be in the category of 'acognitive culture.'" Not simply a new or different type of activity, acognitive culture (in a manner similar to concept art's superceding of structure art) was to supersede, discredit, and ultimately abolish art, along with any conventionally recognized recreation or entertainment. Flynt singled out, in particular, the compositions that he, Conrad, and the circle around Young had been exploring during the previous couple of years. All forms of composition, in their claim to dictate performances, were intersubjective impositions on others (they "are for 'others' to do"). (In this, Flynt was in part working through the implications of Cage's positing of form itself as oppressive.) In the lecture, Flynt additionally specified an opposition to "the post-artistic non-art movement exemplified by such New York post-artistic non-artists as Brecht, Bob Morris, Walter De Maria, [and] La Monte Young, their events, games, environments."[49] (Those of Conrad's word scores that dictated that performance take place *before* composition or cognition were presumably exempt from such a critique.)

Although Flynt denied the value of all conventional cultural activities, he was at pains to point out that acognitive culture was not a manifestation of pure nihilism, but rather a positive concept put forth to replace what it negated. Indeed, the goal of his theory and lecture was to attain for his version of pure recreation a status and respectability by which it could legitimately come to replace (earlier) cultural forms. "The reason for making the analysis, having the concept," he explained, "is . . . to show those who are to give up the discredited activities what replaces them: to show that in giving them up they have not given up doing things just liked. So that they will 'take seriously,' pride themselves on what they do just 'for fun,' doing what they like, would do anyway; rather than being ashamed because they do not contribute to the discredited activities."[50]

• • •

Flynt's acognitive culture was to designate a realm of actions that were not only uncodified, but entirely individual. From any logical standpoint, this was the weakest part of Flynt's argument, for it could not be proven, but only asserted that the most legitimate source of value or enjoyment is entirely intrinsic. "If it fits oneself who's doing the liking, if one allows oneself one's likings, then oneself is the source of value and, it would seem, will as a matter of course like one's creations best," Flynt contended. "Does it make sense for me to appreciate 'great' chess players, poets, pole-vaulters (if their activities are to be regarded as recreation)?" Even Flynt did not seem entirely sure of this point; the closest to certainty he would come was to claim that this perspective "would seem entirely plausible."[51]

Yet more than a potential logical flaw (if that is the level at which one wanted to approach Flynt's argument), Flynt's insistence betrayed the hypertrophied search or claim to presence upon which his position was founded.[52] Indeed, on one level, Flynt's theory of acognitive culture was an attack on representation of any kind, whether manifest in an artwork, a composition, a recording, or, importantly, writing. As Flynt declared, "All this leads to the idea of (one's) acognitive culture as a part of oneself—as within oneself, at least so far as specifications are concerned.... Acognitive culture (being what one would do anyway) would not, it would seem, consist of artifacts built up outside of, separate from, oneself, to be gone back to (for ex. recordings, writings); or specifications one would have to be concerned about remembering." The self-reflexive nature of Flynt's acognitive culture was so much the case, so confined to the individual, in fact, that he explicitly refused to give any examples in the lecture, because that would risk their taking on a general, transindividual character: "Real acognitive culture is not likely to lend itself to reduction to words. And trying to describe examples of acognitive culture cannot but be a tendency to make them into works."[53]

Acognitive culture thus appears as the inverse of a traditional expressive notion of art, wherein a painting, sculpture, composition, or poem is understood to reflect or encapsulate something of the artist's inner being. Although Flynt's idea of acognitive culture was equally if not much more individualistic than the notion of artistic genius, artistic *expressions* were posited as dead, abstracted forms: once objectified, separated from the self, they would seem to become almost entirely meaningless—hence "there is no reason why one's acognitive culture should mean anything to another, or even to oneself at another time."

Flynt has claimed that Young already knew the work of Antonin Artaud by this time.[54] While it is not known whether Flynt himself studied Artaud firsthand (and his analytical lecture lacks Artaud's mad, anarchic violence) the relationship between acognitive culture and expression echoes the sentiments of the French writer, who saw writing as nothing more than oppressive, lifeless forms and even his own words as of little more value than dead traces, excrement.[55] Very much the same sentiment was revealed the next year in Maciunas's elaborate plan to publish Flynt's complete writings as a Fluxus edition. Each essay was to appear as a separate pamphlet, initially issued in provisional or preliminary form, but with a plan for updating that would erase any trace of their incompleteness. When any text was updated, the previous version would have to be returned for supervised destruction before the new one could be received. As detailed in the plan's announcement:

> Henry Flynt's intention is thus that the superceded drafts be extinct and the superceding versions alone be extant: only the resulting canon will communicate what he intends.... It makes sense to buy later-to-be-returned writings; because it is the only way to study Henry Flynt's ideas now: they serve their purpose, and then are superceded. And they do become so obviously worthless that the subscriber might as well return them even if he were not obliged to.... It really would be detrimental to preserve everything; the extinction of the superceded drafts produces a positive effect in the canon, a superior canon—and the canon Henry Flynt intends.[56]

In the announcement's brief full text the term "worthless" appears three times in relation to the outdated works. When no longer animated by the force of intention, it seems, Flynt's writings fell into complete abjection.

A more proximate influence on Flynt's ideas was not Artaud, however, but another of Artaud's readers, John Cage. This was revealed when, during the question-and-answer session of Flynt's Harvard lecture, the audience pressed for an informal example of acognitive culture. In response, Flynt described something that he had liked to do, but did no longer: sitting in a silent, lightless room with his eyes closed and his fingers in his ears.[57] This seemingly idiosyncratic, almost autistic activity had in fact previously been classified as an audart composition and included in the *Anthology of Non-Philosophical Cultural Works* published by Conrad:

> To experience this composition, one must be alone in a quiet, darkened room. Relax, and accustom oneself to breathing slowly so that one's breathing will be as quiet as possible. Then put one's fingers in one's ears and close one's eyes. Listen to the very low sound (subsonic vibration) and the medium high-high noise (the sound of one's nervous system in operation), and "look" at the changing pattern

> of light and dark.... If done properly this should be a very strange experience.[58]

Despite his claims for the autogenic nature of acognitive culture, Flynt's example clearly betrayed its source: Cage's oft-recounted experience in an anechoic chamber at Harvard a decade before. As Cage described the episode in "Experimental Music":

> For certain engineering purposes, it is desirable to have as silent a situation as possible. Such a room is called an anechoic chamber, its six walls made of special material, a room without echoes. I entered one at Harvard University several years ago and heard two sounds, one high and one low. When I described them to the engineer in charge, he informed me that the high one was my nervous system in operation, the low one my blood in circulation. Until I die there will be sounds. And they will continue following my death.[59]

At the Harvard lecture, Flynt's example proved even closer to Cage, as he specifically mentioned "the sound of... blood circulating" in place of the more general "subsonic vibration."

Beyond the specificity of this example, the entire concept of acognitive culture may be understood as a particular development of (or, more specifically, through and beyond) Cage's aesthetic. We have already seen how, for Conrad, the primary lesson of Cage was the expansion of legitimate listening experiences beyond the institutional confines of music (however wide) to the indeterminate, uncomposed realm of uncodified nature. Flynt, too, seems at least for a time to have understood Cage in an analogous fashion, extending this attitude (following Cagean theatricality) toward actions, rather than just sounds. On a certain level, Flynt's acognitive culture seems an attempt to replicate or extend Cage's aesthetic of immanence by importing into ethics what Cage claimed to be doing for sounds. Indeed, aspects of Flynt's project appear as more or less direct transpositions of Cage's desire to free sounds of any and all transcendent structures, including individual preconceptions and traditional artistic forms. Such had been the very motor force behind Cage's aesthetics for decades, one that he often presented as a liberationist project. As Cage explained for instance in the "Lecture on Nothing," he initially took up the cause of noises because they had been excluded from what Flynt would call "Serious" music:

> They [noises] had not been intellectualized; the ear could hear them directly and didn't have to go through any abstraction about them. I found that I liked noises even more than I liked intervals. I liked noises just as much as I had liked single sounds. Noises, too, had been discriminated against; and being American, having been trained to be sentimental, I fought for noises. I liked being on the side of the underdog.[60]

Free of intellectualization (or what Flynt would call "cognitive pretensions") and abstraction (or, more generally, abstract form), Cage's noises could be received, or so he proposed, "directly." Or as he explained in "Composition as Process: Changes," just after recounting his experience in the anechoic chamber, one could receive "each sound just as it is, not as a phenomenon more or less approximating a preconception."[61]

Even more specifically related to Flynt's project, what Cage had discovered in the anechoic chamber was the impossibility of any type of silence understood as the complete absence of sounds. Since sounds are present all the time anyway, if only coming from the inside of one's body, silence had to be redefined, famously, as merely the presence of *unintended* sounds: "the situation one is clearly in is not objective (sound-silence), but rather subjective (sounds only), those intended and those others (so-called silence) not intended. If, at this point," Cage continued, "one says 'Yes! I do not discriminate between intention and non-intention,' the splits, subject-object, art-life, etc., disappear, an identification has been made with the material, and actions are then those relevant to its nature."[62] Flynt's acognitive culture thus seems a strict cognate of Cagean silence, designating actions that are not only understood as "relevant" only to their own nature, in the sense of not conforming to any (external) form, but that also occupy an undecidable position between intention and nonintention. Hence the strangely proleptic structure of acognitive culture, analogous to the structure of some of Conrad's word scores, which had to take place *before* it was cognized as such. To pursue acognitive culture, to valorize or recognize it in the manner that Flynt proposed, is, then, to *intend* to act in ways that are strictly *unintentional* and that are recognized as such only after the fact.

But if Flynt's project was an attempt at the translation (or supersession) of Cage's aesthetic, it ended up vastly different. Cage's theatricality, as well as his view of society, was one of interactive multiplicity, not a nearly autistic confinement or individual isolation. As Conrad understood, Cage's challenge was to transform and expand one's taste, not self-reflexively fold it back onto one's just likings. For Cage, the human subject is always in contact with external influences (ambient sounds being the primary example), the interaction with which he understood as potentially transformative, leading people not to guard their own actions, thoughts, or "likings," but rather, to use Cage's deceptively simple phrase, to change their minds.[63] This change could be either oppressive (when it enforces conformity) or liberatory (when, as an "experimental" action, the outcome is ateleological and undetermined, leading the subject to act transformatively from his or her own center), but it is understood to be continual. For Cage, both the individual life and that of society are in a constant state of transformation. Not surprisingly, then, despite the roots of Flynt's thinking in his own, Cage – when he attended an "improved version" of Flynt's lecture on general acognitive culture – would not approve.[64]

• • •

Flynt, however, did not attempt in his theory of acognitive culture to take up the whole of Cage's thought. As we have seen in previous chapters, doing so seems not to have been a viable critical option at that historical moment for anyone laboring in Cage's shadow.[65] Rather, like so many of the dialogical responses to the Cagean legacy encountered thus far (for example, in Young's various word scores), Flynt sought to pressure or extend one of the composer's presuppositions to such a degree as to transform and thereby surpass or get beyond it. (Flynt would say "annul" it.)

In the case of acognitive culture, Flynt pressured the aspect of Cage's aesthetic that related to Duchamp's readymade, what revolved around the "unmusical" "found" sound, the sound that—whether as a natural occurrence or a noise generated by unconventional procedures—does not normally reside in a concert hall, in much the same way that a urinal or a snow shovel (in Duchamp's *Fountain* [1917] or *In Advance of the Broken Arm* [1915]) transgressed the conventional limits of the gallery or museum. It was one of the unavoidable ambiguities of such a strategy, however, that its transgressive nature is patently undecidable. Does the importation of a ready-made object into the conventional and institutional space of the museum represent an assault on the category of aesthetics as an autonomous realm? Or does it merely result in the aestheticization of the everyday object, its transformation into art? The readymade is, inescapably, on the edge of representation in this way. With the advent of happenings and Fluxus events of the type practiced by George Brecht or Alison Knowles, this ambiguity was imported into the realm of readymade *actions*, such as exiting a room, preparing one's lunch, or applying hand cream (Brecht's *Exit* [Spring 1961], and Knowles's *Proposition #2* (October 1962) ["Make a Salad"] and *Nivea Cream Piece—for Oscar Williams* [November 1962], respectively). It is as though Flynt's response, when faced with the aesthetic (already) beginning to gain the upper hand—when he saw the "post-artistic non-artist such as Brecht" creating art—was to move outside the aesthetic altogether, to obviate or eradicate the existence of form completely and embrace an even more radical anti-art practice that cannot be assimilated, since it cannot, except in retrospect, even be cognized. In taking his position to such an extreme, Flynt so pressured the idea of a gratuitous (theatrical) action, one as free as possible from any extractable form, as to push Cagean multiplicity (the collagelike interaction of many such actions) into *heterology*.

As we saw in Chapter 1 in a somewhat different context, heterology is Georges Bataille's term for the study of the completely other, of what is constitutively inadmissible to conventional forms of thought, whether science, mathematics, or common sense (all of which Flynt, too, railed against). There is little likehood of Flynt's having had access to Bataille's thought or writing, which was almost completely invisible in the United States at that time. And there is as little of Bataille's rage for blood and violence in Flynt's statements as there is of Artaud's madness. Nor is there any echo of Bataille's Nietzschean language or claims to virility and sexual excess (indeed, as we will see, quite the opposite). Nevertheless, their two projects betray a certain kinship.

Flynt's new concept of acognitive culture was to be completely outside any socially or intersubjectively recognized form; it was not high art (Serious Culture), nor was it low art (entertainment or recreation); it sought to escape even the codification of writing, recording, memory, and thought. What Flynt described as acognitive culture was thus some sort of cultural remainder, the refuse that persists once each and every possible form or means of designation has been removed, an action that exists, in its utter individual idiosyncrasy, in, as Bataille would say, "the absence of any possible common denominator."[66] Hence Flynt's ban on giving examples. As Bataille explained, "there is no way of placing such elements in the immediate objective human domain, in the sense that the pure and simple objectification of their specific character would lead to their incorporation in a homogeneous intellectual system, in other words, to a hypocritical cancellation of their excremental character."[67] Even though, as Flynt maintained, such actions were being continually created and practiced, what falls into the realm of acognitive culture is so insignificant, so idiosyncratic, quotidian, or mundane as to appear utterly worthless. (And it did appear worthless to even such close associates as Dick Higgins, who negatively though accurately described Flynt's project as "whatever incommunicable subjective activity one might light on which pleased him, such as shifting one's weight from one leg to the other.")[68] The very proposition to take it seriously was thus a provocation and was received as such at the time by nearly everyone save Conrad and Maciunas. The actions of acognitive culture are too trivial to be considered culture without degrading the category of culture altogether. Not Serious Culture and below even "low" cultural activities such as recreation, acognitive culture was truly formless, *informe*, the lowest of the low.[69]

• • •

It is from this perspective that we can turn back to Flynt's Conrad-sponsored lectures at Harvard. In the second of his two lectures, Flynt presented three chapters of a proposed book entitled *Creep*.[70] Flynt began by characterizing the traits associated with "the creep personality" as weakness, avoidance of competition and the "sophistication-proving" delinquency of adolescence, social awkwardness, and, in particular, the inability to feel comfortable around members of the opposite sex. The creep, he went on,

> may seem self-contemptuous. He may be nervous enough to make others nervous. He is shy. Somatically, he is weak and small. He appears immature, young. He lacks physical courage. He is unathletic. He lacks poise and is awkward. He may seem idiotic. He may be naively emotional, for example, naively enthusiastic. He is unstylish, from a childish lack of desire to be stylish. He childishly lets his hair go and dresses unstylishly, for example, wears unmatching socks.

On account of such characteristics, the creep is persistently looked down upon, excluded and ostracized by mature adults who (in both American and Soviet society, Flynt specified) consider him inferior. "Creepiness is disvalued," he observed. "At best, the creep is pitied as a cripple, a victim of an unprogressive social order to be cured."

Adult human values (what Flynt calls the "adulthood ideal") are hegemonic in society, and childhood is an imperfect or low form of adulthood, a stage in a process – if carried out "correctly" by educational institutions – of molding people into this form (a process of becoming adult). From such a conventional point of view, a creep is the result of an unsuccessful process of education, maturation, and enculturation: a scandalous or pitiable failure, a social abortion. "Creep is American teenager slang for a person who is failing to become an ideal young adult by deviating in the direction of weirdness and weakness." Hence the creep's segregation from hegemonic culture, which presumably increases in proportion as he or she continues to deviate from adult norms. "Society reacts to the surface creep with condescension. In particular by ridiculing him. Society scorns him and excludes him. Thus, society isolates the creep further since, in the presence of others, the creep appears to all as the weak one, cannot hold on to his self-respect but is compelled to feel inferior. The creep actively seeks isolation, withdraws."

However, precisely because creeps remain outside of the socialization process, they are able to maintain (indeed are forced back onto) their own individual thoughts and actions (their "creep acognitive culture"), which can therefore develop uniquely on their own (and possibly return to culture in the form of artistic expressions or accomplishments; Flynt's example is Emily Dickinson).[71] The most important point is that the creep is other: "Isolated from the pressure to give up childishness and become adult and depending on childlike fantasy, the creep is outside the childhood/adulthood dichotomy."[72]

Flynt's proposal advocated a form of creeps' rights or creeps' pride: a raising of the creep personality to a level of, if not respect, acceptability. Importantly, in raising up the creep, Flynt rejected any assimilation to adult human values. Outside the norms of the adult male and rejected on account of his creepiness by the adult female (or vice versa), the creep, or so Flynt proposed, would find solace in biological mutation, the formation of an indeterminate sexual identity, a third (a)sex that would allow creeps to keep their preadolescent attributes and idiosyncrasies. Although Flynt recognized that the prospects for actual biological mutation lay in the future (he estimated at least thirty years), the purpose of describing the alternate, "non-human" organism was to provide a different subjective ideal toward which the creep — the "deliberate creep" who accepts his or her creepiness — could aspire without conforming to existing social dichotomies, hierarchies, and expectations.

Flynt had earlier produced a series of *Ugly Drawings* (1959, only one of which survives), in which — inspired by dada — he sought to reverse the hierarchy of taste, and he presumably did much the same with his performance of "bad" Viennese music at Ono's loft. Rather than a mere reversal, however, Flynt's revaluation of creepiness sought a heterological transvaluation of the devalued attributes: the goal was not just to raise the creep high, but to raise him or her as something other. A deliberate creep was to be regarded "not as a human, crippled and to be cured, but as a precursor of a different species." For Flynt, the elevation of the creep without subsumption to the demands of societal expectations would result in the vindication of attributes rooted in play, imagination, and childlike creativity unfettered from intersubjective pressures. Now biologically and ideologically differentiated, the creep was to exist "sovereignly," outside of the "restricted economy" (as Bataille would put it) of social, cultural, conventional, and biological norms.[73]

• • •

Flynt's project was both profoundly allegorical — of the liberation struggles in Black Africa and the U.S. civil-rights movement, both of which Flynt was already involved in at the time — and starkly personal.[74] Beyond mere personal resonances, however, Flynt's project was vectored against a similar type of "paranoiac" law such as we have encountered in the work of Young and Morris (with both of whom Flynt was in dialogue): a transcendent, hierarchical, repressive authority. Flynt's form of avant-garde, however, models a much more starkly polarized response than Young's disciplinary identification or Morris's subversive dialectics.[75]

Flynt's project implicitly presents power in a manner that can be characterized as "simultaneously distant and close."[76] Social structures are constructions (from afar) that intimately, closely impact upon the individual's being. Likewise, forms of culture are an imposition on individual taste; the institutionally accepted forms of art or recreation are constrictions upon one's own "just likings" (Cage's "cumbersome, top-heavy . . . prohibitions" in a different form).[77] Similarly, for creeps, the strictures of mature adult behavior, and particularly the social codes of interaction and reproduction (real *and* ideological), are felt as impositions upon their being, leading to withdrawal, seclusion, and desires of biological mutation. Like aesthetic forms, social structures are regarded as too distant (they are objective, purely objective forms and thus are unrelated to my personal desire) and simultaneously too close (they confine and restrict me, causing me to be unable to enjoy my just likings without feelings of worthlessness and inferiority). For Flynt, power was conceived along the lines of what Deleuze and Guattari refer to, in passing, as "the great paranoiac": "always on our case yet infinitely distanced from us."[78]

If Flynt's project was largely predicated on a paranoiac form of power, it can also be seen to operate, at the same time, on a more immanent level: not only because acognitive culture necessarily was to occur in bodily actions, as opposed to language or form, but because the idiosyncratic physical activities on which the concept of acognitive culture seems to have been built were precisely those types of behavior that avoid or evade disciplinary normalization. They are *traces* (in Foucault's sense, rather than Derrida's) that prove constitutively *ab*normal, "deviating," as Flynt put it, "in the direction of weakness and weirdness."[79] Flynt's acognitive culture and proposal for creeps, as unconventional as portions of them are, thus prove not entirely distant from the more well-known projects of Morris and, particularly, Young. They were modes of resistance at the intersection of sovereign and disciplinary power. Like Morris's works, they were to subvert the dictates of form while, like Young's, they proposed "counter-conducts" by which disciplinary power could be detourned. Although we will return, below, to how Flynt's understandings of acognitive culture and the creep were transformed into a more overtly political project, we should pause at this point and examine another of Flynt's early proposals, which engaged a more disciplinary power, and Conrad's response to it.

• • •

Flynt's Harvard lecture was not the first time that he proposed to affect or intervene directly on the individual subject. In 1961, he devised a sort of proto-acognitive culture in the form of unartistic activities (not even audart, visart, or any of Flynt's other categories) not yet as uncodifiable as true acognitive culture. Flynt called these activities, first presented on July 15 at the AG Gallery, "Exercise Awareness States." Flynt subsequently discarded his original text, reconstructing it from memory in 1966 as "Mock Risk Games: A Psychological Exploration."[80] In the later presentation, Flynt defined a "mock risk game" as a "game such that the misfortune which you risk is contrary to the course of nature, a freak misfortune; and thus your preparation to evade it is correspondingly superficial." Exercise awareness states or mock risk games derived from Flynt's attempt to systematize or develop those of Young's word scores that instructed improbable occurrences: waiting for a piano to eat a bale of hay, for instance, or pushing a piano through a wall.[81] Such works would subsequently be developed in the direction of even more fantastic or impossible actions in Fluxus works such as Nam June Paik's *Danger Music #5 (to Dick Higgins)* (ca. 1962), which famously instructed the performer to "Creep into the vagina of a living whale," or Takehisa Kosugi's *Music for a Revolution* (1964): "Scoop out one of your eyes 5 years from now and do the same with the other eye 5 years later." Flynt's exercise awareness states / mock risk games proved equally bizarre and pointedly pointless: "You are suddenly upside down, resting on the top of your head on the floor. . . ." "The floor disappears just behind you, leaving you on a precipice. . . ." "Your body is split in half at the waist by a high, foot-thick wall . . ." your partner's "head flies off and hurtles at you like a cannonball. . . . you will be hit unless you jump aside . . . "

These awareness states, which resemble nothing so much as an acting coach setting a (rather odd) mood for improvisation, were not without precedent in the way they understood certain of Young's word scores to be modeling a form of *reception*. At least one early piece by Morris followed a similar path; *Piece #1* (1961) reads: "To be looked at in a state of shock: nearly anything in a state of shock."[82] In a not unrelated manner, Conrad's "Imagined," a notebook entry from the same time, proposes a work in a similarly experiential direction: "Directions: listen to the (imagined) distant music; listen for very small, distant sounds (that are not there). Tell that they are just below threshhold [sic] of hearing, perhaps."[83]

Once again, Conrad and Flynt would prove particularly aligned in their efforts. In addition to "Imagined" and similar proposals, Conrad produced a detailed meditation on the nature of such works. He wrote on November 19, 1961:

> Piece: Yourself during orgasm.
> Example of *varied listening attitude or experience*. Varied type of existential experience + influence on listening. Thus the idea arises of the independence of listening + performing: Performing ("music") determines sounds produced or incident upon listener; listening as an art determines (by "composition" (?)) the type of reception of the sounds (whatever they may be).

Since, Conrad reasons, the act of listening (to the wind, for example, as in John Cale's *Outdoor Piece for Robin Page*) could potentially be decoupled from performance, couldn't the artist's or composer's function be that of modeling the condition of listening as, previously, they had modeled the conditions of performance? This leads to a consideration of what Conrad called "listening compositions": "Various types: (1) varied existential states: orgasm (as above), drunk, high (marijuana, eg), asleep, not present, etc; (2) various 'physiological['] effects: standing on head, with various items stuffed in ears, altering ear response to pitch curve, physical removal or relationship to the performance. (3) Attitudes, as prescribed by Henry, esp; type of listening, mentally + culturally speaking."

Finally, Conrad comes up with a definition for the new mode. "'*Composition*' in listening," he writes, "consists in combining and determining instances of experiences + states such as above, either through prescribing contingencies which will produce the desired effect (as in music the notes or instructions for performance that tell what to do but not what sounds to make directly; 'metacomposition'), or describing the attitudes or listening characteristics directly (as in usual types of musical composition)."[84]

In such cases, the removal of any actual performance opens the way to a direct, unmediated connection between composition (as Flynt understood it, as a relation of force) and reception. As there is, in some sense, no longer any work of art – if by that one means the production of audible sounds or visible images or objects – the artist or composer no longer produces a *representation* for the viewer or listener to receive, but molds the receptive (subjective) situation itself. In such an event, it would seem, the much-vaunted "dematerialization of the art object" (which Lippard would laud as the particular accomplishment of conceptual art) leads not toward nothingness, transcendence, or liberation (from the gallery space or commodity form), but toward the operation of discipline or control. Conrad's "listening compositions" reveal Cage's project of subjective transformation stripped bare, disclosing its essence (whether oppressive or liberatory) as a power effect, a pure technique of power. Flynt's exercise awareness states did much the same thing. It was against this, perhaps, that his concept of acognitive culture turned away, in an about-face from the imposition of any form, including forms of reception. Exercise awareness states, however, in their literal reference to alternate realities (related, no doubt, to "strange culture description") were also antinormative techniques or counter-conducts. Conrad would continue to explore such more or less direct (and potentially dangerous) modes of subjective and corporeal influence in the context of expanded cinema (see Chapter 6). It is thus, perhaps, not uncoincidental that Flynt would revive exercise awareness states as mock risk games in 1966 for publication in *Film Culture*'s special issue on "Expanded Arts."

• • •

In 1963, Flynt, Conrad, and Jack Smith took the iconoclastic program of acognitive culture into the streets (Figures 4.6 through 4.8). On February 27, the three picketed the Museum of Modern Art, the Metropolitan Museum, and Philharmonic Hall at Lincoln Center, carrying signs that advocated their destruction: "Destroy Art!" "Demolish Art Museums!" "Demolish Concert Halls!" "No More Art!" "Demolish Serious Culture!" Flynt's cultural ideas underlay this venture, and the group distributed fliers containing a summary of his position, now termed "Veramusement," and an invitation to a lecture the next evening in Walter De Maria's loft.[85]

Conrad recalled about the genesis of the event:

> The sequence of discussions had begun much earlier, with theoretical developments of Henry's. The idea that there would be a protest actually to back this up and thereby a direct confrontation with the institutions of the culture industry was an eventuation that we were bound to see taking some form or other.... I was a little, I must say, hesitant at first in approaching this whole project of pushing for the actual dismantling of these institutions.... I actually thought about it quite carefully. I thought, do I really want to be involved in this completely anarchic demonstration? But, finally, I decided that, if Henry was willing to go this distance, I would go, too. (I have to say that this is one of the most embarrassing things you can possibly do. It takes a certain amount of stiffness of resolve and purposefulness to outfit yourself with a lunatic sandwich sign and face the passing crowd!)...
>
> To my recollection, we had only very tangential contact with anybody except ourselves. This was a symbolic picket. This wasn't

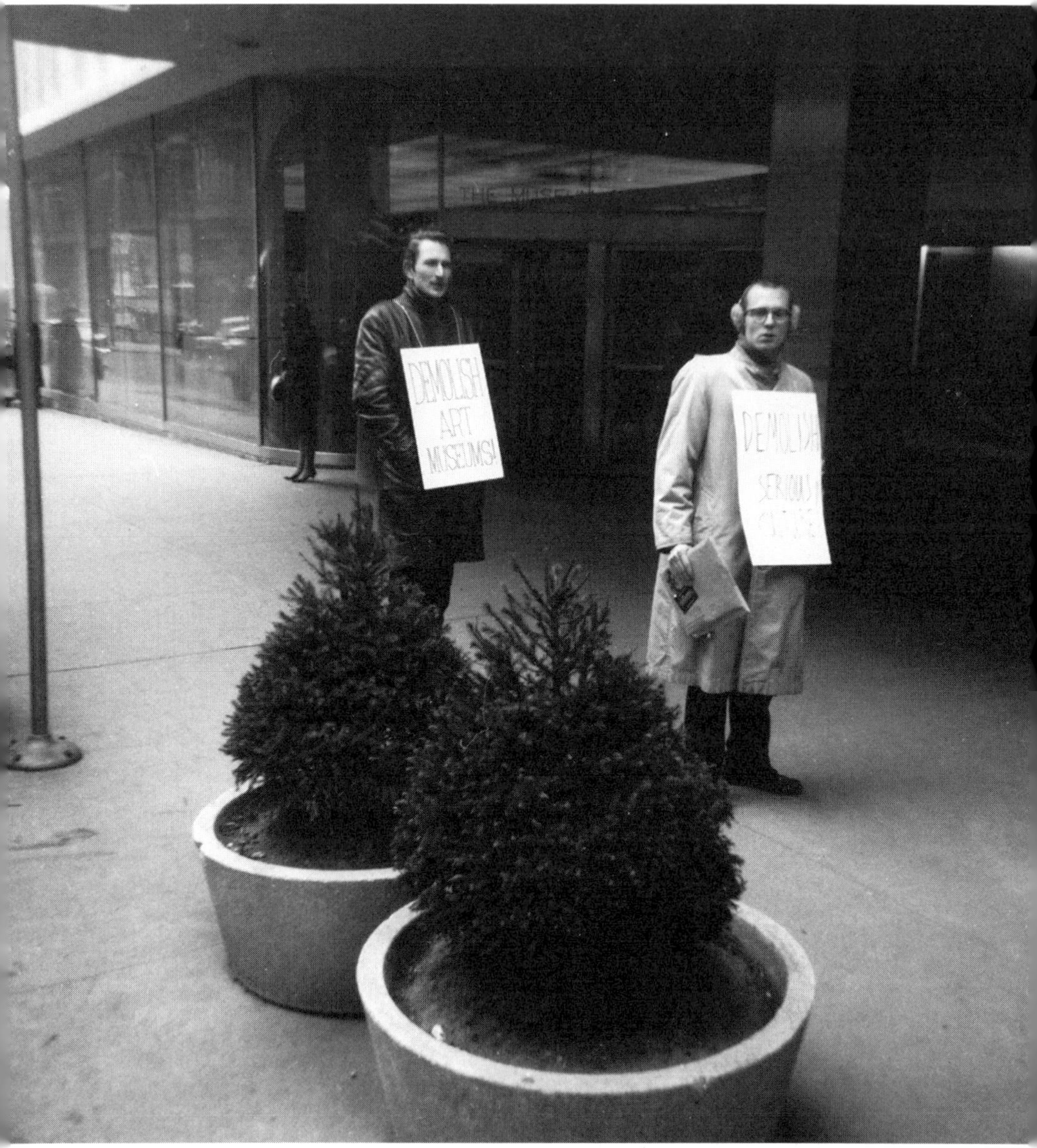

Figure 4.6. Henry Flynt and Jack Smith protesting at the Museum of Modern Art, New York, February 27, 1963. Photo: Tony Conrad. © Henry A. Flynt, Jr. Used by permission of Henry A. Flynt, Jr.

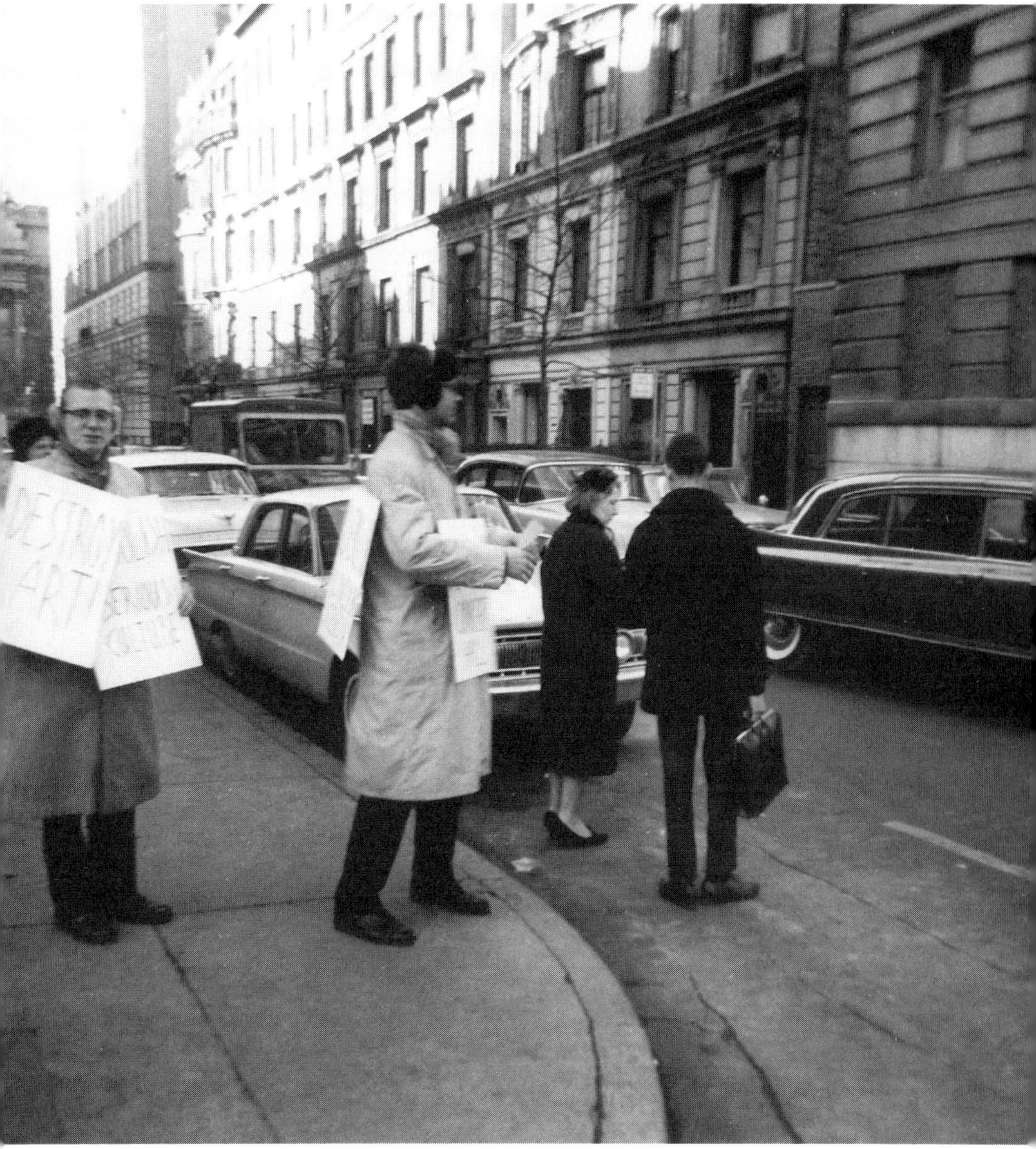

Figure 4.7. Henry Flynt and Tony Conrad protesting at the Metropolitan Museum of Art, New York, February 27, 1963. Photo: Jack Smith. © Henry A. Flynt, Jr. Used by permission of Henry A. Flynt, Jr.

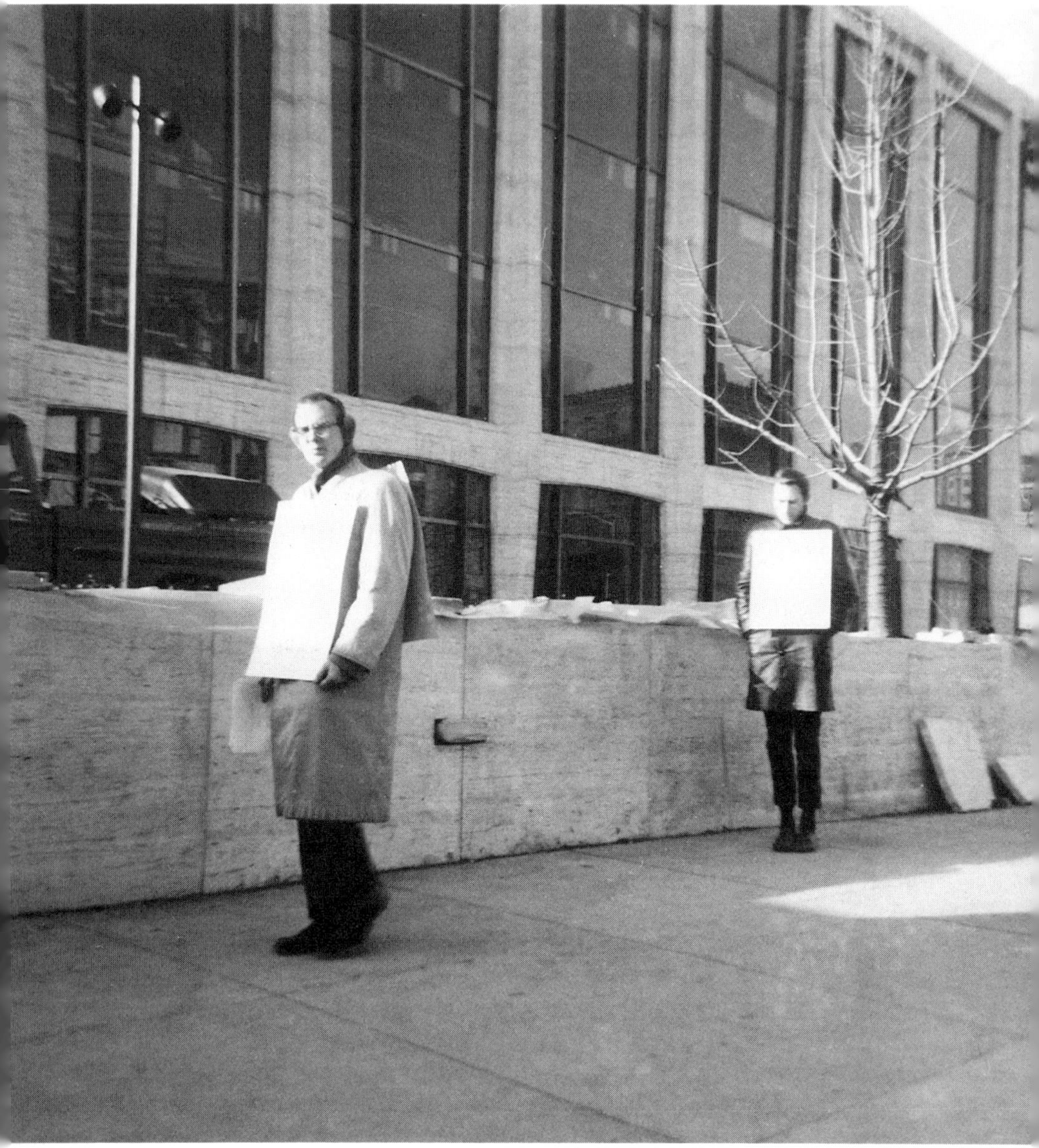

Figure 4.8. Henry Flynt and Jack Smith protesting at Lincoln Center for the Performing Arts, New York, February 27, 1963. Photo: Tony Conrad. © Henry A. Flynt, Jr. Used by permission of Henry A. Flynt, Jr.

> something where you go and have campfires and warm your hands for the next round and stay for two or three weeks encamped in front of the White House or whatever. No, this was symbolic, but I think the fact that it's symbolic also suggests our faith in symbolic efficacy.... In the sort of sociopolitical understanding of the day, the "action"—presence itself—had a standing that was of considerable importance. Like, you could write a piece of music, but the performance was where it came to life, and in a similar way, this [Flynt's critiques of "Serious Culture"] had to be performed to be real.[86]

Flynt's lecture, "From 'Culture' to Veramusement," was more elaborately staged than its predecessor at Harvard (Figure 4.9). Attendees entered by stepping on a poster of the *Mona Lisa*, which had been drawing huge lines at the Metropolitan, where it was on display at the time of the event.[87] It was a debasement of the work—which figured as the very icon of "culture"—that recalled both Duchamp's *L.H.O.O.Q.* (1919; in which a reproduction of the *Mona Lisa* was defaced by graffiti) and, in its turning of the painting into a door mat, Duchamp's "reciprocal readymade" proposal to use a "Rembrandt as an ironing board," as updated by Yoko Ono's *Painting to Be Stepped On* (winter 1960). Surrounding Flynt were some of the placards carried during the march, along with another proclaiming "Veramusement—not Culture." Above Flynt's head was a portrait of Vladimir Mayakovski, the revolutionary Soviet poet, literally held up for identification (against the *Mona Lisa*) as an example of the Communist culture to which Flynt had already begun connecting his ideas.

A year later, Flynt (partially, apparently, at Maciunas's instigation) turned his attention from Leonardo da Vinci to Stockhausen.[88] The protests, entitled Action Against Cultural Imperialism, took place on two occasions, the first when Stockhausen appeared on a program of West German music at Town Hall (April 29, 1964), the second at the premiere of Stockhausen's happeninglike *Originale* at Charlotte Moorman's New York Avant-Garde Festival at Judson Hall (September 8, 1964) (Figures 4.10 and 4.11). Conrad, whose connection to Stockhausen had been much closer than

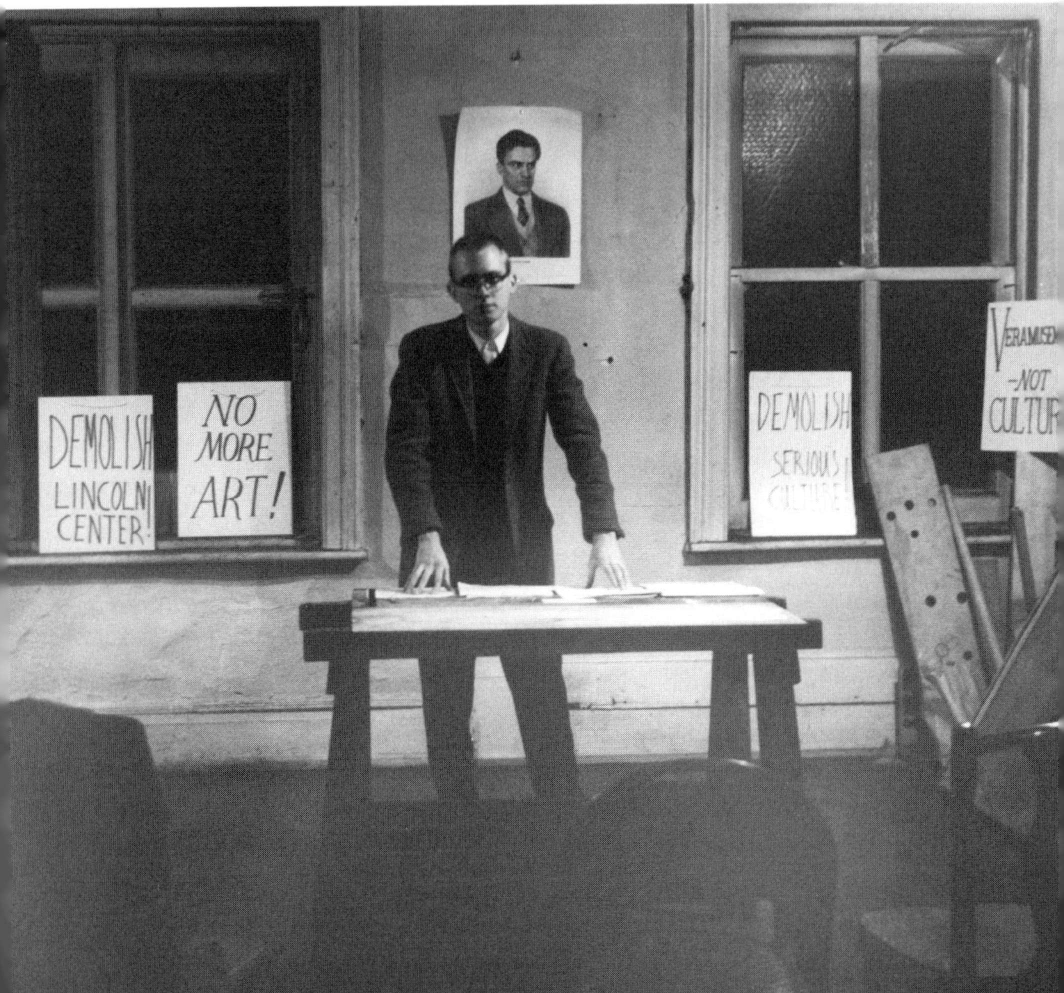

Figure 4.9. Henry Flynt delivering the lecture "From Culture to Veramusement," February 28, 1963. Walter De Maria's loft. Photo: Diane Wakoski. © Henry A. Flynt, Jr. Used by permission of Henry A. Flynt, Jr.

Flynt's, did not participate in the first protest (neither Flynt nor Conrad recalls why), but appeared prominently in the second. It was something of a measure of how much Flynt's and Conrad's aesthetic outlooks had transformed that the first lines of Flynt's flier, which they handed out detailing the protest's rationale, cited none other than the lecture they attended six years before: "'jazz [Black music] is primitive . . . barbaric . . . beat and a few simple chords . . . garbage . . . [or words to that effect]' Stockhausen, Lecture, Harvard University, fall 1958."[89] Conrad recounts of the second round of protests:

> This was contentious from the start in that it was not simply impersonally directed toward some institution. . . . Here, we were asked — I was asked — to enjoin an activity directed at a person, that is, Stockhausen. So that asked a bit more. Also, by this time Henry had stepped up the heat of his language, largely I think in response to his involvement with organized Left politics. He had adopted some of the form and voice of the Marxist Left. This looked more challenging on those grounds. . . . But the idea of Stockhausen as representing a European imperialist cultural effort struck me as a sensible and justifiable critique, as the core critique, in fact. The very fact that the New York avant-garde seemed to be yielding itself up for capture by Stockhausen in the presentation of this very event — the way in which so many artists had pitched in to support and enact Stockhausen's *Originale* score and be involved in his performance — almost seemed to bear out these allegations.[90]

More directly linked, via Maciunas, to Fluxus (members of which could be found on both sides of the picket), the *Originale* protest had more visibility and much wider ramifications than the earlier demonstration by Flynt, Conrad, and Smith. Indeed, the Stockhausen protest has been portrayed as the (first) death of Fluxus, cause of a nearly irrevocable split between those who did and did not take part.[91] But if the *Originale* protest was the death of Fluxus, Flynt's ideas, it must be noted, were part of Fluxus nearly from its birth. Maciunas's "Neo-Dada in the United States"

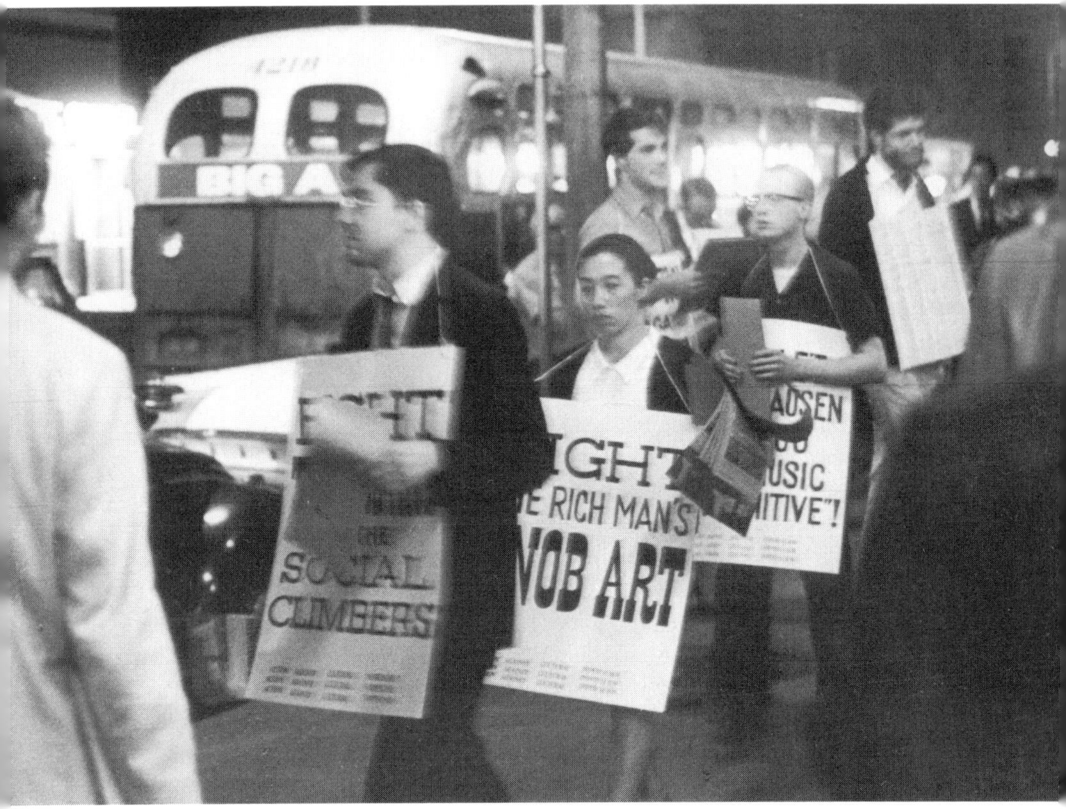

Figure 4.10. George Maciunas, Takako Saito, Henry Flynt, Alan Marlowe (against pole), and Marc Schleifer, in "Action Against Cultural Imperialism," Judson Hall, September 8, 1964. Photo by Peter Moore. © Estate of Peter Moore / VAGA, NYC.

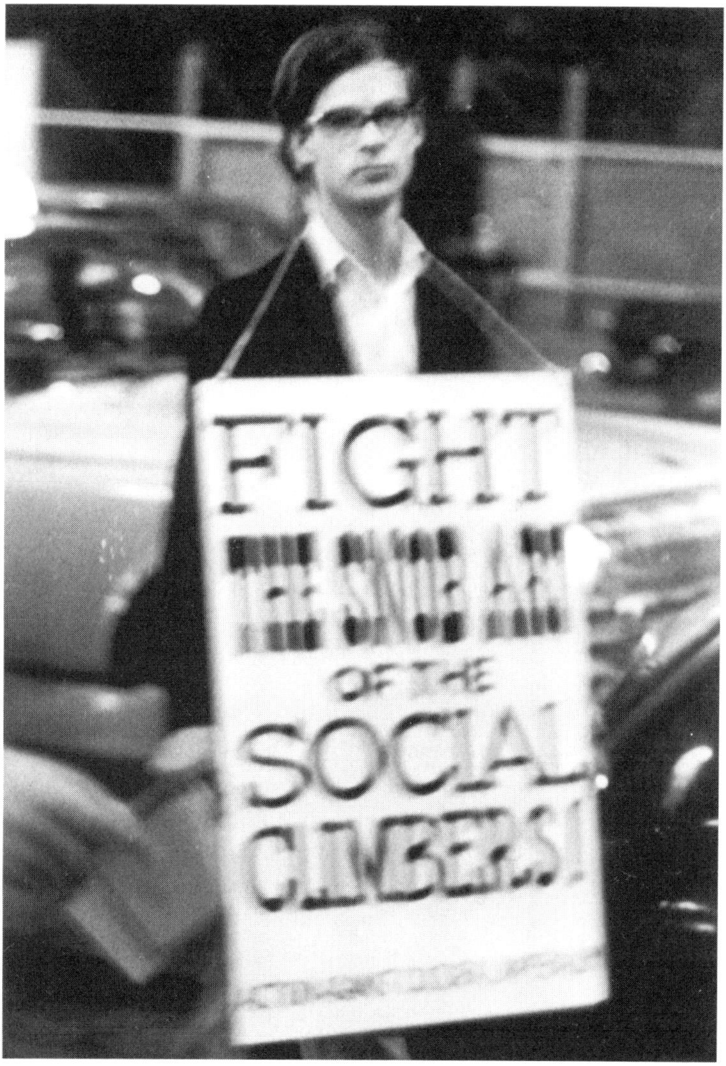

Figure 4.11. Tony Conrad in "Action Against Cultural Imperialism," Judson Hall, September 8, 1964. Photo by Peter Moore. © Estate of Peter Moore / VAGA, NYC.

– the lecture presented at the first public manifestation of Fluxus, the event "Après John Cage" at Galerie Parnass in Wuppertal, Germany on June 9, 1962 – invoked both Flynt's ideas of structure art and his "radical art nihilism," a reference to the concept of acognitive culture, which Maciunas planned to publish in 1962.[92] Maciunas, on the other hand, had spurred Flynt's turn to socialism by introducing him to Soviet productivism shortly after they first met.[93] As is well known, Maciunas looked to the early Soviet avant-garde, in particular that associated with the Left Front of the Arts (LEF), as a model for Fluxus, which he considered but a temporary phase in art's revolutionary elimination. "Fluxus is definitely against art object as non-functional commodity," he explained in 1964 to Tomas Schmit, although "it could temporarily have the pedagogical function of teaching people the needlessness of art, including the eventual needlessness of Fluxus itself."[94] Teaching people the needlessness of art seems to have been Flynt's semiofficial role with regard to Fluxus (whether or not he is considered part of the group). As Maciunas proposed in 1963, the final event of the New York Fluxus Festival was to have been "in largest hall, largest audience – a lecture by Henry Flynt: denouncing all Fluxus festival activities as decadent serious culture aspects & expounding his BREND doctrine & campaign."[95]

Despite the possibility that Maciunas may have initiated them, the Stockhausen protests were integrally related to Flynt's politics. By that time, however, Flynt's anti-art agenda was no longer confined to elevating the individual's "just likings," but concerned the valorization of socially and politically marginalized and denigrated ethnic populations and their music.[96] Flynt desublimated his relation to decolonization and civil-rights struggles, targeting Stockhausen not simply as a representative of high art, but on account of what he saw as incipiently racist views. "THE FIRST CULTURAL TASK IS PUBLICLY TO EXPOSE AND FIGHT THE DOMINATION OF WHITE, EUROPEAN-U.S. RULING-CLASS ART!" the flier for the *Originale* protest screamed in bold headline: "Whatever path of development the non-European, non-white peoples choose for their cultures, we will fight to break out of the stifling bondage of white, plutocratic European Art's domination. STOCKHAUSEN — PATRICIAN 'THEORIST' OF WHITE SUPREMACY," it concluded, "GO TO HELL!"[97] Although Flynt connected his advocacy of civil rights to issues of class struggle (particularly in the first protest's flier), he would never subordinate the former to the latter.[98]

Flynt has suggested that the point would have been better made by protesting representatives of more staid, traditional culture such as Leonard Bernstein.[99] The reason put forth for protesting Stockhausen, however, was quite specific: his ability to produce the legitimating concepts ("invent 'scientific' Laws") that perpetuate Western music's pretension to advancement and supremacy. "Stockhausen's real importance, which separates him from the rich U.S. cretins Leonard Bernstein and Benny Goodman, is that he is a fountainhead of *"ideas" to shore up the doctrine of white plutocratic European Art's supremacy*, enunciated in his theoretical organ *The Series* [*Die Riehe*] and elsewhere."[100]

The mere existence of such ideas, Flynt contended, oppresses "restless," anti-racist white intellectuals as much as the people whose music it denigrates by reinforcing a hierarchy of high and low and an identification, thereby, with "uplifting" cultural values: "The domination of patrician Art — which is aristocrat-plutocrat in origin, as Opera House etiquette alone shows — condemns you to be surrounded by the stifling cultural mentality of social-climbing snobs. It binds you to the most parochial variety of the small merchant mentality, as promoted by *Reader's Digest* — 'Music That Ennobles You to Listen to It.'"[101]

For Flynt, it was exactly what led Cage to dismiss folk and jazz from advanced musical culture — that "they are not cultivated species, growing best when left wild" — that recommended them and other indigenous musics as the legitimate expression of the culture of peoples.[102] (Flynt recalls an argument with Cage on this subject at his first Ono loft concert.)[103] Like acognitive culture, Veramusement, or Brend, such musical expressions were understood as spontaneous, unalienated — indeed bodily — manifestations that already existed and needed only to be recognized and raised up without assimilation to forms of European culture otherwise deemed high.[104] (Like his own audart, such musical expressions did have a structure, but a structure Flynt evidently conceived as implicit, not external, imposed, or extractable as form.) As he explained in another Maciunas-designed broadside, *Communists Must Give Revolutionary Leadership in Culture*:

> In general, for each nation there is a common musical culture which is the spontaneous creation of those farm-workers and later city-workers who are not social climbers and can't quit being poor. *Actually, it is usually a fusion of music, dancing, and lyrics—which is done or watched, but not "performed." Such a dance of one national grouping comes to another nation not on the Concert Stage, but by people taking it up, doing it.* This music-dancing is *already* the indigenous symbol of the oppressed. In a phrase: "street-Negro music."[105]

The rhetoric of the Stockhausen protests thus extended and refunctioned the dialectics Flynt articulated at Harvard. Nonwhite populations, degraded and ostracized, take the place of the creep, while their musical expressions are understood, like acognitive culture, as integrally related to their (social and communal) being—not written (like "Stockhausen Music"), but evolved and passed on, according to Flynt, as an active "doing."

Although Flynt linked his views to Soviet productivism and was included by Maciunas in the overtly Marxist "East European Section" of Fluxus,[106] his cultural politics proved closer, once again, to those of Bataille. Like Flynt, Bataille came to connect his Gnostic/Manichean dialectic of high and low to issues of class struggle. Anticipating Flynt's opposition to the "ennobling," "social-climbing" aims of the Western bourgeoisie, Bataille opposed the raising up of "higher" cultural values as mere ideology.[107] Bataille's sectarian battle was primarily with the surrealists, whom he regarded, despite their alliance with the Communist Party, as clinging to the abstract (and ineffectual) realm of poetic values. "Instead of relying on presently lower forms whose interplay will in the end destroy bourgeois prisons," wrote Bataille, the surrealists' supposedly avant-garde "subversion" "finds itself, scarcely alive, searching for an authority *above* the one that has provoked the revolt. Abused by a system that threatens to crush or domesticate them, individuals have put themselves, in practical terms, at the mercy of what appears to them, through blinding flashes and disheartening attacks of empty verbiage, to be above all the pitiful contingencies of their human existence, for example *spirit, surreal, absolute,* etc."[108]

It had been from the "pitiful contingencies of human existence" that Flynt attempted to forge his paradoxically acategorical category of acognitive culture. The route to political revolution was to follow a similar path: an adherence to the abject, to what had been socially denigrated and excluded from official cultural values (high or low). And necessary as a first step — very much in the way Bataille envisaged it — was lashing out and attacking accepted culture: "there is no possibility for any class until bourgeois principles have become altogether and for everyone principles of derision and general disgust."[109]

Flynt's politics were not assimilationist. They called for the recognition of difference without those types of incorporation that rendered it simply a gradation or degree within a commensurate (homological) hierarchy (a minority understood as an inferior instance of majoritarian standards). Instead, Flynt's project, like Bataille's, sought to keep difference outside homogeneity, outside the common social realm in which, as Bataille explained, there could be no true subversion, but only exploitation.[110] Both Bataille's and Flynt's politics pivoted on the heterological, those politically considered the "lowest of the low" — not the proletariat (low, but part of the system nonetheless), but those excluded from it, rejected on account of race or abject poverty, those, in Flynt's terms, who "can't quit being poor." Flynt's project was on all levels to contest such a racist perception or designation, to refuse it as the necessary precondition of a truly revolutionary political program. In *Communists Must Give Revolutionary Leadership in Culture*, he denounced this exclusion in rhetoric that reached a clarified, fiery pitch:

> For revolutionary leadership, street-Negro music *must be the point of departure*. . . . Now there is no nonsense about bringing this music-dancing to the masses, because they created it. The almost insuperable problem is to bring street-Negro music to the Communists. Personal a[c]quaintance reveals that *in general* the instinct of Communists towards street-Negro music is a revulsion that defies rationality. . . . Communists' faces are turned "up" to old European bourgeois Music, even through they do not know a great deal about it; even though they cannot analyze the *Grosse Fuge* or a Bruckner Symphony — even through they have never heard of the insertion syncopations of *Sumite karissimi* — or of Faugues. Their idea of popular music is European popular music, Anglo-American music, Mitch Miller music. They will fabricate the most tortuous sophistry to prove that street-Negro music is "bourgeois corruption" — but that of course Beethoven's *Solemn Mass in D Major* is not. Communists derive self-respect from being too "high-minded" for those "vulgar, noisy, trashy" dances. They feel threatened by street-Negro music as if it were a bottomless pit of tar.[111]

It was only, for Flynt, from the "bottomless" realm of low culture, beneath that of white popular entertainment ("Mitch Miller music"), that any truly revolutionary artistic practice could emerge. And it was only from there, as well, according to Flynt, that any unadulterated force of social revolt and subversion could be born. As he contended in the second Action Against Cultural Imperialism flier:

> the domination of imperialist white European plutocrat Art condemns you to live among white masses who have a sick, helpless fear of being contaminated by the "primitivism" of the colored peoples' cultures. Yes, and this sick cultural racism, not "primitive" musics, is the real barbarism. What these whites fear is actually a kind of vitality the culture of these oppressed peoples have, which is undreamed of by their white masters. *You lose this vitality.* Thus, nobody who a[c]quiesces to the domination of patrician European Art can be revolutionary culturally — no matter what else he may be.[112]

At the time, Flynt's protests were largely rejected as wrong-headed, divisive, extreme, or, on the contrary, trivial.[113] After several more years of the Vietnam War and the continued struggle for civil rights, however, two of Flynt's early interlocutors would take up similar strategies. On May 22, 1970, Robert Morris would help lead a protest on the steps of the Metropolitan Museum of Art in the name of "Art Strike Against Racism War Repression," calling for a one-day closure in solidarity with concerns over the bombing of Cambodia and the recent death of student protesters at Kent State.[114] Two years after that, Cornelius Cardew launched his attack, first on Cage, in "John Cage; Ghost or Monster?" and then on Stockhausen, in "Stockhausen Serves Imperialism."[115] A decade earlier, Cardew's reaction to Flynt's iconoclastic project had been somewhat less than critical of the institution. In response to "From 'Culture' to Veramusement," Cardew explained, "Since I may be depending on organized culture for my loot & livelihood I can wish you only a limited success in your movement."[116] Once Cardew's views had radicalized (denouncing Stockhausen's "mysticism," for example, "as a tool for suppression of the masses"), his position would still, however, differ from Flynt's.[117] Cardew embraced structure, above all, eventually denouncing his musical experiments with AMM and the Scratch Orchestra, which, as we have seen, proved close to Conrad's understanding of the Theatre of Eternal Music. Cardew's was a more evidently Oedipal struggle against musical "fathers" he now considered "weak" (especially Cage) and insufficiently doctrinaire, and his own compositional energies moved increasingly toward party-sanctioned socialist realism, workers' anthems in a nineteenth-century romantic style.[118] (The party in some sense seems to have become for Cardew the stern father that Cage, in his permissive embrace of chance procedures, had refused to be.) It was Conrad who would take up, so to speak, where Cardew left off. Years later, once he felt that Young had assimilated his musical legacy to "scientific" and spiritual ends akin to those of Stockhausen, he revived the strategy of cultural protest, picketing Young's concert with a flier that declared "Composer La Monte Young does not understand 'his' work."[119]

• • •

Flynt's cultural politics developed in tandem with his musical practice. Flynt's understanding of American roots music had been fundamentally transformed by exposure to Samuel Charters's book *The Country Blues* and its attendant Folkways collections of recordings.[120] It was among such indigenous American voices as Bukka White, Blind Lemon Jefferson, Leroy Carr, and, especially, Robert Johnson that Flynt found the expression of cultural difference that he had not heard in the Angel recording of Ali Akbar Khan, as well as a relation, particularly in the blues, to his own interests in repression, ostracism, and social abjection. (One can well image Flynt's appreciation of how all these factors came together in something like Peg Leg Howell's "Low Down Rounder's Blues" from the first of Charters's Folkways anthologies.) In retrospect, Flynt seems to have been Charters's ideal reader, taking from the socially conscious author all he had hoped to convey. As Charters explained in the 1975 preface to his book, "I was trying to effect a change in the American consciousness by presenting an alternative consciousness."[121]

Flynt's response to this music was not mere emulation, but an association with his own roots in North Carolina and the hillbilly fiddle music of its poor white rural population. He adopted and transposed this tradition by combining it with aspects of modal repetition already present in jazz and early minimalism in such pieces as "Hoedown" (1968) and, later, "Banjo Country" (1976) and "Hillbilly Jive" (1977), eventually combining these with certain influences of Indian music to produce a unique "raga hillbilly jive" in "C-Tune" (1980), "You Are My Everlovin'" (1981), and others.[122] In this, Flynt pursued much the same strategy that had characterized his discussion of the creep: a Bataillian "dialectic" of raising up without transposition what was considered low. Though Flynt's musical efforts are diverse, this aspect of them attempted to valorize hillbilly music as a form of "high" culture without assimilation or compromise with European conventions of high art, but rather by bringing those conventions low:

> For me, innovation does not consist in composing European and academic music with inserted "folk" references. It consists in appropriating academic or technical devices and subordinating them to my purposes as a "folk creature."... I intensify and elevate the American ethnic musics to produce a sophisticated music whose nearest correlative would be Hindustani music. (Or one might simplify by saying that I did for hillbilly music what Ornette Coleman did for jazz.)[123]

It is, no doubt, Flynt's intense personal investment, not only in the political content, but also in the popular forms from which his music is forged, that makes the idiosyncratic protest songs of Henry Flynt and the Insurrections (the group he formed briefly in 1966, with Walter De Maria on drums) more compelling than Cardew's doctrinaire Peoples' Liberation Music.[124]

(In the mid-1970s, Flynt would connect his revolutionary country and blues music to another proletarian group with its own culture: truckers, producing "trucking and trancing" numbers such as "Virginia Trance" [ca. 1975–78].[125] In this, too, he would not be alone. Mayo Thompson of the Red Crayola, associated at the time with the conceptual art group Art & Language, would also — parodically? — extol truckers as a revolutionary force. In a brief article in the conceptual art journal *The Fox*, Thompson denounced the manufactured hit song "Convoy" for the manner in which "10-35 lingo has... been expropriated and translated to disarm it and fuel petty-bourgeois opportunism.")[126]

As seen at this chapter's beginning, Flynt's hybrid "popular" music began with his collaboration with Young, whose version of jazz piano Flynt understood as similarly raising, without transposition, a "high" cultural form out of jazz, combined, as John Coltrane and others had done, with aspects of Indian music. In so doing, it not only obviated the role of a composed structure (or should have; recall Flynt's critique of Young's scientific pretensions in "Art or Brend?"), but sublated the distinction — as had, in a different, but related manner, *arabic numeral (any integer)* to H. F. — between the standard (or tune) and its improvisational variations: "Instead of trying to escape the foundations of jazz into abstraction, Young did the opposite. In the duets he played with Terry Jennings and with me, his piano was the entire 'rhythm.' Dropping the distinction between tune and solo, he isolated a basic 'house' piano à la Horace Silver and repeated the chorus ad infinitum with lapidary variations. There was no tune; the line instrument was all solo."[127]

It would be through the lens provided by Flynt's music and ideas that Conrad (who avowedly lacked any jazz background) understood and instantly wanted to take part in the music performed by Young's ensemble at the 10-4 Gallery in 1962. "That summer," Conrad recalled,

> La Monte started to do this series of concerts at the 10-4 Gallery, and the question on my mind was, "Where do we go now?" after all of these word pieces and basically conceptual work, and all of this stuff that had to do with the challenge of Cage.... When I went to see this thing that La Monte was doing, where he had Marian singing one note, Billy Linich playing the guitar, Angus MacLise playing the hand drum, and he [Young] was just going crazy, you know, I thought, "Fuckin' amazing man! This is like so weird! You know, like *really* weird!" It's obviously got a relation to Indian music, but the thing that captured my attention about it was that it seemed like a way of dealing with the questions that, in a sense, Cage leaves unanswered — like about where you reenter the sound, and the idea that you're not going to use a score or the composer isn't making a score. That the composer is now ... there's the composer! (La Monte is already notable as a composer at this point.) There's the composer! He's sitting out there in the *middle* of the sound! I had no relation to jazz, and it didn't even occur to me ... that La Monte had reverted to his jazz roots. I went to several of these concerts and I used to stay as long as anybody.[128]

For Conrad, such manifestations were on the order of a collective audart, an immersion into the material of sound, devoid of abstract or extrinsic compositional structure. It was thus the opposite of (an opposite that superseded) his word pieces and concept art. Later performances with Flynt, MacLise, and others at the time and afterward would perpetuate Conrad's interest in a contemporary, free-form, "indigenous" downtown music.[129]

• • •

The culmination of Flynt and Maciunas's collaboration (and the high point of Flynt's alliance with communism) was the brochure *Communists Must Give Revolutionary Leadership in Culture* (Figure 4.12). This "new theoretical analysis of communist cultural policy" put itself forward as the "best possibility in culture for the present period." In it, Flynt elaborated a position on all forms of cultural production — theater, literature, film, visual arts, and music — assuming (or usurping) the role of official dictate of the party. The impetus behind such an official tone was not Maciunas (who had previously written to Nikita Khruschev to give the Soviet premier unsolicited advice on cultural policy), but Sam Marcy, the chairman of "the tiny Leftist sect called WWP [Workers World Party]" with which Flynt was involved at the time.[130] The fields of "design engineering" and architecture were left to Maciunas, who designed (and commented on) the brochure and presented an elaborate appendix detailing his own system for prefabricated housing, including construction plans and a chart comparing the relative merits of the "Maciunas system" against competitors, from Buckminster Fuller's geodesic dome, to the tent, to existing Soviet methods of prefabricated housing.[131] (A warning was included that detailed: "Caution: Fuller's general theories are crackpot, and his house and automobile designs are totally inefficient. The dome however really works.")

Throughout most of the brochure, Flynt did not so much propose new forms of revolutionary culture as call the USSR back to the most radical proposals of its historical avant-garde, endorsing

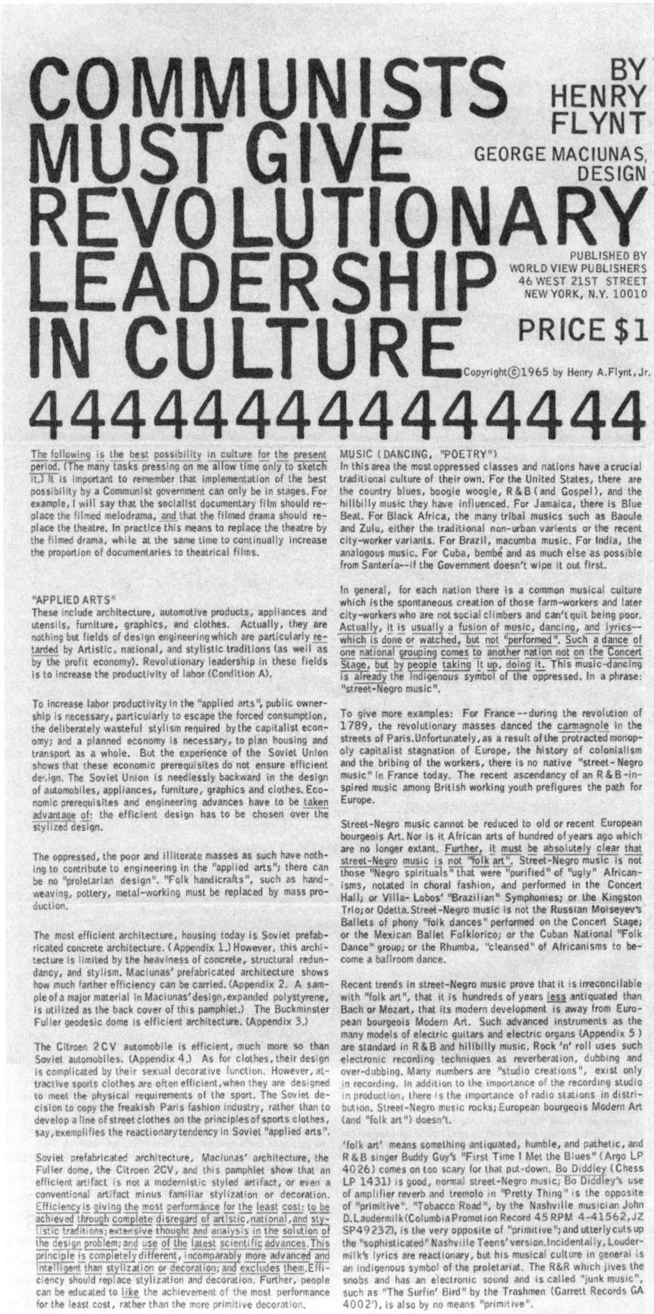

COMMUNISTS MUST GIVE REVOLUTIONARY LEADERSHIP IN CULTURE

BY HENRY FLYNT

GEORGE MACIUNAS, DESIGN

PUBLISHED BY WORLD VIEW PUBLISHERS 46 WEST 21ST STREET NEW YORK, N.Y. 10010

PRICE $1

Copyright©1965 by Henry A.Flynt, Jr.

4444444444444

The following is the best possibility in culture for the present period. (The many tasks pressing on me allow time only to sketch it.) It is important to remember that implementation of the best possibility by a Communist government can only be in stages. For example, I will say that the socialist documentary film should replace the filmed melodrama, and that the filmed drama should replace the theatre. In practice this means to replace the theatre by the filmed drama, while at the same time to continually increase the proportion of documentaries to theatrical films.

"APPLIED ARTS"

These include architecture, automotive products, appliances and utensils, furniture, graphics, and clothes. Actually, they are nothing but fields of design engineering which are particularly retarded by Artistic, national, and stylistic traditions (as well as by the profit economy). Revolutionary leadership in these fields is to increase the productivity of labor (Condition A).

To increase labor productivity in the "applied arts", public ownership is necessary, particularly to escape the forced consumption, the deliberately wasteful stylism required by the capitalist economy; and a planned economy is necessary, to plan housing and transport as a whole. But the experience of the Soviet Union shows that these economic prerequisites do not ensure efficient design. The Soviet Union is needlessly backward in the design of automobiles, appliances, furniture, graphics and clothes. Economic prerequisites and engineering advances have to be taken advantage of: the efficient design has to be chosen over the stylized design.

The oppressed, the poor and illiterate masses as such have nothing to contribute to engineering in the "applied arts"; there can be no "proletarian design". "Folk handicrafts", such as hand-weaving, pottery, metal-working must be replaced by mass production.

The most efficient architecture, housing today is Soviet prefabricated concrete architecture. (Appendix 1.) However, this architecture is limited by the heaviness of concrete, structural redundancy, and stylism. Maciunas' prefabricated architecture shows how much farther efficiency can be carried. (Appendix 2. A sample of a major material in Maciunas' design, expanded polystyrene, is utilized as the back cover of this pamphlet.) The Buckminster Fuller geodesic dome is efficient architecture. (Appendix 3.)

The Citroen 2CV automobile is efficient, much more so than Soviet automobiles. (Appendix 4.) As for clothes, their design is complicated by their sexual decorative function. However, attractive sports clothes are often efficient, when they are designed to meet the physical requirements of the sport. The Soviet decision to copy the freakish Paris fashion industry, rather than to develop a line of street clothes on the principles of sports clothes, say, exemplifies the reactionary tendency in Soviet "applied arts".

Soviet prefabricated architecture, Maciunas' architecture, the Fuller dome, the Citroen 2CV, and this pamphlet show that an efficient artifact is not a modernistic styled artifact, or even a conventional artifact minus familiar stylization or decoration. Efficiency is giving the most performance for the least cost: to be achieved through complete disregard of artistic, national, and stylistic traditions; extensive thought and analysis in the solution of the design problem; and use of the latest scientific advances. This principle is completely different, incomparably more advanced and intelligent than stylization or decoration; and excludes them. Efficiency should replace stylization and decoration. Further, people can be educated to like the achievement of the most performance for the least cost, rather than the more primitive decoration.

MUSIC (DANCING, "POETRY")

In this area the most oppressed classes and nations have a crucial traditional culture of their own. For the United States, there are the country blues, boogie woogie, R & B (and Gospel), and the hillbilly music they have influenced. For Jamaica, there is Blue Beat. For Black Africa, the many tribal musics such as Baoule and Zulu, either the traditional non-urban varients or the recent city-worker variants. For Brazil, macumba music. For India, the analogous music. For Cuba, bembé and as much else as possible from Santería--if the Government doesn't wipe it out first.

In general, for each nation there is a common musical culture which is the spontaneous creation of those farm-workers and later city-workers who are not social climbers and can't quit being poor. Actually, it is usually a fusion of music, dancing, and lyrics--which is done or watched, but not "performed". Such a dance of one national grouping comes to another nation not on the Concert Stage, but by people taking it up, doing it. This music-dancing is already the indigenous symbol of the oppressed. In a phrase: "street-Negro music".

To give more examples: For France--during the revolution of 1789, the revolutionary masses danced the carmagnole in the streets of Paris. Unfortunately, as a result of the protracted monopoly capitalist stagnation of Europe, the history of colonialism and the bribing of the workers, there is no native "street-Negro music" in France today. The recent ascendancy of an R & B-inspired music among British working youth prefigures the path for Europe.

Street-Negro music cannot be reduced to old or recent European bourgeois Art. Nor is it African arts of hundred of years ago which are no longer extant. Further, it must be absolutely clear that street-Negro music is not "folk art". Street-Negro music is not those "Negro spirituals" that were "purified" of "ugly" Africanisms, notated in choral fashion, and performed in the Concert Hall; or Villa-Lobos' "Brazilian" Symphonies; or the Kingston Trio; or Odetta. Street-Negro music is not the Russian Moiseyev's Ballets of phony "folk dances" performed on the Concert Stage; or the Mexican Ballet Folklorico; or the Cuban National "Folk Dance" group; or the Rhumba, "cleansed" of Africanisms to become a ballroom dance.

Recent trends in street-Negro music prove that it is irreconcilable with "folk art", that it is hundreds of years less antiquated than Bach or Mozart, that its modern development is away from European bourgeois Modern Art. Such advanced instruments as the many models of electric guitars and electric organs (Appendix 5) are standard in R & B and hillbilly music. Rock 'n' roll uses such electronic recording techniques as reverberation, dubbing and over-dubbing. Many numbers are "studio creations", exist only in recording. In addition to the importance of the recording studio in production, there is the importance of radio stations in distribution. Street-Negro music rocks; European bourgeois Modern Art (and "folk art") doesn't.

'folk art' means something antiquated, humble, and pathetic, and R & B singer Buddy Guy's "First Time I Met the Blues" (Argo LP 4026) comes on too scary for that put-down. Bo Diddley (Chess LP 1431) is good, normal street-Negro music; Bo Diddley's use of amplifier reverb and tremolo in "Pretty Thing" is the opposite of "primitive". "Tobacco Road", by the Nashville musician John D. Laudermilk (Columbia Promotion Record 45 RPM 4-41562, JZ SP49232), is the very opposite of "primitive"; and utterly cuts up the "sophisticated" Nashville Teens' version. Incidentally, Loudermilk's lyrics are reactionary, but his musical culture in general is an indigenous symbol of the proletariat. The R&R which jives the snobs and has an electronic sound and is called "junk music", such as "The Surfin' Bird" by the Trashmen (Garrett Records GA 4002'), is also by no means "primitive".

Figure 4.12. Henry Flynt, *Communists Must Give Revolutionary Leadership in Culture*, 1965. Design by George Maciunas. © Henry A. Flynt, Jr. Used by permission of Henry A. Flynt, Jr.

factographic reportage over imaginative literature; the cinema over novels, theater, and visual art; and documentary of the type practiced by Dziga Vertov over melodramatic film. To this, Flynt added, as we have already seen, his most expanded and impassioned argument in favor of adopting African-American popular music as the official policy of the Communist Party. On this and only this point, Flynt's cultural program followed the line of reasoning about a posteriori recognition originally developed in Conrad's word scores and Flynt's "New General Theory of Acognitive Culture": "Street-Negro music is *already* a vital symbol of the most oppressed," he contended; "all that is needed is encouragement so that it can become more so." Beyond its being the most vital form of cultural expression, Flynt further contended that African-American musical styles were already the most modern and advanced. As he noted, "Recent trends in street-Negro music prove that it is irreconcilable with 'folk art', that it is hundreds of years *less* antiquated than Bach or Mozart, that its modern development is away from European bourgeois Modern Art. . . . Street-Negro music rocks; European bourgeois Modern Art (and 'folk art') doesn't."

It was at this point, perhaps, that Flynt's cultural project was somewhat betrayed by his collaboration with the party (though one should not, perhaps, overestimate the seriousness of the proposal, which took the form of an anti-art artwork). Flynt and Maciunas not only took up a claim to major power (to advise or become the party), but sought to justify and thereby raise their cultural preferences to superior values in the exact manner Bataille had warned against. In this case, the values were not only modernity and advancement, but the rationalist ideal of efficient production long propounded by Maciunas. (Indeed, Maciunas's argument for the "elimination of the fine arts" was "motivated by desire to stop the waste of material and human resources . . . and divert it to socially constructive ends.")[132] In an analogue (and exacerbation) of Flynt's claims of advancement and modernity, Maciunas's extended series of appendices provided graphic evidence in support of the efficiency of their proposals. Thus, in appendix number five, the superiority of African-American popular music was demonstrated, not on the grounds of its revolutionary cultural force, but on the greater functionalism of the designs of the electric organ and electric guitar (Figure 4.13).

• • •

Despite his acquaintance with Maciunas and his close friendship with Flynt, Conrad's politics would ultimately develop in a different direction. As we will see, the self he sought or modeled was not locked solipsistically into his or her "just likings" (to use Flynt's terms), but was a more Cagean self, open to change. And despite a closeness to Flynt's cultural politics and understanding of music, Conrad would not operate according to the same strategy of low/high opposition, but via a form of immanence that undermined the notion of transcendental authority differently. As we will begin to understand in Chapter 5, Conrad's relation to social difference, oppression, and abjection was inflected not so much by the civil-rights movement — though he was at Martin Luther King Jr.'s "I Have A Dream" speech in Washington, D.C. — but by his relation to the radical (and socialist) queer underground milieu of his partner in the pickets, Jack Smith. None of this would stop him, however, from further collaborations with Flynt.

After the publication of *Communists*, Flynt broke from all but the most fantastic adherence to the orthodox political left, setting his project to take one more twist.[133] In 1968, the very high point of social unrest, he formed his own political party of sorts. Dubbing it (with evident irony) The Realists, Flynt launched a proposal to "Overthrow the Human Race!" In an expression of what many longtime participants in contemporary social struggles must have felt, Flynt proclaimed, "The evidence is overwhelming that humanity is biosocially irrational."[134] Then, in a return to ideas initially put forward in his "Creep" lecture, he proposed: "'Social problems' can only be solved outside the biological limits of human beings as social animals. Loyalty to the human species is absurd." In an extreme (and humorous) response to increasingly

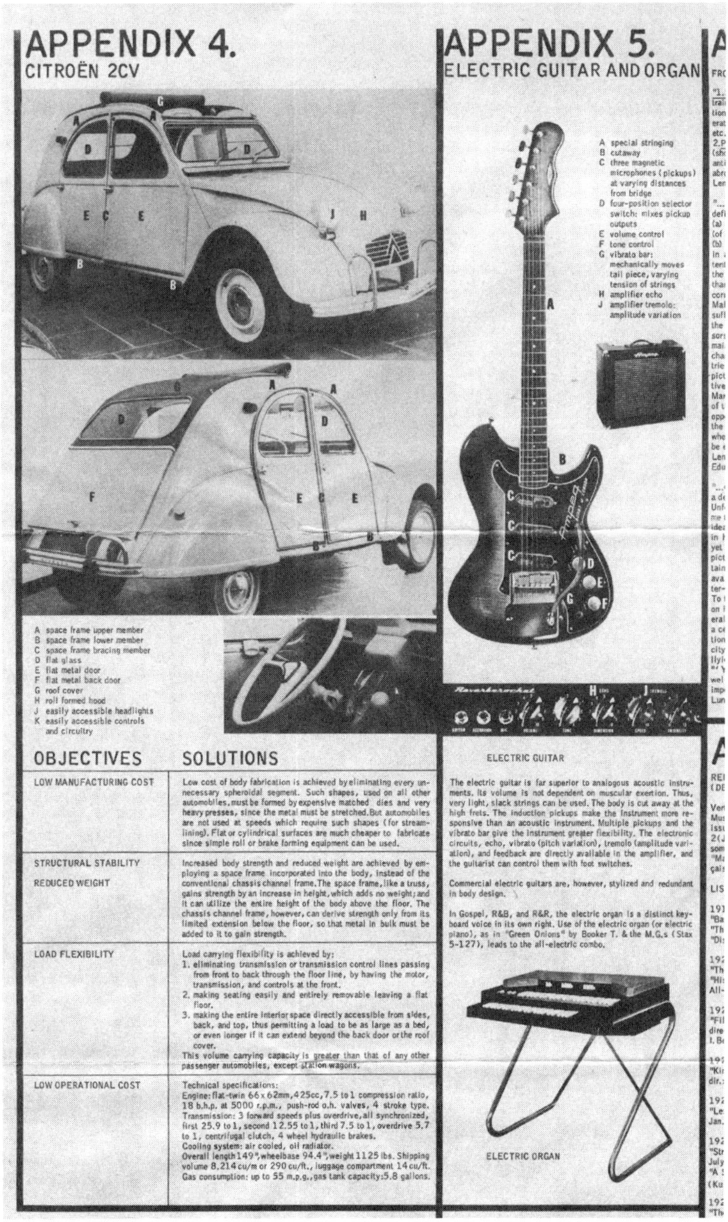

APPENDIX 4.
CITROËN 2CV

A space frame upper member
B space frame lower member
C space frame bracing member
D flat glass
E flat metal door
F flat metal back door
G roof cover
H roll formed hood
J easily accessible headlights
K easily accessible controls and circuitry

OBJECTIVES	SOLUTIONS
LOW MANUFACTURING COST	Low cost of body fabrication is achieved by eliminating every unnecessary spheroidal segment. Such shapes, used on all other automobiles, must be formed by expensive matched dies and very heavy presses, since the metal must be stretched. But automobiles are not used at speeds which require such shapes (for streamlining). Flat or cylindrical surfaces are much cheaper to fabricate since simple roll or brake forming equipment can be used.
STRUCTURAL STABILITY REDUCED WEIGHT	Increased body strength and reduced weight are achieved by employing a space frame incorporated into the body, instead of the conventional chassis channel frame. The space frame, like a truss, gains strength by an increase in height, which adds no weight; and it can utilize the entire height of the body above the floor. The chassis channel frame, however, can derive strength only from its limited extension below the floor, so that metal in bulk must be added to it to gain strength.
LOAD FLEXIBILITY	Load carrying flexibility is achieved by: 1. eliminating transmission or transmission control lines passing from front to back through the floor line, by having the motor, transmission, and controls at the front. 2. making seating easily and entirely removable leaving a flat floor. 3. making the entire interior space directly accessible from sides, back, and top, thus permitting a load to be as large as a bed, or even longer if it can extend beyond the back door or the roof cover. This volume carrying capacity is greater than that of any other passenger automobiles, except station wagons.
LOW OPERATIONAL COST	Technical specifications: Engine: flat-twin 66 x 62mm, 425cc, 7.5 to 1 compression ratio, 18 b.h.p. at 5000 r.p.m., push-rod o.h. valves, 4 stroke type. Transmission: 3 forward speeds plus overdrive, all synchronized, first 25.9 to 1, second 12.55 to 1, third 7.5 to 1, overdrive 5.7 to 1, centrifugal clutch, 4 wheel hydraulic brakes. Cooling system: air cooled, oil radiator. Overall length 149", wheelbase 94.4", weight 1125 lbs. Shipping volume 8.214 cu/m or 290 cu/ft., luggage compartment 14 cu/ft. Gas consumption: up to 55 m.p.g., gas tank capacity: 5.8 gallons.

APPENDIX 5.
ELECTRIC GUITAR AND ORGAN

A special stringing
B cutaway
C three magnetic microphones (pickups) at varying distances from bridge
D four-position selector switch: mixes pickup outputs
E volume control
F tone control
G vibrato bar: mechanically moves tail piece, varying tension of strings
H amplifier echo
J amplifier tremolo: amplitude variation

ELECTRIC GUITAR

The electric guitar is far superior to analogous acoustic instruments. Its volume is not dependent on muscular exertion. Thus, very light, slack strings can be used. The body is cut away at the high frets. The induction pickups make the instrument more responsive than an acoustic instrument. Multiple pickups and the vibrato bar give the instrument greater flexibility. The electronic circuits, echo, vibrato (pitch variation), tremolo (amplitude variation), and feedback are directly available in the amplifier, and the guitarist can control them with foot switches.

Commercial electric guitars are, however, stylized and redundant in body design.

In Gospel, R&B, and R&R, the electric organ is a distinct keyboard voice in its own right. Use of the electric organ (or electric piano), as in "Green Onions" by Booker T. & the M.G.s (Stax 5-127), leads to the all-electric combo.

ELECTRIC ORGAN

Figure 4.13. Henry Flynt, *Communists Must Give Revolutionary Leadership in Culture*, 1965, appendices 4 and 5. Design by George Maciunas. © Henry A. Flynt, Jr. Used by permission of Henry A. Flynt, Jr.

widespread and intransigent violence and repression, both at home and abroad, Flynt proposed the goals of "forming an alliance with a superior life-form from outer space to attack the human race," "causing mutations in animals, producing intelligent species which will rise up against their human oppressors," and "causing mutations in humanity that will transform it beyond recognition."[135] Conrad, who had never followed Flynt into socialist orthodoxy, immediately signed on.[136]

Chapter Five

Primitives and Flaming Creatures

> Be primitives naturally.
>
> — Tony Conrad

On December 3, 1964, the year after Henry Flynt's lecture, "From 'Culture' to Veramusement," Walter De Maria's Bond Street loft would be host to a very different event — a rehearsal and impromptu recording session by the rock group the Primitives (Figure 5.1). The Primitives were Tony Conrad, John Cale, Walter De Maria, Lou Reed, and, on this occasion, if not publicly, "Jimmie," likely Jimmie Sims, a friend of Reed's and fellow songwriter from Pickwick Records. The Long Island City–based Pickwick company produced low-budget pop songs in whatever styles were fashionable at the time — rock and roll, surf music, rhythm and blues — shamelessly hoping to foist a "hit" on an unsuspecting and often undiscriminating public (Figure 5.2)."There were four of us literally locked in a room writing songs," Reed recalled of his time at Pickwick. "They would say 'Write ten California songs, ten Detroit songs,' then we'd go down into the studio for an hour or two and cut three or four albums really quickly."[1]

The Primitives had been created to perform "The Ostrich," written and recorded by Reed and Sims along with fellow Pickwick songwriters Terry Phillips and Jerry Vance and pressed that month as by the (as yet nonexistent) Primitives.[2] Parts of the story are already well known in the annals of rock history: How Reed and the others had recorded "The Ostrich" late one night while high, along with another, similar track, "Sneaky Pete." How, after hearing them, the company thought the two songs, with

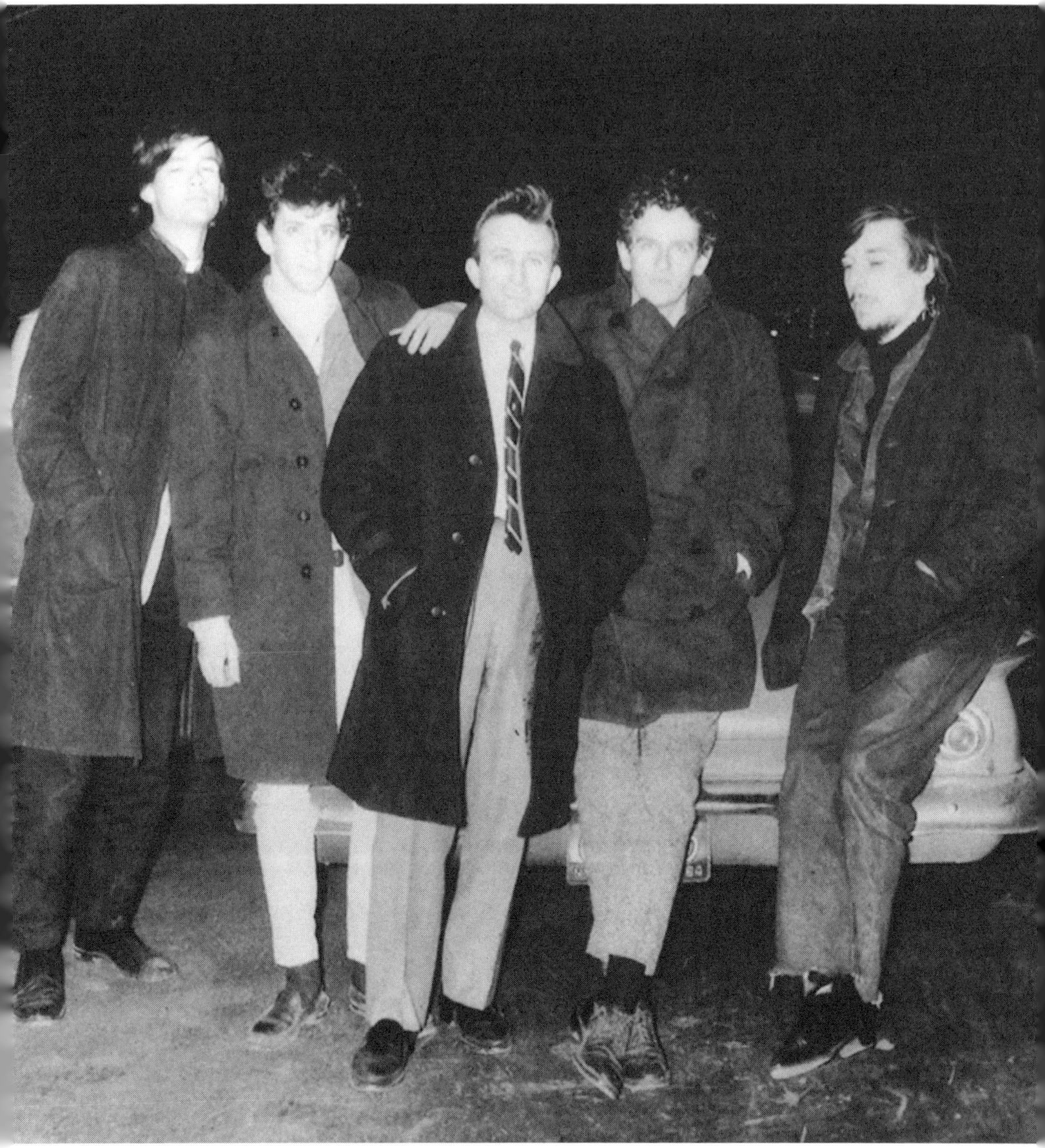

Figure 5.1. The Primitives (Tony Conrad, Lou Reed, unknown, Walter De Maria, John Cale), c. 1965. Photographer unknown.

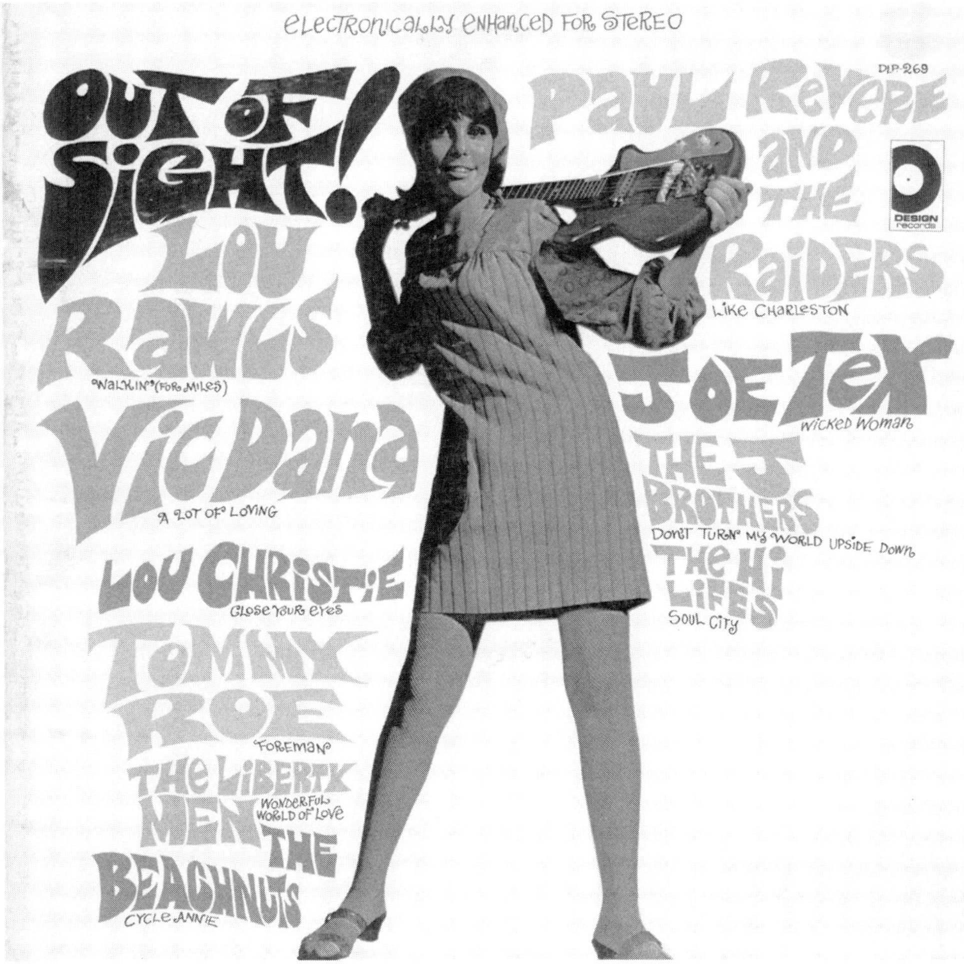

Figure 5.2. Various Artists, *Out of Sight!* LP cover, Design Records (a product of Pickwick International) DLP 269, released 1967.

"The Ostrich" on the A side, could form a viable single, the first to be released on the Pickwick City imprint. How since, as Conrad put it, "some of the guys were 'executive material,' so they were not going to go out on the road," the company was subsequently faced with the task of putting together a suitable band to promote it.[3] How Conrad and Cale had been induced to attend an East Side party by David Gelber (brother of Jack Gelber, playwright of *The Connection*), where they were invited to join the group, their "long" hair signaling to Phillips and the other executives ("hyper-sleazy types from Brooklyn and Long Island City"[4] who probably knew nothing of the downtown avant-garde) that they must be popular musicians. How the company initially (and unsuccessfully) attempted to get Conrad, Cale, and De Maria to sign exclusive contracts forfeiting all creative rights for the next seven years. How the group supposedly appeared on American Bandstand. And how the short-lived promotion of the single was the occasion for the first meeting of Cale and Reed, who would go on to form the Velvet Underground, one of the most influential American rock groups of all time and an integral part of Andy Warhol's multimedia Exploding Plastic Inevitable.[5]

"The Ostrich" has been referred to by some as the first punk rock record on account of the ridiculous and mock-violent nature of the "dance" it was supposedly promoting. "All right, everybody, get down on your face," Reed calls out before the first verse, beckoning the audience to follow.

> Hey, put your head up, upside your knees
> Now, do the Ostrich
> (Do the Ostrich, Do the Ostrich [chorus])
> Yeah, yeah, yeah, yeah, yeah
> Yeah, you take a step forward, you step on your head
> Now, do the Ostrich
> (Do the Ostrich, Do the Ostrich)

Reed continues describing similarly ridiculous, sometimes ambiguous moves until, in the final verse, he instructs:

You take a step forward, put your head onto your knees
(Do the Ostrich, Do the Ostrich)
Ohh, one more time, yeah
Yeah, do just 'bout anything you please
Now, come on
(Do the Ostrich, Do the Ostrich)

In between, there's much screaming and exhortations to the crowd (most notably, Reed's repeated shouts of "Do it" that would resurface three years later in the Velvet Underground's "Sister Ray" from the album *White Light / White Heat*).

The repeated four-syllable chorus, "Do the Ostrich," is delivered in a somewhat grating falsetto screech, in exactly the same manner, in fact, as the chorus of the B side: "Sneaky Pe-ete, Sneaky Pe-ete." Both sides of the single share the shrieking, yelping background vocals and might indeed be understood in relation to the garage rock protopunk of groups such as the Sonics, if it weren't so obviously campy and deliberately over the top. Both the mock hysteria and the camp aspects of "The Ostrich" are further augmented by studio-added crowd noise, a supplement that is as fake as it is energy producing.

When the Primitives returned to De Maria's loft that night, following their first live performance, at the Riverside Plaza Hotel, they ran through "The Ostrich" at least twice, although only playing the chorus and the break, not the verses. Each time, the group's screeches, whoops, yips, and yells build in intensity until they reach a sort of collective ecstasy, obviously the trademark "primitivism" that seems to have been evolving into the group's signature style. (And for Conrad, perhaps, an echo of the "vitality" Flynt had lauded just a few months before in the "primitive" rock and blues on behalf of which they had protested.) A tape recording made by Conrad of the rehearsal, however, does not begin with or even spend the most time on "The Ostrich," but rather focuses on an early version of the song "Why Don't You Smile Now," at this point entitled, "Won't You Smile."

Unlike "The Ostrich," "Won't You Smile" would not be a pure

Pickwick Records production, but the first known collaboration between Reed and Cale (ultimately credited to Phillips, Vance, Reed, and Cale). It would have a surprisingly intense early life, being first released on a seven-inch single by the All Night Workers (friends of Reed's from Syracuse University, where he was an undergraduate) on Round Sound records in 1965, the flip side of a non-Reed-penned minor hit, "Don't Put All Your Eggs in One Basket." Later that year, "Why Don't You Smile Now" would be covered as a smooth R&B track by Donnie Burkes on Decca Records as the B side of "Satisfaction Guaranteed."[6] In 1966, it would appear yet again, this time on *The Rock Sect's In*, the third and final album by the Downliners Sect, a British Rolling Stones–influenced group on the UK division of Columbia Records.[7]

Judging from the stripped-down instrumentation and the tempo at which it's played, the first of the two takes of "Won't You Smile" recorded at De Maria's loft may have been an initial run-through for the group. Reed sings:

> Now you left me, baby, all alone,
> Won't you smile (chorus)
> Yeah, yeah, yeah
>
> You left me for, oh, another guy
> I hope you smile
> Uh uh, huh
>
> I found my friend, my Cadillac car
> I hope you smile

After a couple more verses, the others gradually join in, transforming the chorus, through screeches and screams, into "Primitives"' style. At the end of the take, Reed says to whomever is at the tape recorder, "Hey man, do me a favor. Shut that thing off and play that fuckin' thing back."

After two takes of "The Ostrich" and some working through off-tape, the group decides to make another recording of "Won't

You Smile." The first, partial take ends quickly, when Sims's tambourine fails to enter at the correct spot. The following take, caught on tape, would be the only fully worked song of the evening and the only known song recorded by the now-legendary Primitives – although, not having been released or even heard since that time, it is, in a sense, the sound of history *not* being made:

> Reed, calling the end of the take: "I need a tambourine."
> Cale (although the number of people speaking over one another make his comments difficult to decipher): "The thing is . . . It's a long stretch . . . solo . . . and then back to Tony. . . ."
> Sims (speaking at the same time): "His beat was just picking up perfect. . . . Walter, give it a good shot. . . ."
> Reed: "OK. One . . . . Here we go, ready? John starts."
> Sims: "Announce the song, take one."
> Reed: "OK, cool. 'Won't You Smile,' take one."
> Sims: "Do that again, 'Won't You Smile,' take one."
> Reed: "'Won't You Smile,' take one. Go. Start."

Taken by surprise, the group half starts out of sequence.

> Reed: "No, wait, wait. That's not the way. . . ."
> Sims: "Clean start."
> Reed: "Clean start."
> Sims: "First him and then I'll come in with the tambourine. . . ."
> Reed: "'Won't You Smile,' take one."
> Background voice (probably De Maria at the drums, mockingly yelled through cupped hands): "This is bullshit."
> Cale (good naturedly, in his strong Welsh accent): "Let's obey the orders, shall we, for once."
> Reed (with mock wistful resignation): "Ahhh, 'Won't You Smile,' take one."

Then the group begins playing, Dum, dum-da-dum, dum-da-dum, dum-da-dum, da-dum, da-dum . . . and in comes the shaking tambourine Reed called for at the beginning of the take. The opening is distinctly reminiscent of the beginning Cale and Reed would orchestrate for the Velvet Underground's "All Tomorrow's Parties," where similarly rhythmic guitar chords are met by tambourine (although rhythmic, in that case) and a cantering piano that recalls the shaken tambourine played here. Reed sings:

> You said that you've found another guy
> Now, won't you smile (chorus)
> (warbling echo of the chorus, mainly, it seems, in a somewhat ridiculous falsetto by Sims, but joined by the group: "Won't you smi-i-ile")
> Yeah baby
>
> You said that you were gonna go in style
> Now, won't you smile
> (warbling echo: "Won't you smi-i-ile")
>
> I saw you down in your sequin dress on Broadway
> (others in falsetto: "Broadway, won't you smile")
> Won't you smile
>
> I walked across the street so I wouldn't get in your way
> Won't you smile
> (warbling echo)
> Yeah, yeah, won't you smile
> (warbling echo)
> Oh, whoa, won't you smile
> (warbling echo)
>
> You said that you had had enough of me
> So, won't you smile
> (warbling echo)

The chorus, which has been echoing Reed's "Won't you smile," has been gradually building in intensity and is now accompanied by loud screeches by the group, once again "Primitivizing" the song. Reed continues:

You said that you had other things to do
So, won't you smile
(warbling echo)

At this point in the first take, Reed had broken into a spoken interlude: "There's one thing I must tell you, darling, in all sincerity. You know that love is no laughing matter, and that you must give it with your heartfelt truth." This was followed by a deeper voice (Cale? Conrad?) mumbling several, largely indecipherable lines in a mock pretentious tone. In this take, however, Reed skips the first take's spoken interlude, yet the mumbling, fake-pretentious voice comes in nonetheless. The words are as difficult to make out as previously: "...didn't wear her red dress ...sequins...but I love...." A screaming chorus follows, really over the top now, as is Sims' falsetto "Won't you smi-i-ile."

To this point, the story told by the song is much the same as that on the later, released version of "Why Don't You Smile Now": that of a lover whose girlfriend has left him for another man. As sung by the All Night Workers and Donnie Burkes, the opening lines became:

You didn't care when I begged you to stay
Why don't you smile now?
You laughed at me and walked away
Why don't you smile now?

Although pleading and desperate at the beginning, by the end of the song, the singer has come to enjoy his revenge. His woman has come back, abandoned by her rich boyfriend, and now the full import of the question asked by the chorus becomes clear: Why don't you smile now, the lover asks, like you were smiling before?

Sequined dress, high heeled shoes
Baby, all you got was blues
Why don't you smile now?

Now you're back, you want back in
But baby you just watch me grin
Why don't you smile now? Yeah, yeah, yeah

At De Maria's loft, however, Reed tells a somewhat different story. The singer is not a jilted lover, it seems, but a pimp, and the man that the woman being addressed has left him for is merely a better, more affluent one. It is now less a canned pop story in Pickwick fashion than a darker, distinctly New York one. We're well on the way to the Velvet Underground again, and it is fitting that the guitar now bears more than a passing resemblance to that in the Velvet Underground's "Venus in Furs." Reed continues:

You been a hooker for a long, long while
So, won't you smile
(warbling echo)

You made me hundred dollars in a little while
So, won't you smile
(Sims, apparently getting the joke of what may have been improvised lyrics on Reed's part, now meshes with rather than echoes Reed's chorus with his falsetto)

You got yourself a big Lincoln car
So, won't you smile
(falsetto once again with Reed)

I hope your money's gonna take you real far
So, won't you smile
(warbling echo drops back in place)

So, won't you smile
(warbling echo)

Others in the group now once again augment their screams, someone yelling a loud, vaguely Western sounding "Yehhhhh ha!"

The take ends with a drawn out, ridiculous falsetto "Wo-o-o-o-o-on't you smi-i-i-i-ile," with Reed throwing in, just before the end, "You know you make me want to shout." "Hey, play it back," he says, "just for the hell of it."

Despite the mock resistance they encounter from De Maria (who, it seems, yells "Bullshit take" just before the recorder is shut off so the group can hear the replay), Reed and Sims are clearly the most comfortable of the group in the pop arena. When the recorder comes on again, what we hear is Reed preparing to play more of the Pickwick songs penned by himself, Sims, Phillips, and Vance. "Can we do 'Teardrops . . .' and 'Sad Lonely Orphan Boy,' some of the songs they haven't heard?" he asks Sims. "Teardrops in the Sand" would be released under the group name the Hollywoods on *Soundsville!*, a diverse compilation of would-be teen hits (all cowritten by Reed) on another Pickwick imprint, Design Records, in early 1965. The album also contained the Beachnuts' "Cycle Annie" and the Roughnecks' "You're Driving Me Insane," both sung and played on by Reed.[8] The latter had a bit of the over-the-top aesthetic of the Primitives, with a similar type of ecstatic background yelping added to an impressive example of Reed's early guitar work. "Sad Lonely Orphan Boy" would also be recorded under the name the Beachnuts, but was apparently never released. Reed, however, begins by playing a version of "Johnny Won't Surf No More," which was also on the *Soundsville!* compilation, recorded by Jeannie Larimore with unacknowledged backing by the Liberty Men.

> Johnny can't surf no more
> And I know one to blame
> Johnny can't surf no more
> (wry aside to the group, "the guy drown")
> Oh, oh what a shame

At this point, another voice (possibly De Maria) breaks in: "Did you write that one?"

Reed: "Yeah."
Voice: "That, that'll make it."
Reed (laughing): "I know it will."
Voice: "Why don't you get it out? Get it out."
Reed: "Unfortunately, in the music business. . . ."
Voice: "You gotta get 'em out!"

Reed and Jimmie Sims then perform the campy, sad "Teardrops in the Sand" and "Sad Lonely Orphan Boy," ballads that are such intensely maudlin kitsch that even Reed can't keep a straight face, breaking up at the beginning of the inevitable spoken interlude in "Teardrops," "I really love that surfer girl . . ." (laughing just like in "Foggy Notion"). "That song kills me," he says. "Sad Lonely Orphan Boy" is even more pathetic:

What has happened to that orphan boy,
who was left alone in this cruel world?
He had no one he could call his own
He had no place he could call his ho-o-ome

He's just a [sung in the style of Frankie Valli] sad lonely orphan boy
sad lonely orphan boy

He's on his own
Oh, all alone

[Then, half-spoken]
I never saw him for a couple of years,
and just the other day, I received a card,
and all it said was, "Thank you for those precious memories,"
and it was signed [Frankie Valli again], "Sad Lonely Orphan Boy.". . .

After this detour into the dregs of Pickwick commercialism,[9] Reed breaks into a spontaneous version of what seems to be Jimmy Reed's "Shame, Shame, Shame," on which, extremely unfortunately, Conrad's tape fades in and out. Despite the poor sound quality, however, it is clear that everyone joins in, playing, screeching, and screaming with gleeful abandon. A voice is once again heard: "Yeaahh Ha!"

• • •

Over the course of the Primitives' brief career, the group would travel to a half-dozen or so weekend gigs, mostly in the Lehigh Valley area of Pennsylvania, attempting to break "The Ostrich" on regional radio. They played high schools and a shopping center (sometimes exchanging instruments in the car) and even did a local radio interview. As Conrad recalled:

> Those gigs were completely mindblowing to Walter, John and me. I mean we're riding around in a station wagon goofing on the idea that we're going to be playing rock & roll music, then we're on this stage and we don't know what's going on and none of us have really played this kind of music before, and then there's all this hype and screaming kids and meeting other groups. The whole thing was absolutely unexpected and hypnotizing.[10]

If anything, the sudden plunge into popular culture from the rarified realms of the New York avant-garde was more startling for Cale than it was for Conrad. Conrad had already encountered his friend Henry Flynt's rejection of high musical forms in favor of blues and the rock music of Elvis Presley upon his return from Europe in 1961. Although Conrad was at first somewhat taken aback, learning to expand his tastes to encompass popular music could be comprehended as a consequence, even an imperative, of the lessons he had learned from Cage (even though Cage himself would largely not follow in that direction). Learning not only to appreciate or to understand, but actually to like pop music would ultimately be only one more step along the path that had begun with the epiphany of hearing (and liking) that bit of Bartók that Flynt had played for him and that had stuck in his head. "*My* program was to find things I *didn't* like and then try to like them,"

Conrad explained to Scott McDonald: "The things that I didn't like included, for example, rock and roll music, so I practiced liking rock and roll music until – somewhat to the astonishment of my friend John Cale – I really *did* like [artists such as] DeeDee Sharp, even went to see DeeDee Sharp in person at the Brooklyn Fox Theater, and had a simply ecstatic experience there."[11]

(It was another, less ecstatic, foray into Brooklyn that would give Conrad the confidence to take the stage with the Primitives. As he explained to Tony Oursler: "When I saw Lou Christie . . . all the people from Brooklyn were like this on the stage [gyrates], and they were really cool. And Lou Christie was like this really like wan, white guy, and he sat in his chair, and then he got up and did his song. And I thought, 'Man, if Lou Christie can be a rock star, *I* can be a rock star!'")[12]

It was only when Cale moved into Conrad's apartment at 56 Ludlow Street (leaving the loft Cale shared with Terry Jennings on Lispenard Street soon after he and Young were busted for selling the drugs that were stashed there)[13] that he became exposed to this dimension of Conrad's interests (Figure 5.3). As Conrad remembers: "We had been working with LaMonte for some time doing very austere regimented things which were pretty intense. We had been talking about serious things like intervals, and Indian music and theory and avant-garde music, but when John moved into my place on Ludlow Street it turned out that when I went home I sat around listening to Hank Williams records and was blasting a huge 45 collection."[14]

It was from this point that Cale started to become interested in rock music, he and Conrad eventually becoming "riveted" to Murray the K's evening broadcasts of British pop on 1010 WINS AM.[15] "There was something very liberating about the whole rock thing," Conrad recalled, "and in a sense 56 Ludlow Street came to stand for a lot in terms of some kind of liberating musical influence."[16]

Perhaps the incident concerning the Primitives most referred to in mainstream rock literature details Conrad's and Cale's surprise at learning that, in playing "The Ostrich," all the strings on the guitar were tuned the same (to A$^{\#}$). Conrad recalled:

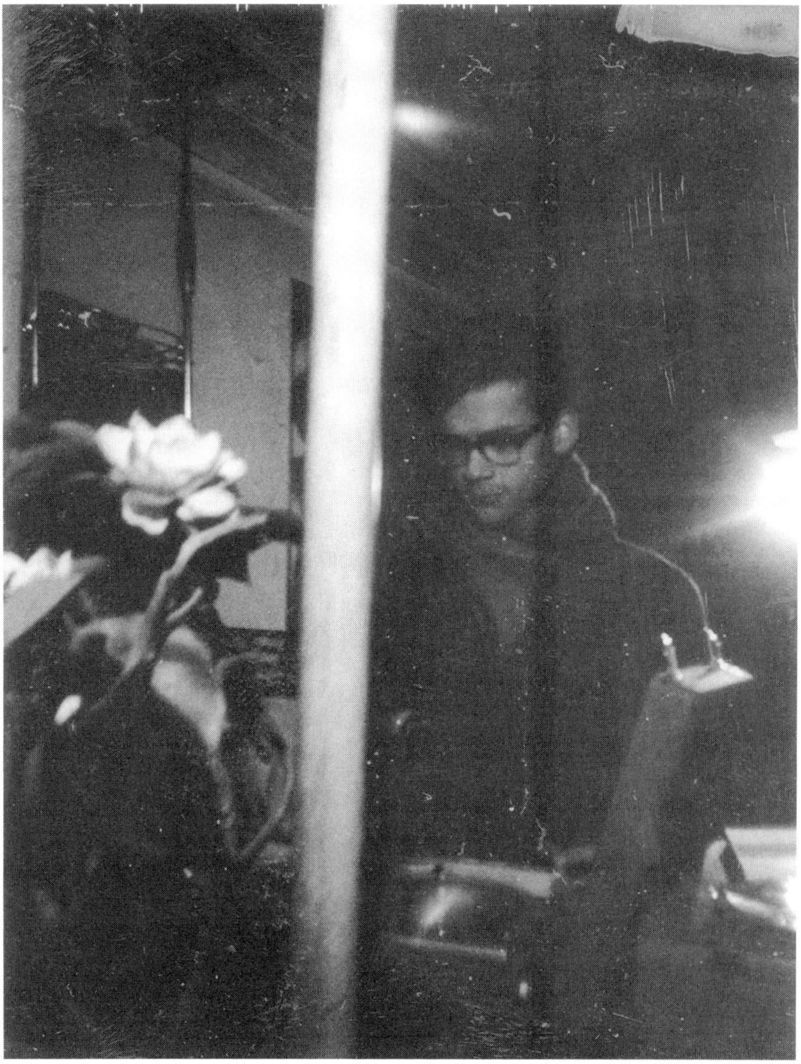

Figure 5.3. Tony Conrad at 56 Ludlow Street, ca. 1964–65. Photo: John Cale. Courtesy Tony Conrad.

> They said, "Don't worry, it's easy to play because all the strings are tuned to the same note," which blew our minds because that was what we were doing with LaMonte in The Dream Syndicate.[17]

> We couldn't believe that they were doing this crap just like in a sort of strange ethnically Brooklyn style, tuning their instruments to one note, which is what we were doing too.... In fact we were tuning to two notes and they were tuning to only one.[18]

Within the canonical history of rock and roll, this anecdote has become emblematic, not only of the meeting of Conrad, Reed, and Cale, but of the subsequent development of the Primitives into the Warlocks, the Falling Spikes, and, eventually, the Velvet Underground, with its melding of Reed's literate rock-and-roll sensibility and the minimalism of the Theatre of Eternal Music—"Heroin," from the Velvet Underground's first album, with Cale's steady, just-intonation viola playing, being the primary example. The actual acoustical record of the Primitives, however, would not seem to fit so neatly within such a linear history. There was nothing "minimal" about the Primitives' shrieking, ecstatic, over-the-top renditions of pop music, and the episode, however brief, represents a deviation from any straightforward trajectory from the Dream Syndicate to the VU. And although in retrospect we might understand the "liberating musical influence" represented by the Primitives as a manifestation of the type of aesthetic relativism often associated with a post-Cagean, postmodern sensibility (the freedom to indulge in high and low musical forms alike), it will not do to comprehend it as the exhaustion of the high arts (including music) and the linear progression (and dissolution) of the avant-garde into an "empirical, chaotic, and heterogeneous" cultural condition in which meaningful aesthetic positions and histories are no longer relevant or can no longer be discerned.[19] However improvised and potentially spur-of-the moment, the Primitives' episode within the trajectory that ran "through the avant-garde and into performance art and then rock" would seem to relate, in a quite specific manner, to the transgressive, camp aesthetic that Conrad, Cale, and De Maria had come to know through their association with underground artist and filmmaker Jack Smith.[20]

• • •

By 1964, Smith had already become well known as the director of *Flaming Creatures* (1962–63), perhaps the most infamous underground film of the 1960s (Figure 5.4).[21] Shot on shoplifted, outdated, black-and-white film stock, frequently overexposed into a sheer, foggy whiteness, with disorienting framing and close-ups and lacking any real narrative continuity, *Flaming Creatures* was a concatenation of seemingly poor technical choices that added up to a hallucinatory new aesthetic vision. Filmed entirely on the secluded rooftop of the Windsor Theater during the summer of 1962, Smith's film was an ecstatic homage to the North African-themed features of the 1940s, such as *Ali Baba and the Forty Thieves* (1944), the sound track for which opens the film. What follows is a series of loosely connected scenes inhabited by Smith's elaborately (but never quite convincingly) costumed "creatures" in various states of disheveled drag, including Rene Rivera (credited as Dolores Flores but soon to be known as Mario Montez), Francis Francine, and Joel Markman. Sheila Bick played the part intended for Marian Zazeela, who had withdrawn from the project on account of her recent connection with La Monte Young and who would ultimately appear only briefly in a Delacroixesque tableau vivant with Young, Angus MacLise, and Irving Rosenthal. Amongst the scenes are numerous creatures, both female and male, some bearded, applying lipstick; a slapsticklike chase of Bick by Francine; and Bick's violation at the hands of a motley mass of creatures, one of whom is similarly ravished, which turns into both an earthquake and an orgy. P. Adams Sitney has aptly described the overall progression of *Flaming Creatures* in terms of a "move toward and away from a central core of three episodes in which the flaming creatures die in an orgy and, after an interval, are reborn."[22] Despite a famous review/defense by Susan Sontag

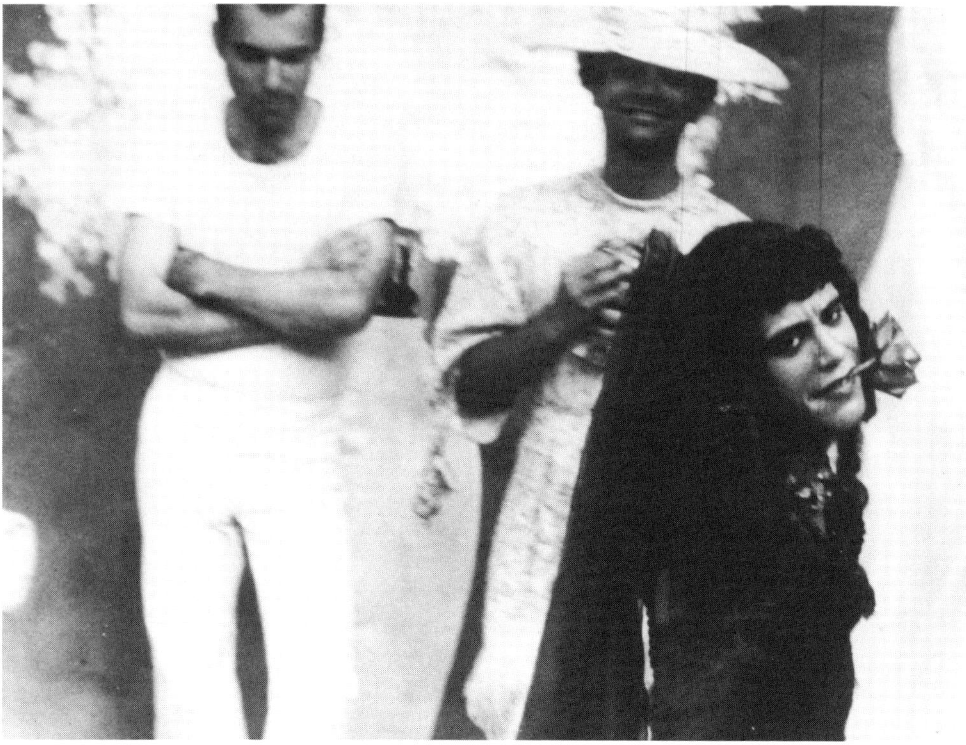

Figure 5.4. Jack Smith, *Flaming Creatures*, 1962–63. 16 mm, black and white, sound, 45 min. Unknown man, Piero Heliczer, and Mario Montez (aka Dolores Flores). Courtesy Anthology Film Archives.

in the pages of *The Nation*, Smith's film would become as much a scandal as a success, seized as pornography in a series of police raids across the country and eventually banned as obscene.

Smith's second feature, which he began shooting in 1963 even as the public scandal around *Flaming Creatures* was erupting, was *Normal Love*. Filmed on location mostly in rural areas around New York, *Normal Love* was a combination of horror movie and Hollywood musical, rendered in extravagant and often stunningly beautiful color (which Warhol once remarked that Smith used "backwards").[23] No more tied to narrative continuity than *Flaming Creatures*, *Normal Love* (or the footage of it that remains, because it was never definitively completed) nevertheless resolves into a series of erotic couplings: between a character named simply the Girl (Diana Baccus) and Uncle Pasty (Arnold Rockwood), the Mermaid (Mario Montez) and the Werewolf (Eliot Cuker), and Cobra Woman (Beverly Grant) and the Mummy (played alternately by MacLise, as the Green Mummy, and Conrad, billed simply as the Mummy). Like *Flaming Creatures*, *Normal Love* ends with a dance sequence, one in which the Chorus Cuties (including Warhol) dance atop a pink cake designed by Claes Oldenburg until interrupted, first by the Mummy's abduction of one of their number (subsequently attacked by Uncle Pasty) and then by the hyperactive Mongolian Child (David Sachs), who runs amok with a broken water-pistol machine gun, killing all of the Cuties, and the Mummy as well, and jumping up and down (and briefly falling) in triumph atop the pink cake.

Conrad initially met Smith via Zazeela, just after she had started living with Young. After graduating from Harvard in the summer of 1962, Conrad arrived at Young's doorstep in New York in need of a place to stay with his girlfriend, Kathryn Erickson (for whom Conrad's *Four Violins* would be recorded, but ultimately never sent). "La Monte would be in there playing Gagaku music, and these people would be lying around, and it was just the weirdest environment in the world."[24] Zazeela offered her old apartment, which she had been sharing with Smith, and on which the rent had been paid even though she was no longer living there. Later, when Erickson had gone back to Wellesley (and then on to California) and Zazeela's rent ran out, Smith and Conrad moved together to the apartment on Ludlow Street that would later be home to Conrad and Cale. It was from there that Conrad and Smith joined Flynt in the protests against the Museum of Modern Art, the Metropolitan Museum of Art, and Lincoln Center. And it was there, as well, that Conrad and Cale would join Smith, Montez, Francine, and others in a series of fantastic recording sessions. "We would sit around Ludlow Street with Angus MacLise, at loose ends but not really, slowly inching up to the point when we could record something," Cale recalled:

> It seemed there was always a magical moment when Angus, who had been wordless since entering the room, would pick up his tom-toms and start flicking away at a rhythm, then Tony would get a level, on bowed guitar, I would strum another guitar or play viola, Jack would have a coughing fit when the tape was running or else he would get the giggles, we would try to control ourselves, and then he would start to speak in that thin, whiny, nasal tone of his, barely audible but nevertheless presented as complementary to the noises coming from us, and suitably twisted too.[25]

A letter from Smith to David Gurin mentions his new living arrangement with Conrad, as well as what he calls their "Peter Pan existence": "when I'm 40 I'll be playing in a sandbox. Androgynous, unconventional, sportif, fascinating creature . . . sometimes momish (momeish?) & waspish but always in the mood for Tropicana orange juice in wax coated golden brazen upturned hindoo containers."[26] Tropicana orange juice was for Smith one of the everyday products that could be endowed with a bit of the fantastic while at the same time an undoubtedly very real luxury for the impoverished Bohemian existence the two were living. Some idea of Smith and Conrad's living situation at the time is conveyed in a letter – simultaneously tragic in its reference to actual poverty and comically overblown – by Smith to Ira Cohen, responding to a request for photographs, likely for Cohen's magazine, *Avant-Garde*. Smith, who had just started shooting *Normal Love*, had to deny Cohen's request:

> You see, I don't have my own lab & would be a whole greek opera to get one — plus, all I ate today was 1 peanut butter sandwich & I noticed that I was very weak and started worrying that I would die from malnutrition. Someday you'll get a whole mess of pix from me tho, I promise. Say hello to Irving & Marc — tell them about my new flic — that it's a color horror musical with a green mummy, a cobra woman, & a pink production number with a 12 foot high pink cake with chorus cuties *on* it & I have lost weight and am down to my skeleton — I expect to die soon.[27]

By the fall of 1962, Smith and Conrad had become close friends and associates; Smith even listed Conrad as his "closest relation" when he was confined to Bellevue mental hospital, where he was transferred for observation after having been sent to The Tombs for attempting to shoplift a department store's entire display of costume jewelry. Smith's correspondence instructs Conrad both to consult his lawyer and not to forget to tend the shrine he had erected in their apartment to his Hollywood muse, the 1940s actress Maria Montez.[28] (Conrad's 45 collection, which would so impress Cale when he moved into 56 Ludlow Street, had actually been shoplifted in partial emulation of Smith. Some years later, in a bit of poetic justice, the entire collection would be stolen out of Conrad's apartment.) Conrad would also prove integral to the most important period of Smith's cinematic production, working closely with him from the onset of filming *Flaming Creatures* (in which Conrad appeared, briefly, in a derriere-exposing, torn backless dress) to the conclusion of shooting *Normal Love*. Under Smith's direction, Conrad would produce the sound track for *Flaming Creatures* ("Anyone who worked with Jack knows what his direction was like: maddeningly unfocused, imprecise, and yet strongly imbued with ideas about the world of the project that it was necessary for all of us to inhabit").[29]

Although the film was Smith's creation, Conrad did suggest

significant touches, such as accompanying Bick's postorgy revival in the arms of the Fantastic Woman (played by Living Theater director Judith Malina) with Bartók's *Solo Violin Sonata*.[30] Conrad was also crucial in helping realize many of Smith's auditory goals, such as the Carnival of Ecstasy "mix" ("made by taking the speaker wires from a whole bunch of phonographs and just twisting them together and running that into the tape recorder") and the horror-house screams of the Earthquake Orgy, produced with the same tape recorder technique that Conrad had devised for *Three Loops for Performers and Tape Recorders*.[31] Conrad was supposed to have been equally integral to the completion of *Normal Love*, for which he was not only to produce the sound track, but also to devise optical effects that would lead to Conrad's first film, *The Flicker*. Before work could be completed on *Normal Love*, however, Conrad and Smith would have one of those falling outs that inevitably marked the end of all of Smith's relationships, although not before Conrad had vacated 56 Ludlow Street (at which point Reed began to room with Cale) to move in briefly with Smith and Mario Montez in the Grand Street loft that was intended to become the home of Cinemaroc Studios.

• • •

At the time Conrad first encountered Smith, the latter's aesthetic was already well developed. Smith had ended a formative period of collaboration with filmmakers Ken Jacobs and Bob Fleischner and "performer" Jerry Sims (concluded in the same type of psychologically fraught break that ended Smith's collaboration with Conrad). That period, which lasted from approximately 1956 through 1961, eventually saw the production of several films, including Jacobs's *Little Stabs at Happiness* (1959–62) and the incomparable *Blonde Cobra* (1959–63), but was dominated by the shooting of Jacobs's long-unfinished magnum opus *Star Spangled to Death* (1956–60/2003–4) (Figures 5.5 and 5.6).[32] In *Star Spangled to Death*, amid literally reels of appropriated footage, including entire television programs and films, Smith, Sims, and others portrayed allegorical embodiments of abstract ideas: Smith, "The Spirit Not of Life But of Living"; Sims, "Suffering"; along with others as "First Evil," "Second Evil," "Misplaced Charity," "The Impulse to Order," "Death," "The Future," and "Oscar Friendly" (the last played by Jacobs). This film and others associated with it, such as *Saturday Afternoon Blood Sacrifice* (1956) and *Little Cobra Dance* (1956), developed in the context of Jacobs and Smith's improvised performances and street theater events, which culminated in *The Human Wreckage Review*, a performance attempted in Provincetown (where Jacobs and Smith had their most significant and lasting falling out) in the summer of 1961.

Smith and Jacobs's endeavors during this time represent an important, but underrecognized facet of the cultural ferment of the late 1950s and early 1960s, one related both to the investigations of the downtrodden underbelly of the American Dream by the Beat artists and poets and to the collage practices of Robert Rauschenberg and the early Claes Oldenburg, particularly the latter's installations and happenings at the Judson Church Gallery and his East Village incarnation of *The Store* (1961–62).[33] For Smith, and especially for Jacobs, the trash aesthetic they developed during this time represented a distinctly political position, an opposition to or critique of the prevailing ideology and ethos of American capitalist culture and a means of acting out rebellious, even revolutionary impulses against it. Jacobs explained to McDonald:

> I was interested in social indictment, and I was disgusted and angry that with few examples Pop Art was going *with* society, was making salable products from sending up its cultural icons. *My* humor was wrathful, destructive; and Pop Art was making the differences in cultural strata very comfortable. . . .
>
> . . . Jack and I would deface posters in the subway, which I called "counter-desecration." At one point, I wanted to make kits for people to attack posters. We had discovered some things you could do with the posters, erasing and adding things. We had a lot of fun. While there was no hope of a real revolution, there could be this playful revolution – a mischievous, little-boy revolution.[34]

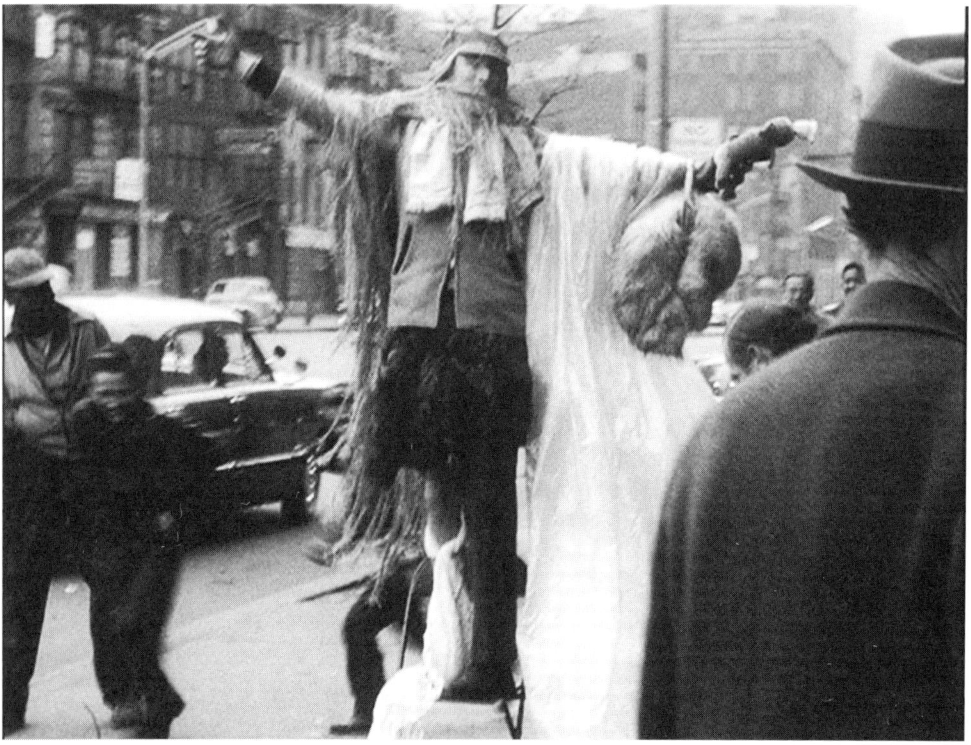

Figure 5.5. Ken Jacobs, *Star Spangled to Death*, 1956–60/2003–4. 16 mm (with video/DVD), black and white and color, sound, 440 min. Shown: Jack Smith.

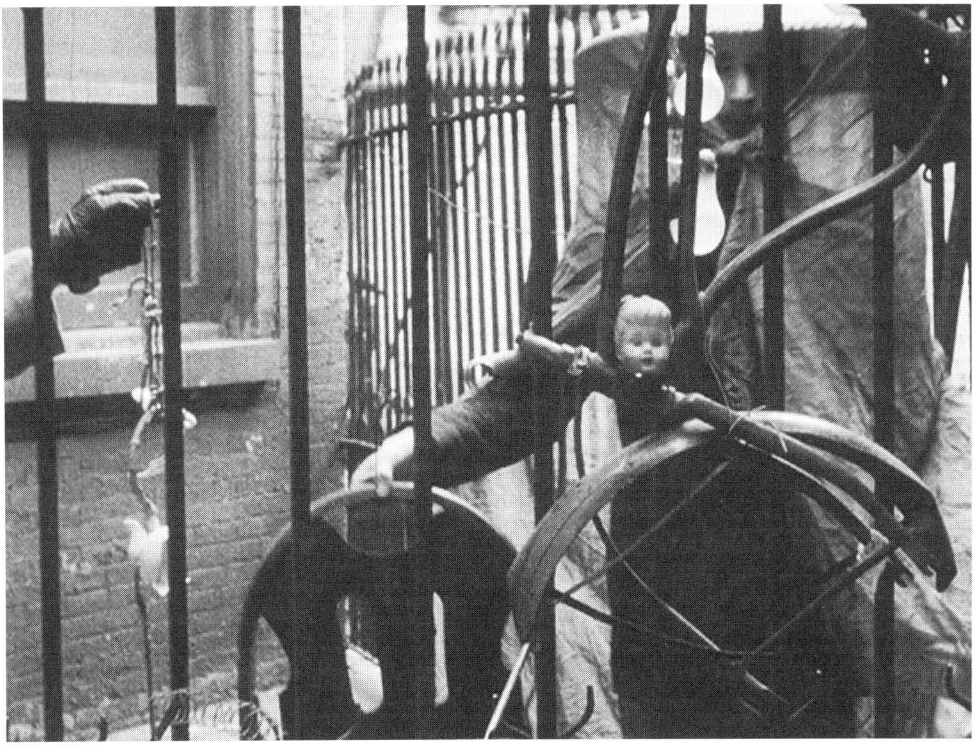

Figure 5.6. Ken Jacobs, *Star Spangled to Death*, 1956-60/2003–4. Shown: Jacobs (hand) and Jack Smith.

Smith and Jacobs' "little-boy revolution" was a Beat-like refusal of the demands of "responsible" adult (Oedipal) normality. It would find a type of confirmation in the more overtly Beat film, *The Flower Thief*, shot in San Francisco in 1960 by Ron Rice (the only underground filmmaker Smith would repeatedly laud) and starring Taylor Mead exploring the city in a series of juvenile antics.[35] That Smith's impromptu performances, such as that for *Saturday Afternoon Blood Sacrifice* (a suggestive imitation of Maria Montez) could attract the attention of the police (who are shown in the film questioning Smith) gives evidence of the type of disturbance such antics could provoke in turn-of-the decade America.

On the day that Conrad and his girlfriend knocked on the door, Smith's current project was *The Beautiful Book*, a photographic homage to his recently departed muse, Zazeela, ultimately published in 1962 (with a cover designed by Zazeela) by Piero Heliczer's Dead Language Press. The book's eighteen photographs were in black and white, developed in the size of contact prints and hand glued without captions onto the muted yellow pages. Throughout, Zazeela appears as an exotic creature, posed in various states of undress, yet often partially veiled by patterned translucent cloths or cast into the darkness of underexposure. Zazeela's portraits alternate with those of others, including Francine, Montez, and Rosenthal, assembled into sexually suggestive, seragliolike scenes that directly prefigure the cinematography of *Flaming Creatures*. "We studied these photographs with keen eye discovering new & more beautiful images hidden in every dissolve & curve of the draperies & silks which ran through these masterpieces like some long lost mysterious fume from byzantium," Ron Rice would declare.[36]

Conrad, by his own admission, was initially unprepared for this aspect of the New York underground. Predicated not on a pursuit of the new, which had governed the musical avant-garde (despite its critique by Flynt),[37] but on an embrace of both the out-of-date and the erotic, Smith's work challenged Conrad's aesthetic sensibilities more profoundly than anything he had yet encountered. (The carnivalesque atmosphere surrounding Smith's activities were not so far removed, however, from the ecstatic minimalism exemplified by Young's 10-4 Gallery concerts, a fact that Conrad later recognized on the *Flaming Creatures* sound track by accompanying the frozen tableau of Zazeela, Young, MacLise, and Rosenthal with a snippet from the August 26, 1962, concert.) Conrad has wryly recollected his earliest reaction to Smith's photographs as "some kind of bizarre, contemptible New York art pornography."[38]

> I recognized very quickly that Jack was one of these "New York artists" that I had heard about, like a "pornography" artist. He was working on these little tiny photographs.... In any case, I had the idea right away that Jack was not a serious artist. I just had no respect for him at all. I had no interest in what he was doing. You know, it was just like I was laughing up my sleeve every time I saw this pathetic creature. And, so...it did astonish me that I had an epiphany in a sense [when I began to appreciate Jack's work].[39]

Although Conrad would soon accompany Smith to the earliest filming session for *Flaming Creatures*—helping carry Smith's large painting of a flower vase, which serves as the film's primary backdrop—his appreciation would take some time. Conrad has described his impressions of that first day's shooting:

> I helped carry the "set," and we went to the Windsor Theater, which was the oldest movie theater standing in New York, though no longer a working movie theater. There was a roof that was next to a loft that this filmmaker, Dick Preston, an Australian, had. And so we set up (or nailed up or hung up) the canvas, and then there ensued a three-hour session of people putting on their costumes and their makeup. Three hours! And I began to think, "Something very weird is going on here" (laughs). I couldn't understand what was happening; I just had no idea. As the afternoon went on, and people were taking more drugs and all of this kind of thing, I thought, "This is *way* out beyond making a movie." Something very strange was happening. These people were putting on cross-dressing costumes, and then

> I allowed myself to be put into one of these costumes too . . . and all I could think is, like, "Geez. If my friends like La Monte could see me now, I would be so embarrassed, because this is like the weirdest shit." But to tell you the truth, the whole experience of this shooting session was *so* mysterious and electrifying that I was really quite turned around.[40]

Conrad's intrigue was undoubtedly sparked in part by his unexpected entry into Smith's branch of New York's queer community, and Conrad's friendships with Smith, Montez, Francine, and others would prove important to him on a variety of levels.[41] Yet as Conrad has recalled, at this time, his intellectual and lifestyle pursuits were insufficiently separable for him not to approach Smith's work in terms of his own aesthetic program and the challenges posed to it:

> I had accepted the fact that maybe Henry could like Elvis Presley or something like that, but this was way beyond that. What was going on with all this stuff, which had to do with sexuality and a retro aesthetic, but which had an incredibly compelling character, seemed not to fit into the Cagean formulation. I very much liked being tempted [by Smith's aesthetic], because it tempted me out of the position of control of the situation. . . . Jack offered something that was very, very different. It wasn't built up or contrived in the same way; it didn't have to do with being the most avant-garde. That set of virtues vanished in this other environment. What happened instead was that you had somebody who lived at the brink of his art, and often splashed around in it in a most egregiously conspicuous fashion.[42]

What Conrad first identified as merely "retro" was Smith's profound engagement with the cast-off, outmoded detritus of capitalist society, an attitude now identified particularly with "camp," but that was also an extension of the trash aesthetic Smith had developed with Jacobs. Smith's attraction to what he called the "musty" or "moldy" was specifically limited to "artifacts of the recent past," objects that were not only "imperfect and ugly" and thus "very rich material to work with," but that were caught in the netherworld between *nouveauté* and "the respectability of antiquarianism."[43] As Smith had told Jacobs, he was nostalgic for the 1940s. ("This is like the mid-fifties! Nostalgia for the forties took a *gift* for nostalgia, because it was such a seedy, dry, dumb period, culturally.")[44] Without the acceptable sheen of antiquarianism or classicism, Smith would explain in his manifesto, "The Perfect Filmic Appositeness of Maria Montez," such moldy cultural artifacts were not simply beneath consideration, they were abject. They called forth feelings of "guilt" and "phoniness," and thus had to be enjoyed secretly, as "secret flix," whether individually or within the semiclosed community to which Conrad was admitted:

> If Maria Montez were still alive she would be defunct. She would be unable to find work . . . She'd be passé, dated, rejected. . . . We punish such uniqueness, we turn against it — give it only about 5 years (the average life of a star). Once lost these creatures cannot be recovered tho their recovery would be agreeable. We wouldn't welcome back Veronica Lake who is by this time a thing in the air, a joke, a tragedy, a suffering symbol of downfall, working as a barmaid at Martha Washington Hotels — shorn. We lose them — our creatures.[45]

Montez, Lake, and other of Smith's pantheon of outmoded movie stars were dejected, cast off, low — refuse, just as much as the actual trash he and Jacobs had used in their earlier collaborations or that would later accumulate into the infamous garbage pile that served as a theater set in the center of Smith's Soho loft.[46]

The tribulations and ultimate impossibility of recovering such outmoded cultural objects and figures were brought to imaginative life in "The First Memoirs of Maria Montez," a performance staged for Conrad's tape recorder on February 24, 1963 by Smith, Conrad, Mario Montez, and David Gurin.[47] In it, Smith describes to hilarious effect the exhumation of the deceased Maria Montez to star in a contemporary feature directed by "Jack Smith, the raging movie director." The partially improvised scenario, in which Montez is played alternately by Mario Montez and Smith and in which Conrad appears as Arthur Lubin (director of *White Savage* [1943] and *Ali Baba and the Forty Thieves*), recounts the decay of the actress's body and the artificial patchwork necessary to repair it. Makeup by Helena Rubenstein (naturally), as well as plaster, is applied to Montez, whose corpse, although she herself remains ravished by its beauty, displays a marked tendency during shooting for pieces to fall off and sink to the bottom of the Pool of Midnight (filled with Montez's favorite: Shalimar perfume). Eventually, the "flaming movie set" is engulfed in actual flames as the flesh of the ever-decaying Montez collapses completely, leaving her a "hideous dancing skeleton." The story, a variation of which was also published in *Film Culture*, illustrates the aesthetic coordinates of Smith's own films, particularly *Flaming Creatures*, which is explicitly cited. The recovery of the Hollywood of the 1940s is possible only in a fragmentary, decaying state, marked by its age and dejected status. Montez's glamour, having become outmoded, is recoverable only as a ruin. (In the published "Memoirs of Maria Montez," the studio sets would crumble into ruin, rather than burst into flame.)

In her article "Notes on 'Camp,'" Sontag (who at times seems to be summarizing Smith's "The Perfect Filmic Appositeness of Maria Montez") would famously discuss aspects of what we have been describing in Smith's aesthetic.[48] Although characteristically perceptive, Sontag's article, as Michael Moon has observed, would largely depoliticize the sensibility and/or strategy of camp.[49] "It goes without saying that the Camp sensibility is disengaged, depoliticized—or at least apolitical."[50] Instead of politics or moralizing (the two, for Sontag, seem to be the same thing), camp offered "sensuous surface," "pure artifice," and "style at the expense of content."[51] "Camp," she wrote, "is wholly aesthetic," its invocation of the past "extremely sentimental."[52] This position largely meshed with (and was influenced by) Sontag's reading of *Flaming Creatures*, which she associated with "pop art" and proclaimed "strictly a treat for the senses."[53] In so doing, however, her definition of camp would seem to have missed the mark of

Smith's work, conflating his "moldy" aesthetic with what he called the "pasty" – the pure relation to surface that unites advertisements, "The World's Fair, Detroit, and amphetamine," and, ultimately, all of conformist, capitalist culture (eventually exemplified, to his mind, by the pop art of his onetime associate, Warhol).[54]

Yet more than sentimental (though there is a relation to childhood), Smith's relation to the past derives from the political and expressly allegorical position he and Jacobs had evolved in the 1950s. Ultimately, Smith's interest in death, decay, overripeness, fragmentation, and ruin would seem to ally him more closely with the allegorical aesthetic defined by Walter Benjamin, one that had its roots in the baroque of the seventeenth century and that would achieve its most cogent formulation in surrealism.[55] Smith would come to describe his work explicitly as baroque, an interest that can be attested in his color photographs of the 1950s, some of which explicitly invoke baroque painting.[56] It was also in the 1950s that Smith and Jacobs had become enamored with the American surrealist Joseph Cornell's *Rose Hobart* (1936), an homage to Rose Hobart, star of Columbia Pictures' *East of Borneo* (1931), made by editing reaction shots of the star and other atmospheric footage without regard to the film's original narrative structure. "We looked at it in every possible way," Jacobs recalled: "on the ceiling, in mirrors, bouncing it all over the room, in corners, in focus, out of focus, with a blue filter that Cornell had given me, without it, backwards. It was just like an eruption of energy."[57]

As famously argued by Benjamin, the surrealists had been

> the first to perceive the revolutionary energies that appear in the "outmoded" – in the first iron constructions, the first factory buildings, the earliest photos, objects that have begun to be extinct, grand pianos, the dresses of five years ago, fashionable restaurants when the vogue has begun to ebb from them. The relation of these things to revolution – no one can have a more exact concept of it than these authors. No one before these visionaries and augurs perceived how

> destitution—not only social but architectonic, the poverty of interiors, enslaved and enslaving objects—can be suddenly transformed into revolutionary nihilism.... They bring the immense forces of "atmosphere" concealed in these things to the point of explosion.[58]

Like the vision of the surrealists, Smith's own vision redeems the outmoded and cast off, brings it back, and, in a sense, elevates it from the abjection into which it had fallen. When the outmoded is brought back, however, it is (like the corpse of Maria Montez) as a ruin. Although redeemed, it is still in essence dejected and, as such, akin to the socially dejected status of marginalized and oppressed peoples, whether on account of sexuality, class, or race (Smith commented repeatedly on Maria Montez's mixed race and dark skin, an attribute shared by Mario Montez).[59] Furthermore, in bringing the outmoded back into play, revealing it in its thoroughgoing and now starkly evident artificiality, what Smith called its "phoniness," Smith's aesthetic points up the evidently constructed (rather than purportedly natural) state of all cultural production, however accepted, normative, and seemingly transparent. "Why can't we enjoy phoniness?" Smith asks about the cinema of the 1940s. "Why resent the patent 'phoniness' of these films—because it holds a mirror to our own, possibly."[60] Outmoded objects of the recent past reveal to us the constructedness of the present moment. As Juan Suárez, who has most thoroughly investigated this aspect of Smith's aesthetic, has argued, "In outdated kitsch, appearances, styles, and gender roles seemed thoroughly artificial, deprived of any overtones of naturalness and normality, and therefore susceptible of being reinvested and revaluated by artists and audiences whose own gender identifications and desires were frequently labeled unnatural and abnormal. Displaced and marginal desires thus found correlative images in materials that had dropped out of the mainstream."[61]

Smith's foregrounding of constructedness was not, of course, simply the result of the return of the outmoded object, a being out of time that allowed for the "dialectical penetration and actualization of former contexts," which Benjamin noted is not historicist, but political.[62] It was also the result of the evidently artificial and assembled character of Smith's work. As opposed to a seemingly natural, purportedly transparent meaning or the seamlessly unified, harmoniously balanced, integrated stylistics of the classical, Smith promoted an aesthetic of the unbalanced, irregular, fragmentary, ruinous, and artificial. The allegorist, to borrow Conrad's terms, reformulates material in an "egregiously conspicuous" fashion. "It is common practice in the literature of the baroque," Benjamin explained of such allegorical procedures, "to pile up fragments ceaselessly, without any strict idea of a goal, and, in the unremitting expectation of a miracle, to take the repetition of stereotypes [a particularly Smithian attribute] for a process of intensification."[63]

• • •

When Conrad accompanied Smith to the set of *Flaming Creatures*, he had had little exposure to the visual arts aside from the "theatrical" post-Cagean and Fluxus-related productions surrounding *An Anthology*. As far as cinema was concerned, although a child of the 1940s era of the weekly matinee, Conrad had given little thought to film as a fine art form.[64] It is thus perhaps not surprising that Conrad would not fully appreciate Smith's work until experiencing his redemptive, allegorical aesthetic effected upon a "moldy" *musical* object. For Conrad, this would occur in the context of helping engineer the sound for Smith's film *Scotch Tape* (1959–62).

Although a modest three minutes in length, *Scotch Tape* "carries considerable conceptual weight," foregrounding much within Smith's aesthetic.[65] Shot in 1959 using Jacobs's camera, *Scotch Tape* shows Sims, Jacobs, and Reese Haire dancing and cavorting in a vacant lot strewn with twisted rebar and pulverized cement (Figures 5.7 and 5.8). The setting attains significant allegorical import, not only as a field of fragments or ruins, the refuse at a demolition site, but as nothing other than the future foundation of Lincoln Center, "ruins in reverse" (as Robert Smithson would

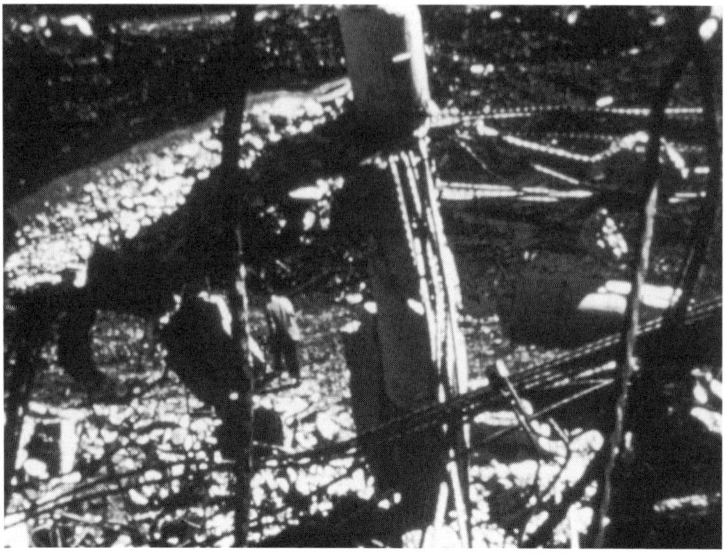

Figure 5.7. Jack Smith, *Scotch Tape*, 1959–62. 16 mm, color, sound, 3 min. Shown: Jerry Sims.

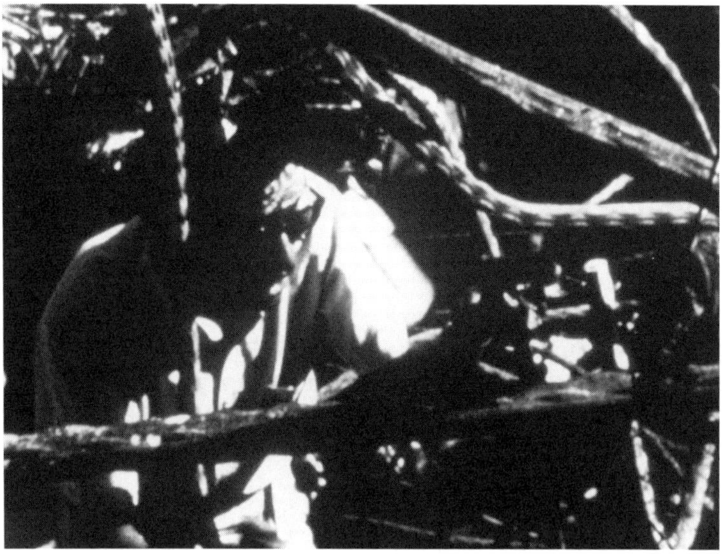

Figure 5.8. Jack Smith, *Scotch Tape*, 1959–62. Shown: Reese Haire.

have called them) of one of the sites of official culture that Smith, Flynt, and Conrad would call to demolish anew in 1963.[66] Like *Flaming Creatures*, albeit more modestly, the figures on screen resurrect, in a partial and incomplete manner, earlier Hollywood archetypes via Haire's Carmen Miranda–like headdress and the comedic dancing of the entire troupe. Nearly every scene, likely edited in-camera on a single one-hundred-foot roll of film, is characterized by scale shifts, some quite dramatic, that sometimes force the audience to search frantically for the actors, who can appear as mere specks within the vast, rubble-strewn grounds. Within this context, the titular piece of dirty Scotch tape lodged inadvertently in Jacobs's camera (also visible in some scenes from *Star Spangled to Death*) provides, as Sitney has noted, a sort of continuity by which to judge the disorienting shifts in scale.[67]

Smith approached Conrad with the problem of how to extend an old 78-rpm record of Eddy Duchin's "Carinhoso" to match the film's length of three minutes. Conrad, who found Duchin's Latin piano rendition disheartening, to say the least, nonetheless gamely extended it to the required length by means of transferring it to magnetic tape and making a couple of primitive splices. He then accompanied Smith to a projection of the film at one of the open screenings at the Charles Theater:

> Not knowing whether there was a tape recorder available, and of course there wasn't, we proceeded to lug the tape recorder over to the theater and set it up. I took the responsibility myself, personally, for the audio-technical side of things.
>
> I set the tape recorder up in front of the theater, waited for the quaint signal to arrive, the lights went down, the film came on, and I pressed the button, and sat back, and suddenly there was something going on that was just simply much more than the sum of the tune that I had been molding and an amorphous frolic in a junk yard. All of a sudden, a commitment emerged, a kind of spectral pleasure that reached out and grabbed the whole scene in a way that was inhabited by a very very special comic presence. And it was on the way to ecstasy, and in fact, it was ecstasy.[68]

This experience would not only open Conrad's eyes to Smith's work, but essentially open his eyes. Previously, Conrad had virtually no interest in movies as an art or in visual art per se; this experience would incite in him the desire to be a filmmaker and, eventually, a visual artist.

Almost certainly, however, it was not the mere coincidence of sound and image that caused such an impact. It was much more likely to have been the allegorical nature of the sound/image juxtaposition — the manner in which the constructed nature of the production was clear, the slight, "spectral pleasure" of the components' distancing — that created the striking comic effect. The field of debris, sometimes shot from directly overhead, almost completely fills each frame of *Scotch Tape*, causing the image to solidify into a nearly depthless square (an effect, as Sitney has noted, that was achieved in *Flaming Creatures* by means of outdated film stock).[69] The shallow space within the frame seems almost to be filled from the bottom up, like a vitrine or an Arman "poubelle" sculpture. In part, it is because Smith's visuals are so full, complete in themselves (like his earlier photographs, especially his color photographs), that the sound seems to function as an addition or overlay, one that coalesces with, but does not suture or subordinate the visuals to an immersive, interpellative whole. The titular square of translucent tape lodged in the picture's lower right corner proves fortuitous, further distancing and ever so slightly alienating the viewer from the depicted scenes. It was no doubt a similarly distanced viewpoint that allowed for the redemption of the outmoded music that Conrad had so despised. "It was an amazing thing that happened," Conrad recalled, "because this incredibly stupid music by this lounge artist, the bottom-of-the barrel scum, just went right to heaven with the picture."[70]

• • •

The experience of seeing *Scotch Tape* and later working on the sound track to *Flaming Creatures* would make available to Conrad a wholly different attitude toward musical material. The allegorical (camp) attitude was unlike the aloof seriousness of Stockhausen or the immersion within one's surroundings of Cage, but was rather a type of distanced immersion that allowed for an engagement with mass culture that, at one and the same time, refunctioned and utilized it for other ends. Such a distanced, but participatory perspective would ultimately allow Conrad, along with Cale and De Maria, to appropriate and play with the conventions of pop music, which Reed, coming from another avenue entirely, was so adept at mimicking and exacerbating, as well. For Conrad, the potentially political aspects of such an attitude would no doubt have been reinforced by his discussions with Flynt around the Stockhausen protests, where the aloof snobbism of "Serious Culture" was criticized in favor of an alliance with what Flynt saw as the "low" and culturally degraded forms of popular African-American rock and blues. For Flynt, however, the popular music he championed was conceived as the spontaneous, even natural expression of oppressed and marginalized peoples, one facet of an organic, integrated culture. With their stylistic imitation, manufactured hype, and in-studio "live" effects, however, there was very little natural about the low, even ersatz pop culture of Reed's Pickwick singles. It was their constructedness and artificiality that opened them to intervention and refunctioning, a self-conscious engagement with the tropes of the form that Mike Kelley and Tony Oursler would later understand as "art rock."[71]

However seriously or not the Primitives took themselves at De Maria's (and one must be cautious in attributing too much to a single late-night recording session, however historic its players were to become), Conrad would continue to be haunted by the venture. His notebooks contain numerous references to pop songs he found noteworthy. At certain points, such as in a note of May 12, 1965 titled "The End in Monster Longings," he appears to contemplate importing further aspects of Smith's aesthetic into rock: "The time is ripe for something like the 'vamp' phenomenon to occur in R&R: Come on evil, sexy, & innocent."[72] In another series of notes, he reflected on the experience of the

Primitives postmortem, self-consciously delving into the constructedness and artificiality of the group's relation to pop music and culture. One note posed the question of how "A 'cultivated' & benign new R&R group sound & style for the masses" should appear on stage: "Should 'Primitives' snarl & growl?" he asks, "or look like frightened animals?"[73] In a remarkable list in which Conrad considered the possible conditions for continuing the group, he proposed further emphasizing the carefully contrived aspect of the group's construction, including the supposed directness and authenticity of their live sound:

(1) Make a bunch of R & R tapes, doctoring the sound as much as desired. Cut demos.
(2) Go to record company, as a group, & push appearance of the group plus look of the group. Press for a single with picture on cover.
(3) For appearances, do a modified "performance" version, approximating only reasonably the true sound. [Example: Shangrilas]
(4) Appeal to the company to manage us; convince them not that we're good, but that we're going to make money.
(5) Stress economic inevitability of a big startling new American group development.

Perhaps most interesting, in light of Conrad's epiphany before Smith's *Scotch Tape* and, as he later described it, "this *place* where picture and sound were conjoined,"[74] was his presentation of the Primitives as an inherently audio-visual phenomenon ("push appearance of group"). Although manufacturing an image is endemic to pop culture, then as now, Conrad sought to take this aspect of the project further into the realm of visual media. Another note recounts a conversation with Stanley Alboum (aka The Turtle) about the possibilities of using the newly imported technology of the Scopitone 16-mm film jukebox:

Sell "The Ostrich" to Scopitone (Zimmerman?) because:
The Ostrich failed as a record due to impenetrability of the too-

strong sound to teeners, but makes it as an in person song, where nature of the effect is made clear.[75]

The Theatre of Eternal music was not, of course, oblivious to its appearance on stage either, especially after their December 1965 performance at "The New Cinema Festival" at the Film-makers' Cinematheque, the first in which they would be bathed in Marian Zazeela's elaborately calligraphic colored light projections. These light shows, however, which would achieve their fullest development in Young and Zazeela's Dream House installations, would be conceived as harmonically interrelated or even aesthetically unified with the music, rather than as allegorically layered.[76] Sometime earlier, in January 1964, Conrad and Cale had proposed an intermedia performance more in keeping with Smith's interests in detritus, overripeness, and rot, to be called "Decomposition of the Master(s)" (Figure 5.9):

> Background projector-illuminated with rotting Van Gogh (P[ainting]): —play in context, using the "Olé technique" of decomposing music:
>
> 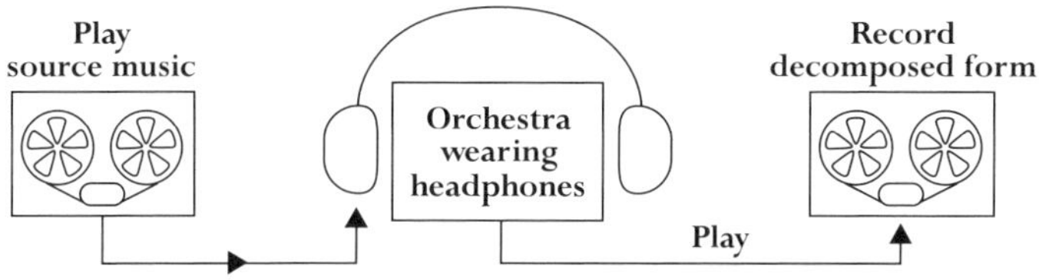
>
>
> Performers instructed either to imitate, play along with, or improvise over the source program.
> Use other rotting backgrounds: Eyes, e.g.
> Backgrounds projected over the performers. Build up the orchestra by overdubbing, possibly.
>
> Multiple decompositions: use decomposed form as source.[77]

Ultimately, Conrad conceived of a project for a faux documentary of the Primitives, one that would share Smith's (and Jacobs's) long-standing interest in an aesthetic of collapse and

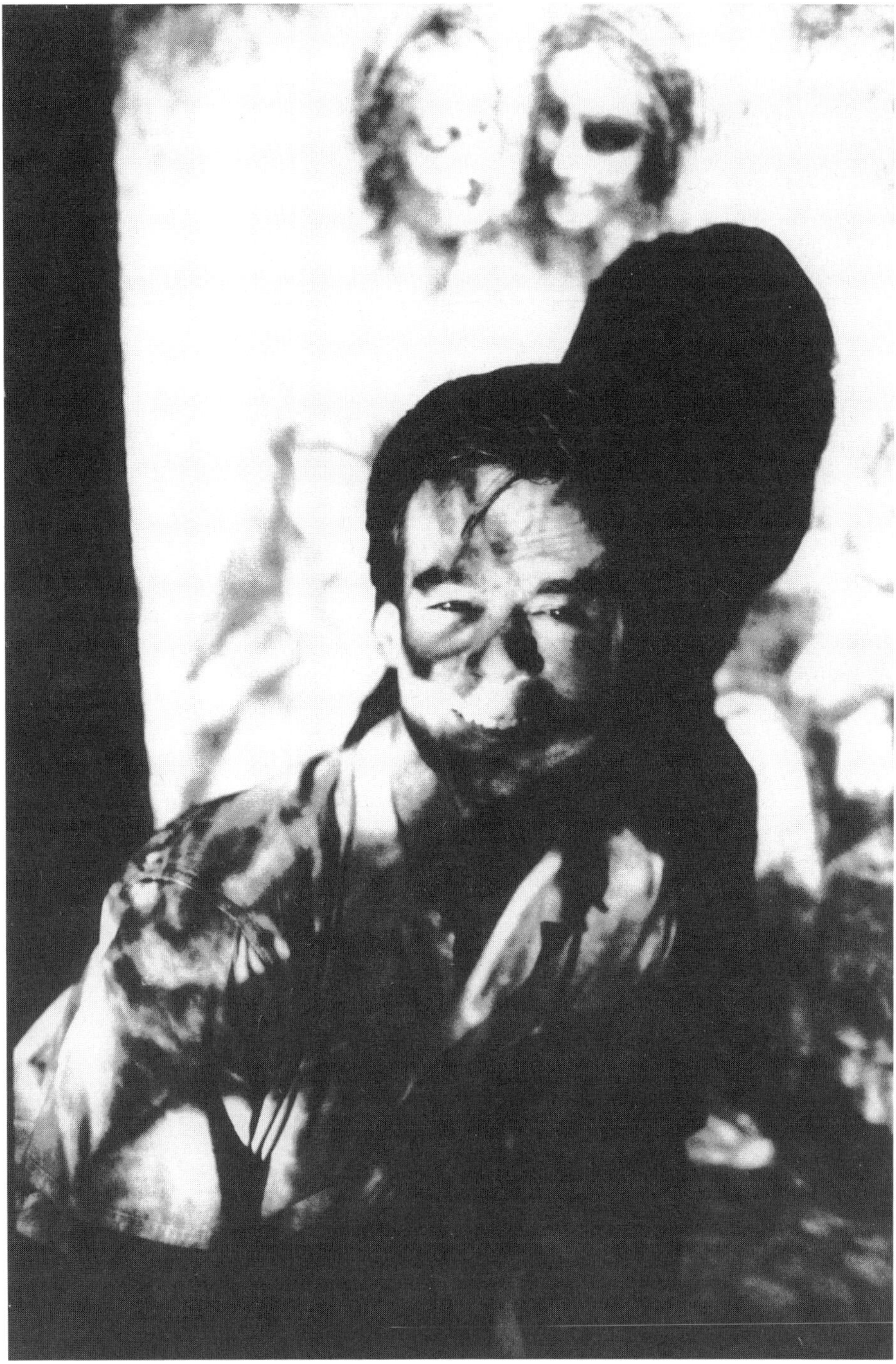

Figure 5.9. Tony Conrad, 1966. Photo: Frederick Eberstadt, used by permission.

incompletion. Another brief, handwritten list details this never-to-be-realized cinematic project:

> Our R & R Movie:
> The story of our R & R Careers:
> Included:
> (1) all the fantasies of what might have been
> (2) all the confusion & bustle of big business in these ludicrous circumstances
> (3) Repeats, bungling, important elements omitted, &c.
> (4) Complete lack of anyone's responsibility for anything; bungling nature of the successes
> (5) All successes are imaginary & real ending is inconclusive

• • •

As profound and important as it is, the constructed aspect of low or popular culture and its possible allegorical redemption explains neither the whole of the Primitives' style nor the entirety (or even, possibly, the core) of Smith's aesthetic. Neither the Primitives nor Smith were simply evidently artificial; both were decidedly over the top. As Conrad later put it in one of his notes, "The way to conquer the 'sophisticated' R & R market: Go 'far out.'" In the Primitives' performances were echoes not only of the artificial crowd noise slathered onto the record by Reed, but perhaps as well of the ecstatic screams let out by Smith during performances such as "Love Is Strange."[78] Indeed, all of Smith's creatures seem perpetually on the verge of "overstimulation," subject to an out-of-control, contagious energy that opens onto a disordered and chaotic vision of the erotic.[79] They do not come back to life simply to exist in frozen, piled-up, allegorical tableaux, but also to come together in Dionysian embraces and polymorphous sexual encounters, manifesting a desire that seems always on the verge of erupting into an excessive, overwhelming outpouring. Pace Sontag, Smith's prose pieces such as "Normal Love," "Red Orchids," or "The White Pig of Medina" approximate the most anarchic scenes in the writings of William S. Burroughs or Antonin Artaud.[80] In them, there is always a confluence of decay – bodies leaking or coming apart and ultimately ending in death – and a polymorphous desire that (very much as in Burroughs's work) literally streams out in all directions: deformed and insulting "babies [who] had enormous heads the size of spoiling watermelons and whispered obscene remarks in sibilant Levantine waterfront pidgin"; the effluvia-spurting backstage electrical grip who violates the ever-younger star, Mavis Davis; the leprous and syphilitic prostitute pig of Medina; and so on.[81] Smith's story, "Normal Love" recounts a film shoot turned "churning carnival of freaky sex": "The little cretin shepardess was now ruined for normal love and she ran amok among the other freaks, inflaming them. Soon the whole hillside was one gigantic, seething, cretin, mongolian and pinhead orgy."[82] In order ultimately to understand the full scope of the lessons Conrad learned from Smith, it will be important to diverge once again to investigate this aspect of Smith's work in more detail.

• • •

Smith's raging, overstimulated vision was exemplified in the Earthquake Orgy from *Flaming Creatures*, where after a shot of a trembling lantern, signal of the onset of the earthquake, the camera begins shaking ever more violently as it films the screaming and struggling Bick being held, prodded, and orally violated. (Smith's vision of the erotic, again not unlike that of Burroughs, is nearly always tinged with violence. This is found not only in the Earthquake Orgy, but in all of the major couplings of *Normal Love*, each one of which resonates with an echo of *Flaming Creatures*' rape scene, even as the comic is simultaneously brought into play via the mud fight between the Werewolf and the Mermaid – who, clothed entirely in white, is literally dirtied in her symbolic deflowering – or in the slapsticklike pursuit of the Girl by Uncle Pasty, who receives a pie in the face that causes him to lose his fake monster fangs.) In the Earthquake Orgy, overly close framing renders the scene a disordered mass of interlocking limbs, faces, genitals, hands, Bick's one exposed breast, and other parts of the creatures' bodies. A mouth shown kissing a foot receives particularly energetic camera jiggling. The lengthy scene is accompanied by Conrad's "Coney Island horror house" audio, which adds to the violence of the depicted scene even as it refuses entirely to meld with it.[83] "The parodistic effect is there, but the horrible sounds are also part of the real violence and sadism of the scene."[84] By downshifting the tape speed halfway through, Conrad lowered the pitch, simultaneously augmenting and distancing the ominousness of the sound. In the end, the flaming creatures, spent by their profligate expenditure of energy, are shown exhausted and dead on the plaster-strewn floor.

The Earthquake Orgy is, however, only the most concentrated site of Smith's interest in the disordered, the excessive, and the erotic. The entirety of the film is characterized by disheveled costumes and revealed body parts, polymorphous erotic interactions (with, as Sontag indicated, the exception of male/female genital relations), and eruptions of frenetic motion, whether in the chase scene between Francine and Bick at the beginning of the film or in the endless eruptions of dancing in the movie's final episodes. (Both *Flaming Creatures* and *Normal Love* end with dance sequences, echoes of the extravagant production numbers in the finales of Hollywood musicals.) In the conclusion of *Flaming Creatures*, twirling bodies careen from one side of the screen to the other or, shot from above, appear as madly spinning tops that, partially through sheer duration, nearly induce feelings of dizziness in the viewers.[85]

Smith's project was to produce not only a cinema of allegory, but a cinema of *excess*. As analyzed and explained in his writings, the opposition is between a cinema of convention, restriction, generality, and reproduction and a cinema of idiosyncrasy, expansion, originality, and a type of direct, affective force. Most explicitly, Smith's aesthetic was opposed to the subordination of film to *language*, both in terms of effects that could be described in words and in the prevalence of narrative or plot. As he explained at some length in the article "Belated Appreciation of V.S.," "In this country the movie is known by its story. A movie is a story, is as good as its story. Good story – good movie. Unusual story – unusual movie. etc. Nobody questions this. It is accepted on all levels, even 'the film is a visual medium' levels by its being held that the visuals are written first then breathed to life by a great cameraman, director."[86] The proof of this, Smith goes on to declare, is found in the fact that even the blind can appreciate most films nearly unhindered. The subordination of film to language in the form of dialogue or plot is not limited solely to Hollywood, either. European art-house films, Smith explained, are similarly beholden; the stories may be less familiar, perhaps, even richer, but no less subsumed beneath the dictates of narrative and dialogue.[87]

As opposed to dialogue or narrative, the visuals within a film, according to Smith, have the capacity to surpass the limitations of words, to take the viewer beyond "explanation plots."[88] As he wrote about the images of his revered Montez:

> She was the bane of critics – that person whose effect cannot be known by words, described in words, flaunts words (her *image* spoke). Film critics are writers and they are hostile and uneasy in the presence of a visual phenomenon.... A spectacular, flaming image – since it threatens their critichood need to be able to write – is bad and they attack it throwing in moral extensions and hinting at idiocy in whoever is capable of visually appreciating a visual medium.[89]

Smith's discussion of film visuals is multifaceted. On one level, the transgressive nature of Smith's images (both those he admired and those he made) had to do with their connection to his sexuality. As he wrote, ostensibly about Josef von Sternberg but clearly equally about himself: "His expression was of the erotic realm – the neurotic gothic deviated sex-colored world and it was a turning inside out of himself and magnificent.... Dietrich was his visual projection – a brilliant transvestite in a world of delirious unreal adventures. Thrilled by his/her own movement – by superb task in light, costumery, textures, movement, subject and camera, subject/camera/revealing faces — in fact all revelation but *visual* revelation."[90]

Because the meanings of the visuals were not spelled out, because they could express or act as evidence of desires that were socially unsanctioned, actively repressed, they served as a refuge for the prohibited. As Smith noted more explicitly in an earlier draft of his article on von Sternberg, "the story that the words of the films tell can't be the same as the visuals (because forbidden themes can be expressed in images, but not in dialogue)."[91] "Having a favorite star has very human ramifications," Smith noted.[92] One of those, undoubtedly, was the manner in which the star could forge or elicit a type of covert connection. All those who shared the same favorite star (Montez, Garbo, Dietrich) formed a potential community with similar desires; no need to express them in words in order to form a connection within the necessarily half-secret world of gay men.

While on one level Smith's perspective on film visuals was inextricably related to his subject position as a gay man, on another, it derived from a particular legacy within the avant-garde. His endorsement of a purely visual, antilinguistic cinema developed certain aspects of Stan Brakhage's *Metaphors on Vision*, which proclaimed in its opening lines "that there is a pursuit of knowledge foreign to language and founded upon visual communication, demanding a development of the optical mind."[93] At the same time, however, Smith's more idiosyncratic, heterogeneous modernism — in its particular insistence that film be a visual medium free from subservience to narrative, its call for film to be itself, rather than merely for a plot — also resonates profoundly with the theatrical writings of Artaud.

Deeply interested in theater, Smith may have come across Artaud in a variety of contexts. Artaud's *The Theater and Its Double*, translated by Mary Caroline Richards at the suggestion of John Cage and published in 1958 by Grove Press, was referred to widely at the time, particularly within the San Francisco Beat circles with which Ron Rice was familiar and in the New York theatrical and, later, happenings milieux.[94] In it, Artaud castigated, in no uncertain terms, theater's subordination to language, whether writing (plot) or speech (dialogue). This critique runs like a leitmotif throughout *The Theater and Its Double*: in the "Theater of Cruelty" manifesto – where Artaud notes "Words say little to the mind; extent and objects speak; new images speak, even new images made with words" – and particularly in the section of the book entitled "No More Masterpieces."

> We must get rid of our superstitious valuation of texts and *written* poetry. Written poetry is worth reading once, and then should be destroyed. Let the dead poets make way for others. Then we might even come to see that it is our veneration for what has already been created, however beautiful and valid it may be, that petrifies us, deadens our responses, and prevents us from making contact with that underlying power, call it thought-energy, the life force, the determinism of change, lunar menses, or anything you like. Beneath the poetry of the texts, there is the actual poetry, without form and without text.[95]

Like Artaud, who maintained that "dialogue – a thing written and spoken – does not belong specifically to the stage, it belongs in books," Smith found language to be foreign to the specificity of the medium of film.[96] "The literature of the film," Smith wrote (in a style that itself strains against grammar), "its words, trite, necessarily so far they are always doing something they shouldn't have to do, they are forced into triteness because they shouldn't be there at all – they should be in novels, anecdotes, conversations, etc. – (NO, movies are not conversations – why should they be so limited!)"[97] The conclusion of this passage – which extols the possibility of dialogue being used as pure rhythm – equally seems to recall Artaud, who proclaimed that the only way to redeem spoken language would be to turn it against the written word and consider it as a "form of *Incantation*."[98] Such would be demonstrated by Artaud in, among other places, the banned radio play *To Have Done with the Judgment of God* (1947). In sections such as "the dance of the TUTUGURI," Artaud erupts into insane cries that, as did the chanting in his imaginary "Native American" dialect, aimed to pierce through language to its outside, revealing there to be "a hundred thousand other sides" than that of merely habitual linguistic expression. Smith would broadcast Artaud's play to accompany a projection of images from *Normal Love* at the New Bowery Theater on St. Marks Place on February 20, 1964.[99]

In *The Theater and Its Double*, Artaud said little positive about film, which to his mind, as a form of mechanical reproduction, necessarily lacked the direct physical presence that he sought from live theater. Nonetheless, what Artaud did extol were "animated hieroglyphs" and "pure stage images" that, like Smith's "pure cinema" images, were liberated from or opposed to plot.[100] Once emancipated from text, both Smith's and Artaud's images were understood to achieve an unmediated impact, what Artaud called "a direct pressure upon the senses" or a "dissociative and vibratory action upon the sensibility."[101] Unlike "thots" [thoughts] which "can be altered to suit & protect," Smith argued, "visual truths are blunt"; the visuals, in films such as von Sternberg's, produce "effects directly through the eye."[102] More importantly, perhaps, Smith's visual images were to give rise to a form of thinking that is distinct – not only more direct, but more idiosyncratic and multiplicitous – from the linguistic and conceptual: "Images evoke feelings and ideas that are suggested by feeling.... It's a very personal process – thoughts via images and therefore very varied.... Images always give rise to a complex of feelings, thots, conjectures, speculations, etc."[103]

Whether Smith was reading Artaud directly, receiving his ideas at some remove, or simply evincing a shared antipathy, his opposition to the hierarchy or priority of the written word, like Artaud's, was merely one aspect of his more general opposition to the entire regime of representation. According to Smith, so-called good acting and good technique are merely terms applied to the predictable execution of preestablished rules, repetitions of norms erected beforehand (even if, in their original incarnations, they were highly innovative), *re*presentations of preset forms every bit as limiting and a priori as an entirely written-out script. (Smith, like Young in "Lecture 1960," was not interested in the "good.") As he wrote of those who could not appreciate Maria Montez's acting:

> Too bad—their loss. Their magic comes from the most inevitable execution of the conventional pattern of acting. What they can appreciate is what most people agree upon—GOOD PERFS. Therefore you can have GOOD PERFS & no real belief. GOOD PERFS that give you no magic—oh I guess a sort of magic, a magic of sustained efficient operation (like the wonder that the car motor held out so well after a long trip).[104]

In Smith's work, the gratuitous, acinematic image, the film visual that overcomes its hierarchical subordination to plot, opposes such efficiency on all levels: by engaging excessive motion, eroticism, or violence (as in the Earthquake Orgy scene); by overstimulated camera movements, undercranking or overcranking the camera to cause fast or slow motion, overexposure, overcrowding the frame, and dirty lenses; but also by excessive stillness, the presentation in the midst of the film of a tableau vivant (as, for instance, in the odalisque scene of Zazeela, Young, Rosenthal, and MacLise) that breaks entirely with any narrative continuity or drive.[105] As Smith declared about the Montez and von Sternberg films that he so admired, "Results of this sort of thing TRANSCEND FILM TECHNIQUE. Not barely—but resoundingly, meaningfully, with magnificence, with the vigor that one exposed human being always has—and with failure."[106]

• • •

Smith's discussion of film visuals brings us back to the thematics of power we have explored in previous chapters and will explore, particularly in relation to Conrad's cinema, in the next. Henry Flynt, as we have seen, in his discussion of acognitive culture, likened forms, all forms, to "work," and saw them as oppressive for the manner in which they establish rules that one would then follow. Flynt railed against forms for much the same reason that Smith railed against good form ("good technique," "good perfs," etc.): They are common, impersonal, objective, rather than idiosyncratic and particular to the individual.[107] Flynt's acognitive culture was to be so specific to the individual, so much an implicit expression of his or her desire, that it would escape entirely the interpersonal and, particularly, the linguistic realms (Flynt refused to put examples into words), realms that were, for him, akin to the type of restrictions imposed by a paranoiac, sovereign power.

Flynt's nascent identity politics, his theorization of the creep personality, was not unrelated to this. The creep was to be a third norm, beyond male and female, falling back on and developing his or her individual idiosyncrasies. Primarily concerned with raising up, without assimilation, the innate characteristics of his or her personality, Flynt's creep was to be distinguished, in part, by an unyielding adherence to childish traits, a pre-Oedipal subjectivity that willfully would refuse to adhere to prevailing sexual and behavioral norms. Smith's position, in some ways, came close to Flynt's. His "Peter Pan existence" was also a refusal of what Flynt had called "adult human values," values that, among other things, were heterosexually normative. The forbidden visuals endorsed by Smith were a part of this refusal. They, too, were forgotten or cast down, excluded from the perspective of adult "normalcy": "We cause their downfall (after we have enjoyed them)," Smith wrote about his secret films, "because they embarrass us grown up as we are and post adolescent / post war / post graduate / post-toasties etc."[108] And yet, although Smith's visuals were individual, particular to their producer (and receiver) — an idiosyncratic manifestation of an unrelinquished desire — they would not lead back to a preestablished identity in the same manner as Flynt's creep. Although being or becoming a creep (a "deliberate creep") was a counter-conduct, a means of subject formation deviating from and vectored against hegemonic norms, it appeared as a development of what Flynt regarded as *intrinsic* characteristics, proclivities, interests, or desires. The deliberate creep would be much the same as he or she was prior to self-realization and empowerment, and it was as a correlate to the creep's self-sufficiency in this regard that he or she would seek biological mutation into an asexual creature, one in which interattraction would be physiologically unnecessary.

Smith, on the contrary, proposed what must be understood as an erotics. Sexual encounters, Smith allowed, are "difficult at best and can be impossible for the sensitive, the neurotic, the badly misinformed, the inexperienced," and others; even so, he claimed, they are nonetheless desirable.[109] Smith's idea of subjectivity was less pre-Oedipal than anti-Oedipal, seeing "normality" (all normality, not just the sexuality of "normals") as a restriction on the inherently polymorphous expression and expanse of desire. Like Flynt's "exercise awareness states" and "mock risk games" or Conrad's "listening compositions," Smith's visuals were to act directly on the receiving subject in an effect of power, rather than of signification; they were to be contagions that would either reinforce "normality" or work against it: "Fantasies now feature weight lifters who think now how lucky and clever they were to get into the movies & the fabulous pay . . . think something like that on camera – it's contagious & you share those thots."[110] The visuals of Smith or von Sternberg, however, which also work "directly through the eye," are idiosyncratic, personal, and multiple, giving rise to a complex of thoughts and feelings and thereby pushing the viewer in multiple directions. Against what Conrad called a "prefigured imaginary" of normative representation (and normative subjectivity), Smith's "thoughts via images" were an excess, beyond the need for any type of return.[111] As Smith wrote toward the end of his article on Maria Montez,

> What is it we want from film?
> *A vital experience*
> *an imagination*
> *an emotional release*

all these & what we want from life
Contact with something
we are not, know not
think not, feel not, understand not,
therefore: An expansion.[112]

John Cage had also put forth an aesthetic of subjective expansion within a realm of indeterminate multiplicity—his compositions were to provide something that, on account of its complexity, we "know not."[113] The multidimensional sound (and increasingly sound-image) space into which Cage's listeners were to be immersed not only went beyond each individual's habitual acoustical experiences (thus setting the "theorizing mind to theorizing" in new and different ways, allowing or inducing listeners to "change their minds"), but was meant to surpass the capacity of any one subject to take it all in, placing him or her within an infinite totality of which any grasp would be partial and thus distinct (although not entirely cut off or separable) from that of any other individual. In this way, what the composer (and conductor and musicians) produce would not push the listener in any one, predetermined or limited direction and thereby would afford them a freedom of response. An audience would become a group of individuals united in their experience, but differing in their reception of it, not a lonely crowd (wherein individuals remain locked in virtual isolation while all receiving the same message), but an anarchic collectivity open to and interpenetrating with their "natural" acoustical surroundings (i.e., the plane of immanence).

For Cage, as we have seen, such a condition was understood as sufficient to undermine, topple, or avoid structures of (sovereign) power. Most often, Cage thought it enough, in order to evade power, to simply walk away from it. Without the energies that sovereign power captures and draws upon (which it detourns from the collectivity itself), power structures would, so Cage seemed to believe, simply collapse, eviscerated from within.[114] For Cage, for instance, protest (a dualistic opposition) does not serve to dismantle, destroy, or undermine power, but merely to fuel it: "Nothing's accomplished in the way of Global Discipline by being angry because the world's angry (i.e., protest against war)," he would write in 1968, "or, rather, what's accomplished is to give further lease on life to divisive structures (nations, politics, finance) that would otherwise die a natural (i.e., technological) death. Recent instance: French riots; de Gaulle's position subsequently strengthened."[115] Cage's project was avowedly utopian in the sense that he thought art could produce a situation by which to model the anarchic world to come beyond power: "Music's not waiting, but sings final dissolution of politics-economics," he noted hopefully: "political organizations . . . will simply fade out of the picture."[116]

Although for Cage the arts were "offerings beyond the law," the law seemed inordinately passive to their surpassing of it.[117] Not so for Smith, who understood much better than Cage that the law (i.e. sovereign power) pushes back and that its surpassing is a much more fleeting and dangerous process, one with consequences. While Cage and Smith, both readers of Artaud, may have agreed that the "topheavy structure of musical prohibitions" resembles the "oppressive" role of plots and stories, Smith regarded that oppression as much more of an active force.[118] This would, of course, be played out with startling clarity in the widespread repression of *Flaming Creatures* that took place in film theaters and on college campuses across the United States and in Europe.[119] Such had all but been predicted in Smith's earliest writings. Those secret, guilt-arousing films of the 1940s that he so admired also brought upon themselves the force of the law. Not only were they, as Smith argued, attacked by writers on the grounds of morality and good sense, but their "irresistibility," according to Smith, "result[ed] in their being cut & stabbed & punished."[120] Failure to follow the rules within the aesthetic realm leads to precisely the same result as refusal to adhere to them within society: Disobedience brings punishment. This was expressed most clearly in Smith's discussion of von Sternberg (published as *Flaming Creatures* was already encountering legal troubles), who was cast out of Hollywood, ostensibly for having violated good technique, but in actuality for visually expressing forbidden themes (most notably, of course, that of gay male desire).[121]

Part of the reason Cage felt that he could step so easily beyond the realm of sovereign power doubtlessly derived from the fact that he sought to leave behind so much that might actually contravene it. Disinterested, dispossessed of the controlling bounds of desire (which, for Cage, was itself a certain type of oppression, an effect of power when it was anything other than indifferently multivalent and omnidirectional), Cage seemed to propose slipping beyond the reach of the law undetected.[122] It was a factor of Cage's aesthetic that did not go unnoticed by Marcel Duchamp. As Cage himself reported, "Asking Duchamp why I accept electronics, refusing chemistry [i.e., drugs], he said, 'It's not against the law!'"[123] This was not the case for Smith, who would assiduously refuse to relinquish his desire, even as he sought its expansion into an unprecedented heterogeneity: "An applying of one's convictions to one's activity obtains a higher excellence in that activity than that attained by those in that activity who apply the rules established by previous successes by others," he wrote. "The more rules broken the more enriched becomes the activity as it had to expand to include what a human view of the activity won't allow it to not include."[124]

Smith had a sophisticated (and prescient) understanding of restricted economy, the manner in which representation, the realm of accepted, codified, comprehendible, rule-bound representations, is related to the political and economic regulations surrounding everyday life. In the modern world, this realm is above all regulated by the imperatives of capitalism, the need to return the maximum profit from the minimum expenditure of resources and energy. Profane existence is subordinated to the imperative to work, and expenditure is limited to that necessary to renew energies and (human) resources and little or nothing more (although with the proviso that in a consumerist economy, consumption itself becomes a form of work, necessary to its continued functioning, with "survival" coded at ever higher levels of consumption).[125] In order to maintain and regulate this imperative to work, force — that is, literally, the police — can be and will be deployed. The "domination of the state" is integrally allied with "the domination of the *possible*."[126]

All facets of this Smith knew well, and they were expressed directly in his writings. The rules of good perfs and good technique are lauded not only by those who follow rules for their own sake, but whether knowingly or not on account of those who have to assure the studios a profitable return.[127] Then as now it is the predictability of profit that necessitates a cinema of general, widespread, middle-of-the-road appeal. Deviations, such as those within the Montez films, are possible only in exceptional situations — such as, Smith notes, the scarcity conditions of the war, when returns are all but inevitable; "when investments must be certain," however, Smith explains, "you must strictly follow banker-logic."[128] In several astounding pages of journal notes, likely written around 1964 after *Flaming Creatures* had been seized, Smith articulated the manner in which economic imperatives underlie the morality enforced by law. After noting how sexual fantasies are "necessary for the propagation of the species and ergo soundness of consumer economy," Smith outlines three tiers within which society separates economies of desire.[129] Most prevalent is the normative economy of the capitalist manufacturers (normative *because* produced by capitalist manufacturers), circulating inextricably via the vast apparatus of advertising:

> the steaming sexual delicatessen counter projection which is not really human but which is multiplied a millionfold almost into truth and which is apparently the ideal of beauty of our masters the manufacturers and which is swallowed whole by their lackeys the censors, the licensers, the police, and increasingly by a public which accepts the pasty foam rubber measurement darlings of panty ads as the consorts and determining image of their sex fantasy lives.[130]

All other sex fantasies that are not, in Smith's terms, "haunted by a can of pork and beans" are forced underground, tolerated if and only if the police, "the money collectors of the municipality," are paid to authorize and allow this realm of supposed criminality (this is the second tier), while all else (the third tier) is prosecuted as obscene.[131] Amid the different economies of desire, there are two that differ in kind – those that (whether licitly or illicitly) can be diverted to support the structure of law and capitalism and those that remain useless to them and are therefore ruled obscene and made the subject of the law.[132]

As Smith well understood, a similar multitiered economy of social and political restriction and repression exists in relation to drugs: some, such as alcohol, being widely socially accepted and legally sanctioned, others, such as for a time LSD, tolerated in a semilegal fashion, and still others, such as marijuana, being subject to sometimes surprisingly harsh police and governmental punishment. Smith's text "Lobotomy in Lobsterland" serves as the counterpart to his journal notes on pornography in exploring (and indicting) this aspect of the social system:

> Marijuana puffing . . . is a quick and easy source of frightened revenues to a jurisprudence of sophistry and its handmaiden a police agency which has assumed . . . a mad dog character itself and in lieu of an adversary worthy of itself has turned upon the public – which process necessitates that more and more matters that affect public life be declared criminal in order to contain insurrection against the Lobster.[133]

Within Smith's social and artistic milieu, illicit sexuality and illicit drug use came together, and it was largely through the latter that Conrad came to know the interrelation of experiences of excess and questions of repression, marginalization, and illegality.[134] (Another shared experience of illegality, as we have seen, was opened up by shoplifting.) Part of what living and working with Smith may have provided Conrad, therefore, is a more complex understanding of the social, cultural, and economic dimensions of the tyranny of sovereign power that Cage (and, at a certain moment, Flynt) saw at work in all abstract forms. And though Conrad would not, by his own admission, fully comprehend the stakes of such a position, not until, in fact, he had himself read Roland Barthes on Bataille, he would nonetheless have through his association with Smith begun to move firmly beyond the bounds of the Cagean paradigm.[135] Most importantly, perhaps, as opposed to Cage – who understood subjective liberation (expansion) in terms of exodus (leaving the law behind) or deterritorialization (expanding past it) – Smith understood such a liberating impulse as a form of *transgression*: a violation and temporary suspension of the law in order to enter a realm of experiences outside or beyond it.

As explained by Bataille, the essence of transgression – the violation, raising, and suspension of the world of profane, everyday regulations – is not so much a single prohibited action (though it is found in that singular transgressive act, as well), but the general overturning of the imperative of work and the taboos and regulations surrounding and guaranteeing it. Transgression opens onto periods of festival or carnival: generalized, communal outbursts of energy expended without reserve. (In 1966, Smith would travel to Rio de Janeiro to film and make a film about Carnival.) Such moments of festival invoke the panoply of forbidden behaviors: from violence and criminality to prohibited sexual acts and encounters to profanation and mocking of all that a culture holds most sacred (elements all found in Smith's writings and films).[136] Yet what the act of transgression puts into question most profoundly is not the rule of (sovereign) law, but the sovereignty of the individual who does the violating. The transgressing subject, opening onto the outside of the restricted economy, beyond the laws governing both representation and political economy alike, enters into a veritable derangement (a world literally "out of order"), wherein linguistic codification gives way to wild cries and ecstatic raptures – moments, in Smith's parlance, of overstimulation. Part of what is dissolved in such transgressive moments is the subject's stable autonomy and self-possession.[137] As in the more general realm of eroticism, transgression opens onto a connection with others, and transgressive eroticism opens onto a realm of multiplicitous interactions (hence its relation to death, the ultimate moment when the subject becomes dispossessed of individuality and returns to the vast continuum of the organic—an outcome also approximated by the effects of certain drugs).[138] For Bataille, the stakes of transgression are exemplified above all in the orgy, the very figure of the diverse interconnectivity of beings, wherein the "contagion" of eroticism overspills the limits of the individual as well as the normative, heterosexual dyad:

> Orgiacal eroticism is by nature a dangerous excess whose explosive contagion is an indiscriminate threat to all sides of life....
>
> ...The refusal implied by taboos confines the individual within a miserly isolation compared with the vast disorder of creatures lost in each other, whose very violence lays them open to the violence of death. From another standpoint the suspension of taboos sets free the exuberant surge of life and favours the unbounded orgiastic fusion of those individuals. This fusion could in no way be limited to that attendant on the plethora of the genital organs.... Wild cries, wild violence of gesture, wild dances, wild emotions as well, all in the grip of immeasurably convulsive turbulence. The perdition ahead would demand this flight into the regions where all individuality is shed, where the stable elements of human activity disappear and there is no firm foothold anywhere to be found.[139]

The Earthquake Orgy in *Flaming Creatures* perfectly exemplifies Bataille's understanding of such a transgressive moment, not only in its bringing together of eroticism, violence (both in the "rape" and in the violent camera movements), and death (the creatures, recall, all die, exhausted, at the end of their expenditure without reserve), but also in its depictions of heterogeneous amalgams of body parts, scenes in which the boundaries of individual bodies are literally overcome, it being difficult to tell to whom each belongs, while each body part is additionally interconnected with others through touch, palpitation, or caress.

• • •

Subjective expansion, the transgressive overcoming of the limits of the autonomous self, would not be confined only to those images depicted on screen. For Smith, as we have seen, visual images, once liberated from the dictates of script (and all the attendant dimensions of restricted economy) were to communicate their effect to the audience as a sort of contagion that, itself idiosyncratic and multiple, would push the viewers in indeterminate and nonnormative directions. On one level, such an effect, as has been argued persuasively by Michael Moon, served as the foundation of Smith's radical queer politics. For Moon, the impact of Smith's films ("the primary source of their power") is found in their being "incitements to his audience not only to play fast and loose with gender roles but also to push harder against prevailing constraints on sexuality. . . . Erotic charges in a work like *Flaming Creatures* do not follow hard-wired gender lines, but move powerfully across circuits of gender and sexual identity in not altogether predictable fashions."[140] This aspect of Smith's work, as we have seen, was clearly evoked in his writings, as for instance in the passage on von Sternberg's presentation of Marlene Dietrich cited above. At the same time, however, Smith also described the evocative power of transgressive images in more formal and abstract terms. As he wrote in his article about Maria Montez,

> The primitive allure of movies is a thing of light and shadows. A bad film is one which doesn't flicker and shift and move through lights and shadows, contrasts, textures by way of light. If I have these I don't mind phoniness (or the sincerity of clever actors), simple minded plots (or novelistic "good" plots), nonsense or seriousness (I don't feel nonsense in movies as a threat to my mind since I don't go to movies for the ideas that arise from sensibleness of ideas).[141]

A "bad film," which Smith had previously defined as one subservient to language and the replication of previously established norms, here finds itself equated (once again, not unlike Brakhage) with a lack of optical effects: flickering and shifting lights, shadows, textures, and contrasts.

It would only be a couple of months after Smith's article on Montez appeared that he would encounter such effects within the very technology of film. On March 5, 1963, during a fantasy session recorded as "Rene and the Flickering Jewel" (subsequently released as "Mario and the Flickering Jewel"), Conrad slowed an old, lenseless 16-mm movie projector to suffuse the seragliolike atmosphere of 56 Ludlow Street with strobe. On the recording, amid gasps of appreciation, Smith can be heard to exclaim in his inimitable drawl, "Have your actual eyes in reality ever seen anything as exaggerated and raging as this?!"[142] Within the squalor of his Lower East Side tenement, Conrad was able to produce something approximating what Smith felt Maria Montez herself had been able to see in the "plaster cornball sets" of Hollywood: "delirious, drug-like hallucinatory beauty."[143] "Neither Jack nor I," recalls Conrad, "had ever seen so compelling and luminous a visionary spectacle."[144]

It would be concluded, practically then and there, that such effects should be incorporated, if possible, into the upcoming project that would become *Normal Love*, which would begin shooting that summer. Several passages in Smith's journal notes seem to make reference to the technique. Entries numbered 194 through 195, labeled as the "CINEMAROC" version and dated to April, 1963, read in part:

> Sun (pink and green) comes up
> creatures come trailing over the hillside
> shot of the green pool pink flowers around it – at end of shot lite starts to flicker faintly
> They go into milk shed
> They milk cows & cast raging glances back and forth, somebody gags on milk as lite starts to flicker

This is followed a few lines later by a brief shot list:

> The green mummy watches the mongo
> The light on the melon flickers in C.U. [close-up]
> The light on the mongo flickers in C.U.

The light on the melon flickers in C.U.
The light on the mongo flickers in C.U.[145]

Before the project could be realized (which, in a sense, it never was), Smith and Conrad would have their falling out. This was precipitated, in part, by the fact that toward the end of the shooting, Conrad and Beverly Grant, who, as the Mummy and Cobra Woman had been paired in *Normal Love*, had begun an actual romantic engagement off the set (Figure 5.10). (Grant seems to have been well cast, being at the time, according to Joan Adler, a bit of a practicing sorceress: "bicycles fell over as she cursed them, men ran screaming from her in the streets, though she wanted to help, and things fell her way at silent bidding." When the python that played the Cobra in some of the most stunning sequences of *Normal Love* died, Grant "threw it into the Hudson at dead of night, with incantations."[146] Labeled by Smith "the queen of the underground, both undergrounds," Grant would later appear in films by Warhol [the unfinished *Batman Dracula* (1964) with Smith] and by Gregory Markopolous.)[147] Against Smith's ideal of a transgressive, heterotopic eroticism (which could and did include heterosexuals), it seems a merely normative, heterosexual coupling, especially with or on the part of one of Smith's actress muses, was an unforgivable act of betrayal.

In considering the manner in which flicker effects could be incorporated on film, two avenues quickly presented themselves. The first was to project intermittent light onto the profilmic scene, as had been the case in Conrad's apartment; the second was to interrupt the image's projection once it had been captured by the motion-picture film. After the end of their collaboration, Smith continued to pursue the first method within the theatrical, expanded cinema productions to which, during the latter part of the 1960s, he increasingly devoted the footage he had shot for *Normal Love*. Conrad's notebooks reveal his reaction to one such presentation:

> Aug 19 [1965]. At a benefit at the Astor Playhouse, Beverly & I saw a fantastic Jack Smith production — Angus [MacLise] & Walter [De

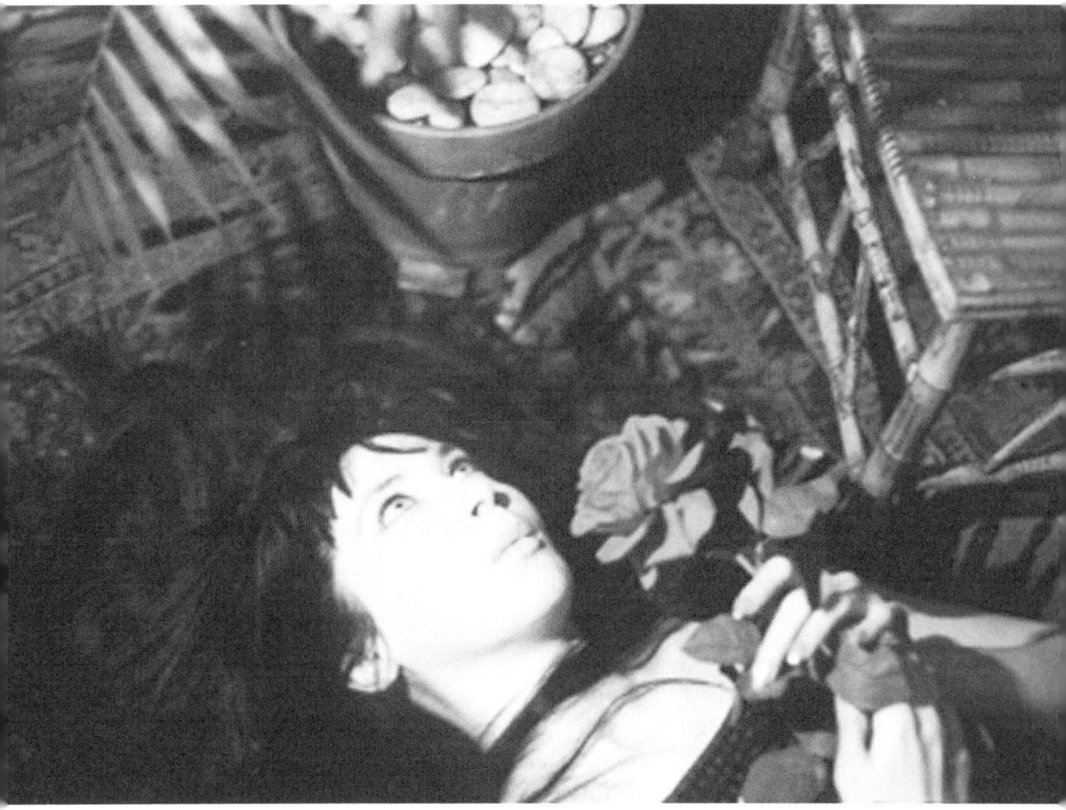

Figure 5.10. Beverly Grant, 1965. Photographer unknown (possibly Robert Adler). Courtesy Tony Conrad.

> Maria] made pounding music while Suzanne [De Maria], Jack, Mario [Montez], John V. [Vaccaro], Bill V. [Vehr], Jeanne Philips &c danced and trailed floating & suspended fabrics & goosies, all in hypnotic poses and motions, while the red scenes & cobra scene from NL [*Normal Love*] were projected on them—one of the most evocative, hypnotic & richly psychedelic & strongest visual events I ever saw. A hallucinatory sensory banquet & the richest production for the eye & mind's eye and mind. I am still stunned by the unexpected richness of this thing, that grows I am sure from Jack's at last having a projector & pursuing the psychedelic direction of IFIF from the inspiring precedent of "Rene & the Flickering Jewel."
>
> I had a lot of thoughts about the light effects that were occurring to provoke such images, & their relationship to double exposure & to printing 2 films simultaneously.[148]

As indicated by the end of this passage, Conrad had primarily chosen to investigate the second avenue for producing perceptible flicker in film, that of interrupting the projection. The primary result, of course, would be *The Flicker*. Indeed, as Conrad has noted, "*The Flicker* began as a library of masking filmstrip patterns that could be used to produce various flicker effects" over or in combination with representational footage.[149]

The project of utilizing flicker within—or, rather, following Smith's aesthetic position, *against*—narrative film would come to fruition, however, only in Grant and Conrad's *Coming Attractions*, the feature-length movie completed in 1970, the same year as their purely abstract film *Straight and Narrow*. Throughout the later 1960s, largely in dialogue with Grant (who had been working in Off-Off Broadway experimental theater, as well as taking conventional acting classes) and partially with Flynt (who, in the spring of 1968, would be enrolled in New York University film courses, in which he would derive a formula for the "Universal Film"), Conrad explored ideas for suitable flicker-filled narratives, reflecting back in part on his understanding and continued appreciation of Smith's work. (A note from October 10, 1967, describes "Acting in which the actor struggles for *SIZE* & *fails* ludicrously, as in 'Flaming Creatures.'")[150] Considered ideas include a psychological drama ("They get into one adventure too deep & she wakes him up each time to the next one. End with repeated wakeups speeding up to flicker") and a potentially Kuchar Brothersesque erotic science-fiction movie that had been pitched by De Maria:

> **FILM**
>
> People sitting in front of color TV (in 1983) for the color strobe hypnotic-sex show. Japanese announcer intro's & builds up the zap. Long shot. Couple sitting in their plush love-&-TV-seat with aluminum body-suits.
>
> Lights zap out at them & they sweat & pant faster & faster, climax: wriggling goes to ripping off the aluminum. A super-fireplace replaces the TV. Costumes do zap-shifts to exotic & sexy tropical costumes. Color strobes go over to zap woman, who zaps the audience with "You Think You're Watching Me, But I'm Watching *You!*" To super-strobe climax in which movie audience mingles with TV audience in relationship to the hyp-zaps.[151]

At least one of Conrad's early propositions – "Flicker-intercut 2 versions of the same scene – same location, but with actor portraying 2 sides of the character – light & dark, good & evil, placid & screaming, &c." – would find realization in *Coming Attractions*, in which related scenes were edited back and forth at the rate of a flicker effect.[152] Conrad, who by the time of the film's production had built his own printing lab in his apartment, also incorporated checkerboard and other patterned flicker mats and color flicker filters into the film's final cut.

Coming Attractions was directed by Grant, with Conrad taking credit for production (financed by a grant from the Rockefeller Foundation) and photography, which included special effects (Figure 5.11). Involving what Conrad calls a "loosely-woven narrative context," *Coming Attractions* ostensibly recounts the fictional "past loves and experiences of an aging transsexual," played

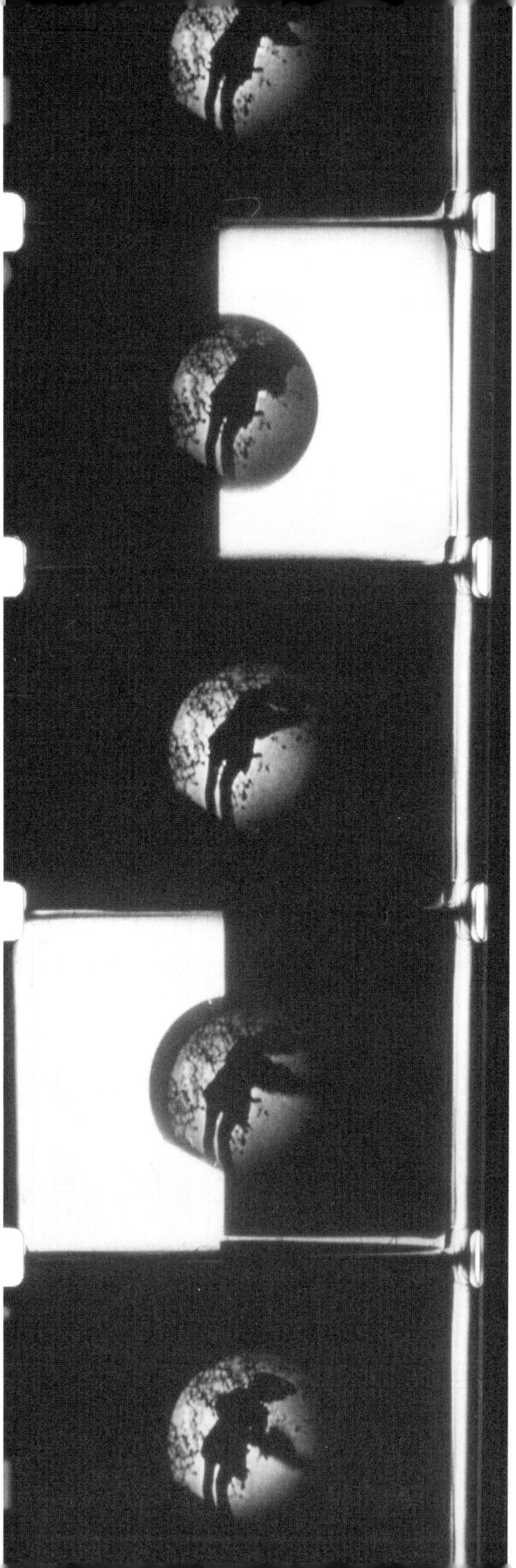

Figure 5.11. "Baby" Bettie Moses in Beverly [Grant] and Tony Conrad, *Coming Attractions*, 1970.

as Mae by Francis Francine.[153] *Coming Attractions* also starred Smith veterans Joan Adler, Tally Brown, and Arnold Rockwood, along with Conrad's Harvard classmate Lewis Oliver, his wife Rosanne, and others. Although somewhat leaden in parts (as are portions of the surviving footage for *Normal Love*), the film was intended as an extension of Smith's aesthetic, a sort of homage and culmination of the lessons Grant and Conrad had learned, particularly from the allegorical aspects of Smith's work, and a realization of the type of effects originally intended for *Normal Love*. As Conrad describes it,

> *Coming Attractions* used allegorical figures to simplify the narrative and emphasize the contextualizing features of music, visual organization, and special effects. This effort to distance and iconicize the elements of the film, while still looking for them to hang together on an immediate (if exaggerated) level of accessibility and affect, cut across every aspect of *Coming Attractions,* from its haphazard original script (by teenager Andrew Lamy) and the distractedly quirky cast to the contrived production design and the music.[154]

The musical score was to embrace and extend the general allegorical thrust, although it may not have been audible to an audience who did not intimately know the performers. Each musical contributor was asked to, in a sense, play themselves, appropriating something from their past with which they had been identified but were not currently known. The classically trained Cale (only recently departed from the Velvet Underground) played a Chopin *Étude*, Terry Riley (credited with the film's score) performed some of the honky-tonk piano he had played for money in bars and army bases in the early 1960s, and Young, a proud Westerner, sang a remarkable, long, slow rendition of the cowboy song "Bury Me Not on the Lone Prairie (The Dying Cowboy)," which Conrad further extended by means of a tape delay. (Charlemagne Palestine, yet to be identified as a minimal musician, contributed the carillon that he played at St. Thomas's Church.)[155] Although benefiting from years of optical experimentation, it would not be

Coming Attractions that would become Conrad's definitive statement and use of intermittent light, but his earlier (indeed, first) autonomous foray into cinema, *The Flicker*, to which we will now turn.

Chapter 6

Flicker

> Occasionally some fascinatingly mysterious device manages to creep out of the obscurity of mathematics to claim a place for itself in the everyday world.
>
> —Anthony S. (Tony) Conrad

On February 12, 1966, Tony Conrad completed *The Flicker*, a thirty-minute film that, aside from its opening titles, consists entirely of black-and-white (or, rather, clear) frames, alternating in a series of patterns to create stroboscopic effects (Figure 6.1).[1] *The Flicker* premiered at a private screening at the New York Cinematheque the next day and made its public debut shortly thereafter. Early audiences' reactions to the film ranged from disorientation, temporary hypnosis, and intense experiences of colors, patterns, and even hallucinogenic imagery—familiar to Conrad from his experiments with the lensless projector at his Ludlow Street apartment—to headaches and violent bouts of nausea, all seemingly caused by the pulsating light's interaction with the brain's alpha waves. By the third week in March, Jonas Mekas would report in the *Village Voice* that *The Flicker* had become "one of the most violently discussed movies in town."[2] Its reputation would be cemented that September when it was featured in the program Film and Vision in the Fourth New York Film Festival at Lincoln Center (Figures 6.2 and 6.3). (Conrad marked his entry into the halls of "Serious Culture" that he had earlier lobbied to destroy by reading a two-page statement protesting the festival's creative and economic exploitation of independent film.)[3] At least one of the Lincoln Center viewers would term the experience of watching the film "masochistic."[4]

Figure 6.1. Tony Conrad, *The Flicker*, 1965–66. 16 mm, black and white, sound, 30 min. Courtesy Anthology Film Archives.

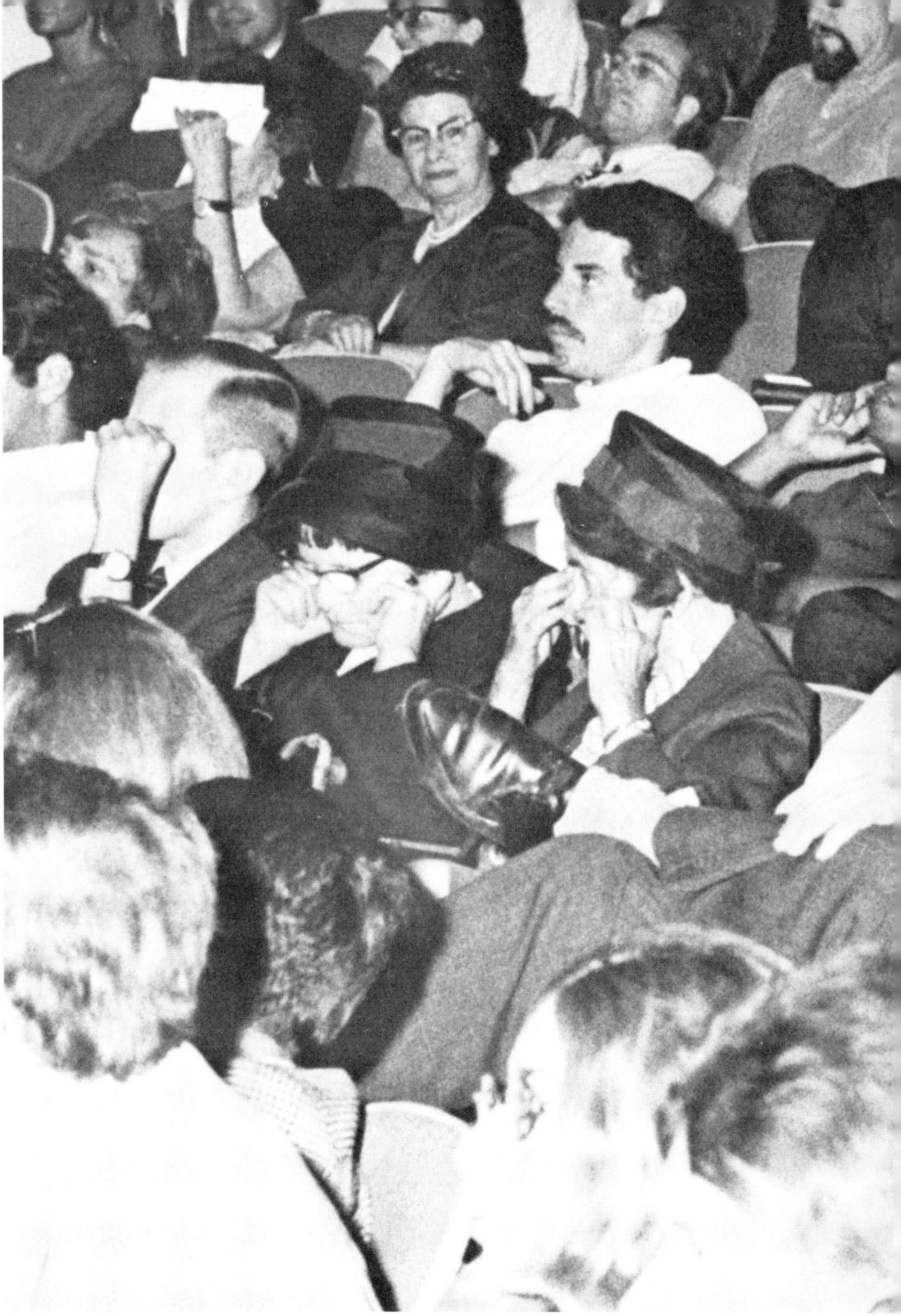

Figure 6.2. Audience at showing of Tony Conrad, *The Flicker*, 1965–66. Fourth New York Film Festival at Lincoln Center, September 15, 1966. Photo: Elliott Landy. © Elliott Landy / Landyvision.com

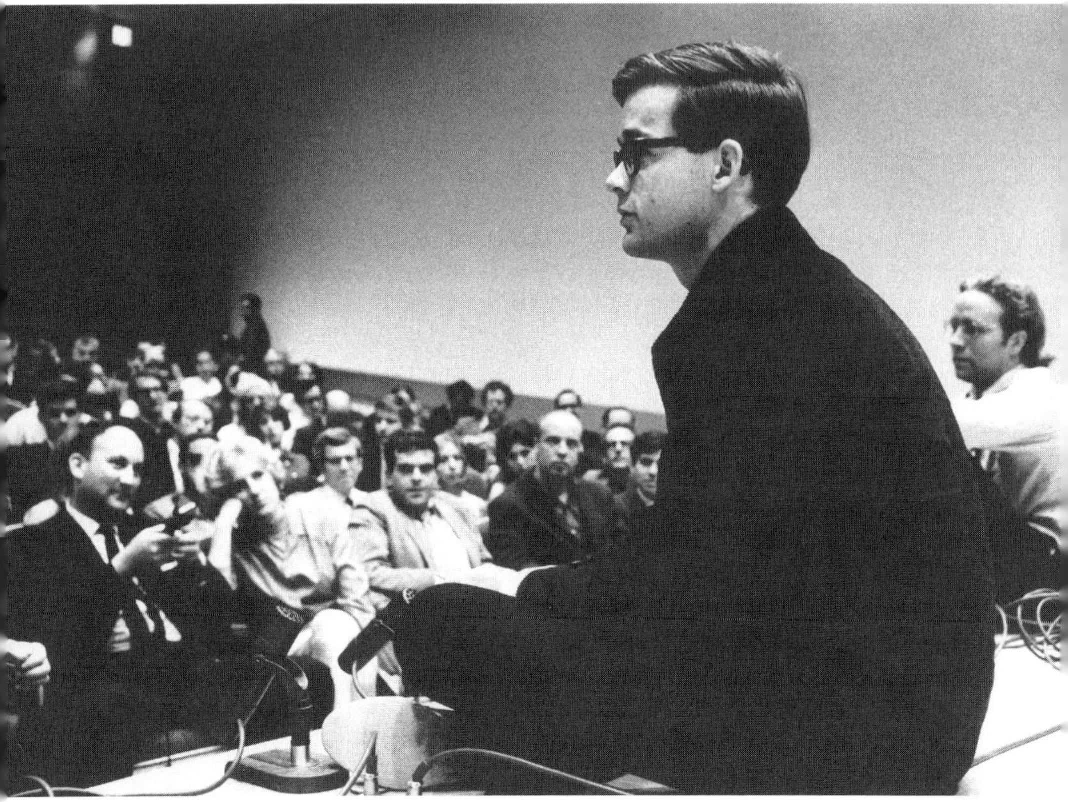

Figure 6.3. Tony Conrad and Victor Grauer at the Fourth New York Film Festival at Lincoln Center, September 15, 1966. Photo: Frederick Eberstadt, used by permission.

Although still capable of inducing such reactions, *The Flicker* is today something of a perceptual artifact. As Mekas noted as early as 1967, audiences were already becoming accustomed to its once overwhelming speeds and intensities of visual assault. "When I first screened *The Flicker*," he wrote, "two-thirds of the people walked out. Today they ask for a repeat screening. It still provokes some heated discussions, but the objectors are being fought down by their own colleagues – there is nothing for me to do."[5] The historicity of *The Flicker* is, as we will see, an important component not only of its current experience and reception, but also of its original significance and meaning.

By the time Conrad attended Jack Smith's optical-effects-filled performance at the Astor Playhouse, he was already well into production of his own film. A bill from Movielab on West Fifty-fourth Street dated July 12, 1965 documents the processing of the film's original six rolls of material at a total cost of $20.22 (paid with a check by Mekas). Conrad's earliest idea for a stroboscopic film separate from his collaboration with Smith seems to have been recorded in a note dated to late November 1964: "Flicker Movie: Gradually lengthening alternate white & black areas on the film. (Go toward shorter end also?)"[6] A quick pen sketch accompanying the note indicates what was perhaps Conrad's initial conception: exposing increasingly longer lengths of film with areas of black and white without regard for the delimitation of actual frames. He would ultimately not adopt such a procedure until 1975, when he made *Articulation of Boolean Algebra for Film Opticals*, which consists of interlocking series of horizontal bands (rather than solid blocks of black and white) printed across the entire strip of film, both on the area intended for image projection and that reserved for the optical sound track: "the whole film, *Articulation of Boolean Algebra for Film Opticals*, was produced as a film *strip*, without marked frame lines. I indicated this feature by signing the finished film on the leader end, rather than using traditional titles. In one sense *Articulation of Boolean Algebra for Film Opticals* is a very long thin photograph, 16mm x 1/2 mile."[7]

Whatever Conrad's original plan for *The Flicker*, its actual production proved complex, involving nearly seven months of painstaking calculations, graphs, and shot breakdowns. In-depth preparation and planning for the film seems to have commenced around the beginning of April 1965. Initially, the task remained that of producing a working library of flicker patterns such as Conrad had envisioned using in *Normal Love*. Conrad set about carefully counting and graphing out numbers of "flickers per cycle," "frames per cycle," and, ultimately, flickers per second as produced at a standard sound-film projection speed of twenty-four frames per second. After generating two detailed charts, Conrad recalculated the film's patterns to take into account the "inter-frame interval of 'dark' projection," in other words, the intermittence of darkness mechanically caused by the closing of the projection shutter, which effectively halves the actual duration of projected light per frame, making it one-forty-eighth of a second, rather than one-twenty-fourth. On June 15, 1965, Conrad set up his lensless projector once again, this time at the loft of Harvard friend (and future *Coming Attractions* cast member) Lew Oliver. There, he sought to test and reconfirm the most effective rates of flicker by which to produce colors, images, and hallucinations. "Synching flicker speeds with a metronome & audio generator to the time flashes proved more difficult than expected," Conrad noted:

> The more vivid effects occur at frequencies below the lowest projector setting, yet some flicker of a gentle & satisfying type is found at this setting. The lowest setting was estimated at 14–17 f.p.s., the highest at 40–42 f.p.s. The approximate normal range is thus 15–40 f.p.s.
>
> In the artificially slowed flicker, ranging down to arbitrarily low frequencies, the hallucinatory effects were pronounced at 5–6 f.p.s., still good at 4 f.p.s., though 4 seemed to be on the edge of the best effects. At 2 and 3 f.p.s., some effect remained, but most of the hallucinatory nature of the phenomenon disappeared.[8]

Having determined the optimum range of flicker effects to lie between six and sixteen flashes per second, Conrad concentrated *The Flicker*'s final manifestation primarily on those frequencies. "Lew noticed advantage in using slightly longer black than white flashes. So, use one more black than white frames on odd-length cycles, the same # of each for even-length frame cycles, even at lightest intensity."

In the end, Conrad derived a set of forty-seven patterns, running from twenty-four flashes per second to three. The intervening patterns of black and white frames varied from fairly simple (flashes per second rates of four, six, eight, nine, etc.) to much more irregular and complex (rates, for example, of ten and two sevenths, eleven and seven nineteenths, and seventeen and five elevenths flashes per second). Conrad then used a borrowed camera to shoot these patterns anywhere from one and a half to five times (exposing a white piece of paper for each of the clear frames and adding the lens cap for each of the dark ones), had them developed and printed multiple times in both positive and negative, and finally set about assembling the final version of the film by means of nearly six hundred crude tape splices, done by hand at a rate of nearly ten minutes a piece. Before completing the work, Conrad projected an early version of the film at the Cinematheque facilities at three in the morning on December 14, 1965.

As previously mentioned, Conrad produced the sound track (what P. Adams Sitney described as "a single blast of stereophonic buzz")[9] on a homemade electronic instrument that generated a continuous range of metronomelike clicks that, with the addition of a mild effect of reverb, exploited the type of rhythm/pitch interactions he had been interested in since his earliest tape experiments of 1959.[10] Drawing upon the stereo effects partially explained to him by Stockhausen, Conrad sought to "expan[d] the filmic space" in a manner that "gives unexpected birth to a sense of aural vastness," creating an acoustical virtual reality to augment and complement the hypnotic and possibly hallucinatory effects of the flickering light—"providing rich enough musical material to actually evoke specific imagery in each viewer."[11] At the time that he was working on the film, Conrad also hoped to pursue a similar type of aural suggestibility within a different context: An early page in one of Conrad's production notebooks records his desire to "Work with Walter [De Maria] on a concert of OP Music & use also the hallucinations of natural sounds (tie in natural sounds with the performance, which must somehow also be live)."[12] The idea of merging "natural sounds" with a musical performance was one that De Maria had already realized in "Cricket Music" (1964) and would explore again in "Ocean Music" (1968), the sound track to his film *Hardcore* (1969). Somewhat conflating the natural and performed, Conrad would later propose releasing a version of *The Flicker*'s sound track as a "hit song" purred by his cat, Peggy O'Fay.[13]

Before encountering either the stroboscopic visual patterns or the buzzing, stereophonic sound, audiences of *The Flicker* find themselves presented with a lengthy opening sequence. Most notable is the infamous liability waiver with which the film begins, disclaiming responsibility for "physical or mental injury," warning of possible "epileptic seizures" or "mild symptoms of shock treatment," and cautioning moviegoers to "remain in the theater only at [their] own risk" (Figure 6.4). In fashioning this warning, which also states that a medical doctor should be present at all times, Conrad extensively consulted with the Epilepsy Association of America and The Neurological Institute of New York, as well as psychoanalyst Dr. Sandor Rado, for whom Beverly Grant occasionally worked. Although flickering light has the ability to produce attacks in, as Conrad estimated, less than .01 percent of the population, he felt the threat to be real enough that procedures for what to do in case of epileptic seizure still accompany the film at every showing. His friend Oliver, a lawyer, had turned up at least two cases in New York State of theater owners being sued by epileptics likely affected by the silent film projector rate of sixteen frames per second, one of the frequencies that *The Flicker* employs.[14]

At the same time, however, Conrad's warning is somewhat undermined by the fact that it remains on screen for what seems an inordinately long time (nearly three minutes) and is accompanied by the jaunty ragtime tune "Raggedy Ann." Evidently taped off of an old 78-rpm record, the music so undercuts the projected announcement as to make it seem, in the words of Lindley Page Hanlon, merely a "sarcastic suggestion."[15] For Cinematheque audiences of the time, it would likely also have brought to mind Conrad's association with the "moldy," outmoded aesthetic of Jack Smith. Before the music draws to a close, hand-lettered title cards reading "Tony Conrad presents" and "The Flicker" appear in a somewhat psychedelic script, adding to the opening sequence an additional set of connotations already by that time unavoidable in the context of strobe lights (Figures 6.5 and 6.6). Although Conrad ultimately produced the titles himself, an early entry in his notebook reads: "Contact Ted about his inimitable writing. It has drug & op & psychological orientation that might prove useful to the new art movement."[16]

Even after the title sequence concludes, *The Flicker*'s visual effects build extremely slowly. Conrad based its overall temporal structure on his experience with the Theatre of Eternal Music, feeling that the initial moments in which little or nothing appeared on the screen would help produce a receptive audience:

> I decided that what I wanted to do was to start off my film with a long section in which nothing would happen. Because I knew from our performances that there was a certain pattern of response that audiences would have — one that I participate in, in some ways, that I sense I can feel. . . .
>
> We would play for like two or three minutes, and when nothing happens and it stays exactly the same, people begin to get nervous because they think they're being jerked around, and they're wondering what's going to happen, and they get increasingly anxious, and then after about seven minutes they leave. Some of them leave, and others lull themselves into a kind of atmosphere of resignation. It takes about that long. And along about nine minutes to eleven minutes after you've started, you've kind of weeded out the people who are going to get angry and who are, like, going to rebel. And the people who have given up have settled in for a long winter's nap,

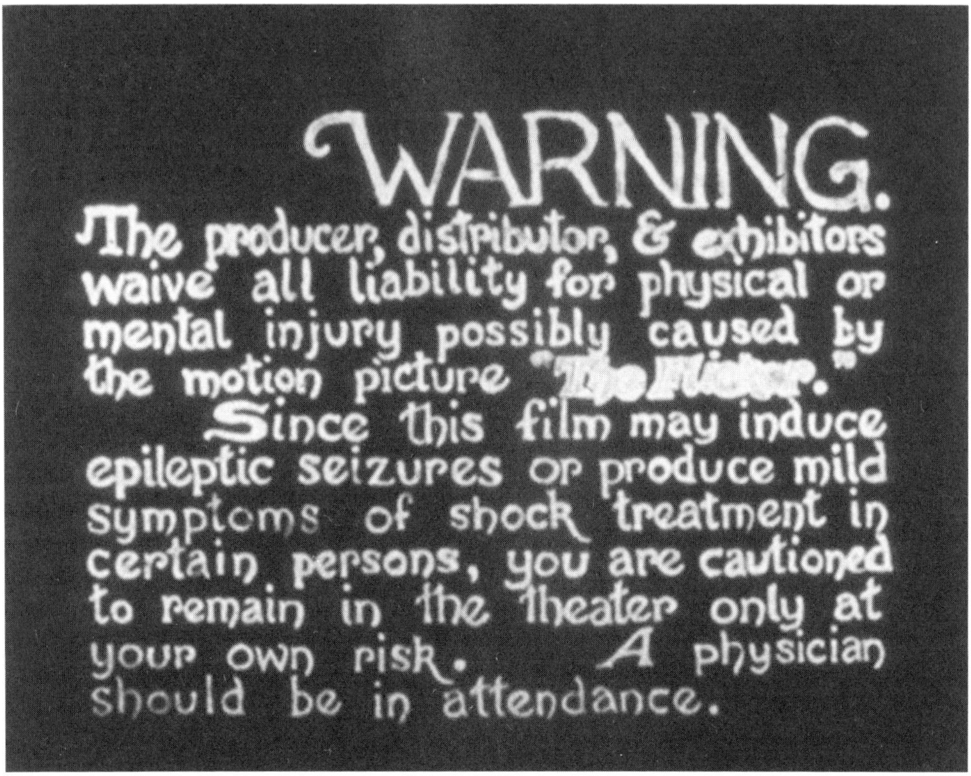

Figure 6.4. Tony Conrad, *The Flicker*, 1965–66. Warning.

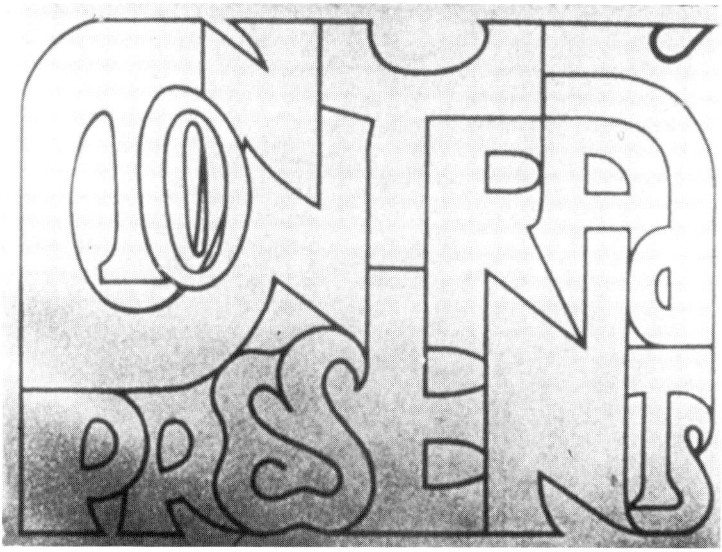

Figure 6.5. Tony Conrad, *The Flicker*,
1965–66. Title sequence.

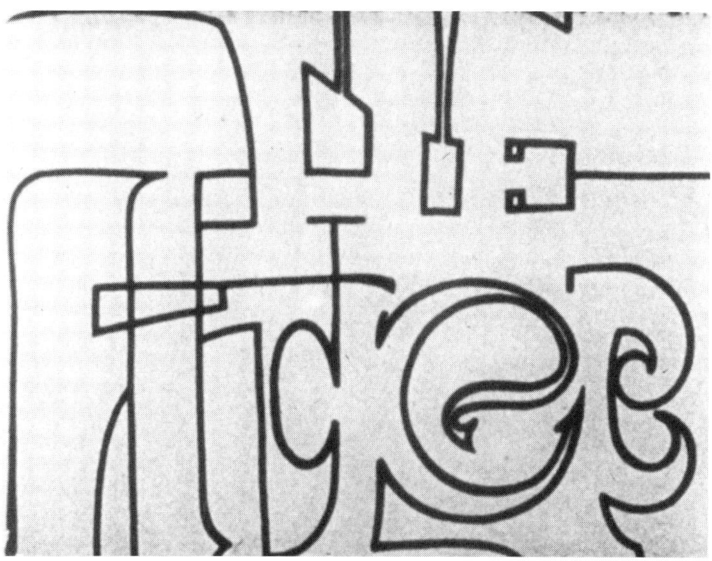

Figure 6.6. Tony Conrad, *The Flicker*,
1965–66. Title sequence.

> and they begin to discover their own experiences, because they no longer have any imposed expectations.[17]

Conrad was highly protective of his flicker patterns, not only on account of possible liability issues (he wondered at one point whether *The Flicker* might be "an illegal form of *hypnotism*"),[18] but also because he thought they were unique and therefore patentable in their production of light-born flicker harmonics. "The greatest part of the film is composed of patterns of the black & white frames which form complex rhythmic structures all relating to the basic beat of the projection frequency," Conrad explained:

> In this case, since perception of flicker is frequency-related rather than actually rhythmic, it is more fitting to speak of the projection frequency as a "tonic." Each pattern is then seen to suggest a "chord" related to the "tonic." The patterns used were, in fact, constructed in such a way that each one contains visible components contributed by up to three related frequencies. These flicker-triads represent, to my knowledge, the first meaningful extension of harmonic principles to the visual sense.[19]

The specter of "visual music" associated with the idea of optical harmonies and the symbolist aesthetics associated with it would be difficult to escape, and Conrad would not entirely do so for some time. Although Conrad did not, in the end, pursue such an avenue (and was too close a reader of the nineteenth-century German physicist Hermann von Helmholtz to believe in any visual harmonics of color), his brother Daniel, to whom he demonstrated the effects of his flickering lensless projector, would go on to produce the abstract film *Circles* (1969) and create and perform on the Chromaccord — a color organ in the lineage of Louis Bertrand Castel's *Clavecin oculaire* (1734) and Thomas Wilfred's *Clavilux* (1920s) — developing a sophisticated exploration of the effects of colors and retinal afterimages.[20]

• • •

Although Sheldon Renan would declare *The Flicker* "the ultimate to date in the nonobjective film," Amos Vogel would proclaim it "a great film," and Mekas would call it "one of the few original works of cinema," there was initially some controversy over whether it could be considered a film at all. Other possibilities included "optical experiment," "medical text for the eyes," or "a detector of the photogenic migraine." Even Conrad himself contended that "I don't think of *The Flicker* as a movie as we know it today," but rather as "a piece of film that is experienced by a group of people in various ways—depending on how they choose to approach it."[21] As late as 1989, Conrad would still describe *The Flicker* as "a library of peculiar visual materials, referenced to the frame-pulse at 24 frames per second."[22]

Despite such uncertainties, *The Flicker*'s primary reception has been as a structural film. As defined by P. Adams Sitney in 1969, structural film markedly differed from the predominant sensibility of American avant-garde cinema up to that point. As opposed to a general trend toward increasingly fast, complex, and organic editing, structural film was characterized by a relaxed temporal expansion and the presence of an intelligible overall outline or structure that Sitney termed "shape." "Theirs is a cinema of structure," he wrote, "wherein the *shape* of the whole film is predetermined and simplified, and it is that shape that is the primal impression of the film."[23] Although Sitney later declared that Michael Snow's *Wavelength* (1967) led him to the idea of structural film, his original article cited *The Flicker* (along with Paul Sharits's color flicker film *Ray Gun Virus* [1966]) as the clearest instance of content's subordination to overall shape—a feature that the "Exposure Timing Sheet" Conrad published in *Film Culture* seemed to literalize by distilling the film into a somewhat optical, moirélike, synchronic form (Figures 6.7 and 6.8).[24] (The "Exposure Timing Sheet" was in fact a three-dimensional plastic object produced after *The Flicker* so as to reveal but also to obscure the film's underlying patterns so they would be difficult to copy.) Moreover, it was to Conrad that Sitney turned for "the most articulate expression of the consciousness of structural form of any published record of the film-makers involved."[25] By this he referred to Conrad's description of *The Flicker* as "static" in relation to the static form developed by the Theatre of Eternal Music. Sitney went on to explain, "The structural film is static because it is not modulated internally by evolutionary concerns. In short, there are no climaxes in these films. They are visual, or audio-visual objects whose most striking characteristic is their over-all shape."[26]

It was on this basis that Sitney differentiated Conrad's aesthetic from that of Peter Kubelka, whose *Arnulf Rainer* (1960) had preceded *The Flicker* in being composed entirely of black-and-white frames.[27] *The Flicker*'s overall structure of what Sitney described as "one long crescendo-diminuendo" contrasted with *Arnulf Rainer*'s much more varied modulation. Despite the similarity of their components, the visual effects of the two films are, as Sitney suggests, quite different. *Arnulf Rainer* does not maintain stroboscopic patterns long enough to create the type of hypnotic or hallucinatory visual effects characteristic of *The Flicker*. There is no absorption into its patterns. The experience is instead one of brief pauses followed by short, patterned bursts that continually blast viewers back from the screen, distancing them from the experience with each staccato eruption of light or white noise, which Kubelka meticulously composed in analogy with the musical dissonance of the Vienna School—or, as Conrad once characterized it, "extending the infinitely anal art-style of Anton Webern into 'the cinema.'"[28]

Although Sitney acknowledged structural film's relationship to the contemporary "aesthetics of painting and music" and subsequently noted its connection to both the broader "constellation" of minimalism (including La Monte Young, Terry Riley, and Yvonne Rainer) and the advent of artists' films (by Robert Morris, Richard Serra, and Bruce Nauman), he was primarily concerned to situate and comprehend the emergent genre within the "major" history of avant-garde cinema as a distinct aesthetic realm.[29] In a response to Sitney's article (which characteristically took the form of a chart), George Maciunas contested such a separation.

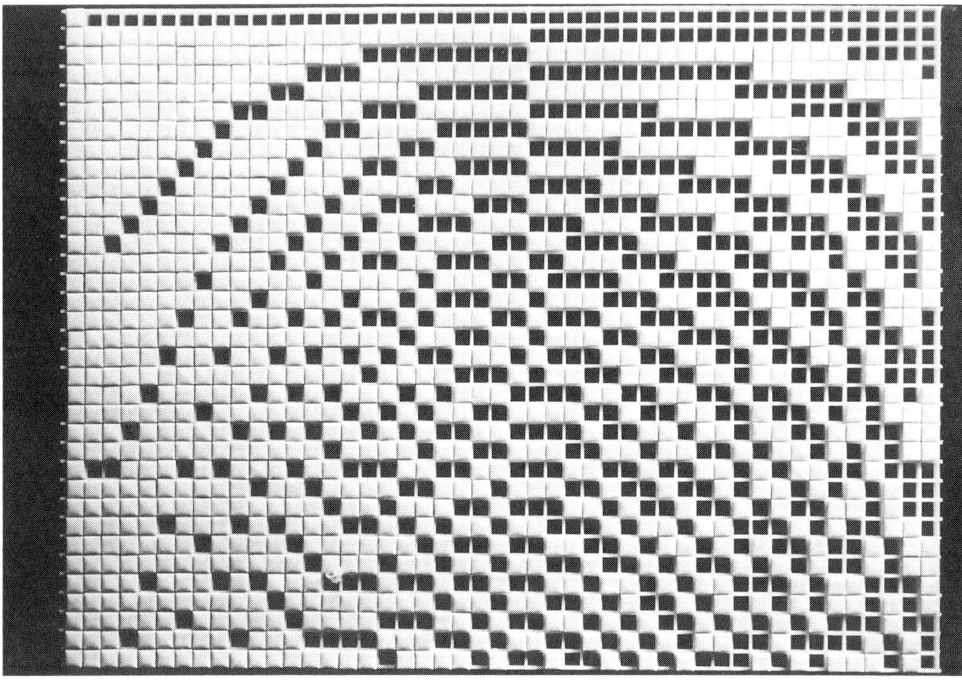

Figure 6.7. Tony Conrad, "Exposure Timing Sheet" for *The Flicker*, 1966. Photo: Robert Adler. Courtesy Tony Conrad.

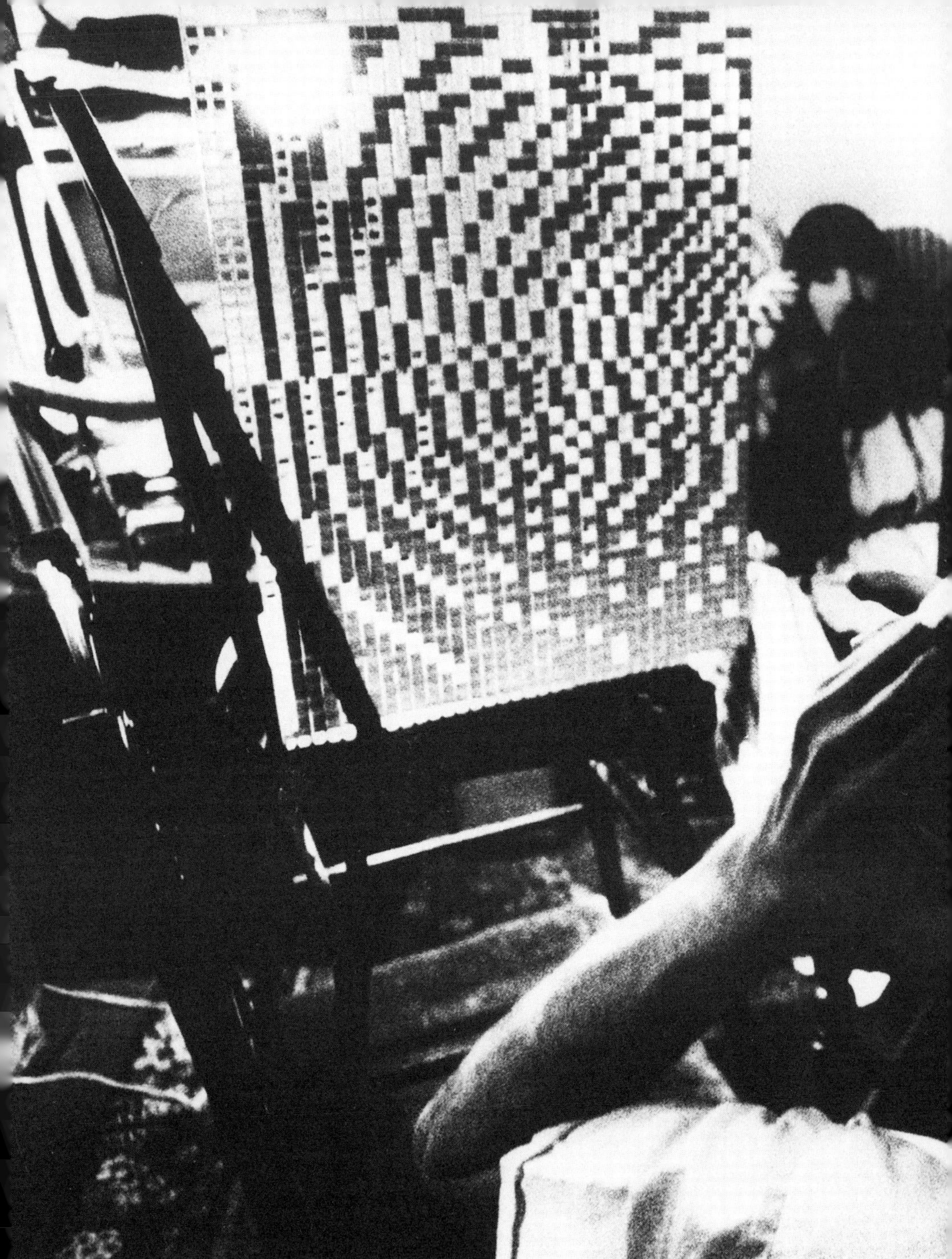

Figure 6.8. Tony Conrad and Beverly Grant with "Exposure Timing Sheet" for *The Flicker*, 1966. Photo: Frederick Eberstadt, used by permission.

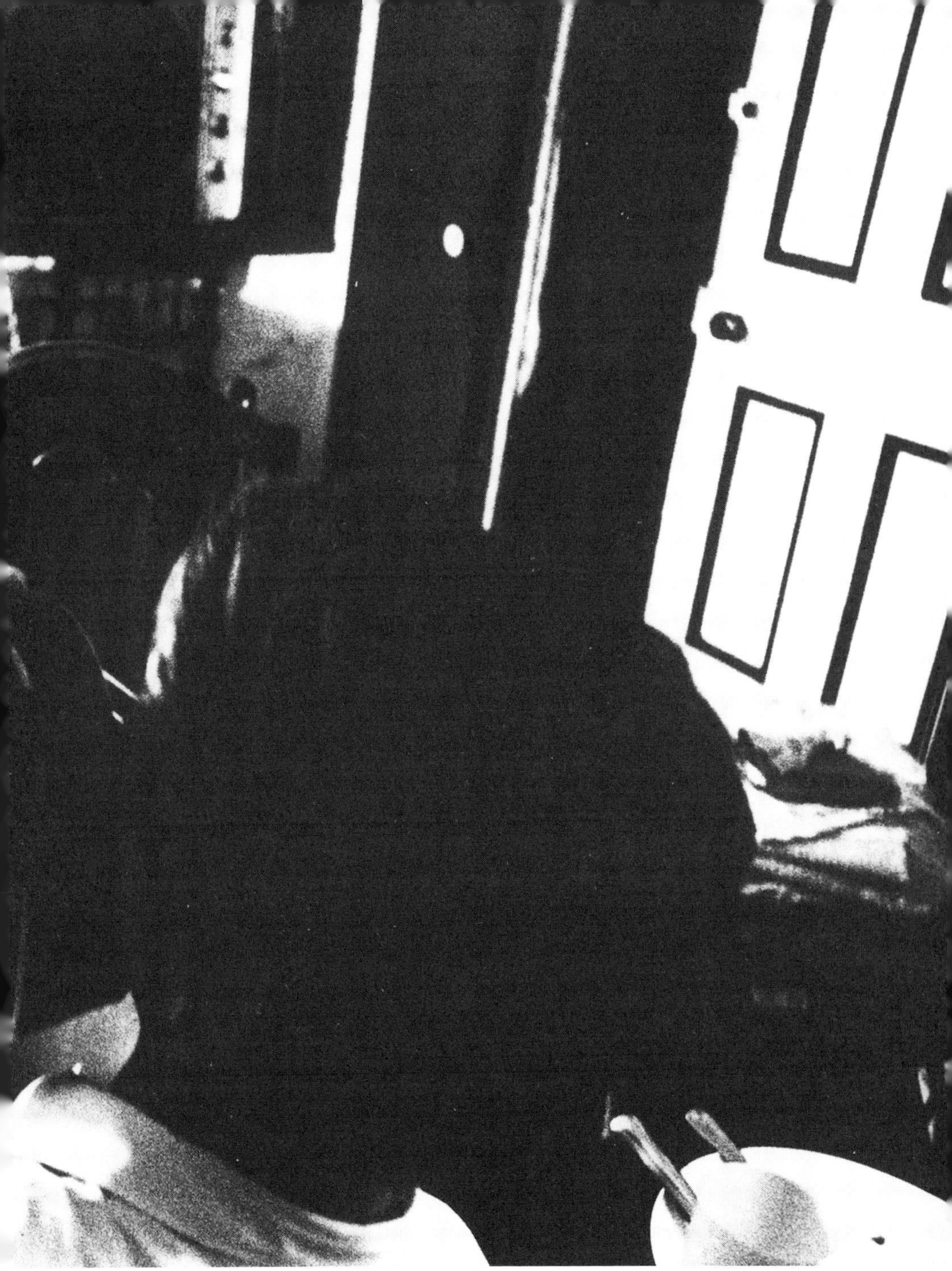

Although he allowed that Sitney had correctly characterized *The Flicker*'s overall structure as a crescendo-diminuendo, he placed Conrad's film (and structural film generally) back into the much wider and more heterodox post-Cagean milieu encompassing Young, Morris, De Maria, George Brecht, Nam June Paik, Chieko Shiomi, Ben Vautier, "etc. etc. etc. etc."[30] Maciunas further criticized Sitney's choice of the label "structural film" since, he contended, the term "structure" in no way implies the simplicity of the single, overarching shape by which Sitney wished to define the genre. As examples of complex structures, Maciunas offered "fugue, sonata, serial form, indeterminate statics of concrete frame, desoxyribose [sic] nucleic acid molecule." As the "cause" of Sitney's "error," Maciunas listed "misplaced dictionary" as well as ignorance of Henry Flynt's notions of structure art and concept art. Proposing the alternative labels of "monomorphic structure" or, in reference to the "Expanded Arts Diagram" he had published in *Film Culture* 43, "Neo-Haiku," Maciunas explained, "this monomorphism tends to border on *Concept-art*, since it emphasizes an image or idea of generalization from particulars rather than particularization (arrangement into particular design or pattern) of generalities." Partisan as ever to Flynt's (anti)aesthetic position, Maciunas went on to advocate a conceptual understanding of structural film by which its material realization would ultimately be irrelevant, "since it is an art of which the material is *concepts* (closely bound with language), rather than particular forms of film, sound, etc."

Spurred by Maciunas's response, as well as by the appearance of other works he wanted to consider (in particular, Ken Jacobs's *Tom, Tom, the Piper's Son* [1969]), Sitney extended his discussion of structural film for inclusion in the *Film Culture Reader* later that year. Whereas Sitney's original article had primarily been concerned with the new sensibility or genre's morphological description, he now emphasized questions of function, explaining that structural film was not merely conceptual in nature, but integrally linked to perceptual concerns. Drawing on the Russian formalist criticism of Victor Shklovsky, Sitney aligned his viewpoint with the strategy of perceptual estrangement: the pursuit of a "de-automatized perception" that would interrupt and prolong the habitual processes of vision and thus render them newly conscious, transforming perception into apperception. "The technique of art is to make objects 'unfamiliar,'" Sitney quoted, "to make forms difficult, to increase the difficulty and length of perception because the process of perception is an aesthetic end in itself and must be prolonged."[31] Ultimately, Sitney's interrelation of the notion of shape with that of perceptual estrangement came to resonate closely with Morris's presentation of minimal sculpture. Viewing a structural film would entail judging or comparing one's experience of the movie as projected in time against its ideal or intuited overall shape (Morris's "constant shape . . . held in the mind . . . against which the literal changing perspective views are related").[32] The outcome, explained Sitney with reference to Snow, was a manifest "apperceptive acknowledgment of the cinematic materials and circumstances" apparent during viewing—not the "illusionary participation" of traditional narrative or even visionary cinema, but a "transcendentalism [that] is always grounded in a dialogue between illusion and its unveiling."[33]

British filmmaker and theorist Malcolm Le Grice would approach *The Flicker* from a similar perspective. However, like his associate, Peter Gidal, Le Grice criticized Sitney's notion of shape as a vestige of formalism and emphasized the audience's cognitive and phenomenological interactions with the film in real time. "This shift in attitude, where the film becomes, as it were, perceptual raw material," he explained, "makes way for a reflexive engagement by the viewer, where his own, rather than the filmmaker's perception and reaction become the primary content."[34] Situating *The Flicker* as the privileged example within his discussion of "perceptual film," Le Grice described it as "conceived entirely in terms of retinal response":

> It explores different stroboscopic systems first, and then systematic interactions between them. The result is a film which enables awareness of changing modes of response to recognizably different strobe

> conditions — awareness of how the autonomic response begins to shade off into pattern recognition as the black and white units increase in length; how the different systems interact; how the difference in colour after-image relates to different strobe rates; and possibly becoming aware of other physiological changes as the retinal activity affects the rhythm of other areas of the nervous system.[35]

Central to Le Grice's understanding of *The Flicker* was much the same static quality that Sitney had focused on, the measured and deliberate approach to and withdrawal from the most intense periods of stroboscopic bombardment. "In Conrad's *The Flicker*," he wrote, "the overall experience is due to awareness of gradually changing modes of perception."[36] For Le Grice, it was this gradual approach that not only separated Conrad's work, once again, from Kubelka's, but also allowed for an authentic apperception — opposed on the one hand to the interpellations of conventional cinema ("spurious pictorial or narrative involvement") and on the other to earlier avant-garde strategies of fast cutting and single framing (precisely what Sitney had also seen structural film reacting against).[37] Yet as Le Grice himself observed, the type of perceptual stimulation invoked by *The Flicker* could have effects on levels other than the cognitive or apperceptive: "Action on the autonomic system seeks to create a nervous response which is largely pre-conscious, the psychological reactions sought being a direct consequence of physiological function."[38]

As an apperceptive aesthetic or technology, then, the flicker film, no matter how gradual, walks an exceedingly fine line: between an entirely autonomized, preconscious or subconscious, physiologically determined perception, on the one hand, and a type of anti-ideological, self-reflexive, and truly apperceptive cognition by which "we may genuinely study ourselves and our reactions," on the other. As Jean-Claude Lebensztejn has noted about the flicker film's play with the "fascistic manipulation [of the viewer] and the anti-fascistic exposition of fascism, the margin is perhaps narrow, fluid, and impure. To play with the thresholds of perception is to play with fire, from whichever side one takes."[39] Nevertheless, for Le Grice, as for the theory of structural (and later, structural/materialist) film in general, the phenomenological, apperceptive realization of perceptual embodiment (one predicated on the same type of detailed and potentially disciplinary interrogation of one's own perceptual processes as involved in Morris's minimal sculpture) was conceived as a source of provisional autonomy, if not of revolutionary liberation.

Conrad, however, seems not to have regarded the production of a purely apperceptive viewing subject as his film's primary motivation or effect. "I viewed this as a situation in which I would mediate the power of the flicker as a tool," he explained:

> My idea was that basically this would just knock people's socks off, and I wanted them to understand that they were being run by the power of this film. That it was not coming from them even though the experience of the film happened inside of their body and not really in the space. A lot of different things seem to be happening in their body, but if they think they have control over this experience I will then gradually withdraw it so that they can watch it go away, and if they feel like they'd like to hold on to it and stay in that space, they can try but they won't be able to. At the end it will have brought them back. People who wrote about it said I was very gentlemanly in bringing people back carefully from the most turgid part of the film experience. Not at all. I wanted to really give people a chance to pretend that they were in control of the situation, but then to make it very painfully and slowly clear—as though you're slicing them very slowly—that it's the film that is in control of what is going on.[40]

Although the denouement ultimately makes the audience aware of *The Flicker*'s impact, the viewing experience proves more complex than an active structuring or continuous apperception. As a process that asserts itself as not fully of the viewing subject, *The Flicker* would seem to question one's sense of autonomy as much as it confirms it. Plugged into the black-and-white patterns as though wired to the flow of alternating current, viewers seem on the verge of dissolving into a circuit with the technology, although perhaps also being aware of their position on this edge.

• • •

By 1972, Conrad would come to embrace *The Flicker*'s reception as a structural film as one of several legitimate understandings. The audiences' reactions, explained Conrad to Gérard Langlois, "are of three sorts, each one of which is valid, if you will. Either they accept the experience as a new type of spectacle, or they ask themselves questions about the very functioning of cinema, through the demystification of the apparatus of projection . . . or they create their own mental experience and come out of their passivity."[41]

Most important for Conrad was the interaction of the first two reactions: how *The Flicker*'s particular use of cinema's material components produces an environmental transformation not simply of the screen, but of the entire space of the theater. "Nothing new can be made without work upon the medium itself," he continued,

> and cinema is an extraordinary medium because it directly creates a total environment, the atmosphere that is in the room, by the combination of its elements (sound and light), whereas graphic art or music can only, themselves, create a limited environment, by a single notion of space. People, however, never ask themselves what makes the atmosphere that surrounds them when they find themselves in a cinema, preferring to project themselves into the story being told. That's why I had the idea of making *The Flicker*, to confront them directly with the elements that make up this atmosphere (light and sound), telling myself that the strangeness of this new environment could become, in its turn, a source of spectacle.[42]

When Conrad made these comments, he and Beverly Grant had already explored cinema's environmental dimension further in *Four Square* (1971), a four-projector film in which each wall of the room becomes a projection screen. "The audience," explained

Conrad, "seated in the four corners of the room, can take in at once all four screens (the light reaching their brains via four points on their optic nerve) and [the light from] two of the projectors, of which one is situated just in front of them."[43] Yet even before such an explicit development, Conrad had discussed *The Flicker* in similar terms. "First let me clarify," he wrote in 1967, "that *The Flicker* certainly is intended as a medium for the communication of atmosphere, though the removal of the viewer is to a decidedly unspecified & unusual environment." And while, as "an abstract environment, the theatre & audience themselves provide [the] basis for imagery or composition," when the stroboscopic bombardment gains in intensity, "the atmosphere gradually & inevitably develops away from the purely 'real' situation of the theatre simply lit from the screen."[44]

Somewhat in contrast to this emphasis on *The Flicker*'s material components (quoted above), Conrad's earliest pronouncements pointedly fail to privilege cinema in any manner. Instead, Conrad consistently discussed it within a much broader context that included op art, psychedelia, popular happenings and rock concerts (particularly those staged in Brooklyn by Murray the K), medical research, and even the "treatment of battle neuroses."[45] Furthermore, prior to 1968, Conrad's working notebooks reveal surprisingly little meditation on film per se. In leafing though their pages, it becomes clear that *The Flicker* arose out of a much wider and more diverse investigation into techniques of perceptual and neurophysiological stimulation — techniques including film and tape loops, broadcast television and other deployments of cathode-ray-tube technology, telephone transmission, ultrasound, gestalt psychology, photo-signal alternators, and pharmaceutical hallucinogens.[46] Of particular interest were subliminal messages, a topic that first arose while Conrad was establishing *The Flicker*'s preliminary set of patterns: "When shooting, leave an extra frame in at end of each cycle to use for indexing purposes when editing. Let this frame have a photo of a subliminal message on it."[47] As Conrad's thoughts on the subject developed, he came to consider a peculiar, self-reflexive manifestation in which he would "incorporate *subliminal* advertising &/or criticism *of the film* in it." Whereas one version of the movie would contain suggestions such as "This is a great film" or "Good movie," a different one would "alter [the] tone of the same film by using different titles and different subliminal messages."[48]

Ultimately, *The Flicker* seems to have been but one possible realization of Conrad's ideas. Alternatives included a "Neon Hula Hoop," "Eyelid-lite Environment Simulators" that would flash directly onto closed eyes, and devices for aural and visual electroecephalograph (EEG) feedback to induce "a convulsive quasi-epileptic seizure that could be used to replace electric shock treatment therapy."[49] Once completed, *The Flicker* was afforded little sanctity as a film, either. Conrad noted how it could be "viewed" — even most effectively — with eyes closed, as well as how it could be deployed as a lighting effect.[50] ("I think it is equally interesting to use the film to complement any other activity or object, so long as no new light sources are introduced.")[51] Conrad even endorsed a viewing position not toward the screen, but rather watching the audience as a screen, a feature he explored in an installationlike showing that projected the film onto one-half of the audience, who were wearing frosted plastic glasses, subjecting them to a direct dose of flicker while the other half of the audience observed the effects.[52] If anything, Conrad's statements indicate that he initially considered *The Flicker* a particular application of *strobe*. And if, as he told Toby Mussmann, "the possibilities of what I believe is an entirely new medium seem unlimited," it was no doubt because intermittent light (which is in essence binary code) proved inherently polymorphous — not wedded to its material substrate, but extractable on the one hand as pure information (perhaps, as Maciunas suggested, as structure or concept art) and on the other as neurophysiological impact.[53] "There is a variety of effects that I am investigating," Conrad explained to Mekas:

> effects that act on your eyes so as to produce the actual imagery directly within the observer rather than in a normal way of having

> the eye interpret the light patterns on the screen.... Most of the details, most of the impact, most of what people find in it, what they take away with them from having watched the film, wasn't there, was conjured up only when they watched this film: It didn't exist before, it doesn't exist on film, it wasn't on the screen.[54]

Although *The Flicker* clearly had an impact on the viewer, precisely *where* in the body the effect was located remained notably unclear. "We don't know exactly how the film affects the mind," explained Conrad, "which seems to be partly through the eye and partly through the brain." "The brain itself is directly involved in all of this; it is not coincidental that one of the principal brainwave frequencies, the so-called alpha-rhythm, lies in the 8 to 16 cycles per second range. Hence the central nervous system itself must here be considered as a kind of sensory mechanism, though its role is not explicitly understood, to my knowledge."[55]

This ambiguity, as we will see, is telling, for it is *The Flicker*'s impact upon heretofore untapped areas of subjectivity that is ultimately at stake. More particularly, Conrad's invocation of the central nervous system's transformation into a sense organ brought him squarely within the contemporary discourse of Marshall McLuhan. For McLuhan, the externalization of the central nervous system bespoke a new stage in the development of electronic media, where, after "the outering of all five senses, we turn to the outering of mental operations in computers."[56] As he put it in *Understanding Media*, "Our private and corporate lives have become information processes just because we have put our central nervous systems outside us in electronic technology."[57] For McLuhan, such observations (cited repeatedly by Cage at the time) bespoke the onset of what we now know as post-Fordism, characterized by informatization, automation, immaterial and affective labor, and the flexible managerial involvement of the worker's entire personality.[58] They also foretold a new and highly ambivalent vocation for the arts. Viewed as indicators, if not instigators, of new perceptual modalities or sense ratios, artistic developments were to be followed not only for their liberatory potentials, but also as more sophisticated forms of market research, forecasting new realms of profit and providing lessons "in the world of management design."[59]

• • •

It was *The Flicker*'s challenge to its medium that led Gilles Deleuze, in a short but insightful passage from *Cinema 2*, to note its role in inaugurating a "third epoch" of cinema: a "cinema of expansion without camera, and also without screen or film stock," a cinema in which "anything can be used as a screen, the body of a protagonist or even the bodies of the spectators; anything can replace the film stock, in a virtual film which now only goes on in the head, behind the pupils."[60] Deleuze was not, of course, the first to see a new age of cinema in its expansion. It had been conceived as such by, among others, Jonas Mekas, who assiduously chronicled the transformations being undergone by "the expanding eye" across a range of sites, from underground film and what would be called "expanded cinema" to commercial television (particularly subliminal advertising) and the corporate pavilions of the 1964 New York World's Fair.[61] Reporting on the diffusion of the projected image across multiple surfaces (screens or not), as well as on the dissolution of film stock altogether, Mekas regarded the locus of such developments as lying in the perceptual and attentive transformation and retraining of the viewer. "Our eye has expanded, our eye reactions have quickened. We have learned to see a little bit better.... We need an audience that is willing to educate, to expand their eyes. A new cinema needs new eyes to see it. That's what it's all about."[62] Although Mekas sometimes characterized these transformations, both undergone and needed, as physiological ("Our eye is undergoing physical changes"), he knew full well that they reside on the level of adaptive reflexive temporalities and habitual psychological associations: "It comes more to removing various psychological blocks than to really changing the eye."[63] In all cases, it was a matter of opening the human subject up to external influences by which their physical, perceptual, and even mental operations were altered in an as-yet unspecified manner:

> What are all these lights doing? What is the real meaning of the strobes? Where is all this coming from or going to? Do any of the artists know the meaning and effect and power (both healing and damaging) of colors and lights? I have noticed, very often, how suddenly, during certain surges of colors and lights, I become electrified, my nerves become jumpy as if somewhere deep inside I were pierced with a knife; or, at other times, suddenly the peace surrounds and takes me over. The same with the new sounds.[64]

Mekas sensed that what was at stake was some sort of subjective transformation, one that he attempted several times to bring into focus and that, like Lebensztejn, he found to be profoundly ambivalent: "Sometimes, I am afraid, the [new] consciousness is being confused with ability to see more color images, with the expanded eye, with the quickness of the eye. But as the quickness of the hand can be used to thrust a knife into one's heart, so the quickness of the eye, the simultaneity of seeing can be used by both Devil and God."[65]

While Mekas's considerations drew upon transformations within a number of artistic, social, and technological arenas, at the base of his thinking lay the articles that Brion Gysin and Ian Sommerville published in *Olympia* magazine concerning their invention of the Dream Machine (1960) (Figure 6.9).[66] Although often understood in purely aestheticizing, even mystical contexts, the Dream Machine was actually associated with the ongoing theorization of "control" by William S. Burroughs, whom Mekas also cited at the time. For Burroughs, control, famously, is the effect of a "virus" that resides within "the central nervous system . . . manipulati[ng] . . . speech centers, throat muscles and vocal cords."[67] The symbiosis of host and virus, according to Burroughs, results in "association lines" of speech, thought, and behavior that tend toward monopolistic standardization, the establishing and perpetuation of a norm.[68] Communication is thus understood as a

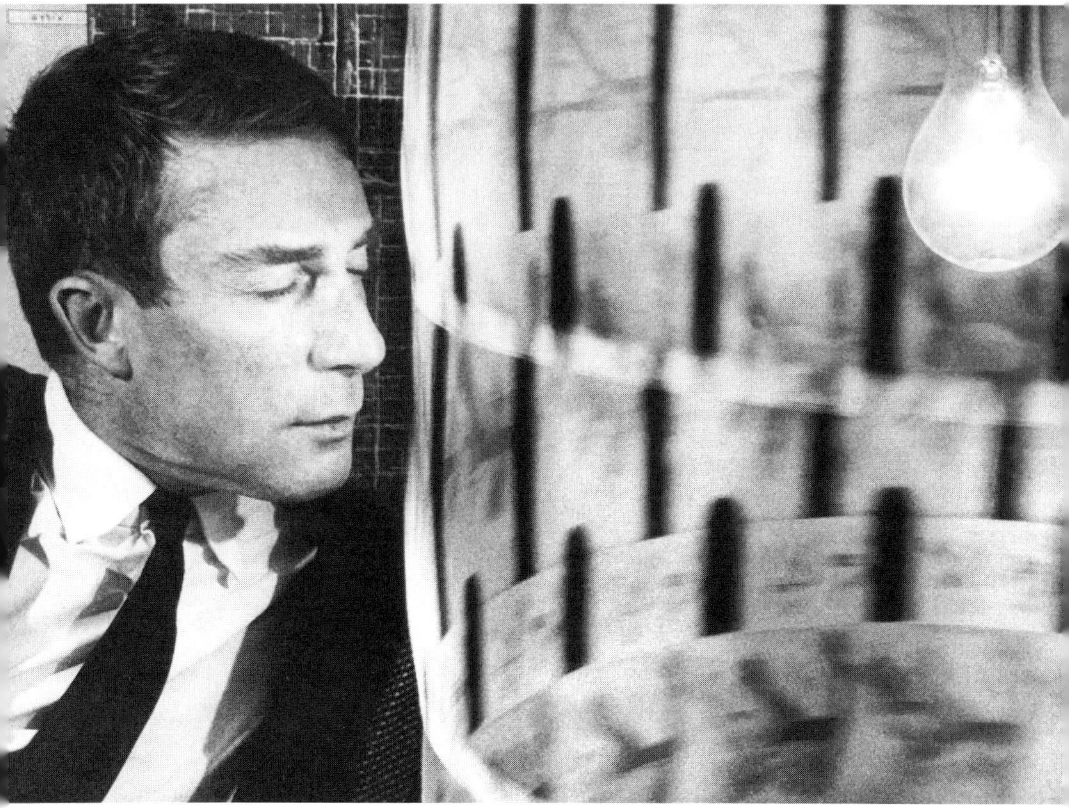

Figure 6.9. Brion Gysin with Dream Machine, ca. 1960. Photo: Harold Chapman. © Harold Chapman / Topham / The Image Works.

power relation, conceived not as a top-heavy prohibition, but as a force of regulation by which the virus seeks to replicate itself at the point of reception.[69] From Burroughs's point of view, human beings are irredeemably infected vessels, and their subjective autonomy is only a distant possibility; absent total deconditioning or escape into outer space (two of Burroughs's sci-fi goals), the human subject is fully situated within relations of power and resistance, where the operative question is "Who are you an agent for?"

Although Burroughs's virus resonates primarily through semiotic networks, it can also operate on the central nervous system directly, opening onto techniques such as subliminal and waking suggestion. It can also, apparently, be propagated through light. "Change," Burroughs noted, "is a function of number and, today in the electronic age, our only interesting constant is 186,000 miles per second; the speed of light, which the speed of electricity does not reach let alone surpass."[70] In "Dream Machine" (the article read by Mekas), Gysin discusses the dissolution of the art object – in particular, the industrially manufactured commodity of the Duchampian readymade – into a realm of luminous perceptual stimulation and subjective transformation: "the one and only thing which cannot be taken from the picture is light – everything else can be utterly transmuted or can go."[71] Sommerville brought the issue directly into cinema. Anticipating Conrad's projector experiments, he noted that "Flicker may play a part in cinematic experience. The frame speed of film is three to four times faster than the average alpha rhythm but the film viewed may include flicker frequencies as a sub-harmonic."[72] The ultimate threat, Sommerville contended, was that "films and TV impose external rhythms on the mind, altering the brain waves which are otherwise as individual as finger-prints. It is entirely possible that the EEG records of a generation of TV watchers will be similar, even identical – although differing from those which present research reveals."[73]

Burroughs, Gysin, and Sommerville all drew their understanding of strobe from the work of British physiologist W. Grey Walter. Walter's book *The Living Brain* was a speculative and sometimes spectacularized account of his research into the ana-

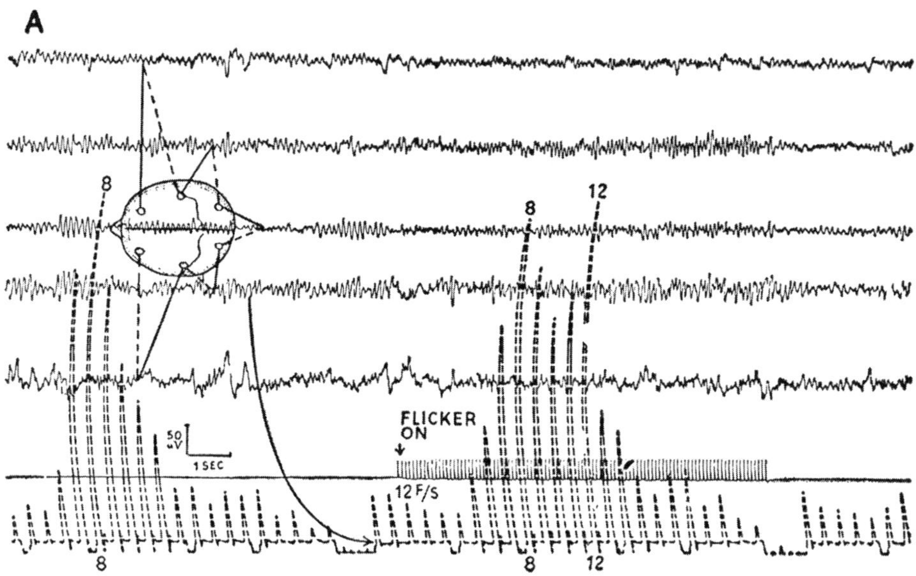

Figure 9. ". . . strange patterns, new and significant, emerged . . ." (a) The resting rhythm is at 8 c/s and flicker evokes another rhythm at 12 c/s.

Figure 6.10. W. Grey Walter, figure 9 from *The Living Brain* by W. Grey Walter.

lysis of brain waves by electroencephalograph and their manipulation via stroboscopic light (Figure 6.10).[74] The effects he described included not only those produced within strict laboratory conditions, but also the occasionally hypnotic impact of driving or bicycling past rows of regularly spaced trees at sunset (an experience that had occurred to Gysin in 1958) and a particularly bizarre case of susceptibility to normal film projection wherein "a man found that when he went to the cinema he would suddenly feel an irresistible impulse to strangle the person next to him."[75] The more normal and less dramatic effects Walter described were those reported as the experience of both *The Flicker* and the Dream Machine: "a sort of pulsating check or mosaic, often in bright colours. At certain frequencies – around 10 per second – some subjects see whirling spirals, whirlpools, explosions, Catherine wheels."[76] The roots of Walter's neurophysiological research lay in wartime investigations into radar and cybernetics, an influence that led him to understand the brain in analogy with electronic and informatic devices.[77] The alpha rhythm, in particular, was understood to manifest the operation of something like an internal "scanning mechanism":

> Put in this attenuated form, and given the proviso that the required mechanism has to be contained in the human head, a communications engineer would jump to the only conclusion which would seem possible to him: a scanning mechanism. The most familiar example of such mechanism is in television, where a space-pattern is most economically converted for transmission into a time sequence of impulses by the scanning mechanism of the camera.[78]

Walter's interest in flicker was far from aesthetic. He regarded the study of stroboscopic light as a means of gaining access not only to layers of neurophysiology, but more importantly, to hitherto unavailable aspects of subjectivity. According to Walter, brain waves are determinant of a wide range of subjective attributes: imagination, curiosity, adaptability, memory, emotions, affective states, and even desire, all of which were now to be not only chartable, but potentially available for harnessing and manipulation by means of flashing light.[79] It is almost certainly no coincidence that each of these formerly "private" attributes were to become central to the types of immaterial and affective, post-Fordist labor that began to emerge as the dominant forms of production at the same historical moment. Walter's stroboscopic research bespoke the passage from an industrial subject to an informatic one, wherein new realms of cognitive, perceptual, and affective forces could be cathected to capital.[80]

In spite of the futurism with which Walter generally imbued his research (as well as his science-fiction writings), the Dream Machine's inventors sought to counter the effect of neurophysiological regulation by recovering an outmoded technology.[81] As is evident in its earliest version, the Dream Machine is essentially a zoetrope – a nineteenth-century optical device for producing animation by viewing sequential images through the slots of a rotating cylinder – only modified so that, like a magic lantern or, more proximately, television, its main light source emanates from within. Like a zoetrope, the Dream Machine permitted unlimited interaction, allowing viewers to exceed normative regulation and enter states of fatigue approximating hypnosis or visual breakdown.[82] Later versions also allowed for modulation through multiple speeds, different layers of openings being calibrated to differing strobe rates. Deconditioning via such techniques was Burroughs's artistic ideal, and he saw it operating in much of Gysin's production. As he commented about Gysin's calligraphic paintings, "The viewer has to learn how to flicker back and forth between a telescopic and a microscopic point of view" or to discern "worlds . . . illuminated by each individual color."[83] The result, as with certain procedures Burroughs practiced in the street, was like "using an arbitrary preconceived scanning pattern, in order to break down automatic scanning patterns."[84]

Although the Dream Machine was an "induced experience," much like film and television, its aim was not to reinforce the norm, but rather to counter it.[85] "External resonators, such as flicker," Sommerville maintained, "tune in with our internal rhythms and lead to their extension."[86] As such, the Dream Machine paralleled the group's experiments with other media technologies in which processes such as tape recording were modulated to states beyond the norm. Speeding up, slowing down, inverting, or "inching" recorded words or phrases aimed to decondition imposed or inherited "association locks."[87] "If 'control,' or, as engineers say, negative feedback, is the key to power in this century," Friedrich Kittler writes about these experiments, "then fighting that power requires positive feedback. Create endless feedback loops until VHF or stereo, tape deck or scrambler, the whole array of world war army equipment produces wild oscillations."[88] For the circle around Burroughs, the Dream Machine figured as part of a wider tactical battle between emerging forces of perceptual and subjective regulation. "It's the opening of a whole new territory," Gysin explained, "which in a way is a threat to very many people who are using the same means for control or are using the same means to make great sums of money."[89] As a tool for counterconditioning, Gysin imagined the Dream Machine as destined for "every suburban home, in the spot formerly occupied by the television set."[90]

While the elementary viral unit, according to Burroughs, is the single compound of word and image, thought is characterized in analogy with cinema: "Like a moving film the flow of thought seems to be continuous while actually the thoughts flow stop change and flow again. At the point where one flow stops there is a split-second hiatus. The new way of thinking grows in this hiatus between thoughts."[91] Burroughs's "split-second hiatus" refers to the discontinuity of cinematic editing, the interstice between frames that allows for the imposition of a cut.[92] Whereas cinema normally utilizes the cut to produce continuity via unitary diegesis or more dialectical montage, Burroughs's interstice dissociates itself from the material on either side. It functions as what Deleuze termed an "irrational cut," opening to an "irreducible difference" or "fissure" between associations. Thus, it works like the Burroughsian cut-up to sever automatic connections and habitual associations. "It is not a matter of following a chain of images, even across voids," notes Deleuze, "but of getting out of the chain or the association." As he explains further,

> But cinema and mathematics are the same here: sometimes the cut, when called *rational*, forms part of one of the two sets which it separates (end of the one or beginning of the other), and this is the case with "classic" cinema. Sometimes, as in modern cinema, the cut has become the interstice; *it is irrational and does not form part of either set, one of which has no more an end than the other has a beginning.*[93]

For Burroughs, Gysin, and Sommerville, the Dream Machine was to bring about a "threshold experience," so exceeding perceptual norms and parcelizing habitual association lines as to open up a complex, variegated, and differential form of perception and, ultimately, thought that would effectively counter perceptual and ideological standardization. As Sommerville describes it:

> "Flicker" vision is a threshold experience produced by altering the speed of light to accommodate the maximum range of our *alpha* rhythms. "Flicker" creates a dazzling multiplicity of images in constantly altering relationships which makes the "collages" and "assemblages" of so-called "modern" art appear utterly ineffectual and slow. Art history as the enumeration of individual images ended with the direct introduction of light as the principal agent in the creation of images which have become infinitely multiple, complex and all-pervading. Art history has come to an end. Light writes in Space. Art is the tail of a comet. The comet is light.[94]

• • •

Conrad consulted Burroughs's article "Points of Distinction Between Sedative and Consciousness-expanding Drugs" while working out the preliminary strobe patterns for *The Flicker*.[95] In it, Burroughs argued that "anything that can be done chemically can be done in other ways, given sufficient knowledge of the mechanisms involved."[96] Although he did not mention the Dream

Machine, flicker—and in particular the work of Walter—served as his primary example of a nonchemical means of expanding consciousness. Although Conrad duly noted Burroughs's report, he had already encountered Walter's ideas directly in a neurophysiology course taken at Harvard.[97]

Derived from similar principles, *The Flicker* and the Dream Machine operate in similar ways. Like the Dream Machine, *The Flicker* primarily deploys the cut as an antirepresentational, disarticulating device. Thus, according to Deleuze, *The Flicker* helps usher in cinema's third epoch, one in which "the black or white screen stands for the outside of all the images, when the flickerings multiply the interstices like irrational cuts."[98] *The Flicker* also similarly allows for modulation through a variety of nonnormative perceptual states. This was to occur not only on the "horizontal" level of the film's running through different rhythms, but on a "vertical" one, as well, because Conrad structured the film's most complex patterns to provide up to three layers of photic driving, a factor he emphasized in all of his earliest discussions. Due to "the ambiguities of frequency, or of harmonic relationships," Conrad explained to Mussman,

> there are many patterns in the film which suggest alternative interpretations in terms of frequency. This ambiguity interests me because it allows you to see the film on a number of different levels .... Instead of a regular off-on pattern, one particular pattern can suggest up to three visual interpretations at the same time. The actual levels of interpretation are at this time rather obscure because we don't know exactly how the film affects the mind, which seems to be partly through the eye and partly through the brain. That is, the brain or eye can respond to one or more patterns at the same time.[99]

In the battle of emerging perceptual technologies that is both expanded cinema and control, *The Flicker* lined up alongside the Dream Machine. The aim was to induce an experience that was not only antinormative, but characterized by multiplicity and differentiation.

When, in 1966, Conrad discussed the aspect of *The Flicker* that Sitney would later characterize as its "shape," he specifically related it to the work of Jack Smith: "I want to stress," Conrad told Mussman, "that I was after a continuity, an overall unity of structure (something let's say like Jack Smith's coloristic formalism). I was not attempting to shock people or irritate them. I liked the idea of going from an absence or minimal sense of impression to one of a complete battering of the senses."[100] Conrad's reference to Smith's "coloristic formalism" – the coding of each sequence in *Normal Love* with a single, overriding tone (green for the Cobra Woman, pink for the giant cake sequence, etc.) – would seem to indicate that at stake in *The Flicker* was something akin to the goals of his former collaborator: the ability of a purely visual phenomenon, the flickering play of light and shadow, to overcome – resolutely and with magnificence, if one were particularly attuned to it – the limitations of what normally appears on the screen. Whereas in Smith's case, these limitations were understood to be those of conventional narrative, acting, and direction ("'good' plots," "good perfs," and "good film technique"), for Conrad, they were understood as abstract form: "One motive for *The Flicker*," he has explained recently, "was the idea that abstract art, barren in its elitist formalism, might be subverted by a wholly nonobjective film that would nevertheless function as a 'movie,' would transport the viewer psychically much as a narrative film does. In this regard *The Flicker* was to function less as an 'anti-film' film, and more as an 'anti-art' film."[101] The dialectic of structural film would thus seem to be modified, if not inverted. Instead of an intuited grasp of the film's overall shape or structure – a constant against which to judge the viewing experience – *The Flicker*'s "hallucinatory trip through unplumbed grottos of pure sensory disruption" sought, like Smith's work, to achieve a moment of transgression, something akin to Sommerville's "threshold experience."[102]

As when watching one of Smith's films, but now on a physiological rather than imaginary or even libidinal level, the audience of *The Flicker* was to be delivered to a realm of ecstatic, unique, and multiplicitous visions — a cinema of excess (not unrelated to the experience of drugs), different for each viewer on account of the particulars of their neurophysiology and different even for the same viewer on different occasions on account of the multiple registers on which the most complicated patterns were to be seen. From a Cagean perspective, *The Flicker* (with its strip of celluloid understood as a "score") was indeterminate with regard to reception.[103] As an entirely personal optical experience, uncontrollable and uncodifiable in advance (although experienced as part of a heterotopic community), Conrad's film could even be understood as an instance of Flynt's visual acognitive culture or visact. Indeed, in 1970, Flynt would incorporate flicker effects into his *Visual Composition*: "With eyes closed, look at bright sunlight. Spread the fingers of both hands. Wave — or actually, vibrate — the hands in front of the eyes so that the spread fingers cross rapidly. By varying the angle and speed of vibration, you should be able to obtain in succession many colors of the spectrum as well as shapes like piled-up boxes or Pueblo dwellings."[104] As though to counter the type of uniformity Burroughs and his associates feared, *The Flicker* connects the viewer to a counterhegemonic device that, like the Dream Machine, provides a different and ultimately unregulated pace, rhythm, temporality, and layering of perceptual stimuli, detourning or deterritorializing contemporary training and attentive norms.[105]

• • •

Conrad would invoke Smith's aesthetic even more explicitly in the little-known first version of his second film, *The Eye of Count Flickerstein* (1966–67; reedited and released in 1975). As in *The Flicker*, the reference to Smith's work appears most prevalently in the opening, both on account of the artisanal, hand-made production of the titles and in the allusion to the type of Hollywood horror movies to which *Normal Love* was devoted. Following an opening title card reading "Conrad Presents" comes a brief section of footage from *The Flicker*, keying the audience to the filmmaker's identity and priming them, perhaps, for visual effects similar to those of his earlier film. (The production of the two films was integrally related; Conrad had shot and had the footage for both developed at the same time.) Next appears a title card reading "The Eye of" held by the hand of an unidentified person who peers through the cut-out middle section of the "o" (Figure 6.11). Conrad zooms in on the eye in close-up before cutting to the final title card, hand lettered in a simultaneously psychedelic and mock-Gothic script, that reads "Count Flickerstein" (Figure 6.12). The film then cuts to an enigmatic shot of two people in a Lower East Side tenement apartment, followed by a shot of a man with a parrot on his shoulder. The horror-movie reference returns in the ensuing shot of the man in a classic vampire pose, his empty hand covering his face as though shielding it with a cape or collar (Figure 6.13). For a second time, Conrad moves in on the eye in close-up, at which point the film cuts to black leader and then to a streaming waterfall of static shot off of a television set at a ninety-degree angle to the camera. The remainder of the nearly ten-minute film, save for the "Count Flickerstein" title card that reappears as an end credit, is composed of several shots of streaming electrons beamed forth from the television's cathode-ray tube (Figure 6.14).

As Conrad's camera zooms for a second time in toward Count Flickerstein's "TV eye," it passes metaphorically into his brain, the "boiling swarm"[106] of static inside figuring as an image of cerebral processing. Such was, as we have seen, precisely the analogy proposed by Walter, who surmised that the alpha waves, so responsive to flickering light, indicate the presence of something akin to an automated mental scanning mechanism. In *The Living Brain*, Walter had gone on to characterize the hallucinatory effects of strobe upon the brain as the result of a type of interference:

> The interference of flicker with a normal process of scanning would be shown on a television screen by illuminating the television studio with a flickering light. The effect of this on the picture would be most unpleasant, indeed hard to bear; blobs of light would dart

> giddily about the screen. Similar confusion in the brain is seen in our records and toposcopic observations, when the conflict between the two time patterns, the inherent scanning rhythms of the brain, and the flicker, produce a brain storm as wild as any distortion on the television screen.[107]

It was, perhaps, something of the sort that Conrad sought to produce by setting the film camera, with its inherently intermittent mode of recording a visual image, against the continuous scanning mechanism of television's cathode-ray tube. Yet while the process involved in *The Eye of Count Flickerstein* does lead the otherwise homogeneous flow of televised static to waver, beat, or gently break apart in time to produce subtle abstract patterns and an ambiguous optical space, the result is rather decorative. Far from psychedelic pyrotechnics, the film's cascade of mildly spatial static achieves something like the cinematic equivalent of a Jules Olitski spray painting. Conrad initially considered it somewhat of a failure, dropping it from his filmography after a single screening.[108]

(Conrad's interest in what we might call reverse remediation – opposing or investigating a newer medium, such as television, by means of a supposedly "older" one, like film – would not, however, disappear. Once again confronting the underlying presuppositions of different media, in this case film and video, Conrad and his students at Antioch College produced *Film Feedback* [1974] via an elaborate procedure devised to process, project, and reshoot just-exposed film [Figures 6.15 and 6.16]. By running the exposed footage through trays of developer and of fixing solution in a darkened room and then under a door to a backlit screen that would be shot again from the darkened side of the partition, Conrad successfully, and with a certain comic effect, produced "feedback" – a visual *mise-en-abyme* of space and time – commonly understood as one of the medium-specific attributes of video.)

Some measure of Conrad's original intentions for *The Eye of Count Flickerstein* is perhaps given in an early note about the project: "FILM: Out-of-town TV station, with sound. Photograph

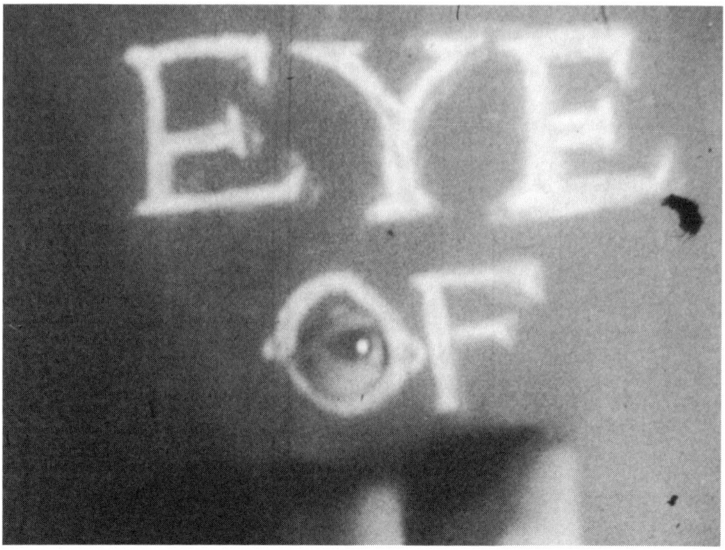

Figure 6.11. Tony Conrad, *The Eye of Count Flickerstein* (first version), 1966–67. 16 mm, black and white, sound, 9 min. 45 sec. Title sequence.

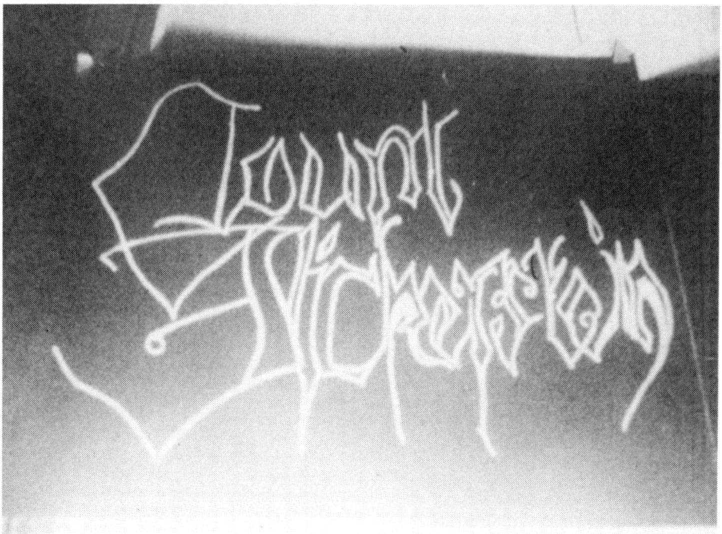

Figure 6.12. Tony Conrad, *The Eye of Count Flickerstein* (first version), 1966–67. Title sequence.

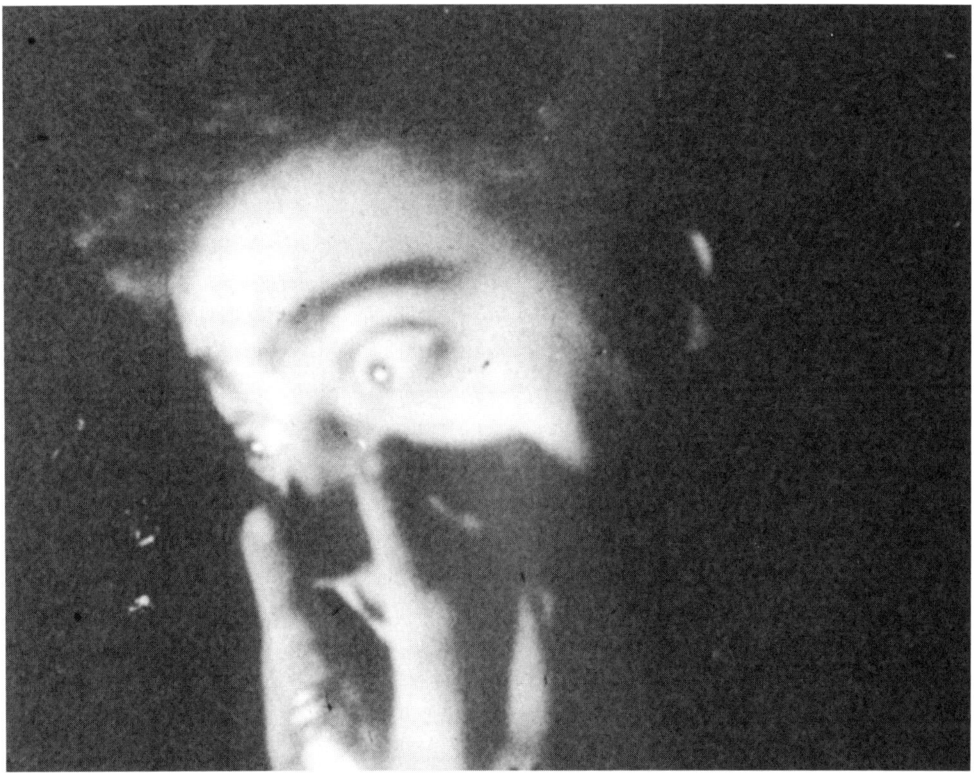

Figure 6.13. Tony Conrad, *The Eye of Count Flickerstein* (first version), 1966–67.

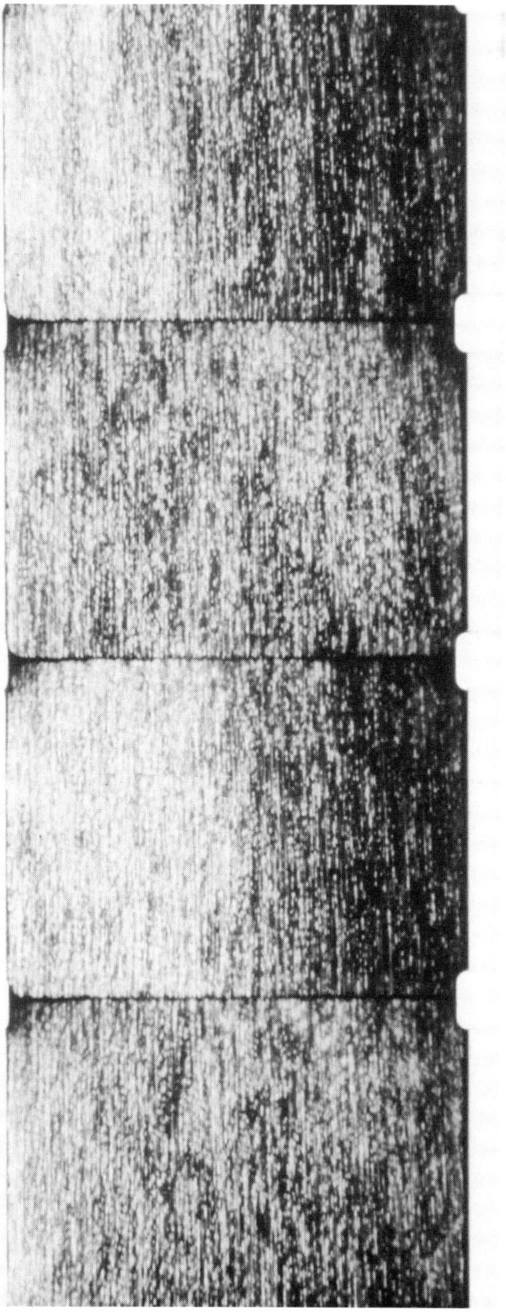

Figure 6.14. Tony Conrad, *The Eye of Count Flickerstein* (first version), 1966–67.

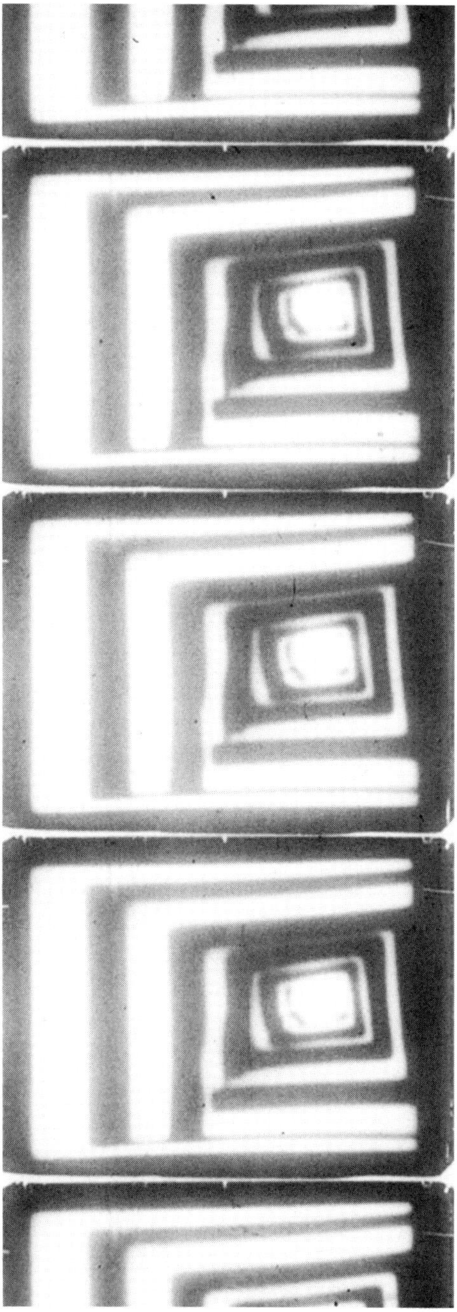

Figure 6.15. Tony Conrad, *Film Feedback*, 1974. 16 mm, black and white, silent, 14 min.

FILM FEEDBACK PRODUCTION DIAGRAM

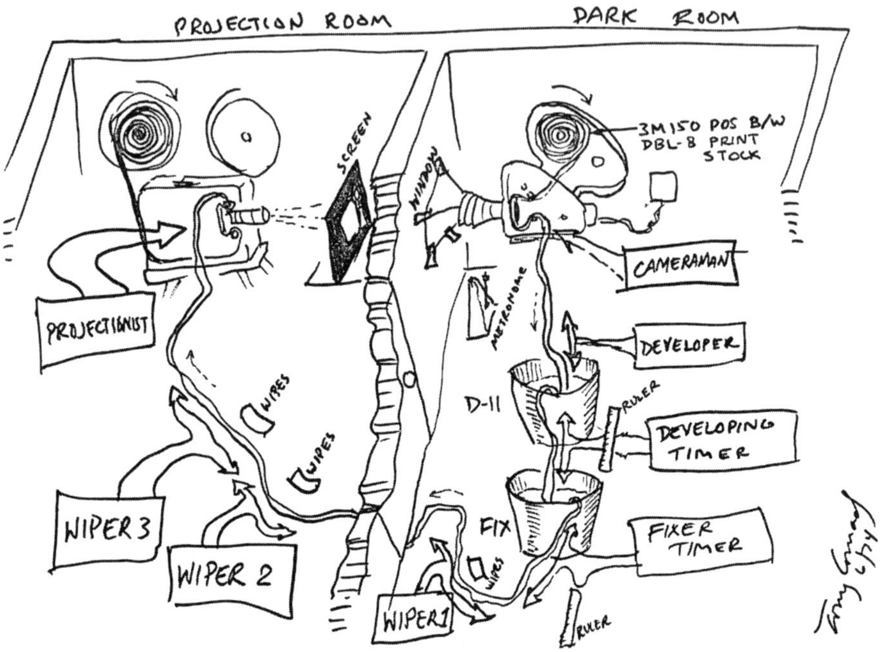

Figure 6.16. Tony Conrad, *Film Feedback* production diagram, June, 1974. Courtesy Tony Conrad.

sideways, to destroy 'TV' appearance."[109] In the manner in which Conrad pitted film against television (not to "alter" or "modify," but to "destroy"), *The Eye of Count Flickerstein* continued a polemic that had already been characterized in Smith's "The Perfect Filmic Appositeness of Maria Montez." There, Smith had described the manner in which Montez films, when sold to and shown on television, were submitted to rather violent aesthetic and commercial constraints. "All are now safe from Maria Montez outrages!" Smith wrote:

> I suppose the color prints are destroyed now. Still, up until about 5 yrs. ago (when they were bought up by T.V.), Montez reissues cropped up at tiny nabes [neighborhood movie theaters] — every week one or another of them played somewhere in N.Y.C. At that time they were 12 to 17 years old. When they are shown now on T.V. they are badly chopped up, with large chunks missing. The pattern being repeated — their irresistibility resulting in their being cut & stabbed & punished. All are now safe from Montez embarrassment — the tiny nabes are torn down, didn't even make supermarkets — the big nabes have to get back investments so can't be asked (who'd ask) to show them.[110]

In order to profit from the Montez films, to guarantee a return on the purchase or investment, they had to be shorn of their "embarrassing" visual excess. TV here functions as a metonym or harbinger of the restricted economy that the multiplicitous, heterotopic visuals of Smith's cinema (and Montez's original films before it) were to transgress. The confrontation figured in *The Eye of Count Flickerstein*, therefore, goes beyond that of merely two different media (television and film) to figure as an opposition of two distinct socioeconomic regimes: restricted and general economy.[111] Though perhaps unsuccessful as an agent of perceptual transgression, *The Eye of Count Flickerstein* may nonetheless be seen as an indicator or chart of the terrain within which *The Flicker*, and with it what Deleuze termed the third epoch of cinema, emerged: where new technological means (from the electronic eye of television to the multiscreen corporate pavilions of the World's Fair) brought forth new modes of bodily enervation and new realms of micropolitical subjection.[112]

• • •

As previously mentioned, the locus of this micropolitical confrontation, the place in which *The Flicker* operated, was the viewing subject, functioning in some uncertain manner between eye, brain, and central nervous system. Conrad's interest in producing effects directly within the body, however, antedated *The Flicker*, initially arising within the acoustic sphere with an instrument or "composition" called *String Loop* (1962). In it, the performer runs a length of string from a point on the floor in front of him or her around the head and across both ears, over which have been placed a pair of sound-transmitting "pegs." The resulting loop—tied with a nooselike sliding knot that allowed it to be adjusted from just under the chin all the way to the floor—was to be played in a manner only the performer would be able to hear, because the sound was channeled in stereo directly into the ears:

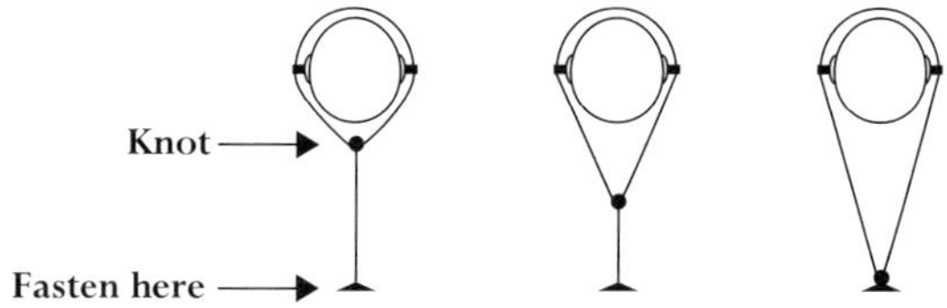

> Bow on either leg of the loop, on the strand to fixed point, or on knot. Make knot adjustable as shown. Vary string tightness using pressure of back of head and bow pressure. Bow using various techniques—fast, very slow, sideways, etc.[113]

The goal of propagating sound waves directly into the body would prove an oddly persistent one for Conrad. It would recur in 1968 in the guise of *Ear String*, a "stereo ear instrument" in which a cord tied between two drumsticklike or chopsticklike lengths of wood held to the performer's ears would be set to vibrate by being plucked or blown across, rather than bowed.[114] Four years earlier, Conrad had pursued a not dissimilar effect with *Ear Glasses* (1964), in which glass tumblers held over the ears (rather than pegs or sticks on them) would propagate acoustical resonances directly into the auditory canals. The tumblers, according to Conrad, could potentially also be fitted out with microphones to capture and rebroadcast the resonant harmonics:

> Experiment with moving glasses in relation to ears & sound. Try hands &c also, as well as other shapes of resonators (e.g. bowls). Try putting the mikes in the resonators into a P.A. system, to test for resonance frequency of the resonator in various positions. [*Also* try feedback effects.] Then try producing various pitches to locate the resonant frequency. With higher P.A. gain, it should be possible to adjust the pitch of the resonance-induced feedback tones – in effect, to play on them – by changing the position of the resonator or mike.[115]

These seemingly idiosyncratic compositions, instruments, or techniques (however one might conceive them) foreshadow *The Flicker*, not only in the investigation of stereophonic (and therefore spatial) audio effects, as employed in *The Flicker*'s sound track, but also in the production of these effects within the listener's physiology (as would occur more clearly in *The Flicker* on the visual, rather than on the acoustical register). It was thus perhaps not coincidental that Conrad's thoughts turned back to *String Loop* on the day *The Flicker* was previewed at the Cinematheque. A notebook entry made on the same date (December 14, 1965) records Conrad's proposal for a "Happening": "Stereo string loops over everyones [sic] ears & from all the ears into a knot, which could be fastened to a sound source or otherwise made to vibrate."[116] Wired to a giant apparatus by which stimuli would be propagated directly into their bodies, the audience of Conrad's "happening" would be structurally identical to that of his "film."

Eventually, Conrad would develop the technique initially devised for *String Loop* into *Bowed Film* (1974), a paracinematic work in which the same nooselike loop is attached to the floor, run around the ears, and played with a violin bow (Figure 6.17). In place of string, however, Conrad substituted a strip of film that (self-reflexively) depicted on each of the "legs" of the loop "a pan [shot] of a bow, as long as the bow."[117] The representation of the bow not only served as the film's iconic content, but transformed the strip of celluloid into a "score" – a visual instruction as to how the piece was to be performed. As with *String Loop*, *Bowed Film* generated a hermetic, private performance in which only the instrumentalist heard the stereophonic sound and saw the stereoscopic imagery (the filmstrip being projected onto the eyes by means of the ambient, flickering light of a movie projector). The result, for the performer, was composed of "the vibration of the strip, the intermittent interchange among the frames, the full-dynamic-range high fidelity live stereo sound track, [and] the kaleidoscopic reflections of the filmstrip back and forth across the angle of the noose knot."[118]

Conrad discussed *Bowed Film* at some length in "INTEGER: Bulldozing a foundation in the culturescape of sound, media, and performance," an article devoted to the possibilities of categorizing *asignifying* sounds and images that nonetheless achieve somatic impacts – stimuli that affect the different senses and even the internal pulsations of desire. In it, Conrad proposed a type of bastard semiology addressed to the "integrative" sensory functions prior to or outside language and any other conventional signifying system, the components of which were to be termed (in analogy with the semiotic categories of signifier, signified, and sign) "integratus," "integrandus," and "integer."[119] According to Conrad, the necessity for such an investigation into modes of "recognition without signification" arose in order to come to terms critically with the path beyond Cage taken by the Theatre of Eternal Music as he understood it: an abandoning of the era of scores (even indeterminate ones) for one of more direct acoustical manipulations.

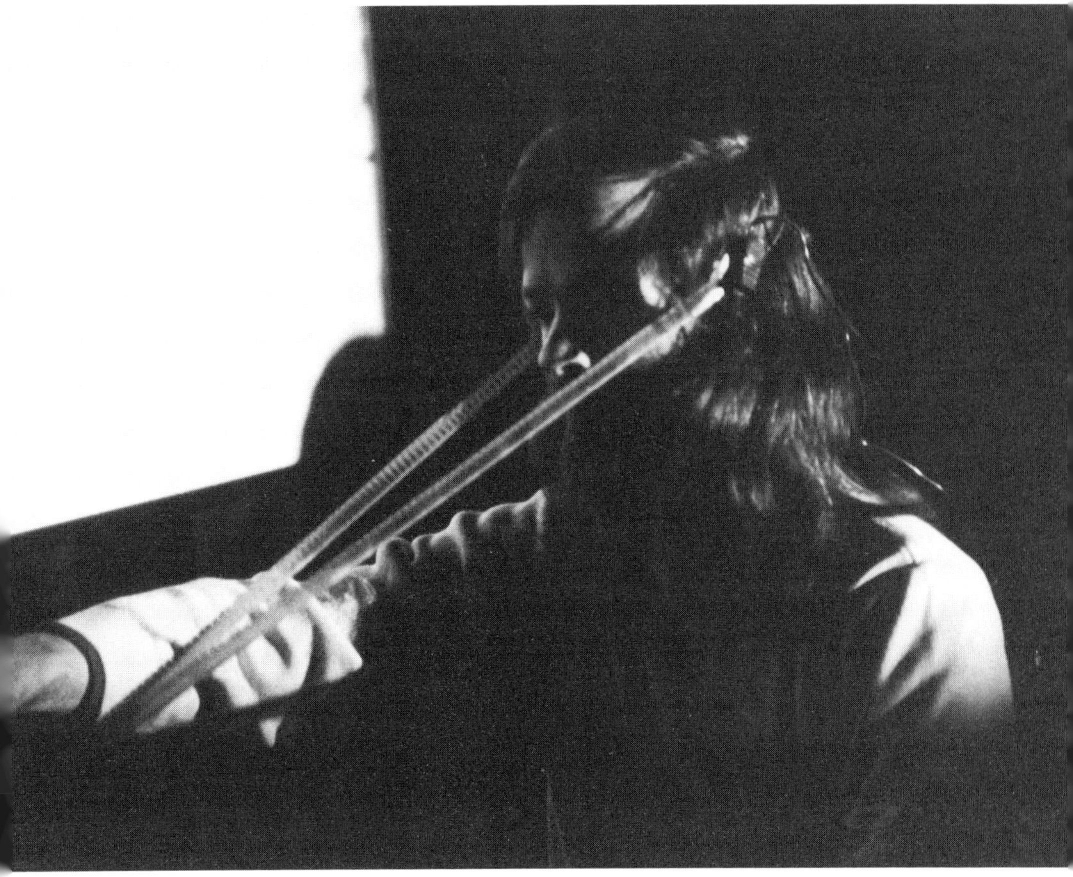

Figure 6.17. Tony Conrad, *Bowed Film*, 1974. Performed at Berks Film-Makers' Cooperative, Reading, Pennsylvania, 1976. Photo: Linda Adlestein, used by permission.

> John Cage's extension of the modernist understanding of composition during the 1950's posed a crisis for composers; the activity of composition was resituated to the critical level, and the esthetics of the listening experience was recast as a kind of split-level exercise in attentiveness: on the one hand, chance methods suggested to the listener that affect and music must bear a strictly relativistic relation to one another, putting audience responsibility at an all-time high level. On the other hand, the listener was authorized to take the work entirely at the value of its strategic or critical practice, and to ignore the sound altogether [the path taken by concept art]. The response of the author and of others attentive to this situation was to shift composition as an activity strongly in the direction of the integratus, the *sound.*[120]

Sound, as Conrad goes on to clarify, was to be approached as acoustic *material*, rather than and in place of traditional symbolic counters: "In the course of a collaboration begun in 1962 with La Monte Young," writes Conrad, "the author was one of a small circle of composers to renounce the score and supplant it by the integratus, the perceptual material of sound."[121]

Bowed Film was to push cinema into a position analogous to post-Cagean composition. Conrad's intention was thus to separate the perceptual experience (had by the filmmaker/performer alone) from the critical or analytic one to which the audience (deprived of both cinematic images and performed sound track) now had recourse. The filmmaker/performer serves here as:

> a surrogate for the audience, which is unexpectedly excluded from the sights, the sounds, the kinetic expression, and the integrative synthesis among these components, that construct—at the moment of performance—that which the film is to *appear to be*. . . . Under circumstances like these, the audience is defined only by its social setting; but it intersects at the same time a province of exclusion which calls the audience's own identity into question.

The resultant condition, in which the audience is thrown back onto itself (a variant of the "social turn" pioneered in certain of Young's word scores), can be resolved only by recourse to a different interpretive register: "the system of absences, which a witness discovers, can only be resectioned, to reform a unitary response, through the audience's resort to a meta-integrative *guesswork*: a performance [on the audience's part] which comprises a complementarity to the performance of the work itself."[122]

Bowed Film would prove one of Conrad's most intriguing and multifaceted interventions into the discourse surrounding structural and structural/materialist film — a discourse that, by the 1970s, had largely been assimilated into a modernist (even neo-Greenbergian) position that Conrad sought to pitch into its endgame. Here, however, we are interested less in the audience's critical compensation for the particular (non)impact of *Bowed Film* upon it than in the peculiarly hermetic impact that it has upon the performer. Whereas the audience finds itself thrust back upon metacritical description and guesswork, the cinematic spectacle properly speaking takes place upon a screen now literally become the performer/spectator's eyes, while the sound resonates through what seems to be the center of the brain. Much the same pertained to *String Loop*. There, however, the performer/listener was instructed to shut his or her eyes while both ears were blocked up by the sound-transmitting pegs, a circumstance that betrays the work's genealogical relation to Cagean silence and, perhaps more specifically, to Flynt's 1961 *Audart Composition*, in which one closes one's eyes and places one's fingers in one's ears to experience the sights and sounds of one's own physiology. As Cage had realized within Harvard's anechoic chamber and Flynt in his darkened Harvard dorm room, in the absence of outside sounds, "so-called silence" resounds with the noise of one's central nervous system and circulating blood. Whereas for Cage this led to an opening of the subject ("the splits, subject-object . . . disappear, an identification has been made with the material"), the goal of Flynt's composition was very close to that of Le Grice's materialist cinema: achieving a conscious, apperceptive grasp of one's perceptual and even autonomic processes.[123] This Flynt explained carefully: "Try to have maximum awareness of both sounds until the low one [the sound of blood circulating] becomes difficult to hear. Then concentrate on the high one [the sound of the nervous system], being aware that it is the sound of oneself listening to it (and of oneself being aware that it is the sound of oneself listening to it)."[124] From the perspective of Flynt's acognitive culture, the experience led to the valorization of one's own "just likings," inviolable manifestations of subjective autonomy.

The performer of *String Loop*, by contrast, finds himself or herself opened to "external" stimuli (the sounds of the resonating string), which are nonetheless received as though indistinguishable from those produced by his or her own physiology. With the reverberating string playing in (or out of) tune with the ringing in one's ears, internal and external sounds become entwined, if not indistinguishable. An identification is made with the material such that the listener's "inside" and "outside" relate to each other as a topological membrane; the human subject is interconnected with another apparatus, positioned as merely one point or node within a larger feedback mechanism (a factor made explicit in Conrad's discussion of *Ear Glasses*). Stereophonically situated between *String Loop*'s two pegs, the performer/listener inhabits a virtual environment defined and determined by an acoustical simulation of spatiality. In pursuing this effect, the resemblance of *String Loop* to stereo headphones is not fortuitous, for it functions in a way that is structurally and experientially identical to the endpoint of that paradigm Friedrich Kittler has defined as "media":

> An unimaginable closeness of sound technology and self-awareness, a simulacrum of a feedback loop relaying sender and receiver. A song sings to a listening ear, telling it to sing. As if the music were originating in the brain itself, rather than emanating from stereo speakers or headphones.
>
> That is the whole difference between arts and media. Songs, arias, and operas do not rely on neurophysiology. Voices hardly

> implode in our ears, not even under the technical conditions of a concert hall, when singers are visible and therefore discernible. For that reason their voices have been trained to overcome distances and space. The "sound of music in my ear" can exist only once mouthpieces and microphones are capable of recording any whisper. As if there were no distance between the recorded voice and listening ears, as if voices traveled along the transmitting bones of acoustic self-perception directly from the mouth into the ear's labyrinth, hallucinations become real.[125]

With the sound of *String Loop* propagated though the pegs directly into the ears, Conrad had no need of the electronics he would nonetheless soon incorporate into *Ear Glasses*. However, *String Loop* must be understood within the same paradigm as any hi-fi stereo system, one in which media technologies allow the "extension and intensification of micro-powers."[126] Is it coincidence that Terry Riley – who would go on, even more extensively, to investigate the mediamatic processes of feedback and tape delay – was drawn to the same startlingly odd idea for a composition at the same historical moment? Drawing upon the amplified frictional improvisations he and Young had performed in California, Riley's *Ear Piece* (ca. 1961) instructs that "the performer takes any object(s) such as a piece of paper cardboard plastic etc and places it on his ear(s)" and "then produces the sound by rubbing scratching tapping or tearing it or simply dragging it across his ear."[127] In both *Ear Piece* and *String Loop*, the distance that still inhered between listener and sound in the almost agonistic relationship described by Young in "Lecture 1960" would be collapsed into symbiotic interaction. The listener is now not only "inside" the sound, the sound is "inside" the listener. Henceforth, *2 Sounds* would take place in the center of the brain. In 1964, Conrad would even rewrite and respond to Young's *Composition 1960 #7* in a manner that pushed it into the realm of media and physioacoustics. In a small word piece, *Loop*, Conrad proposed a tape loop of a "simple emotive sound" infinitely repeated (Figure 6.18).

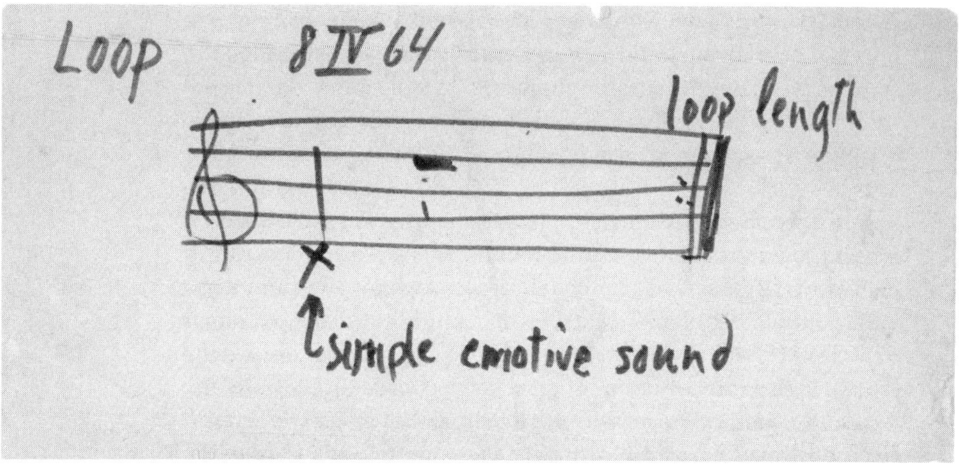

Figure 6.18. Tony Conrad, *Loop*, April 8, 1964. Courtesy Tony Conrad.

• • •

As Young would come to understand it, the music he produced, beginning in the Theatre of Eternal Music, would operate directly upon the listener's neurophysiology. Drawing on concepts associated with Indian modal music and ideas put forth in the pages of the *Psychedelic Review* by musicologist Alain Daniélou, Young regarded harmonics produced in just intonation as directly generative of, indeed ultimately identical to, internal affective states.[128] "There is evidence," he told Richard Kostelanetz, "that each time a particular frequency is repeated it is transmitted through the same parts of our auditory system. When these frequencies are continuous, as in my music, we can conceive even more easily how, if part of our circuitry is performing the same operation continuously, this could be considered to be or to simulate a psychological state."[129] The result, as developed in Young and Marian Zazeela's Dream Houses or "frequency environments" was what Young referred to as a "drone state in the nervous system, establishing periodic patterns which are the internal representations of the external air molecule patterns vibrating the eardrums and sending pulses throughout the nervous system in these periodic relationships."[130] The result is a type of affective programming, explicitly conceived on the model of information technology. "Through this system" of just intonation, Young noted, "we can, first, catalogue each feeling with its corresponding rational number, and then actually create, store, retrieve and, finally and most importantly, repeat the feeling, relative to the musician's ability to tune the intervals."[131] The "human mechanism" becomes a "recording organism."[132] "Finally, by this precise control of the total harmonic structure of my music, I can attain the ultimate goal, which is to have a more precise control over the nature of the psychological state that the music produces in the listeners."[133]

For Conrad, as well, the resounding frequency environments that the Theatre of Eternal Music produced had an effect of subjective reprogramming. This was not, however, according to Conrad, a result of the unity of harmonic ratios, affective states, and cosmic truth, but a function of a perceptual retraining effected by the group's alternate tuning system, one ultimately tied not simply to the mathematical ratios of just intonation, but to the resonant frequency of the electrical grid. The "second dream" of the Theatre of Eternal Music, the one brought to it by Conrad, was that of "the high-tension line step-down transformer."[134]

The Dream Syndicate's evolution was bound to electronics and electronic media. Their particular development of just intonation, in which performers were conscious of and interacted with a variety of harmonic partials and the sum tones and difference tones produced by their interaction, was all but impossible without microphone pickups and electronic amplification to make them audible (not to mention recording and storage of the results on magnetic tape). As Conrad commented in "Inside the Dream Syndicate," "Ours is the first generation with tape, with proper amplification to break down the dictatorial sonority barriers erected by the master instruments of the cultures. It is no longer necessary to press upon groaning mechanical instrumentation to produce the terrific power and sonority necessary for dealing with partial complexity and without shattering the all important sound — the throbbing reverberance that has fixed musical attention on consonance and formal design."[135]

In order to perfect such an exacting acoustical consonance (and to neutralize interference produced by the amplification system itself), the group began tuning to the frequency of the electrical current coming out of the wall and its resonances within electronic mechanisms such as the engine running the aerators in the tank of Young and Zazeela's pet turtle (ultimately dubbed, as an instrument, the "turtle motor"). Thus, as Conrad noted in "Inside the Dream Syndicate," the "high harmonic-content timbre complexes" adopted and manipulated by the group had been suggested by "machines." As he explained further:

> Alternating current is pouring into this building; we only alter, modify, store and use it as our energies direct. We treat it with the respect of machines for the source of all power, and it gives us the

> 6th partial of our Tonic, 10 c.p.s. It is in the air. Outside the domain of 60 cycle current, our music will fall less resonantly on the city ear, the most tonal of all cultures. This strikes true reflection in the rhythms of the deserted shore. After the years pass, we fail to have consciousness of the changes: the voices sound like something else, the violin is the echo of the saxophone, the viola is by day frightening rock 'n roll orchestras, by night the sawmill. The necessary changes have occurred.[136]

In this passage, Conrad presents the conditioning relationship between sound and the human subject not as a one-to-one correspondence of affect and acoustical vibration, but as a form of perceptual retraining mastered and accommodated gradually via habit. After years of almost daily practice, those within the group have assimilated the alterations to their perceptual habituation to a degree such that they are no longer conscious of the effects.[137]

Repeatedly throughout his career, Conrad has commented on the defining relation between media technologies (from amplified instruments to video monitors) and the underlying pulse of electric current, perhaps nowhere more extensively than in "On 60 Cycles," a text written for a Rhys Chatham program of music and video that is worth quoting at length:

> All we do is take 60 cycle power out of the wall and do different things with it to the purposes of our own gratification. "There are a few isolated cases of other frequencies. For example, in southern California the frequency of 50 cps was in general use, but the 60-cycle power that is transmitted from Hoover Dam has necessitated changing a large proportion of the power systems to this frequency.... the Interborough Rapid Transit in New York and the Metropolitan Transit Authority in Boston...operate at 25 cps. For most power purposes, however, the frequency of 60 cps is quite satisfactory. Moreover, incandescent lamps when operated at 25 cps have a distinct flicker which is not noticeable at 60 cps." But the true tonic of our social lives, though it does lie above fusion, has been pointedly handed down to us principally through the

> primary machinations of the primitive machines. 60 cycles is a compromise between the desires of motors and transformers and the reactance of long-line power transmission. Throughout our lives we hear with unresponsive insouciance the groans of the machines, ineffectively complaining on the long electromechanical wave band of their 60 cycle burden. Their wavelength is buried down there with the whistlers; one wave spans our continent. The revenge is simple: 60 cycles is the ideal killer frequency for biochemical lifeforms....
>
> There is another way to tune in to 60 cycles. Keep the power away from you by transmitting it though the air. Use your ears as transducers. Convert from analog to digital. Join the most constant universal life event on our continent. Hum at 60 cycles, way down at the end of the Fletcher-Munson curve. Slip in between the molecules in the body and learn about being a clock....
>
> There truly is such a thing as perfect pitch, both alive and in the legendary dead ears of such as Mozart.... The least precocious child alive today can hardly miss 60 cycles... the largest, most careful melody ever played. 60 cycles is pumping and surging all about the heart of the civilization.... with [my] ear pointing in the right direction, it will hear far far past the future, into the current of the living present.[138]

Whether or not one responds consciously to the machines' moaning—as did the Dream Syndicate, humming or playing along with their resonant drones—the frequency of electric current, Conrad suggests, functions as a metonym of a larger realm of micropolitical perceptual regulation, not only resonating along with the ringing in one's ears, but also setting the indiscernible, flickering pulse of artificially illuminated vision.[139] Thus are "the molecules of the body" infiltrated by a constant ambient regulation.

In 1965, Conrad's invocation of electricity was by no means eccentric within the context of avant-garde music. It was at precisely the same moment that John Cage, long interested in electronic music, began to speak explicitly about the electrical grid and other utilities (gas, water, telephone) that span the North American continent. For Cage, who would prove increasingly susceptible to the technocratic influence of Buckminster Fuller, such utilities — because they are not, from Cage's perspective, hierarchically imposed forms — function in an inherently neutral manner, free from and even opposed to government and politics (i.e., the structures of sovereign power). "Divisiveness is being weakened by technology," he noted: "Electrical power, by means of new dielectrics permitting 1,500-mile radius of transmission, now exceeds national boundaries."[140] "Do not fear that as the globe gets utility organized your daily life will not remain (or become as the case may be) disorganized, characterized by chaos, illuminated anarchically."[141] Although Cage understood and indeed explicitly commented on the capacity of electronics to alter physiological systems (as in forms of shock treatment), he considered its effect inherently indeterminate and thus salutary: "Russian chickens had diseased muscles. Chemical therapies failed. Suddenly, the chickens were healthy. The muscular tissues'd been reduced to chaos, disorganized by electrical means."[142]

Cage's discussion of utilities once again betrayed his ultimate incapacity or utopian refusal to come to terms with modes of power that operate in anything other than sovereign form. Nevertheless, his attention to networks that operate across expanses as vast as the continent might itself be considered symptomatic of the emergence of a society of control wherein both the hierarchical towers of sovereign authority and the discrete institutions of disciplinary regimes were increasingly being outflanked, surrounded, passed through, and reconditioned by more deterritorialized systems of "distribution and regulation."[143] What Cage foresaw as the topography resulting from the evisceration of such structures (neither of which, of course, collapsed entirely, since both were redeployed and potentially even revivified as archaisms with a contemporary function) was an entirely smooth, focusless, but differentiated field.[144]

By contrast, Conrad's discussion of electrical current, the "one wave [that] spans our continent," opens onto a realm of power relations in which the forces of micropolitical regulation operate wholly on an immanent plane. Although still engaged in the production of a certain set of harmonics in a bodily, even disciplinary manner, the performer is not, from Conrad's perspective, subsumed beneath a hierarchical, transcendent ideal (as seemed to be the case within Young's conception), but rather plugged laterally into a modulating, regulating force communicated via a network that operates continuously across a continental expanse. Such regulation does not press down upon subjects in a sovereign manner or lord over them as an ideal, disciplinary goal so much as it passes through them within an articulated feedback loop, the forces of which (whether electrical current or the resonance of a vibrating string) do not limit themselves to the contours of the individual body, but fold out into larger virtual apparatuses or machinic assemblages. If, from Young's perspective, the Theatre of Eternal Music can be understood to lie on the border between sovereign ideal and disciplinary practice, from Conrad's, it would seem to operate between the disciplined body and the regulating feedback circuits of control.

Within the context of his later work in film and, particularly, video, Conrad would explicitly critique and oppose the artist's dependence on the corporate interests behind both the utilities and the mechanisms through which they operate:

> A large corporation manufactures a monitor. Another manufactures the energy that comes out of the wall. Plug it in. Inefficiently, it pumps a stream of electrons onto a phosphor plate, and you sit and watch it.... The meditative experience of slow change is hard to reach for when creation happens out at the end of the long string of electronic identities. Then it is time to take the manufacturing process out of the hands of the big corporations and sit inside of the monitor the creator builds himself.[145]

Although a certain amount of anticorporate sentiment was already at play in the mid-1960s (as in Conrad's intervention at the New York Film Festival at Lincoln Center), Conrad's earliest discussions of electrical current relate to it as something like a media or technological unconscious.[146] Amplified so as to create an enveloping acoustical environment, the normally unnoted hum of electrical machinery and the complex mosaic of harmonics built upon it become within the Dream Syndicate a vast and unsuspected realm within which perceptual habits and expectations are gradually transformed. According to Walter Benjamin, such an accommodation to technologically engendered perceptual milieux contained an inherently utopian potential; adaptation to higher technological orders entails an implicit promise of liberation, the possibility of which the subject would not only be able to glimpse, but would make into a political demand.[147] There is little evidence within Conrad's statements of the time that he harbored any such conception (which proves closer to Cage's utopianism). Nevertheless, like Young, Conrad did seem to regard the practice of the Dream Syndicate as a counterhegemonic one, a counter-conduct opposed to the dominant cultural codification of sound as represented by Western harmony: "The crashing howl of possibilities at last here at the end of a wire are wiping the orchestras slowly from substantial earthing into the swamp of eclecticism. No ill wishes to them; all we could ask of the embodiment of their institutional ramparts, their reviewers, is that they deal our independence impartial tones synchronous with the steady flow of communicant response they will find in brushing against the tortoise."[148]

Part of what separated the Theatre of Eternal Music from conventional orchestras was the potentially unlimited number of pitches that could be derived from their just-intonation "scale" of 3s and 7s. As Young explained to Kostelanetz,

> I haven't taken a count; but just glancing over at Tony Conrad's chart on the wall here, I can see, roughly, in *O*-tonalities we have used about twenty-seven frequencies to the octave, which is more than double the number used in the twelve-note system. Of course, there is no limit upon the number we can eventually squeeze into an octave, because we don't necessarily hear them as one coming after another,

> filling up an octave. We hear them as various relationships to a pitch we have established very clearly in our ears and minds. We approach each new pitch, which then provides another identification point in an octave, from some very simply established interval. That is, every new pitch very simply relates to the previous point of departure.[149]

As the group continued to practice and evolve, they derived ever new harmonic ratios, each one more exotic and less connected to the habitual Western scale: a collaborative process that progressively (though at the pace of the tortoise invoked in their titles) differentiated itself from the hegemony of Western tuning and its perceptual training, moving ever farther away on a line of escape. As Young put it, "We can go on infinitely in one dimension with these numbers."[150]

The Flicker does something analogous. Predicated on the surreptitious flicker of alternating current and the rhythm of the projector shutter (both of which it brings into consciousness), it envelops the audience within an overriding sensory environment in order to lead them to a counterhegemonic perceptual experience. *The Flicker* differs from the Theatre of Eternal Music, however, as we have seen, in one important way. Although partly based on the notion of stasis or static form developed within the group, *The Flicker* sought to bring the audience into a transgressive and indeterminate threshold experience, one that, in the final instance, was uncontrolled, even though induced by interaction with an external resonator — less a line of flight than a transgressive, heterotopic encounter with the outside, an instance of positive feedback that induces wild perceptual oscillations.

• • •

In 1969, *The Flicker* entered the laboratory, when an enterprising New York University student, Jetta Bernier, utilized Conrad's film — minus the title sequence, but with sound track intact — for a clinical psychology study entitled "The Flicker Phenomenon."[151] Bernier subjected forty-four introductory psychology students (twenty-three female, twenty-one male) to the experience one at a time, showing the film to them individually in a small room with the projector "covered by a screen to prevent any examination of the reel by the subjects." Each of the test subject's reactions were then recorded by means of a twenty-four-part questionnaire, a somewhat imperfect method, given the results Bernier hoped to find. Information solicited included a general description of the perceptual experience; listing the number, type, sequence, and combination of colors seen, if any; and calculating the level of tenseness or relaxation. The final question was simply, "Do you wish you had never seen the film?" (Five respondents answered yes.) Test subjects were also asked to plot their "predominant reaction to the film" as a line graph in relation to time.

Respondents reported seeing no colors at all to seeing as many as six in combinations of up to three at a time, as well as perceiving forms and patterns – amorphous forms, simple geometric and nongeometric forms, simple or complex geometric patterns, and so on. More hallucinatory perceptions included seeing various types of insects (fly, roach, beetle), a large eye that rolled its pupil, and even "a lady and boy in garb of old frontier, standing by a stream, apart from a wagon train." Bernier's goal was to study the viewers' physiological and affective responses and particularly the film's potential "power of addition." Respondents were asked to rate their affective reactions from "pleasant" to "exciting" to "relaxed" to "tense." Although many found the experience rather calming, a number expressed a marked fear of potentially controlling effects: "fear of becoming hypnotized," a "mesmerized effect" – one subject declared, "I thought that if I really got into it I would eventually black out or fall asleep." Bernier rendered all of the responses into a set of forty-two numerical variables, computerized the information, submitted it to chi square and elementary linkage analysis, and sought its correlation into various interrelated "syndromes."

Bernier's project was no doubt inspired by her advisor, Arnold M. Mordkoff, who corresponded with Conrad about the results. Mordkoff, while a researcher at the University of California,

Berkeley, had helped pioneer the use of a motion picture in the study of physiological and psychological stress.[152] A few years earlier, he and his associates, most notably Richard S. Lazarus, had conducted a much larger and more sophisticated series of experiments on the "psychological and autonomic effects of a motion picture stressor."[153] In that study, which gave rise to several papers, the "stressor film" was the silent documentary *Subincision*, by Hungarian-born ethnologist and psychoanalyst Géza Róheim (a former associate of Sandor Rado and fellow student with him of Sandor Ferenczi), which depicted a ritual scarification procedure carried out with a sharpened piece of flint on the penis and scrotum of adolescent males of the Aranda (Arunta) people of Central Australia.[154] (The "control film" was *Corn Farming in Iowa*.) *Subincision* had previously been used as the basis of empirical studies of psychoanalytic theories of the castration complex.[155] The goal of the Berkeley experiments, conducted on both undergraduate psychology students and a group of "middle-level airline executives,"[156] was to access psychophysiological stress levels as betrayed by increasingly sophisticated technological means of monitoring subjects' heart rates and galvanic skin reflex (GSR) (two of the three primary autonomic indicators utilized by lie detectors). According to the researchers, the motion picture was valuable precisely for its interpellative effect, the fact that it causes viewers to identify with events taking place on screen: "Despite the fact that the subjects are in no way physically involved in the procedures, nor are they required to perform during the film, stress is produced through the mediation of psychological process related to the meaning of the stimulus events."[157]

The Berkeley group performed separate studies to attempt to evaluate the effects of "film-produced disturbance" on different personality types and to test the "ego-defense theory" of stress reduction (adding, in one study, different sound tracks, which would either point up or play down the discomfiting events on screen).[158] The most conclusive findings, however, were largely methodological. As primarily reported in "The Relationship Between Autonomic Indicators of Psychological Stress," Mordkoff and his senior associates argued that it was unsatisfactory for their purposes to approach the effects of stress on the level of the individual, as a reaction conveyed verbally by a subject to the event as a whole. Satisfactory experiential correlations between the stressor film's impact and the subject's response were obtained only by charting autonomic responses as they fluctuated temporally and only as they occurred "within a given physiological unit, i.e., within the subject."[159] Dealing with the subject as a psychological entity (accessed via a verbal recollection of the event and imbued with conscious and unconscious components) resulted in little more than a finding that the reaction was "complex."[160] For the goal of understanding and, ultimately, of influencing "behavioral indicators," the Freudian subject had to be dissolved into a "physiological system," mappable according to those psychophysiological factors that betrayed relevant and perceptible real-time responses.[161] The experimenters openly lamented the fact that "electronic data processing programs that could perform such an extensive analysis" directly and in real time on psychological indicators, rather than just on autonomic, physiological ones, had not been perfected at the time of their experiments.[162] Nevertheless, they made clear that such a means of continuous monitoring was their eventual goal.[163] From their point of view, "large individual differences" — that is, differences on the level of an autonomous subject, particularly as revealed in "verbal self-report techniques" — proved to be little more than errors, idiosyncrasies to be weeded out and corrected for.[164] Once broken down into individual components, the final subject was then reassembled, as their methodological article indicated, as a type of information avatar, the data received "intra-individually" across different subjects combined into a statistical type.[165] As an interpretive method, the last vestiges of psychoanalysis, the "talking cure," with its model of an individual recounting the memory of a stressful and possibly traumatic event, were to be eliminated. If psychoanalysis, as Michel Foucault argued, could be understood to effect a certain mode of resistance to the more intensive extension of micropowers by retreating into "the trappings of the old order of power" —

what he called "retro-version," or, in the terms of Deleuze and Guattari, recourse to an "archaism with a contemporary function" – this was now to give way.[166] Rendered into data and delivered over to informatic processes, the subject was to be placed more fully within the contemporary regime of control.

Although Bernier's analysis of *The Flicker* was limited to the much cruder apparatus of the questionnaire (and thus, unavoidably, to the level of the individual), her aims tended in the same direction. Hence her request for subjects to provide a graphic account of their response to the film across time. Deprived of the dermohmeters and cardiotachometers available to her advisor, Bernier could only ask her "physiological units" to chart their own autonomic reactions across time by means of pencil and paper, no doubt lamentably clouding the results with the idiosyncrasies of individual memory and psychology. Nevertheless, what had previously been indeterminate, multiplicitous, and even transgressive visual experiences predicated on individual neurophysiological differences were rendered into statistics to be reformulated into computerized "syndromes." Such is the fate of the subject in the age of electronic media: "So-called Man is split up into physiology and information technology."[167] Thus, too, would the Cagean paradigm opened within the anechoic chamber come to a close – with the low sound of one's blood in circulation and the high one of one's central nervous system connected to sensory mechanisms and turned into modulating flows of information.

• • •

Around the same time as Bernier's experiment, the implications of *The Flicker* phenomenon would be brought back into the realm of composition under the rubric "Bio-Music," which was nothing other than a doggedly medium-specific term for the mode of biopower coincident with media technologies. According to Manford L. Eaton (whose treatise, *Bio-Music*, was the last book to appear on Dick Higgins's Something Else Press), the goals of biomusic were essentially identical to those posed by Young and Burroughs:

> Bio-Music is the term used by ORCUS [Operational Research Company Universal Systems] Research to describe a class of electronic systems that use biological potentials in feedback loops to induce powerful, predictable, repeatable, physiological/psychological states which can be elegantly controlled in real time. The types of states that can be programmed are as powerful as chemical (drug) states, and the hallucinogenic powers of electronic sensory feedback systems can be controlled and guided with a precision utterly impossible with chemical methods.[168]

Eaton's text goes on to describe a number of biomusical techniques, mechanisms, and apparatuses, including sensory deprivation, sensory bombardment, aural stimulation via rhythmic sounds, photic stimulation (expressly citing W. Grey Walter), and emotional stimulation ("a term for non-abstract information").[169] Aspects of the "Physiological Program" of biomusic—that is, the monitored output of the stimulation—include conscious statements, respiration, EKG, EEG, GSR, and eye movements. This data was not simply to be recorded—"on a multiple track magnetic tape recorder (8-track minimum)"—but used to operate a series of implements, from "flash lamps" to "audio and video signals" generators to "conventional color organs" (all things that Conrad had envisioned or planned between 1965 and 1968).[170] Of everything considered, Eaton found the stimulation and EEG measurement of alpha waves to be the most prominent area of utilizable "bio-potentials." "ELECTROENCEPHALOMUSIC" was to some degree biomusic's initiator and privileged form.[171]

The essence of Eaton's system, as he explained in his "Philosophy of Bio-Music," was "the real-time feedback loop" (Figure 6.19).[172] Placing the "listener" into such a system, as his description makes clear, was basically submitting them to control:

> As the physiological program progresses, the real-time program memory feeds updated information into the SRM [Statistical Reaction Memory] to refine the physiological program. If the subject frequently breaks out of the feedback loop, and it is necessary for the

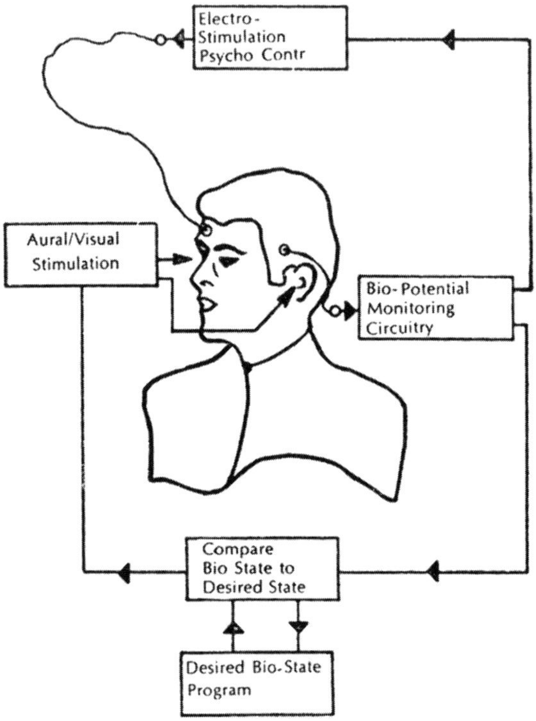

Figure 6.19. Manford L. Eaton, Basic Elements of a Bio-Music System, from *Bio-Music*, 1974.

> control mechanism to pursue him, the programmer for the composition needs to do more homework on how to compose biological music; and/or, the system designer needs to do more work on his Biological Music System design.[173]

Despite certain caveats on Eaton's part, biomusic ultimately aimed for nothing other than an individual's regulation to such a degree as to be rendered into an automaton or somnambulist, virtually (and at times literally) narcotized into submission. From this perspective, the dissolution of ego boundaries Cage found within the anechoic chamber (where the splits between "intention and non-intention" and "subject-object" disappear) becomes the optimum condition for manipulation.[174] By means of "such techniques as electro-narcosis," Eaton noted, "we want to induce an alpha rhythm characteristic such as one might achieve in a quiet room with his eyes closed, in a state of repose with no internally generated intellectual stimuli. It is into this type of alpha state [a Consciousness Field] that we inject a sensory stimulus."[175]

Although, as Eaton explains, "'Classical music' for the 20th Century psyche is a very weak feedback loop," he nonetheless situated his endeavors within the realm of music because it was, to his mind, the art most aligned with the "real-time organization of sensory stimulation."[176] Although Eaton neglects any discussion whatsoever of cinema, he privileges the example of broadcast television. In television could be found—albeit via the relatively crude and "definitely inferior" means of letters to the station and door-to-door opinion polls—an instantiated system of feedback and control: "In the case of TV, we have the situation where many viewers could be controlled to have the same responses to any given work of Bio-Music.... In this situation we could have elicited responses rather than only the physical aspects of the stimuli itself, and this is where its [biomusic's] great power lies."[177]

Although Eaton halfheartedly holds out the idea that a biomusical television would allow for greater audience "participation" (in the form of biological and possibly communicative indicators being fed back into the system in real time), liberation by such means is by no means inherent to his agenda. Understood not only as a perceptual technology, but as the overall regulatory feedback circuit that includes advertising, opinion polls, and Nielsen ratings (not to mention more recent information-gathering techniques such as focus-group "dial testing" and other moment-to-moment response studies and, most recently, passive data collecting devices such as TiVo), television figures as a particularly prominent node within control's ascension to hegemony as a process of the continuous extraction, regulation, and feedback of information for the purposes of production, capitalization, and profit.[178] It is within this social and technological network or assemblage that TV would come to act in what Deleuze calls its "social function" as "social engineering in its purest form."[179] Even McLuhan would be cautious enough to forewarn: "Once we have surrendered our senses and nervous systems to the private manipulation of those who would try to benefit from taking a lease on our eyes and ears and nerves, we don't really have any rights left."[180]

• • •

With *The Flicker*, Conrad was already operating within (and opposing) this "biomusical" realm in which what is at stake is the manipulation not only of the physiology of perception, but affect, behavior, and thought. Unlike Eaton, however, Conrad did not seek to keep his "subjects" within a negative feedback loop, but rather to push them, via positive feedback, into a transgressive moment beyond the pursuit of the "control mechanism." Implicit at the time, the stakes of *The Flicker* would perhaps be made fully explicit only a decade later in Conrad's article, "A Few Remarks Before I Begin." Reacting, in part, against the almost complete reliance of film and video theory on semiotics, Conrad suggested that "the film scholar has never been up to dealing efficaciously with the problem of *anticipation, suspense, temporal composition*." At the base of the experience of film, television, and video, however, he declared, is the fact that "people respond with their attention in ways which can be *programmed*."[181]

As Conrad continued in greater detail, not only does the regulation of attention prove a means of regulating thinking itself, but attentive regulation is a site of contestation between competing cultural interests: between the "common practice *program*" of mainstream cinema and television, on the one hand (devoted, as Conrad's analysis makes clear, to "the making of money, within the economic reality of our capitalist-socialist world"), and those artistic and cultural counter "programs" that would contend with them, on the other. Modes of attentive and perceptual transformation thus hold an important function: "We know that *attention* is the key item in linking experience to thought: it stands to reason."[182] As presented by Conrad, new speeds, patterns, and modes of attention would seem to be necessary for new types of thinking, as well as for new types of control. "Consequently," he noted, "it is safe to say that very probably human thought requires constant renewal and alteration. In fact, the variety of thought available to humans is almost directly a function of the number of scales of attentiveness which are achieved within the individual."[183] It was, no doubt, something akin to the multiplication of such "scales of attentiveness" that Conrad had initially attempted in his indeterminate and multiplicitous "flicker-triads" that could be absorbed on more than one level at a time. *The Flicker* was thus perhaps the first work in a lifelong career to oppose an emerging force of regulation with a new type of thought, one that would "have to be (metaphorically speaking) cloudlike, holistic; unsystematic to be sure."[184] As Conrad concluded his "Few Remarks" (with a pointed ambiguity), "*Attention* needs guideposts for focus. Exploration of alternative attentiveness is a valuable cultural commodity."[185]

• • •

In perhaps his final moment of intersection with the "minor" history that this book has been charting, Robert Morris would argue in "Notes on Sculpture, Part 3" of 1967 that minimal sculpture's turn toward external structural and contextual relations had written an end to the insular, linear ("major") history of artistic form.

Revising somewhat his earlier emphasis on sculpture's inherent spatial and volumetric properties, Morris argued that minimalism's uniqueness "lies in the kind of order that underlies the forming of this work. This order is not based on previous art orders, but is an order so basic to culture that its obviousness makes it nearly invisible. The new three-dimensional work has grasped the cultural infrastructure of forming itself that has been in use, and developing, since Neolithic times and culminates in the technology of industrial production."[186]

Regarded in this manner, minimal sculpture breaks from the realm of artistic modernism to adopt the morphology of industrial manufacture and the syntax of serial production. "The imagery involved is referential in a broad and special way: it does not refer to past sculptural form. Its referential connections are to manufactured objects and not to previous art."[187] Freed from indigenous artistic legitimation, a minimal artwork is relevant and valid – it "'sticks' and 'holds'" or not, contended Morris – "by virtue of its relationship to this infrastructure."[188]

As Morris realized, however, the industrial "infrastructure" that he saw extending into prehistory was being superseded at precisely that historical moment. "New conditions under which things must exist," he observed, "are already here. So are the vastly extended controls of energy and information and new materials for forming. The possibility for future forming throws into sharp relief present forms and how they have functioned."[189] Although Morris's own antiform sculptural experiments were just beginning, their "refusal to continue estheticizing the form" would involve more than anti-idealism.[190] The morphological instability and continual redeployment of Morris's felt wall hangings and threadwaste scatters – which he discussed in terms of "automation" and "media" – responded to an era in which earlier modes of industrialization were beginning to "become obsolete with a thoroughgoing automation of production involving a high degree of feedback adjustments."[191]

Born of the same historical moment, *The Flicker* ultimately proves homologous with a whole series of transformations in what Morris would label "infrastructure." With the dissolution of artistic form written by feedback and automation (Morris), on the one hand, and the mediamatic processes of light (Gysin and Sommerville), on the other, control moved to operate directly within and upon individual subjects, positing them as nodes within affective, perceptual, regulating networks. Born of the types of neurophysiological experiments conducted by Walter and ultimately destined for the psychological studies of Bernier, *The Flicker*—Conrad's "piece of film that is experienced by a group of people in various ways"—emerged as part of a socioeconomic transformation (one that it helped to make visible and conceivable) in which human mental and physiological faculties were being rendered into data and input into similar circuits of automation and feedback, operating in networks that stretch beyond the limitations of disciplinary institutions and sovereign forms. As an external resonator, albeit dedicated to indeterminate perceptual transgression rather than to biomusical feedback, *The Flicker* acted as both harbinger and disruptor of this new "infrastructure" of control. As such, Conrad's first aesthetic production "beyond" the boundaries of the Dream Syndicate, product of the minor history we have been tracing, acts in much the same way that Deleuze and Guattari have described a "minor" art: "it consists in prolonging, in accelerating, a whole movement that already is traversing the social field. It operates in a virtuality that is already real without yet being actual ([articulating] the diabolical powers of the future that for the moment are only brushing up against the door)."[192] It would be wrong, however, to see *The Flicker* as merely a passive symptom, simply and seamlessly submerged within its historical context. Minor assemblages, as Deleuze and Guattari argue, have "a double function: to translate everything into assemblages and to dismantle the assemblages. The two are the same thing."[193]

Who are you an agent for? From the perspective of the infrastructure of control within which *The Flicker* may already be seen to be functioning, the operative distinction is no longer subversion against sovereign form or autonomy against the strictures of the disciplinary institution, but rather the connection of biopolitical forces to either hegemonic apparatuses of normalization or heteronomous apparatuses of countercontrol. Negative feedback can be countered only by positive feedback and practices of regulation by practices of multiplicity, indeterminacy, and differentiation, operative wholly on a plane of immanence. What Conrad attempted with *The Flicker* was to remake cinema in a similar manner as the Theatre of Eternal Music had remade music, to call forth a "new kind" of viewer whose central nervous system had been outered by means of electronic media, a subject residing on the microthin division separating two real, but virtual futures: either, as Deleuze would characterize it, "a disturbed brain-death or a new brain which would be at once the screen, the film stock and the camera, each time membrane of the outside and the inside."[194]

Conclusion

For nearly a decade after having completed *The Flicker*, Conrad would pursue, as one strain within a consistently bifurcated or multiplicitous artistic project, investigations into the materials and discursive properties of structural and structural/materialist film. As this facet of his work developed, he would increasingly come to explore alternative modes or paradigms of film processing and projection. This began with the series of *Yellow Movies* (1972), which employ neither film stock nor projection, but were merely "screens," generally painted with an emulsion of cheap house paint—for example, "Gull white flat interior latex, Magicolor No. 3011-11"—which changes in time to produce a "cinematic" experience (a time-based art form of an image on a screen) with an extremely long duration (because the paint can take years to change appreciably) (Figure 7.1). Immediately afterward, by foregrounding the manner in which film could be "exposed" and developed via heat, pressure, or electricity, rather than merely by light and developer fluid, Conrad moved to produce a "material" paracinema.[1] In *4-X Attack* (1973), Conrad struck a roll of celluloid with a hammer in a darkroom (Figure 7.2). "The material being brittle," Conrad noted, "it was not only left with stress-bearing deformations, but was compressed in points, scraped and sheared in others, and generally speaking completely totalled [sic]."[2] Once the film was fractured into myriad pieces, Conrad

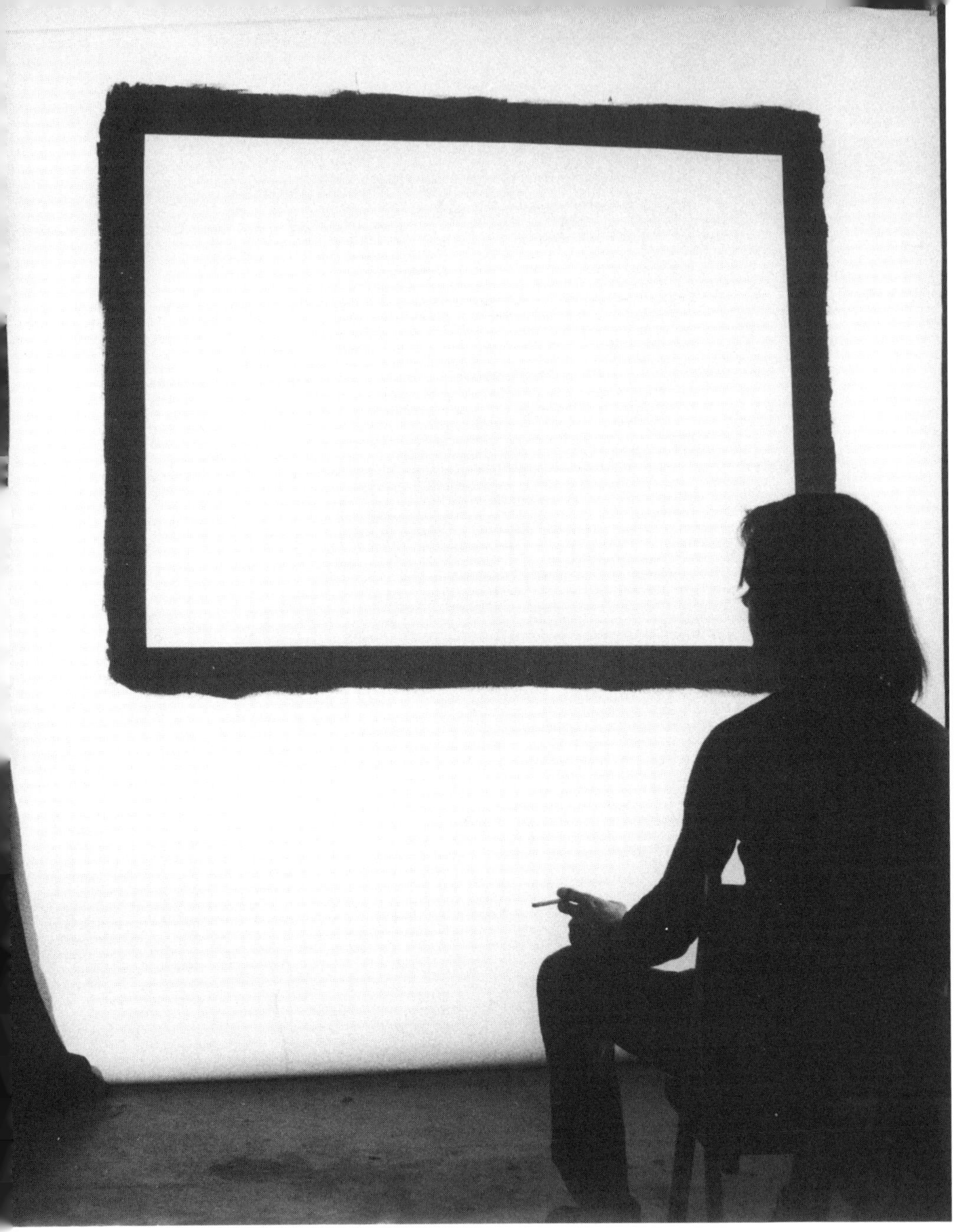

Figure 7.1. Tony Conrad, *Yellow Movie*, 1972. Photographer unknown. Courtesy Tony Conrad.

Figure 7.2. Tony Conrad, *4-X Attack*, 1973. 16 mm, black and white, silent, 1 min.

swept them back together, "flashed the film once with a strobe, so as to activate the latent stress record," developed it in a cheesecloth sack, and then painstakingly, even archaeologically, reconstructed the roll (it is, after all, an "edited" film) into a projectable movie.[3] As a visual experience, *4-X Attack* resembles nothing so much as a Stan Brakhage film, a fast, abstract, time-condensed event. Taking Brakhage's abstract expressionist aesthetic, in some sense, one step further, Conrad produced an "action" film by means of his swinging hammer (an engagement, once again, with a contemporary structural film theory that had been assimilated to a neo-Greenbergian formalism). In the next year, Kodak 4-X film would suffer further at Conrad's hands in *Electrocuted 4-X, Brine Damaged* (1973), *Deep Fried 4-X* (1973), and *Electrocuted 4-X, Second Series* (1974).

In a response, of sorts, to Birgit and Wilhelm Hein's *Roh Film* study of 1968, Conrad began a series of "Cooked Films" in 1973. Folding social and political concerns into the process in an explicit manner, Conrad—who at the time was serving as primary caregiver to his and Beverly Grant's child, as well as professor of film at Antioch—adapted the practice of filmmaking to the stereotypically female role of domestic cook.

> It happened that I was actually then burdened, you might say, by home care; in other words, I had a baby; I'm babysitting at home.... And I think, "Well, I'm in a position that women have found themselves in for millennia.... Why is it that this is like a prison that locks one away from cultural progress?" So, I decided that I would take advantage of that rather than be retained by it. I decided to use cooking, specifically, as a paradigm for film processing.... I had a curry recipe. So, I took a roll of film and curried it. And when I went back over, I showed it to my class... my curried film looked really nice.[4]

Usually substituting "raw" film in the place where different recipes called for onions, Conrad "processed" the footage in various manners on his countertop or stove. The showing of the first projectable work, *Curried 7302* (1973), produced colorful and aesthetic patterns on screen (once again recalling nothing so much as certain works of Brakhage) (Figure 7.3). "It was this gorgeous mottled yellow, abstract thing," Conrad recalled.[5] The second work in the series was a film chicken creole, the projection of which caused – through the thick alimentary residue still clinging to the celluloid – gate slipping and other effects simulated in structural films such as those of Annabel Nicholson or the Heins (Figure 7.4).[6] As a set of actual difficulties for the projectionist (whom Conrad recalls swearing at his task from the booth), Conrad's creoled film also included unrepeatable variations in showing (the slippages not occurring in the same place twice), while the projector and the normally unnoted act of projecting also became an evident and integral part of the visual experience – not unlike Jack Smith's later film performances, in which he manipulated and even edited the footage during the screening. "So I made this creole and I took that over," Conrad related:

> Well, this was very interesting because the meat ran all over the projector, and it was full of grease and chicken. It slipped in the gate, and it stunk because the lamp heated it up, and it was like really an olfactory experience, and it tested the skill of the projectionist, who is covered in slime. . . . But it was very interesting because of the way that it created this other site of action. Suddenly the projectionist becomes like an actor. Instead of being concealed, the projectionist and the projection activity become a part of the show.[7]

Conrad would subsequently, and with a more apparent parodic thrust, accentuate the performative in other paracinematic pieces such as *7360 Sukiyaki* (1973), where the "processed," cooked film was literally thrown (pro-jected) against the screen (Figure 7.5).

All of these developments, in some manner or another, were articulated with an examination of the power hierarchies underlying them: from the place of film within the structure of industrial capitalism, which alternate processing techniques could indicate and partially avoid, to the role and valorization of traditionally female domestic labor. Conrad would explicitly invoke such social

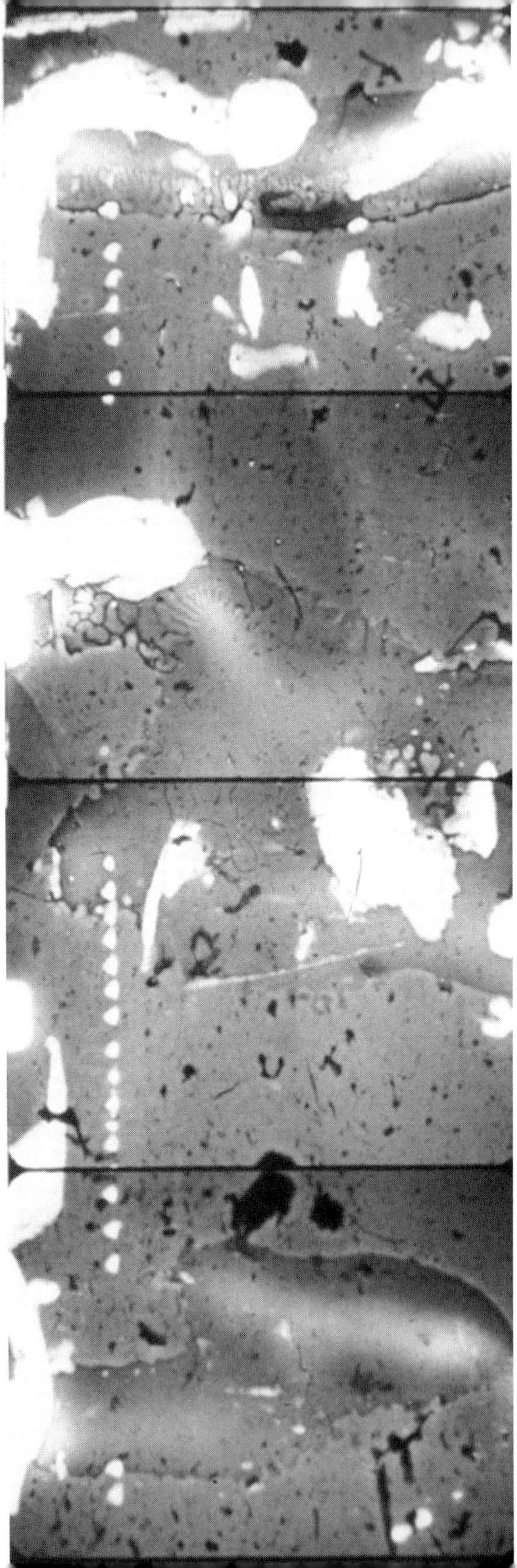

Figure 7.3. Tony Conrad, *Curried 7302*, 1973. 16 mm, color, silent, 2 min.

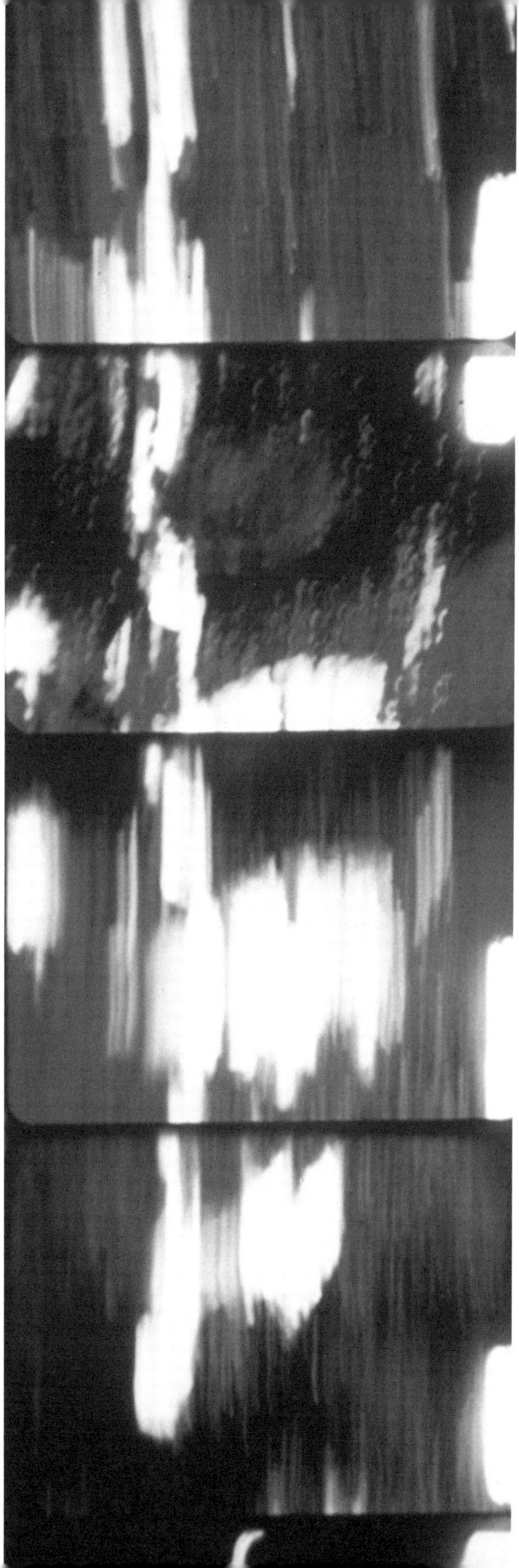

Figure 7.4. Tony Conrad, *7302 Creole*, 1973. 16 mm, color, silent, 1 min.

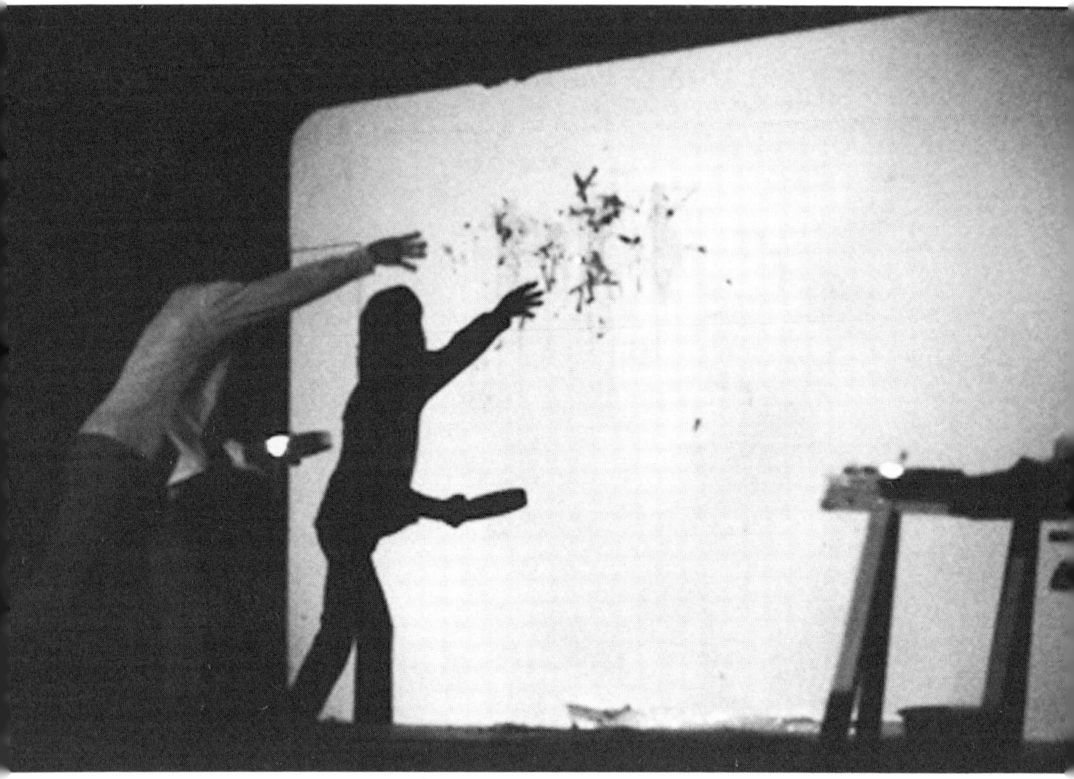

Figure 7.5. Tony Conrad, *7360 Sukiyaki*, 1973. Performed in 1977. Photographer unknown. Courtesy Tony Conrad.

dimensions as indispensable for any continuation of the avant-garde within even his most abstract and formal cinematic production, *Articulation of Boolean Algebra for Film Opticals* (1975). As he stated in "for INTRO to Boolean Alg.," a note originally written in 1973 for pronouncement at screenings of the film:

> What is ART?
>
> | | |
> |---|---|
> | – An abstract value? | – No. |
> | – A personal goal? | – No. |
> | – The NEW? | – No. |
> | – A social systematization? | – Yes. |
>
> What is the NEW?
>
> | | |
> |---|---|
> | – The latest? | – No. |
> | – Application of principles? | – Not directly. |
> | – Revolution in person, style, content, &c. | – Not directly. |
> | – The new *is* what *functions* within the societal context of Art as influence-style-language *determining*; a societal imperative. | |
>
> Hence the importance of an historical and functional understanding of the societal context for art discourse.[8]

Conrad would not, however, give up his investigations into perceptual stimulation as examined in his earliest cinematic work. As he notes further within the same document, "I have hoped, ever since my first non-representational, metaphor denying, relationally impoverished film, 'The Flicker,' to find a substantiation in terms of physiological and psychological phenomena for a direct and inherently human sound-vision relational interaction."[9]

In 1980, Conrad would begin to address questions of social and political power relations in a different manner in his "army movie" project (Figures 7.6 and 7.7). Edited and titled in different versions as *Hail to the Fallen* (1981), *Combat Status Go* (1981), and *Beholden to Victory* (1983), Conrad's film (and video) project sought to allegorize power relations on a number of different

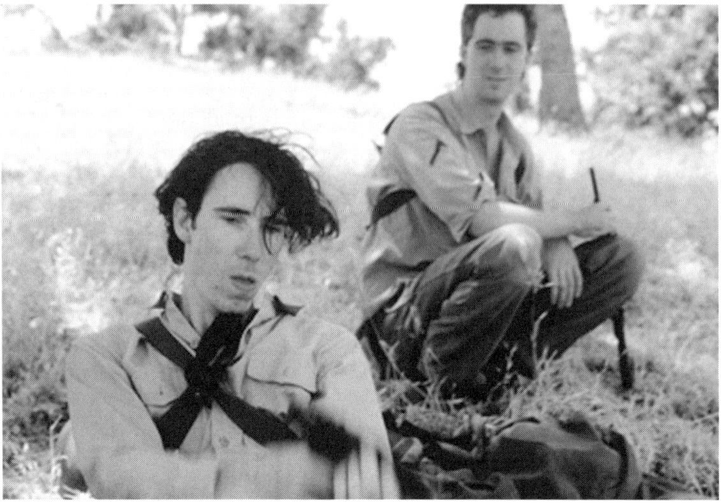

Figure 7.6. Mike Kelley and Tony Oursler on the set of Tony Conrad, *Beholden to Victory*, 1980–83/2007. Photograph by Tony Conrad, 1980. Used by permission.

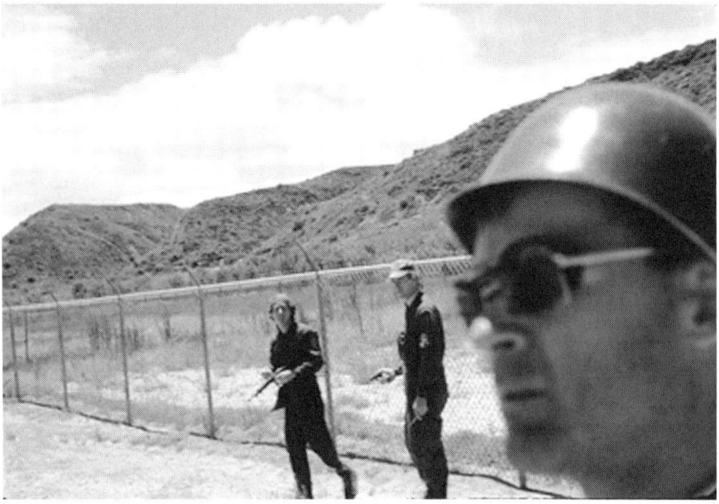

Figure 7.7. Charles Rotter, Louis Hock, and Tony Conrad (directing in costume) on the set of Conrad, *Beholden to Victory*, 1980–83/2007. Photograph by Tony Conrad, 1980. Used by permission.

levels.[10] Devoid of a script, the actors were instead provided with a set of functional subject positions and associated character traits as either superiors or subordinates. Those in the superiors' roles were to be haughty, domineering, and imperious, while those in the inferior positions were to improvise the characteristics of shiftlessness and insubordination. Devoid of actual characters to play, acting was transformed into a sort of characterologial task-performance activity, a fictional exacerbation and presentation of the social dynamics of power. The "army movie," as Conrad explained, "has a *game*, not a story—the game of an Officer and a Private."[11] The overall army theme and setting (the genre context of the war movie) serves here as the metonymic indicator of a wider set of social hierarchies, which extend within the film from officers and enlisted men to teachers and students, parents and children, and the like. Drawing upon his much earlier associations with Jack Smith and Henry Flynt, Conrad's film project was both allegorical and related to the heterotopic exaltation of subordinated subject positions habitually considered "low."

Conrad extended the thematic of power relations onto the formal level, as well, in the guise of a series of preset camera positions and movements identified as either dominant or subordinate, an oscillation in point of view that worked against the audience's habitually seamless identification with the camera: "the idea here was to open a pathway into a new (and more dignified) culture, in which the viewer is aware of efforts to sway their attitudes, and respects (in return) opportunities which are afforded for them to control these affinities themselves."[12] In certain screenings, the power divide was extended further into the audience's attitudes by providing elements of costuming (which identified each person with either "officer" or "private") and imposing a choice between officers and enlisted solders which had to be made upon choosing one's seat within an auditorium that was divided, the way families are at a wedding ceremony, into opposing aisles. Such provisional role playing—somewhat like the infamous Stanford Prison Experiment—further inscribed hierarchical power relations into the audience's experience of the film.[13] In an expressly anti-interpellative gesture – an opposition to the normally "subordinated" audience watching a conventional narrative film – Conrad sought to situate the viewer within a "dominant" position, from or across which (depending on which "side" they were on) their identification with the actors would take place:

> *Combat Status Go* is a work designed within an economy of distrusts and of abuses of authority; in particular, the respective abuses of our authoritarian roles as *director* (on the 1 hand) and as *viewer* (on the other).
>
> *Combat Status Go*, *Beholden to Victory*, and *Hail the Fallen* are scintillating failures – they transfer the "Officer" attitude effectively to the audience. The normally-ductile viewer (complicitous with the narrative) responds appropriately with contempt for the *film*(!) on the basis of their disapprobation of the childlike Soldier characters. Some viewers who were actual war veterans, though, reported that the demeaning atmosphere of the film was "accurate."[14]

As we have seen in Chapter 1, much of the "army movie" was shot in Southern California, shortly after Conrad first met Mike Kelley and Tony Oursler. The two made a star turn in the film, appearing as shiftless privates temporarily separated from the rest of their company and patrol. Whereas many of the other actors assigned to the subordinate category, according to Conrad, resorted to already-known character types from the movies (they tended, he recalls, to imitate Jerry Lewis), Kelley and Oursler fully understood the aesthetic of "failure" Conrad was after. Like the comic-book character Sad Sack, whom Kelley has invoked in art works from his *Garbage Drawings* (1988) to the collaboration with Paul McCarthy, *Sod and Sodie Sock* (1998), Kelley's and Oursler's two clueless enlisted men are paragons of dysfunction. Clumsily climbing over a fence into an abandoned "desert" field, they throw and drop their weapons and other belongings, mock their superiors, and wander about aimlessly. Kelley has recalled that "we were informed of what we were not allowed to do and were left to struggle with what we could do."[15] Further expressing their "low" status, they fall to the ground, play in the dirt, occasionally emit guttural groans and howls, and indulge in adolescent and infantile behavior. At the same time, as befitting the inverted "heroic" status that Conrad wanted, after all, for the enlisted soldiers, Kelley and Oursler manage to form a sympathetic and even identificatory bond with the audience, an effect not far, to Conrad's mind, from goals sought over two decades earlier by Flynt's exaltation of the "creep." Kelley's and Oursler's performances would have been at home on the stage of a Poetics concert, where certain aspects of heterotopic dysfunction were also being explored. In retrospect, Conrad's "army movie" would prove a particularly fortuitous intersection of two generations and the first of many collaborative endeavors within a minor history that is still ongoing.

Notes

Chapter One: What Is a Minor History?

1. Tony Conrad, "The Eye and the Asshole: Otto Muehl and the Extremes of Vienna, 196–," *The Underground Film Bulletin* 5 (1986): 54–74. Conrad also presented in the film programs of Documenta V (1972) and Documenta VI (1977). The films *Straight and Narrow* and *Four Square* are credited to Tony and Beverly Conrad; *Coming Attractions* is credited as directed by Beverly Conrad, with production and photography (including editing and special effects) by Tony Conrad.

2. David Fricke, liner notes to Tony Conrad with Faust, *Outside the Dream Syndicate*, Thirtieth Anniversary Edition, Table of the Elements / The Sandwalking Company; Tony Conrad, interview with author, Buffalo, NY, August 15–16, 1995. Conrad and Cale colloquially referred to the Theatre of Eternal Music as the Dream Syndicate, a designation dated in Conrad's notebooks to May 1965 (yellow *Flicker* notebook, p. 4). This should not be confused with the California rock group of the early 1980s, the Dream Syndicate, named after the by-then already mythic 1960s group.

3. Tony Conrad, "Inside the Dream Syndicate," *Film Culture* 41 (Summer 1966): 5–8.

4. Reviewer Ken Johnson wrote: "what this disorienting hodgepodge of crude paintings, sculptures, found objects, tediously digressive and mostly inaudible video interviews, raw sound and cacophonous music says about history remains mysterious." Ken Johnson, "Art in Review: Tony Oursler and Mike Kelley, 'The Poetics Project: 1977–1997,'" *New York Times*, June 19, 1998, sec. E, pt.

2, p. 39. The most complete discussion of *The Poetics Project* is found in "Mike Kelley and Tony Oursler Discuss *The Poetics Project*," transcript of an unpublished interview conducted at the Watari Museum of Contemporary Art, Tokyo, 1997.

5. On Throbbing Gristle and its earlier incarnation as a performance art group, see Simon Ford, *Wreckers of Civilisation: The Story of Coum Transmissions and Throbbing Gristle* (London: Black Dog Publishing, 1999).

6. A section of the Documenta version of *The Poetics Project* included *Why I Love Guitar* and *Why I Love Drums*, two canvases with inset speakers blaring solos by Arto Lindsay and Mike Kelley, respectively. These were later sold to the Cartier Foundation separate from the installation.

7. Mike Kelley, "The Poetics: Remixes of Recordings from 1977 to 1983," in Tony Oursler and Mike Kelley, *Poetics Project* (Tokyo: On Sundays / Watari Museum of Contemporary Art, 1997), n.p.

8. On Destroy All Monsters, see Mike Kelley, liner notes to *Destroy All Monsters 1974–1976*, three-CD boxed set released by Father Yod and Ecstatic Peace in 1994, which includes Mike Kelley, "What Destroy All Monsters Means to Me" and "Destroy All Monsters Interviews Itself" (1976). See also Destroy All Monsters, *Geisha This* (Oak Park, MI: Book Beat Gallery, 1995).

9. "Destroy All Monsters Interviews Itself." On Loren's interactions with Jack Smith, see Branden W. Joseph, "Son of the Creature: An Interview with Cary Loren," *Grey Room* 12 (Summer 2003): 116–25.

10. Kelley and Oursler divide the production of the Poetics into an organ-dominated period and a guitar-dominated "rock" period. Only the first incarnation is represented in the released CD set, *The Poetics: Remixes of Recordings 1977–1983*, Compound Annex 1–3. The rock incarnation of the Poetics consisted of Kelley, Oursler, Bill Stobaugh (later replaced by Miller), John Arnheim, and Simon (whose last name has been forgotten). Certain of the tracks included on the CD set of the Poetics are in fact taken from Oursler's videos of the time.

11. Kelley, "The Poetics, Remixes of Recordings from 1977 to 1983," in Oursler and Kelley, *Poetics Project*, n.p. Oursler similarly recalled: "In this early working process Mike and I discovered that we shared amongst other things, a love for the Ex-Catholic experience in all its mystical, sexual, and angst-ridden designs. And formally the organ seemed best to evoke the drama, ritual, incense, and bended knee." Tony Oursler, "Poetics Memories," in Oursler and Kelley, *Poetics Project*, n.p.

12. Oursler, in Mike Kelley, "An Endless Script: A Conversation with Tony Oursler," in *Introjection: Tony Oursler Mid-Career Survey 1976–1999*, ed. Deborah Rothschild (Williamstown, MA: Williams College Museum of Art, 1999), p. 43. On Suicide, see Clinton Heylin, *From the Velvets to the Voidoids: A Pre-Punk History for a Post-Punk World* (New York: Penguin, 1993). Suicide famously caused a near riot at the Ancienne Belgique ballroom in Brussels, Belgium, in 1978, an event captured on tape and released as "23 Minutes over Brussels," *Suicide*, Mute 9104CD.

13. See Kelley's description of the group's performance in Long Beach before a group of hard-core punk fans in Kelley, "The Poetics: Remixes of Recordings 1977 to 1983," in Oursler and Kelley, *The Poetics Project*, n.p.

14. Elizabeth Janus, "Talking Back: A Conversation with Tony Oursler," in *Introjection: Tony Oursler Mid-Career Survey 1976–1999*, p. 84.

15. Oursler, "Poetics Memories," in Oursler and Kelley, *The Poetics Project*, n.p.

16. *Ibid.*

17. For the text of this project, see Mike Kelley, *Plato's Cave, Rothko's Chapel, Lincoln's Profile* (Venice, CA: New City Editions, 1986). The performance was released as Mike Kelley, *The Peristaltic Airwaves and Plato's Cave, Rothko's Chapel, Lincoln's Profile*, High Performance Audio, audio cassette, 1987. From the running leitmotif of underground caverns to the final description of activities in "Remembrances of Camp P.O.W. Ow!" themes of lowness run throughout Kelley's text. More than simply illustrating an untransposable lowness—an antiformal, unmolded, ambiguous, unshaped, or indeterminate substance—as even the best discussions have emphasized, Kelley's work deals with the specific conflicts and transpositions of a "heterological" dialectic of high and low or allowable and repressed aspects of cultural production. On Kelley's relation to Bataille, see Pamela M. Lee, "Mike Kelley's Name Dropping," *Word and Image* 11, no. 3 (July–September 1995): 300–319; Yve-Alain Bois and Rosalind E. Krauss, *Formless: A User's Guide* (New York: Zone Books, 1997); and Hal Foster, "Obscene, Abject, Traumatic," *October* 78 (Fall 1996): 107–24.

18. Georges Bataille, "The Use Value of D. A. F. de Sade (An Open Letter to My Current Comrades)" (1929), trans. Allan Stoekl with Carl R. Lovitt and Donald M. Leslie, Jr., in *Visions of Excess: Selected Writings, 1927–1939*, ed. Allan Stoekl (Minneapolis: University of Minnesota Press, 1985), p. 95. Kelley included an excerpt from this article in *Mike Kelley* (London: Phaidon, 1999), pp. 108–10.

19. See Yve-Alain Bois's similar claim for his and Rosalind Krauss's Bataille-inspired "Formless" project. Bois and Krauss, *Formless*, p. 21.

20. Mike Kelley, "Introduction to an Essay which is in the Form of Liner Notes for a CD Reissue Box Set," in Oursler and Kelley, *Poetics Project*, n.p. This statement appeared, slightly abridged, in Paul Szulman, "Mike Kelley / Tony Oursler," in *Documenta X Short Guide*, ed. Françoise Joly et al. (Ostfildern-Ruit: Cantz, 1997), pp. 114–15.

21. These interviews were later released by Tony Oursler as separate videotapes under the title *Synesthesia* (1997–2001). The other individuals interviewed were David Byrne, Arto Lindsay, Lydia Lunch, and Thurston Moore.

22. Conrad also played an underhanded art dealer opposite Karen Finley in Gibbons's film, *The Genius* (1993). Gibbons had been a student of Conrad's in the film section of the Art Department at Antioch College, and the two collaborated on the performance *Laughter and Defecation* (1986).

23. Victor Bockris and Gerard Malanga, *Up-Tight: The Velvet Underground Story* (London: Omnibus Press, 1983), p. 21. Sterling Morrison, apparently erroneously, attributes the book's finding to Piero Heliczer in Sterling Morrison, "Going Back in Time to Piero Heliczer," *Little Caesar* 9 (1979): 223–31.

24. *Ten Years Alive on the Infinite Plain* debuted on March 11, 1972, at The Kitchen in New York: Tony Conrad (violin), Rhys Chatham (long-string drone), Laurie Spiegel (pulsing bass), with live video processing performed by Woody and Steina Vasulka from a film source by Tony and Beverly [Grant] Conrad. *The Fundamental D Flat Group* was performed at Antioch College on April 22–23, 1972: Conrad (violin, horn, string drone), Chatham (flute, organ, string drone), Palestine (voice, pipes, brandy snifter).

25. Conrad's discussion could be understood as an extended answer to the seventh question posed by Oursler, "Can popular culture be subversive?"

26. Tony Conrad, *Early Minimalism, Volume One*, four-CD boxed set, Table of the Elements 33, 1997. *The Poetics Project* also included a multiple-CD boxed set as part of its act of historical recovery. The allegorical nature of the format was commented on by Kelley: "The very mode of the music's presentation is of the present – cd box sets did not exist in the Seventies; the packaging itself tears the music from its historical frame. Thus the music is revealed as not being 'popular,' that is – designed to produce instant gratification, since it gratifies fifteen years too late. Instead it is art, it is facade." Kelley, "Introduction to an Essay which is in the Form of Liner Notes," n.p.

27. Each of Conrad's *Early Minimalism* compositions for various string ensembles is subtitled with a different date, which refers to the period to which they relate as a historical echo. The *Early Minimalism* CD set included compositions subtitled *April 1965*, *May 1965*, and *June 1965*, along with *Four Violins*, a multitracked solo performance recorded on December 19, 1964. *Early Minimalism: December 1964* premiered on March 22, 1987, at the Experimental Intermedia Foundation in New York, a performance space directed by fellow minimalist composer and videomaker Phill Niblock.

28. Conrad's conflict with Young has served as the focus of numerous articles and interviews. See Peter Margasak, "Amid the Drone, a Feud over Who Composed It," *New York Times*, August 13, 2000, sec. 2, p. 27, and Rob Young, "Slapping Pythagoras: The Battle for the Music of the Spheres," in *Undercurrents: The Hidden Wiring of Modern Music*, ed. Rob Young (London: Continuum, 2002), pp. 71–79. This conflict also forms the subtext of Conrad's own writings: see, for example, Tony Conrad, "Capping Nostalgia," in *The Kitchen Turns Twenty: A Retrospective Anthology*, ed. Lee Morrissey (New York: The Kitchen, 1992), pp. 31–35; Tony Conrad, liner notes to *Slapping Pythagoras*, compact disc, Table of the Elements 23, 1995; and Tony Conrad, liner notes to *Four Violins (1964)*, vinyl record, Table of the Elements 17, 1996; repr. in *Halana* 2 (1996): 5–15 and in *Early Minimalism, Volume One*. Conrad's picketing was noted in Herman Trotter, "Concert Is Marked by Some Odd Notes: Ex-colleague Pickets Outside," *Buffalo News*, April 8, 1990, sec. B, p. 23. Young has responded to Conrad's writings in La Monte Young, "Notes on The Theatre of Eternal Music and *The Tortoise, His Dreams and Journeys*" (2000), twenty-seven-page PDF document (2000) posted in the La Monte Young section of the Web page for the MELA Foundation, www.melafoundation.org (last accessed June 22, 2007).

29. The most detailed discussion of the Theatre of Eternal Music is found in Keith Potter, *Four Musical Minimalists: La Monte Young, Terry Riley, Steve Reich, Philip Glass* (Cambridge: Cambridge University Press, 2000), pp. 56–76. Performance dates can be found in Young's resumé, copies of which are located in the John Cage Archive, Northwestern University Music Library, Evanston, IL; The New York Public Library for the Performing Arts, composers' files; and Conrad's archive.

30. Conrad, "Four Violins." Conrad's description of the 10-4 concert should not be taken to mean that it was wholly amorphous. As Potter has noted,

tapes of the group's performance reveal a tense interrelation of improvisation and repetition, freedom and control. Potter, *Four Musical Minimalists*, p. 61.

31. This can be heard on recordings of *19 X 63 NYC fifth day of the hammer B flat Dorian Blues, 24 XII 63 NYC third day of yule Early Tuesday Morning Blues*, and *21 I 64 AM NYC the first twelve Sunday Morning Blues*. The titles of these works, some of which have circulated in unauthorized recordings, refer to the calendar date of their recording, as well as to MacLise's poem *Year* (1961), which renamed each day of the calendar (e.g., "fifth day of the hammer"). Young would explore the production of a sonic "cloud" more thoroughly in his *Well-Tuned Piano*, begun in June 1964.

32. This is a point of particular contention between Young and Conrad. Young has acknowledged Conrad's role in the adoption of just intonation and the exploration of harmonic integer relations in Edward Strickland, *American Composers: Dialogues on Contemporary Music* (Bloomington: Indiana University Press, 1991), p. 65; Cole Gagne, *Soundpieces 2: Interviews with American Composers* (Metuchen, NJ: The Scarecrow Press, 1993), p. 495; and William Duckworth, *Talking Music* (New York: Schirmer Books, 1995), p. 241.

33. For a concise overview of just intonation, see David B. Doty, *The Just Intonation Primer: An Introduction to the Theory and Practice of Just Intonation* (San Francisco: The Just Intonation Network, 1994).

34. An examination of Conrad's working notebooks, particularly "Music Notes II," begun at Darmstadt, Germany in March 1961, leaves no doubt that Conrad was extremely interested in and knowledgeable about the effects of different harmonics and alternate tuning systems. One of the earliest entries reads: "With scordatura, 7th harmonic, good intonation at weird intervals is made possible using harmonics alone." "Music Notes II," p. 5 (entry 10, "Harmonics," dated March 12, 1961). On Young's later work with harmonics, see Kyle Gann, "The Outer Edge of Consonance: Snapshots from the Evolution of La Monte Young's Tuning Installations," in *Sound and Light: La Monte Young, Marian Zazeela*, ed. William Duckworth and Richard Fleming (Lewisburg, PA: Bucknell University Press, 1996), pp. 152–90. Conrad also elaborated the harmonic practices begun in the Theatre of Eternal Music. See his discussion in the liner notes to Tony Conrad with Faust, *Outside the Dream Syndicate* (1972), Table of the Elements CD 3, 1993.

35. Tony Conrad, interview with the author, Buffalo, NY, August 15-16, 1995.

36. Conrad had investigated Varèse's and Hába's alternative scales in Europe. See Chapter 2.

37. John Cage, "Indeterminacy" (1958), in *Silence* (Middletown, CT: Wesleyan University Press, 1961), p. 261.

38. Conrad, "Inside the Dream Syndicate," p. 6.

39. Alan Licht, "The History of La Monte Young's Theatre of Eternal Music," *Forced Exposure* 16 (1990): 66.

40. Young provides the decibel figure in Richard Kostelanetz, *The Theatre of Mixed Means* (1968; New York: RK Editions, 1980), p. 212.

41. Conrad, interview with author, Buffalo, NY, August 15–16, 1995.

42. MacLise would die in Nepal in 1979. He had returned to New York in 1965, however, where he played again with the Theatre of Eternal Music on a recording released in 2000 as John Cale, Tony Conrad, Angus MacLise, La Monte Young, and Marian Zazeela, *Inside the Dream Syndicate Volume One: Day of Niagara (1965)*, Table of the Elements compact disc 74.

43. The Velvet Underground consisted of Lou Reed, John Cale, Sterling Morrison, and Moe Tucker (the latter, famously taking MacLise's place after he refused the expectation of having to show up for concerts and play on time). The program of the Expanded Cinema Festival (officially titled "New Cinema Festival I") listed the Theatre of Eternal Music's performances as "La Monte Young Marian Zazeela / Dream Music: a Light Sound production," a Special Closing Program for December 4 and 5, 1965. The Velvet Underground appeared as part of *Rites of the Dreamweapon*, which was listed as "A seven-part Manifestation of the Presence, —Coordinated by Angus MacLise. Movement * Light * Sound * Word * Darkness * Silence * Dance * Liturgy * Noise * Stillness. Rites of the Dreamweapon—revealed by the Lords of the Dreamweapon—the Dreamweapon of life for the healing of all wounds." Film-makers' Cinematheque press release for "New Cinema Festival I," copy located in the text archives of Anthology Film Archives. The entire *Rites of the Dreamweapon* program seems to have been a multipart production: part I, "The Tremor Rite" (November 1, 1965) and part III, "The Mysteries of the Essence Chamber" (November 4, 1965), were listed as by Angus MacLise. Other sections were presented by Jerry Joffen, Don Snyder, and John Vacarro and also included (as part V) Jack Smith's *Rehearsal for the Destruction of Atlantis* (November 7, 1965). Contrary to some reports, none of the sections are listed as by Piero Heliczer.

44. Kate Lloyd, "... And One Evening When Listeners 'Floated Away,'" *Vogue*, May 1966, p. 242.

45. Conrad, "Capping Nostalgia," p. 32. A single example of the disputed

recordings was released as John Cale, Tony Conrad, La Monte Young, and Marian Zazeela, *Inside the Dream Syndicate*. On Dreyblatt's role, see Arnold Dreyblatt, "An Open Letter to La Monte Young and Tony Conrad" (2000), available at www.dreyblatt.net/html/music.php?id=68&more=63#more, and partially reproduced as "*Niagara* Squalls," in *The Wire*, 199 (September 2000), p. 6. See also Tony Conrad, "Tony Conrad's Response to *An open letter to La Monte Young and Tony Conrad*," (2000), also available at www.dreyblatt.net/html/music.php?id=68&more=63#more (last accessed June 22, 2007).

46. Diedrich Diedrichsen, "The Primary: Political and Anti-Political Continuities between Minimal Music and Minimal Art," in *A Minimal Future? Art as Object, 1958–1968* (Los Angeles: The Museum of Contemporary Art, Los Angeles, 2004), p. 125.

47. Which is how it is presented by Margasak in "Amid the Drone, a Feud."

48. Wim Mertens, *American Minimal Music: La Monte Young, Terry Riley, Steve Reich, Philip Glass*, trans. J. Hautekiet (London: Kahn & Averill, 1983); Edward Strickland, *Minimalism: Origins* (Bloomington: Indiana University Press, 1993); K. Robert Schwarz, *Minimalists* (London: Phaidon, 1996); and Potter, *Four Musical Minimalists*.

49. The best counter to this is Edward Strickland's *Minimalism: Origins*, which must be credited for undertaking a history of minimalism traced through art and music. However, although broader in its ambitions, the historical assumptions of Strickland's study are largely the same: The progression of musical minimalists primarily follows the same linear path from Young to Glass. While Strickland's discussion of minimal music remains one of the most valuable, his discussion of minimal art (which he largely conflates with formalist painting) can be faulted for reasons partially detailed in this book.

50. Michel Foucault, "Nietzsche, Genealogy, History" (1971), trans. Donald F. Bouchard and Sherry Simon, in *Language, Counter-Memory, Practice*, ed. Donald F. Bouchard (Ithaca, NY: Cornell University Press, 1977), p. 152.

51. Strickland, *Minimalism*, pp. 153–54, and Potter, *Four Musical Minimalists*, p. 23. See also Schwarz, *Minimalists*, pp. 16–19. Jeremy Grimshaw traces Young's aesthetic back to his Mormon roots; see Jeremy Grimshaw, "The Sonic Search for Kolob: Mormon Cosmology and the Music of La Monte Young," *Repercussions* 9, no. 1 (Spring 2001): 77–120.

52. On form of content and form of expression, see Gilles Deleuze and

Félix Guattari, *Kafka: Toward a Minor Literature*, trans. Dana Polan (Minneapolis: University of Minnesota Press, 1986), p. 3.

53. Potter, *Four Musical Minimalists*, p. 23. Potter also analyzes *Trio for Strings* as based on the "Dream Chord," p. 35. Strickland, by contrast, on account of *Trio*'s underlying serial structure, does not see it as properly forming part of minimalism at all.

54. Though he relies upon Young's own quotes, Potter cites minimal music's relation to "universal truths" or "universal structures" no fewer than five times in the chapter devoted to Young (pp. 41, 57, 65, 67, 78).

55. Hence, Potter can write: "Just as the world had become conceptualised as 'a single gigantic performance of *Poem*,' so *Composition 1960 #7* can be considered to encompass Young's entire output," and he continues: "This can also be said of *Composition 1960 #10*." *Four Musical Minimalists*, p. 52; internal quote from Cornelius Cardew, cited in *Four Musical Minimalists*, p. 46.

56. Strickland opens his book with a discussion of the institutionalization of minimalism, pp. 1–14.

57. Conrad, letter to Peter Yates, November 13, 1965 (copy of original located in Conrad's archive); published in Peter Yates, "Music," *Arts and Architecture* 83, no. 2 (February–March 1966): 45. In a letter to Henry Romney of November 11, 1965, Conrad insisted as well on his and Young's "long collaboration" and describes "the work that La Monte and I (and John Cale and Marian Zazeela) have done in harmony." Conrad, "Tony Conrad on 'The Flicker,' from a letter to Henry Romney, dated November 11, 1965," *Film Culture* 41 (Summer 1966): 1. In a lecture on October 15, 1965, "A Comparative Exposition of Eastern and Western Musical Systems Offering Foundational Points of Departure for Dream Music and the Earlier Work" at the Carnegie Institute of Technology, Young spoke while Conrad, who had produced the chart to which the group referred during practices, presented the visual diagrams.

58. Young, "Notes on The Theatre of Eternal Music," p. 17.

59. Morton Feldman and La Monte Young, "A Conversation on Composition and Improvisation (Bunita Marcus, Francesco Pellizzi, Marian Zazeela)," *Res* 13 (Spring 1987): 162.

60. Foucault, *Nietzsche, Genealogy, History*, p. 150.

61. There is a bit of this in "Four Violins," where Conrad declares, for example, that he "introduced the sustained drone of just-intonation into 'minimal' music in 1962."

62. *Panopticon* was shown in the exhibition Media Buff. / Media Art of Buffalo, New York at the Herbert F. Johnson Museum of Art, Cornell University, September 9–November 12, 1988.

63. Michel Foucault, "What Is an Author?" (1969), trans. Donald F. Bouchard and Sherry Simon, in *Language, Counter-Memory, Practice*, ed. Donald F. Bouchard (Ithaca, NY: Cornell University Press, 1977), p. 131.

64. The particular irresolution regarding the status of musical minimalism is reflected in Timothy A. Johnson, "Minimalism: Aesthetic, Style, or Technique?," *The Musical Quarterly* 78, no. 4 (Winter 1994): 742–73. Questions of the status of musical minimalism also inform Elaine Broad, "A New X? An Examination of the Aesthetic Foundations of Early Minimalism," *Music Research Forum* 5 (1990): 51–62, and Jonathan W. Bernard, "The Minimalist Aesthetic in the Plastic Arts and in Music," *Perspectives of New Music* 31, no. 1 (Winter 1993): 86–132. More recently, artistic minimalism has been approached as a discourse in James Meyer, *Minimalism: Art and Polemics in the Sixties* (New Haven, CT: Yale University Press, 2001). Although Meyer's book is an invaluable study of artistic minimalism, he does not investigate the relations of or question the distinctions between minimal art and music.

65. Foucault, "What Is an Author?" p. 135.

66. The omission of Conrad from the discourse of minimalism reached its apogee when K. Robert Schwarz, whose book *Minimalists* is probably the most widely distributed account of musical minimalism, simply omitted Conrad from the Theatre of Eternal Music altogether (p. 37). The result was not only a falsification of history, but a misleading analysis, because Schwarz recounted that "in *The Four Dreams of China* (1962), [Young] assigned each of the four members of the Theatre a single pitch to sustain indefinitely," which would indicate that Angus MacLise, whom Schwartz noted in lieu of Conrad, sustained a pitch on the hand drum (p. 38).

67. This term is found in promotional material surrounding the release of *Early Minimalism, Volume One*.

68. Conrad met Sherman and Longo in Buffalo in 1976, when they ran Hallwalls, organizing exhibitions and lectures by their peers and artists of earlier generations in whom they were interested. Conrad encountered the films of Jack Goldstein at Hallwalls in November 1978 and was also impressed by, though he did not entirely agree with, an early, still-unpublished, talk given by David Salle at SUNY Buffalo on that occasion. (Goldstein was invited not by

Sherman and Longo, who had by this time already moved to New York City, but by Patrick O'Connell, then director of Hallwalls.) Although Conrad has discussed the roots of postmodernism as arising in post-Cagean music much earlier than in the visual arts (see liner notes to *Early Minimalism*, p. 73), he recognized in the visual-art practices of this generation a means to reengage that legacy within a musical context that had become increasingly conservative.

69. Conrad, "Capping Nostalgia," p. 33. Conrad's piano project echoed the postminimal transformation of the work of individuals such as Yvonne Rainer, who, involved in appropriation since *Terrain* (1963), began incorporating practice into her dances in *Performance Demonstration* (1968) and increasingly allegorical procedures into performances and eventually into films in the 1970s. As Conrad recalls, "*Music and the Mind of the World* was an improvisatory venture that combined the recording process with me and the piano. From the first, *Music and the Mind of the World* was designated *open*; it allowed physical memory, it allowed practicing, it denied perfection by being all inclusive, it hoped for the incorporation of expression as much as formal devices and inventions, and inventiveness of any kind. It permitted all tactics without emphasizing novelty; reciprocally, it explored my body and my body's fluctuating capacity for performance as much as my body explored the capacity of the piano.... I began to sense an expanded spectrum of issues dealing with control, power, manipulation, institutional memory, and authorship or authority. And as I began to see the way in which music as a whole had functioned, or had been manipulated in respect to these larger social forces, or had proved useful in certain respects, I also began to see how these relationships could find their way into the broader palette of opportunities that filmmaking provided." Tony Conrad, "Progress 4," unpublished text, August 1, 2003.

70. See Young's comments to Edward Strickland: "When I sit down to play *The Well-Tuned Piano* I basically pray that I can become the servant of this source of information that comes through me, that I will be able to realize it in the most pure and direct way, and that I will be able to have the energy and strength to perform what comes to me. I follow the dictates of this stream, source of information that comes through me, and I don't get in the way of it." Edward Strickland, *American Composers: Dialogues on Contemporary Music* (Bloomington: Indiana University Press, 1991), p. 65. See also Ramon Pelinski, "Upon Hearing a Performance of the Well-Tuned Piano: An Interview with La Monte Young and Marian Zazeela, 78 1 x 22 4:58:25 – 7:15:00 PM NYC," *Parachute* 19 (Summer

1980): 10, and Cole Gagne, *Soundpieces 2: Interviews with American Composers* (Metuchen, NJ: The Scarecrow Press, Inc., 1993), p. 475. By contrast, Conrad writes of *100 Songs*: "Beth recorded an auxiliary sound tape that yelled snide remarks at me. 'If you can't play any softer than that, I'd rather not hear you at all!' 'The right hand doesn't know what the left hand is doing!' 'This doesn't sound like a song to me. Are you sure this is right?'" "Capping Nostalgia," p. 33.

71. Detractors might liken Conrad's appropriation more closely to that of Sherrie Levine, who rephotographed and exhibited as her own the work of signature artists such as Edward Weston. While conceding authorship to Young in a manner that Conrad does not, such a reading would not necessarily detract from the provocative nature of Conrad's project.

72. Douglas Crimp, "Pictures," *October* 8 (Spring 1979): 78. Crimp is describing Goldstein's *Two Fencers* (1977). Not unimportantly, Crimp points out that the work of the "Pictures" generation derived from the legacy of minimalist "theatricality."

73. Conrad, liner notes to *Early Minimalism*, p. 67.

74. Foucault, "What Is an Author?" p. 135, and Conrad, liner notes to *Early Minimalism*, p. 68.

75. Conrad, liner notes to *Early Minimalism*, pp. 36–37.

76. Conrad, "Four Violins." For a discussion of some of the political implications of this view, see Diedrichsen, "The Primary."

77. Conrad, "Slapping Pythagoras."

78. Kelley, "Introduction to an Essay which is in the Form of Liner Notes," n.p. See also Oursler's comments in Janus, "Talking Back," pp. 82 and 84. Compare Foucault's discussion of history and fiction in Michel Foucault, *Remarks on Marx: Conversations with Duccio Trombadori*, trans. R. James Goldstein and James Cascaito (New York: Semiotext(e), 1991), p. 36.

79. Tony Conrad, letter to Mike Kelley, October 6, 1982, copy located in Conrad's archives. Conrad accurately predicted Kelley's ascension over then-prevailing modes of painting: "Give me a break, and I'll try to break into it a little deeper. There's a lineage to the performance pieces here which relies on metonymies, on formal themes of shape, context, and such, and these goodies are a big part of the seduction: the seduction that *replaces* the now-inevitable neo-expressionist paint surface and so on that we have to look at everywhere." Conrad's acumen as an art critic was not limited to Kelley. See, for instance, the early appreciation of "No Wave" cinema in Tony Conrad, "At Last Real

Movies: Super-8 Cinema from New York," *Journal: Southern California Art Magazine* 27 (June–July 1980): 50–53, or the prescient critique of the "projected image" in contemporary art in Tony Conrad, "People Will Come If the Pictures Move: New Opportunities in Video Installation Art," *The Squealer* [newsletter of Squeaky Wheel, Buffalo, New York] (Spring–Summer 1997): 29–31.

80. Kelley, "Introduction to an Essay which is in the Form of Liner Notes," n.p.; repr. in *Documenta X Short Guide*, pp. 114–15.

81. On the "minor," see Deleuze and Guattari, *Kafka*, pp. 16–27; Gilles Deleuze, "Control and Becoming," in *Negotiations, 1972–1990* (New York: Columbia University Press, 1995), pp. 173–74; and Gilles Deleuze and Félix Guattari, *A Thousand Plateaus: Capitalism and Schizophrenia*, trans. Brian Massumi (Minneapolis: University of Minnesota Press, 1987), pp. 100–110, 291–98, 362–74. Deleuze's most concise statement appears as Gilles Deleuze, "Philosophie et minorité," *Critique* (February 1978): 154–55, parts of which appear in *A Thousand Plateaus*.

82. The major "appears twice, once in the constant and again in the variable from which the constant is extracted." Deleuze and Guattari, *A Thousand Plateaus*, p. 105.

83. *Ibid.*

84. *Ibid.*, p. 292.

85. Foucault, *Nietzsche, Genealogy, History*, p. 139, and Foucault, "What Is an Author?" p. 137.

86. Deleuze and Guattari, *A Thousand Plateaus*, p. 298.

87. *Ibid.*, p. 101.

88. A minor history is never "homogenized matter, but is essentially laden with singularities (which constitute a form of content)." *Ibid.*, p. 369.

89. *Ibid.*, p. 101.

90. *Ibid.*, pp. 369, 372.

91. *Ibid.*, pp. 106.

92. Tony Conrad, letter to Gerald O'Grady, October 23, 1975, p. 4, copy located in Conrad's archive. Conrad is contrasting himself to Paul Sharits: "On the other hand, Mr. Sharits is one of a very few filmmakers whose work as a whole can readily be approached as a tangibly holistic body." More recently, Robert Morris (whose work is discussed in Chapter 3) has discussed his own apparent artistic "inconsistency" in Robert Morris, "Professional Rules," *Critical Inquiry* 23, no. 2 (Winter 1997): 298–322.

93. Hubert Damisch, "Concert (Portrait of an Artist as Michael Snow)," in *Michael Snow: Panoramique* (Brussels: Société des Expositions du Palais des Beaux-Arts de Bruxelles, 1999), p. 24.

94. Though it will also miss some. In the case of a history predicated on following Conrad, the monumental significance of the Judson Dance Theatre in the development of all aspects of minimalism — the one connection beyond the field of the visual arts consistently (though still insufficiently) acknowledged within canonical art history — finds itself shortchanged. Conrad had little if any interaction with Judson, one of the many important aspects of which — in the work of Trisha Brown, Simone Forti, Yvonne Rainer, Carolee Schneemann, and others — was to bring to the fore issues of gender and feminism, even before many of its protagonists identified themselves as feminists. Conrad's own exposure to and embrace of feminism would largely begin at the outset of the 1970s, particularly in the context of his work with Beverly Grant, following earlier engagements with differences in subject position via the queer aesthetics of Jack Smith and questions of race broached by Henry Flynt (see Chapters 4, 5, and Conclusion). Although Judson's importance has been recognized within art history, it has generally been treated as an influence, not made to question the distinction between the disciplines of dance and the visual arts: Rainer's and Forti's "dances," for example, are usually, if implicitly, separated from Robert Morris's "performances" and Robert Rauschenberg's "happenings." For a productive questioning of these divisions, see Carrie Lambert, "More or Less Minimalism: Six Notes on Performance and Visual Art in the 1960s," in *A Minimal Future? Art as Object 1958–1968*, ed. Ann Goldstein (Los Angeles: The Museum of Contemporary Art, Los Angeles, 2004), pp. 103–109. On the role of Judson more generally, see also Sally Banes, *Democracy's Body: Judson Dance Theater, 1962–1964* (Durham, NC: Duke University Press, 1993), and Sally Banes, *Greenwich Village 1963: Avant-Garde Performance and the Effervescent Body* (Durham, NC: Duke University Press, 1993).

Chapter Two: The Social Turn

1. Conrad's job was received from a researcher at the Research Institute for Advanced Science (RIAS), Baltimore, Maryland, with whom he had worked while still in high school. The work allowed Conrad to be anywhere, and he chose California solely out of personal interest. The next summer's position in Copenhagen was also obtained through the same research contact.

2. La Monte Young, letter to Tony Conrad, March 19, 1960. Unless otherwise identified, all letters cited are located in Conrad's personal archive.

3. Tony Conrad, interview with the author, Buffalo, NY, August 15–16, 1995. All unattributed quotes are from this source.

4. "I had this experience which blew my mind, where I found that after I had actually dutifully bought the records and played them to myself over and over again because I knew I was supposed to, I found that I liked them. I had this éclat, this incredible epiphany. Actually, it was really just like a tune in my head, but an uncharacterizable tune – a sound that I could only claim as an internal construction and could not identify until I listened to the Bartók record, and then I realized that that's where it came from. Then, subsequent listening brought the whole thing out for me. So soon I liked the whole thing. But my focus then turned to the fact that I had had this change which to me was the element of greatest significance." Conrad, interview with the author, Buffalo, NY, August 15–16, 1995.

5. Conrad's archives contain programs for Harvard-Radcliffe Music Club concerts from February 21, 1958; November 23, 1958; March 5, 1959; May 18, 1959; and February 14, 1962. The program for Karlheinz Stockhausen's lecture dates it to November 5, 1958. According to Henry Flynt, the lecture largely derived from sections IV and VIII of Karlheinz Stockhausen, "Electronic and Instrumental Music" (1958), in *Audio Culture: Readings in Modern Music*, ed. Christoph Cox and Daniel Warner (New York: Continuum, 2004), pp. 370–80. Telephone conversation with Flynt, December 15, 2006. Conrad also attended a lecture and demonstration by Stockhausen at MIT the previous day. Conrad recalls the Cage and Tudor lecture and performance occurring around the same time; although Conrad does not recall the title, he is certain that it was not "Indeterminacy."

6. Detailed notes from the Kolisch lectures occupy several loose pages interleaved in Conrad's "Music Notes I," a handwritten notebook begun, according to a notation on the first page, on January 5, 1961, now located in Conrad's archives.

7. Henry Flynt, *Fragments and Reconstructions from a Destroyed Oeuvre, 1959–1963* (New York: Backworks, 1982), p. 1.

8. Conrad, interview with author, Buffalo, NY, August 15–16, 1995.

9. Young acknowledges receipt of the tape in a letter to Conrad (undated, but some time before April 11, 1960). On the date of Young's retuning the piano for the *Well-Tuned Piano*, see La Monte Young, "Notes on The Theatre of Eternal

Music and *The Tortoise, His Dreams and Journeys*," twenty-seven-page PDF document, (2000), p. 4, available in the La Monte Young section of the MELA Foundation Web page: http://www.melafoundation.org/lmy.htm (last accessed June 22, 2007).

10. Conrad's time in Cologne is recorded in a handwritten notebook entitled "Music Notes II" (actually written on the back of the notebook, "Music Notes I"), which was begun in Darmstadt in March 1961, but includes notes transcribed from as early as the summer of 1959. Conrad's comment on Eimert is found on page 20 (entry 41, "People," dated April 14, 1961).

11. Conrad, "Music Notes II," p. 34 (entry 58, "End Köln," dated April 20, 1961).

12. Conrad, in "Tony Conrad on the Sixties," in Scott MacDonald, *A Critical Cinema 5: Interviews with Independent Filmmakers* (Berkeley: University of California Press, 2006), p. 72.

13. Conrad wrote: "Back to pulse rhythms, Stockhausen said he had experimented with fast rotation, with the table, and discovered the obvious fact that pulses so generated give a directionless tone at high enough frequency. He wants to use this in a piece—weird sounds that are generated 'by the air itself.' It will mystify everyone, he says. Actually, the effect is somewhat related to the difference (or more accurately, summation) tone phenomenon, but will be influenced, I think, by the relative phase of the sounds used. That means that the location of the listener will be critical, because of the speed of sound and the changing distance of the loudspeakers, which will give phase differences, especially noticeable in lower sounds, that will change the entire sound character (possibly from one ear to the other!). The intensities of the component sounds will also be important, giving a large-scale variation with location. The basis of the phenomenon, essentially, is the summation, out of phase, of a number of low tones to give one higher tone. Near one speaker the high tone will be lost. Since Stockhausen has apparently *tried* this only with low low tones, he might not have noticed any of the above-noted effects, especially due to the 'spreading' and echoing effect with low tones." "Music Notes II," pp. 31–32 (entry 54, "Recordings," April 18, 1961).

14. Friedrich A. Kittler, *Gramophone, Film, Typewriter*, trans. Geoffrey Winthrop-Young and Michael Wutz (Stanford, CA: Stanford University Press, 1999), p. 100.

15. Conrad, interview with author, Buffalo, NY, August 15–16, 1995. Con-

rad notes having first heard *Kontakte* in "Music Notes II," p. 19 (entry 41, "People," dated April 14, 1961).

16. Tony Conrad, *(Prelude and) Fugue for Strings for 18 Solo Instruments*, handwritten score, 1961, p. 3.

17. John Cage (ed.), *Notations* (New York: Something Else Press, 1969), n.p.

18. Conrad, "Music Notes II," p. 37 (entry 66, dated November 8, 1961). Conrad's mention of "Cage radios" refers to Cage's *Imaginary Landscape No. 4* (1951), scored for twelve radios.

19. Conrad, *Three Loops for Performers and Tape Recorders*, typed and handwritten score, November 8–21, 1961, p. 8.

20. R. S., "New Music at Harvard," *Christian Science Monitor*, December 19, 1961, clipping located in Conrad's archives.

21. K. Robert Schwarz, *Minimalists* (London: Phaidon, 1996), p. 36. Keith Potter notes Riley's use of tape loops in late 1960 and into 1961: Potter, *Four Musical Minimalists: La Monte Young, Terry Riley, Steve Reich, Philip Glass* (Cambridge: Cambridge University Press, 2000), p. 98.

22. Conrad, "Music Notes II," p. 37 (entry 66, "Resonance," dated November 8, 1961).

23. Conrad, "Music Notes II," p. 40 (entry 78, "Feedback," dated November 20, 1961): "This summer I produced some fascinating whistling + sighing using tape recorder feedback, swinging the mike back + forth or in circles in front of the speaker. A very good sound!"

24. Conrad, "Music Notes II," p. 14 (entry 39, "USA," dated March 22, 1961).

25. John Cale, "Dream Interpretation" (with Conrad), track one of *Dream Interpretation: Inside the Dream Syndicate II*, Table of the Elements compact disc 79.

26. Tony Conrad, "Inside the Dream Syndicate," *Film Culture* 41 (Summer 1966): 7.

27. Tony Conrad, "Tony Conrad on 'The Flicker': From a Letter to Henry Romney, Dated November 11, 1965," *Film Culture* 41 (Summer 1966): 1.

28. Although Cage was not himself in residence, Stockhausen was extolling his thought and music, and David Tudor participated, as well.

29. Richard Kostelanetz, *The Theatre of Mixed Means* (1968; New York: RK Editions, 1980), p. 191.

30. John Cage, "Preface to *Indeterminacy*" (1959), in *John Cage: Writer*, ed. Richard Kostelanetz (New York: Limelight Editions, 1993), p. 78.

31. Young, letter to Conrad, September 22, 1959.

32. This was actually the second major phase of Cage's development. The first revolved around percussion. Cage's work would transform again in the 1960s, a transformation that Henry Flynt suggests was, in part, brought forth by the developments in the circle around Young. Henry Flynt, "La Monte Young in New York, 1960–62," in *Sound and Light: La Monte Young, Marian Zazeela*, ed. William Duckworth and Richard Fleming (Lewisburg, PA: Bucknell University Press, 1996), p. 77.

33. The best critical study of Cage's work remains James Pritchett, *The Music of John Cage* (Cambridge: Cambridge University Press, 1993). I have attempted to chronicle certain aspects of Cage's development in detail elsewhere. See my "'A Therapeutic Value for City Dwellers': The Development of John Cage's Early Avant-Garde Aesthetic Position," in *John Cage: Music, Philosophy, and Intention, 1933–1950*, ed. David W. Patterson (New York: Routledge, 2002), pp. 135–75; "John Cage and the Architecture of Silence," *October* 81 (Summer 1997): 80–104; and "White on White," chapter 1 of *Random Order: Robert Rauschenberg and the Neo-Avant-Garde* (Cambridge, MA: MIT Press, 2003), pp. 25–71.

34. John Cage, "Composition: To Describe the Process of Composition Used in *Music of Changes* and *Imaginary Landscape No. 4*" (1952), in *Silence* (Middletown, CT: Wesleyan University Press, 1961), p. 59.

35. John Cage, "Composition as Process II: Indeterminacy" (1958), in *Silence*, p. 36.

36. Gilles Deleuze and Félix Guattari, *A Thousand Plateaus: Capitalism and Schizophrenia*, trans. Brian Massumi (Minneapolis: University of Minnesota Press, 1987), pp. 266–67.

37. John Cage, "On Film" (1956), in *John Cage: An Anthology*, ed. Richard Kostelanetz (New York: Da Capo, 1970), p. 115; John Cage, "Where Are We Going? And What Are We Doing?" (1961), in *Silence*, p. 194. In this as in all cases, I have chosen not to reproduce Cage's typographic experimentations.

38. Cage, "On Film," in *John Cage: An Anthology*, p. 115.

39. Cage, "45′ for a Speaker" (1954), in *Silence*, p. 161.

40. Cage, "Composition as Process II: Indeterminacy," in *Silence*, p. 38.

41. John Cage, "Composition as Process I: Changes" (1958), in *Silence*, p. 31.

42. Cage, "Composition as Process II: Indeterminacy," in *Silence*, p. 38.

Cage comments further on dualism and dialectics in "Program Notes" (1959), in *John Cage: Writer*, pp. 81–82.

43. Cage, "Where Are We Going? And What Are We Doing?" in *Silence*, p. 237, and Cage, "On Robert Rauschenberg, Artist, and His Work" (1961), in *Silence*, p. 98.

44. Daniel Charles, *Gloses sur John Cage* (Paris: Union Générale d'Éditions, 1978), pp. 91–109, and Gilles Deleuze and Félix Guattari, *Anti-Oedipus: Capitalism and Schizophrenia*, trans. Mark Seem, Robert Hurley, and Helen R. Lane (Minneapolis: University of Minnesota Press, 1983), pp. 370–71.

45. Liz Kotz, "Post-Cagean Aesthetics and the 'Event' Score," *October* 95 (Winter 2001): 59 and 59 n. 10.

46. John Cage, "Experimental Music" (1957), in *Silence*, p. 10.

47. Cage, "On Robert Rauschenberg, Artist, and His Work," in *Silence*, p. 108.

48. Cage, "Where Are We Going? And What Are We Doing?" in *Silence*, pp. 224–26.

49. John Cage, "History of Experimental Music in the United States" (1959), in *Silence*, p. 72.

50. John Cage, "Form is a Language," *Art News*, April, 1960; repr. in *John Cage: An Anthology*, p. 135. The history of Cage's relation to anarchism remains to be written. For a hint at the environment in which it operated, see Judith Malina, "Remembering Jackson Mac Low," *Performing Arts Journal* 80 (2005): 76–78.

51. John Cage, "Experimental Music: Doctrine" (1955), in *Silence*, p. 14.

52. *Ibid.*, p. 12.

53. Cage, "45′ for a Speaker," in *Silence*, p. 149.

54. Michael Fried, "Art and Objecthood" (1967), in *Art and Objecthood: Essays and Reviews* (Chicago: University of Chicago Press, 1998), p. 164.

55. *Ibid.*, p. 152.

56. *Ibid.*, p. 166.

57. Fried specifically mentions music, particularly Cage, in *ibid.*, p. 164.

58. *Ibid.*, pp. 168–69 n. 6.

59. See Michel Foucault's critique of "the 'institutional-centric' approach" ["*institutionnalocentrisme*"] in *Security, Territory, Population: Lectures at the Collège de France, 1977–1978*, ed. Michel Senellart, trans. Graham Burchell (New York: Palgrave Macmillan, 2007): "This kind of method entails going behind the insti-

tution and trying to discover in a wider and more overall perspective what we can broadly call a technology of power. In the same way, this analysis allows us to replace a genetic analysis through filiation with a genealogical analysis . . . which reconstructs a whole network of alliances, communications, and points of support. So, the first methodological principle is to move outside the institution and replace it with the overall point of view of the technology of power" (p. 117).

60. La Monte Young, "Lecture 1960," in *Ubi Fluxus ibi motus, 1990–1962*, ed. Achille Bonito Oliva (Milan: Nuove edizioni Gabriele Mazzotta, 1990), p. 198. The various published versions of "Lecture 1960," not all of which are identical, are discussed below.

61. Cole Gagne, *Soundpieces 2: Interviews with American Composers* (Metuchen, NJ: Scarecrow Press, 1993), pp. 484–85.

62. La Monte Young, *Vision*, score, November 12, 1959. Copy located in the Research Library, The Getty Research Institute, Los Angeles, California, David Tudor Papers (940073), box 12, folder 3.

63. Cornelius Cardew, "One Sound: La Monte Young," *Musical Times* (November 1966): 960. Cage had advocated unusual materials, including an amplified phonograph cartridge, as part of his sound collages in "Lecture on Nothing" (1950), in *Silence*, p. 117.

64. Young, letter to Conrad, before April 11, 1960; Allan Kaprow, "One Chapter from 'The Principles of Modern Art,'" *It Is* 4 (1958): 51–52.

65. Kaprow, "One Chapter," p. 52.

66. *Ibid.*

67. This is evinced in the "musical" setting of George Maciunas's earliest manifesto pronouncement, "Neo-Dada in Music, Theater, Poetry, Art," read by Arthus C. Caspari at the concert Après John Cage, at the Galerie Parnass, Wuppertal, West Germany, on June 9, 1962; repr. in Clive Phillpot and Jon Hendricks, *Fluxus: Selections from the Gilbert and Lila Silverman Collection* (New York: Museum of Modern Art, 1988), pp. 25–37.

68. Michael Nyman, "An Interview with George Brecht," in *An Introduction to George Brecht's Book of the Tumbler on Fire*, ed. Henry Martin (Milan: Multhipla, 1978), pp. 106–7. Brecht makes reference to nuclear physics and Zen philosophy as influencing his idea of the eventlike nature of all physical objects (p. 106). John Cage had come to much the same conclusion about the relation of objects and processes. See Cage's comments in John Cage and Daniel Charles, *For the Birds* (New York: Marion Boyars, 1981), p. 220.

69. Kaprow, "One Chapter," p. 52.

70. Program notes, University of California, Berkeley, Department of Music, "Noon Concerts," May 11, 1960, copy in Conrad's archives. Alternate titles for *Poem* are given in Young, letter to David Tudor, July 5, 1960, located in the Research Library, The Getty Research Institute, Los Angeles, California, David Tudor Papers (940073), box 13, folder 11.

71. Young, letter to Conrad May 19, 1960. Whether known to Young at the time or not, such theatrical scores had been preceded by Cage's Black Mountain College Event of 1951.

72. Young, letter to Tudor, July 5, 1960.

73. *Ibid.*

74. Young's "Lecture 1960" has been published in several versions, including: La Monte Young, "Excerpts from 'Lecture 1960,'" *Kulchur* 3, no. 10 (Summer 1963): 18–21; La Monte Young, "Lecture 1960," *Tulane Drama Review* 10, no. 2 (1965): 73–83, repr. in *Happenings and Other Acts*, ed. Mariellen R. Sandford (London: Routledge, 1995), pp. 72–81; in La Monte Young and Marian Zazeela, *Selected Writings* (Munich: Heiner Friedrich, 1969), n.p.; in Oliva (ed.), *Ubi Fluxus ibi motus*, pp. 198–204; and as "Lecture, Summer–Fall, 1960," in Jon Hendricks (ed.), *What's Fluxus? What's Not! Why.* (Detroit: The Gilbert and Lila Silverman Fluxus Collection Foundation, 2002), pp. 75–83. Although an early version of the lecture was presented in July 1960 at Halprin's workshop (accompanied by a tape recording of Young's *Trio for Strings*), sections of the published lecture were added later that year.

75. Young, "Lecture 1960," *Tulane Drama Review*, p. 83.

76. *Ibid.*, p. 75.

77. *Ibid.*, p. 79. See also Flynt's discussion of Young's position toward Cage in Flynt, "La Monte Young in New York," pp. 52–53 and 57.

78. An inserted page in the middle of the conjoined notebook sections of "Music Notes I" and "Music Notes II" reads:

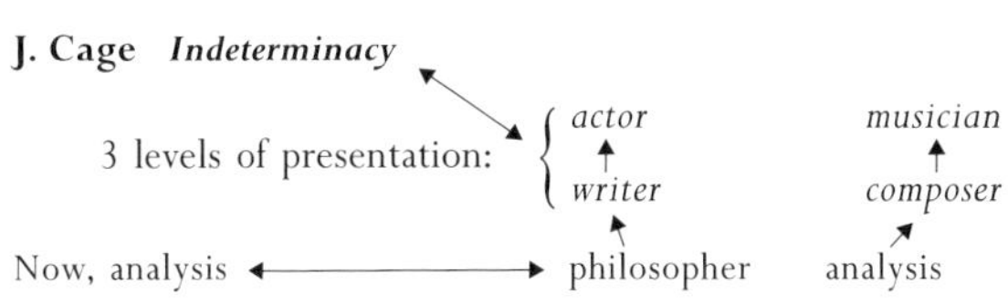

> A composition will here denote the effects prescribed by the composer either directly or by implication, or as a part of an accepted tradition. Other aspects are called indetermined (see anecdote about Wolff playing)[.] All other aspects may be in a sense considered determined.
>
> Determination: Indetermination is new form.

Although this note is found amid several call slips labeled "Deutsche Staatsbibliothek Musikabteilung," Conrad recounts that he must have heard *Indeterminacy* prior to this moment and certainly not at the Staatsbibliotek. Conversation with author, January 6, 2007.

79. Young, letter to Conrad, before April 11, 1960. Flynt has stated that Conrad's reference to the piece, *IS* was likely referring, in actuality, to either *Poem 1* or *Poem 2*, both now destroyed. Flynt, telephone conversation with author, December 15, 2006.

80. La Monte Young (ed.), *An Anthology* (New York: La Monte Young and Jackson Mac Low, 1963), n.p.

81. Kostelanetz, *The Theatre of Mixed Means*, p. 195.

82. On Young's collaborations with Warhol, see my "'My Mind Split Open': Andy Warhol's Exploding Plastic Inevitable," *Grey Room* 8 (Summer 2002): 80–107.

83. Edward Strickland, *Minimalism: Origins* (Bloomington: Indiana University Press, 1993), p. 138.

84. Potter, *Four Musical Minimalists*, p. 41.

85. Young was particularly interested in the limits to which indeterminacy could be taken. See, for instance, the discussion between Young, Dennis Johnson, and Richard Maxfield, in Young, "Lecture 1960," *Tulane Drama Review*, pp. 76–77.

86. In addition to the work's (once again, almost conventional) theatrical aspect, *Piano Piece for Terry Riley #1* focused on the role of the body (and physical exhaustion), a line taken up, as we will see, in Young's *arabic numeral (any integer)* (April 1960) to H. F. [Henry Flynt] and echoed later in the physically demanding musical and performance-art activities of Charlemagne Palestine.

87. Young emphasizes the visual aspect of the work in Kostelanetz, *The Theatre of Mixed Means*, p. 192.

88. Young, "Lecture 1960," *Tulane Drama Review*, p. 75 (answering the

question of whether, when a tree falls in the forest and there is no one there to hear it, it can or cannot be considered music).

89. To my knowledge, only Michael Nyman has noted the piece's relation to *4'33"*. See Nyman, "An Interview with George Brecht," p. 119 n. 5.

90. In this, they resemble the work of Marcel Duchamp, in which (unlike George Brecht) Young, who as his dedications to Richard Huelsenbeck shows was aware of dada, has never professed any interest. Duchamp's example would nonetheless have been received by Young, if in no other way, mediated via Cage and, later, Robert Morris.

91. In this manner, they can be understood, much like the Duchampian readymade, to operate simultaneously on the level of *parole*, the individual linguistic utterance, and *langue*, the overall structural conditions of a language.

92. Strickland, *Minimalism*, p. 142.

93. Dick Higgins, "open letter" to George Maciunas, November 19, 1974, located in the Research Library, The Getty Research Institute, Los Angeles, California, Dick Higgins Papers (870613), box 20, file F-65/I/Maciunas, George.

94. Ken Friedman, (ed.), *The Fluxus Performance Workbook*, a special edition of *El Djarida* magazine, Trondheim, Norway, vol. 9 (1990), pp. 11, 13. The fourth part of Bozzi's *A Piece for Chieko Shiomi* entails letting fall "a glass of water from horizontal outstretched arm while standing on a stool or on the top of a ladder."

95. Friedman, (ed.), *The Fluxus Performance Workbook*, p. 47. See also Conrad's *Imagined* and Brecht's discussion of "borderline art," cited in Chapter 4, note 82.

96. Alison Knowles, *By Alison Knowles* (New York: Something Else Press, 1965); variant in Friedman, (ed.), *The Fluxus Performance Workbook*, p. 34.

97. Young comments on the reaction of the audience in Cole Gagne, *Soundpieces*, p. 485.

98. Cage, "Experimental Music: Doctrine," in *Silence*, p. 13.

99. On this general goal, see, for instance, John Cage, *Conversing with Cage*, ed. Richard Kostelanetz (New York: Limelight Editions, 1994), p. 234, and John Cage, in C. H. Waddington, *Biology and the History of the Future* (Edinburgh: Edinburgh University Press, 1972), p. 45.

100. See Cage's discussion of the opening up of the ego as he learned from Daisetz Suzuki in, for example, *Conversing with Cage*, p. 229.

101. John Cage, "Letter to Paul Henry Lang" (1956), in *John Cage: An Anthology*, pp. 117–18.

102. Kostelanetz, *The Theatre of Mixed Means*, pp. 193–94.

103. Program flier for A Program of Sound Improvisation, California School of Fine Arts, May 6, 1960; copy located in Conrad's archives.

104. Young, "Lecture 1960," *Tulane Drama Review*, p. 80.

105. Friedman (ed.), *The Fluxus Performance Workbook*, p. 54. Ono's *Audience Piece* is described in Midori Yoshimoto, *Into Performance: Japanese Women Artists in New York* (New Brunswick, NJ: Rutgers University Press, 2005), pp. 93–94.

106. Young, "Lecture 1960," *Tulane Drama Review*, pp. 77–78.

107. Conrad, "Music Notes II," p. 39 (entry 75, "Mattress," dated November 19, 1961).

108. Young, "Lecture 1960," *Tulane Drama Review*, p. 76.

109. *Ibid.*, p. 77.

110. Liz Kotz perceptively argues for the importance of Cage's typographic score in "Post-Cagean Aesthetics," pp. 55–89.

111. Conrad, "Music Notes II," p. 39 (entry 77, "Audiences," dated November 19, 1961).

112. *Ibid.* The mathematical indication, *n!* signifies the factorial, which, for a positive integer n is defined as: $n(n\text{-}1)\ldots2\cdot1$.

113. Conrad, "Music Notes II," p. 37 (entry 69, "Audience Res.," dated November 15, 1961).

114. Young, letter to Conrad, July 7, 1960.

115. Tony Conrad, liner notes to *Four Violins (1964)*, Table of the Elements 17 Cl, vinyl record; repr. as "LYssophobia: on *Four Violins*," in *Early Minimalism, Vol. 1*, and as "Four Violins (1964)," *Halana* 2 (1996): 5–15 (quote appears on p. 10).

116. Conrad, interview with author, Buffalo, NY, August 15–16, 1995.

117. Sally Banes, *Greenwich Village 1963: Avant-Garde Performance and the Effervescent Body* (Durham, NC: Duke University Press, 1993), pp. 65–73.

118. Cornelius Cardew, "Towards an Ethic of Improvisation," in *Treatise Handbook* (London: Edition Peters, 1971), p. xviii.

119. La Monte Young, "Notes on The Theatre of Eternal Music and *The Tortoise, His Dreams and Journeys*," (2000), p. 25. It should be noted that Conrad does not consider the Theatre of Eternal Music to be an improvisation, either. As he explained to Jérome Noetinger of *Metamkine* magazine, "our collective relationship with the sound did not rely on melody or rhythmic continuity, whose absence depleted the referential vocabulary necessary for 'improvisation.'

This is to say that I had never properly regarded our work together as either improvisation or the work of a composer, but as a very direct challenge to both conceptions, and the founding of a different principle in the organization of musical sound." Conrad, eight-page typescript in response to interview questions sent by Jérome Noetinger for *Metamkine* magazine, October 27, 1995, pp. 3–4, located in Conrad's archives.

120. As Cardew wrote in the first line of his discussion of La Monte Young's *arabic numeral (any integer)* (April 1960) to H.F.: "The writing down of music is in the process of disintegrating." Cornelius Cardew, "On the Role of the Instructions in the Interpretation of Indeterminate Music," in *Treatise Handbook* p. xiv.

121. The tape is discussed in Cardew, "One Sound: La Monte Young," pp. 959–60.

122. Conrad, interview with author, Buffalo, NY, August 15–16, 1995.

123. *Ibid.*

124. Tony Conrad, liner notes to *Slapping Pythagoras*, Table of the Elements 23 V, compact disc. Conrad's concerns with radical democracy were broached earlier in Tony Conrad, "Capping Nostalgia," in *The Kitchen Turns Twenty: A Retrospective Anthology*, ed. Lee Morrissey (New York: The Kitchen, 1992), p. 35.

Chapter Three: The Tower and the Line

1. This and all of Young's word scores are published in La Monte Young (ed.), *An Anthology* (New York: LaMonte Young and Jackson Mac Low, 1963), n.p. The chapter epigraph comes from a personal communication with the author, Buffalo, NY, August 15–16, 1995.

2. Ken Friedman (ed.), *The Fluxus Performance Workbook*, a special edition of *El Djarida* magazine, Trondheim, Norway, vol. 9 (1990), p. 29.

3. Jon Hendricks, *Fluxus Codex* (New York: The Gilbert and Lila Silverman Fluxus Collection, in association with Harry N. Abrams, 1988), p. 358.

4. Yoko Ono, *Grapefruit: A Book of Instructions and Drawings* (1964; New York: Simon and Schuster, 2000), n.p.

5. Tony Conrad, "Music Notes II," p. 37 (entry 71, "Draw Line," dated November 19, 1961).

6. Hendricks, *Fluxus Codex*, p. 102.

7. Henry Flynt would explicitly extend Young's implicit critique of "newness" in the lecture "The Supererogatory, Misleading Notion of 'Newness,'" delivered at Young's Bank Street apartment on June 3, 1961.

8. See discussion and reproduction of the evening's program in Henry Flynt, "La Monte Young in New York, 1960–62," in *Sound and Light: La Monte Young, Marian Zazeela*, ed. William Duckworth and Richard Fleming (Lewisburg, PA: Bucknell University Press, 1996), pp. 59–63.

9. William Weber in the Harvard *Crimson*, April 11, 1961, quoted in Flynt, "La Monte Young in New York," p. 63.

10. Flynt, "La Monte Young in New York," p. 63 (emphasis in the original). For a different discussion of the passage to "art in general" that focuses on mainstream minimal and conceptual art, see Thierry de Duve, *Kant after Duchamp* (Cambridge, MA: MIT Press, 1996), especially chapter 4, "The Monochrome and the Blank Canvas," pp. 199–280.

11. John Cage, letter to David Tudor, [May, 1961], Research Library, The Getty Research Institute, Los Angeles, California, David Tudor Papers (940073), box 13, folder 2. Cage would be kept apprised of Young's proclivity for extended duration through a letter sent by Diane Wakoski detailing Young's playing his "Young's Blues" at a party long after everyone had wanted to leave. Diane Wakoski, letter to John Cage, November 26, 1961, John Cage Archive, Northwestern University.

12. La Monte Young, letter to David Tudor, 1961, Research Library, The Getty Research Institute, Los Angeles, California, David Tudor Papers (940073), box 13, folder 11. On Robert Morris's *Site*, see Maurice Berger, *Labyrinths: Robert Morris, Minimalism, and the 1960s* (New York: Harper and Row, 1989), pp. 81–82.

13. Richard Kostelanetz, *The Theatre of Mixed Means* (1968; New York: RK Editions, 1980), p. 205.

14. From the beginning, Young's sound experiments at Halprin's seem to have been considered potential sources for a type of electronic music, or more accurately, "tape music," akin perhaps to certain of Maxfield's pieces such as *Cough Music* (1959).

15. Jacqueline Caux and Daniel Caux, "John Cage: 'Une experience qui a changé ma façon d'entendre,'" *Chroniques de l'art vivant* 30 (May 1972): 26, my translation wherever cited. See also Cage's comments in Jean Vanden Heuvel, "The 'Fantastic Sounds' of La Monte Young," *Vogue* 147 (May 1966), p. 198, and in John Cage, *Conversing with Cage*, ed. Richard Kostelanetz (New York: Limelight Editions, 1994), pp. 203–4.

16. Walter Benjamin, "Little History of Photography" (1931), trans. Edmund Jephcott and Kingsley Shorter, in *Walter Benjamin: Selected Writings,*

Volume 2, 1927–1934, ed. Michael W. Jennings, Howard Eiland, and Gary Smith (Cambridge, MA: Harvard University Press, 1999), p. 512. The preceding quote about "human consciousness" occurs on p. 510.

17. Walter Benjamin, "The Work of Art in the Age of Its Technological Reproducibility: Third Version" (1936–38), trans. Harry Zohn and Edmund Jephcott, in Walter Benjamin: *Selected Writings, Volume 4, 1938–1940*, ed. Howard Eiland and Michael W. Jennings (Cambridge, MA: Harvard University Press, 2003), p. 265. Benjamin specifically extends this unconscious to the "auditory" realm, as well, in the wake of the development of sound film (p. 265).

18. John Cage and Daniel Charles, *For the Birds* (New York: Marion Boyars, 1981), p. 150.

19. Unlike Benjamin, Cage did not relate to the technological unconscious according to the presuppositions of psychoanalysis. For Benjamin (at least for a certain aspect of his argument), the traces of the uncoded "real" that are captured by media technologies are ultimately to be read as symptoms; they are "meaningful," albeit "covert," and the role of the camera (via enlargement, etc.) is to bring them to perceptibility. Caught by the camera are the lapses (*lapsus*) of the imaginary, those moments when the real erupts into the visual field. Uninterpreted (unenlarged, unseen, i.e. remaining "covert"), they are "magic"; made visible and interpretable, they are revealed as "a thoroughly historical variable" and hence, as Benjamin writes in "The Work of Art" essay, open up vast fields or areas of human intervention. Cage, by contrast, does not seek to deliver the newfound possibilities made available by the acoustical unconscious to symbolic interpretation (à la psychoanalysis). Indeed, as he explained to Jacqueline and Daniel Caux, "If you listen to [Young's] work with intelligence rather than your ears [i.e., on the level of the symbolic, rather than the real, in the parlance of Friedrich Kittler], you could think that you don't hear anything, but if you listen to it with your ears, you can hear this complexity that I just mentioned." Caux and Caux, "John Cage," p. 26. For Cage, each object (even a symbolic object, i.e., a linguistic sign) is an artificially frozen moment in an otherwise ongoing process. Electronic technologies, therefore, not only open up the unconscious of "objects" (via enlargement or amplification), but dissolve them into commutable (infinitely transmutable) processes, precisely what Paul Virilio would later observe about the electronic transformation of the means of production and, via television, the visual realm. See Paul Virilio, *The Lost Dimension*, trans. Daniel Moshenberg (New York: Semiotext(e), 1991).

20. Cage and Charles, *For the Birds*, p. 150.

21. La Monte Young, "Lecture 1960," *Tulane Drama Review* 10, no. 2 (1965): 81.

22. Young's comments at the beginning of the section are particularly redolent of Cage's ideas and phraseology. See, for instance, John Cage, "Experimental Music" (1957), in *Silence* (Middletown, CT: Wesleyan University Press, 1961), p. 10.

23. This phenomenon is best explained in La Monte Young and Marian Zazeela, "Dream House," in *Selected Writings* (Munich: Heiner Friedrich, 1969), n.p.

24. Richard Kostelanetz, "Conversation with John Cage," in *John Cage: An Anthology*, ed. Richard Kostelanetz (New York: Da Capo, 1970), p. 26.

25. Young, "Lecture 1960," *Tulane Drama Review*, p. 82.

26. John Cage, "A Composer's Confessions" (1948), in *John Cage: Writer*, ed. Richard Kostelanetz (New York: Limelight Editions, 1993), p. 41.

27. John Cage, "Memoir" (1966), in *John Cage: An Anthology*, p. 77.

28. Young, "Lecture 1960," *Tulane Drama Review*, p. 81. The experience of getting inside a sound, as experienced in the work of Young and the Theatre of Eternal Music more generally, could, and perhaps should, be understood more radically by stressing the aspect of negation — the distinction and distancing from the habitual (auditory) environment — though that aspect is only hinted at, not emphasized, by Young.

29. Caux and Caux, "John Cage," p. 26 (ellipsis in original).

30. John Cage, *A Year from Monday* (Middletown, CT: Wesleyan University Press, 1967), p. 16. See Marian Zazeela's comments on this passage in Ljerka Vidic, "Meet the Composer: La Monte Young and Marian Zazeela," *EAR: New Music News* 12, no. 3 (May 1987): 26. Cage's judgment, however, did not stop him, toward the end of his life, from developing certain aspects of Young's aesthetic in his late compositions.

31. On Kaprow, see Michael Kirby and Richard Schechner, "An Interview with John Cage," *Tulane Drama Review* 10, no. 2 (Winter 1965): 69; repr. in Mariellen R. Sandford, *Happenings and Other Acts* (New York: Routledge, 1995), p. 69.

32. Caux and Caux, "John Cage," p. 26.

33. Such is Theodor Adorno's critique of Cage. See, for example, Theodor W. Adorno, "Vers une musique informelle" (1961), trans. Rodney Livingstone,

in *Quasi una fantasia* (London: Verso, 1994), pp. 269–322. Wim Mertens attempts to extrapolate Adorno's perspective from Cage to the main line of minimalist composers in the last chapter of his *American Minimal Music: La Monte Young, Terry Riley, Steve Reich, Philip Glass*, trans. J. Hautekiet (London: Kahn & Averill, 1983), pp. 113–24.

34. Flynt, "La Monte Young in New York," pp. 60–61. Flynt further recalled that *Box with the Sound of Its Own Making* was played during the intermission and perhaps before the concert, and that Morris was upset that it was mistakenly left off the flyer. Henry Flynt, e-mail to author, November 21, 2006. Morris corresponded with Cage about the happeninglike *Wind Ensemble* in letters dated August 8, 1960 and February 27, 1961. See Robert Morris, "Letters to John Cage," *October* 81 (Summer 1997): 70–73.

35. Morris, "Letters to John Cage," pp. 71–76.

36. Robert Morris, interview with Jack Burnham, November 21, 1975, in Robert Morris's archive, partially quoted in Berger, *Labyrinths*, p. 31.

37. The score for *Variations V* was referred to as "thirty-seven remarks re an audio-visual performance." Kostelanetz (ed.), *John Cage: An Anthology*, p. 218. James Pritchett refers to this as "'*a posteriori*' scoring." James Pritchett, *The Music of John Cage* (Cambridge: Cambridge University Press, 1993), p. 144.

38. On the work of Walter De Maria and Robert Morris's contributions to *An Anthology*, see Barbara Haskell, *Blam! The Explosion of Pop, Minimalism, and Performance, 1958–1964* (New York: Whitney Museum of American Art, 1984), pp. 91–103. On De Maria, see also Jane McFadden, "Toward Site," *Grey Room* 27 (Spring, 2007): 36–57. On Morris, see also Flynt, "La Monte Young in New York," p. 78.

39. Quoted in Morris's letter to Cage of February 27, 1961. Morris, "Letters to John Cage," p. 73.

40. Morris, "Letters to John Cage," p. 75.

41. *Ibid.*, p. 74.

42. See, for instance, Carrie Lambert's discussion of Judson Dance's hybridization of dance and sculpture in Carrie Lambert, "More or Less Minimalism: Six Notes on Performance and Visual Art in the 1960s" in *A Minimal Future? Art as Object 1958–1968*, ed. Ann Goldstein (Los Angeles: The Museum of Contemporary Art, Los Angeles, 2004), pp. 103–9. In George Maciunas's *Expanded Arts Diagram*, published in *Film Culture* 43 (Winter 1966): 7, nearly all of the major categories of artistic production would be labeled as variants of "theatre":

"Kinesthetic Theatre," "Acoustic Theatre," "Happenings / Neo-Baroque Theatre," and so on.

43. Riley's sculpture is reproduced in Stephen Bann, "The Magic Theater," *L'Oeil* (August–September 1968): 40–45.

44. Bruce Nauman's *Violin Film #1 (Playing the Violin as Fast as I Can)* (1967–68, parts of which would end up on *Record* [1969]), *Playing a Note on the Violin While I Walk around the Studio* (1967–68), and *Violin Tuned D.E.A.D.* (1969) were all made in dialogue with the music made in the Theatre of Eternal Music. See Michael Kimmelman, "Two Who Define Today Amble in the Past: At the Met with Susan Rothenberg and Bruce Nauman," *New York Times*, February 21 1997, sec. C, p. 26; and Bruce Nauman, *Please Pay Attention Please: Bruce Nauman's Words*, ed. Janet Kraynak (Cambridge, MA: MIT Press), pp. 245–46, 306. Although Nauman explicitly mentions only Young, rather than the whole of the Theatre of Eternal Music, his use of the violin is most clearly related to Conrad's presence in the group.

45. See Simone [Forti], "Instructions for a Dance," in *An Anthology*, n.p. – in which one dancer is told to "lie on the floor" without moving, while a second is instructed to "tie the first man to the wall," establishing a conflict in which the work's stated intentions necessarily remain unfulfilled – and Yvonne Rainer, "A Quasi Survey of Some 'Minimalist' Tendencies in the Quantitatively Minimal Dance Activity Midst the Plethora, or an Analysis of Trio A," in *Minimal Art: A Critical Anthology*, ed. Gregory Battcock (Berkeley: University of California Press, 1995), p. 270.

46. Morris, "Letters to John Cage," p. 76. In this version, Morris's *Column* is related to his more evidently sexual work, *Footnote to the Bride* (1961). Yvonne Rainer has recently related the original production of *Column* to the context of her dance work. Yvonne Rainer, *Feelings Are Facts: A Life* (Cambridge, MA: MIT Press, 2006), p. 235. Some accounts have Morris's *Column* toppled by another person, he being treated for his injury at the time of the performance.

47. Rosalind E. Krauss, *Passages in Modern Sculpture* (Cambridge, MA: MIT Press, 1977), pp. 201–3.

48. Berger, *Labyrinths*, pp. 47–48.

49. Robert Morris, "Notes on Sculpture, Part 2" (1966), in *Continuous Project Altered Daily* (Cambridge, MA: MIT Press, 1993), p. 20.

50. The reception of Duchamp is perhaps the major distinction between Young and George Brecht, who wrote on Duchamp in *Chance-Imagery* even

before fully absorbing the example of Cage. See George Brecht, *Chance-Imagery* (1957; New York: Something Else Press, 1966).

51. Morris's exposure to Duchamp came from the 1959 monograph by Robert Lebel. Berger, *Labyrinths*, p. 28. Cage, however, had also referred to "The string Duchamp dropped" in a lecture of 1961 and possibly earlier in the "Lecture on Nothing," Cage, *Silence*, pp. 195 and 150.

52. Morris, "Notes on Sculpture, Part 2," pp. 16–17.

53. Robert Morris, "Notes on Sculpture, Part 3: Notes and Non Sequiturs" (1967), in *Continuous Project Altered Daily*, p. 28.

54. Krauss, *Passages*, p. 267.

55. Morris, "Letters to John Cage," p. 73.

56. Annette Michelson, "Robert Morris: An Aesthetics of Transgression," in *Robert Morris* (Washington, D.C.: Corcoran Gallery of Art, 1969), pp. 7–79. The term "presentness" derives from Michael Fried, "Art and Objecthood" (1967), in *Art and Objecthood: Essays and Reviews* (Chicago: University of Chicago Press, 1998), pp. 167–68. To date, it is Michelson who has best articulated the relation between Morris's work and that of Cage.

57. Hal Foster, *The Return of the Real* (Cambridge, MA: MIT Press, 1996), pp. 56 and 54 (emphasis in the original).

58. Robert Morris, "Notes on Sculpture, Part 1" (1966), in *Continuous Project Altered Daily*, p. 3. Foster's text emphasizes Soviet productivism, rather than the constructivism that Morris recovers. Foster addresses this distinction in minimalism's reception of the Russian avant-garde in "Some Uses and Abuses of Russian Constructivism," in *Art into Life: Russian Constructivism, 1914–1932* (New York: Rizzoli, 1990), pp. 248–49. The dialectical aspect of Morris's use of constructivism is most evident in Michelson, "Robert Morris."

59. Robert Morris, "Three Folds in the Fabric and Four Autobiographical Asides as Allegories (or Interruptions)" (1989), in *Continuous Project Altered Daily*, p. 263.

60. Morris, "Notes on Sculpture, Part 1," p. 6. Although the elements of sculpture's literal and tactile nature are mentioned, it is important to note how, by the article's end, they are largely supplanted or overcome by an emphasis on the wholeness and unity of parts. See also Morris's comments in "Three Folds in the Fabric," p. 279.

61. Foster notes the primacy of the ideal form in Morris's work in *Return of the Real*, p. 47.

62. James Meyer, *Minimalism: Art and Polemics in the Sixties* (New Haven, CT: Yale University Press, 2001), p. 158.

63. See, for instance, Carl Andre and Hollis Frampton, *12 Dialogues 1962–1963* (Halifax, Nova Scotia and New York: The Press of the Nova Scotia College of Art and Design and New York University Press, 1980), p. 43.

64. Morris, "Notes on Sculpture, Part 4" (1969), in *Continuous Project Altered Daily*, p. 64.

65. Michelson makes the latter point, "Robert Morris: An Aesthetics of Transgression," pp. 23–25. It might be noted here that Edward Strickland presents late modernist formal painting as connected with early musical minimalism, seeing the two as consistent and both as opposed to sculptural minimalism. Such a perspective (erroneous, to my mind) seems to follow from an unquestioned adherence to Young's understanding of minimalism and transcendence that is at odds with the more consequential and political aspects of minimal sculpture and dance. Edward Strickland, *Minimalism: Origins* (Bloomington: Indiana University Press, 1993).

66. See Robert Morris, "American Quartet" (1981), in *Continuous Project Altered Daily*, p. 245: "One of the central aspects of Abstract Expressionism and Minimalism is the projection of an aura of power and domination over the viewer. The production of icons with an intense presence that projected authority has been one of the ambitions of these types of work. Higher authority or force is, of course, the basis of the transcendent."

67. Fredric Jameson, "Periodizing the 60s," in *The Sixties without Apology*, ed. Sohnya Sayres et al. (Minneapolis: University of Minnesota Press, 1984), p. 190.

68. John Cage, "Goal: New Music, New Dance" (1939), in *Silence*, p. 87.

69. As Morris wrote in an unpublished text of 1970, "the repressive structures within the art world parallel those outside it." Quoted in Berger, *Labyrinths*, p. 109. See also p. 118.

70. Berger, *Labyrinths*, p. 123.

71. *Ibid.*, p. 146.

72. Morris, "Notes on Sculpture, Part 1," p. 8. Thus, as Berger observes about Morris's late-1960s landscape works, "The expansive landscape of Holland [sic] or Nazca offered no ideological resistance for Morris to work against; he would have to return to the world of repressive institutions in order to critique them more convincingly" (p. 148). The risk of this sort of institution critique,

which remains within and potentially strengthens the institution as much as it critiques it, has been noted by Hal Foster in *Return of the Real*, p. 196. Such a dynamic, in which critique can only ever remain inside, was long ago discussed by Susan Buck-Morss, "The Dialectic of T. W. Adorno," *Telos* 14 (Winter 1972): 137–44.

73. Gilles Deleuze and Félix Guattari, *Kafka: Toward a Minor Literature*, trans. Dana Polan (Minneapolis: University of Minnesota Press, 1986), pp. 75–76.

74. Morris's political actions, as Berger makes clear, aimed toward greater artist involvement in institutional affairs, forging "emergency cultural government[s]" and the like (*Labyrinths*, pp. 111–13). It is thus not simply an "irony" that Morris's actions "mostly took place in the very institutions he deplored: the museum and the gallery" (p. 93).

75. Jean-Jacques Nattiez (ed.), *The Boulez-Cage Correspondence* (Cambridge: Cambridge University Press, 1993), p. 143, and Berger, *Labyrinths*, p. 120.

76. See Giorgio Agamben, *Homo Sacer: Sovereign Power and Bare Life*, trans. Daniel Heller-Roazen (Stanford, CA: Stanford University Press, 1998), and Judith Butler, *Precarious Life: The Powers of Mourning and Violence* (London: Verso, 2004), especially "Indefinite Detention," pp. 50–100.

77. Deleuze and Guattari, *Kafka*, p. 75.

78. The most important theorist of power in this manner is, of course, Michel Foucault. As he noted: "So, there is not a series of successive elements, the appearance of the new causing the earlier ones to disappear. There is not the legal age, the disciplinary age, and then the age of security. Mechanisms of security do not replace disciplinary mechanisms, which would have replaced juridico-legal mechanisms. In reality you have a series of complex edifices in which, of course, the techniques themselves change and are perfected, or anyway become more complicated, but in which what above all changes is the dominant characteristic, or more exactly, the system of correlation between juridico-legal mechanisms, disciplinary mechanisms, and mechanisms of security. In other words, there is a history of the actual techniques themselves." Michel Foucault, *Security, Territory, Population: Lectures at the Collège de France, 1977–1978*, ed. Michel Senellart, trans. Graham Burchell (New York: Palgrave Macmillan, 2007), p. 8. See also Deleuze and Guattari, *Kafka*, pp. 72–76 and, on the related issue of the heterogeneous nature of contemporary economic regimes, Paolo Virno, "The Ambivalence of Disenchantment," in *Radical*

Thought in Italy: A Potential Politics, ed. Paolo Virno and Michael Hardt (Minneapolis: University of Minnesota Press, 1996), pp. 18–19.

79. Discipline is most fully discussed in Michel Foucault, *Discipline and Punish: The Birth of the Prison*, trans. Alan Sheridan (New York: Vintage, 1977). According to Berger, Morris read this book as soon as it was translated into English (*Labyrinths*, p. 163 n. 9). Traces of Morris's reception of Foucault's concern with power, specifically power-knowledge, however, seem perceptible in his writings much earlier in the 1970s. See, for example, "Some Splashes in the Ebb Tide" (1973), in *Continuous Project Altered Daily*, p. 121. It is interesting or worthwhile to note that Morris's move toward emphasizing disciplinary power and its internalization within the subject (as opposed to repression of the subject in a sovereign manner) brings with it a certain questioning of institutional boundaries "beyond studios and even factories." Robert Morris, "Some Notes on the Phenomenology of Making: The Search for the Motivated" (1970), in *Continuous Project Altered Daily*, p. 92. On sexuality as a site, not of liberation, but of power effects, see Michel Foucault, *The History of Sexuality. Volume 1: An Introduction*, trans. Robert Hurley (New York: Pantheon, 1978).

80. Michel Foucault, *Psychiatric Power: Lectures at the Collège de France, 1973–1974*, ed. Jacques Lagrange, trans. Graham Burchell (New York: Palgrave Macmillan, 2006), p. 55. Interestingly, it was none other than Michael Fried who intuited this point about Morris's minimal sculpture: "It is the explicitness, that is to say, the sheer persistence with which the experience presents itself as directed at [the beholder] from outside . . . that simultaneously makes him a subject — makes him subject — and establishes the experience as something like that of an object, or rather, of objecthood." Fried, "Art and Objecthood," p. 159.

81. Berger, who discusses Morris's relation to Foucault, largely presents the idea of discipline as conforming to the Marcusean ideas of repression and desublimation with which Foucault's work is distinctly at odds (though Morris may have initially understood it this way himself). Discipline, however, as Foucault continually emphasized, is primarily productive — which makes it "one of bourgeois society's great inventions" — and as such must be located not on the "oppressive" side of ideal form, but on the "liberated" side of the viewing subject (though it is precisely this idea of liberation that Foucault questions so profoundly). Indeed, in *Discipline and Punish*, Foucault would go so far as to posit that the very idea of a free or liberated subject is itself an effect of disciplinary power, not its opposition. The above quote on discipline and bourgeois society is found in Michel Foucault,

"Society Must Be Defended": Lectures at the Collège de France, 1975–76, ed. Mauro Bertani and Alessandro Fontana, trans. David Macey (New York: Picador, 2003), p. 36. Michael Hardt and Antonio Negri have argued for the interrelation of sovereignty (what I would call neosovereignty) and discipline in *Empire* (Cambridge, MA: Harvard University Press, 2000), pp. 83–88, 330–31.

82. This is argued in Berger, *Labyrinths*, pp. 153–59, where he discusses it in relation to Deleuze and Guattari's *Anti-Oedipus*.

83. Caux and Caux, "John Cage," p. 26. Cage's reference to school had a precedent in "45′ for a Speaker," where "trying things out in school" had been his description of the artificial separation of music from the larger and more inclusive realm of theater. *Silence*, p. 189.

84. This idea is found in its most interesting and anodyne form in Young's discussions of tuning as a function of time in "Notes on the Continuous Periodic Composite Sound Waveform Environment Realizations of 'Map of 49's Dream The Two Systems of Eleven Sets of Galactic Intervals Ornamental Lightyears Tracery,'" in *Selected Writings* (Munich: Heiner Friedrich, 1969), n.p.

85. See, for example, Young's comments in "La Monte Young: Good Vibrations," *Flash Art International* 25, no. 167 (November–December 1992): 54. Both Cage and Young refer to Young's practice as that of a yogi. Jacqueline Caux and Daniel Caux, "La Monte Young: '. . . Créer des états psychologiques précis,'" *Chroniques de l'art vivant* 30 (May 1972): 27, my translation wherever cited, and Caux and Caux, "John Cage," p. 26. Accordingly, Young and Zazeela would soon disciple themselves to Indian Kihrana singer Pandit Pran Nath, who became their—as well as Terry Riley's—guru and master in the early 1970s.

86. Kostelanetz, *The Theatre of Mixed Means*, p. 218.

87. Young's remark to the *Crimson* is quoted in Flynt, "La Monte Young in New York," p. 63. On Cage and Young as opposites, see Caux and Caux, "La Monte Young," p. 27, and Caux and Caux, "John Cage," p. 26.

88. Tony Conrad, interview with the author, Buffalo, NY, August, 15–16, 1995.

89. Tony Conrad, "Inside the Dream Syndicate," *Film Culture* 41 (Summer 1966): 7 (ellipses in original).

90. Tony Conrad, liner notes to *Four Violins (1964)*, Table of the Elements 17 Cl, vinyl record, repr. as "LYssophobia: On *Four Violins*," in *Early Minimalism, Volume One*; and as "Four Violins (1964)," *Halana* 2 (1996): 5–15 (quote on p. 11).

91. Deleuze and Guattari, *Kafka*, pp. 57–60.

92. Foucault notes: "If the objective of the pastorate is men's conduct, I

think equally specific movements of resistance and insubordination appeared in correlation with this that could be called specific revolts of conduct, again leaving the word 'conduct' in all its ambiguity. They are movements whose objective is a different form of conduct, that is to say: wanting to be conducted differently, by other leaders (*conducteurs*) and other shepherds, towards other objectives and forms of salvation, and through other procedures and methods. They are movements that also seek, possibly at any rate, to escape direction by others and to define the way for each to conduct himself." Foucault, *Security, Territory, Population*, pp. 194–95 ("counter-conduct" is discussed on p. 201). Compare Cage's comments: "And [Young's] attitudes are rather extraordinary, because he does not find that the daily life of the majority of people suits him. He sleeps at special hours, he changes each day the time during which he sleeps, lives, works. He makes a yoga of his life, and the people he attracts adapt themselves to this rhythm." Caux and Caux, "John Cage," p. 26.

93. Young, score for *arabic numeral (any integer)* (April 1960) for H. F., titled as "Variably Titled Piece (for Henry Flynt), 1960," Research Library, The Getty Research Institute, Los Angeles, California, David Tudor Papers (980039), box 14, folder 9; see also Young, letter to Tudor, 1961.

94. The last is how the piece is currently listed on La Monte Young's works list in the Web page for the MELA Foundation, http://www.melafoundation.org/lmyresum.htm#works (last accessed July 22, 2007).

95. Cage, letter to Tudor, [May 1961].

96. Cage, *Conversing with Cage*, p. 203.

97. For more on the interaction of Cage and Young in the context of the *Vexations* concert, see my "The Play of Repetition: Andy Warhol's *Sleep*," *Grey Room* 19 (Spring 2005): 22–53.

98. John Cale and Victor Bockris, *What's Welsh for Zen: The Autobiography of John Cale* (London: Bloomsbury, 1999), p. 47.

99. Cornelius Cardew, "On the Role of the Instructions in the Interpretation of Indeterminate Music," in *Treatise Handbook* (London: Edition Peters, 1971), p. xv.

100. Deleuze and Guattari, *Kafka*, p. 76.

101. Cardew, "On the Role of the Instructions," p. xiv.

102. *Ibid.*

103. Cornelius Cardew, "The Unity of Musical Space," *New Departures* 1 (Summer 1959): 56.

104. A different, but not unrelated effect would be courted in Yvonne Rainer and Steve Paxton's collaborative dance, *Word Words* (1963). In it, both choreographers, nude except for the G-strings and, in Rainer's case, pasties required by law, performed identical solos and then repeated them together as a duet. While the distinctions between the two presentations (and bodies) would not have been separable from that of sexual difference (and the gender inequalities socially entailed), neither would they be wholly reduced or subsumed to them, as reviews of the performance bear out. The result was a "metaphoric toppling" of the stereotypical gender roles in traditional ballet and modern dance, as well as the hierarchical priority of the male body — the immanent contingencies of bodily repetition partially undoing the hierarchical relations of subordination. See Sally Banes, *Democracy's Body: Judson Dance Theater, 1962–1964* (Durham: Duke University Press, 1993), pp. 88–90.

105. Cornelius Cardew, "Criticism of *The Great Learning*," in *Stockhausen Serves Imperialism and Other Articles* (London: Latimer, 1974), p. 100.

106. Cornelius Cardew, liner notes to *The Great Learning*, Deutsche Grammophon LP 2561 107 (1971), released on CD by the Cortical Foundation, CORTI 21 (2000). Cardew is also critiquing what he saw as Cage's apoliticism; "nature has no goals," and so Cage's work succeeds too easily.

107. Cage, "45′ for a Speaker," in *Silence*, pp. 170–71.

108. John Cage, "Letter to Paul Henry Lang" (1956), in *John Cage: An Anthology*, pp. 116–17.

109. Conrad, score for *Sextet for Metronomes and Violins* (ca. 1959). This provision was later revised in *Sextet for Violins and Metronomes* (ca. 1959) as a call for "3 violins to be played by persons who have studied the violin less than 3 years."

110. Tony Conrad, liner notes to *Slapping Pythagoras*, Table of the Elements 23, compact disc. Conrad's critique accompanies his reproach of "Pythagoras" for codifying harmony, for having, in fact, made number into a royal science — an abstract, conceptual ideal: "To effectuate and reinforce the Idealization of Number (which is the Pythagorean heritage in music, mathematics, and astronomy), Pythagoras substituted a Theology of Number for the pragmatics of counting." Cardew's repudiation of *The Great Learning* occurs in "Self-Criticism: Repudiation of Earlier Works," in *Stockhausen Serves Imperialism*, pp 78–103. The Scratch Orchestra is referred to in terms of "ultra-democracy" in Rod Ely, "A History of the Scratch Orchestra," in Cardew, *Stockhausen Serves Imperialism*, p. 18.

Chapter Four: Concept Art

1. Tony Conrad, interview with the author, Buffalo, NY, August 15–16, 1995. Young replies to Conrad's mention that Flynt had quit composing in a letter to Tony Conrad, July 7, 1960, located in Conrad's archives. The epigraph to this chapter is from Henry Flynt, "On Social Recognition" (1973), in Henry Flynt, *Blueprint for a Higher Civilization*, ed. Germano Celant (Milan: Multhipla edizioni, 1975), p. 179. Flynt and Conrad no longer work together so closely.

2. Henry Flynt, "La Monte Young in New York, 1960–62," in *Sound and Light: La Monte Young, Marian Zazeela*, ed. William Duckworth and Richard Fleming (Lewisburg, PA: Bucknell University Press, 1996), p. 64. At their first session (April 2, 1961), Flynt played song flute; in New York (January 9, 1962), he played violin (p. 71).

3. Conrad, interview with the author, Buffalo, NY, August 15–16, 1995. Conrad tells much the same story in "Bowing and Light: Project Introduction," three-page typescript, June 1977, located in Conrad's archives.

4. La Monte Young, letter to Tony Conrad, before April 11, 1960.

5. Henry Flynt, interview with Kenneth Goldsmith, WFMU, February 25, 2004, archived in realaudio on www.wfmu.org/playlists/shows/10521, "Henry Talks about Indian music etc." (last accessed July 6, 2007).

6. Conrad, "Music Notes II," p. 36 (entry 62, "Æolean," dated October 22, 1961), located in Conrad's archives.

7. Conrad, interview with author, Buffalo, NY, August 15–16, 1995.

8. For historical information on Flynt's life and work, see Henry Flynt, *Fragments and Reconstructions from a Destroyed Oeuvre, 1959–1963* (New York: Backworks, 1982); Henry Flynt, "Mutations of the Vanguard: Pre-Fluxus, During Fluxus, Late Fluxus," in *Ubi Fluxus ibi motus, 1990–1962*, ed. Achille Bonito Oliva (Milan: Nuove edizioni Gabriele Mazzotta, 1990), pp. 99–128; and Flynt, "La Monte Young in New York," pp. 44–97.

9. Flynt, "Mutations of the Vanguard," p. 105. Young also considered this of interest. See Richard Kostelanetz, *The Theatre of Mixed Means* (1968; New York: RK Editions, 1980), p. 204. Flynt invoked a similar temporal inversion several times, from "Demonstration to Be Held Before It Is Called" (March 4, 1968), repr. in Flynt, *Fragments*, n.p., to "Show in Advance of Its Existence," (1990; unrealized, documentation under that title at www.henryflynt.org, last accessed on July 22, 2007).

10. Henry Flynt, *Concerto for Kitchen Sink and Monkey Orchestra*, repr. in *Dimension* 14 (Ann Arbor, MI, 1963), p. 75.

11. George Maciunas, *Diagram of Historical Development of Fluxus and Other 4 Dimentional* [sic], *Aural, Optic, Olfactory, Epithelial and Tactile Art Forms (Incomplete)* (Lund, Sweden: Kalejdoskop, 1978), n.p.; repr. in Jon Hendricks, *Fluxus Codex* (New York: The Gilbert and Lila Silverman Fluxus Collection in association with Harry N. Abrams, 1988), pp. 329–32, and in Astrit Schmidt-Burkhardt, *Maciunas' Learning Machines: From Art History to a Chronology of Fluxus* (Berlin: Vice Versa Verlag, 2003), pp. 122–25. Flynt's concerts took place on February 25–26, 1961.

12. Flynt, "Mutations of the Vanguard," p. 107.

13. *Ibid.*

14. *Ibid.*, p. 110.

15. Flynt, "La Monte Young in New York," pp. 56–57.

16. *Ibid.*, p. 69 (program reproduced on p. 74). According to Flynt's account of the taped performance, Young announced "This piece is only a title," which (inadvertently) echoed some of Conrad's word pieces (see below). Flynt, "Mutations of the Vanguard," p. 110. The ONCE Festival took place on February 9, 1962.

17. A. S. Conrad, "The Flexagon," RIAS [Research Institute for Advanced Science] Miscellaneous Report, Baltimore, February, 1960 (later renamed "The Theory of the Flexagon," RIAS Technical Report 60-24, 1960), and Anthony S. Conrad and Daniel K. Hartline, "Flexagons," RIAS Technical Report 62-11 Baltimore, Maryland, May, 1962. Both papers can be found at http://delta.cs.cinvestav.mx/~mcintosh/oldweb/pflexagon.html.

18. Conrad's word scores are found in "Music Notes II," esp. pp, 41–43 and in a series of separate sheets and three-by-five cards in his archive. Unless otherwise noted, all works are dated summer 1961.

19. Conrad, interview with author, Buffalo, NY, August 15–16, 1995.

20. Michel Foucault, "What Is an Author?" (1969), trans. Donald F. Bouchard and Sherry Simon, in *Language, Counter-Memory, Practice*, ed. Donald F. Bouchard (Ithaca, NY: Cornell University Press, 1977), p. 130.

21. Cage's *0'00"* reads: "In a situation provided with maximum amplification (no feedback), perform a disciplined action"; its first performance consisted of Cage, his pen connected to a contact microphone, writing out a copy of the score. Flynt speculates on *0'00"* being a response to the younger generation's word scores in "La Monte Young in New York," pp. 76–77.

22. Ken Friedman, ed., *The Fluxus Performance Workbook*, a special edition of *El Djarida* magazine, Trondheim, Norway, vol. 9 (1990), p. 20.

23. Maciunas, *Diagram of Historical Development.* In 1990, Flynt considered the only "endorsed" concept art to have been produced by himself and (in the 1970s) Christer Hennix. "Mutations of the Vanguard," p. 128 n. 9. In 1996, he reconsidered this view, regarding a series of related word scores and other pieces to have been part of the genre. "La Monte Young in New York," p. 69.

24. Henry Flynt, "Essay: Concept Art (Provisional Version)," in *An Anthology*, ed. La Monte Young (New York: La Monte Young and Jackson Mac Low, 1963), n.p.; repr. with slight revisions as Henry Flynt, "Essay: Concept Art," in *An Anthology*, ed. La Monte Young (New York: Heiner Friedrich, 1970), n.p. (all citations from the second version).

25. Henry Flynt, "Structure Art and Pure Mathematics" (1960), in *Fragments*, n.p.

26. *Ibid.*

27. Flynt refers to Young's *2 Sounds* (as *Cans on Windows*) in "Essay: Concept Art," n.p. Flynt's "Central Park Transverse Vocals" were released on Henry Flynt, *Raga Electric: Experimental Music, 1963–1971*, Locust Music 6, compact disc.

28. Flynt, "Structure Art and Pure Mathematics," n.p.

29. Flynt, "Essay: Concept Art," n.p.

30. Conrad, "Music Notes II," p. 41 (entry 81, dated November 6, 1961), and on a separate three-by-five card with the same date. Another explicit reference to Flynt's concept art occurred in Conrad's note "*AUDIENCES,*" "Music Notes II," p. 39 (entry 77), quoted in Chapter 2.

31. Conrad, "Music Notes II," pp. 37–38 (entry 72, "Complex-Absurd," dated November 19, 1961); square bracketed insert in original.

32. Flynt, "Essay: Concept Art," n.p.

33. Henry Flynt, "Art or Brend?" in Henry Flynt, *Down with Art* (New York: Fluxpress, 1968), n.p., repr. in Henry Flynt, *Blueprint for a Higher Civilization*, ed. Germano Celant (Milan: Multhipla edizioni, 1975), pp. 63–73. Compare Tony Conrad, liner notes to *Slapping Pythagoras*, Table of the Elements 23, compact disc. Conrad expanded on this connection: "I thought Henry's work was very important because of what it did to the entire structure of truthfulness as a logical predicate. . . . If we can demonstrate ways of casting doubt on these things, it may mean that we can begin to dismantle some of the idealism that has always attached itself to number, or at least since the time of Pythagoras. . . . It is, in fact, Pythagoras who imports the idealism of number into Greek thought at a

precise moment which is identifiable as the invention of philosophy. . . . So in this structure — this system of musical accommodation to number systems, numerical relationships among frequencies, and all of this — it finally becomes kind of an urgent matter to refine our discrimination in such a way that we can see exactly where the idealism enters the picture and accept it or reject it. And it occurred to me that the most radical way to do that would be to reconceive number as a structure, not having its basis in counting, but having its basis in *measuring*. I proposed this to Henry Flynt late in our interaction . . . [and] I'm still very attached to this idea that there might be a discrimination between measuring and counting." Conrad, interview with author, Buffalo, NY, August 15–16, 1995.

34. Flynt, "Essay: Concept Art," n.p. Flynt's invocation of "meaning, expression, and emotion" is found in "Structure Art and Pure Mathematics," n.p.

35. Flynt, "Structure Art and Pure Mathematics," n.p.

36. Flynt, "Essay: Concept Art," n.p.

37. Marcel Duchamp, quoted in Calvin Tomkins, *The Bride and the Bachelors* (New York: Penguin, 1968), p. 18. This quote is found in a clipping (likely from Tomkin's original *New Yorker* article) affixed to a three-by-five card of the same time and format as several of Conrad's 1961 word pieces. Duchamp further related art making to a drug in "Apropos of 'Readymades,'" in *The Writings of Marcel Duchamp*, ed. Michel Sanouillet and Elmer Peterson (New York: Da Capo, 1973), p. 142.

38. Henry Flynt and Tony Conrad, untitled prospectus for *The Journal of Indeterminate Mathematical Investigations*, November 1967, one-page mimeographed statement, located in Conrad's archives. Conrad was to be the editor; the prospectus text seems mostly to be Flynt's writing.

39. Flynt warrants no mention in Alexander Alberro and Blake Stimson (eds.), *Conceptual Art: A Critical Anthology* (Cambridge, MA: MIT Press, 1999), nor is there any reference in Alexander Alberro, *Conceptual Art and the Politics of Publicity* (Cambridge, MA: MIT Press, 2003). Flynt does appear in a footnote in Benjamin H. D. Buchloh, "Conceptual Art 1962–1969: From the Aesthetic of Administration to the Critique of Institutions," *October* 55 (Winter 1990): 105–43; Buchloh notes the relation of terms and possible lineage and also notes the refusal of this connection by Kosuth and others (p. 107 n. 1). Flynt is mentioned in Ken Friedman, "Notes on Concept Art" (1971), in Lucy R. Lippard

(ed.), *Six Years: The Dematerialization of the Art Object from 1966 to 1972 . . .* (1973; Berkeley: University of California Press, 1997), pp. 258–59. Interestingly, in the book's chronology, Lippard briefly notes the republication of Flynt's concept art essay in Heiner Friedrich's 1967 reprint of *An Anthology*; it was in late 1967 that she and John Chandler wrote "The Dematerialization of Art," published in the February 1968 issue of *Art International* (repr. in *Conceptual Art: A Critical Anthology*, pp. 46–50). Lippard's sole mention of Flynt in the forward to the 1997 republication of *Six Years* erroneously attributes to him an interest in Duchamp (p. ix). More recent considerations, which relate the history of conceptual art to Fluxus, largely continue to bypass Flynt's work. See Peter Osborne (ed.), *Conceptual Art* (London: Phaidon, 2002); Flynt would not allow republication of his essay in that book. For a consideration of concept art in the context of conceptual art, see my "Concept Art and Instrumental Reason," *Texte zur Kunst* 15, no. 60 (Winter 2005): 74–87, which derives from the material in this chapter.

40. Buchloh, "Conceptual Art," pp. 105–43. On the idea of a logical, but not rational practice in conceptual art, see Rosalind E. Krauss, "LeWitt in Progress," in *The Originality of the Avant-Garde and Other Modernist Myths* (Cambridge, MA: MIT Press, 1985), pp. 245–58.

41. See Alexander Alberro's very accurate comment on the difference between Fluxus and conceptual art in Alexander Alberro, Yve-Alain Bois, et al., "Conceptual Art and the Reception of Duchamp," *October* 70 (Fall 1994): 132.

42. Henry Flynt, "Implications — Concept Art Version of Colored Sheet Music No. 1 3/14/61 (10/11/61)" and "Concept Art: Innperseqs (May–July 1961)," in *An Anthology*, n.p.

43. Joseph Kosuth, "Art After Philosophy," in *Conceptual Art: A Critical Anthology*, pp. 158–77.

44. Flynt, "Essay: Concept Art," n.p.

45. In an undated letter (ca. 1962–63) reproduced in *Fragments*, Flynt notes his repudiation of everything he published in *An Anthology*.

46. Henry Flynt, "The Supererogatory, Misleading Notion of 'Newness'" (April 1961), in *Fragments*, n.p. (the surviving version was preserved by Conrad). Flynt's lecture "The Cognitive" was destroyed. Flynt, e-mail to author, July 18, 2005.

47. Henry Flynt, "My New Concept of General Acognitive Culture," tape

recording by Tony Conrad of original lecture, May 15, 1962, located in Conrad's archives; published as Henry Flynt, "My New Concept of General Acognitive Culture," *décollage* 3 (December 1962); consulted on-line at www.henryflynt.org/aesthetics/acogcult.html (last accessed July 22, 2007).

48. Flynt, *Fragments*, n.p.

49. Flynt, "My New Concept of General Acognitive Culture," tape recording.

50. In this, Flynt's reasoning recalls that of John Cage: "nothing was lost when everything was given away. In fact, everything is gained." John Cage, "Experimental Music" (1957), in *Silence*, p. 8.

51. This point was, however, flatly rejected by Robert Morris in a letter dated August 13, 1962: "If I need concentration, which I do, I can't think of anything on my own as good as chess. One accepts language, one accepts logic." Quoted in Henry Flynt, *Down with Art*, n.p.

52. The notion of (metaphysical) presence – the idea that existence, thoughts, and intentions can be wholly present to the individual, without mediation – has been most thoroughly discussed and critiqued by Jacques Derrida. See, for instance, Jacques Derrida, *Speech and Phenomena and Other Essays on Husserl's Theory of Signs*, trans. David B. Allison (Evanston, IL: Northwestern University Press, 1973).

53. In this, Flynt's acognitive culture resembles Walter De Maria's "meaningless work": "to be fully understood, meaningless work should be done alone or else it becomes entertainment for others." De Maria, "Meaningless Work" (March 1960), *An Anthology*, n.p.

54. Flynt, "La Monte Young in New York," p. 52. Young recounts knowledge of Artaud in Richard Kostelanetz, *The Theatre of Mixed Means*, p. 216.

55. See, for instance, Antonin Artaud, "Correspondence with Jacques Rivière," in *Selected Writings*, ed. Susan Sontag, trans. Helen Weaver (Berkeley: University of California Press, 1988), pp. 31–49, and Antonin Artaud, *The Theater and its Double*, trans. Mary Caroline Richards (New York: Grove Weidenfeld, 1958). On the relationship of Artaud to expression and presence, see Jacques Derrida, "La parole soufflée" and "The Theater of Cruelty and the Closure of Representation," in *Writing and Difference*, trans. Alan Bass (Chicago: University of Chicago Press, 1978), pp. 169–95 and 232–50.

56. *Fluxus Preview Review* (ca. July) 1963, quoted in Hendricks, *Fluxus Codex*, p. 249. The announcement was itself "numbered to take into account the possibility that the plan may be changed."

57. Flynt, question-and-answer session after "My New Concept of General Acognitive Culture" lecture at Harvard, taped by Conrad, in Conrad's archive.

58. Henry Flynt, "Audart Composition (May 1961)," in *Anthology of Non-Philosophical Cultural Works* (Cambridge, MA: published by Tony Conrad, 1961), p. 2. Facsimile on-line at www.henryflynt.org//overviews/artworksphotos_new.html. p. 2 (last accessed July 22, 2007).

59. Cage, "Experimental Music," in *Silence*, p. 8.

60. John Cage, "Lecture on Nothing" (1950), in *Silence*, pp. 116–17.

61. John Cage, "Composition as Process I: Changes" (1958), in *Silence*, p. 23. For the most trenchant critique of this facet of Cage's aesthetic, see Theodor W. Adorno, "Vers une musique informelle" (1961), trans. Rodney Livingstone, in *Quasi una fantasia* (London: Verso, 1994), pp. 269–322.

62. John Cage, "Experimental Music: Doctrine" (1955), in *Silence*, pp. 13–14.

63. John Cage, "Where Are We Going? And What Are We Doing?" (1961), in *Silence*, p. 194. Although Cage, as an anarchist, endorsed a society in which "many centers can interpenetrate without obstructing one another, ways people can do things without being told or telling others what to do" (John Cage, "Afterword," in *A Year from Monday* [Middletown, CT: Wesleyan University Press, 1967], p. 166), he had, since as early as 1956, advocated moving away from "private human concerns towards the world of nature and society." John Cage, "In This Day . . . " (1956), in *Silence*, p. 95. Both realms, for Cage, are in a state of continuous change. Cage, "Afterward," in *A Year from Monday*, p, 166.

64. Flynt presented "My New Concept of General Acognitive Culture: Improved Version" at 49 Avenue D in New York, on July 5, 1962. Cage and Virgil Thomson were both in attendance. On Cage's reaction, see Flynt, "Mutations of the Vanguard," p. 110.

65. Hal Foster has made a not dissimilar observation about the 1950s neo-avant-garde artists' relationship to Duchamp. Hal Foster, "The Crux of Minimalism," in *The Return of the Real* (Cambridge, MA: MIT Press, 1996), pp. 21–22.

66. Georges Bataille, "The Use Value of D. A. F. de Sade (An Open Letter to My Current Comrades)," trans. Allan Stoekl, Carl R. Lovitt, and Donald M. Leslie, Jr., in *Visions of Excess: Selected Writings, 1927–1939*, ed. Allan Stoekl (Minneapolis: University of Minnesota Press, 1985), p. 98.

67. *Ibid.*

68. Dick Higgins, "Something Else about Fluxus," *Art and Artists*, London,

October 1972, p. 18, quoted in Henry Martin, *An Introduction to George Brecht's Book of the Tumbler in Fire* (Milan: Multhipla, 1978), p. 15.

69. On this concept within the visual arts, see Yve-Alain Bois and Rosalind E. Krauss, *Formless: A User's Guide* (New York: Zone Books, 1997).

70. Henry Flynt, "Creep," lecture, May 15, 1962. Audiotape by Conrad located in Conrad's archives.

71. In a later text, also entitled "Creep," published in *Blueprint for a Higher Civilization* (pp. 182–86), Flynt revisits his Harvard lecture. The extensive critique he devotes to it, however, loses much of the original talk's character, most regrettably through a markedly misogynistic strain absent from the Harvard lecture, in which Emily Dickinson was the primary (indeed sole) affirmative example of a creep personality that Flynt provided.

72. Flynt anticipates similar observations by Mike Kelley, who found in certain strains of 1960s counterculture an attempt to raise dysfunction as a protopolitical project. Their common source was, no doubt, the relation between adolescence and rock music. See, for instance, Mike Kelley, "Jutta Koether," *Journal of Contemporary Art* 7 (Summer 1994): 8, 15–16.

73. In addition, Flynt suggested, the goal of biological mutation – of a difficulty, he proposed, akin to that of the space program – would bring about a form of collective creep consciousness. Even through they were different, and in their isolation guarded their idiosyncratic uniqueness, creeps, according to Flynt, would need collective action to alter society such that it would devote the needed resources to their quest.

74. When asked at the Harvard lecture whether he considered himself a creep, Flynt unhesitatingly responded in the affirmative. In "Concept Art," he also characterized his opposition to conventional mathematics in personal terms: "for reasons of taste I wanted to deemphasize discovery in mathematics. . . . I wasn't good at such discovery, and it bored me." Flynt, "Essay: Concept Art," n.p. Years later, he described the "insight which has propelled all of my work" as "my ability to direct all of my merciless perceptions of vulnerability outward and not onto myself." Flynt, "Mutations of the Vanguard," p. 114.

Flynt's first of several journalistic writings on liberation struggles in Africa appeared the day after the "Creep" lecture: "The Black and the White" (unsigned article), *Eastern Nigeria Guardian*, May 16, 1962 (I have been unable to access a copy). Flynt also published Henry Flynt, "Behind the Crisis in Zimbabwe ('Rhodesia')," *The Partisan* 2, no. 1 (March 1966): 28–31, and, under the pseudonym, Henry Stone, "Program for Genocide in South West Africa," *Workers World*, March 19, 1964, 3 (which reported on South Africa's racist actions in Namibia). On June 5 and July 3, 1966, Flynt would be a guest, along with the Zambian ambassador to the United Nations, Fwanyanga Mulikita, on radio station WLIB, New York. Information in Flynt, *Fragments*, n.p. Flynt briefly refers to an involvement in the sit-ins in his home town of Greensboro, North Carolina, in 1962 in Flynt, interview with Kenneth Goldsmith. Benjamin Piekut relates that Flynt "observed" the demonstration, which likely occurred in 1963 (rather than 1962), and sent a letter to *Workers World*, published under a pseudonym as Charles Henry, "I Saw the Birth of Freedom in Greensboro, N.C.," *Workers World*, May 25, 1963. See Benjamin Piekut, "Taking Henry Flynt Seriously," *Institute for Studies in American Music Newsletter*, 34, no. 2 (Spring 2005): 6–7 and 14, on-line at http://depthome.brooklyn.cuny.edu/isam/NewsletS05 /Piekut.htm (last accessed on July 22, 2007).

75. At the time, Robert Morris noted the lack of dialectical mediation in Flynt's presentations. See comments reproduced in Flynt, *Down with Art*, n.p.

76. Gilles Deleuze and Félix Guattari, *Kafka: Toward a Minor Literature*, trans. Dana Polan (Minneapolis: University of Minnesota Press, 1986), p. 77.

77. In "Art or Brend?" Flynt explicitly refers to the social realm as a cruel despotism ("the general repressiveness of society") and starkly and without nuance relates "the likes of the community" to "ideological deception." For Flynt, this posed a strangely symptomatic and insurmountable contradiction, particularly within aesthetics. The aesthetic object "supposedly has a value which is entirely subjective and entirely within you, is a part of you" (i.e., the object is close). "Yet—the object can exist without you, is completely outside you, is not you or your valuing, and has no inherent connection with you or your valuing. The product is not personal to you" (i.e., the object is too distant). "Art or Brend?" in *Down with Art*, n.p.

78. Deleuze and Guattari, *Kafka*, p. 77. "The infinitely distant law emits hypostases, sends emanations that always come closer and closer." *Ibid.*

79. On the "trace," see Michel Foucault, *Discipline and Punish: The Birth of the Prison*, trans. Alan Sheridan (New York: Vintage, 1977), pp. 130–31.

80. Henry Flynt, "Mock Risk Games: A Psychological Exploration," *Film Culture* 43 (Winter 1966): 5; repr. in Flynt, *Blueprint for a Higher Civilization*, pp. 153–59. Flynts' original proposal can be found in Harry Flynt, "Exercise Awareness Status," *Ikon* 11 (1990): 71–75.

81. Flynt refers to *Piano Piece for Terry Riley #1* in Flynt, interview with Kenneth Goldsmith.

82. Morris, letter to John Cage (February 27, 1961), in Robert Morris, "Letters to John Cage," *October* 81 (Summer 1997): 76.

83. Conrad, "Music Notes II," p. 43 (entry 88, dated June 18, 1962). This work might be understood as a reworking of Young's *Composition 1960 #15* (the whirlpools in the middle of the ocean). Resembling Mieko (Chieko) Shiomi's *Boundary Music*, Conrad's *Imagined* also recalls George Brecht's idea of "'Borderline' art": "Sounds barely heard. Sights barely distinguished. 'Borderline' art. (See which way it goes.) (It should be possible to miss it completely.)" Brecht, "Events: Scores and Other Occurrences," two-page typescript dated December 28, 1961, Research Library, The Getty Research Institute, Los Angeles, California, Jean Brown Papers (890164), box 3, folder I.331, "Brecht, George: corresp."

84. Conrad, "Music Notes II," p. 38 (entry 74, "Orgasm," dated November 19, 1961). Conrad's term, "'listening' 'composition,'" comes on p. 39 (entry 76, "Titles") of the same date. Such experiential compositions anticipate Lee Lozano's conceptual art pieces, such as *Grass Piece* and *No-Grass Piece* (both 1969), which Dan Graham would mention in his consideration of conceptual art, "Subject Matter," in *Rock My Religion: Writings and Art Projects, 1965–1990*, ed. Brian Wallis (Cambridge, MA: MIT Press, 1993), pp. 38–51.

85. De Maria's relation to Flynt, Conrad, and Smith was quite close at the time. Jack Smith wrote an essay on De Maria's sculpture: Jack Smith, "Ammonia Pits of Atlantis: Evil in the Art World or WALTER VERSUS THE GIANT KNICK KNACKS" (1966), in *Wait for Me at the Bottom of the Pool: The Writings of Jack Smith*, ed. J. Hoberman and Edward Leffingwell (London: Serpent's Tail, 1997), pp. 97–101.

86. Tony Conrad, interview with the author, December 25, 2006.

87. Flynt mentions "the fools lined up to worship" the painting in the press release he issued in 1963, repr. in Flynt, *Down with Art*, n.p.

88. Flynt mentions Maciunas's instigation of the second protest in "Mutations of the Vanguard," p. 114. Maciunas had disliked Stockhausen since as early as 1963, calling him a "Nationalistic Megalomaniac." Emmett Williams and Ann Noël (eds.), *Mr. Fluxus: A Collective Portrait of George Maciunas, 1931–1978* (London: Thames and Hudson, 1997), p. 62.

89. Henry Flynt, "Picket Stockhausen Concert!" leaflet for September 8, 1964 picket (ellipses and bracketed insertion in original). According to Flynt,

Stockhausen's statement was likely made as an oral embellishment at or near the pronouncement about "melodic inventions within a given basic rhythmic and harmonic scheme in jazz" in Karlheinz Stockhausen, "Electronic and Instrumental Music," in *Audio Culture: Readings in Modern Music*, ed. Christoph Cox and Daniel Warner (New York: Continuum, 2004), p. 378. "In the live talk," Flynt notes, "this came across as far more patronizing or deprecatory that [sic] it seems in print." Henry Flynt, letter to author, December 16, 2006.

90. Conrad, interview with author, December 25, 2006.

91. On the aftermath of the Stockhausen picket, see Dick Higgins, "Auszug aus 'Postface,'" in *Happenings, Fluxus, Pop Art, Nouveau Réalisme*, ed. Jürgen Becker and Wolf Vostell (Reinbeck bei Hamburg: Rowohlt Taschenbuch Verlag, 1965), pp. 189–92; Dick Higgins, "A Child's History of Fluxus" (1979), in *Horizons: The Poetics and Theory of Intermedia* (Carbondale, IL: Southern Illinois University Press, 1984), pp. 87–91; and Williams and Noël (eds.), *Mr. Fluxus*, pp. 107–9.

92. George Maciunas, "Neo-Dada in the United States," quoted in Hendricks, *Fluxus Codex*, p. 23. Although Flynt's text was supposed to be published by Maciunas, it appeared instead, much to Maciunas's consternation, in Wolf Vostell's magazine *décollage*. For Maciunas's reaction to Vostell's publication, see Hendricks, *Fluxus Codex*, p. 248. Recently, the relation of Flynt and Maciunas has been discussed at length in Cuauhtémoc Medina, "The 'Kulturbolschewiken' I: Fluxus, the Abolition of Art, the Soviet Union, and 'Pure Amusement,'" *Res: Anthropology and Aesthetics* 48 (2005): 179–92.

93. Flynt, "Mutations of the Vanguard," p. 112.

94. Maciunas, letter to Tomas Schmit, January, 1964, quoted in Williams and Noël (eds.), *Mr. Fluxus*, p. 104.

95. Maciunas, in *Fluxus Newsletter* no. 7, May 1, 1963, repr. in Jon Hendricks et al. (eds.), *Fluxus etc., Addenda 1* (New York: Ink &, 1983), p. 157.

96. The relation between blues and an earlier Popular Front politics of the 1930s was noted by Marybeth Hamilton, "In Search of the Blues," lecture delivered at "Tangled Roots: A Workshop on American Folk and Field Recordings," Princeton University, November 22, 2002.

97. Flynt, "Picket Stockhausen Concert!"

98. "Stockhausen was a well-known symbol of contempt and disdain for every kind of workers', farmers', or non-European music, whether the music of Black Americans, East European peasants, Indians, or even most of the music

that West German workers themselves like." Henry Flynt, "Fight Musical Decoration of Fascism!" leaflet for April 29, 1964 picket.

99. Susan Goodman, "Anti-Art Pickets Pick on Stockhausen," *Village Voice*, September 10, 1964, p. 8, and Flynt, "Mutations of the Vanguard," p. 114.

100. Flynt, "Picket Stockhausen Concert!" Emphasis in the original.

101. *Ibid.*

102. John Cage, "Forerunners of Modern Music" (1949), in *Silence*, p. 63.

103. Flynt, interview with Kenneth Goldsmith.

104. Although he greatly admired John Coltrane and Ornette Coleman, Flynt did not like the jazz of, for instance, Albert Ayler, Archie Shepp, or Pharoah Sanders as represented on ESP Records, which he saw as jazz's pursuing a modernization "parallel" to that of modern European music: "You already had it with Cecil Taylor. I mean, Cecil Taylor sounded to me like somebody trying to play Bartók by ear.... I actually though it was a mistake, because, I thought that they [jazz musicians] had already won. They had won and now they decided that was not good enough and maybe they needed to lose." Flynt, interview with Kenneth Goldsmith.

105. Henry Flynt and George Maciunas, *Communists Must Give Revolutionary Leadership in Culture* (New York: World View Publishers, 1965), n.p. (quotation by Flynt), emphasis in the original. Flynt himself claims always to choreograph dance movements to go with his music.

106. Hendricks, *Fluxus Codex*, pp. 120–21. Flynt was joined in the East European Section by Young's old friend Joseph Byrd, scheduled to contribute such articles as "Critical Analysis of the Theories of Zhadanov" and "Critical Analysis of Current Marxist Estheticians (in Regard to Lack of Dialectic Approach)."

107. "Even when ... ideas have a low origin, they are no less elaborated *in a high place*, in high intellectual spheres, before taking on a universal value." Georges Bataille, "The 'Old Mole' and the Prefix *Sur* in the Words *Surhomme* [Superman] and *Surrealist*," trans. Allan Stoekl, Carl R. Lovitt, and Donald M. Leslie Jr., in *Visions of Excess*, p. 36. The claim of (merely) bourgeois values to universality (what Flynt would call their pretension to being "the real right thing to do") is the signature move of ideology.

108. *Ibid.*, p. 33.

109. *Ibid.*, p. 43.

110. Georges Bataille, "L'abjection et les formes misérables," in *Oeuvres complètes II: Écrits posthumes 1922–1940* (Paris: Gallimard, 1970), pp, 217–21. A

translation (with several mistakes) appeared as Georges Bataille, "Abjection and Miserable Forms," trans. Yvonne Shafir, in *More & Less*, ed. Sylvère Lotringer (Pasadena: Art Center College of Design, 1999), pp. 8–13. Rosalind Krauss has argued for a certain separation of the Bataillian terms "abjection" and "formless" (*informe*) on the basis of their usage in contemporary art criticism. Rosalind Krauss, "The Destiny of the *Informe*," in *Formless: A User's Guide*, pp. 235–52. Nevertheless, my use of the term "abject" remains close to her use of "formless," as is the case as well with Hal Foster's use of the term "abject" in Hal Foster, "Obscene, Abject, Traumatic," *October* 78 (Fall 1996): 107–24.

111. Flynt and Maciunas, *Communists Must Give Revolutionary Leadership in Culture*, n.p. See also Flynt's elaboration of these themes in Henry Flynt, "3. European-U.S. Cultural Imperialism," six page typescript, Research Library, The Getty Research Institute, Los Angeles, California, Jean Brown Papers (890164), box 17, folder 2, "Flynt, Henry."

112. Flynt, "Picket Stockhausen Concert!" Bataille proposed a remarkably analogous (and equally problematically primitivizing) relation to the vitality of dominated racial and ethnic groups. Black communities, he argued, would be a necessary component within postrevolutionary organizations on account of their relation to "ecstasy and frenzy," in opposition to the "abominable inhibitions paralyzing" the white race. Bataille, "The Use Value of D. A. F. de Sade," in *Visions of Excess*, p. 102. Flynt's position reflects aspects of what Sally Banes has discussed as "positive primitivism," which one might see in more problematic terms than she tends to do. Sally Banes, *Greenwich Village 1963: Avant-Garde Performance and the Effervescent Body* (Durham, NC: Duke University Press, 1993), pp. 206–21.

113. A reporter from the *Village Voice* noted, with barely concealed condescension, that Flynt "considers it outrageous that [conservatories] only teach European music." Goodman, "Anti-Art Pickets," p. 3.

114. On Morris's political actions, see Maurice Berger, *Labyrinths: Robert Morris, Minimalism, and the 1960s* (New York: Harper and Row, 1989), pp. 107–27; and Julia Bryan-Wilson, "Hard Hats and Art Strikes: Robert Morris in 1970," *Art Bulletin* 89, no. 2 (June 2007): 333–59.

115. Cornelius Cardew, *Stockhausen Serves Imperialism and Other Articles* (London: Latimer, 1974), pp. 34–40 and 46–55.

116. Cardew (June 7, 1963), in Flynt, *Down with Art*, n.p.

117. Cardew, *Stockhausen Serves Imperialism*, p. 49.

118. References to Cage's weakness (and his former "toughness") are found in Cardew, *Stockhausen Serves Imperialism*, pp. 33–40. Before moving toward socialist realism, Cardew passed through a phase of integrating banners with slogans such as "SMASH THE DECAYING IDEOLOGICAL AND CULTURAL SUPERSTRUCTURE!" and "DOWN WITH IMPERIALISM!" into Scratch Orchestra performances. *Stockhausen Serves Imperialism*, p. 32. Interestingly, Cardew insisted on presenting Flynt's Stockhausen protests as radical student manifestations against Cage, even after having been corrected on this point. *Stockhausen Serves Imperialism*, p. 35 and p. 111 n. 18.

119. Tony Conrad, "Silence = Death," flier handed out at Young's appearance at the North American New Music Festival, Buffalo, NY, April 1990. Point number four of Conrad's flier denounced Young's "misunderstand[ing]" of just intonation "as neo-Pythagorean rationalism (after the scientific idealism of Helmholz)."

120. Samuel B. Charters, *The Country Blues* (1959; New York: Da Capo, 1975). Charters edited two volumes of *Country Blues* on Folkways records (Folkways F-RF1 and F-RF9). Flynt mentions the importance of Charters and that he ordered at least one Folkways collection in Flynt, interview with Kenneth Goldsmith.

121. Charters, *The Country Blues*, pp. ix–x.

122. These titles can be found on Henry Flynt, *New American Ethnic Music, Volume 2: Spindizzy*, Recorded 006, compact disc; Henry Flynt, *C-Tune*, Locust 3, compact disc; and Henry Flynt, *New American Ethnic Music, Volume One: You Are My Everlovin' / Celestial Power*, Recorded 003, compact disc. Other examples have been released as Henry Flynt, *Back Porch Hillbilly Blues* vols. 1 and 2, Locust 14 and Locust 16, compact discs, both 2002.

123. "The Meaning of My Avant-Garde Hillbilly and Blues Music" (1980/2002), on-line at http://www.henryflynt.org/aesthetics/meaning_of_my_music.htm (consulted April 28, 2003; last accessed July 7, 2007). See also, Henry Flynt, "The Politics of 'Native' or Ethnic Music" (1975), in *V Tre May 2, 1976*, ed. Robert Watts, Sara Seagull, and Fluxus Editorial Council for Fluxus; consulted in typescript at Research Library, The Getty Research Institute, Los Angeles, California, Jean Brown Papers, (890164), box 17, folder 2, "Flynt, Henry." In his identification with an impoverished rural white population ("hillbillies"), Flynt—although he, himself, grew up at some remove from this milieu—found "a people" and a means to connect to a "*collective assemblag[e] of enun-*

ciation." Deleuze and Guattari, *Kafka*, p. 18. Flynt's musical and political relation to such rural populations has been discussed further by Ben Piekut in "The Whiteness of Henry Flynt," conference paper presented at "Music, Performance, and the Racial Imagination," New York University, March 2005.

124. Henry Flynt and the Insurrections, *I Don't Wanna*, Locust Music 39, compact disc; Cornelius Cardew, *We Only Want the World: The Peoples' Liberation Music Tapes 1973–78 and Other Songs*, Music Now compact disc, MNCDX004 (2001). Further information on the PLM can be found at www.musicnow.co.uk/plm (last accessed July 7, 2007).

125. Released on Henry Flynt, *Graduation and Other New Country and Blues Music*, Ampersand, Ampere8, compact disc.

126. Mayo Thompson, "Review: Convoy," *The Fox* 3 (1976): 96–97. Thompson continued, "The FCC was down on 'Convoy' because they feared it might promote lawless ratchet-jaws in eighteen-wheelers to view the five-five, chicken-coops with comic-books, bears with ears, etc. as just more of, part of the Uncle Sam fat load that could be cleaned up by getting the hammer down; even though [Bill] Fries [the musician and business executive that recorded the song] explained 'Convoy' as '. . . fun and games . . .' it was temporarily banned in Iowa" (p. 97, ellipses in original).

127. Flynt, "La Monte Young in New York," p. 71.

128. Conrad, interview with author, Buffalo, NY, August 15–16, 1995.

129. For an example, see "Dreamweapon Benefit for the Oklahoma City Police Department," parts 1 and 2, recorded at the Film-makers' Cinematheque, 1968, on Angus MacLise, *Braindamage in Oklahoma City*, Quakebasket/Siltbreeze SB-81, compact disc (2000). Musicians include Tony Conrad, Henry Flynt, Angus MacLise, Hetty MacLise, and Jackson Mac Low.

130. Henry Flynt, "George Maciunas and My Work with Him," *Flash Art* 84–85 (October–November 1978): 49. On Maciunas's corresponding with Khruschev, see Flynt, "Mutations of the Vanguard," p. 112; Williams and Noël (eds.), *Mr. Fluxus*, p. 92; and Cuauhtémoc Medina, "The 'Kulturbolschewiken' II: Fluxus, Krushchev, and the 'concretist society,'" *Res: Anthropology and Aesthetics* 49–50 (Spring–Autumn 2006): 231–43.

131. For more on Maciunas's architecture and design, see Cuauhtémoc Medina, "Architecture and Efficiency: George Maciunas and the Economy of Art," *Res: Anthropology and Aesthetics* 45 (Spring 2004): 274–84. Flynt described Maciunas's design as "an innovative, integrated, functional solution which com-

bines quality with the possibility of mass production of components — and which allows both centralized and decentralized construction." "George Maciunas and My Work with Him," p. 49.

132. Maciunas, letter to Schmit, in Williams and Noël (eds.), *Mr. Fluxus*, p. 104.

133. See, for example, the conversation about Communist burial rites in Flynt's avant-country song "Graduation," on Flynt, *Graduation and Other New Country and Blues Music.*

134. Henry Flynt, "Overthrow the Human Race!," one-page broadsheet, ca. 1969, provided by Flynt.

135. Flynt, "Overthrow the Human Race!" Flynt's fifth and final goal was more frightening (and probable): a nuclear war that would transform consciousness and biology.

136. Conrad's archives contain a recording of a conversation between him and Flynt, "Organizational Phone Call — Effort to Overthrow Human Race," dated March 29, 1969, and another, dated the same year, titled "Henry Flynt, Tony [Conrad], and Beverly [Grant]: Discussion up to 'Realist' Conversation."

Chapter Five: Primitives and Flaming Creatures

1. Victor Bockris and Gerard Malanga, *Up-Tight: The Velvet Underground Story* (London: Omnibus Books, 1983), p. 17. This book remains the best history and prehistory of the Velvet Underground. Epigraph from an undated note, ca. 1964, in Conrad's archives.

2. The Primitives, "The Ostrich" b/w "Sneaky Pete," seven-inch single, Pickwick City PC-9001, dated December 1964 in the matrix by the pressing plant. For general information on Lou Reed's early career, including a discography, see http://olivier.landemaine.free.fr/prevu/lrprevu.html (consulted August 25, 2006 and last accessed July 8, 2007).

3. Conrad, in Jim Condon, "Three Interviews: Tony Conrad, Henry Flynt, Terry Riley (1983)," in *The Velvet Underground Companion: Four Decades of Commentary*, ed. Albin Zak (New York: Schirmer Books, 1997), p. 39. On the history of the Primitives, see Bockris and Malanga, *Up-Tight*, pp. 17–20.

4. Conrad, in Condon, "Three Interviews," p. 39.

5. On the Exploding Plastic Inevitable, see my "'My Mind Split Open': Andy Warhol's Exploding Plastic Inevitable," *Grey Room* 8 (Summer 2002): 80–107.

6. The All Night Workers, "Don't Put All Your Eggs In One Basket" b/w "Why Don't You Smile Now," seven-inch single, Round Sound RS-1, 1965; Donnie Burkes, "Satisfaction Guaranteed" b/w "Why Don't You Smile Now," seven-inch single, Decca 32134, 1965.

7. The Downliners Sect, *The Rock Sect's In*, LP, Columbia (UK) 1745, 1965. The Downliners Sect, who also covered Rufus Thomas's "All Night Worker," may have been attracted to the first single on account of the group's name. In any case, it is the All Night Workers' cut that they clearly listened to, not that of Donnie Burkes.

8. Various Artists, *Soundsville!*, LP, Design DLP 187 (mono) SDLP 187 (stereo), 1965. The Beachnuts' "Cycle Annie" would also find its way onto the Design record *Out of Sight!* (DLP-269), alongside Lou Rawls, Lou Christie, Paul Revere and the Raiders, and, as usual, a number of Pickwick creations.

9. Perhaps not the dregs. The other song on *Soundsville!* credited to the Beachnuts, the mock Beach Boys' "I've Got a Tiger In My Tank," by Reed, Phillips, Vance, Sims, and Robert W. Motta, began life as a commercial Vance had written for the Esso Corporation. It would be recorded and released again in 1965 as a single on Epic Records, this time as by the Intimates, with the even more kitsch addition of tiger roars.

10. Conrad, in Bockris and Malanga, *Up-Tight*, p. 18.

11. Scott MacDonald, "Tony Conrad on the Sixties," in *A Critical Cinema 5: Interviews with Independent Filmmakers* (Berkeley: University of California Press, 2006), pp. 60–61.

12. Tony Oursler, *Synesthesia: Tony Conrad*, video recording, 1997–2001.

13. John Cale and Victor Bockris, *What's Welsh for Zen: The Autobiography of John Cale* (London: Bloomsbury, 1999), p. 64.

14. Bockris and Malanga, *Up-Tight*, p. 14.

15. Cale and Bockris, *What's Welsh for Zen*, p. 65.

16. Bockris and Malanga, *Up-Tight*, p. 14.

17. *Ibid.*, p. 17.

18. Conrad, in Condon, "Three Interviews," p. 39.

19. Fredric Jameson, *Postmodernism or the Cultural Logic of Late Capitalism* (Durham, NC: Duke University Press, 1991), p. 1.

20. Conrad, in Bockris and Malanga, *Up-Tight*, p. 18.

21. The critical literature on Jack Smith is of a particularly high level. On account of the trajectory through his work that I want to chart in relation to

Conrad, it is not possible to deal with the previous writing on Smith in detail. Nevertheless, the reader is referred to the essays in Edward Leffingwell, Carole Kismaric, and Marvin Heiferman (eds.), *Jack Smith: Flaming Creature, His Amazing Life and Times* (London and Long Island City, New York: Serpent's Tail and The Institute for Contemporary Art / P.S. 1 Museum, 1997); the dossier "Jack by Popular Demand: Jack Smith in Retrospect," *Artforum* 36, no. 2 (October 1997): 66–75 (still the best source for Smith's early color photography); Michael Moon, "Flaming Closets," *October* 51 (Winter 1989): 19–54; Juan A. Suárez, *Bike Boys, Drag Queens, and Superstars: Avant-Garde, Mass Culture, and Gay Identities in the 1960s Underground Cinema* (Bloomington: Indiana University Press, 1996); Ken Jacobs, "Thanks for Explaining Me: Jack Smith at P.S. 1," *Aperture* 152 (Fall 1998): 74–76; and Jerry Tartaglia, "The Perfect Queer Appositeness of Jack Smith," in *Experimental Cinema: The Film Reader*, ed. Wheeler Winston Dixon and Gwendolyn Audrey Foster (London: Routledge, 2002), pp, 163–72. The best documentation and discussion of Smith's films is J. Hoberman's excellent *On Jack Smith's* Flaming Creatures *and Other Secret-flix of Cinemaroc* (New York: Granary Books / Hips Road, 2001). P. Adams Sitney's *Visionary Film: The American Avant-Garde, 1943–2000*, 3rd ed. (Oxford: Oxford University Press, 2002) remains indispensable. See also David E. James's discussion of Smith in "Introduction: Socialist Questions in a Rented World," in *Power Misses: Essays across (Un)Popular Culture* (London: Verso, 1996), pp. 1–24. A special issue on Jack Smith appeared in the French journal *Exploding: Revue d'analyse de l'expérimentation cinématographique* 8 (May 2002).

22. Sitney, *Visionary Film*, p. 335.

23. David Ehrenstein, "An Interview with Andy Warhol" (1965–66), in *I'll Be Your Mirror: The Selected Andy Warhol Interviews*, ed. Kenneth Goldsmith (New York: Carroll and Graf, 2004), p. 67.

24. Tony Conrad, interview with the author, Buffalo, NY, August 15–16, 1995.

25. Cale and Bockris, *What's Welsh for Zen*, p. 62. Conrad has released two tracks from such sessions featuring Cale: "Silent Shadows on Cinemarock Island" (September 5, 1964), track six of *Silent Shadows on Cinemarock Island*, compact disc, Table of the Elements 47, 1997; and "Cold Starry Nights" (undated), track four of *Les Evening Gowns Damnées*, compact disc, Table of the Elements 46 (Audio ArtKive 01), 1997.

26. Jack Smith, "O David" [letter to David Gurin, early fall 1962], in *Wait for*

Me at the Bottom of the Pool: The Writings of Jack Smith, ed. J. Hoberman and Edward Leffingwell (London: Serpent's Tail, 1997), p. 164 (ellipses in the original).

27. Jack Smith, one-page, handwritten letter addressed "Dear Ira," no date, but likely early 1963, located in Conrad's archives. Smith's photographs would eventually appear as "Brain Damage: Sorcery as Art," in *Avant Garde* (1968). Ira Cohen's film *The Invasion of Thunderbolt Pagoda* (1968) would feature "The Universal Mutant Repertory Company," which included Conrad, Flynt, MacLise, and Jackson Mac Low, as well as Loren Standlee, Ziska Baum, and Raja Samayana. Other members of the company included Smith and Beverly Grant. See *The Invasion of Thunderbolt Pagoda* DVD (Bastet) and "Cross Platform: Ira Cohen," in *The Wire* 271 (September 2006): 18.

28. Jack Smith, letter to Conrad, December 12, 1962, located in Conrad's archives. The Montez shrine would later appear to the side of Mario Montez's milk-bath pool in *Normal Love*.

29. Tony Conrad, statement in David Reisman, "In the Grip of the Lobster: Jack Smith Remembered," *Millennium Film Journal* 23–24 (Winter 1990–91): 65.

30. MacDonald, "Tony Conrad on the Sixties," p. 63. It is a measure, once again, of how far Conrad's aesthetic had come that he chose to include Bartók—previously, for him, the epitome of the avant-garde—in what, as we will see, he regarded as Smith's "retro" aesthetic.

31. *Ibid.*, p. 62. Ken Jacobs once suggested that it may have been Conrad's discipline that allowed Smith to complete *Flaming Creatures*, the only major film production he ever finished. Jacobs, unpublished interview by Federico J. Windhausen, July 2006.

32. *Blonde Cobra* was edited by Jacobs from footage shot by Fleischner, with a sound track by Smith, added during a moment of détente in their relationship.

33. According to Jacobs, *Star Spangled to Death* "came out of a collage aesthetic," both in its use of trash as setting and décor and in its apparently haphazard and self-undermining structure: "it's a movement towards order arguing *with* order every inch of the way." Scott MacDonald, "Ken and Flo Jacobs," in *A Critical Cinema 3* (Berkeley: University of California Press, 1998), p. 371. Film critic Parker Tyler, not wholly sympathetic to Jacobs's film, nonetheless recognized its roots within contemporary art: "the use of the trash pile as a source of costume and décor, and the infantile-neurotic style of Smith and minor characters in this film, stem from classic avant-garde painting (that of Schwitters, for

example) and especially from the step from the object-collagist, Robert Rauschenberg to the Happening-inventor, Allan Kaprow." Parker Tyler, *Underground Film: A Critical History* (New York: Da Capo, 1995), p. 79. Jacobs mentioned his admiration for the earliest works of Claes Oldenburg to Windhausen.

34. MacDonald, "Ken and Flo Jacobs," pp. 368 and 370.

35. Sitney, *Visionary Film*, p. 335. Jacobs recounts his reception of *The Flower Thief* in MacDonald, "Ken and Flo Jacobs," pp. 368–69. Smith lauds Rice in "The Perfect Filmic Appositeness of Maria Montez" (1962–63), in *Wait for Me at the Bottom of the Pool*, pp. 30 and 32, and in "Belated Appreciation of V.S." (1963–64), in *ibid.*, p. 42. Smith would appear with Mead in Rice's unfinished *The Queen of Sheba Meets the Atom Man* (1963).

36. Ron Rice, promotional statement for *The Beautiful Book*, reproduced in Leffingwell, Kismaric, and Heiferman (eds.), *Jack Smith: Flaming Creature*, p. 109.

37. Flynt delivered "The Supererogatory, Misleading Notion of 'Newness'" at Young's Bank Street apartment in New York on June 3, 1961; Conrad was not in attendance.

38. Conrad, in Reisman, "In the Grip of the Lobster," p. 63.

39. Tony Conrad, interview with the author, Buffalo, NY, August 15–16, 1995.

40. *Ibid.*

41. See Conrad's comments in MacDonald, "Tony Conrad on the Sixties," pp. 59–60.

42. Tony Conrad, interview with the author, Buffalo, NY, August 15–16, 1995. Conrad has also connected his reception of Smith to the challenge of Cage in Reisman, "In the Grip of the Lobster," p. 64.

43. Gerard Malanga, "Interview with Jack Smith," *Film Culture* 45 (Summer 1968): 13, and Smith, "The Perfect Filmic Appositeness of Maria Montez," p. 33.

44. MacDonald, "Ken and Flo Jacobs," p. 372.

45. Smith, "The Perfect Filmic Appositeness of Maria Montez," p. 31.

46. On the trash-pile set within Smith's loft theater, see Jonas Mekas, "Jack Smith, or The End of Civilization" (July 23, 1970), in *Movie Journal: The Rise of a New American Cinema, 1959–1971* (New York: Collier Books, 1972), pp. 388–97.

47. Jack Smith, with Mario Montez, Tony Conrad, and David G., "The First Memoirs of Maria Montez" (February 24, 1963), track 2 of *Silent Shadows on Cinemaroc Island*. A different version was published as Jack Smith, "The Memoirs

of Maria Montez or Wait for Me at the Bottom of the Pool," in *Wait for Me at the Bottom of the Pool*, pp. 37–39.

48. Susan Sontag, "Notes on 'Camp,'" in *Against Interpretation* (New York: Farrar, Straus and Giroux, 1966), pp. 275–92.

49. Moon, "Flaming Closets," pp. 35–36.

50. Sontag, "Notes on 'Camp,'" p. 277.

51. *Ibid.*, pp. 278 and 281.

52. *Ibid.*, pp. 287 and 280.

53. Susan Sontag, "Jack Smith's *Flaming Creatures*," in *Against Interpretation*, p. 229.

54. Malanga, "Interview with Jack Smith," p. 13. Smith's later antipathy toward Warhol was manifest in a variety of places. To cite only one example, see Jack Smith, "Remarks on Art & the Theater" (1988), in *Historical Treasures*, ed. Ira Cohen (Madras and New York: Hanuman Books, 1990), p. 123. Although Cale, of course, would come to work closely with Warhol, Conrad shared Smith's antipathy, even at one point suggesting an "*Artistic Revolution*" against Warhol: "Study the early politics of the pre-revolution CP [Communist Party] in Switzerland to find out how to conduct effective artistic revolution against the established representatives of the publicity machines of the artistic aristocracy." Conrad, yellow *Flicker* notebook entry, dated March 12, 1966, p. 56. See also Conrad's comments on Warhol in Reisman, "In the Grip of the Lobster," pp. 67–69.

55. The allegorical dimension of Smith's aesthetic has been discussed in Suárez, *Bike Boys, Drag Queens, and Superstars*, pp. 181–213.

56. Smith describes his work as baroque in a letter to Heiner Ross, July 1987, in *Wait for Me at the Bottom of the Pool*, p. 150, and in "Remarks on Art & the Theater," in *Historical Treasures*, p. 115. Before the 1980s, Smith seemed to refer to this aspect of his work as "Romantic." It is interesting to compare Smith's interest in decay, in, for example, "The First Memoirs of Maria Montez," with certain passages cited by Walter Benjamin from seventeenth-century baroque tragic dramas. See, for example, Walter Benjamin, *The Origin of German Tragic Drama*, trans. John Osborne (London: Verso, 1977), p. 190.

57. Jacobs, in Sitney, *Visionary Film*, p. 331. On *Rose Hobart* and what Smith may have taken from it, see pp. 330–33. On Smith and surrealism, see J. Hoberman, "Jack Smith: Bagdada and Lobserrealism," in Smith, *Wait for Me at the Bottom of the Pool*, pp. 14–23.

58. Walter Benjamin, "Surrealism: The Last Snapshot of the European Intelligentsia" (1929), in Walter Benjamin: *Selected Writings, Volume 2, 1927–1934*, ed. Michael W. Jennings, Howard Eiland and Gary Smith (Cambridge: Harvard University Press, 1999), p. 210.

59. On Maria Montez, see Ronald Tavel, "Maria Montez: Anima of an Antediluvian World," in *Jack Smith: Flaming Creature*, pp. 88–104; on Mario Montez and for a polemical discussion of the issue of race in queer theory, see Hiram Perez, "You Can Have My Brown Body and Eat It, Too!" *Social Text* 23, nos. 3–4 (Fall–Winter 2005): 171–91. The role of gender within the redemptive (as distinct from the defamiliarizing) dimension of Smith's aesthetic seems somewhat more problematic. For a discussion of some of the relevant issues, see Caryl Flinn, "The Deaths of Camp," *Camera Obscura* 35 (May 1995): 53–84. My thanks to Bliss Cua Lim for this reference.

60. Smith, "The Perfect Filmic Appositeness of Maria Montez," p. 33.

61. Suárez, *Bike Boys, Drag Queens, and Superstars*, p. 203.

62. Walter Benjamin, *The Arcades Project*, trans. Howard Eiland and Kevin McLaughlin (Cambridge, MA: Harvard University Press, 1999), p. 392.

63. Benjamin, *The Origin of German Tragic Drama*, p. 178.

64. MacDonald, "Tony Conrad on the Sixties," p. 57.

65. Hoberman, *On Jack Smith's* Flaming Creatures, p. 81.

66. The location of the scene in *Scotch Tape* is identified by Hoberman, from information by Jacobs, in *ibid.*

67. Sitney, *Visionary Film*, p. 323.

68. Conrad, in Reisman, "In the Grip of the Lobster," pp. 64–65.

69. "The narrowing of the tonal range [by the washed-out texture of outdated raw film] obscures the sense of depth, which Smith capitalizes on by cluttering the panning frame with actors and with details of limbs, breasts, a penis, and puckered lips so that not only depth disappears but the vertical and horizontal coordinates as well." Sitney, *Visionary Film*, p. 335.

70. Conrad, interview with the author, Buffalo, NY, August 15–16, 1995.

71. The difference between Conrad's attitude and Flynt's would be illustrated by a proposal in Conrad's notebook, "Music Notes II," dated ca. August 3, 1964. Titled "*Ethnic Fraud*," it proposed "Make phoney [sic] ethnic tapes to sell to record producers (like Folkways)" (p. 50, entry 106). Cale would ultimately find the sophistication of pop music, in particular the harmonies in the Everly Brothers' "Dream," to be of interest and importance equal to or greater than the

music he had done with the Theatre of Eternal Music, ultimately leading him out of the high-cultural avant-garde. Cale and Bockris, *What's Welsh for Zen*, p. 65. According to Cale, the term "dream" for the Dream Syndicate derived in part from the Everly Brothers' song.

72. Conrad, yellow *Flicker* Notebook, p. 4, dated May 12, 1965. On the relationship of the vamp to Smith, see Moon, "Flaming Closets," p. 40.

73. Unless otherwise noted, all quotes in this section derive from a small collection of loose, handwritten notes dated approximately 1965, located in Conrad's archives. Square bracketed insertions in original.

74. MacDonald, "Tony Conrad on the Sixties," p. 61.

75. Scopitone films originated in France around 1960 and were imported into the United States in mid-1964. For a listing of Scopitone films, see http://www.scopitonearchive.com/ (last accessed July 9, 2007).

76. At around the same time, Conrad would propose projecting "Polarized light on plastic costumes, with polarized camera filter, so that actors are dressed in stress patterns." Yellow *Flicker* notebook, p. 35; entry dated ca. December 1965.

77. Conrad, "Plan for Cale-Conrad Concert Collaboration," "Music Notes II," pp. 58–59 (entry 124, "J.C. & I," dated January 16, 1964).

78. Jack Smith (with Francis Francine and Tony Conrad), "Love is Strange," track two of *Les Evening Gowns Damnées*.

79. This is particularly true of the least cerebral of Smith's creatures: the "cretins," "pinheads," and, especially, "mongos," who seems almost continually in a state of overexcitement. Clearly, such designations are far from present-day conceptions of political correctness and are only one of many places where Smith's archetypes come dangerously close to stereotypes (as often in his casting of African Americans). As Conrad once noted at the showing of the restored *No President* (1967–70), one starts to notice that something in the picture is not right, but its only when you realize that nothing is quite right that you begin to get anywhere. In 1959, Smith shot a film entitled *Overstimulated* (1959–63).

80. Jack Smith, "Normal Love," "Red Orchids," and "The White Pig of Medina," in *Wait for Me at the Bottom of the Pool*, pp. 51–52, 61–75. Smith's hysterical reading of the "Pfeffernus Flavored Aspirin" section of "Red Orchids" was released as "The Horrors of Agony," track 7 of *Silent Shadows of Cinemaroc Island*. Sontag strictly separated the avant-garde legacy (which included Artaud) from the camp attitude (in which Smith would be located) in "Notes on

'Camp,'" p. 287. Jonas Mekas would connect Smith's aesthetic to that of Burroughs in "On the Baudelairian Cinema" (May 2, 1963), in *Movie Journal: The Rise of a New American Cinema, 1959–1971* (New York: Macmillan, 1972), pp. 85–86, and would later connect Smith to Artaud in "On the Expanded Cinema of Jack Smith..." (November 18, 1965), in *Movie Journal*, pp. 211–12.

81. Quote from Smith, "Red Orchids," p. 61.

82. Smith, "Normal Love," pp. 51–52. The story ends with God exacting corporeal punishment on the perpetrators, only to find himself in turn overcome with desire. Much the same would happen in the section of Smith's sound track to *Blonde Cobra* devoted to Madame Nescience's dream of Mother Superior and Sister Dexterity. See Smith, "Soundtrack of Blonde Cobra," in *Wait for Me at the Bottom of the Pool*, p. 159.

83. David Packman, "Jack Smith's Flaming Creatures: With the Tweak of an Eyebrow," *Film Culture* 63/64 (1977): 54.

84. Ken Kelman, "Smith Myth," in *Film Culture Reader*, ed. P. Adams Sitney (New York: Praeger, 1970), p. 282.

85. In the final scenes of Ron Rice's *The Queen of Sheba Meets the Atom Man*, dancing would specifically be labeled transgressive, as the cast dances (sometimes in same-sex pairs) in a bar beneath a "No Dancing" sign.

86. Smith, "Belated Appreciation of V.S.," p. 41.

87. Smith, "The Perfect Filmic Appositeness of Maria Montez," p. 32.

88. Smith, "Belated Appreciation of V.S.," p. 41.

89. Smith, "The Perfect Filmic Appositeness of Maria Montez," pp. 28–29.

90. Smith, "Belated Appreciation of V.S.," p. 42.

91. Smith, *Wait for Me at the Bottom of the Pool*, p. 169.

92. Smith, "The Perfect Filmic Appositeness of Maria Montez," p. 29.

93. Stan Brakhage, "From *Metaphors on Vision*," in *The Avant-Garde Film: A Reader of Theory and Criticism*, ed. P. Adams Sitney (New York: New York University Press, 1978), p. 120. Smith likely knew Brakhage's text, which was written in 1960, but published in *Film Culture* 30 (Fall 1963), one issue after Smith's "The Perfect Filmic Appositeness of Maria Montez." My thanks to David James for reiterating Brakhage's importance.

94. On the reception and availability of Artaud, see Douglas Kahn's excellent chronicle, "Artaud in America," in *100 Years of Cruelty: Essays on Artaud*, ed. Edward Scheer (Sydney: Power Publications and Artspace, 2000), pp. 237–62.

95. Antonin Artaud, *The Theater and Its Double*, trans. Mary Caroline

Richards (New York: Grove Weidenfeld, 1958), pp. 87 and 78. See also pp. 110–11.

96. *Ibid.*, p. 37. In his disdain for language, Smith was like many enthusiasts of silent film, though Smith extended this enthusiasm to the sound films of the 1940s. Smith would later come to describe his work as an extension of silent film. *Wait for Me at the Bottom of the Pool*, p. 150.

97. Smith, "Belated Appreciation of V.S.," p. 41.

98. Artaud, *The Theater and Its Double*, p. 46.

99. J. Hoberman recounts that Smith "projected *Normal Love* production slides to the accompaniment of a taped radio speech by Antonin Artaud" in Hoberman, "The Big Heat: Making and Unmaking *Flaming Creatures*," in *Jack Smith: Flaming Creature*, p. 162. This radio play was undoubtedly *To Have Done with the Judgment of God.* For a translation, see Antonin Artaud, *Watchfiends and Rack Screams*, trans. Clayton Eshleman (Cambridge, MA: Exact Change, 1995), pp. 281–308 (quote from p. 297). A translation of Artaud's text by Guy Wertham had been circulating in translation since the mid-1950s, particularly among the Beat circles of San Francisco, and would appear in print in the Fall 1963 issue of *Northwest Review*. Kahn, "Artaud in America," pp. 249–50.

100. Artaud, *The Theater and Its Double*, pp. 54 and 61; Smith, "The Perfect Filmic Appositeness of Maria Montez," p. 33. See, however, Artaud's positive comments about film (but against language) in "Sorcery and the Cinema" (1927), in Sitney, ed., *The Avant-Garde Film*, pp. 49–50.

101. Artaud, *The Theater and Its Double*, pp. 125 and 89, respectively.

102. Smith, "The Perfect Filmic Appositeness of Maria Montez," p. 34 and "Belated Appreciation of V.S.," p. 42.

103. Smith, "The Perfect Filmic Appositeness of Maria Montez," p. 33. See also Smith's remarks on thinking and ideas on p. 30 and in "Belated Appreciation of V.S.," p. 42.

104. Smith, "The Perfect Filmic Appositeness of Maria Montez," p. 25.

105. On the roles of the "mobility of the support" (e.g. camera movement) and the stasis of the "tableau vivant," see Jean-François Lyotard, "Acinema," trans. Paisley N. Livingston, in *Narrative, Apparatus, Ideology*, ed. Philip Rosen (New York: Columbia University Press, 1986), pp. 356–57. Lyotard's text was first cited in reference to Smith's cinema (which it seems to describe perfectly), in David E. James, *Allegories of Cinema: American Film in the Sixties* (Princeton, NJ: Princeton University Press, 1989), p. 120.

106. Smith, "The Perfect Filmic Appositeness of Maria Montez," p. 30.

107. See Smith's comments on particular and general in "The Perfect Filmic Appositeness of Maria Montez," p. 28.

108. *Ibid.*, p. 30.

109. Smith, "The Adorable and Pasty Creatures," in *Wait for Me at the Bottom of the Pool*, p. 77.

110. Smith, "The Perfect Filmic Appositeness of Maria Montez," p. 28 (ellipses in original).

111. Conrad, liner notes to *Slapping Pythagoras*, Table of the Elements 23, compact disc.

112. Smith, "The Perfect Filmic Appositeness of Maria Montez," p. 34.

113. See, for instance, Cage's comments on the minimum number of events needed to achieve multiplicity in *Silence* (Middleton, CT: Wesleyan University Press, 1961), pp. 173, 186.

114. On power's drawing of energy from the collective, see Roger Caillois, "Power," in Denis Hollier, ed., *The College of Sociology, 1937–39* (Minneapolis: University of Minnesota Press, 1988), p. 132.

115. John Cage, "These Days" (1968), in *John Cage: An Anthology*, ed. Richard Kostelanetz (New York: Da Capo, 1970), p. 179.

116. John Cage, "Seriously Comma" (1966), in *A Year from Monday* (Middletown, CT: Wesleyan University Press, 1967), p. 27, and "Diary: How to Improve the World (You Will Only Make Matters Worse) 1965," *ibid.*, p. 13.

117. Cage, "Where Do We Go from Here?" (1963), in *A Year from Monday*, p. 92.

118. Smith refers to preset story lines as "oppressive" in "The Perfect Filmic Appositeness of Maria Montez," p. 32. Cage also, undoubtedly following Artaud, opposed subservience to language. As he wrote "We are not, in these dances and music, saying something. We are simple-minded enough to think that if we were saying something we would use words. We are rather doing something. The meaning of what we do is determined by each one who sees and hears it," Cage, "In This Day . . ." (1956), in *Silence*, p. 94. See also *Silence*, pp. 10 and 176.

119. Incredibly, the repression of *Flaming Creatures* would involve all three branches of the U.S. government: not only the executive and judiciary, in police raids and subsequent obscenity trials, but even the legislative, in debates within the halls of Congress. On the repression of *Flaming Creatures*, see J. Hoberman, "'Crimson Creatures,'" in *On Jack Smith's* Flaming Creatures, pp. 34–51.

120. Smith, "The Perfect Filmic Appositeness of Maria Montez," p. 28.

121. Smith, "Belated Appreciation of V.S.," p. 43.

122. On the controlling bounds of desire, see, for example, Cage's comments on emotions in *Silence*, pp. 253–54 and in John Cage and Daniel Charles, *For the Birds* (New York: Marion Boyars, 1981), pp. 56–57.

123. John Cage, "Diary: How to Improve the World (You Will Only Make Matters Worse) Continued 1966," in *A Year from Monday*, p. 60.

124. Smith, "The Perfect Filmic Appositeness of Maria Montez," p. 34.

125. Georges Bataille, *Erotism: Death and Sensuality*, trans. Mary Dalwood (San Francisco: City Lights, 1986), p. 68: "Taboos are there to make work possible; work is productive; during the profane period allotted to work consumption is reduced to the minimum consistent with continued production." This idea is developed most thoroughly in Georges Bataille, *The Accursed Share, Volume 1*, trans. Robert Hurley (New York: Zone Books, 1988).

126. Georges Bataille, *The Unfinished System of Nonknowledge*, ed. Stuart Kendall, trans. Michelle Kendall and Stuart Kendall (Minneapolis: University of Minnesota Press, 2001), p. 86.

127. Interestingly, Artaud's *To Have Done with the Judgment of God* opened with a remarkable figuration of restricted economy, one in which nothing, including nature and desire (represented by the fantastic tale of the American government's extraction of schoolchildren's sperm), would escape the "triumphant replacement products" of American capitalism. Artaud, *Watchfields and Rack Screams*, p. 285.

128. Smith, "The Perfect Filmic Appositeness of Maria Montez," p. 27. Smith would continue to have a vision of films (and film sets) as places for visual offerings beyond the thought of a return on investment. See Smith, "Taboo of Jingola" (1972), in *Wait for Me at the Bottom of the Pool*, p. 102.

129. Smith, "The Adorable and Pasty Creatures," p. 77.

130. *Ibid.*, p. 78.

131. *Ibid.*, pp. 77–78.

132. On the "diversion of illegality for the illicit circuits of profit and power of the dominant class," see Michel Foucault, *Discipline and Punish: The Birth of the Prison*, trans. Alan Sheridan (New York: Vintage, 1977), p. 280. Smith had a prescient understanding of the uses of illegality. See, for example, his presentation of the wino in his "Rehearsal for the Destruction of Atlantis," at the 1965 New York Film-makers' Cinematheque Expanded Cinema festival ("New Cinema Festival I"), in *Wait for Me at the Bottom of the Pool*, pp. 90–95.

133. Jack Smith, "Lobotomy in Lobsterland" (ca. 1965), in *Wait for Me at the Bottom of the Pool*, p. 82. The differential legalities of alcohol and marijuana are also invoked in Smith, "Rehearsal for the Destruction of Atlantis."

134. Although much of the history of drugs in the New York art world remains unrecorded, Conrad emphasized its importance in a telephone conversation with the author, December 31, 2006. As Conrad noted, unlike Smith's sexuality, drug use was an experience of excess, illegality, and the potentially repressive force of law that he shared not only with Smith but also with Cale and Young. Denizens of much the same underground milieu, whom Smith called "the scum of Baghdad," would form the community to whom Conrad's own psychedelic, countercultural film, *The Flicker*, would originally be directed.

135. Conrad discusses his reading of Roland Barthes, "The Metaphor of the Eye," in *Critical Essays* (Evanston, IL: Northwestern University Press, 1972), pp. 239–47, in "Progress 2," unpublished manuscript (2003) in Conrad's archive.

136. Bataille, *Erotism*, pp. 65–70. Bataille is drawing from Roger Caillois's text "Festival" (1939), in Denis Hollier, ed., *The College of Sociology*, pp. 279–303, where among other things, excess is marked by orgies, "verbal excesses," and moments when "one dances until exhaustion and spins until dizzy" (p. 298).

137. "The whole business of eroticism is to destroy the self-contained character of the participators [this would be better translated as: "the closed structure of the individual being"] as they are in their normal lives." Bataille, *Erotism*, p. 17.

138. *Ibid.*, pp. 83–90.

139. *Ibid.*, pp. 113–14.

140. Moon, "Flaming Closets," pp. 41–42. On transgression, see also Tartaglia, "The Perfect Queer Appositeness of Jack Smith," pp. 163–72.

141. Smith, "The Perfect Filmic Appositeness of Maria Montez," p. 33.

142. Jack Smith and Tony Conrad, "Mario and the Flickering Jewel" (March 5, 1963), released as track four of Jack Smith, *Silent Shadows of Cinemaroc Island*. Earlier, Conrad apparently erroneously dated his involvement with flicker to 1962, in Tony Conrad, "Tony Conrad on 'The Flicker': From a Letter to Henry Romney, Dated November 11, 1965," *Film Culture* 41 (Summer 1966): 2. On the initial flicker session, see also John Geiger, *Chapel of Extreme Experience: A Short History of Stroboscopic Light and the Dream Machine* (Brooklyn: Soft Skull Press, 2003), pp. 73–74.

143. Smith, "The Perfect Filmic Appositeness of Maria Montez," p. 25.

144. Conrad, "Progress 2."

145. Smith, "Journal Notes on *Normal Love*," in *Wait for Me At the Bottom of the Pool*, p. 48.

146. Joan Adler, "On Location," in Stephen Dwoskin, *Film Is: The International Free Cinema* (Woodstock, NY: Overlook Press, 1975), p. 15.

147. Smith's reference to Grant is made in Malanga, "Interview with Jack Smith," p. 15. Smith's previous break with Jacobs had possibly also been precipitated by the latter's relationship with his future wife, Flo, in whom Smith had shown an artistic interest. According to Conrad, Smith had also come to harbor an intense dislike for Young (whom Smith "used to call evil names") after the onset of his relationship with Zazeela. Conrad, interview with author, Buffalo, NY, August 15–16, 1995.

148. Conrad, yellow *Flicker* notebook, pp. 17–18. Conrad's thoughts about the implications of Smith's performance continue for several pages.

149. Conrad, "Progress 2."

150. Conrad, yellow *Flicker* notebook, p. 60 (Flynt's formula for the "Universal Film" appears on p. 61). Interestingly, in light of the reflections on media to be explored in Chapter 6, Conrad's next note reads: "McLuhan's 'Hot' vs. 'Cool' media as a measure of SIZE (in *acting* sense)," p. 60 (entry dated to October 10, 1967).

151. Conrad, yellow *Flicker* notebook, pp. 68 and 66, respectively. The film idea, attributed to De Maria, is dated December 6, 1967.

152. Conrad, yellow *Flicker* notebook, p. 79 (entry dated December 7, 1967).

153. Conrad, "Progress 2" and press release for "World Premiere Engagement" of *Coming Attractions* at the Whitney Museum of American Art New American Filmmakers Series, December 31 – January 6, 1971, located in Conrad's archives.

154. Conrad, "Progress 2." Despite its intentions, *Coming Attractions* is not, at least in the judgment of this author, entirely successful. Not only were Conrad and Grant unable to coax the type of performances out of their actors that Smith engendered, but in their hands, allegory too often turns over into stereotype or, perhaps worse, archetype (as in the flickering appearance of an angel at the film's end). Perhaps most disappointing is an extended erotic sequence that entirely lacks the Smith's transgressive vision (being far too much an expression of the sexuality of "normals") and that appears as desultory period soft-core porn.

155. Conrad, who first met Palestine in that capacity, recalls: "It was clear that something very strange was going on up there [in the St. Thomas bell tower] because it sounded like John Cage was ringing the bells, and then the next time it would sound like some kind of Indonesian thing or something." Conrad, interview with the author, Buffalo, NY, July 31, 2001.

Chapter 6: Flicker

1. Information on *The Flicker* is found in two notebooks located in Conrad's archives. The "blue" notebook relates most directly to the film's production, containing elaborate shooting and editing notes. Another notebook, referred to below and in the notes to the preceding chapter as the "yellow" notebook, collects a more diverse set of notes dating from May 1965 to May 1968. The epigraph to this chapter comes from Anthony S. Conrad, "The Theory of the Flexagon," RIAS Technical Report 60–24, 1960, p. 1.

2. Jonas Mekas, "An Interview with Tony Conrad: On the Flickering Cinema of Pure Light" (March 24, 1966), in *Movie Journal: The Rise of a New American Cinema, 1959–1971* (New York: Macmillan, 1972), p. 228.

3. Tony Conrad, "Statement Concerning the Relationship between the New York Film Festival and Independent American Film-makers," two-page typescript (1966), in Conrad's archives. Although Conrad's authorship is referred to in Fred Wellington, "Towards Understanding of 'Subversion,'" *Film Culture* 42 (Fall 1966): 24, the statement was published without attribution and with a mistakenly truncated title as "Statement Concerning the Relationship between the New York Film Festival," *Film Culture* 42 (Fall 1966): 115–16. Conrad refers to the event as "the Lincoln Center Scandal" in a letter to Stan Brakhage, attempting, with only moderate success, to enlist the elder filmmaker's support for his cause. Letter from Conrad to Stan Brakhage, September 19, 1966, located in Conrad's archive. In it, Conrad explained that he had the "implicit support" of Mekas and Dick Preston for his intervention in the Lincoln Center festival.

4. Ken Dewey, Henry Geldzahler et al., "Expanded Cinema: A Symposium, N.Y. Film Festival 1966," *Film Culture* 43 (Winter 1966): 2.

5. Jonas Mekas, "On the Changing Eye" (November 9, 1967), in *Movie Journal*, p. 296. Mekas continued: "It's clear that we tend to incredibly underestimate our real capacities—our capacities to see, to hear, to learn, to perceive, to accumulate; and to hate, to murder, to violate."

6. Loose, handwritten note dated by Conrad to late November, 1964, found in blue *Flicker* notebook. Another loose note, which Conrad also dates to 1964, reads: "flicker film. do in reduced length c̄ 5th bowed guitar track, print many times & splice together."

7. Tony Conrad, "Progress 2," unpublished manuscript in Conrad's archives.

8. Blue *Flicker* notebook, three-page section entitled "'Flicker' Research," n.p.

9. P. Adams Sitney, "Structural Film," in *Film Culture Reader*, ed. P. Adams Sitney (New York: Praeger, 1970), p. 343. Sitney's original article appeared in *Film Culture* 47 (Summer 1969): 1–10. It was reproduced in full in *Film Culture Reader* with additional material inserted in square brackets.

10. Conrad would write in the blue *Flicker* notebook: "For short cycles, gradual density changes are bought about by changing rhythms of cycle densities. Pulse rhythm composition (à la Kontakte): Do on film & record photoelectronically."

11. Tony Conrad, "Midsummer 1967," program notes, August 25, 1967, n.p., and Tony Conrad, "Tony Conrad on 'The Flicker': From a Letter to Henry Romney, Dated November 11, 1965," *Film Culture* 41 (Summer 1966): 1. See also Toby Mussman, "An Interview with Tony Conrad," *Film Culture* 41 (Summer 1966): 5.

12. Conrad, blue *Flicker* notebook, n.p.

13. Conrad, yellow *Flicker* notebook, p. 33 (November 18, 1965) and p. 45 (December 1966). Walter De Maria's "Cricket Music" and "Ocean Music" were released as the compact disc *Drums and Nature* (2000). Conrad recalls another version of De Maria's "Ocean Music" dating to before 1968. While making *Coming Attractions*, Conrad, inspired by De Maria, made field recordings of the ocean and the Bronx Zoo aviary, taking along with him Irv Teibel, who possessed a stereo tape recorder. Based upon the recordings Conrad made, Teibel would go on to produce an influential series of "Environments" records (the first one, *Environments®: New Concepts in Stereo Sound, disc 1* [Atlantic LP SD66001] was released in 1969, featuring "The Psychologically Ultimate Seashore" b/w "Optimum Aviary"). Conrad, conversation with the author, January 6, 2007. La Monte Young and Marian Zazeela would also record themselves singing with the ocean for Columbia Records, which was never released.

14. Conrad, blue *Flicker* notebook, n.p. Conrad surmised that they had been affected by silent projection, since they both occurred nearly a quarter of a cen-

tury before. Conrad's notebook also contains a reprint of M. H. Charlton and Paul F. A. Hoefer, "Television and Epilepsy," *Archives of Neurology*, 11 (September 1964): 239–47.

15. Lindley Page Hanlon, in *A History of the American Avant-Garde Cinema* (New York: The American Federation of the Arts, 1976), p. 115. Hanlon provides the most detailed discussion of *The Flicker* to date.

16. Conrad, yellow *Flicker* notebook, p. 11 (May 17, 1965).

17. Conrad, interview with the author, Buffalo, NY, August 15–16, 1995.

18. Conrad, blue *Flicker* notebook, n.p.

19. Conrad, "Midsummer 1967," n.p.

20. See Daniel Conrad, "The Dichromaccord: Reinventing the Elusive Color Organ," *Leonardo* 32, no. 5 (October 1999): 393–98, and Lee Gardner, "Pigments of His Imagination: How Daniel Conrad Learned to 'Play' Colors," *Baltimore City Paper*, July 4, 2001, consulted on-line at http://www. citypaper. com/music/printready.asp?id=8290 via http://www.citypaper.com/ music/ on September 2, 2006 (last accessed July 10, 2007). Conrad discusses the impossibility of color visual harmonics in "Letter to Henry Romney," p. 1. Conrad would, nonetheless, speculate on more complex "flicker-compositions" in "Midsummer 1967."

21. Sheldon Renan, *An Introduction to the American Underground Film* (New York: E. P. Dutton, 1967), p. 31; Amos Vogel, quoted in Wellington "Towards Understanding of 'Subversion,'" p. 16; Mekas, "An Interview with Tony Conrad," pp. 228 and 231; and Conrad, quoted in Mekas, *ibid.*, p. 229.

22. *Film-makers' Cooperative Catalogue*, vol. 7 (New York, Film-makers' Cooperative: 1989), p. 116.

23. Sitney, "Structural Film," *Film Culture Reader*, p. 327.

24. P. Adams Sitney, "Michael Snow's Cinema," in *The Essential Cinema*, ed. P. Adams Sitney (New York: New York University Press, 1975), p. 221, and Sitney, "Structural Film," in *Film Culture Reader*, pp. 327, 343–44. Sitney deleted his initial, prominent mention of *The Flicker* in later versions of his discussion. See Sitney, *Visionary Film: The American Avant-Garde, 1943–2000*, 3rd ed. (Oxford: Oxford University Press, 2002), pp. 347–70. Conrad's "Exposure Timing Sheet" was originally reproduced in *Film Culture* 41 (Summer 1966): n.p.

25. Sitney, "Structural Film" in *Film Culture Reader*, p. 343.

26. *Ibid.*, p. 344.

27. Conrad had not seen *Arnulf Rainer* and apparently learned of it only

after the material for his own film had already been shot. On one page of his working notebook concerned with cataloging the flaws in the third film roll appears the word "Kubelka." *The Flicker* was in fact only one of several flicker films to appear in 1966, including Paul Sharits's *Ray Gun Virus*, Victor Grauer's *Archangel*, and John Cavanaugh's *Blink* (aka *Flicker*). The first film composed entirely of solid frames, in color, rather than in black and white, was likely Dwinell Grant's *Color Sequence*, 1943.

28. Tony Conrad, "The Eye and the Asshole: Otto Muehl and the Extremes of Vienna, 196–," *The Underground Film Bulletin* 5 (1986): 66.

29. Sitney, "Structural Film," in *Film Culture Reader*, pp. 330, 346; Sitney, "Michael Snow's Cinema," p. 220. Responding to his critics, Sitney avers in "Structural Film" that he explicitly "tried to define and describe a prevalent tendency within the avant-garde cinema" (p. 329).

30. George Maciunas, "Some Comments on 'Structural Film' by P. Adams Sitney," in *Film Culture Reader*, p. 349. This context was certainly apposite for Conrad and potentially so for Sharits and George Landow (aka Owen Land). Both Sharits and Landow contributed to Maciunas's series of Fluxfilms and had other films distributed under the auspices of Fluxus. Sharits also produced a number of nonfilm Fluxus works. See Jon Hendricks, *Fluxus Codex* (New York: The Gilbert and Lila Silverman Fluxus Collection in association with Harry N. Abrams, 1988), pp. 304–5, 467–74.

31. Sitney, "Structural Film," in *Film Culture Reader*, pp. 335–36.

32. Robert Morris, "Notes on Sculpture, Part 2" (1966), in *Continuous Project Altered Daily* (Cambridge, MA: MIT Press, 1993), pp. 16–17. The relation of Sitney's structural film to minimalism has been noted by Paul Arthur (who specifically discusses Morris) in "Structural Film: Revisions, New Versions, and the Artifact. Part Two," *Millennium Film Journal* 4–5 (Summer–Fall 1979): 122–34, and by David E. James, in *Allegories of Cinema: American Film in the Sixties* (Princeton, NJ: Princeton University Press, 1989), pp. 240–41.

33. Sitney, *Visionary Film*, p. 359.

34. Malcolm Le Grice, in *Structural Film Anthology*, ed. Peter Gidal (London: British Film Institute, 1976), p. 60. Le Grice is discussing the structural films of Kurt Kren.

35. Malcolm Le Grice, *Abstract Film and Beyond* (Cambridge, MA: MIT Press, 1977), p. 106.

36. *Ibid.*, p. 107.

37. *Ibid.*, p. 108.

38. *Ibid.*, p. 106.

39. Jean-Claude Lebensztejn, *Écrits sur l'art récent: Brice Marden, Malcolm Morley, Paul Sharits* (Paris: Éditions Aldines, 1995), p. 153, my translation.

40. Conrad, interview with author, Buffalo, NY, August 15–16, 1995. See also Mussman, "An Interview with Tony Conrad," p. 4.

41. Gérard Langlois, "Les soirées underground du C.J.C.: Entretien avec Tony Conrad," *Cinéma* 171 (December 1972): 11. My translation, as are all quotes from this source.

42. *Ibid.*, pp. 10–11.

43. *Ibid.*, p. 11.

44. Conrad, "Midsummer 1967," n.p.

45. Conrad, "Letter to Henry Romney," 2. See also Conrad, "Midsummer 1967," Mussman, "An Interview with Tony Conrad," and Mekas, "An Interview with Tony Conrad."

46. Conrad's working notebooks make several references to drugs. On the same page of Conrad's yellow *Flicker* notebook, and dated to the same day (May 17, 1965) as Conrad's first mention of a self-reflexive "Flicker shot" ("Superimpose flicker & shot of the projector light receding from the camera" [p. 9]) is the proposal "Make fast-edited documentary film on every way to use grass, including all techniques of burning, eating, rolling, making pipes, &c." Yellow *Flicker* notebook, p. 9. A similar juxtaposition would occur in notes dated December 11. After a note proposing to record the noise of the camera as a possible (self-reflexive and medium-specific) film sound track, Conrad immediately proposes another "Dope flic." Yellow *Flicker* notebook, p. 35. In 1967, Conrad would consider a very different type of drug film to be titled *Grass Grows in Brooklyn*: "Use millions of hippie extras—Benefit communal population by 30% of profit of film, to go to their community. Portray Brooklyn run by a hippy governm't. LSD in city water supply as imperial military maneuver of Bklyn." Yellow *Flicker* notebook, p. 48.

47. Conrad, blue *Flicker* notebook, n.p.

48. Conrad, yellow *Flicker* notebook, p. 10 (May 17, 1965); see also pp. 6 (May 14, 1965), 9 (November 21, 1965), and 28 (November 4, 1965). Conrad would also plan (independently of Sharits) to produce a "Flickering film composed entirely of words forming images sequentially scrambled," an idea that he would not realize. Yellow *Flicker* notebook, p. 28 (November 4, 1965).

49. Conrad, yellow *Flicker* notebook, pp. 89–91 (August 11–13, 1967), and 34 (November 26, 1965). Even when thinking about *The Flicker* as a film, Conrad was concerned to monitor its distribution tightly, not only on account of potential liability, but in order to "prevent its use as a technique" for other purposes: "'Flicker': Give Jonas [Mekas] distribution for a %age but HOLD ONTO THE FILM! Give it out *each time* for showings. (To prevent its use as a technique or piracy of a print)." Yellow *Flicker* notebook, p. 4 (May 12, 1965).

50. "Angus [MacLise] liked 'The Flicker' better seen with eyes closed than with eyes open." Conrad, blue *Flicker* notebook, n.p.

51. Conrad, "Midsummer 1967," n.p.

52. On watching the audience, see Mekas, "An Interview with Tony Conrad," pp. 231–232. Conrad's alternative showing of *The Flicker* took place at Millennium Film Workshop, New York, in the early 1970s. Conrad, conversation with author; confirmed by e-mail November 24, 2004. The idea, however, seems to have occurred much earlier. In an undated note from the 1960s titled "Projection ideas for 'Flicker,'" Conrad wrote: "'Be Screen' – project on the audience," and in another note dated May 2, 1966, "Flicker is ideally viewed thru translucent glasses." Blue *Flicker* notebook, n.p.

53. Mussman, "An Interview with Tony Conrad," p. 5. Conrad explained to Mekas that "there is a numerological way of thinking about" *The Flicker*. Mekas, "An Interview with Tony Conrad," p. 229. As Steve Durkee of the intermedia group USCO explained to Mekas, "Strobe is the digital trip. In other words, what the strobe is basically doing, it's turning on and off, completely on and completely off." Mekas, "More on Strobe Light and Intermedia" (June 16, 1966), in *Movie Journal*, p. 245.

54. Mekas, "An Interview with Tony Conrad," pp. 229, 232. Conrad further explained: "The seeing with your eyes closed is a very different type of sensory experience from the visual impressions that you get with your eyes open, when your eyes are focused on an object. The only way to have such impressions is to use a devise [sic] that produces them – doesn't project them, but actually produces them in the eye" (p. 229).

55. Mussman, "An Interview with Tony Conrad," p. 5, and Conrad, "Letter to Henry Romney," p. 2.

56. Marshall McLuhan, "The Electronic Age – The Age of Implosion" (1962), in *Media Research: Technology, Art, Communication*, ed. Michel A. Moos (Amsterdam: G+B Arts International, 1997), p. 29.

57. Marshall McLuhan, *Understanding Media: The Extensions of Man* (New York: McGraw-Hill, 1964), p. 52.

58. See, for instance, McLuhan, "The Electronic Age." On post-Fordism, see Paolo Virno, "The Ambivalence of Disenchantment," in *Radical Thought in Italy: A Potential Politics*, ed. Paolo Virno and Michael Hardt (Minneapolis: University of Minnesota Press, 1996), pp. 13–34; Maurizio Lazzarato, "Immaterial Labor," in *Radical Thought in Italy*, pp. 133–47; and Michael Hardt and Antonio Negri, *Empire* (Cambridge, MA: Harvard University Press, 2000), pp. 280–303. For Cage's citations of McLuhan, see, for instance, comments in Michael Zwerin, "A Lethal Measurement" (January 6, 1966), in *John Cage: An Anthology*, ed. Richard Kostelanetz (New York: Da Capo, 1970), pp. 163–64, and John Cage, "Diary: How to Improve the World (You Will Only Make Matters Worse) 1965," in *A Year from Monday* (Middletown, CT: Wesleyan University Press, 1967), p. 10.

59. McLuhan, "The Electronic Age," p. 23.

60. Gilles Deleuze, *Cinema 2: The Time-Image*, trans. Hugh Tomlinson and Robert Galeta (Minneapolis: University of Minnesota Press, 1989), p. 215 (translation modified). Deleuze is also discussing the work of George Landow and Lettrist cinema.

61. On the new cinematic and perceptual developments at the World's Fair (including Mekas's reaction to them) and their role in the birth of expanded cinema, see Beatriz Colomina, "Enclosed by Images: The Eameses' Multimedia Architecture," *Grey Room* 2 (Winter 2001): 6–29; Branden W. Joseph, "'My Mind Split Open': Andy Warhol's Exploding Plastic Inevitable," *Grey Room* 8 (Summer 2002): 80–107; and Branden W. Joseph, "Plastic Empathy: The Ghost of Robert Whitman," *Grey Room* 25 (Fall 2006): 64–91.

62. Jonas Mekas, "On the Expanding Eye" (February 6, 1964), in *Movie Journal*, pp. 119–20.

63. Jonas Mekas, "Spiritualization of the Image" (June 25, 1964), in *Movie Journal*, p. 144, and Mekas, "On the Expanding Eye," p. 118. For the most important discussion of the subject's perceptual transformation under the conditions of modernity, see Jonathan Crary, *Suspensions of Perception: Attention, Spectacle, and Modern Culture* (Cambridge, MA: MIT Press, 1999).

64. Mekas, "More on Strobe Light and Intermedia," p. 244.

65. Jonas Mekas, "On the Psychedelic Explorations of Timothy Leary, on Chance, Strobe, and Cinema" (July 22, 1965), in *Movie Journal*, p. 199.

66. Brion Gysin, "Dream Machine," in *Olympia Magazine* 2 (1962); repr. in *The Best of "Olympia": An Anthology of Tales, Poems, Scientific Documents and Tricks which Appeared in the Short-lived and Much Lamented* Olympia Magazine, ed. Maurice Girodias (London: New English Library, 1966), pp. 18–20; Ian Sommerville, "Flicker," in *Olympia Magazine* 2 (1962); repr. in *The Best of "Olympia,"* pp. 25–27. Mekas discusses both articles in "On the Expanding Eye," pp. 118–20.

67. William S. Burroughs, in Daniel Odier, *The Job: Interviews with William S. Burroughs* (New York: Penguin, 1974), p. 222. The idea of control would be taken up by Gilles Deleuze in "Postscript on Control Societies," trans. Martin Joughin, in *Negotiations, 1972–1990* (New York: Columbia University Press, 1995), pp. 177–82.

68. Burroughs, in Odier, *The Job*, pp. 15, 170.

69. *Ibid.*, p. 206.

70. *Ibid.*, pp. 173–74. Although Burroughs seems to refer to Gysin, this passage appears amid quotes from Ian Sommerville, "Flicker," and Ian Sommerville, "Dreammachine," quoted in Robert A. Sobieszek, *Ports of Entry: William S. Burroughs and the Arts* (Los Angeles: Los Angeles County Museum of Art, 1996), p. 78.

71. Gysin, "Dream Machine," p. 19. Gysin continues: "The Dream Machine may bring about a change of consciousness inasmuch as it throws back the limits of the visible world and may, indeed, prove that there are no limits" and, in a gloss on Nietzsche's *Übermensch*, concludes, "The ape became a man. It must be possible to become something more than a man" (pp. 19–20). Gysin's discussion of the dematerialization of the art object would seem the basis of Mekas's discussion of expanded cinema's dematerialization of film stock. See "Spiritualization of the Image," p. 145.

72. Sommerville, "Flicker," p. 26.

73. *Ibid.*, partially quoted in Odier, *The Job*, p. 360.

74. W. Grey Walter, *The Living Brain* (New York: W. W. Norton, 1953).

75. *Ibid.*, p. 98. Walter even went so far as to speculate on the phylogenetic impact that flicker produced by the sun beaming through the leafy canopy of the jungle may have had upon human evolution: "Perhaps . . . with their slowly swelling brains and their enhanced liability to breakdowns of this sort, our arboreal cousins, struck by the setting sun in the midst of a jungle caper, may have fallen from perch to plain, sadder but wiser apes" (p. 100).

76. *Ibid.*, p. 101.

77. Rhodri Hayward, "The Tortoise and the Love-Machine: Grey Walter and the Politics of Electroencephalography," *Science in Context* 14, no. 4 (Winter 2001): 624–25.

78. Walter, *The Living Brain*, p. 108.

79. *Ibid.*, pp. 152, 188, 211–12, 223–24. See also Hayward, "The Tortoise and the Love-Machine," p. 621: "While physical reflexes and animal habits might have remained open to academic investigation, there was always an inner spiritual territory that exhausted the finite tools of rational description.... This was the territory on which Walter now set his sights."

80. See T. J. Clark's discussion of such a colonization of new areas of subjectivity in terms of "the bad dream of modernism." T. J. Clark, *Farewell to an Idea: Episodes from a History of Modernism* (New Haven, CT: Yale University Press, 1999), pp. 306–8.

81. In W. Grey Walter's science-fiction novel *The Curve of the Snowflake* (New York: Norton, 1956), he, like Burroughs, describes subjective transformation in terms of the effect of a virus.

82. On the zoetrope and the regulation of attention and fatigue, see Jonathan Crary, *Techniques of the Observer: On Vision and Modernity in the Nineteenth Century* (Cambridge, MA: MIT Press, 1990).

83. Burroughs, quoted in Barry Miles, *The Beat Hotel: Ginsberg, Burroughs, and Corso in Paris, 1957–1963* (New York: Grove Press, 2000), pp. 159 and 157.

84. Burroughs, in Odier, *The Job*, p. 186. That this practice derived from Gysin's paintings seems clear from comments in Miles, *Beat Hotel*, p. 157.

85. Burroughs, in Odier, *The Job*, p. 174.

86. Sommerville, "Flicker," p. 26.

87. Burroughs, in Odier, *The Job*, p. 161.

88. Friedrich A. Kittler, *Gramophone, Film, Typewriter*, trans. Geoffrey Winthrop-Young and Michael Wutz (Stanford, CA: Stanford University Press, 1999), p. 110.

89. Gysin, quoted in Miles, *Beat Hotel*, p. 261.

90. John Geiger, *Chapel of Extreme Experience: A Short History of Stroboscopic Light and the Dream Machine* (Brooklyn: Soft Skull Press, 2003), p. 66.

91. Burroughs, in Odier, *The Job*, p. 91.

92. As Peter Kubelka argued in "The Theory of Metrical Film," it is not between two shots, but between two frames that the "collision" basic to cinema occurs. Peter Kubelka, "The Theory of Metrical Film," in *The Avant-Garde Film:*

A Reader of Theory and Criticism, ed. P. Adams Sitney (New York: New York University Press, 1978), p. 141. Conrad noted much the same thing in Mussman, "An Interview with Tony Conrad," p. 5.

93. Deleuze, *Cinema 2*, pp. 180–81 (translation modified; emphasis in original).

94. Sommerville, quoted in Sobieszek, *Ports of Entry*, p. 78; partially quoted in Odier, *The Job*, p. 174.

95. William S. Burroughs, "Points of Distinction Between Sedative and Consciousness-expanding Drugs," *Evergreen Review* 8, no. 34 (December 1964): 72–74, partially reproduced in Odier, *The Job*, pp. 128–34. Burroughs's article is noted three times in Conrad's blue *Flicker* notebook. "Points of Distinction" seems to have been Burroughs's contribution to the conference organized by Timothy Leary on psychedelic drugs for the American Psychological Symposium in Boston in 1961. Burroughs would ultimately prove unimpressed with the undisciplined nature of Leary's supposed investigations: "Burroughs had not come to Harvard to join psychedelic encounter sessions or to listen to blatherings about love and cosmic unity. He wanted to talk about neurological implants and brain wave generators." Ted Morgan, *Literary Outlaw: The Life and Times of William S. Burroughs* (New York: Henry Holt and Company, 1988), p. 381. When Burroughs volunteered to work on flicker instead of pharmaceuticals, Leary withdrew his conference funds, including his return ticket.

96. Burroughs, "Points of Distinction," p. 73. Compare Mekas's paraphrase in "On the Expanding Eye," p. 118.

97. Renan, *An Introduction to the American Underground Film*, pp. 33 and 138. See also Geiger, *Chapel of Extreme Experience*, pp. 73–74. Conrad recalls that while he may have become aware of the Dream Machine via associates of Jack Smith, he did not feel the need to pursue the device on account of his familiarity with its underlying principles. Conrad, conversation with author, Buffalo, NY, August 14–18, 1995.

98. Deleuze, *Cinema 2*, p. 215.

99. Mussman, "An Interview with Tony Conrad," p. 5.

100. *Ibid.*, p. 4.

101. Tony Conrad, "Progress 1," unpublished text, 2003.

102. Conrad, "Letter to Henry Romney," p. 1. None of this is to say that Jack Smith approved of the intellectual and anti-iconic nature of Conrad's production. He didn't. As Smith noted sarcastically in 1971 in reference to the Rockefeller grant Conrad received in 1966: "I know of someone who received

thousands of dollars from a foundation to make a movie that's main claim to fame was it gave people epileptic fits." Jack Smith, *Wait for Me at the Bottom of the Pool: The Writings of Jack Smith*, ed. J. Hoberman and Edward Leffingwell (London: Serpent's Tail, 1997), p. 167. Like Smith's work and that of Burroughs, Gysin, and Sommerville, *The Flicker* was also related to the psychedelic experience. See, for example, Jud Yalkut, "The Psychedelic Revolution: Turning on the Art Trip," *Arts Magazine* (November 1966): 22–23.

103. Conrad has discussed certain aspects of films in relation to scores, for instance with regard to the "frozen films" and diagrams of Paul Sharits. Interview with author, Buffalo, NY, August 15–16, 1995. Conrad was referring to his lecture "Paul Sharits: Prescription and Collapsed Temporality," delivered at Albright-Knox Art Gallery, Buffalo, March 9, 1976; materials in Conrad's archive. As late as 2006, Henry Flynt, when presenting his "Flynt Films" at the Emily Harvey Gallery, New York, referred to the scenarios/treatments as "scores."

104. Henry Flynt, *Fragments and Reconstructions from a Destroyed Oeuvre, 1959–1963* (New York: Backworks, 1982), n.p.

105. "*The Flicker* employs harmonic relations, speeds, pulses, and patterns different from those used until now." Conrad, in Mekas, "An Interview with Tony Conrad," p. 230.

106. Sitney, "Structural Film," in *Film Culture Reader*, p. 344. Sitney's brief mention in this article would prove the only reference to Conrad's second film within the literature.

107. Walter, *The Living Brain*, pp. 111–12.

108. It was only in 1975, when the discourse of North American structural film had largely fallen under the sway of the modernist aesthetic of the art critic Clement Greenberg, that *The Eye of Count Flickerstein*, shorn of its title sequence, would reappear as a purely formal film.

109. Conrad, yellow *Flicker* notebook, p. 73 (May 5, 1965).

110. Jack Smith, "The Perfect Filmic Appositeness of Mria Montez" (1962), in *Wait for Me at the Bottom of the Pool*, p. 28.

111. Beyond its "brief Dracula parody" (Sitney, "Structural Film," in *Film Culture Reader*, p. 344) and reminiscence of *Normal Love*, the opening sequence of *The Eye of Count Flickerstein*, it is perhaps worth noting, contains another interrelated reference. The zooms toward the eye peering though the "o" in the "Eye of" title card and that of the "Count" were conceived as retorts to the

famous title sequence of Alfred Hitchcock's *Vertigo* (1958), done by Saul Bass and John Whitney, in which the close-up of an eye gives way to the spiraling lissajous swirls of Whitney's computer graphics. As such, Conrad alludes not only to Hollywood narrative cinema, but also to the work of Whitney, an experimental filmmaker whose own version of "visual harmonics" continued the mystical modernist aspirations of the nineteenth century. Conrad's outmoded, handcrafted aesthetic would thus seem to be juxtaposed against both narrative film and a symbolist method, the latter, in Whitney's case, somewhat ironically produced with analogue computers and World War II artillery firing directors.

112. Deleuze describes the confrontation of film and electronic imagery (characteristic, once again, of the third epoch of cinema) in terms of "a battlefield where art and thought launch together with cinema into a new domain, while the forces of control try to steal this domain from them, to take it over before they do, and set up a new clinic for social engineering . . . the convulsive confrontation of cinema and television, where hope mingles with the worst of all possibilities." Gilles Deleuze, "Letter to Serge Daney: Optimism, Pessimism, and Travel" (1990), trans. Martin Joughin, in *Negotiations, 1972–1990*, p. 77.

113. Tony Conrad, "Music Notes II," p. 43 (entry 92, dated "June 23 [idea: Spring '62]").

114. Conrad, "Music Notes II," p. 62 (entry 146, dated January 29, 1968).

115. Conrad, "Music Notes II," p. 56 (entry 114, dated September 6, 1964). Inserted square bracket in original.

116. Conrad, yellow *Flicker* notebook, p. 37.

117. Tony Conrad, "INTEGER: Bulldozing a foundation in the culturescape of sound, media, and performance," *Cinematograph* 2 (1986): 24.

118. *Ibid.*, p. 33.

119. *Ibid.*, pp. 28–29.

120. *Ibid.*, p. 30.

121. *Ibid.*

122. *Ibid.*, p. 33.

123. Cage's comments appear in "Experimental Music: Doctrine" (1955), in *Silence* (Middletown, CT: Wesleyan University Press, 1961), p. 14.

124. Henry Flynt, *Anthology of Non-Philosophical Cultural Works* (Cambridge, MA: published by Tony Conrad, 1961), p. 2.

125. Kittler, *Gramophone, Film, Typewriter*, p. 37. In the end, Conrad's *String Loop* had resonances with the same wartime stereo technologies that underlay

Stockhausen's *Kontakte* and his own sound track to *The Flicker*. As Kittler notes of the Nazi Heinkel pilot, strapped into the audio range-finding equipment of his bomber: "Historically, he had become the first consumer of a headphone stereophony that today controls us all" (p. 100). On the role of the subject as a "human servo-mechanism" within such wartime technologies, see David A. Mindell, *Between Human and Machine: Feedback, Control, and Computing before Cybernetics* (Baltimore: Johns Hopkins University Press, 2002).

126. Kittler, *Gramophone, Film, Typewriter*, p. 94. This applies equally, I am arguing, to *The Flicker*, which, within Kittler's analytic framework, dissolves cinema's "imaginary" into the "real" he associates with acoustical media technologies.

127. Terry Riley, "Ear Piece," in *An Anthology*, ed. La Monte Young (New York: La Monte Young and Jackson Mac Low, 1963), n.p. Conrad, who had access to *An Anthology* before publication, may have come across Riley's piece before formulating *Ear String*.

128. Alain Daniélou, "The Influence of Sound Phenomena on Human Consciousness," *Psychedelic Review* 7 (1966): 20–26. Young's ideas about audition were profoundly influenced by Daniélou's text. In it, Daniélou connected the manifestation of acoustical vibrations (particularly in just intonation) both to the production of specific emotions and to the manifestation of a cosmic, universal truth. Like Daniélou's article, much within Young's subsequent understanding and presentation of his work and that of the Theatre of Eternal Music resonates strongly with the type of New Age mysticism that emerged within the psychedelic movement. Indeed, it would be via Ralph Metzner, associate of Timothy Leary and editor of the *Psychedelic Review*, that Young and Zazeela would come to find their guru, Pandit Pran Nath, to whom they discipled themselves until his death. Frank J. Oteri, "La Monte Young and Marian Zazeela at the Dream House," *New Music Box [The Web Magazine from the American Music Center]* 5, no. 6 issue 54 (October 2003): 19–20, accessed on-line at http://www.newmusicbox.org/page.nmbx?id=54fp00 (last accessed July 14, 2007). The goal of direct affective influence was one widely pursued under the auspices of psychedelia. "If we really understood human sensibility," Metzner would proclaim, "we would be able to affect consciousness." Jud Yalkut, "Prophet-eer? Celebrations of T. Leary Under the Auspices of the League for Spiritual Discovery," *Arts Magazine* (February 1967): 23. On the relation of Conrad's and Young's work to psychedelia, see Diedrich Diederichsen, "The Primary: Political and Anti-Political

Continuities between Minimal Music and Minimal Art," in *A Minimal Future? Art as Object 1958–1968*, ed. Ann Goldstein (Los Angeles: The Museum of Contemporary Art, Los Angeles, 2004), pp. 111–31.

129. Young, in Richard Kostelanetz, *The Theatre of Mixed Means* (1968; New York: RK Editions, 1980), pp. 217–18.

130. Ramon Pelinski, "Upon Hearing a Performance of the Well-Tuned Piano: An Interview with La Monte Young and Marian Zazeela, 78 1 x 22 4:58:25 – 7:15:00 PM NYC," *Parachute* 19 (Summer 1980): 6. Zazeela describes her environmental light installations in a similar manner: "Part of the projection falls upon us as we play and re-programs us." Quoted in Kostelanetz, *The Theatre of Mixed Means*, p. 216.

131. La Monte Young, "Notes on *The Well-Tuned Piano*," in *The Well Tuned Piano 81 X 25* Record Program Booklet (New York: Grammavision, 1987), p. 6. As Young explained further to Pelinski, "It's the basic principle for any system of information, or any system of language because it depends on the fact that you can repeat things, and that's what the system of just intonation provides" (p. 7).

132. Ljerka Vidic, "Meet the Composer: La Monte Young and Marian Zazeela," *EAR: New Music News* 12/3 (May 1987): 26; Antonin Artaud, *The Theater and its Double*, trans. Mary Caroline Richards (New York: Grove Weidenfeld, 1958), p. 13.

133. Jacqueline Caux and Daniel Caux, "La Monte Young: '... Créer des états psychologiques précis," *Chroniques de l'art vivant*, no. 30 (May 1972): 28, my translation. As previously discussed, Young's conception of the intense, disciplinary practice of the Theatre of Eternal Music effectively places it under the sign of a transcendent ideal: on the most proximate level that of the authority of the score and composer and, on a higher level, the universal structural harmony to which the composer would have access. Like the performer, the listener, too, comes to be disciplined by the acoustical environment to approach the ideal of a pure affective response, a relationship taken to such a degree within Young's discussion that it begins to approach something like discipline's utopian ideal of a complete identification, whereby the sign and its effect would be instantaneously connected. Michel Foucault discusses this idea in the evolution of discipline in *Discipline and Punish: The Birth of the Prison*, trans. Alan Sheridan (New York: Vintage, 1977), pp. 104–31.

134. The reference is to the Theatre of Eternal Music's *The Second Dream of the High-Tension Line Step-Down Transformer* (1962). On Conrad's making Young

aware of the name of this device, see William Duckworth, *Talking Music* (New York: Schirmer Books, 1995), p. 241. In a note dated November 21, 1965, Conrad writes: "Get catalogues of professional sawmill supplies (blades &c.) &/or hi-tension line stepdown transformer parts." Yellow *Flicker* notebook, p. 33.

135. Tony Conrad, "Inside the Dream Syndicate," *Film Culture* 41 (Summer 1966): 8.

136. Conrad, "Inside the Dream Syndicate," pp. 7–8.

137. Not, at least, until after the rehearsal. As Conrad related, "All of us had experiences with sound overload that left us with acoustic afterimages. Like, I would go out in the street after we would rehearse and I would hear the sound of the music in my head, ringing in my ears, for a long time. It would merge with the sound of the city, because we were using 60 cycles as a reference; it would merge with the sound of transformers in the subway and the buzzing of fluorescent lights and so forth, and replicate and continue the sound through this kind of subjective perceptual anomaly." Interview with the author, Buffalo, NY, July 31, 2001.

138. Tony Conrad, "On 60 Cycles," two-page typescript, annotated as "Program Notes for Rhys Chatham video-electronic music piece," May 21, 1972. Copy located in Conrad's archives. Internal quotation cited to "*Industrial Electricity*, p. 15." Conrad's statement that "one wave spans our continent" refers not only to the ubiquity of 60-cycle current within North America, but also to the calculation of 60 cycles/second divided by 186,000 miles/second (the speed of light), which provides a measurement of the length of the wave form at 3100 miles (i.e., approximately the length of the United States). Conrad, conversation with author, January 6, 2007.

139. "The glow of light alternates fifty times per second in European lightbulbs, sixty times in American ones: the uncomplicated, and hence imperceptible, rhythm of our evenings and of an antenna called the body." Kittler, *Gramophone, Film, Typewriter*, p. 122.

140. John Cage, "These Days" (1968), in *John Cage: An Anthology*, p. 179.

141. Cage, "Diary: How to Improve the World (You Will Only Make Matters Worse) 1965," pp. 15–16.

142. John Cage, "Diary: How to Improve the World (You Will Only Make Matters Worse) Continued 1966," in *A Year from Monday*, p. 54. Cage discusses the experiment further in John Cage, "The Cage Around Us," *Connection: Visual Arts at Harvard* 4, no. 2 (Spring 1967): 24. Cage's discussion was part of his

polemical preference for electronics over pharmaceuticals, as commented on by Duchamp (see Chapter 5). The limitations of Cage's "sunny disposition" and inability to conceive of any type of control other than sovereign power would be clear not only in his embrace of electroshock therapy, but also in his temporary flirtation with ideas of eugenics. See, for instance, Cage's comments in Richard Kostelanetz, "Conversation with John Cage," in *John Cage: An Anthology*, p. 34; Cage, "These Days," in *John Cage: An Anthology*, p. 179; and "Diary: How to Improve the World (You Will Only Make Matters Worse) Continued 1966," p. 54.

143. Jonathan Crary, "Eclipse of the Spectacle," in *Art After Modernism: Rethinking Representation*, ed. Brian Wallis (Boston: David R. Godine, 1984), p. 284.

144. Deleuze tends to present the succession from sovereign power, to discipline, to control as a linear succession. Deleuze, "Postscript on Control Societies." In contrast, see Michel Foucault, *Security, Territory, Population: Lectures at the Collège de France, 1977–1978*, ed. Michel Senellart, trans. Graham Burchell (New York: Palgrave Macmillan, 2007), pp. 6–9.

145. Tony Conrad, "Yellow Movies, a forty monitor show," press release for The Gray Gallery, Antioch College, April 15–20, 1976. Copy located in Conrad's archives.

146. Conrad's oppositional stance toward mainstream commercial and corporate culture was the subject of his profile in *Look* magazine as part of their special issue on the American man: "Underground Man: The Social Dropout," *Look* 31, no. 1 (January 10, 1967): 70–71. Although it was written by Isabel Eberstadt, she removed her name from the piece on account of differences over the article's editing.

147. Walter Benjamin, "The Work of Art in the Age of Its Technological Reproducibility: Second Version" (1936), trans. Edmund Jephcott and Harry Zohn, in *Walter Benjamin: Selected Writings, Volume 3*, ed. Howard Eiland and Michael W. Jennings (Cambridge, MA: Harvard University Press, 2002), pp. 101–33.

148. Conrad, "Inside the Dream Syndicate," p. 8.

149. Young, in Kostelanetz, *The Theatre of Mixed Means*, p. 206.

150. *Ibid.*, p. 208.

151. Jetta Bernier, "The Flicker Phenomenon," New York University Department of Psychology study, 1969, n.p. Copy located in Conrad's archives.

152. Mordkoff, who was a United States Public Health Service research fellow at Berkeley, was subsequently employed at the Department of Psychology, Neurology, and Behavioral Sciences at the University of Oklahoma Medical Center before becoming an assistant professor at New York University. He died in a swimming accident off the coast of Norway in 1971. See, Richard S. Lazarus, "In Memorandum: Arnold M. Mordkoff, Ph.D., 1936–1971," *Psychophysiology* 9, no. 1 (January 1972): 155.

153. Richard S. Lazarus, Joseph C. Speisman, and Arnold M. Mordkoff, "The Relationship Between Autonomic Indicators of Psychological Stress: Heart Rate and Skin Conductance," *Psychosomatic Medicine* 25, no. 1 (1963): 21.

154. On Róheim, see Paul A. Robinson, *The Freudian Left: Wilhelm Reich, Geza Roheim, Herbert Marcuse* (New York: Harper and Row, 1969), pp. 75–146.

155. A. Aas, *Mutilation Fantasies and Autonomic Response* (Oslo: Olso Univeristy Press, 1958), and Bernard J. Schwartz, "An Empirical Test of the Two Freudian Hypotheses Concerning Castration Anxiety," *Journal of Personality* 24, no. 2 (December 1955): 318–27. These are discussed in Joseph C. Speisman, Richard S. Lazarus, Les Davison, and Arnold M. Mordkoff, "Experimental Analysis of a Film Used as a Threatening Stimulus," *Journal of Consulting Psychology* 28, no. 1 (1964): 23–33. Róheim's interpretation of the subincision ritual is found in Géza Róheim, *The Eternal Ones and the Dream: A Psychoanalytic Interpretation of Australian Myth and Ritual* (New York: International Universities Press, 1945), esp. pp. 68–79.

156. Joseph C. Speisman, Richard S. Lazarus, Arnold M. Mordkoff, and Les Davison, "Experimental Reduction of Stress Based on Ego-Defense Theory," *Journal of Abnormal and Social Psychology* 68, no. 4 (1964): 369.

157. Richard S. Lazarus, Joseph C. Speisman, Arnold M. Mordkoff, and Leslie A. Davison, "A Laboratory Study of Psychological Stress Produced by a Motion Picture Film," *Psychological Monographs: General and Applied* 76, no. 34 (whole no. 553) (1962): 20–21. Film replaced actual physical discomfort or techniques of psychological manipulation such as telling subjects they had failed an important test.

158. Lazarus, Speisman, Mordkoff, and Davison, "A Laboratory Study of Psychological Stress," p. 27; Speisman, Lazarus, Mordkoff, and Davison, "Experimental Reduction of Stress Based on Ego-Defense Theory."

159. Lazarus, Speisman, and Mordkoff, "The Relationship Between Autonomic Indicators of Psychological Stress," p. 21.

160. Speisman, Lazarus, Davison, and Mordkoff, "Experimental Analysis of a Film Used as a Threatening Stimulus," p. 32.

161. Lazarus, Speisman, and Mordkoff, "The Relationship Between Autonomic Indicators of Psychological Stress," pp. 28 and 24.

162. Speisman, Lazarus, Mordkoff, and Davison, "Experimental Reduction of Stress Based on Ego-Defense Theory," p. 376.

163. Lazarus, Speisman, Mordkoff, and Davison, "A Laboratory Study of Psychological Stress," p. 27: "Thus it is apparent that, for the subject population as a whole, the variation in level of disturbance is not random but is closely tied to the attributes of the film itself. Yet, when self-report measures of disturbance were sought, these were in the form of a single-type score for each subject summarizing this very complex patterns of ups and downs. Our means of understanding response to lifelike stressor conditions will be immeasurably improved when we are able to obtain continuous records for behavioral variables such as those which are now obtained for the autonomic nervous system, and when intraindividual analyses have been performed, and patterns of reaction are related to known personality dispositions or stimulus conditions."

164. *Ibid.*, p. 25; Speisman, Lazarus, Mordkoff, and Davison, "Experimental Reduction of Stress Based on Ego-Defense Theory," p. 379: "In any event, we would still argue ... that when stress reactions to a complex film stimulus are being studied, continuous, point-to-point measurement of the reaction is more defensible where possible and appropriate, than procedures which average the reaction over the entire period of changing levels of threat, or depend upon recall of a complex and remote psychological experience." In other words, the psychoanalyst's couch on which the patient recounts his or her trauma is to be replaced by the manipulation and recording of psychological indicators modulating in time. As Kittler noted, "With technological media, a knowledge assumes power that is no longer satisfied with the individual universals of its subjects, their self-images and self-representations — these imaginary formations — but instead registers distinguishing particulars." *Gramophone, Film, Typewriter*, p. 83.

165. Lazarus, Speisman, and Mordkoff, "The Relationship Between Autonomic Indicators of Psychological Stress," p. 24.

166. Michel Foucault, *The History of Sexuality. Volume 1: An Introduction*, trans. Robert Hurley (New York: Pantheon, 1978), p. 150. On the relation to media, see Kittler, *Gramophone, Film, Typewriter*, p. 94. The psychoanalytic project of Róheim, who made the *Subincision* film, explicitly and combatively

argued for an understanding of power in sovereign form; see Robinson, *The Freudian Left*, p. 124: "Roheim extended this line of reasoning by arguing that the adored [political] leader must be thought of as a symbolic penis. The body politic was inconceivable without a political phallus." (It might be noted that Robinson's book itself, published in the same year as Bernier's study, was an attempt to explore the resistant potentials of psychoanalysis.) Conrad would later argue that psychoanalysis is, in fact, a prolongation of the "scientific" project of knowledge and power. Conrad, "The Invocation of Freud's Name Must Be Recognized as the Battle Cry of the Sciento-Technological Orthodoxy," three-page typescript, n.d., located in Conrad's archives.

167. Kittler, *Gramophone, Film, Typewriter*, p. 16.

168. Manford L. Eaton, *Bio-Music* (Barton, VT: Something Else Press, 1974), preface. Eaton's text first appeared in *Source: Music of the Avant-Garde* 9 (vol. 5, no. 1) (January 1971). Perhaps his earliest publication was M. L. Eaton, *Bio-Potentials as Control Data for Spontaneous Music* (Kansas City, MO: ORCUS Research Technical Publication TP-3001, 1968).

169. Eaton, *Bio-Music*, p. 39.

170. *Ibid.*, pp. 48–49, and 17.

171. M. L. Eaton, *Electronic Music: A Handbook of Sound Synthesis and Control* (Kansas City, MO: ORCUS Research Technical Publication TP-3003, 1969), pp. 60–61.

172. Eaton, *Bio-Music*, p. 64.

173. *Ibid.*, p. 48.

174. Cage, "Experimental Music: Doctrine," in *Silence*, p. 14.

175. Eaton, *Bio-Music*, p. 11 (bracketed insertion in original).

176. *Ibid.*, p. 53 and preface.

177. *Ibid.*, p. 64.

178. On the evolution of this aspect of control, beginning in the nineteenth century, see James R. Beniger, *The Control Revolution: Technological and Economic Origins of the Information Society* (Cambridge, MA: Harvard University Press, 1986). Although Beniger does not discuss television, he argues that the "basic societal transformation from Industrial to Information Society had essentially been completed by the late 1930s," a date that, perhaps not unimportantly, coincided with television's public debut at the 1939 New York World's Fair (p. 293).

179. Gilles Deleuze, "Letter to Serge Daney," p. 74. On the network function of television, see Crary, "Eclipse of the Spectacle."

180. McLuhan, *Understanding Media*, p. 68.

181. Tony Conrad, "A Few Remarks Before I Begin," in *The Avant-Garde Film*, ed. P. Adams Sitney (New York: New York University Press, 1978), p. 266.

182. *Ibid.*, pp. 267–68.

183. *Ibid.*, p. 269.

184. *Ibid.*, p. 268.

185. *Ibid.*, p. 274.

186. Robert Morris, "Notes on Sculpture, Part 3: Notes and Non Sequiturs" (1967), in *Continuous Project Altered Daily*, p. 27. Morris expressly opposes his analysis to many of the common ideas about minimalism's innovations: "It is not in the uses of new, exotic materials that the present work differs much from past work. It is not even in the nonhierarchic, non-compositional structuring, as this was clearly worked out in painting."

187. *Ibid.*, p. 27.

188. *Ibid.*, p. 38.

189. *Ibid.*, p. 39.

190. Robert Morris, "Anti Form" (1968), in *Continuous Project Altered Daily*, p. 46.

191. Morris, "Notes on Sculpture, Part 3," p. 27. On "media," see Morris, "Notes on Sculpture, Part 4" (1969), in *Continuous Project Altered Daily*, p. 70 n. 3, and on "automation," see Morris, "Some Notes on the Phenomenology of Making: The Search for the Motivated" (1970), in *Continuous Project Altered Daily*, pp. 86–87. On related engagements with cybernetics at this time, see Pamela M. Lee, "'Ultramoderne': Or, How George Kubler Stole the Time in Sixties Art," *Grey Room* 2 (Winter 2001): 46–75.

192. Gilles Deleuze and Félix Guattari, *Kafka: Toward a Minor Literature*, trans. Dana Polan (Minneapolis: University of Minnesota Press, 1986), p. 48.

193. *Ibid.*, p. 47.

194. Deleuze, *Cinema 2*, p. 215.

Conclusion

1. On Conrad's "paracinematic" work, see Jonathan Walley, "The Material of Film and the Idea of Cinema: Contrasting Practices in Sixties and Seventies Avant-Garde Film," *October* 103 (Winter 2003): 15–30. Walley sees this work as "conceptual" in nature, rather than material. For a more recent discussion of this work on Conrad's part, see Tony Conrad, "Is This Penny Ante or a High Stakes

Game? An Interventionist Approach to Experimental Filmmaking," *Millennium Film Journal* 43–44 (Summer–Fall 2005): 101–9.

2. Conrad, quoted in Bruce Goldstein, "Independent Film Maker: Tony Conrad," press release for Film Section of the Museum of Art, Carnegie Institute, Pittsburgh, PA, November 13, 1974. Copy located in Conrad's archives.

3. Conrad, quoted in Goldstein, "Independent Film Maker."

4. Conrad, interview with author, Buffalo, NY, August 2, 2001. Conrad had long recognized the domestic work that Beverly Grant had done, crediting her equally in part for that reason on the structural films, *Straight and Narrow* and *Four Square*.

5. *Ibid.*

6. Indeed, *Curried 7302* seems a literalization of Malcolm Le Grice's discussion of the Heins' *Roh Film* and his own *Little Dog for Roger* (1967/1968): "The two films . . . create much of their experience through evident tactility and evident process: traces of the films' handling are deliberately retained. They attack the implicit alienation in the film process which loses contact with the vital stages of image transfer and chemical development, and both are the result of contact between the film-maker and film at all stages." Malcolm Le Grice, *Abstract Film and Beyond* (Cambridge, MA: MIT Press, 1977), p. 118. Le Grice discusses Conrad's cooked films in Malcolm Le Grice, "Vision," *Studio International* 188, no. 968 (July–August 1974): 42–43 (review supplement, pp. 2–3).

7. Conrad, interview with author, Buffalo, NY, August 2, 2001.

8. Tony Conrad, "Articulation of Boolean Algebra for Film Opticals," six-page typescript, November 2, 1975, p. 5; quotation also in "Visiting Filmmaker: Tony Conrad," press release for Walker Art Center, statement dated November 2, 1975. Copy located in Conrad's archives.

9. Conrad, "Articulation of Boolean Algebra for Film Opticals," p. 5; also in "Visiting Filmmaker: Tony Conrad."

10. Although shot on super-8 film, versions of Conrad's "army movie" have been transferred and shown on video and, more recently, DVD and other digital projection technologies.

11. Conrad, program notes for "Authorized to Surrender: Tony Conrad 1977–90, A Video Retrospective," exhibition at The Kitchen, New York, February 5 – March 5, 1991, p. 3.

12. *Ibid.*, p. 4.

13. After shooting his army movie, *Beholden to Victory*, Conrad began work

on a "jail movie" project, utilizing the genre of the women in prison film (the quintessential example of which, Jonathan Demme's *Caged Heat* of 1974, boasted a soundtrack by John Cale). Conrad's still-unfinished project included appearances by Mike Kelley and Tony Oursler. Kelley's monologue "Slow Boat to Lesbos" was written and performed for Conrad's film. Mike Kelley, "Slow Boat to Lesbos," *Barney: The Modern Stone-Age Magazine* 4 (Spring 1984): 20–21.

14. Conrad, "Authorized to Surrender," p. 4.

15. Mike Kelley, *Minor Histories: Statements, Conversations, Proposals* (Cambridge, MA: MIT Press, 2004), p. 181.

Index

Zone Books series design by Bruce Mau
Image placement and production by Julie Fry
Typesetting by Archetype
Printed and bound by Maple-Vail on Glatfelter acid-free paper